Art and Creative Development for Young Children

THIRD EDITION

Robert Schirrmacher

University of California, Santa Cruz Education Extension

Monika Weis

Delmar Publishers

I(T)P® An International Thomson Publishing Company

Albany • Bonn • Boston • Cincinnati • Detroit • London • Madrid • Melbourne
Mexico City • New York • Pacific Grove • Paris • San Francisco
Singapore • Tokyo • Toronto • Washington

NOTICE TO THE READER

Cover Design: Publisher's Studio

Delmar Staff

Publisher: William Brottmiller
Administrative Editor: Jay Whitney
Associate Editor: Erin O'Connor Traylor
Project Editor: Marah Bellegarde

Production Coordinator: Sandra Woods
Art and Design Coordinator: Timothy J. Conners
Senior Editorial Assistant: Glenna Stanfield

COPYRIGHT © 1998
By Delmar Publishers
an International Thomson Publishing Company

The ITP logo is a trademark under license.

Printed in the United States of America

For more information, contact:

Delmar Publishers
3 Columbia Circle, Box 15015
Albany, New York 12212-5015

International Thomson Publishing Europe
Berkshire House
168-173 High Holborn
London, WC1V 7AA
England

Thomas Nelson Australia
102 Dodds Street
South Melbourne 3205
Victoria, Australia

Nelson Canada
1120 Birchmount Road
Scarborough, Ontario
Canada, M1K 5G4

International Thomson Editores
Campos Eliseos 385, Piso 7
Col Polanco
11560 Mexico D F Mexico

International Thomson Publishing GmbH
Konigswinterer Strasse 418
53227 Bonn
Germany

International Thomson Publishing Asia
221 Henderson Road
#05-10 Henderson Building
Singapore 0315

International Thomson Publishing—Japan
Hirakawacho Kyowa Building, 3F
2-2-1 Hirakawacho
Chiyoda-ku, Tokyo 102
Japan

   4 5 6 7 8 9 10 XXX 03 02 01 00 99 98

Library of Congress Cataloging-in-Publication Data

Schirrmacher, Robert, 1946–
      Art and creative development for young children / Robert
   Schirrmacher. — 3rd ed.
            p.   cm.
      Includes bibliographical references and index.
      ISBN 0–8273–7639–1
      1. Art—Study and teaching (Early childhood)—United States.
   2. Creative ability—United States. 3. Child development—United
   States. 4. Creative activities and seat work. 5. Curriculum
   planning—United States.   I. Title.
   LB1139.5.A78S35   1997
   372.5'044—dc21   96-46234
                              CIP

CONTENTS

PREFACE

Young children, art, and creativity are very compatible. Young children are often noisy, active, and messy. Art too can be noisy, active, and messy. Art can also be quiet and meticulous like a child who sits motionless while small fingers try to glue together pieces of paper, yarn, and ribbon. Art allows children to experiment and explore, to see what they can create. It is fun even though the finished product might not resemble anything in the real world. With older children, art begins to approximate reality more closely, as in the picture drawn by Lea. Lea, who lives in South Africa, created a very detailed elephant including long trunk, tusks, and what appears to be a bug or animal hitching a ride.

What is your earliest recollection of art? Perhaps you remember painting in preschool and going to the easel, like the girl in the photograph. She spent a lot of time using colorful strokes of paint to fill her canvas. Or maybe you remember getting glue all over your fingers while doing a collage in kindergarten and then having fun peeling it off when it dried. You might have made something like the sample shown in the photograph. It was fun to do but really doesn't resemble anything. The artist who created the collage in the photograph used paint, paper, and markers. Maybe your artwork found its way into your baby book or onto your bedroom wall. Maybe it was hastily thrown away. You may remember carefully coloring the pages in a coloring book, making sure to stay within the lines. The author remembers a kindergarten experience of being unable to sew together two pieces of red netting to make a Christmas stocking and being removed from the group. Inability was, and is, no reason to be put in time out.

This book journeys back to our childhoods as budding artists and forward to our futures as professional early childhood educators who will help young children reach their creative and artistic potential. It is written for practicing early childhood educators and those preparing to work with children in a public or private preschool, child care, and kindergarten through third grade setting. Teachers of infants, toddlers, and older children will also find this book useful. Sound principles and basic art media are appropriate regardless of the age of the artist.

The book is written from three different perspectives. It attempts to synthesize the author's training and experience as an artist, teacher of young children, and teacher educator. The book is neither a cookbook of activities nor a review of theory and research. It is readable and practical.

There is a systematic attempt to merge theory with practice. Knowing what and how to provide for an art activity is as important as knowing why. The book, therefore, is based on a developmental perspective. Knowing about child development, the nature of children's art, creativity, artistic elements, sensory stimulation, and aesthetics forms a backdrop for how one approaches the teaching and discovery of art. The teacher plays a key role as facilitator within a recommended art center approach, maximizing creative expression, responsible freedom, decision making, and discovery. The book closes with several helpful appendices.

FEATURES

Special features of the text include chapter objectives, summaries, and review questions. Abundant class-tested activities are included throughout the book. Age ranges are provided for many activities; however, these should be regarded as guidelines only. A teacher's knowledge of a particular child's developmental level must be the main guide in determining the appropriateness of any activity.

There is an old saying that goes, "If it's not broken, don't fix it!" Positive response to the first two editions has led the author to "leave alone what was working." In the third edition, however, several new features have been added. Many new photographs depict infants, toddlers, preschoolers, kindergartners, and school-age children engaged in producing art. The author believes it important that the book address an age range from birth through age eight. The photographs depict the ethnic diversity found in our homes, schools, and centers. They also give an international perspective, with samples of children's art from around the world.

The eighteen chapters are clustered around five main sections. Each section contains three or more chapters and uses photographs and questions to introduce the chapters that follow. The addition of sections connects the material, helping the chapters to flow and develop cohesively.

Each chapter has an opening section that includes a case box with a photograph and several thought-provoking questions. The purposes of this section are to stimulate thinking, foster group discussion, and motivate the reader.

This third edition can be used in early childhood teacher education programs at two- and four-year colleges. The text reflects an art focus, emphasizing child-directed (as opposed to teacher-directed) activities and outlining an art center approach. It is presently being used in courses such as Early Childhood Art or Creative Activities for Young Children. It will be useful in your work with toddlers, preschoolers, kindergartners, and children in the primary grades. This third edition reflects a major revision and the reader will find the following new features:

NEW   Chapters replace units. The order of the chapters has been reworked. The text begins with a discussion about creativity as a foundation for art-related classroom activity. Creativity and creative expression form the basis for art and artistic expression.

NEW   Media and art activities from former Units 18 and 19 have been distributed into individual chapters. Instructors can use their class meetings to overview the chapter contents and conduct workshops in specific art media. The activities are provided as suggestions to enhance and supplement, rather than replace, child-directed art activity.

NEW   Potentially unsafe and high-risk art activities using rubber cement, bleach, dye, powder tempera and electrical appliances have been deleted. Even adequate supervision cannot guarantee a safe experience.

NEW   Many new child-centered art activities have been added, including simple ways to make your own paper.

NEW   Separate chapters on Creative Experiences and Art Assessment have been added.

NEW   Sections on multicultural arts-and-crafts ideas, multiple intelligences, and the Reggio Emilia experience have been added.

NEW Icons are used to indicate the age appropriateness of art activities as follows:

T = Older toddlers and Twos

P = Preschoolers or Threes and Fours

K = Kindergartners or Fives

S = School-age children or Fives through Eights

The NAEYC guidelines for Developmentally Appropriate Practices (DAP) have been expanded to focus on art practices. They are listed in the front and back inside cover pages. Guidelines for DAP are cross-referenced throughout the text. The icon **N** indicates a statement supported by the NAEYC position paper on Developmentally Appropriate Practices.

SUPPLEMENTS

An Instructor's Manual listing answers to review questions is available free upon classroom adoption of the text.

ACKNOWLEDGMENTS

To:

Amanda Brooke and Lauren Taylor with love.

David Black, professional photographer, Mobile, Alabama.

Vincent Justin West

Smithfield families, Mobile, Alabama.

Marie Lynch, former graduate student and kindergarten teacher, Mobile, Alabama.

Anne Brandon, Directress. The Montessori Academy, Mobile, Alabama.

Leslie Welch, Director. L'Ecole School for the Gifted and Talented; Mobile, Alabama.

Christ United Methodist Church Preschool and Mothers' Day Out, Mobile, Alabama.

Wendy McEarchern, owner and director of Green Fields School, Mobile, Alabama.

Margaret Mactavish, former Director, and her teachers. First Congregational Early Childhood Center, Winter Park, Florida.

Children and parents with whom I have worked in Michigan, Illinois, Florida, Alabama, and California. All former and present students of child development and early childhood education who have helped me refine my thinking on children's art.

Karen Lavroff-Hawkins, former Delmar editor.

Vera L. De Pass and her staff at the Center for Employment and Training, Montessori Child Development Center, San Jose, California.

Barbara Rodriguez, High/Scope trainer, San Jose, California.

Child Development Inc. Centers: Green Valley and Bachrodt, San Jose, California.

Christie Van Staden, Faculty of Education, University of South Africa.

Louise Derman-Sparks, Anti-Bias Project, Pacific Oaks College, Pasadena, California.

Florence Pirofski, Child Study Department, West Valley College, San Jose, California.

Aline D. Wolf, Pennsylvania Montessori Academy, Altoona, Pennsylvania.

Faculty, staff, parents, and children at our two child-development centers: San Jose City College and Evergreen Valley College. A special thanks to the teachers and director for making the commitment to an art center by providing a room and resources.

Jay S. Whitney, early childhood education editor at Delmar Publishers and friend. Thanks for the extra time to polish this third edition.

Staff at Delmar Publishers for your expertise in once again turning a stack of photos and pages of material into a creative work of art.

The Art & Creative Materials Institute, Inc. for providing the material for Appendix F. Readers are encouraged to contact the Institute at 100 Boylston St., Suite 1050, Boston, MA 02116 for free materials on art safety.

The reviewers, whose advice and enthusiasm made this finished book possible, are Linda Aulgur, Stephens College, Columbia, Missouri; Kristin G. Congdon, University of Central Florida, Orlando, Florida; Jill E. Fox, Virginia Commonwealth University, Richmond, Virginia; and Jan McLanahan, North Shore Community College, Lynn, Massachusetts.

ABOUT THE AUTHOR

Robert Schirrmacher is Program Coordinator for Early Childhood Education at the University of California, Santa Cruz Education Extension Department. He also is a full-time Instructor with the San Jose/Evergreen Community College District. Currently, he teaches and supervises Early Childhood Education majors at two on-campus laboratory child development centers (San Jose City College and Evergreen Valley College). His teaching responsibilities include early childhood education, child development, child guidance, and curriculum courses. The author received his Ph.D. in Early Childhood Education from the University of Illinois. His experience includes teaching preschool, kindergarten, and first grade. He has also assisted in Montessori schools, directed programs for young children, and taught early childhood education at the undergraduate and graduate levels. He continues to serve as consultant to parent groups and public and private early childhood programs. As an advocate for developmentally appropriate education and quality care for young children, the author is actively involved in professional organizations at the local, state, and national levels.

NAEYC GUIDELINES FOR DEVELOPMENTALLY APPROPRIATE ART PRACTICE

Curriculum planning emphasizes learning as an interactive process. Teachers prepare the environment for children to learn through active exploration and interaction with adults, other children, and materials.

Workbooks, worksheets, coloring books, and adult-made models of art products for children to copy are *not* appropriate for young children, especially those younger than six.

Basic learning materials and activities for an appropriate curriculum include (among others) supplies of paper, water-based paint and markers, and other materials for creative expression.

Adults provide opportunities for children to choose from among a variety of activities, materials, and equipment; and time to explore through active involvement. Adults facilitate children's engagement with materials and activities and extend the child's learning by asking questions or making suggestions that stimulate children's thinking.

Children of all ages need uninterrupted periods of time to become involved, investigate, select, and persist at activities. The teacher's role in child-chosen activity is to prepare the environment with stimulating, challenging activity choices and then to facilitate children's engagement.

Once we understand that toddlers learn by active involvement with people and by manipulating objects, it becomes clear that such activities as coloring books, worksheets, and models made of clay or other materials that children are expected to imitate are *inappropriate*.

Appropriate for Toddlers

Toddlers are given appropriate art media such as large crayons, watercolor markers, and large paper. Adults expect toddlers to explore and manipulate art materials and do *not* expect them to produce a finished art product. Adults *never* use food for art because toddlers are developing self-regulatory skills and must learn to distinguish between food and other objects that are not to be eaten.

Inappropriate for Toddlers

Toddlers are "helped" by teachers to produce a product, follow the adult-made model, or color a coloring book or ditto sheet. Tactilely sensitive toddlers are required to finger paint or are given edible finger paint or play dough because they will probably put it in their mouths.

Appropriate for Threes

Adults provide many materials and opportunities for three-year-olds to develop fine motor skills such as crayons, brushes, paints, markers, play dough, blunt scissors. Although the scribbles of three-year-olds are more controlled than those of toddlers, and they will create designs with horizontal and vertical strokes, and will sometimes name their drawings and paintings, adults do not expect a representational product. Art is viewed as creative expression and exploration of materials.

Inappropriate for Threes

Adults expect children to demonstrate fine motor skills by cutting out figures or shapes, by coloring within the lines in coloring books or on ditto sheets, or by following the teacher's directions and models to create identical art products. When children draw or paint pictures, teachers ask, "What is it?" and lead children to believe that only a representational picture is valued.

Appropriate for Fours and Fives

Children have daily opportunities for aesthetic expression and appreciation through art and music. Children experiment and enjoy various forms of music. A variety of art media is available for creative expression, such as easel and finger painting and clay.

Inappropriate for Fours and Fives

Art and music are provided only when time permits. Art consists of coloring predrawn forms, copying an adult-made model of a product, or following other adult-prescribed directions .

Appropriate for School-Age Children

Art, music, movement, woodworking, drama, and dance (and opportunities for other physical activity) are integrated throughout each day as relevant to the curriculum and as needed for children to express themselves, aesthetically and physically, and to express ideas and feelings. Specialists work with classroom teachers and children. Children explore and experiment with various art media and forms of music.

Inappropriate for School-Age Children

Art, music, and physical education are taught as separate subjects only once a week. Specialists do not coordinate closely with classroom teachers. Representational art, evaluated for approximation to reality, is emphasized. Children are expected to follow specific directions resulting in identical projects. So-called "crafts" substitute for artistic expression.

Creativity

*T*he author believes so strongly in creativity that it will be explored as a separate aspect of development in Chapter 4. Others would include creativity under cognition, since creativity depends on thinking. What is creativity? Can you give an example? Creativity is an elusive term; although we all would agree it's important, we might not all agree on what it is. Because creativity peaks during the early years, it seems fitting that Chapter 1, Understanding Creativity, should contain extensive discussion on the nature of creativity.

Look at the toddlers in the photograph. What are they doing? Is anything creative happening?

The children have been given play dough and an array of clay tools. What are they using? Can you locate the tortilla press, garlic press, pizza cutter, cookie cutter, hard-boiled-egg slicer, detergent bottle lid, rolling pin, masher, and pie crimper? Kitchen drawers hold many objects that can be combined creatively with play dough. The kitchen tools are being used in different ways: this is creativity. One girl is forsaking all tools and is about to use her hands. Tools should always supplement but not replace the actions of the fingers and hands. Look at the boy with the rolling pin. What is he doing? He is being creative by using his rolling pin in a novel way. Rather than rolling, he is poking the handle into the play dough. The children are engaged in creative processing with kitchen tools and play dough.

Look at the photograph depicting children's sculptures displayed on paper plates. How creative! Each sculpture is unique, as is the artist who created it.

Look at Sue Ann's picture. What do you see? She has taken creative liberty by giving the sun facial features, including a wide smile. Rays warm the monkeys who swing from forklike trees and are oblivious to the zebra who appears to be dwarfed by the tall grass. Sue Ann's interpretation of wildlife in her South African home is personally meaningful and creatively rendered.

Chapter 2, Creative Thinking, identifies the components of creative thinking, also called divergent production, and activities that easily can be incorporated into small or large group times.

Besides art, how else can children express their creativity? Chapter 3 identifies Creative Experiences in the areas of play, language, music, and movement which incorporate creative expression throughout the day.

CHAPTER 1

Understanding Creativity

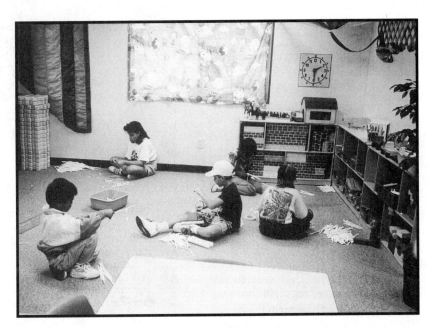

Would you give children a handful of straws and roll of masking tape and ask them to make whatever they want? At what age could they do this? Why would a teacher provide this type of art experience?

The school-age children in this photograph enjoy the challenge of getting the straws to stay together while making the resulting structure look like something. They have chosen to work independently. Each child's straw structure will be different. Each child will have a creative end product.

OBJECTIVES

After studying this chapter, the student will be able to

- Explain creativity as an attitude, process, product, skill, set of personality traits, and set of environmental conditions
- Compare and contrast creativity with conformity and convergent thinking
- Discuss the relationship between creativity and intelligence
- Discuss ways adults can facilitate children's creative expression
- Explain the concept of multiple intelligences

INTRODUCTION

What or who do you associate with creativity? Do you think of architecture by Frank Lloyd Wright, a play by Shakespeare, a painting by Picasso, Henry Ford's Model T, or the *Nutcracker Suite?* These are classic examples of the creative works of some very creative individuals. You probably had other examples. Children were not included in this list. Were they included in yours? Let us focus on creativity and see how it specifically relates to young children.

Consider This:

Having converted their spacious basement into several play spaces, the Cliffords are involved in family day care. Today, Mika has put a hair roller on each one of her fingers, saying, "See my rings, me pretty." Yoshi has taken a spare roll of toilet paper and is wrapping up the dolls. He says, "Got hurted, fix." Rhonida is putting the teddy bear counters into a bowl atop the play stove saying, "Mmmm, hot soup; it's good for you. Sit and eat." Cassie has found an empty shoe box and is planning to make a boat for the small plastic family. She says, "They are rich and famous movie stars and live on one of those yok (yacht) things on the ocean, and way up in the mountains." The Cliffords do not dismiss these episodes as humorous but unimportant. They see these playful behaviors as indicators that the children in their care are developing creatively. The children are fortunate to have adults like the Cliffords who accept, value, and plan for their creative expression.

Reflection

Identify someone whom you would call creative. What is it about this person that earns the title of creative? Think about yourself. What is it about you that makes you unique, different, and special? What do you do creatively? There is at least one thing. Is it cooking, gardening, home decorating, writing poetry, or sewing? Think about your skills and talents. Is it a special dish that you cook, a way of decorating your home on a limited budget, or a gift of putting colors and clothes together? Upon reflection, you are probably more creative than you realize. Celebrate your own creativity. It is the first step in nurturing children's creativity.

FIGURE 1–1   *Creative expression begins early in life.*

BEGINNINGS OF CREATIVITY

Creative expression begins early in life (see Figure 1–1). Babies manipulate toys, explore space, discover their body parts, test hunches about their immediate world, and even solve problems. For example, Lea wants a toy rattle that she has accidentally kicked to the foot of her crib. Through trial-and-error behavior she discovers that she can get the toy by tugging at the blanket it rests on.

YANI: ART PRODIGY

According to Newman (1990), Wang Yani can be considered an art prodigy. Yani, the daughter of Chinese oil painter Wang Shiqiang, began painting when she was only two and had her first exhibit at age four. Two years later she had completed some 4,000 paintings. Her works have been exhibited throughout the world. Perhaps you have heard about her or viewed her exhibit.

Yani began painting like most children, smearing paint and making unrecognizable shapes. Yani's father credits her success to her drive, not to talent. Frustrated and annoyed that her pictures bore so little resemblance to her mental images, at age three Yani proceeded to cram many years of artistic development into several months. She painted for hours on end, improving her skills through trial and error. Although Yani believed she was just having fun, her father believes she was refining her craft (Newman, 1990).

Yani's art is filled with delightful creatures. Her favorites are monkeys, and many people believe that Yani identifies with monkeys and their antics. By age six, however, Yani had expanded and began painting birds, flowers, landscapes, and people. Monkey antics gave way to children and landscapes of the scenic region of Southern Chin where Yani lives with her family.

Is Yani naturally talented or was she taught? Yani's father claims he did not teach her the way art is typically taught in Chinese schools. He gave up his own painting in oils so as not to influence her style. Instead, Yani's father guided her into developing her sense of perception and into discovering techniques for controlling her brushes, ink, and water. As of 1990 Yani's father works full-time as her manager and curator of her works. Yani is now in her teens. Her artwork is not for sale.

The steps to Yani's rapid development as a gifted artist appear so simple that one wonders why there are not more child art prodigies. Yani had the concentration, drive, determination, and motivation to master painting and to develop her own technique. She received support from her artistic father, who provided space, materials, and encouragement. Still, one cannot dismiss the role of natural talent and teaching in cases involving child prodigies.

There are many examples of creativity in adults and young children. Merely identifying examples, however, does not help us understand the nature of creativity. Just what is creativity? How will we know if something or someone is creative? One way to attempt to understand creativity is by defining it.

DEFINING CREATIVITY

There are many ways to define creativity. Perhaps this has added to the confusion, misunderstanding, and mystique surrounding it. People have different definitions for the same term. How would you define creativity? Some generally accepted definitions are

- the ability to see things in new ways
- boundary breaking and going beyond the information given
- thinking unconventionally
- making something unique
- combining unrelated things into something new

How does your definition compare with these? Torrance (1963), a pioneer in creativity, has chosen to define creativity as the process of sensing problems or gaps in information, forming ideas or hypotheses, and communicating the results. For example, two five-year-olds, Missy and Eric, want to build a school, but they have no blocks or pieces of wood. They consider using shoe boxes, which are fairly durable and stackable, for a base.

Although our attempts to define creativity may provide us with some general feel for the concept, there are other ways to better understand and explain creativity.

EXPLAINING CREATIVITY

Although there is no single definition of creativity, there are different ways to explain it. Creativity can be explained as a(n)

1. attitude
2. process
3. product
4. skill
5. set of personality traits
6. set of environmental conditions

Creativity Is an Attitude Not an Aptitude

For young children it may be more helpful to view creativity as a way of doing things. Creativity is a special and different way of viewing the world in which there are no right or wrong answers, only possibilities. Think of creativity as an attitude rather than an aptitude. Children demonstrate a creative attitude when they:

- try out new ideas and different ways of doing things
- push boundaries and explore possibilities
- manipulate and transform ideas and materials
- take things apart and put them back together in different ways
- physically play with objects
- imagine, engage in fantasy, or just daydream
- solve problems or try to figure things out
- ask questions or challenge accepted ways of thinking or acting

Creativity Is the Process of Doing

The previous examples view creativity as a process. A visit to an early childhood center should find children engaged in creative processing as they manipulate and play with objects. For example, Mr. Omar wants his preschoolers to engage in creative processing. At the art table he has put out play dough, ice cream sticks, cookie cutters, small toy dinosaurs, and large buttons. He provides options without overwhelming the children with an endless array of props. The children creatively process by combining the materials with play dough. Adding the props has extended the creative range of possibilities and moved play dough from a simple to a more complex activity. There are many possibilities and combinations. Mr. Omar knows that creative processing might lead to some creative products. Xandra prefers to alternate between rolling and flattening her play dough while disregarding the other objects. Mr. Omar accepts Xandra's preferences for processing and does not force or expect her to make

FIGURE 1–2   Creative processing by painting with a twig

something. Using one's hands to work play dough is an important skill in itself.

A process approach to creativity holds that a person can engage in the creative process even though it may not result in a finished product. All people are capable of creative processing (see Figure 1–2). Creative processing includes thinking, speaking, playing, writing, dancing, singing, playing a musical instrument, experimenting with objects, transforming materials, and manipulating ideas and objects. Therefore, the artwork of young children can be considered creative according to this process explanation. Artists, whether young or old, engage in the same processes when pounding clay, drawing, mixing colors, painting, weaving, and making a collage. In the early years, children's creative functioning emphasizes a process orientation. The emphasis is on making and doing rather than on completing a project. For example, children may paint but end up throwing the picture away or not claiming it to take home. The primary satisfaction is in the processing, the smearing with paint, rather than in what it turns out to be.

Creativity May or May Not Result in a Finished Product

Sometimes, the creative process results in a product. Creative processing with an idea might result in making something new or different. In Mr. Omar's example, three other children were seated with Xandra at the art table. Pauley shoved his ice cream stick through three balls of play dough. He said, "That's my caterpillar. He's very hungry just like in our story." Shameer buried her dinosaurs in play dough and announced, "They're hiding." B-Jay flattened his play dough while embedding several buttons into his pancake shape. Different processing resulted in different products, each one unique and special just like their creators. Mr. Omar accepted the fact that some children like Xandra are process-oriented while others like Pauley, Shameer, and B-jay are more interested in making a finished product. All children were successful in this creative endeavor.

The light bulb was Edison's creative product. Bell invented the telephone. Both creators made a unique product that revolutionized society. Other creative products could include a musical score, medical cure, work of art, or scientific principle. Gifted creators include Mozart, Plato, Galileo, Newton, and Einstein, among others. Focusing exclusively on revolutionary products restricts creativity to a small core of gifted elite. Most of us are truly uncreative by comparison.

According to this view, creative functioning is not accessible to the masses. Only a small percentage of the general population, the gifted elite, can be considered creative as judged by their unique works.

This product view of creativity automatically excludes children, because few, if any, produce something that is truly novel or that contributes significantly to the advancement of society. Still, most adults would consider young children capable of creativity. For example, from a product perspective, there is nothing unique about mixing red and blue paint at the easel and creating purple. Either young children are uncreative or the product explanation for creativity is too narrow. Perhaps the product explanation should be qualified to state that the object created must be unique or new to the creator. If so, the swirling of purple paint may be considered creative for Brad, a toddler who has not yet discovered that red paint mixed with blue makes purple. Modifying a product explanation to reflect personal originality extends creativity to the activities of young children.

Young children are often product-oriented. Three-year-old Lisa delights in finishing her art projects and often insists on taking several examples home. Some children may have learned that a completed art product will bring praise from adults. Pictures that look like something may even get taped to the refrigerator door. It is hoped that young children will not abandon a creative process orientation in favor of making art products that look like something solely to please adults. This is not the essence of creativity. Artistic processing may not produce a souvenir. Evidence of a finished art product often justifies a child's existence in school. The finished picture shows what he or she did today. Young children should engage in artistic processing and product making for themselves. The child who fails to bring home a finished painting may be no less productive or creative than the one who insists on finishing a picture.

The product and process explanations for creativity are not mutually exclusive. Choosing the creative process over the product or vice versa should not be an either-or decision. The process and product are complementary. If it were not for the creative process, the production of creative products would be impossible. Creative products are built through creative processing. Rome was not built in one day! It is unfair to acknowledge only the creative product. If the creative product remains the sole criterion for assessing creativity, it is obvious that creativity must be reserved for the gifted elite.

Creativity As a Skill

Although all children are capable of creativity, the potential to create remains dormant without practice. With practice, the potential to create becomes a reality. For example, the skill of playing tennis is quickly lost without practice. Good tennis players practice frequently. So too the skill of creativity requires exercise to grow. Without practice, the ability to write, make music, sing, dance, and paint would be lost. Creativity as a potential and skill requires exercise.

When a discussion of creativity arises, many adults are prone to state, "I'm just not creative." Everyone seems to have a friend or relative who is creative, but not all people believe themselves to be creative. In part, this relates to the old idea of a creative elite and a product explanation for creativity. Still, all people evidence some degree of creativity, whether in writing, sewing, cooking, making crafts, pursuing hobbies, home decorating, or even teaching! It is important to find a creative outlet and practice the process or skill involved. What is your creative outlet?

Still, why do some adults feel themselves uncreative when by contrast young children are consid-

ered highly creative? What has happened between early childhood and adulthood? Research on creativity suggests that the child reaches a peak of creative functioning during the early childhood years. Torrance (1965) plots the degree of creative functioning versus age. Creativity peaks at about four to four and a half years of age and is followed by a sharp drop upon entrance into elementary school. Perhaps the push for conformity, accountability, and academics in elementary school accounts for this sharp drop. Yet this drop is not inevitable. Environmental conditions and practice can keep the spirit of creativity alive.

Creativity As a Set of Personality Traits

The personality approach attempts to identify the personality profile of highly creative individuals. Researchers have identified highly creative individuals and attempted to identify personality traits that these individuals share. Some of these include

- an openness to the new and unexpected
- a tolerance for ambiguity
- a willingness to experiment and take risks
- impulsivity
- curiosity
- a preference for complexity
- being highly intuitive
- sensitivity
- flexibility
- introversion
- individualism
- nonconformity, daring to be different
- independence
- playfulness
- a sense of humor
- preference for being alone, may be unsocial or very social

The list of personality traits is extensive, and not every highly creative individual will possess all the traits. Also, the list of personality traits will vary depending on the researcher. Torrance (1962) identified the following seven indicators of creativity that may be useful in identifying and explaining the behavior of the highly creative young child.

Curiosity   The child's questioning is persistent and purposeful. Curiosity can be either verbal: "What is that?" or "Why?"—or nonverbal: manipulation and active exploration.

Flexibility   If one approach fails, the creative child will try a variety of different approaches.

Sensitivity to Problems   The child is quick to see gaps in information, exceptions to the rules, and contradictions in what is seen and heard.

Redefinition   The child sees hidden meaning in statements that others accept at face value. New uses are found for familiar objects. The child sees connections between things that appear unrelated to others.

Self-Feeling   The child has a feeling of self-importance and individuality. Self-direction permits the child to work alone. Merely following directions or conforming results in boredom.

Originality   The child has surprising, uncommon, interesting ideas.

Insight   The child has access to realms of the mind that the less creative visit only in their dreams. Much time is spent toying with ideas and possibilities.

Identifying the one typical personality pattern of the highly creative individual may be impossible. There is too much variation among creative individuals. Still, a set of global traits may provide some assistance in identifying these individuals and understanding the nature of creativity.

Creativity As a Set of Environmental Conditions

If creativity is an inherent potential, there must be things that can be done to enhance or retard its development. Environmental conditions include people, places, objects, and experiences. Children do not create out of a vacuum. They need a source of

Profile of a Gifted/Talented/Highly Creative Child

Think of a child that you have observed or worked with that you would call creative. What words would you use to describe this child? While the following traits describe creative children, no one child will perfectly match this tentative profile. Creative children tend to be

1. original, imaginative, spontaneous, resourceful, and uninhibited.
2. sensitive to sensory stimuli and have heightened awareness. They are open to new ideas, see things afresh, and are intuitive.
3. curious, alert, impulsive, risk taking, adventurous, and into everything.
4. independent in thinking and social behavior. They can appear aloof and may prefer older peers and adults to friends their own age.
5. developmentally advanced, precocious, fast learners. They have good memories, extensive vocabularies, and are interested in books, often learning to read by themselves at an early age.
6. perfectionists with a good sense of humor; they ask "why" questions.
7. persistent, with a long attention span; they can stick with a plan or idea.
8. nonconforming and unconventional; they question or challenge the status quo.
9. inventive and innovative, and good at solving problems.
10. not overly concerned with being neat or prompt; they may be easily bored with routine and mundane tasks.

inspiration or an experiential background from which to draw. For example, a child who has never visited an airport or been aboard a plane will have difficulty discussing these concepts or incorporating them into block play, dramatic play, movement, art, and other creative activities. By contrast, a child who has visited an airport and flown on a plane will be able to discuss these experiences and use them as pivots for creative expression. Parnes (1967) draws an analogy between a kaleidoscope and creativity. The more numerous and colorful the pieces in the drum of a kaleidoscope, the greater the variety of resulting shapes, colors, and patterns. Likewise, in creative expression, the greater one's background of experiences with people, places, and objects, the greater the range of possibilities to draw from in creative activity.

Home Environment   Obviously, the home environment is a critical factor in a child's development of creativity. Is there a home environment that optimizes the development of creativity? In MacKin-non's (1962) study of creative adults, he found that the following family variables operated during their childhoods:

- Parents respected their child.
- Parents had confidence in their child's ability.
- Parents granted their child unusual freedom to explore and make decisions.
- Discipline was almost always consistent and predictable.
- Family values stressed integrity, quality, intellectual and cultural efforts, success, and ambition.

The above factors and behaviors can be practiced in home and school settings to foster children's creative development (see Figure 1–3).

The Creativity Equation

Children will be creative on their own but there are conditions or factors that nurture creativity. They can be combined into the following equation:

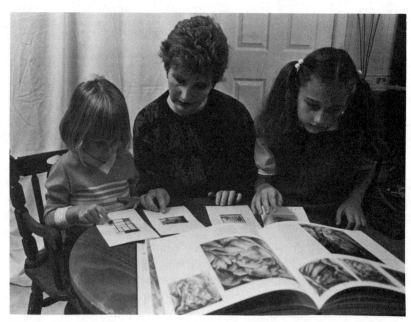

FIGURE 1–3   Parents can discuss art with their children.

```
┌─────────────────────────────────────┐
│        Unconditional Love from        │
│           Significant Adults          │
│      Acceptance, Encouragement,       │
│            and Nurturance             │
└─────────────────────────────────────┘

                   +

┌─────────────────────────────────────┐
│         Autonomy and Freedom          │
└─────────────────────────────────────┘

                   ↓

┌─────────────────────────────────────┐
│       Competence and Self-Esteem      │
└─────────────────────────────────────┘

                   ↓

┌─────────────────────────────────────┐
│       Risk Taking and Creativity      │
└─────────────────────────────────────┘
```

Children need unconditional love, acceptance, encouragement, and nurturance from adults who are significant in their lives. These include family members, relatives, friends, and teachers. Children need adults who empower them to exercise responsible freedom to do things on their own and to make things happen. In turn, this develops competence and enhances their self-esteem. Competence and self-esteem are reciprocal. Making something on their own makes children feel good about what they accomplished. Good feelings about themselves motivate children to keep trying new things and become even more competent. In turn, children will feel safe to take risks and trust their creative impulses to venture out and dance to the beat of their own drummers.

OBSTACLES TO CREATIVITY

Just as a stimulating environment and family factors can enhance creativity, negative conditions can restrict it. Four environmental conditions that provide potential obstacles to creativity are

- parents
- school
- sex roles
- society, culture, and tradition

Parents

Parents often have certain expectations for their children. Unfortunately, creative children may not conform to these expectations. Highly creative children often question authority, limits, adult logic, and

---

ACEI Position Paper on Children's Right to the Arts

The Association for Childhood Education International (Jalongo, 1990) believes that children have a right to the expressive arts. In order to reaffirm the importance of the expressive arts in school, educators must accept the following beliefs.

1. Every child has a right to opportunities for imaginative expression.
2. Educating the child's imagination is education for the future.
3. The educated imagination is the key to equity and intercultural understanding.
4. Children's creative productivity is qualitatively different from adults'.
5. Creative expression should permeate the entire curriculum.
6. Imagination is the key to artistry in teaching and excellence in our schools.
7. We must refashion our schools for the twenty-first century.

explanations. These children act and behave differently. Parents may view these creative behaviors as misbehavior. They may perceive and treat their creative child as odd, immature, abnormal, or naughty. Parents may need to be informed and educated about the nature of creativity through classroom observation, readings, and informal sessions in which they discuss creativity and engage in creative processing themselves.

School

The teacher may not understand, encourage, or value the creative child. Too often the creative child must operate in a school situation based entirely on conformity and convergent thinking. The child is taught that black is the color of night when he or she has experienced it as purple-blue or licorice. With the current emphasis on academics in early childhood education, there is a concern that less time will be spent on creative activities. It is also possible that some children feel confined in noncreative classrooms and "shut down" or rebel to protect their creative integrity. It is important for teachers to understand, value, and encourage creativity by providing an abundance of curricular activities that foster it.

Sex Roles

Sex roles limit boys and girls to certain types of behavior on the basis of gender. Creative functioning, however, transcends sex role barriers. Forcing children to conform to sex roles denies them their optimal development as individuals. We do children a disservice when we expect boys to be active, independent, and rugged, and girls to be passive, dependent, and gentle. If sex roles were to dictate, boys would be denied access to quieter expressive activities and girls would be denied access to reactive manipulative experiences. Either way someone loses, since both types of experience are vital to creative processing.

Society, Culture, and Tradition

Society, culture, and tradition are distinct concepts, but each dictates a certain set of behaviors, values, and attitudes. These are transmitted to children at a very early age in the form of expectations. Unfortunately, creative children may operate with a different agenda. Problems arise for highly creative children in a milieu where adults have all the answers and children are expected to fit into a rigid behavioral mold or pattern. Often, the rationale includes, "That's the way it's done in our family" or "If it was good enough for me, it's good enough for you." It is important to respect, reinforce, and uphold the expectations of society, tradition, and one's culture without sacrificing individuality in the process.

CHILDREN NEED ADULTS WHO FACILITATE CREATIVE EXPRESSION

The following strategies send a message to children that their creative expression is valued.

1. Celebrate creativity.

Help children identify with creative heroes. For example, bring in telescopes or visit a planetarium on Galileo's birthday. Read books about creative individuals. Discuss their accomplishments. Ask, "What if we didn't have lights?" Turn off the lights and light candles. Discuss the importance of the light bulb. Point out creativity when you see it: "A Velcro lunch box, now that's a creative idea." Accept and celebrate your own creative side.

2. Value children's creativity.

View creative development as a vital component of the whole child. Allow them the freedom to think and act differently. Accept their uniqueness. Accept their attempts at creative processing which might not result in a finished product. Advocate on behalf of creativity and inform others. Discuss the importance of creativity with children, parents, staff, and administrators. Speak up against budget cuts for the arts or attempts to replace play with academics.

3. Be a creative partner.

Empower children by making yourself available to enter their creative worlds. Be a play partner who follows the lead of children rather than imposing your own plot, sequence, and script.

4. Provide time and space for creative expression.

Children need plenty of space to lay out materials and work alone or together to give form to their ideas. Time and space should be fluid and flexible. Tables, chairs, and movable units may need to be arranged to meet the demands of the activity at hand. Creativity may entail noise, excitement, movement, and clutter. Perhaps this is why young children and creativity are so compatible. An excessive concern for constant cleanliness, quiet, or neatness inhibits creative "messing about."

5. Provide toys and materials conducive to creativity.

Let children creatively use and transform toys and materials. Accept the fact that small building blocks from the manipulative center will be transported to the house area and used as food or money. Clean smocks from the art center might find their way into the dress-up area where they will be used as capes for superheroes. Provide props for pretend and fantasy play as well as recycled junk. Do not feel that you must impart a specified purpose or use. Children will turn safe and clean trash into creative treasures. In choosing and providing toys and materials, *open-ended* items are more conducive to creative expression than *closed-ended* ones. Open-ended materials are loosely structured and do not require one right or correct way to work. They have multiple rather than single outcomes. For example, water, sand blocks, play dough, and building pieces are open-ended in that they empower children to use them in creative ways. There is no one preset right way to build with blocks or play with water. By contrast, a puzzle is an example of a closed-ended material in that it is designed with a single outcome or correct purpose, to fit the pieces together in a predetermined pattern. Although one can use puzzle pieces creatively, for example, as food or money, that is not their intent. A comparison and contrast of open- and closed-ended toys and materials is found in Table 1–1.

Toys and play materials can also be categorized as simple and complex. Simple toys and materials foster some degree of creative expression whereas complex toys and materials extend the potential for creativity. Toys and play materials that offer some degree of creativity can be made complex. For example, blocks alone are considered simple in that they can be creatively combined. Block play can be made more complex by adding props, including small containers, vehicles, and animals. The same is true for water and sand play. Adding kitchen containers to water and sand play expands the creative possibilities.

OPEN-ENDED	CLOSED-ENDED
are conducive to creativity	are conducive to conformity
have multiple outcomes	have single outcomes
have many uses	have a singular use
are multipurpose	have only one purpose
are used in many "right" ways	are used in only one right way
are flexible: have a use and purpose determined by child	are inflexible: have a use and purpose predetermined by adult
reflect unlimited range of possibilities or options	reflect very limited range, only one possible way

TABLE 1–1   Comparison of Open-Ended and Closed-Ended Materials

6. Provide a psychological climate conducive to creativity.

Children flourish in a psychologically safe setting which respects, trusts, and empowers them to act autonomously without the fear of criticism, rejection, failure, or pressure to conform. Children need to make choices and decisions, and to do things on their own in their own ways. By providing an array of materials and activities from which to choose, the environment can be set up to foster children's autonomy. An overly structured day revolving around teacher-directed activities impairs children's creative development. They quickly learn to override their drive for creativity and autonomy and instead become dependent on others for right answers or solutions.

7. Weave creativity and creative expression throughout your curriculum.

Creativity should not be approached as an isolated skill that must be scheduled into an already over-crowded day. Children cannot magically turn on their creativity to fill a half-hour time slot on alternating Fridays. The curricular areas provide ample opportunities for children to use both sides of the brain. For example, children may need to learn about the food groups and making healthy choices, but there are also creative ways to plan menus and make posters for healthy eating. A resourceful teacher will find ways to integrate creativity into the curriculum.

COMPARING AND CONTRASTING CREATIVITY

Another way of attempting to understand and explain creativity is through comparison and contrast. One way to learn about a concept is by comparing and contrasting it with other concepts that are either similar or different.

Creativity vs. Conformity and Convergent Thinking

Convergent, or noncreative, thinking and behavior based on conformity are built into our educational system and reflected in our school goals. There are facts and bodies of knowledge that we want all children to possess. For example, children need to know that up is the opposite of down, that a triangle has three sides, that wheels are round, that STOP on the traffic sign does not mean to run, and that there are five pennies in a nickel. This type of knowledge involves memory and convergent thinking in that all children are expected to come up with the one right answer. Beyond this, conformity in school often entails behaving in a certain way, with an emphasis on sitting still, speaking only when spoken to, obeying, not challenging authority, not questioning, compliance, and doing what is generally expected. Obviously, conformity is important if groups of people are to get along, whether in school or in the wider society. When it is carried to extremes, however, an emphasis on conformity and convergent thinking can kill the creative spirit.

Creativity vs. Intelligence

Creativity can also be compared and contrasted with intelligence. It has sometimes been erroneously assumed that a high IQ is needed to be creative. Research, however, indicates that high scores on tests of creativity are not correlated with high scores on IQ tests. A high IQ says something about intelligence, but it cannot guarantee high creativity. This is easy to understand, since answering items on an IQ test requires remembering bits and pieces of factual information and involves convergent or noncreative thinking. Thus, it is possible for a child with a high IQ to be quite uncreative compared with other children of average intelligence. It does seem, however, that some basic level of intellectual functioning and an average IQ near 100 is required for creativity. For example, a child must have some basic knowledge of the properties of a milk carton and transportation before he or she can creatively transform an empty milk carton into a moving van. Therefore, using tests of intelligence to screen highly creative children must be done judiciously. Such tests are merely one of many tools, including teacher observation and parental reports, that can be used. According to Torrance (1962), if we were to identify children as gifted solely on the basis of IQ tests, we would eliminate approximately 70 percent of the most creative. In summary, although some amount of intelligence is a prerequisite for creativity, a high IQ does not guarantee high creativity. In turn, average intelligence does not necessarily mean mediocre creative ability. Intelligence is merely one factor influencing creativity.

Because children's thinking is a vital concern of early childhood educators, it may be interesting to pursue further the relationship between intelligence and creativity. It appears that the profiles for the highly intelligent child and that for the highly creative child do not match. Nor does the profile for the child of low intelligence match the profile for the child of low creativity. Wallach and Kogan (1965) studied the interplay of intelligence and creativity in school-age children. Four patterns emerged.

1. High intelligence and high creativity—These children were flexible and could be serious at one time and playful at another. They could easily adapt to different learning environments. They were very self-confident and displayed high attention and concentration for school tasks. They also engaged in attention-getting and disruptive behavior.
2. Low intelligence and high creativity—These children were frustrated and had a difficult time in traditional schools. This probably tended to make them feel unworthy and inadequate. They were cautious, lacked self-confidence, and engaged in disruptive behavior.
3. Low intelligence and low creativity—These children did not appear to understand what school was all about. They spent their time in either intense physical activity or passive retreat.
4. High intelligence and low creativity—These children were devoted to achieving in school. They had high attention spans and high self-confidence. They were unlikely to act up in school and were well liked by their teachers.

Teachers were later asked to identify their ideal pupil from these four profiles. Which one would you select? Teachers overwhelmingly selected children characterized as highly intelligent but low on creativity. The behavior problems that could arise from creativity (or its stifling), as in 1, appear to outweigh any advantages or assets. It may be understandable why teachers in this study favored high intelligence over high creativity. Highly intelligent children follow directions, work independently, listen, pay attention, obey, and conform. On the other hand, the highly creative child is often viewed as a problem requiring individual attention. According to the general personality profile, highly creative children tend to be daydreamers, independent, nonconforming, impulsive, outspoken, challenging, and questioning individuals who test limits. It comes as no surprise that Getzels and Jackson (1962) also found that teachers favored high IQ but less creative children because they were easier to manage.

Multiple Intelligences   According to Gardner (1993), intelligence is not a single concept. He believes there are many ways of demonstrating one's intelligence. Gardner (1993) defines intelligence as the capacity to solve problems or make things that are valued by one's culture. Multiple intelligences include bodily-kinesthetic, musical-rhythmic, interpersonal, visual-spatial, verbal-linguistic, logical-mathematical, and intrapersonal. We all have some of each intelligence as well as particular strengths. Everyone can be characterized as smart in one or more of the intelligences. The multiple intelligences, related "smarts" and corresponding strengths and interests are depicted in Table 1–2.

All Children Are Creative but Not All Are Labeled Gifted or Talented   All children have the potential to create but some are more creative than others. What accounts for this difference? First, some children have had their creativity nurtured; others have not. Ways of nurturing children's creative potential are discussed in this chapter as well as in Chapters 2 and 3. Second, intelligence influences creative expression. Children of high intelligence who also demonstrate high creativity are labeled gifted. Children with creative aptitude for art, music, drama, or dance are labeled talented. In some schools children who are considered gifted and/or talented receive

INTELLIGENCE	"SMART"	STRENGTHS AND INTERESTS
bodily-kinesthetic	body	sports, movement, dance, acting, dramatics, large motor and playground activities
musical-rhythmic	music	singing, dancing, playing a musical instrument, listening to music
interpersonal	people	making friends, socializing, cooperative projects, being a leader, resolving peer conflicts
visual-spatial	pictures	art, looking at pictures, daydreaming, puzzles, maps, charts
verbal-linguistic	words	speaking, reading, writing, listening, telling stories, thinking in words, discussions, memorizing, word puzzles, word games
logical-mathematical	math	math, reasoning, logical and abstract thinking, problem solving, patterns, working with numbers, computers
intrapersonal	self	understands self, knows strengths and accepts limits, works alone, pursues own interests, reflective, self-paced learner

TABLE 1–2 Gardner's Multiple Intelligences (1993)

enrichment to challenge them and to supplement their regular courses of study. Chapter 5 continues our discussion of gifted and talented children.

CREATIVITY AND CHILD DEVELOPMENT

What is the relationship between creativity and a child's development? Are there any developmental benefits to a child's creative functioning? Whatever the form that creativity may take, the child develops large and small muscle skills through handling and manipulating the appropriate tools or apparatus. Musical instruments are played, paint is mixed and spread, clay is pounded, and the body moves to music and song. Creative expression can enhance physical development. Socially, it can also help children come to terms with themselves and others. At times creativity involves solitary thinking or grappling with a problem. At other times social skills, including sharing, taking turns, and entertaining other points of view, are practiced. Creative expression fosters emotional development and positive

mental health by validating the uniqueness of the individual. Juan, age three, made a clay dinosaur with two legs and an oversized head. He was proud of his accomplishment, and it did not matter if dinosaurs had four legs. Juan felt good about himself and the dinosaur he had created. Creativity fosters success and mastery, since there is no one right way involved. In turn, successes accumulate and enhance a positive self-concept. Children feel worthy and competent, knowing that they can have an effect on their environment. Creativity fosters mental or cognitive development. It involves a wide range of higher-level thinking skills, including observation, problem solving, discovery, analysis, hypothesizing, predicting, testing, and communicating, among others (see Figure 1–4). In the school setting, creativity can enhance and reinforce learning in the traditional curricular areas of math, science, social studies, listening, speaking, pre-reading, pre-writing, and other expressive arts. Beyond individual development, creativity advances civilization and society by addressing and attempting to solve the global problems of hunger, poverty, disease, war and pollution.

FIGURE 1–4 Rocky's Rock Restaurant makes a personally creative statement.

SUMMARY

The mystery sounding creativity was addressed in this chapter. Creativity can be viewed as making a unique product. Children, however, may make or create things that are new or original only to them. These were considered creative on the basis of their creative processing, which may or may not result in a finished product. Creativity was also viewed as a skill requiring practice. Environmental conditions can either foster or hinder creativity, and an optimal home environment was identified. Creativity was also compared and contrasted with conformity, convergent thinking, and intelligence. It was found that a high IQ did not guarantee a high degree of creativity.

Creative children should be viewed as a national asset. We must not allow them to become an endangered human resource. Expect them to wonder, question, and challenge conventional wisdom or traditional ways of doing things. They may enjoy doing their own thing rather than "playing the game of school." The creative traits cluster around a personality which goes beyond the status quo and thrives on daring to be different and nonconformist. And this is exactly the type of person on which the future depends. We need creative individuals who will not settle for givens, but instead strive to fulfill themselves while making the world a better place to live for all people.

Suggested Activities

1. Identify or develop at least one thing you do creatively. Practice and continue to refine it. Document your own creative development, including setbacks, frustrations, and successes, with a diary or journal.

2. Make a resource list of local businesses and contacts that are good sources of free (or inexpensive) and recyclable materials. Include the name, address, phone number, and contact person.

3. Spend one morning observing a teacher's use of time, space, and curriculum, as well as his or her teaching behavior. List specific recommendations for how each could be modified to further enhance creativity.

4. Write your own definition of creativity. Ask five other individuals to do the same. Note similarities and differences. Are there gender, race, or ethnic influences in the differences?

Review

A. What is the relationship between creativity, convergent thinking, and intelligence?

B. Name three different ways of understanding creativity.
1.
2.
3.

C. Pretend that you are speaking to your parent group on creativity. They ask you for important things that they can do at home to enhance their child's creativity. Specifically, what do you recommend?
1.
2.
3.

D. List major obstacles to creativity.
1.
2.   4.
3.   5.

E. Are young children more process- or product-oriented in their creative expression? Explain your position.

F. Complete the Creativity Equation:

$$\boxed{} + \boxed{} \rightarrow \boxed{} \rightarrow \boxed{}$$

and Creativity

G. Is intelligence a single concept confined to thinking? Include a discussion of multiple intelligences to justify your position.

CHAPTER 2

Creative Thinking

What do you see happening in this picture? Is this something you would do with children?

Miss Casey and her group of three-year-olds are playing with water, funnels, and clear plastic tubing. The children are engaged in an informal science activity. The teacher asks open-ended questions to stimulate their language and thinking. "What do you see happening?" "How can we get the water to come out?" "How else can we hold the tube?" "What else can we do to keep the water from coming out?" "How can we make the water come out faster or slower?"

OBJECTIVES

After studying this chapter, the student will be able to

- Discuss creativity as a function of the brain
- Discuss creativity as a mental operation
- Identify and explain the four components of divergent thinking and production
- Compare and contrast right and left brain thinking
- Discuss ways adults can facilitate children's creative thinking

INTRODUCTION

There are many ways of being creative. These outlets or modes of creativity include play; the expressive arts: art, music, movement, dance, drama, and mime; and thought and language. For example, play is an excellent opportunity for creative expression. A young child building with blocks relies on past experiences in transforming pieces of wood into a train, airport, or castle. Putting on an oversized coat helps four-year-old Beth become a business executive, queen, or pilot. Children can use their bodies to creatively move like animals, robots, or astronauts. They can also use paint, markers, clay, and paper to give form to their innermost thoughts and substance to their experiences. Young children also creatively transform standard English. Darrell, age three, felt that "carage" made more sense than garage. Tanya, age four, announced to her preschool class that Santa Claus has a team of "snowdeer," not reindeer. Swiss made no sense to five-year-old Kyle, shopping with his grandmother. He insisted on having "hole cheese" in his sandwiches. Young children also engage in creative thinking, although this particular mode is often given less emphasis and less of a role in the early childhood curriculum.

Just what is creative thinking? Creativity has been identified as a cognitive process or way of thinking. DeBono (1970) identified two types of thinking: vertical and lateral. Vertical thinking involves learning more about something or arriving at a conventional, accepted, convergent answer. For example, when Ms. Bell asked her preschoolers, "What time of the day do we eat breakfast?" Lin answered, "In the morning." But if the object is to find unusual, divergent, creative solutions for problems, lateral thinking is appropriate. Lateral thinking is the way of using one's mind or mental processes that leads to creative thinking or products. For example, Katie, who was playing alone at the sandbox, decided to creatively use sticks and twigs to keep her company.

Children Express Their Creativity Through Thinking

Art is not the only way to express one's creativity. Being able to think in creative ways is another. Some may believe that creative thinking is abstract and reserved for adults. Creative thinking is not confined to authors, artists, scientists, and inventors. Young children can and should engage in creative thinking. Creative thinking is a skill that not only helps children solve problems in their daily lives, but also prepares them for life in the twenty-first century. If we are to solve social, economic, political, and environmental problems it will be through efforts at creative problem solving. Using the same old solutions to persistent problems has not worked. Children who grow up valued as creative and original thinkers will have the necessary skills to confront and solve problems facing them in the twenty-first century.

Consider This:

The children we work with today will become the world citizens of tomorrow. If we do a good job of nurturing and educating them, they will thrive. What will life in the twenty-first century be like? What if we were able to rid civilization of all its negative features? What if future children found

- affordable housing instead of homelessness
- employment and equal opportunity instead of welfare and unemployment
- peace instead of war and violence
- lawfulness instead of lawlessness and crime
- preventive medicine, cures, and affordable health care instead of life-threatening diseases, terminal illnesses, and AIDS
- love and friendship instead of gangs and hate
- equality and acceptance of diversity instead of discrimination
- conservation and environmental protection instead of pollution and depletion of natural resources
- positive self-esteem and self-respect instead of substance abuse

This "wish list" can be a reality if individuals are encouraged to approach these problems in new and different ways using creative thinking. Children can be encouraged to think creatively at an early age. As adults they will be better able to address and solve community and global problems.

Creativity and the Brain

Creativity can also be discussed as a function of the brain. According to Galin (1976), the human brain houses two separate but interacting thinking systems, or hemispheres. The right and left hemispheres are joined by the corpus callosum, a thick branch of nerves that serves as a communication system between them. The hemispheres have different specializations. The left hemisphere houses the thinking abilities traditionally associated with school: reading, writing, math, and rational and logical thinking. The right hemisphere specializes in nonrational, intuitive thinking and spatial relations—in short, creative ways of processing information. Dominance is not established at birth, and it is imperative that children be provided with experiences that capitalize on and integrate the functioning of both sides of the brain. Although schools are set up to emphasize conformity and convergent thinking, or left-brain functioning, Galin believes that at an early age the right-brain or creative function is dominant. Early childhood educators are in a key position to open the vistas of thinking for young children by planning experiences that engage both left- and right-brain functioning.

Why Does the Left Brain Have to Be Right?   Seen from above, the human brain resembles a walnut. The two halves or cerebral hemispheres, right and left, are connected at the center by the corpus callosum which provides communication between the two hemispheres. The nervous system is connected to the brain in a crossed-over fashion. The left hemisphere controls the right side of the body; the left side of the body is controlled by the right hemisphere. The two hemispheres of the brain are specialized and process information differently (see Table 2–1). Each side possesses capacities for certain mental processes which are independent of each other. The right hemisphere operates in a mode which is nonverbal, subjective, intuitive, and global. The left hemisphere operates in a mode which analyzes, abstracts, verbalizes and uses logic.

The old view held that the two hemispheres competed and never worked together to process information. According to Edwards (1979), the two hemispheres can and do work together in a number of ways. Sometimes they cooperate and divide the task with each half contributing its special abilities in doing what it does best. The hemispheres can also work singly; one hemisphere dominates and is "on" while the other is "off." The hemispheres may also compete and try to do what it knows the other half can do better. For example, Zena is standing at the easel painting a picture. She is trying to paint her family. How might her brain approach this task? The left side of her brain reacts logically telling Zena she needs four figures, two male and two female. If the left side dominates, her father would be painted with his beard and depicted taller than her mother. Zena would plan to paint herself smaller than her older brother. If the right side of her brain

LEFT BRAIN	RIGHT BRAIN
analytical	intuitive
logical	impulsive
aware of time	unaware of time
sequential and linear	nonsequential, holistic
can break down whole into parts	focuses on whole, not parts
verbal	nonverbal
uses language	uses touch, kinesthetic
mathematical, calculating	recognizes faces, 3-D shapes, patterns
responsive to positive moods	responsive to negative moods
can write music scientifically	processes tones and sounds
cognitive	sensory, affective, creative
factual	processes imagery, dreams
reality-bound	fantastical

TABLE 2–1   *Two Sides of the Brain*

predominates, Zena might react emotionally rather than logically. She could become engrossed in mixing colors and making designs to highlight clothing. Or, her mother could be painted larger than life and wearing a crown while her older brother might appear in the background, lacking facial features.

Although schools pay lip service to creativity, most are set up according to left-brain functioning. Curricular implications based on brain specializations are listed in Table 2–2. In left-brain-oriented schools, teaching is sequenced and time schedules are rigidly followed. Children sit in desks aligned in straight rows. Teachers reward convergent thinking with letter grades. Reading, writing, and math (the three R's) form the core of the curriculum. Right-brain pursuits including art, music, and movement do not receive equal time, attention, and funding, and may be the first areas eliminated when the budget is cut. This is unfortunate. Jane Alexander, chairwoman for the National Endowment for the Arts (1995), advocates restoring arts education to the school curriculum as a means of enhancing students' creativity, helping their development, and curbing violence. She believes that some individuals who do not have a way to express themselves creatively do so violently. Is graffiti one example?

Creativity As a Mental Operation

Guilford (1977) was one of the original investigators of creativity as a mental process or operation. He conceptualized a "Structure of the Intellect" consisting of three dimensions: contents, products, and operations. Operations include knowing, discovering, or being aware (cognition); retrieving information from storage (memory); the generation of multiple responses (divergent production); coming up with the one right answer (convergent production); and judging the appropriateness of information or decisions (evaluation).

Characteristics of Divergent or Creative Thinking

What makes divergent or creative thinking different from uncreative thinking? Creative or divergent thinkers share the following mental qualities.

LEFT BRAIN SPECIALIZES IN	RIGHT BRAIN SPECIALIZES IN
handwriting	spatial relationships
language	shapes and patterns
reading	color sensitivity
phonics	singing, music, dance
locating details and facts	art
following directions	creativity
listening	feelings and emotions
math	visualization

TABLE 2–2   Brain Specialties

They are

1. FLUENT thinkers who have many ideas and solutions
2. FLEXIBLE thinkers who have different ideas which cross categories or break boundaries
3. ORIGINAL thinkers who have unique and unusual ideas
4. ELABORATE thinkers who add details to the ideas

The divergent thinking of creative children is fluent, flexible, original, and elaborate, although not all four qualities appear in each thought or action.

When confronted with a problem, creative or divergent thinkers are able to come up with a long list of possibilities or options. This characterizes fluency or fluent thinking. For example, ask children for their ideas on celebrating the upcoming December holidays. Their fluent replies might include parties, baking cookies, playing in the snow, exchanging gifts, making cards, taking a field trip to the mall, singing songs, putting on a play, making presents for family members, writing letters to Santa, giving a gift to Santa, or giving gifts to needy children. The sheer quantity of responses indicates fluency. They reflect a good job of brainstorming for many ideas, and all ideas should be accepted and respected.

The above responses indicate flexibility. Flexibility is the ability to mentally push boundaries, shift categories, and take mental detours. It results in a varied and diverse array of responses. One's thinking can be fluent without being flexible. The children's thinking was fluent in that it generated several party-type suggestions. It was flexible in that their options went beyond the scope of party-type ideas for themselves to include Santa, parents, and the less fortunate. These options reflect flexible thinking.

Giving a gift to Santa is one original idea, especially for a young child. Originality refers to uniqueness. Original ideas are uncommon, unusual, different, and unexpected. By contrast, the other party-type suggestions are not wrong but quite obvious and common.

Creative individuals have elaborate ideas and express themselves in complex ways. Elaboration involves a lot of detail and rich expression. For example, in her letter to Santa, Arden merely requested a new doll and did not elaborate. By contrast, Beau was elaborate in requesting a "new robot, it's awesome, with arms and wings that move around and can do things. It has batteries and rockets that shoot out sideways." Beau was able to stretch and expand his thought. Creative children embellish their artwork with colors and decorate their speech with fancy words. Creative children at play build elaborate constructions out of blocks which may be embellished with masking tape for roads and string for power lines.

Edwards and Nabors (1995) apply the components of divergent thinking and production to the creative act of finger painting in the following ways. Finger painting allows children to experience fluency between a medium, the child's body, and the child's ideas. The activity is flexible and gives children freedom to experiment and explore with color, motion, design, and physical movement. Since there is no one right way to finger paint, the activity encourages originality. Finger painters elaborate on their paintings by adding new colors, details, or incorporating other materials, such as brushes or combs.

Whole Brain, Whole Learning

Few would argue that schools should not stress conformity and convergent thinking. Still, a better balance is needed between creativity and individuality vs. conformity and convergent thinking. We need to balance left- and right-brain learning. Our educa-

tional goals, curriculum, and practices should exercise many modes of learning and different styles of processing information. Certainly, we do not want children to creatively read the word "shoe" as anything other than what it is. Nor would we want children to creatively add 2 + 3 and come up with 32. Still, children should not be spoon-fed knowledge, nor have their left brain overworked and their right brain left to atrophy. The author observed a kindergartner being corrected for stating that the color of the sun was "white hot." It appeared that the teacher was looking for convergent thinking to produce the one acceptable answer of "yellow." Conformity and convergent thinking can be taken to extremes. Over time, children come to reject divergent thinking as incorrect or useless. And as an aside, your right brain is correct; the sun is not yellow.

Not all creative-thinking activities provide the opportunity to assess all four components of divergent production. The following sample item from a test of creativity will help us practice informally evaluating a child's thinking for originality and elaboration. In the following example, children are asked to complete an open-ended drawing similar to the one in Figure 2–1. Obviously, there is no one right way to complete this picture, and many possibilities exist. How would you complete it? Carefully examine the finished product in Figure 2–2. What can you say about this

FIGURE 2–1   Open-ended drawing

FIGURE 2–2   Completed drawing by a six-year-old

FIGURE 2–3   Completed drawing by a six-year-old

FIGURE 2–4   This five-year-old's drawing of a park is detailed and elaborate.

six-year-old's originality and elaboration? The author would rate this low on both originality and elaboration. The completed picture is rather stereotyped, unimaginative, mundane, and not very original. Details are minimal, and the picture lacks elaboration. From only this one sample, the author is not in a position to make a strong statement about this child's level of creativity. It does indicate, however, that this particular child needs practice and encouragement in divergent production. On the other hand, consider a drawing completed by a different six-year-old (Figure 2–3). What can you say about this six-year-old's originality and elaboration? The author believes that this completed drawing evidences a high degree of originality and elaboration.

Not every creative activity will or should lend itself to evaluation for fluency, flexibility, originality, and elaboration. Fluency and flexibility may be more appropriate to games of creative thinking. Originality and elaboration can be applied to children's art (see Figure 2–4). The informal rating scale in Table 2–3, adapted from Guilford's 1967 work, can be used to assess divergent production. Again, our intent is not to grade or label creativity, or to include it on a child's report card. Discretionary use of the following instrument will help us keep track of progress as we strive to reach our goal of helping young children to demonstrate fluency, flexibility, originality, and elaboration in their creative processing and production.

LOW	FLUENCY	HIGH
• few different		• many different

FLEXIBILITY		
• lacks variety		• wide variety
• rigid		• flexible
• limited range		• wide range

ORIGINALITY		
• stereotyped		• unique
• unimaginative		• imaginative
• common		• unusual

ELABORATION		
• lacks detail		• very detailed
• unelaborate		• elaborate
• simple		• complex

TABLE 2–3   Rating Scale   (Source: J. P. Guilford, *Way Beyond the IQ,* Buffalo, NY: The Creative Education Foundation, 1967.)

Children Need to Engage in Convergent <u>and</u> Divergent Thinking

What is creative thinking? When is thinking creative and what makes creative thinking different from uncreative thinking? Creative thinking can be equated with divergent thinking. Thinking is divergent when many possibilities or options result. Divergent thinking is open-ended, allowing for an array of possibilities. For example, you can engage in divergent thinking when planning a creative curriculum. Ask yourself, "What can I provide for the children that will enhance their creativity?" There is no one piece of material or specific activity. There are endless possibilities, including experiences in art, play, language, music, and movement, among others. By contrast, convergent thinking results in one correct answer. Much of what is learned in school requires convergent thinking, especially when taking tests. Convergent thinking is required to produce the one right answer to the following questions:

- Do dogs have puppies or kittens?
- What is the name of the largest dinosaur?
- What comes out at night, the sun or the moon?
- Name the months of the year in proper order.
- What shape is our classroom door?
- What is the opposite of hot?
- How many fingers am I holding up?
- What is the sum of three plus five?
- What is the capital of the United States?

Both modes of thinking, convergent and divergent, are very important. Children who lack opportunities to engage in convergent thinking will lack access to a core body of knowledge needed for school success and academic achievement. Acquiring a body of factual information is not enough, however. Children also need opportunities to engage in creative thinking. Children denied access to creative processing and divergent thinking will become conforming individuals who do not realize their creative potential. The problem arises when conformity and convergent thinking dominate the curriculum at the expense of individual and divergent thinking.

ACTIVITIES FOR CREATIVE THINKING

Sample items taken from tests of creativity (Torrance, 1966) and modified for use with young children provide suggestions for activities to foster creative thinking. Some general guidelines are in order. You may want to try out these activities yourself first. Record and evaluate your responses. Allow yourself and your children plenty of "think time" to grapple with the problem posed. The activities can be conducted with individual children or with small or large groups. Creative thinking games can be played at any time during the day and can easily become part of one of the following routines: arrival time, opening activity, small group time, circle time, snack time, story time, transition time, indoor recess, indoor rainy-day activity, and predismissal time, among others. Explain the nature of these creative thinking games. You are looking for unusual responses, and there will be no one right answer. This may be unsettling to some children. Participation should be voluntary, and some children will feel more comfortable with these activities than others. Try to reward and encourage thinking rather than acceptable answers. Children may get silly, and some answers may bear no relation to the question asked. These children may simply be testing your commitment to creativity and suspending conformity. Initially, the games should be kept short. Stop when the children show signs of restlessness or lack of interest. Because the games are so open-ended, they may create some initial mental discomfort, especially to children who have been led to believe that all questions have one right answer.

Since young children vary in their level of creative thinking and verbal ability, it is difficult to recommend specific age ranges for the following creative thinking activities. Activities that require some degree of verbal fluency can be successfully used with kindergartners and children in the primary grades. Activities requiring a verbal response can also be used with preschoolers who demonstrate strong oral language skills. Activities requiring a nonverbal response, such as drawing, can also be used with younger children. Older children can be challenged to write their responses, thereby making creative thinking a literacy event. There is no upper age limit on the thinking games.

Finish My Picture

Ask the children to complete one of the pictures in Figure 2–5. The pattern could be drawn on the board at child level or run off as a photocopy. The advantages of using a photocopy are that children may be less prone to copy other children and that later they can share their products with one another. In this way they come to see that there are many, many possible responses.

Picture Possibilities

Draw one of the line or pattern pictures in Figure 2–6 on the board or on a transparency for the over-

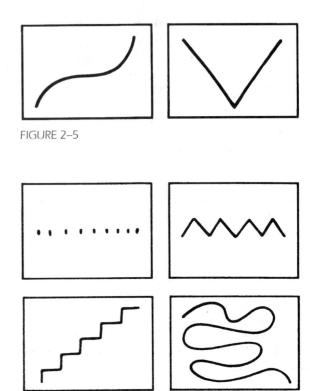

FIGURE 2–5

FIGURE 2–6

head projector. Allow the children time to think about possible meanings. Ask them to give you a possible title or interpretation. "What do you see in this picture?" "What else could it be?"

What Would Happen If?

Ask the children to listen very carefully as you ask them one of the following. What would happen if

- refrigerators ate food?
- bathtubs could talk?
- you could be invisible?
- cars could drive by themselves?
- toys were real?
- dreams came true?
- you never had birthdays?
- pets went to school?

Young children might enjoy using the tape recorder to tape their responses. Print the above sentences on index cards and place them in a learning center.

Unusual Uses

Bring in the following items. Encourage the children to inspect each one carefully and to handle them all. Ask them to think of many things to do with these items.

- shoe
- shoe box
- cork
- dish
- newspaper
- balloon
- juice can
- napkin
- golf tee
- brick
- paper clip
- rubber band

Just Suppose

Ask the children to listen carefully to a short story. Have them "just suppose" an end to your story. Examples might include

- Just suppose you found $1 million. What would you buy?
- Just suppose you met a moon child in an empty field. What would you say or do?
- Just suppose you could be somebody else. Who would you be?
- Just suppose you could be the teacher. What would you do?
- Just suppose you found a magic flying carpet. Where would you go?
- Just suppose you could be invisible for one whole day. What would you do, and where would you go?
- Just suppose you could be any animal. Which would it be? Why?

Your Own Book Ending

Assemble a small group of children for story time. Ask them to listen quietly while you read a class favorite. *Where the Wild Things Are* by Sendak is one possibility. Slowly read the story, stopping just before the end. Close your book. Ask the children to think up a different way to end the story.

Some children may insist on giving back the predetermined ending. Encourage them to come up with their own even though it will be different from the book ending. As children gain experience at supplying their own endings, you can stop reading earlier in the story and require them to supply a greater part of the creative ending.

Tell Me About My Picture

Seat a small group of children in a close circle. Hold up an interesting picture you have clipped from a magazine. Try to find pictures that are vague and have a variety of possible meanings. Ask the children to examine the picture carefully and

- give different names or titles for the picture. What else could we call it? What else could this story be about? What happened to cause this? What might happen next?
- tell their very own stories about this picture.

Beginning writers can be encouraged to dictate or even print their own story lines. Individual children might enjoy taping their own story at a learning center.

How Many Ways

Seat a small group of children in a close circle. Ask them to listen very carefully as you ask the following questions. How many different ways can you

- celebrate your birthday?
- scare your brother or sister?
- get into trouble?
- make a new friend?
- be happy?
- go on a vacation?
- spend Saturday?
- surprise Grandma or Grandpa?
- earn some money?
- be naughty?

Descriptives

Seat a small group of children in a close circle. Hold up one of the following objects. Encourage each child to inspect it carefully as it is passed around the circle. Ask the children to tell you many different words that describe a

- flag
- umbrella
- cereal box
- key
- toy
- sock
- gerbil
- lunch box
- pencil
- coin

Encourage children to use descriptive terms, including references to color, shape, size, use, form, texture, weight, composition, and so on.

Make Up a Story

Seat a small group of children in a close circle. Ask the children to listen very carefully to the beginning of a story. Then, ask them to finish your story. Three very simple story starters are:

- Once upon a time there was a little girl who wanted her very own horse. But her Mommy said there was no money to buy one. So one day the little girl . . .
- One morning Marco was waiting for the school bus. He waited and waited, but it didn't come. So Marco decided to . . .

- Kitten wanted to go to school. But Billy said, "Kittens don't go to school. They stay at home." So one day Kitten . . .

Encourage children to make up their own beginnings to share with their friends.

Picture Guess

The open-ended designs in Figure 2–7 can be sketched on the board one at a time. Ask the children to study the shape carefully. Allow plenty of "think time," and do not encourage quick shouting out. Have the children tell you many different things each of the pictures could be.

Make It Better

Seat a small group of children in a close circle. Hold up a familiar toy, such as a stuffed animal or race car. Encourage each child to inspect it carefully as it is passed around the circle. Ask the children

- How could we make it a better toy?
- What could we do to make it more fun to play with?

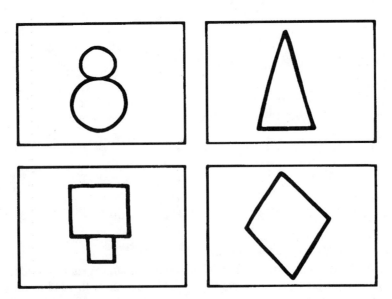

FIGURE 2–7

What Would . . . If It . . . ?

Seat a small group of children in a close circle. Ask them to listen very carefully to your question and then think up their own answers. Here are some sample questions.

- What would taste better if it were sweeter?
- What would be more fun if it went faster?
- What would be scary if it were bigger?
- What would be happier if it could escape?
- What would be funny if it were alive?

What All

Seat a small group of children in a close circle. Ask them to think of many things that

- are round
- make noise
- sink
- are wet
- smell
- have horns
- shine
- roll
- are green
- hurt
- are square
- stick
- squeak
- ring
- fly

Pretend

Seat a small group of children in a close circle. Ask them to carefully listen to a "Pretend . . ." sentence. Examples might include

- Pretend you didn't have a paintbrush. What else could you use to paint the walls?
- Pretend you didn't have a present. What else could you take to a friend's birthday party?
- Pretend you didn't have a friend to play with. What else could you do?
- Pretend you didn't have any money for your play store. What else could you use?

FACILITATING YOUNG CHILDREN'S CREATIVE THINKING

Although children will act and think in creative ways without prompting, adults can facilitate the process by providing time, space, and resources, as well as setting the stage.

Provide a Psychological Climate Conducive to Creativity

Children flourish in a psychologically safe setting which trusts and empowers them to act autonomously without the fear of criticism, rejection, or failure. Expectations for children's behavior are positive yet appropriate. Autonomy involves exercising one's freedom, or acting freely but in responsible ways. Children need to act autonomously by making choices, decisions, solving problems, and making things happen on their own. By providing an array of materials and activities from which to choose, the environment can be set up to foster children's autonomy. An overly structured day, in which choices regarding activities are made for the children, impairs their creative ability. They quickly learn to override their creative impulses and autonomous drive while becoming overly dependent on others for answers and solutions.

Creative Thinking Takes Time

Children need large blocks of time to engage in activities that involve thinking. Exploring and exhausting possibilities takes time. Time should be viewed as fluid and flexible. Your daily schedule should be divided into a few large blocks of time rather than several short blocks. Larger blocks provide enough time to think, plan, and try out possibilities, and then to leave, return, and begin again by trying out different ways. Children who are rushed are not only denied adequate time to think and do but may also resist by misbehaving. Children need time to daydream and reflect, at times to do nothing but sit and think. Let creativity and creative thinking permeate your day. Engage children in creative thinking activities throughout the day. Use individual and small group times, snack, transition, and early morning/late afternoon to play games requiring creative thinking. Sometimes creativity is unpredictable and will evolve into something unplanned requiring additional time. The flexible teacher is able to flow with the "teachable moment" as well as to bring closure when warranted.

Teachable Moments

Teachable moments are those unplanned events which open the door to high-interest activity and a burst of learning. Seize those teachable moments and capitalize on their potential for learning. Two examples illustrate the concept of teachable moments. A group of three-, four- and five-year-olds found spiders out on the playground. They informally organized a spider hunt. They requested bug houses to catch them. The teacher provided plastic cups with clear plastic wrap for lids. She offered magnifying glasses for good measure. One child wanted to kill his spider, which led to a discussion on the value of life. Another child said, "Don't hurt it; it might be somebody's mama." The children compared their spiders while focusing on size, shape, color, and markings. Legs were counted. One child expressed dismay at the "poor trapped spiders." The group voted to release the spiders to their natural habitat before coming indoors. The teacher decided to forego her book on colors to continue the discussion on spiders. She was sure that writing spider stories and making books would dominate the afternoon. Her flexible approach to planning allowed her to capitalize on this teachable moment.

A week later, Mindy's mother brought her baby sister to school. The teacher asked if she could visit with the children. The children were told to look with their eyes and to touch by gently stroking the baby's arms and legs. They talked about size and age differences. One child asked if the newborn could stay and play. This fostered a discussion of infant capabilities and helped the children see how much they had grown and developed in only a few short years. Mindy wanted the children to see the baby's funny belly button. This prompted an informal discussion of reproduction and the origins of maternal attachment. The interest in babies continued in the dramatic play area long after the baby left. The teacher used a small group time to graph names of children who had a baby sister or brother versus those who did not. The teacher was amazed at how much the children learned from these unplanned activities or teachable moments. She wished more of her planned activities generated this level of excitement. Be responsive to possible teacher moments and capitalize on their learning potential. Chapter 12 continues our discussion of incorporating teaching moments into a spontaneous or emergent approach to curriculum development.

Children Need Space in Which To Be Creative

Children need plenty of space to lay out materials and to work alone or together to complete their plans. Like time, space should also be fluid and flexible. Creative thinking may require private, enclosed, solitary space for private thinking and daydreaming. Other creative activities may require larger open spaces for group involvement. Tables, chairs, and movable units may need to be arranged to meet the needs of the activity at hand. Creativity may entail noise, excitement, movement, and clutter. An excessive concern for constant cleanup or neatness inhibits creative "messing about." Perhaps this is why creative expression and young children are so compatible.

STRATEGIES TO FACILITATE CREATIVE THINKING

The following strategies will help children feel that their attempts at creative thinking are valued.

1. Build creative thinking into your program.

Provide a variety of ways for children to think creatively. Integrate your curriculum. Avoid an overemphasis on conformity and convergent thinking. Children who are led to believe that there is only one right way or correct answer will have their creativity stifled. Expect that creative children will question and challenge your ideas and ways of doing things. Provide opportunities for children to explore creative options and possibilities, to play with their ideas.

2. Model creative thinking.

Be a creative thinker and model the process. Share your creative solutions to problems. For example, you promised the children that they will be able to finger paint in the morning. You promised, however, before discovering that there is no more paint. You announce the problem and model how you engaged in creative thinking to come up with a solution: "We ran out of paint so I thought of what else we could use. I'll put shaving cream into each of these four trays and we can use that for finger painting." Also share your frustration and setbacks. Let children know it took you several tries to find a way to keep the door closed so the classroom pet would not escape at night. Try new ways of doing things. Let children know that if one way does not work out, you simply think again and try another.

3. Recognize, encourage, and value creative thinking and problem solving.

Reward the process of thinking creatively rather than the idea itself. In the previous classroom pet cage example, the teacher should also recognize her accomplishments by saying, "I like my idea of an open padlock and it seems to be working. It took some good hard thinking." This is not the same as boasting or bragging. Encourage children to be creative thinkers. In the former shaving cream example, Carlos gets the liquid watercolor and says, "Let's make colors." Reply, "Carlos wants to add coloring to our shaving cream. Good thinking."

4. Help children value their own creative thinking.

Help them stand up for their ideas in the face of criticism and peer pressure. Say, "That was your idea and it's OK if your friend doesn't agree with you." For example, what if the children do not like Carlos' idea and say, "No, that's yucky." The teacher could say, "I think Carlos has an idea. If you don't want color just say so." "Carlos, it's OK if your friends don't like your idea." In turn, help children respect the ideas of others. Help them see that it's OK to be different and to have different ideas.

5. Pose problems requiring creative solutions.

For example, to a group of school-age children who want to go on a field trip, say, "How can we raise money to go?" Look for many and different ideas. Help children build on each other's ideas. Provide ample "think time" during which you remain silent and wait for them to reply. Defer judgment and evaluation. Avoid saying, "That won't work," or "Let's think of a better idea." Resist the temptation to step in too soon and shield children from manageable amounts of frustration and even failure at times. Help children test out their hunches and rethink possibilities. Encourage critical thinking. Discuss the pros and cons of the ideas generated.

6. Engage children in critical thinking.

For example, once again Miss Tina finds herself reading the story of *Goldilocks and the Three Bears* to a small group of preschoolers. It is a favorite and she always provides puppets, stuffed animals, costumes, character headbands, and a set of felt pieces for children to use later, retelling the story in their own words. She approaches today's reading with a different goal in mind—critical thinking. Before reading she asks the children to listen carefully and decide who is good or nice as opposed to who is bad or naughty. Devlin says the bears are bad, especially Papa Bear because he scares the little girl and she has to run away. Afi thinks that Mama Bear is good because she cooks for her family and won't let them eat the food if it's too hot. Rosa thinks that Baby Bear is bad because he woke up Goldilocks. She adds that she gets into trouble at home if she wakes up her new baby sister. Kalmir disagrees. He believes Goldilocks is naughty because she broke Baby Bear's chair. Nan adds that Goldilocks ate the porridge and that wasn't right because she didn't ask first. Sergio says that Goldilocks is the "baddest" because she walked right into the house; the bears could call the police and take her to jail. The children are thinking critically about the characters in simple terms like good vs. bad and naughty vs. nice, that they easily understand. Miss Tina was able to help the children look beyond the labeling and see the bigger issue of safety and intent. She agreed that Goldilocks did something that could be called bad or naughty because it was unsafe and very dangerous. She asked the children if it is okay to go into a stranger's house. Fay said it would be okay if she knocked first. Miss Tina asked the other children what they thought. And so the critical thinking continued.

7. Ask open-ended questions.

Open-ended questions are worded in such a way that there is no one correct answer. They invite an array of possible responses. They require children to engage in divergent or creative thinking and to operate at a higher mental level in formulating answers. Examples of open-ended questions include:

- When reading a story, ask, "What do you think will happen next?"
- When solving a peer-related problem, ask, "Well, what do you think we can do to solve this problem?"
- When frustrated with blocks that won't stack up or nature items that won't stay glued, ask, "How else could you get that to work?"
- When listening to sounds or looking at partially covered magazine pictures, ask, "What else could it be?"
- When planning a walk around the block, ask, "What are some things we need to think about to make sure we have a safe trip?"
- When keeping a roof on a block building from caving in, ask, "Who can show us a different way?"

- To a child who wants to snatch a prized toy from another, ask, "What else could you do instead of grabbing the toy?"

By contrast, closed-ended questions aim for one right answer. Either you know it or you don't. Closed-ended questions require low-level or convergent thinking based on recall. Answers to closed-ended questions are stored in memory as bits and pieces of unrelated information. Examples of closed-ended questions include:

- What color is the sun?
- If you have two pennies and I give you two more, how many pennies will you have all together?
- What shape is the clock on the wall?
- How many wheels are there on a tricycle?

See Table 2–4 for comparison and contrast of different types of questions.

Let's apply our study of questioning to Miss Tina's reading of *The Three Bears*. If she wanted children to engage in low-level thinking and give back factual information she could ask the following closed-ended questions:

- How many bears were there in our story?
- What was the name of the little girl?

CLOSED OR CONVERGENT QUESTIONS	OPEN OR DIVERGENT QUESTIONS
seek the one right answer or correct response	seek many possible answers
invite a quick response	take time to think about and formulate a response
require low-level thinking, e.g., names and facts	require higher level thinking, e.g., reasoning and problem solving
require answers previously stored in child's memory	invoke child's imagination, and are actively constructed
involve simple answers and responses	involve complex answers and responses
involve answers known to adults	involve responses unknown to adults
ask what, who, when, and where	ask how, why, or tell me about

TABLE 2–4 Types of Questions

Creativity and the ECE Curriculum

It would be fair to say that a general misunderstanding pervades the concept of creativity and its role in the curriculum. With the present emphasis on accountability, basic academic skills, testing, reform, and budget cuts, creativity may be eyed suspiciously by parents, taxpayers, and even teachers, who often report that they believe creativity to be important yet find little time to encourage it. The elusive nature of creativity merely complicates the issue. Reporting to parents that their child is reading at level X may convey more information than saying their child is highly creative. Some believe that doing well in math is a more marketable skill than high creativity. At a parent meeting, one father asked, "If creativity is so important, why doesn't it appear on my child's report card and school record?" He went on to state that he didn't recall creativity being part of his school career and felt he had become a success in spite of it. His point may reflect wider public opinion. This is another reason why parent education, teacher education, and arts advocacy are critical.

- Why was she called Goldilocks?
- What did Mama Bear cook in the morning?
- Where did Baby Bear find the girl?
- Why did the bears go for a walk?
- Did they find the girl upstairs or downstairs?
- How many bowls were on the table?
- What got broken?

She knows that these questions will be easy for her children and will not engage them mentally. By contrast, children will be engaged in higher level thinking as they actively construct answers to the following open-ended questions:

- Let's give the bears first names. What could we call them?
- Let's change the story. Who can share a different ending?
- Why do you think Goldilocks ran away from the bears' house?
- What do you think about going into a stranger's house?
- How could we help Baby Bear and Goldilocks become friends?
- What else could Mama Bear cook for breakfast?

Asking open-ended questions led to an involved discussion with most of the children wanting to contribute different ideas. It is also important to provide "think time." Children need time to reflect on the question while mentally and verbally formulating one or more answers. Do not become impatient and answer your own question. This disrespectful practice sends a negative message to children. It tells them you will not invest the time in waiting to hear what they have to say. They may interpret this to mean that you really don't care about them or their ideas.

SUMMARY

There are many ways to express one's creativity. Play, the expressive arts (art, music, movement, dance, dramatics, and mime), language, and thought are just a few that are relevant to early childhood. Creativity, or divergent production, was viewed as a thinking skill or mental operation within Guilford's "Structure of the Intellect." Creative thought and production are characterized by fluency, flexibility, originality, and elaboration. A rating scale and sample activities were provided for the adult reader to use with young children.

Suggested Activities

1. Do several of the creative thinking activities. Record your own responses. Use the rating scale to informally evaluate your divergent thinking and production. Record your strengths and weaknesses in fluency, flexibility, originality, and elaboration.

2. Do one of the creative-thinking activities with a small group of young children. Record their responses. Practice using the rating scale to evaluate their creative thinking.

3. Check out tests of creative thinking from the library and review them. Begin a card file of creative-thinking activities. Be creative and modify the test items rather than merely copying them.

Review

A. List the major mental operations.

   1.
   2.
   3.
   4.
   5.

   Place an asterisk in front of the one that is generally equated with creativity.

B. List the components of divergent thinking and production.

   1.
   2.
   3.
   4.

C. Match each term with its description.

   1. elaboration   coming up with many possibilities
   2. originality   the uniqueness of an idea
   3. flexibility   making an idea rich or complex
   4. fluency   coming up with very different responses

D. Fill in five specializations for each side of the brain.

Left Brain: Right Brain:

1.   1.
2.   2.
3.   3.
4.   4.
5.   5.

E. List five ways adults can facilitate children's creative thinking.

1.
2.
3.
4.
5.

CHAPTER 3

Creative Experiences

What do you see in this picture? Is this child at work or at play? What are the criteria that characterize play?

Play takes on many forms, and this chapter examines physical play, constructive play with blocks, dramatic play, play with natural materials, and games. The concept of play and its contrast to work will be explored in depth.

OBJECTIVES

After studying this chapter the student will be able to

- Explain how children express their creativity through play
- List at least three criteria that characterize play
- List the five different types of play
- Discuss how young children use language creatively
- Develop creative experiences in music and movement
- Discuss three different ways adults can facilitate children's creative expression

INTRODUCTION

Chapter 1 introduced the reader to creativity in its widest sense. Chapter 2 focused the discussion on creative thinking. This chapter begins our discussion of various art media by examining the process of mark making, as well as some activities to help children make creative marks. It also outlines other ways that children express their creativity. These include play, language, and music and movement.

Consider This:

Margo is a first-year kindergarten teacher in a suburban school. She has spent the last few weeks of summer meeting with the kindergarten and primary teams. Personally, she believes she will fit in and be able to get along. Professionally, however, she has some concerns. Margo is trying to reconcile what she learned in her classes about developmentally appropriate practices. Her co-teachers tease her about her "book learning" and remind her that although preschoolers can spend their days playing, kindergarten means work. She becomes even more concerned as the kindergarten reading-readiness and math workbooks arrive. Margo found blocks, a water table, and dramatic play props in storage. She would like to set up centers but wonders where, because tables and chairs take up most of the space. She asks herself, "What is the role of play and creative expression in programs for young children, kindergartners in particular?"

This chapter explores the concept of play, contrasting it to work, and identifying criteria which characterize play. Play takes many forms and this chapter examines physical play, constructive play with blocks, dramatic play, play with natural materials, and games. Language and the components of music and movement are two other major ways that children express their creativity. Ideas for setting up centers in these curricular areas along with recommended materials and suggested activities are also presented (see Figure 3–1). Chapter 3 closes with a review of ways teachers can enhance and facilitate children's creative expression.

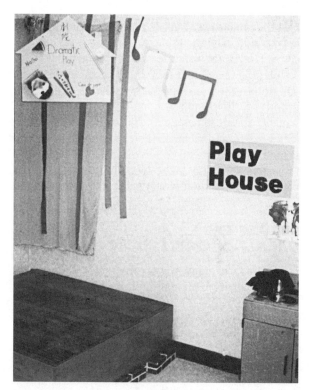

FIGURE 3–1   A center for creative play

CREATIVITY ENHANCES CHILDREN'S DEVELOPMENT

Creativity and creative expression, whether demonstrated through art, thinking, play, language, music, or movement, foster the development of the whole child, including the physical, social-emotional, cognitive, and creative domains. For example, Tearra wants to use the unit blocks to make a house for her doll family. Physically, she must lift, carry, manipulate, and position the blocks. Her eyes and hands work together as her small fingers carefully stack and straighten the large blocks. Initially, Tearra works alone. Creativity respects the child's right to privacy. Later, she invites Portia to help. Socially, they work together practicing cooperative skills, including turn taking and sharing. They practice language skills as they talk and listen to each other. Planning a house to accommodate four dolls takes much thinking and planning. At first they make a wall around their dolls but become dissatisfied saying it looks more like an animal cage. They want separate rooms for each doll. The problem is posed and they think of some different solutions—they are problem solving. They are proud of their joint accomplishment which enhances their self-esteem. Although their house lacks sides and a roof, their compartmentalized structure is their own creative idea. They run to get their teacher, who takes two photographs which will be added to their portfolios.

MODES OF CREATIVE EXPRESSION

There are many ways (or modes) to express one's creativity. Thinking and art have been introduced and will be discussed throughout the chapters. Chapter 3 introduces the reader to the following additional modes of creative expression:

1. play
2. language
3. music and movement

CHILDREN EXPRESS THEIR CREATIVITY THROUGH PLAY

What is play? Play is a difficult concept to understand because it lacks a precise definition. One person may define play as children's work, while another defines play as frivolous activity lacking purpose. A variety of behaviors are labeled play, ranging from what infants do with their bodies and toys to games, hobbies, sports, recreational pursuits, and creative activities like art, music, and dance. Although play cannot be precisely defined, perhaps it can be contrasted with work. Historically, play has been viewed as the opposite of work. It was the Puritan work ethic which gave impetus to this work-play dichotomy. Adult work was considered earnest, serious, worthwhile, productive activity. By contrast, children's play was viewed as idle, frivolous fun bordering on evil. The present impact of this thinking is evident when a child is said to be "just" playing. The qualifying "just" connotes a lack of purpose and worth. Rarely does

one complain about a child who "just" reads or behaves, for these behaviors are valued. This negative attitude toward play is reflected by the parent, or educators like Margo's peers, who feel that children must work rather than play if they are to learn. The following example, however, shows that work and play are not opposites. The young child thoroughly absorbed in carefully stacking blocks to build a tower displays the same careful precision and effort of the adult builder at work. The positive qualities associated with work are also found in play. A further distinction between work and play examines the process and product of each. Play is process oriented while work is product oriented. One plays for the sake of playing; one works for the end product of one's endeavors. Examples of creative processing through play include:

- building with blocks, stacking or fitting them together
- playing with empty boxes
- filling and emptying containers with water
- using kitchen tools and containers to scoop, sift, and mold sand
- pounding and hammering nails into soft wood; sawing and gluing wood pieces together
- pretending to serve lunch to the baby dolls using pretend food
- making up a new version of tag, hide-and-seek, hopscotch, or jump rope
- using poker chips as money at the outdoor fast-food drive-through

So, what is play? Garvey (1990) identifies the following five criteria that define play.

1. Play is pleasurable and enjoyable. Children play because it is fun.
2. Play has no extrinsic goals. Children are intrinsically motivated to play. They play because they want to and in the absence of any tangible reward.
3. Play is spontaneous and voluntary. Play empowers children to make decisions about what to play, who to play with, where and how to carry it out, as well as when to start and finish.
4. Play involves some active engagement on the part of the player. Young children are active learners and play is an active process. Play can be

intense and captivating, thereby disproving the myth that children have short attention spans and cannot stay with an activity for a long period of time.

5. Play is linked with non-play areas. Play fosters the development of the whole child and fosters learning in the early childhood curricular areas. During play, children are physically and mentally active, socializing and talking with their peers and feeling good about what they have playfully made happen. Since there is no right or wrong way to play, children are creative and successful at play, and their self-esteem is enhanced. Play also allows children to express and master their feelings and emotions. They think and form concepts while playing.

Creative Play with Boxes, Cartons, and Accessories

Children can be creative with just about anything they find. Play materials need to be safe, clean, and sturdy, but need not be expensive to foster creative play. Commercial toys which are costly might not enhance creativity, despite their labeling. Empty cardboard boxes and containers are great props for fostering creative play because they

- are safe, sturdy, and durable
- are lightweight and easy to move about
- are recycled items
- are free and can be discarded without a financial loss
- can be personalized using tape, paint, crayons, or markers
- come in a variety of sizes and shapes
- can be many things depending on what the children decide
- are versatile and can be used indoors or outdoors

Large appliance cartons can easily become structures, such as a house, school, castle, restaurant, store, or hospital, as well as vehicles like a rocket ship or bus. Turning the carton on its side converts it into a tunnel or a cave. Cut doors and windows for the children but do not suggest what the box should become. Let the children impart their own meaning

while you serve as a resource to the project. Children may want to paint or decorate the interior and exterior. Providing an array of boxes and cartons in different sizes will help children see possibilities and make connections; they may use the small boxes for furniture or control panel instruments. Problems may arise if you provide only one carton to a large group. Providing more than one large appliance carton fosters small group cooperative play in which individual children have space and a part to play. Play with boxes requires supervision. Some children do not like being enclosed in a small area. Help children see that segregating play with one carton for the girls' house and another for "boys only" is discriminatory and not fair. Your commitment to anti-bias will prohibit exclusion based on gender. It also violates your classroom rule for playing together without hurting others. Adding props or accessories like old sheets and a steering wheel increases the range of creative possibilities. Use cartons to enhance your language and literacy program. A carton decorated like a house sets the stage for dramatizing classic books like *Goldilocks and the Three Bears*. A carton-turned-bridge facilitates the acting out of *The Three Billy Goats Gruff.*

Creative Play with Plastic Pipe (PVC)

Children enjoy constructing with lengths of plastic pipe and several of the following fittings:

- elbows, pipes which come in 45- or 90-degree bends
- couplings, short pipes which join two other pipes in a straight line
- tees, T-shaped joints with three openings
- crosses, X-shaped joints with four openings

Children impart meaning to the materials; the connected pieces become whatever the children decide. Buy lengths of plastic pipe (PVC). Precut lengths are inexpensively priced, or lengths can be cut with a saw. Buy a variety of fittings that allow children to assemble lengths or connect pieces into angles. Connectors without internal threads are easier to assemble. Pieces are priced according to diameter and it is important to purchase all pieces in the same diameter. Adults may want to consider using plastic pipe to make a puppet stage or a four-sided structure that can be suspended from the ceiling with fishing line.

Types of Play

Play takes many shapes and forms. These overlapping categories include:

1. physical play
2. constructive play with blocks
3. dramatic play
4. play with natural materials
5. games

Ⓝ **1. Physical Play**

As its name implies, physical play involves motor activity and movement. Physical play entails both gross motor (large muscle) activity and fine motor (activity involving the small muscles and eye-hand coordination). Outdoor play activities like running, climbing up and going down a slide, riding tricycles, and jumping involve gross motor or large muscle activity. Large muscle play can occur indoors but limited space may restrict it. Still, indoor climbing structures do provide for gross motor activity, especially on days when the weather keeps children inside. Activities like stringing beads, pegs and pegboards, parquetry and design blocks, puzzles, small blocks, sewing and lacing cards, and table toys which lead to sorting or being taken apart and put back together involve fine motor or small muscle activity as well as eye-hand coordination. These are referred to as manipulatives. Since young children are physical beings, physical play is a high priority. Infants grasp and release soft toys and shake rattles. For a toddler, physical play means repeatedly filling and dumping toys into a plastic bucket while wandering about the room. Preschoolers enjoy fitting Legos and bristle blocks together. Whether they actually make something is secondary to the process of fitting together and taking apart. Kindergartners have mastered puzzles with many pieces and may build complex structures with connecting blocks while dramatizing with small people and vehicles. School-age children who have mastered running, catching, throwing, and skipping may progress to competitive games involving races and tests of physical prowess.

Ⓝ *Physical Play on the Outdoor Playground*   Rarely does one have enough outdoor space or equipment for outdoor play. Space is often at a premium and some sites have only a blacktop or small yard with which to work. Others must share space with different age groups or have inherited outdated equipment. Quality playground equipment is expensive. If children were to have their say, however, they would probably allocate most of the annual operating budget and daily schedule to playing outdoors (see Figure 3–2). Your input regarding the design, modification, or improvement of a children's playground may be sought at some point in your professional career. Assuming that space is not restricted and cost is not an issue, what outdoor play areas would you like to see? Suggested areas and recommended materials are listed below.

- water: water table, dishpans or tubs, kitchen gadgets, and containers
- sand: sandbox or sand table, dishpans or tubs, kitchen gadgets, and containers
- water + dirt or sand = mud!
- carpentry or woodworking table with sturdy tools, goggles, lightweight woods
- flexible, multipurpose, multilevel climbing equipment for an array of large muscle activities like climbing, jumping, and sliding
- riding vehicles (simple and complex, one- and two-passenger) and a clearly defined one-way path, traffic cones and signs
- art materials on an art cart and easels that are freestanding or attached to a fence
- music and movement materials, including dance props, rhythm instruments, recorded music and player
- pets or small animals and cages
- garden and gardening tools
- playhouse, dress-up clothes, bridge, stage, elevated platform or other structure for dramatic play
- shady area for looking at books or listening to and telling stories

FIGURE 3–2   Creative play outdoors

- obstacle course stations to jump on and off, crawl through, etc.
- construction materials: large and small blocks, barrels, boards, planks, lumber, old sheets, crates, cardboard boxes, appliance cartons, large sheets of cardboard, tires, tree stump, etc.
- assorted props: balance beam, balls in a variety of sizes, jump ropes, bean bags, hoops, ring toss, parachute, flat wooden ladder, cargo net, low basketball hoop and net, etc.
- storage shed or area that can be locked

2. Constructive Play with Blocks

Building with blocks is a good example of constructive play. Children are not only physically active as they build with blocks but may also dramatize. Blocks serve all facets of a child's development as seen in the play of Tearra and Portia. Physically, blocks are lifted and carried about enhancing development and coordination of small and large muscles. Socially, children may choose to interact and talk with others as they build. This involves cooperative group effort and social give and take. Emotionally, children feel good about what they have successfully created. Destruction may bring emotional release and more joy than construction. Cognitively, children think, plan, and learn about balance,

height, shape, space, cause and effect, architectural forms, and even gravity when tall towers give way to an unsturdy base. Since block play is open-ended, they foster a child's creative development.

Types of Blocks   There are several types of blocks: unit, large hollow, cardboard bricks, and miscellaneous, including smaller table blocks and those made of soft foam. Wooden blocks, including unit and large hollow, are an expensive but sound investment. If properly cared for, they should last many years. Wooden unit blocks are built to scale, e.g., square or half unit, unit, double unit, and quadruple unit, so children encounter mathematical concepts as they compare blocks by length. There are also an array of block shapes, including curve, ellipse, switch, triangle, ramp, column, buttress, arch, and pillar that supplement the lengths of unit blocks. Older block builders may rely on some of the additional shapes but do not feel obligated to purchase multiples of each and every shape, especially for younger and beginning block builders.

Block Center   Block play requires ample space and protection from foot traffic. Building on a carpet reduces the noise level. Blocks require storage and should never be randomly placed in a box or storage bin. This damages the finish, edges, and corners.

Blocks should be arranged on low open shelves according to size, length and shape so they are easily found and put away. Reserve a bottom shelf for the heavier pieces with lightweight props on the top. Providing an outline of the block shape will help in matching and cleanup. Trace the shape of the block onto colored construction paper, cut it out, and attach it to the back of the appropriate shelf. Provide props like animals, small dinosaurs, small people, vehicles, and traffic signs to enrich block play, as well as small sheets for roofs, boards for ramps, blue construction paper for water, Plexiglas, and masking tape for streets or sidewalks. Similar props like cars and trucks can be kept together in clear tubs or baskets. Remember to rotate block props and to include items that reinforce what you are studying. For example, be sure to include toy fish and blue fabric when studying sea life. There is nothing more frustrating to young builders than having their construction "accidentally" knocked down. This can be avoided by reminding children not to build too close to each other or too close to the storage shelves. To make cleanup less chaotic, remind children to only take a few blocks out at a time and then use them before going for more. Also, dismantling buildings from the top down eliminates unnecessary noise and accidents. (See Figure 3–3.)

Whereas unit blocks stress fine motor and eye-hand coordination, large hollow blocks provide a gross motor and large muscle challenge. They also allow children to build larger, child-proportioned structures. Be sure to include steering wheels for children who make child-sized vehicles. Smaller unit blocks encourage children to build in miniature, which is why small props are provided. Blocks foster active play and you may need to set guidelines regarding safety issues like how high children can build. Children may also need this reminder: "Blocks are for building, not throwing. They are heavy and can hurt." These printed words can appear as signs in your block centers. Keep an instamatic camera loaded with film and ready to photograph individual or group block constructions. Take dictation or encourage children to write if they have words that accompany their building. The dated photo can be included in the child's portfolio. Children may need

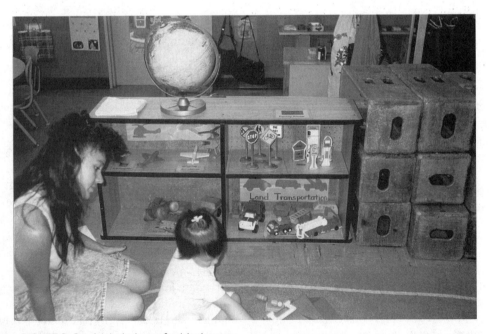

FIGURE 3–3   A labeled area for block props

your assistance in making signs such as "Please do not knock down" or "Keep up." Reserve a shelf in your block area for books on construction and building, along with papers and writing instruments. This will connect block play with literacy. Along with labeled shelves, include photographs of multicultural homes and neighborhoods as well as males and females involved in block-play-related pursuits like construction, farming, and transportation.

Cardboard bricks are a third type of block. They are inexpensive and not sturdy. They are large but lightweight which inhibits complex building like making high towers and may frustrate the skilled builder. On the positive side, they make less noise when they tumble. On the negative side, children enjoy walking on them which quickly destroys them. Cardboard bricks are a good choice for the very young, who can later graduate to heavier wooden blocks. Make your own blocks by covering shoe boxes or milk cartons with contact paper. Other types of blocks include rubber, foam, and small table blocks. Rubber and foam blocks are lightweight, inexpensive, and recommended for young and beginning block builders. Table blocks, which are smaller than unit blocks, involve small muscle control and eye-hand coordination and result in construction on a smaller scale. Different types of blocks can also supplement each other during constructive play.

3. Dramatic Play

Dramatic play is also referred to as play that involves fantasy, imagination, or make-believe. Children engage in dramatic play alone or with others and usually with props. A child who is dressing a baby doll is engaging in dramatic or symbolic play. Toddlers learn that the doll symbolically represents a real baby. A preschooler may use a box as a table. Children who engage in dramatic play have attained representational ability. Children practice language and social skills, as well as planning and decision-making skills, in dramatic play. They can rehearse family roles and learn about community helpers. Children re-create what they know through dramatic play. A child who has been loved and nurtured will act out this scenario in dramatic play. A child

who talks harshly to or even spanks a baby doll tells you something very different about what he or she knows or has experienced. Children will also use dramatic play to work through emotional issues like sibling rivalry, fear of abandonment, or impending hospitalization. In contrast to dramatic play, sociodramatic play is a more organized, cooperative type of fantasy play engaged in by older preschoolers, kindergartners, and young school-age children in which roles are divided and players have different parts. For example, in playing house, there may be a mommy, a daddy, twin babies, and a pet dog. Each child has a role, function, and speaking part to play.

Dramatic Play Center   A dramatic play center can be located next to the block area since both invite loud, active, imaginative play. Similar items should be organized, grouped together, and labeled. Providing furniture that resembles a home, including table and chairs, cooking and eating equipment, kitchen appliances, food, multiethnic dolls and clothing, stuffed animals, mirror, cash register, microphone, camera, puppets, walkie-talkies, and telephones sets a familiar and comfortable stage. Props enhance dramatic play by expanding the realm of creative possibilities. Be sure to include clothing that represents what both men and women, as well as uniformed community helpers, wear in your locale. Children are learning about their social world, so expect boys to try on half-slips and jewelry and girls to play being the daddy. Providing open-ended props like a sheet or a length of rubber hose will challenge older preschoolers.

Connect dramatic play to your curriculum. Providing "money," such as Styrofoam pieces or strips of green construction paper, facilitates counting; grouping food in the grocery store builds classification skills. Include books on multiethnic families and the occupations under study. Children can only re-create what they know so they will have difficulty dramatizing being a banker, astronaut, travel agent, or circus performer. Make sure that they have directly experienced what you want them to act out. Invite in a mother who is a dentist and then set the stage for dental play in your dramatic play corner. Or, go on a field trip to a local fast-food restaurant.

FIGURE 3–4   Young chefs being creative at play

Set up your own version with clothing and props upon your return. Encourage sociodramatic play by building prop boxes for dramatic play around a theme (see Figure 3–4). For example, collect clothing and props related to a veterinary hospital and place in a large box labeled with symbols (e.g., pictures of animals and the words "Veterinarian" or "Animal Doctor"). Keep an inventory of the contents taped to the inside lid. For instance, include stuffed animals, lab coats, surgical gowns and masks, and red-cross armbands for doctors and nurses; lab coats for office workers and dress-up clothes for pet owners; doctor tools and medical bag, Band-Aids, and gauze or lengths of white fabric; boxes, baskets, bowls, and brushes for sick pets. Introduce your prop box with a book or better yet a field trip or class visit by a vet. Connect your prop box and dramatic play area to literacy. Include writing instruments, clipboards, stamps, papers, envelopes, cookbooks and magazines. Specific literacy props for dramatizing a veterinary hospital include an appointment book, old x-rays, a prescription pad, a doctor's In/Out sign, magazines for the waiting room, empty medicine containers, and books on animals, first aid, or veterinarians. Including papers and writing materials will encourage children to write letters, lists, receipts, and to send and receive mail.

Favorite books and stories can be acted out in the dramatic play area. This will work better with children who have interacted together in sociodramatic play. Start with a simple nursery rhyme like "Humpty Dumpty," moving on to short stories with a few characters, simple plots, and manageable speaking lines. Provide simple costumes and props to ease children into the role. For example, Humpty Dumpty may wear a fancy bathrobe and a simple crown, and horses may hold simple masks. Girls can play the part of the king's men and take creative liberty to change the rhyme to include "all the king's women."

4. Play with Natural Materials

Adults who appreciate a walk on the beach, splashing in the waves, soaking in a bathtub, or smelling and feeling sawed wood will understand how play with water, sand, and wood appeal to young children. Play with natural materials is sensory-rich, soothing, and therapeutic. Since our world is made up of water and sand, children gradually develop concepts about bodies of water like oceans and land forms like deserts. Although water is wet and sand is dry, both hold great sensory appeal and lead children to similar discoveries; for example, both can be poured and measured. Children can also discover that water, sand, and wood have unique properties. Unlike sand, water can freeze and melt. Wood can be sawed into small pieces and attached with either glue or hammer and nails. Natural materials are open-ended and provide unlimited creative possibilities, while also supporting physical, social, emotional, cognitive, and language development. Along with the obvious physical challenge, carpentry and woodworking foster children's verbal and social interaction. They develop skills in observation, problem solving, measurement, and hypothesizing.

Water/Sand Play   Water and sand need large containers that will provide ample room for small group play. Water/sand play tables with lids are commercially available and a sound investment. They tend to be large enough to accommodate four children and come with a drain plug. Alternatives include:

- dish pans or baby bathtubs
- shallow flat containers like photographic developing trays
- shallow wading pool or plastic sandbox
- plastic boat
- large tractor or truck tire

Place your table near the sink and cover surrounding floor area with a vinyl shower curtain or old towels that can be thrown in the dryer when wet. Cleanup equipment for mopping up water or sweeping up spills should be kept on an adjacent storage shelf along with accessories. Provide waterproof smocks and remind children to roll up their sleeves. Children should also keep a change of clothing in their cubbies. Limit the number of children based on the size of your water or sand table. Discuss guidelines and limits and set them in positive terms: "We play with sand and water and keep it in the table. Splashing water gets our friends wet." "Throwing sand is dangerous and can hurt the eyes." Give children a choice of either upholding the guidelines or playing somewhere else. Remind children that part of the cycle of playing with water and sand is cleaning up.

Water/sand play can occur both indoors and outdoors. Some teachers prefer to have an indoor sensory table that rotates contents between water (with and without soap bubbles), sand, shaving cream, nature specimens like shells, pebbles, stone, or flower petals, snow, shaved ice, aquarium gravel, marbles, sawdust, birdseed, or cornstarch and water. It is of foremost importance that children experience the tactile quality of the contents. Later, add props and accessories to supplement tactile exploration. Choose those that are appropriate for contents. Eliminate glass, sharp or rusty items, and those which are breakable, or are too small and tempting to put in one's mouth.

Water/sand play accessories include:

- animal figures, aquarium nets
- balloons, bicycle pump, blocks, boats, bowls, brushes (e.g., bottle, spray, squirt, shaving), bulb basters, buttons, buckets
- clothespins, colanders, condiment bottles, containers (with holes and without in graduated sizes), cookie cutters, corks, cups, cars, construction vehicles
- dish detergent, dish mops, dolls and clothes
- egg beaters
- film cans, fishing bobbers, funnels (alone or attached to ends of plastic tubing)
- golf balls and tees
- hose with spray nozzle
- ice, ice-cream scoop, ice-cube trays
- Jell-O molds
- kettle
- ladles, liter bottles (with holes punched around the base to create a fountain)
- magnets, margarine tubs with lids, marbles, measuring cups and spoons, medicine droppers, milk cartons, muffin tins
- nesting cups
- pail, pans, paintbrushes, people figures, pie tin, Ping-Pong balls, pitchers, plastic eggs, plastic hoses and tubes, plastic straws, Popsicle sticks, pots, plastic containers
- rocks, rolling pin, rubber washers
- salt shakers, scoops, scrub brush, shells, sieve, sifters, slotted spoons, small boats, snow, soap (bar), sponges (e.g., alphabet and numeral), spools, stones, strainer, Styrofoam packing, syringe, shovels
- teapot, thermometers, thimble, tinfoil (flat pieces and balls) tongs, tongue depressors, toothpicks, tubing
- water wheels, watering can, whisk, wood scraps, wooden blocks, wooden spoons

Activities for water play include:

washing—Provide shells, paintbrushes, small furniture, vehicles, bar soap, scrub brush, and washboard. Discuss how items look before and after washing.

dish washing—Periodically have children wash the dishes and play food in the dramatic area.

doll washing—Provide dolls of color along with bar soap, washcloths, and brushes. Help children see that dark skin does not equate with dirty. Skin color is a given and constant that does not change with washing. Dirty baby dolls with light skin stay light skinned, but clean, after washing; dirty baby dolls with dark skin stay dark skinned, but clean, after washing.

measurement—Provide measuring cups and container of water. Encourage children to discover how many small containers are needed to fill a larger container.

magnetism—Provide small fishing poles and magnetic fish.

melting—Place a block of ice, ice cubes, snow, or shaved ice in a container outdoors in the sun. Encourage children to see what happens over time. Does one form melt faster than the others?

temperature—Engage in play with water of different temperatures. Leave the water out in the sun before playing. Later, add ice cubes. Discuss the similarities and differences.

absorption—Provide Q-tips, paper towels, sponges, and an array of nonabsorbent materials. Encourage children to discover which ones absorb water.

evaporation—Provide large paintbrushes, house painter's gear and buckets of water. Encourage children to paint the sidewalk, building, windows, and clean the riding vehicles. Observe what happens to the painted-on water over time.

evaporation—Have children wash doll or baby clothes and hang them on a clothesline outdoors to dry. Or, use several wet sponges—alphabet and numerals are good choices because they connect water play with literacy. Encourage them to check back over time. What happened and why?

freezing—Children pour water into ice-cube trays. Place one in freezer; leave others in the room or in the sun. Have children notice any differences. What happened and why?

freezing—Have children wash doll or baby clothes. Place in freezer and check over time. What happened and why?

coloring water—Provide eye droppers and place drops of food coloring or liquid watercolor into water. What change takes place? What if different colored waters are mixed? Begin by providing one or two primary colors at a time.

coloring water—Have children place strips of crepe paper or tissue paper in clear plastic tumblers. Note what happens to the water.

coloring water—Add colored ice cubes to a container of water and watch what happens.

dissolving—Provide materials including Jell-O, salt, sugar, dirt, pebbles, marbles, paper scraps, etc. Have children place each in water and observe which ones dissolve.

sink and float—Provide an array of objects that sink (e.g., marbles, pebbles, nuts, bolts) and items that float (e.g., corks and twigs). Encourage children to predict and then test out their hunches by placing the objects in water.

sink and float—Provide materials like wooden craft sticks, small wooden scraps, or sheets of tinfoil for making boats.

sink and float and dissolving—Place bars of soap in water. Observe what happens over time. Have children observe the size of the soap and consistency of the water.

mixing—Have children make mud pies by combining water with sand or dirt.

mixing—Add liquid soap to water and provide rotary egg beaters.

making music—Assemble eight identical glass tumblers or bottles. Fill the containers with water at varying levels. Gently strike each with a rhythm stick or pencil and listen.

conservation—Provide containers that hold the same volume or amount but are of different sizes and shapes. Encourage children to fill and compare but do not verbally impose adult logic. Avoid saying, "See, it's still the same amount."

Although water may be more versatile in terms of potential activities, children can also use sand in the above activities involving measurement, absorption (of water), coloring (with chalk), mixing, (with paint) and conservation. Wet sand is good for sculpting; children can use their fingers to practice printing their name or favorite letters in dry sand.

Carpentry or Woodworking The thought of carpentry or woodworking and young children concerns some educators. It may be a safety issue or one's own discomfort level based on a lack of knowledge and skills in using tools. Tools empower boys and girls as well as provide opportunities in refining large muscle and fine motor skills as well as eye-hand coordination. Carpentry and woodworking also allow for emotional release. An angry child who has difficulty verbalizing his or her feelings can hammer or saw them out. It does not address the heart of the problem but it does relieve pent-up anger. Tools must be individually introduced through modeling, with children practicing the correct way to hold and use a tool. Safety is a foremost consideration. Carpentry or woodworking takes very close supervision with a maximum of four children participating at a time, one per corner. Children should wear aprons and safety goggles. Provide real tools in smaller sizes as opposed to toy tools which can easily bend and snap. Tools can be displayed on the Peg-Board with the outlines of each drawn around it. Tables can be commercially purchased but a handyperson could easily make one to your specifications, or simply cut the legs off a wooden kitchen table. Sawhorses with a sturdy plank or old door that has been securely attached can also be used. Height is very important—the bench should be waist-high to the children, neither too high nor too low. Along with a sturdy workbench, recommended tools include:

- claw hammers (12-oz. weight)
- C-clamps (to hold the wood steady while sawing)
- vises mounted at opposite corners of the workbench (to hold the wood steady while sawing)
- pliers
- screwdrivers: slotted and Phillips
- hand drill, brace, and bit (better for older children since it involves downward pressure with one hand while other hand turns a circle)
- saws: crosscut with 10–12 teeth per inch (10- or 12-point) and 16- to 18-inch blade
- nuts, bolts, washers, screws, and nails
- wood scraps (soft woods including fir, white pine, and balsa)
- wood craft sticks
- doweling

- wood glue
- large Styrofoam pieces
- sandpaper and sandpaper blocks

Young children will approach carpentry or woodworking activities with a process orientation. They want to see what they can do with tools, wood, and fasteners. Sawing wood and hammering nails are pleasurable in and of themselves. Older children will be more interested in making something and may even plan their finished product in advance. Encourage them to make blueprints or simple sketches of what they plan to make. Invite children to

- hammer nails into layers of cardboard which have been glued together
- hammer nails into a tree stump
- hammer golf tees into Styrofoam
- hammer nails into Styrofoam
- hammer nails into a jar lid
- hammer nails into a block of plasticene or clay
- tighten screws on toys, tricycles, and furniture
- use sandpaper on rough edges of blocks of wood or on old wooden toys and blocks
- use tools to make block props
- glue wood scraps into a wood collage

Hint Help children use a hammer by showing them how to hold it. Young children tend to grasp the hammer near the head. Holding the handle farther back, however, provides greater leverage and pressure. You may want to tap a nail to help children begin hammering. Or, push the nail through an index card or sturdy strip of paper with the child holding the end of the card or paper as they strike the nail. This way fingers and thumbs stay clear of the hammer. When the nail is adequately pounded, they can pull the paper away.

Hint Provide nails that are short with broad heads. Roofing nails work well. Longer nails take too long to hammer in and often bend in the process.

Hint To help children use a saw, secure wood in vise or C-clamp. Help the child hold the saw at a 45-degree angle and use light pressure to rhythmically move the saw downward in a back and forth motion.

Hint Reserve the hand drill for use with school-age children. It is difficult to operate since one hand applies downward pressure while the other makes it go around. Also, young children tend to make it turn backwards, which only loosens the drill bit.

Hint Make a game out of cleanup. Provide whisk brooms and dustpans for sweeping up sawdust. Magnets work well for picking up fallen nails, nuts, bolts, and screws. Always match up tools to their outline on the Peg-Board. Tools lying around pose potential safety problems.

Games Think back to your own childhood and reflect on the games you played. Do you remember playing "tag," "hide-and-seek," or an informal game of ball? Do you recall winning or never getting picked for the team? Have you ever observed a teacher trying to play "Duck, Duck, Goose" with a group of young children? They play out of turn and often do their own thing. Young children have difficulty playing games. Their egocentric side may keep them from waiting, taking turns, and playing by the rules. They may change and break the rules at whim to make it work for them. This is not cheating, but rather reflects their inability to hold to rules which protect others and may keep them from winning. With years of social interaction, older children see how rules protect the rights of all individuals and may ostracize a child whom they believe is "cheating." Games are competitive, usually resulting in a winner and loser. This may be difficult for even older children to face. Depending on your group it may be wise to modify games. For example, in "Musical Chairs," the play is ongoing but no chairs are removed so there are no losers; everyone gets to play every round of the game. School-age children, however, become socially competitive as they test their mental prowess with card and board games, involving memory, strategy, or chance. They compare their physical abilities like aiming, racing, chasing, or hiding, and in sports like baseball, soccer, basketball, and kickball. You may want to intro-duce them to cooperative games which foster team building and working together rather than winning at the expense of others.

CHILDREN EXPRESS THEIR CREATIVITY THROUGH LANGUAGE

The profile of the creative child reminds the author of two famous characters in children's literature. First, like the little boy in *The Emperor's New Clothes,* creative children are able to see what others do not. They are also able to stand up for their beliefs and not yield to social pressure, whereas others may change their opinions to conform and not appear different. Second, like the Ugly Duckling who becomes the beautiful swan, children can trust their creativity to help them become the unique individuals they are destined to become. Help children acknowledge and accept their creative uniqueness by identifying with characters in literature.

The early years are a time of rapid language development. Language is caught rather than taught. Children learn an extensive collection of words or vocabulary which helps them communicate with others. The infant who says "bobba" will be given a bottle by an adult who knows the infant is asking for a bottle. Saying "bobba" will not get a ride in the car although saying "go" might. Much of language development entails learning that words refer to specific objects and actions. Children also creatively invent their own words as evidenced in the following examples:

- Sahid calls his brother's convertible a "top-down car."
- When served pancakes for breakfast, Jocelyn exclaims, "Oh good, flat cakes; my favorite."
- Gabrielle asks her teacher for some "cutters" as she points to the empty scissors rack.
- Daryl asks his mother if he can talk to his grandma on the "hello phone."
- Amira walks with a doll in the stroller as she announces, "I'm getting a baby pusher like this for my birthday."
- During lunch Cory argues that they are drinking "cow juice," not milk.

- Mrs. Lo is doing a food activity with her small group. She passes around an uncut pineapple. When it is Orin's turn he remarks, "Oh, Christmas-tree fruit."
- Scott puts on his jacket but does not get it fastened. While pointing to the Velcro fasteners he asks, "Can somebody stick me together?"
- McKenzie's parents pack a slice of pepperoni pizza in her lunch box. Her friends look on with envy as she exclaims, "Oh, cold meatzza for lunch again!"

Language is actively constructed. Children will invent words and creatively err when forming plurals or verb tenses. They are constructing the rules of language and may overgeneralize in the process. Knowing that you add an "s" to the end of words to form plurals leads children to talk about "geeses" and "fishes." Since "ed" is added to the end of a word to signify past tense, children proudly announce, "I wented home," or "I goed to school." Adults who have learned English as a second language will testify that English is a complex language with more exceptions than regularities. Express interest as children creatively construct and invent words that work and make sense to them. There is no need to correct. Instead say, "Meatzza—that's a clever name for meat pizza." In this way McKenzie learns that her creative expression through language is valued but that conventional alternatives also exist.

Informal Creative Language Activities

A child's waking day offers a wealth of opportunities for fostering language development (see Figure 3–5). Children in school learn language while interacting with peers and adults. Consider these two recommendations. First, children who are vertically grouped with a range of ages are exposed to a wider array of vocabulary and language patterns than children who are grouped by identical chronological age. Second, teachers must model and provide opportunities for speaking, listening, reading, and writing. Some informal creative language activities include the following:

- Provide oral language props including puppets, telephones, and walkie-talkies. These props help

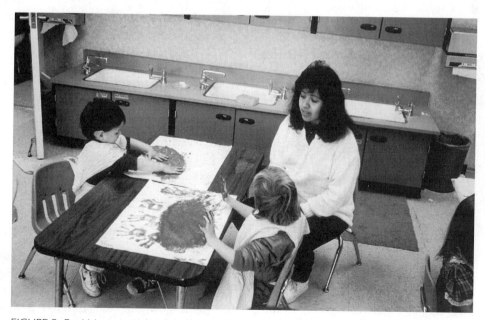

FIGURE 3–5   *Using words to describe*

shy children and those beginning to learn English.

- Tell stories in novel ways using unusual props. Invite children to tell you stories or "read" the pictures in books.

- Make storytelling props like felt or pellon (interfacing) pieces available to children. Tell them how much you enjoy being at the receiving end of a good story.

- Take creative liberty with traditional and contemporary literature. Add, change, or delete characters. For example, invent new wild things for *Where the Wild Things Are.*

- Take dictation. Ask children if there are words or a story to go along with their artwork. Carefully listen, write, and read it back. Encourage the child to read along with you (see Figures 3–6, 3–7, 3–8).

- Observe opportune times to get involved and facilitate children's play. For example, children who are simply sitting in the dramatic play area may be waiting for a good idea. Facilitate play by suggesting that the babies appear hungry and might want to go out to eat before their afternoon nap. Stay involved as long as necessary but without dominating or imposing your way of doing things.

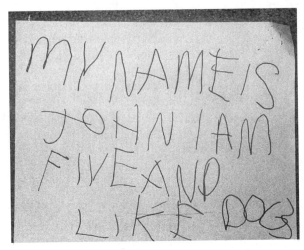

FIGURE 3–7   John wrote his own story.

FIGURE 3–8   Mark wrote his own book.

Using Literature to Facilitate Children's Creative Expression

There are many examples of children's books that foster creative expression. Following are some good books and creative activities to extend the stories:

- After reading *The Napping House* by Audrey Wood, ask the children to come up with their own napping story. Change the location to create a napping story set on a farm, at a zoo, or in outer space.

- *Pretend You're a Cat* by Jean Marzollo is a good lead-in to a creative movement activity. Have the children move or make noises like the animals in the story. What other noises or movements does

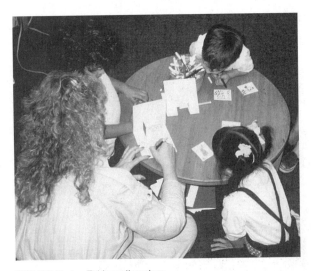

FIGURE 3–6   Taking dictation

each make? Pretend you are an animal that doesn't appear in the story. What noise or movements does it make? What else might it say or do?

- After reading *Imogene's Antlers* by David Small, have the children brainstorm for other possible uses for Imogene's antlers.
- In *Bearymore* by Don Freeman, Bearymore, a performing circus bear, is told by the ringmaster to come up with a new act. What could it be? Ask the children to help Bearymore think of new and different ways to perform.
- Discuss the dilemma in *Doctor DeSoto* by William Steig. How can the mouse-dentist treat his wolf-patient without being eaten in the process?
- After reading *A House Is a House for Me* by Mary Ann Hoberman, ask the children to identify things that could be a house for something else. For example, a Band-Aid could be a house for a cut. What could be a house for a butterfly? Try to have the children come up with many different possibilities.
- After reading *Can I Keep Him?* by Steven Kellogg, have the children identify unusual pets and brainstorm potential problems with keeping that animal for a pet. For example, an alligator might be a good pet but it would have too many teeth to brush.

Refer to the cover and color insert for other creative language activities.

CHILDREN EXPRESS THEIR CREATIVITY THROUGH MUSIC AND MOVEMENT

Music and movement begin early in life when parents sing lullabies and dance with infants in their arms. Children may grow up with grandparents who sing to them and older siblings who dance about the house. They learn that people use music and movement to communicate. In turn, they sing when happy, often repeating TV jingles and familiar songs. They will sing while at play, in the bathtub, on the potty, or when falling asleep. They will creatively make up their own words to familiar tunes. See Table 3–1 for Pica's (1995) Developmental Stages of Musical Experiences.

As with motor development, every child progresses through the stages of musical development at his or her own pace. Although the sequence of developmental stages remains the same for all children, the ages at which they reach and pass through each stage can vary from child to child.

2-YEAR-OLDS

- Use their bodies in response to music, often by bouncing up and down
- Can learn short, simple songs
- Show increasing ability to follow directions in songs
- Respond enthusiastically to favorite songs, often asking to hear them repeatedly
- May sing parts of songs (often not on pitch), but seldom sing with a group
- Enjoy experimenting with sounds, with everything from household objects to musical instruments
- Can discriminate among songs

3-YEAR-OLDS

- Have greater rhythmic ability
- Can recognize and sing parts of familiar tunes, though usually not on pitch
- Make up their own songs
- Walk, run, and jump to music
- Enjoy dramatizing songs

4-YEAR-OLDS

- Can grasp basic musical concepts like tempo, volume, and pitch
- Show a dramatic increase in vocal range and rhythmic ability
- Create new lyrics for songs
- Enjoy more complex songs
- Love silly songs
- Prefer "active" listening (singing, moving, doing fingerplays, accompanying music with instruments)

TABLE 3–1   Developmental Stages of Musical Experiences

(continued)

5- TO 6-YEAR-OLDS

- Can reproduce a melody
- Begin to synchronize movements with the music's rhythm
- Enjoy singing and moving with a group
- Enjoy call-and-response songs
- Have fairly established musical preferences
- Can perform two movements simultaneously (e.g., marching and playing a rhythm instrument)

7- TO 8-YEAR-OLDS

- Are learning to read lyrics
- Can learn simple folk dances taught by adults
- Enjoy musical duets with friends
- May display a desire to study dance or play an instrument
- Can synchronize movements to the beat of the music
- Can compare three or more sounds

TABLE 3–1 (continued)
(Courtesy of Pica, R. 1995. *Experiences in Movement.* Reprinted with permission from Delmar Publishers.)

Music and movement complement the developing child who is naturally talkative and constantly in motion. A child's singing and body movement indicate mood. A happy child will sing and actively move his or her body. An overly quiet, sullen child with halting, limited movements may signify a different mood, such as an "off-day" or possible problem. As with art, there is a human need to make music and move to it. This need crosses time and culture. People have been making music and dancing since day one in caves and may one day do the same in outer space. Music and movement are lifelong pursuits. Adolescents appear addicted to music and dance while adults are known to hum, whistle, sing in the shower or while driving, play an instrument, and dance. The interest and love for music and movement compensate for any perceived lack of innate talent or ability.

Why Music and Movement Are Important

Creative experiences in music and movement serve two major purposes. First, they meet the needs of the whole child: physically, socially, emotionally, cognitively, creatively, and in the area of language. Second, they help integrate and enrich the early childhood curriculum. When moving to music, children are involved in physical activities—stretching, bending, reaching, hopping, crawling, and leaping, to name a few. Small muscle and fine motor control as well as eye-hand coordination are needed to play musical instruments. Socially, young children may choose to sing and dance with others. This involves taking turns, cooperating, and sharing musical instruments—all important social skills. Multicultural songs and dances extend children's social horizons and help them see the universality among people— all people everywhere sing and dance. An acceptance of how children sing and move fosters their self-acceptance and promotes positive self-esteem. Emotionally, they are also able to express their feelings. Music can have a calming effect on an upset child or provide an outlet for feelings of frustration or anger. For example, children can sing in mad voices or use their bodies to show how mad they are feeling. Cognitively, music helps children develop concepts of fast-slow, high-low, colors, animals, shapes, the alphabet, and numbers, as in counting songs. The patterns heard in music prepare the child for the patterning that underlies math and reading. Learning about themselves and their world can be done in developmentally appropriate ways through the use of music and movement, as opposed to a didactic academic approach. Adults who accept children's attempts at singing and dance send a message that there is no right or wrong way. In turn, this nurtures children's creative development. The language arts, speaking, listening, reading, and writing, are also enhanced through music and movement. Because singing is speech set to music, children's oral language development is also enhanced. Children practice listening and auditory skills like discrimination and memory when learning the words to new songs or attending to music's repetition, rhythm, and rhyme. Music is intimately connected to a young child's emerging literacy. Children can compose and even draw-write their own songs or dance steps. They may also want to write their own books about a favorite song. Song charts based on simple repetitive favorites like "There Were Ten in the Bed" can facilitate word recognition, reading, and math.

Components of Music and Movement

There are four vital components to a comprehensive music and movement program. These include listening to music, singing, playing instruments, and moving to music.

1. Listening to Music

Listening to a song is a good preparation for singing. It allows children to learn the words and rhythm. Provide a variety of music for children to listen to. Play music throughout the day. Music with an upbeat tempo will facilitate cleanup. Lullabies by Brahms will set a quiet relaxed tone for rest. Provide more than just children's songs. Introduce children to folk music, jazz, classical music, and music from different cultures. Provide a tape recorder with a jack and multiple headsets for more than one child to use at a time. Color-code instructions (e.g., green dot on play and red dot on stop) to foster children's independent use. Include children's songbooks on tape. Children will enjoy having their individual or small group singing recorded for future playbacks. By listening to a variety of music, children come to learn that music

- can be fast or slow, just like when they walk as opposed to run
- has tempo, as they compare a lullaby with a march
- can be loud or soft (they can also sing in a loud or soft voice)
- has a beat, like a clock or their heart

2. Singing

Although children's singing does not occur in stages, Wolf (1994) believes that children progress from listening to tagging on, which is followed by joining in, and culminates in independent singing. According to this framework, children learn to sing by first listening to songs sung to them. Toddlers soon start to "tag on" to songs that they hear and like. They may echo bits and "catchy parts" while at play. Preschoolers join in singing as part of a group. Eventually most young children not only enjoy singing with a group but are equally comfortable singing alone. This usually occurs by kindergarten. Children can sing alone, with others, or while listening to a record or tape. Since music and movement are closely related, choose songs that are accompanied by activity. For example, children enjoy hammering with their fists while singing "Johnny Works with One Hammer" and the finger and hand motions that accompany the "Itsy Bitsy Spider" or "Wheels on the Bus." It is not required that the teacher be a gifted singer. Children are more interested in an enthusiastic model who loves to sing. Children are not critical if you cannot sing well, because they have a very limited singing range (a few notes above middle C) and often sing off-key when notes are too high or too low. Begin by learning the song well before presenting it to the children. When introducing a new song, sing slowly and clearly, repeating the song. Then invite the children to sing along. Select songs that you like and ones based on your children's interests, abilities, and developmental stage. Young children enjoy songs that are silly and involve body actions or their names. Select short, simple, active songs with a limited musical range, repetition, and simple rhythms. Examples include "Do You Know the Muffin Man?" and "If You're Happy and You Know It." Each of these allows for creative improvisation. Have parents teach you songs in other languages and help translate songs learned in English into a second language. Sing throughout the day during transitions and routines like arrival time, group time, play time, cleanup time, and departure time. Continue singing when outdoors. Plan for music but also allow for spontaneity. Break into a song when it begins raining or when welcoming back a child who has been hospitalized. Sing familiar songs but encourage children to creatively invent their own. Work with small groups in creatively changing the words to familiar songs just for fun or to fit a routine or transition. For example, to the tune of "Are You Sleeping, Brother John?" try singing "Are you cleaning, are you cleaning, Jay and Kate, Leslie and Don?" Or, "This is the way we clean up our room, clean up our room, clean up our room. This is the way we clean up our room on Monday morning." Become familiar with a host of child-oriented popular recordings by Steve & Greg, Raffi, Sharon, Lois & Bram, Burl Ives, Sesame Street, Barney, Ella Jenkins, Hap Palmer, Wee Sing, and Disney, among others who offer a variety of records, tapes, and CDs for sale. How to choose? According to Wolf (1994), look for in-tune singing, children's voices, easy-listening adult vocals, and simple instrumentation. Songs can integrate and extend into other curriculum areas. Singing "Old Macdonald Had a Farm" can tie in with a discussion of animals or life on a farm. "The Wheels on the Bus" can introduce a unit on transportation or vehicle safety. "Mary Had a Little Lamb" can lead to a discussion of rough and soft with children decorating their own lambs with cotton balls. This activity extends a music-based book into the realm of art. A book-based curriculum connects literacy with the creative arts.

3. Making Music with Rhythm Instruments

Children love to make music, as evidenced by the popularity of banging on pots and pans. Do not overlook the body as a musical instrument. Children enjoy clapping hands, shaking body parts, stamping feet, slapping thighs, and snapping fingers to music. There are different types of musical instruments which are commercially available. Include both rhythm and melodic instruments. Drums, tambourines, sticks, triangles, maracas, cymbals, and sandpaper blocks are examples of percussion instruments that make a single sound and can be used to make and keep a beat. Children can play a tune on melodic instruments including a xylophone, a piano, a keyboard, and tone bells. Be sure to include other items that make sounds, including kitchen gadgets, keys, musical toys, music boxes, a metronome, or sound containers. Although commercially available, rhythm instruments can be inexpensively made. This not only empowers the children but provides an incentive for using them. Music is integrated with art when instruments are creatively decorated. Instructions for how to make a few simple instruments follow.

Rattles—Place dry gourds on a windowsill, turning them every few days. After a few weeks the seeds inside will dry and fall away from the inner skin.

Drums—Children can rhythmically pound any of these: milk cartons, coffee cans, oatmeal boxes, wooden bowls, pots, pans, empty house-paint cans, stainless steel mixing bowls.

Shakers—Put beans or pebbles between two paper plates and staple the edges together. Or fill a margarine tub (or any plastic container with a removable lid), paper bag, or plastic stocking eggs with beans or pebbles.

Maracas—Place rice or gravel in an empty, clear plastic shampoo or detergent bottle.

Rhythm sticks—Children can rap together two pencils or dowel rods.

Spoons—Use any two metal spoons.

Bells—String jingle bells on a piece of elastic and tie the ends. Wear on wrists or ankles. Or attach to plastic six-pack rings, or through holes punched in toilet paper tubes. Bells can also be sewn onto ribbon strips.

Cymbals—Bang together two pot lids or pie tins.

Banjo—Stretch several different-sized rubber bands over the bottom of a shoe box and strum.

Sand blocks—Glue sandpaper to two wooden blocks.

Baton—Roll up a newspaper to make a drum major or orchestra conductor's baton.

Gong—Hit an old license plate with a toy mallet.

Children need experience with rhythm if they are to successfully use rhythm instruments. Having young children listen to music and clap out the beat with their hands or tap it out with their feet is a good introduction to rhythm instruments. Provide ample experiences in clapping rhythm patterns to their names, simple poems, and nursery rhymes. For example, Ida's name involves two claps: I (clap) da (clap). When introducing a rhythm instrument, first listen to the music for its rhythmic patterns and then match the beat with the instrument. It is wise to have multiples of rhythm instruments and introduce them one at a time, for example, four tambourines in a small group. This prevents children from just creating noise by playing a group of unrelated instruments together with no regard for rhythm. Children also enjoy having a parade or playing in a band. Children can take turns using the baton to lead the orchestra. Sing "Old MacDonald had a band, ee-i-ee-i-o. And on that band he had a (add instrument)." Or, sing "The Farmer in the Dell" with the instruments choosing each other. Or, "This is the way we play our bells," etc.

4. Moving to Music

Large motor actions like walking, hopping, swaying, marching, and galloping can be paired with music. Children enjoy moving like animals, vehicles, or characters in a favorite story. Model movement and dance. You need not be a gifted dancer. It is more important to share your love of music and the way your body moves to music. Props help the unsure or shy child. Include hoops, crepe paper streamers, scarves, hats, crowns, fancy costumes, ribbons, magic wands, grass skirts, fans, soft batons for leading the band, pom-poms, and lengths of sheer fabric. Streamers taped to outstretched arms make dancing wings. Creative movement gives children an outlet for their physical energy, encouraging them to express their feelings and creativity in nonverbal ways. Creative movement activities can be either totally open-ended or teacher-guided. In open-ended activities, children move in ways that are individually meaningful. For example, a teacher can play a tape of *Swan Lake* and watch the children dance, however the music moves them. In teacher-guided activities, the adult provides the stimulus or frame which subtly structures the movement activity. Examples include asking children to move

- like a familiar animal or pet
- like a familiar vehicle, e.g., motorcycle
- like a familiar community helper, e.g., fire fighter or truck driver
- creatively, like a flying car
- in ways that enact a nursery rhyme like "Jack Be Nimble" or a simple story like "The Three Little Pigs"
- in pantomime to waking up, getting dressed, eating, or falling asleep
- in ways that are angry, sad, happy, scared, or surprised
- as if they were trees swaying in the wind, toast in a toaster, clothes in a dryer, water going down the bathtub drain, or food in a blender
- with imaginary wings and fly away
- by making their body grow very tall or shrink very small
- by staying in one spot and wiggling all over and then becoming perfectly still

- by moving around hula hoops in slow and quiet ways
- by using their hands and arms to make rainbows in the sky
- by becoming very crooked or very soft and squishy

Solicit children's input in other ways to move. They will tell you ways they know how to move, for example, wiggly. They will suggest concepts, like dinosaurs, for movement. In planning movement activities, keep developmental appropriateness in mind. It will be impossible for a child to move like a helicopter or an elevator if he or she has never directly experienced one. Remember that images of helicopters or elevators in books or on TV are symbolic images. The symbolic images of cows in books are small, flat, mute animals who do not smell. As such, these vicarious experiences do not advance a child's knowledge of cows. You will be more successful if you structure movement experiences around things children know and have experienced. Children living in rural areas may have well-developed concepts of farm animals, whereas city children may not.

Children also need ample space, including their own personal space in which to move. By extending their arms out around them, children can define their personal space which others must respect. Remember to move with the children without telling or showing them how to move. There is more than one way to move like a snake. Above all else, remember to provide a psychologically safe environment in which children feel comfortable to trust their creative impulses and move in ways that makes sense to them. As with singing, respect the right of children to refrain from participation, especially for those who are shy or unsure.

Moving with a Parachute in Creative Ways A parachute is a good investment and a piece of movement apparatus that has many uses. Get a small parachute; if unavailable, use a tablecloth or sheet. Tie knots at the corners and midpoints to signify places and something to hold. Use with a small group of children to reinforce spatial, directional, and temporal concepts. Some parachute activities include having the children

- hold the parachute high (above their heads) or low (down on the ground):
- lift their arms and parachute as high as possible, release, and then watch as it floats to the ground
- move the parachute slowly and then very fast
- bounce lightweight objects like balloons or balls on top of the parachute (either try to keep them on or try to have them bounce off)
- make the parachute get small by walking to the middle and then get big by walking back to their places
- walk to the right and then to the left while holding the parachute waist high
- run under the parachute without getting caught
- extend arms upward and while still holding on, turn around and sit on the ground while the parachute covers them up

Music and Movement Center Provide a soft, comfortable place for one or more children to listen to and make beautiful music. Include a record player and records as well as tapes and songs on tape. Hang your rhythm and musical instruments on a Peg-Board and draw an outline around each to show children where to store them. Cup hooks under a shelf are good for hanging small items like castanets and triangles. Include homemade rhythm instruments. You may want to place this center close to your active areas and away from the quiet corner. Hang pictures of children and adults singing, dancing, playing instruments, and listening to music. Include dancers and musicians from many cultures. Provide ample time for children to discover and make music. Include books on music, musicians, and songs, as well as visuals like songs on charts. A small selection of papers and writing tools will encourage children to combine art with music as they make their own songbooks or sheet music. Provide movement props like scarves, streamers, and lengths of fabric. The center must have ample space if children are to freely dance and move about (see Figure 3–9). If inside space is very limited you may want to think about an outdoor music and movement center. To round out your music and movement program, take children on field trips where they can hear music and see dance performed. If not possible, invite in family members and community volunteers who sing, dance, or play musical instruments. This is a good way to have family members share their cultures' music and dance.

FIGURE 3–9 A creative place for music and movement

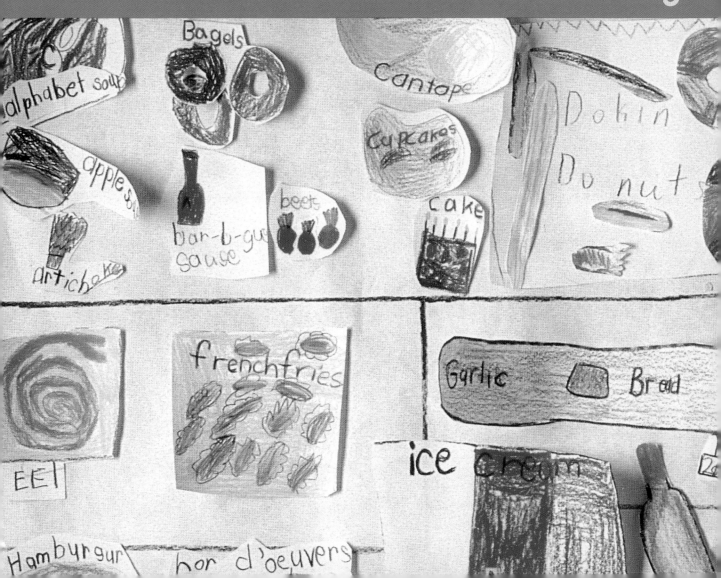

Math Cards

Students will use colored pencils to create their own dominos or sorting games. After drawing pictures of objects, children can match patterns or sort the cards according to attributes.

Alphabet Pop Up Mural

Foods drawn with colored pencils can be cut out and placed on a huge refrigerator mural. Reading Ruth Tilden's pop up alphabet book, <u>What's in the Fridge</u>, can start this activity.

Pattern Books
or Cause and Effect Stories

Read stories that are strong in establishing repetitive patterns and demonstrate cause and effect, such as <u>Fortunately</u> by Remy Charlip or <u>The Happy Tale</u> by Dorothy Butler.

Then have students create their own simple pattern stories that deal with cause and effect. Illustrate and write with colored pencils and crayons.

Fortunately he found a bike to ride to New York.

Unfortunately the bike got a flat tire.

Unluckily the hat was wet and fell out of the lady's hand

Luckily the hat was plastic and floated

Recipe Chart

After reading the class Marcia Brown's <u>Stone Soup</u>, create a class recipe chart. Students can invent a new soup recipe and use colored pencils to draw the ingredients that are attached to large, lined chart paper. Reinforce math concepts by having them make and display the correct number of ingredients and measuring utensils.

Story Extensions

After reading Verna Aardema's <u>The Three Wishes</u>, have students use story paper and colored pencils to write and illustrate original stories that deal with their personal three wishes or create a new ending to the classic story.

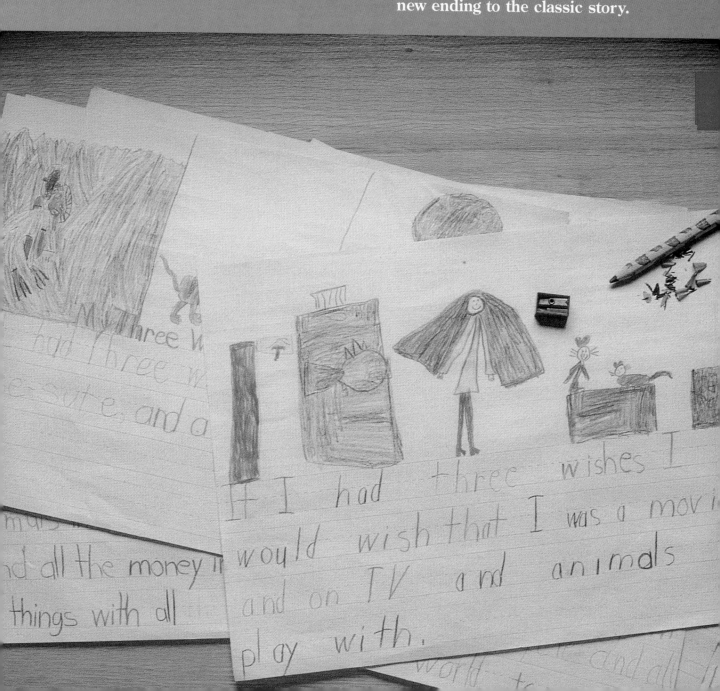

Sequence Story

Build off Ruth Krauss's <u>The Carrot Seed</u>. Discuss plant growth and have children identify the steps in the planting and growing sequence. Each child will then write and illustrate a section of the class planting story. After each child has completed a section, assemble the planting story according to the sequence of events.

Card Making

After reading the class Ahlberg's <u>The Jolly Postman</u>, divide the students into small groups. Each group selects a favorite story and uses colored pencils to create cards that would be correspondence between characters of the story. Urge the students to fold their cards in interesting ways to create gatefold, die-cut and pop-up cards. The correspondence between the storybook characters should relate to the plot and feelings communicated in the story.

Bed Time Stories

After reading bedtime stories, such as <u>There's a Nightmare in my Closet</u>, <u>There's an Alligator Under My Bed</u> and <u>No More Jumping on the Bed</u>, children will use colored pencils to write and illustrate their own imaginative bedtime stories dealing with their bedtime routines or overcoming their fears of imaginary creatures who emerge from the dark.

Special thanks to the teachers and children who helped us create this insert: Margaret Seip - George Wolf Elementary, Sharon Czekner - Washington Elementary, Ann Benner - Our Lady of Hungry, Mary Phillips - Roosevelt Elementary, and Mary Richards - Truman Elementary.
Author: Cheri Sterman Product Manager: Rahael Strauss Publication Design: Rob Schneider

FACILITATING CHILDREN'S CREATIVE EXPRESSION

Teachers can build on children's creative drive by implementing the following strategies.

1. Provide ample blocks of time for creative expression. Children need large blocks of time to create and re-create. Being hurried or pressured to begin or finish works against the creative impulse. Children also need time to start, change, and return to their creative processing.
2. Provide ample space indoors and outdoors for children to express their creativity (see Figure 3–10). Space should be fluid and flexible allowing for spontaneous activity which may extend between learning centers. For example, block building may extend into dramatic play.
3. Provide resources including open-ended toys, props, materials, and creative junk. Children cannot create from workbook pages.
4. Set the stage for creative expression by providing a psychologically safe environment. Be accepting of children's processing. Give them permission to be different and to do things their way, as long as their health and safety are not at risk.

FIGURE 3–10   Provide ample space for creative expression.

5. Play a variety of roles. Observe and record individual children as they create (see Figure 3–11). Be a player and participant in children's play, without taking over.

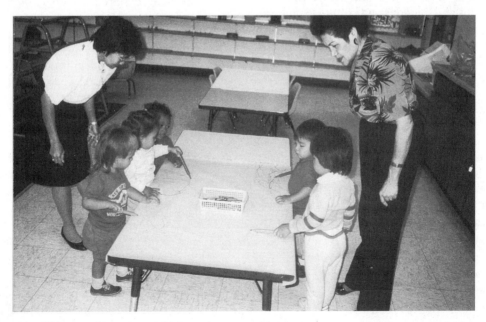

FIGURE 3–11   Observing children as they create

MARK MAKING

Mark making is a term used to refer to the variety of artistic marks that young children make. Young children begin by making scribbles or unrecognizable marks and progress to recognizable shapes and forms. Scribbling is important both in itself and as practice for later printing, writing, and drawing. Scribbling is to drawing and printing or writing as babbling is to talking and crawling is to walking. Most young children will have some experience with using crayons, pencils, markers, or pens at home.

Children need large sheets of paper to make movements with the entire arm. Later, they will develop hand coordination and fine motor control. Crayons are recommended for the beginning mark maker. Colored pencils are too long and thin and have a soft point. They are hard to control, and the points break easily. The advanced mark maker can be given colored pencils for making precise drawings. Scribblers need crayons, but not a wide array of colors. Often, one dark color is enough for making marks. Their interest will be in making marks and strokes rather than using a variety of colors. Crayons will be peeled, sucked, and broken. Actually, scribblers need peeled crayons so that they can use both the tips and the sides and bottom to make a variety of marks.

There is no one best position for mark making. Older infants and toddlers enjoy sprawling on the floor on their tummies and marking with crayons on a large piece of paper. This setup can accommodate four mark makers at any one time, one at each side of the paper. Others may enjoy kneeling on the floor while marking. Easels are not just for painting. Some children may be most comfortable standing while making marks. Others will prefer to stand or sit at a table. The seated position is most appropriate for the older, experienced mark maker, since it requires more-restricted small-muscle movement. Standing, reclining, and kneeling permit greater whole body involvement and movement while marking.

Children make marks with a variety of tools:

- pencils
- crayons
- chalk
- markers

Pencils

colored—for advanced mark makers

drawing—#2 for making marks

erasers—to be used sparingly, not in striving for perfection

grips—three-sided pencil holders, more important for printing than for artistic mark making

lead—#2 for making marks

primary—thick; may be too heavy for smallest hands

Chalk

chalkboard—good for marking with long, sweeping strokes

colored—for marking on chalkboard and on black, white, and colored construction paper

pastels—leave a soft, smooth, velvety line; not recommended for beginners. Use to draw on cloth or paper but not chalkboard. Pastels provide the best of chalk and crayons. They are powdery but do not rub off like chalk. They are not as hard as crayons but are just as colorful and brilliant.

white—for marking on chalkboard and on black and colored construction paper

Hint Chalk can be used wet or dry. Chalk is messy, and older children will enjoy blending colors made with chalk. Chalk needs a fixative. Brushing liquid starch or buttermilk on the paper first will help the chalk adhere. Chalk can also be dipped into either of these fixatives and then applied. Children tend to dislike the smell of buttermilk. Spraying with hair spray will help the chalk adhere. Use outdoors and sparingly.

Hint Chalkboard paint is available at hardware stores. You can paint on your own chalkboard surface.

Hint Like crayons, chalk will quickly break, especially if loosely thrown into a box. A piece of foam rubber can make a chalk holder. Use a scissors point to carefully bore small holes or openings into the foam rubber. Insert one piece of chalk in each hole. Make sure that the chalk fits tightly in an upright position.

Crayons and Accessories

Chunk-o-Crayon—a small, square stick of heavily pigmented color; comes in primary colors, black, and a rainbow of colored specks; good for wide strokes and rubbings

Cray Away—washable crayons, water-soluble. Or dip in water for watercolor effects.

crayon melter—commercially available

crayon sharpener—save the colored shavings!

Easy-Grip or Chubbi Stump—look like small ice-cream cones and fit tiny hands

Easy-Off—can be removed from washable surfaces, e.g., walls; good for use at home

fabric—for marking directly on cloth, or use on paper and then transfer to fabric with a hot iron

fluorescent—bright, vibrant colors

food-warming tray—for special melted-crayon activities

grater—for shaving crayons

hexagonal—six-sided crayons; will not roll and are a good size for little hands

jumbo or extra large—may be too big and heavy for youngest

nonroll—for children working on slanted surfaces or who find the major use of crayons is for rolling

So Big—first crayons for older infants and toddlers

standard size—thin and prone to break with pressure

thick or large—sturdier than standard

triangular—long, three-sided, good for wide, sweeping strokes

Hint Young children do not need large boxes of crayons with every color under the sun. Colors, shades, and tints can be made by using the basic set. Children or parents assume that more and bigger is necessarily better. This is not the case with crayons.

Hint Some children enjoy keeping their own basic set of eight crayons in a cigar-box-type container in their cubbies. However, some teachers feel that it is important to provide a mass of crayons and encourage children to share. Add exotic and metallic colors like silver, gold, copper, and bronze.

Hint Never throw away a broken crayon. They can be melted down and made into new ones. Place several small, peeled, broken crayon pieces into a nonstick muffin tin resting in a skillet of boiling water. Or line metal muffin tin openings with tinfoil to eliminate sticking. The skillet rests on a hot plate. Colors can be kept separate or creatively combined in the muffin tins. Remember the principles of color mixing. Mixing purple and brown will yield a dark color. Let cool. Carefully remove and use as a fat crayon. Remember, never melt crayons directly over heat; they are highly flammable. Or place the muffin tin in the oven at 250°F until the crayons have melted. Turn off the oven when crayons are completely melted. Remove the muffin tin when the oven is cold. Remove crayon cookies by pushing on the bottom of the muffin tin. Remind children that these tempting cookie-type creations are made of wax and are not to be eaten.

Layers of different melted colors can also be poured into a film container or pill bottle. Carefully pour from a muffin tin or use an old pot, making sure to wipe it clean between color meltings. Let harden between layers of color. Put it in the refrigerator to hasten hardening. Gently tap the bottom to remove, or quickly dip in hot water to loosen. The result will be a lipstick-shaped crayon that produces stripes and rainbow colors when used on its side. Or broken crayons can be slowly melted together in a plastic egg carton placed on a cookie sheet in the hot sun. Or pour melted crayon wax into a sturdy paper cone. Wrap several layers of sturdy paper into an ice cream cone shape. Tape securely. Pour in layers of colored wax. Carefully unwrap the paper when the colored cone is hard. Small colored cones will fit nicely into small hands. Remind children that these are special crayons and not food.

Hint To make a Crayon Egg, carefully poke a pin through both ends of an egg. Blow out the yolk and white of the egg. Place in the egg carton. Enlarge the opening on the top of the egg so you can pour melted crayon wax into the empty egg. To melt wax, place unwrapped, broken crayons or stubs in an empty coffee can. Place the can in a pan of boiling water. When melted, pour into egg mold. (Do not do this part with children.) When crayon wax has hardened, peel off eggshell.

Hint Children will inevitably break crayons to hear the pleasurable popping noise and peel the paper off. It is a way for them to exhibit their power over objects. They can break a crayon in two with their own bare hands! Thicker crayons are harder to break, but are also more difficult to manage. Removing the paper allows children to use the sides in wide, sweeping strokes. Many parts of a crayon other than the pointed tip can be used. Children may also quickly discard the box, since fitting the crayons back in once they have been removed is difficult and frustrating.

Hint There is no one best way to store crayons. Montessori might advocate grouping a mass of crayons by color and sorting each in its own container—for example, all the reds together. She would most likely provide only the primary colors and encourage children to mix these basic three to get all others.

Hint Children who use vigorous hard strokes when coloring with crayons can have their colorful marks polished. Use a paper towel over a pointer finger and polish the crayon marks until they smear together, blend, and sparkle.

Hint Peeled, broken crayon stubs can be recycled into Crayon Creatures. Cover the bottom of one to six cookie cutters with two layers of heavy-duty tinfoil to prevent leaking of melted crayon. Place on a cookie sheet. Fill each cookie cutter with peeled, broken crayon bits and pieces. Mixing colors is an option. Place the cookie sheet in a warm oven for about 10 minutes or until crayons melt and float but are not totally liquid. Place the entire cookie sheet with cookie cutters into the freezer for about 30 minutes. Carefully remove Crayon Creatures from cookie cutters. Use like crayons. Wash cookie cutters with hot soapy water.

Hint Soap Crayons can be made using mild powdered laundry soap, food coloring or liquid watercolor, and water. Add 1 cup of laundry soap to bowl. Add several drops of color. Slowly add water by the teaspoon until soap is liquid. Stir well. Pour into ice-cube trays. Set in sunny, dry spot for a few days. Allow crayons to harden. Great for writing on sinks or bathtubs.

Markers

Markers are popular mark making tools for young children, as they can make bright strokes with little pressure. They come in a variety of colors and tip styles and are indispensable to any early childhood art program. Some drawbacks are their relative expense compared to crayons and the fact that they dry out and must be replaced.

Hint Markers and their tops or caps get easily separated. A Marker Cap Keeper will also help very young children or those with physical disabilities who may have trouble pulling off the caps. To make a Marker Cap Keeper, collect deep plastic meat trays and fill them with plaster of paris (inexpensively purchased from hardware and building supply stores). While it's wet, press in about eight markers, caps down. If the caps are smooth, try wrapping rubber bands around them first. Let dry. This creates a keeper for the markers, makes it easier for children to use them, and avoids the problem of lost tops.

Items to accompany mark-making tools include

- ruler
- stencils
- pencil compass
- protractors
- lids and tops (to trace)

Here are some activities for mark making.

Scribbling

Older infants, toddlers, and preschoolers scribble. They make marks for the sheer joy of moving a tool across paper and seeing what happens. They need a variety of mark-making tools and large sheets of paper.

Crayons   Crayons are a preferred medium. They are colorful, responsive to children's movements, and fairly inexpensive. They are always ready for use and do not require mixing or special preparation. Most young children will have experience with them and will automatically be drawn to them. Young children will have their color preferences. Vibrant colors, such as silver, gold, and hot pink, will quickly lose their pointed tips. Young scribblers do well with only the basic primary colors. Yellow is difficult to see when used on white paper.

Crayons are composed of pigmented wax. Dark crayons contain more wax, are softer, and will leave an opaque mark. Light crayons contain less wax, are harder, and will leave a transparent mark. The older mark maker discovers that if you color dark over light, e.g., brown over yellow, the lighter color will not show. The younger mark maker, however, will not be that concerned with color mixing and planning.

Marking with crayons or scribbling will progress in stages. Young scribblers push, pull, and drag their crayons across the paper, resulting in horizontal, vertical, diagonal, and circular marks. The crayons will not be lifted off the paper, and the resulting marks will be continuous, with little or no variation. Beginning scribblers will often look away while marking, being more interested in the muscular activity itself than in the finished product. Details and small marks will be largely absent because of limited fine muscle development and control. With time, practice, and control, shapes and symbols begin to be included. Details and variations appear. Some variations on the use of crayons include

- scribbling with a crayon in each hand
- marking with a crayon in the nondominant hand—e.g., righty uses a crayon with left hand

- using two or more crayons that are tied together with a rubber band
- making notches or grooves in a peeled crayon and using it in a sideways, swirling, or up-and-down motion
- mixing colors by blending or overlaying crayons on white paper
- using crayons on colored construction paper
- varying the pressure on crayons, coloring heavily or lightly, and noticing the effects of pressure on the types of marks
- polishing crayon marks by rubbing them with a tissue to make a shiny surface
- using all sides of the crayon: the point for small dots; the flat end for larger round circles; the side for sweeping, wide strokes; and holding the crayon in the middle and rotating it to make bows or large circles
- using only dots made with a crayon to form a picture, outline, or design

Musical Scribbling

Children also enjoy scribbling or mark making to music. Make a mark or stroke that shows how the music makes you feel. Most of the previous suggestions also apply to musical scribbling. Make a simple doodle to music. Stop and turn the paper in a different direction. Attempt to continue the design or to complete a picture that the doodle suggests. For example, a mass of looping lines might suggest a snake. A tail and head could be added. Or, it could be spaghetti, with the child drawing a fork and plate.

Drawing or Sketching

Older children develop from random scribbling to more purposeful drawing or sketching that is often systematically planned out in advance. Some children may enjoy drawing or sketching

- each other
- objects in the room
- a very simple display, such as two stuffed animals

- school or center experiences, such as a field trip or outdoor play
- people, places, and things at home
- numbers, letters, and words
- using only geometric shapes
- a new animal made up of two very different ones, for example, a "turtlephant" with a turtle's head and an elephant's body
- items brought for show-and-tell

Chalk and Pastels

Older children will appreciate the possibilities of marking with chalk. It is messy, but the colors produced are beautiful, and the possibilities for blending are endless. Children can mark

- with light chalk on dark paper, e.g., white on black for a snow scene
- with colored chalk on white paper
- with dry chalk on wet paper
- with wet chalk on dry paper
- with the tip and/or side of the chalk
- by rubbing or blending chalk dust on a cotton ball (scrape with a dull knife or Popsicle stick)
- on rough, textured paper that responds to chalk
- by dipping the chalk in liquid starch before marking
- with chalk sticks soaked in a solution of ⅓ cup sugar to 1 cup water for five to ten minutes before use. The colors will appear more brilliant and tend to resist smudging.
- on paper wet with buttermilk or a combination of canned milk and liquid starch, to add sparkle
- outdoors on sidewalk and blacktop (it washes away with rain)
- with pastels, which provide a compromise between crayon and chalk. They are fairly solid and come in brilliant colors, but are slightly expensive.

Recipe for Sidewalk Chalk

1 cup of plaster of paris (do not pack)
about ½ cup of cool water
liquid tempera paint

Pour plaster into a disposable margarine container or large paper cup. Stir in most of the water. Add 2–3 tablespoons of liquid tempera. Mix well, especially at the bottom. Add a little more water as the mixture thickens. Stir well and pour into small paper cups. Peel paper off when the chalk is dry. Use to mark on sidewalks.

Mural P K S

Making a mural involves many social skills and decision making. How will we share the entire mural space? Who will make what, and where? Murals can revolve around a theme, such as outer space. Young children, however, often depart from the theme. There may be three planet Earths in the mural or animals floating about in space. Often, there will be a second bottom baseline at the top of the mural. This is to be expected. Murals can be the focus of a group story or dictation. Provide a long strip of paper. Place it on the floor in an out-of-the-way spot and encourage each child to make his or her unique contribution. Letters, names, numbers, and words can also be added to the art picture story.

Me Marks P K S

Most young children are interested in talking and learning about themselves. This can be part of social studies or a unit on "me." Some related mark-making activities include

- a self-portrait
- drawing, making marks, or making self-sketches that show being happy, angry, sad, scared, hurt, lonely, or silly
- a "me" book that shows things that make me feel one of the previous ways—for example, a separate page with "happy" on it

A wall mirror will help children notice details, including eye and hair color, clothing, and the presence or absence of freckles and front teeth. Still, even though young children can visually see, they will not necessarily represent realistically.

Object Trace-Over

Much of the artistic junk (see Appendix A) will have a characteristic shape and outline, often geometric in nature. Lids, tops, caps, boxes, and containers can be traced over. The shapes can be creatively combined. Some can be repeated in a sequence or pattern. Some children may prefer to make something out of their traced objects. For example, a series of traced-over circular lids might suggest a caterpillar or wheels on a bulldozer.

Architect's Art **S**

You will need a ruler, pencil, protractor, and pencil compass. Older children can make a number of lines with a ruler and pencil by tracing the arc of a protractor or by using a pencil compass. An interesting design with lines, circles, and arcs will result. Children can add their own designs. (See Figure 3–12.)

Graph Paper Cube Design **S**

Buy graph paper with large squares. Or make a series of 1-inch squares on a sheet of paper and photocopy it. Children can be encouraged to think of an object that has a square or rectangular shape or is composed of small boxes. For example, it would be more difficult to make a round swimming pool than a rectangular skyscraper. Sketch out the

FIGURE 3–12   Architect's art

exterior outline. Fill in the individual squares to complete the picture.

Run, Mark, Run **P K**

Children will enjoy using markers on paper towels or thin fabric on which they will blend and run. Place newspaper or cardboard underneath.

Sandpaper Art **K S**

Children can use crayons to make heavy marks or a design on a small 4- to 6-inch square of sandpaper. Use fine or medium grade rather than coarse. Press hard, and make solid-colored forms. When the sandpaper is fairly well covered with crayon marks, it can be heated in a warm oven at 250°F for ten to fifteen seconds until the crayon melts. The crayon wax will harden and produce an interesting effect. Also, this activity can be a good tie-in to discussing the effects of heat and temperature change. What happens if we leave our crayons in the sun or on the heater? Will the same thing happen to our pencil? Who knows why?

Glue Design **K S**

Make a design using a bottle of liquid white glue on wax paper. Make thick masses, shapes, or forms. Let dry until hard and clear. Decorate the dried glue with thin or fine-line felt-tip pens. The dried and decorated shapes can be carefully peeled off, laced with thread, and hung overhead or worn as jewelry.

Crayon Shavings **K S**

Old, broken crayons can be recycled for this activity. Carefully scrape a dull plastic knife or Popsicle stick along the crayon and catch the shavings. Place them on a piece of wax paper and arrange them into a design. Add glitter, ribbon, tissue paper, and a piece of string if a hanging is desired. Place another piece of wax paper on top. An adult can press with a warm iron to melt the wax and seal it. Cut the excess wax paper off or snip it into an interesting shape. Use black construction paper for the outer frame. Hang it over the window and let the light shine through.

Coffee Filter Art

Crayon shavings can also be placed on a flattened paper coffee filter. Place a sheet of construction paper on top. An adult can press with a warm iron. You will get two pieces of art. The heat will melt the crayon wax, and you will have a colored design on a round white background. You will also get a print of that design on your piece of construction paper. (See Figure 3–13.)

Iron Art

Fold a sheet of drawing paper in half. Mark or color dark and solid on one half. Refold the paper with the colored design inside. An adult can press with a warm iron to make a print. Open. A colored image or print will appear on the other half.

Fabric crayons can be used in a similar way. Mark with fabric crayons on white paper. Color heavily. Place the paper face down over fabric. An adult can transfer the picture onto the fabric by ironing the paper with a warm iron. The wax will melt, and the heat will set the colors into the fabric.

Fabric crayons are designed to be used with fabric. Locate some material scraps—prewashed muslin, an old T-shirt, or white sheet. Staple a small square of old sheet or muslin to cardboard to keep the fabric from slipping. Use the fabric crayons to make heavy marks or a design. Place paper on top and press with a warm iron. The heat will melt the colored wax and set the design. Individual squares could be sewn together into a quilt.

Crayon Etching

Probably everyone has done at least one crayon etching. Older children can fill up a piece of manila paper with a crayon design. Leave no space empty. Polish with a paper towel to help the layer of color adhere. Next, using black crayon, color darkly over the entire surface. Polish again. Last, use a Popsicle stick to etch out a design. A fairly thick etched line will reveal a rainbow of colors beneath. This activity is recommended only for older children who have the patience and muscular strength to color dark over an entire sheet of paper and stay with this activity through its several steps.

FIGURE 3–13   Coffee filter art and print

Crayon Melt

Crayon melting activity needs a food-warming tray. The tray will remain warm but not dangerously hot. Still, children need to discuss the dangers and take precautions. Place a large sheet of paper on the warming tray. Children can slowly draw a picture or design. Remind them to keep their hands and arms off the warming tray. The heat from the warming tray will melt the wax, leaving a melted impression. This activity is not dangerous but needs supervision.

Rub-a-Dub-Rub

Rubbing a marking tool over a textured surface produces an interesting rubbed effect. Some people do this over gravestones while studying family or local history. Visitors make rubbings of family and friends whose names are listed on the Vietnam Memorial. Crayons are recommended for children, although chalk could also be used. Hold a piece of paper in place while rubbing. Possible textured surfaces include

- wood grain
- tree bark
- fabric
- cement and concrete
- flocked wallpaper
- leaves and other flat nature specimens
- screens and grills
- brick
- signs with raised letters
- comb
- sandpaper
- mosaic tile
- leather
- buttons
- paper clips

Some of the author's favorite textured surfaces are

- embossed greeting cards
- keys
- license plates
- coins
- corrugated cardboard
- paper lace doilies and Valentine's Day placemats

Bingo Marker Art

Bingo markers are large markers used to mark off cards at bingo games. Unlike markers with a narrow pointed tip, bingo markers have larger round heads. Their surface is fragile and can easily be ruined if children pound with them. Show children how to gently push down. Bingo markers come in a variety of colors. Use them on coffee filters, paper towels, or paper doilies for an interesting effect.

Lazy Susan Art

Find a base that revolves. Place a round sheet of paper on the round turntable or base. Gently spin the base while holding a marker on the paper. Children will discover that too much pressure will stop the turntable. This is recommended for older children with good coordination because it involves doing two things at the same time. Children can also work in pairs with one spinning and the other marking, and then change jobs.

Record Player Art

An old record player can be used with close adult supervision. Place a paper plate on the turntable and turn on the record player. Have the child hold a marker on the plate as it turns around. The marker can be moved about to create interesting line designs. The child may want to change colors or use more than one marker at a time, perhaps one in each hand. A windup toy record player would be a good alternative to an electric one.

Kaleidoscope Art

Accordion-fold any white absorbent paper like coffee filters, white tissue paper or one-ply paper towels. Then fold in half. Use markers to color along the edges and then dip in water. Squeeze out excess moisture. Let dry first before attempting to unfold and open.

Doorknob Hangers ![PKS]

Draw and cut out several basic hanger shapes similar to the ones found on hotel room doors requesting privacy or maid service. Encourage children to use markers to customize their own with pictures or designs. Discuss the concept of privacy, personal space, and ownership. Older children may write messages like "Do Not Disturb" or "Keep Out," especially if they have siblings.

Paper-Bag Backpacks ![PKS]

Make your own backpack using a large brown grocery sack, cut down and folded over at the top several times for strength. Use the strips that are cut off the top as shoulder straps. Staple them firmly in place. Children can use markers to decorate their backpacks. If a backpack tears and cannot be repaired, a new one can be easily made. Miniature versions of the backpacks for dolls and teddy bears can be made using brown paper lunch bags.

Sun Visors ![TPKS]

Use a cloth tape measure and find the children's average head size. Measure approximately two-thirds of the way around the forehead, for this is the area that holds the visor. Create a U-shaped visor pattern in this size and trace and cut individual visors out of poster board. Visors can be decorated using markers. Cut a piece of elastic about 10 inches long. Staple one end to the visor. Adjust it to fit each child's head snugly. Staple the other end to the visor. Trim away excess elastic or visor. This is a good activity on a hot day or a summer field trip.

Pass-It-On Picture ![S]

Fold a piece of white paper into quarters with the top fourth folded down and the bottom fourth folded up. One child uses the top to draw a head. The paper is turned over and passed to a second child who draws the middle. The third child uses the unused portion to draw legs. When the paper is opened, a creative combination of head-middle-bottom ap-

pears. Children may need to practice this activity a few times to understand the process.

Magnet Marker ![KS]

You will need a marker, nut, ½-inch washer, duct tape, clear Plexiglas, magnet, and blocks for elevation. Place uncapped marker through nut. Place nut and marker on top of washer so that the tip of the marker is exposed. Secure marker, washer, and nut together with duct tape. Place Plexiglas on top of blocks to make a bridge. Plexiglas needs to be elevated high enough for child's hands to move easily underneath. Tape a piece of paper to Plexiglas. Stand marker up on paper. Make sure the washer lies flat against the Plexiglas. Slowly and carefully move magnet underneath the Plexiglas to begin mark making on paper.

SUMMARY

This chapter continued our discussion of creativity and introduced the reader to three major modes of creative expression other than art. These included play, language, and music and movement, which was further broken down into listening to music, singing, making music with instruments, and moving to music. Play was examined as an elusive term; it was not easily defined. Nor could it be simply contrasted with work, for children work very hard at their play. Instead, criteria for characterizing play were identified. A discussion of play in its many forms covered physical play, constructive play with blocks, dramatic play, play with natural materials, and games. Ideas for creative play using cardboard boxes, cartons, and accessories, as well as plastic pipe, were suggested. As with play, information on centers, materials, and activities in the curricular areas of language and music and movement were also provided. The chapter closed with suggested ways adults can facilitate and enhance children's creative expression by providing space, time, and resources, along with setting the tone and playing different roles.

Suggested Activities

1. Observe a room of same-age children. Note the expression of individual differences within the same age range. Record your findings.

2. Observe or volunteer to work with young exceptional children who have been mainstreamed.

3. Observe or volunteer to work in an early childhood bilingual or multicultural program.

4. Spend one morning in an early childhood classroom looking for examples of diversity or bias. Examine the books, music collection, wall displays, as well as the clothing, props, dolls, and tools in the house area. Do the curriculum and room environment reflect the cultures of the children present? Explain and offer suggestions.

5. Provide children with a multicultural art experience.

6. Observe children at play. Capture a creative episode by writing down what transpired. Use words to objectively record words and actions. Analyze your observation and justify why this episode was "creative."

7. Work with a small group of children in implementing one of the following creative activities discussed in this chapter:
   a)   boxes, cartons, and accessories
   b)   plastic pipe (PVC)
   c)   parachute

8. Implement one of the water play activities discussed in this chapter with a small group of children.

9. Work with a partner and implement one of the movement activities discussed in this chapter. This can be done informally during play time or large group time.

Review

A. List three modes of creative expression other than art.

B. Identify at least three criteria that characterize play.

C. Name five different categories or types of play.

D. List the four components of music and movement.

E. Discuss three different ways adults can facilitate children's creative expression.

SECTION TWO

Young Children As Artists: A Developmental View

hy is art important for young children? Is there more to art than just enjoyment? Pretend you are teaching and a parent complains that there is too much emphasis on art in your program. You show her your schedule reflecting an array and balance of activities, but she's still not satisfied. Although her daughter loves art, the mother asks, "Why is art so important?" How would you respond?

Let's review what we know about the developing child and connect this to art. What is the relationship between art and child development? Does art foster the development of the young child physically, socially, emotionally, cognitively, and creatively? Chapter 4, Art and the Developing Child, attempts to answer these questions. Although the child is fragmented into developmental pieces for individual analysis, the focus is on an interactive model of the whole child.

Examine the photograph of the earthquake picture drawn by a school-age child. Earthquakes are a reality and a source of stress for children living in California. Expressing fear makes it more manageable by getting it out in the open where one can deal with it. Children cope with their fears in different ways. Some can talk about their fears; others prefer to draw them out. The child who drew this picture expressed her dislike or hate in words and symbols representing the damage to cars, buildings, and streets that she witnessed. In this example, art helped Lauren's emotional development by giving her the vehicle to legitimately vent and express her feelings and fear. It provided something tangible to talk about. Art helped her cope.

Examine the dolls and books in the picture. The photograph depicts anti-bias materials displayed by Louise Derman-Sparks. Children, like the dolls in the photo, come in all sizes, shapes, colors, and conditions. Many are physically challenged. Each child is unique, and our job is to recognize, accept, value, and nurture each child's uniqueness. Chapter 5, Children Are Unique Individuals, provides general guidelines for working with children with special needs and celebrating multicultural backgrounds within the broader context of anti-bias.

Chapter 6, Children's Artistic Development, attempts to explain art by examining different theories and stage sequences. Theories provide explanations for the how, what, and why of children's art. Stages provide a sequence or progression in children's artistic development. Over time, beginning scribbles become more controlled, shapes are combined and detailed, and pictures become recognizably realistic.

CHAPTER 4

Art and the Developing Child

*C*hase will soon turn three. He will move from a Montessori toddler room to the three-year-old room. What do you see in this photo?

Chase is involved in a printmaking activity. Each of the objects can be dipped in paint and pressed onto paper to leave a print. Study Chase's posture. Notice his fixed gaze and the position of his hands. What does this tell you about Chase's development? Does he appear to be coordinated and to have fine motor control? Do his eyes and hands appear to work together? What kind of art supplies are on the table? What has Chase made? Does this picture tell you anything else?

OBJECTIVES

After studying this chapter, the student will be able to

- Discuss how art fosters child development
- Use an art example to portray a wholistic model of development
- Discuss the developmental progression in a child's use of scissors and how to meet the needs and abilities of young cutters
- Critique the use of food in art activities
- Provide experiences for children to process with art materials and tools

INTRODUCTION

This chapter provides a developmental overview of the young child: physically, socially, emotionally, cognitively, and creatively. According to our wholistic model of child development, these aspects influence and are influenced by one another. Ideally, we can act on this knowledge in planning art activities. Our present analysis attempts to answer the following question: How does art foster the development of the whole child? Our purpose is twofold: first, to help understand how art can foster a child's development; and second, to use what we know about art and child development in planning our art program and justifying it to ourselves and others. Providing a justification is more than giving a defensive reply: "Art is important, and that's why we spend a lot of time doing it!" If art is important (and it is), we should be able to provide a rationale for studying it. Relating art to a child's development provides one rationale.

DEVELOPMENTAL MODEL

One way to get a working knowledge of young children is to build a model for studying development in the following areas:

- physical—including large muscle or gross motor, small muscle or fine motor, perceptual-motor or eye-hand coordination, and sensory development, good health, self-care.
- social—including a development of the self and relations with others (Figure 4–1)
- emotional—including feelings about self and emotional expression as well as personality and temperament
- cognitive—including thinking, problem solving, discovery, language, curiosity, reasoning, and learning
- creative—including original thinking, imagination, and verbal and nonverbal expression

FIGURE 4–1   Art can be a physical and social experience.

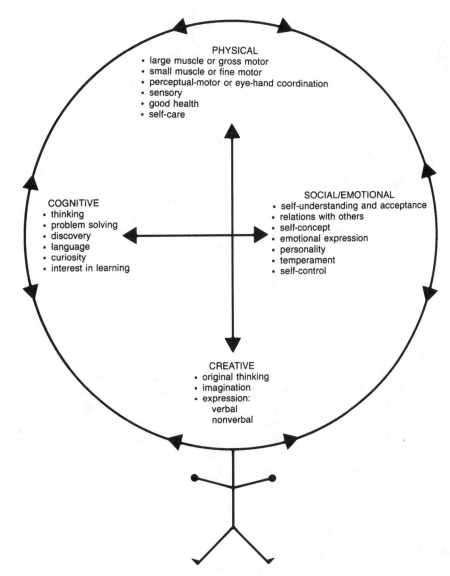

FIGURE 4–2   Wholistic model of child development

This model of development is depicted in Figure 4–2 Still, this neat division or separation is too simplistic. A pie or pizza can be neatly cut into five pieces or slices, but a child's development cannot. Aspects of development interact; they are interdependent and interrelated. It is impossible to study a child's physical development in isolation. Physical development is influenced by and also directly influences social, emotional, cognitive, and creative development. For example, five-year-old Joey has been mainstreamed midyear into a regular kindergarten classroom. Muscular dystrophy has left him confined to a wheelchair. It influences what he can and cannot do physically. However, it is not the only influence on his overall development. Joey's physical state affects and is also affected by his social, emotional, cognitive, and creative functioning. Initially Joey was treated as an outcast. He was shunned by his peers and misunderstood by his teacher. Slowly, he withdrew. Emotionally, Joey began feeling sorry for himself, wishing he was like his peers. His self-concept suffered, and he began to doubt his own personal worth. Cognitively, he began to avoid school tasks, shunned class discussion, and refused to work. Creatively, however, Joey channeled his energies into making original pictures of outer space. Interestingly, Joey always drew himself as the space captain, with massive, powerful legs and strong arms. As in Joey's case, development is uneven, reflecting developmental spurts and lags. Fortunately, Joey's teacher recognized the problem and her lack of knowledge and enrolled in a course on mainstreaming. She worked closely with Joey, his mother, his peers, and his resource teacher. The students openly discussed handicaps and how all people have strengths and weaknesses, assets and limitations. Over time, the children accepted Joey and welcomed him into their activities. In fact, they became overprotective, and Joey regressed to an earlier stage of helplessness. Continual discussion, support, and encouragement helped Joey become more independent. He began to show improvement in his schoolwork and eagerly reported to his mother what he was learning. Joey became very well liked by his peers, and his self-concept improved.

DEVELOPMENTAL PROFILE

Providing a detailed description of child development is beyond the scope of the present chapter. Instead, a general overview of a young child's physical, social, emotional, cognitive, and creative development will be presented.

Physical Development

Young children are physical beings characterized by much activity and energy. Physical development depends on adequate rest, exercise, sleep, and good nutrition. Young children are intrinsically motivated to make an effect on their environment. They do this primarily through motor activity and sensory exploration.

Infants develop prehension, or grasping, and a pincer grasp that allows them to hold objects between their fingers and opposing thumb. Older infants can hold a stubby crayon and be guided into making marks on paper. Young children are more adept with large muscle or gross motor skills than with small muscle or fine motor skills. They will master easel painting with large brushes before they can use a small brush with watercolors. By age three, most preschoolers can hold a crayon with their fingers, as opposed to the earlier clenched-fist grip. Young children are good doers, talkers, and movers. They have difficulty sitting still, listening, and remaining silent.

Art and Physical Development   Art activities provide experience and practice in developing and refining gross motor or large muscle skills. Art involves physical and manipulative activity. While easel painting, children use their entire arms and upper torsos in making large, sweeping motions with paintbrushes. Large, long-handled, wide-bristle brushes facilitate this movement. The muscles of the hand are developed while working with clay— tearing, rolling, twisting, coiling, pounding, pinching, and flattening it. Whole hand and arm motions are involved in hand painting, with paint spread and worked with the fingers, whole hand, nails, knuckles, fist, palm, and back of the hand. These gross motor or large muscle skills are perfected before fine motor or small muscle skills. Using the smaller watercolor brush with its shorter handle and narrow point involves greater precision and fine motor control. All the manipulative movements involved in art help develop the hand and finger muscles that are needed to properly hold and use a pencil. Although making children into early printers or writers is not the main purpose of art, art does facilitate the development of this skill.

Scissoring is another physical activity that involves a patterned "open-close" rhythmical movement. Cutting with scissors on a line fosters eye-hand coordination and visual acuity, with the eyes and

Cutting with Scissors

Cutting with scissors is a difficult developmental task for many young children. Using scissors gives children a feeling of power and mastery. Scissors, once a taboo or "no-no," now become an acceptable tool if used properly. Some guidelines for helping children cut and for selecting proper equipment include the following:

1. Tearing paper is a good starting point for young children. Torn pieces can be pasted on paper or cardboard to form a collage, as seen in Figure 4–3. Tearing paper is itself an important skill that need not be eliminated when a child learns to cut.

2. Cutting thin, pliable Play-Doh is a good introduction to using scissors.

3. Snipping or fringing paper is a beginning step in using scissors with paper. Give children a narrow ¼- or ½-inch-wide paper strip. Show them how to make a single cut or snip into the paper. Children enjoy snipping off small pieces that can be pasted. Small snips into a wider 1-inch strip will produce fringe. Hole-punched computer paper sides are ideal for snipping and fringing. Paper ribbon has more body than paper and is easily cut into confetti.

4. With practice, the young child will be able to make repeated snips in a sequence or line. Draw a thick, straight line on paper, and show the children how to follow it while cutting. It does not matter if the children stray from the line. The aim is to help them coordinate repeated snips into a continuous cutting action.

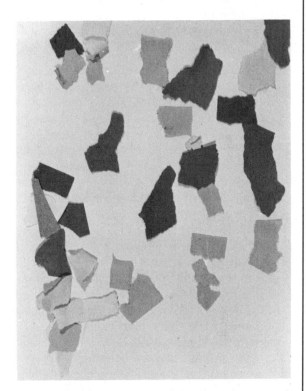

FIGURE 4–3   *Tearing paper is an alternative to cutting with scissors.*

5. Advanced cutters can practice cutting wavy, bending, or angular lines. Children can also practice cutting out geometric shapes.

6. Cutting along interior lines, such as the eyes in a mask or paper-bag puppet, is too difficult. It is also potentially dangerous, since children are prone to begin the hole by poking with the point of the scissors.

continued

Cutting with Scissors, continued

7. Rules for the proper use of scissors need to be established, discussed, and posted in words or pictures or both. Rules include:

    - Scissors are used only for cutting paper.
    - Walk when carrying the scissors. Running with scissors is very dangerous. If you fall while running with scissors, you or someone else could get poked or stabbed.
    - There is a right way to hold and pass scissors. Hold the closed points in your own hand, pointed down, when carrying scissors or passing them to someone else.

8. A scissors rack provides safe storage for scissors. Metal stands are commercially available at a modest cost. Scissors are easy to get and return to their upright position. Scissors that are merely placed in a box tend to tangle together. An egg carton or a coffee can with a plastic lid can substitute for a metal scissors rack. Over time, however, the holes will tear from repeated use, and the makeshift rack will need to be replaced.

9. A variety of types of scissors are commercially available. Blunt scissors have rounded ends. Clip-type scissors have one pointed and one rounded end. Sharp scissors have two pointed ends. There are different scissors for different cutting needs and abilities. For example, smaller 4-inch scissors with rounded tips are safe for use by young children. Their blades are fairly dull, but their metal handles may pinch or irritate the skin.

10. Scissors with rubber-coated finger holes are more comfortable and will not hurt.

11. Plastic safety scissors are lightweight, inexpensive, comfortable, and easy to use.

12. Squeeze-type scissors have an easy-grip, continuous-loop handle. A gentle squeeze with two hands, the fingers and palm of one hand, or the thumb and fingers of one hand will cut. The two blades are blunt and fairly small. They are good for snipping and fringing. Extensive cutting will take more squeezing and hand activity than when using scissors with longer blades.

13. Some young children, including those with special needs and/or poor fine motor coordination, have more difficulty learning to cut than others. Merely observing someone else cut or trial-and-error practice may not be enough. Try using double-handled training scissors with four rubber-coated finger holes. The teacher and child cut together as one. Over time, these children may graduate to using a single pair of scissors.

14. Both right- and left-handed scissors should be made available. It is very difficult and frustrating for a "lefty" to hold and cut with scissors designed for a "righty."

15. Children's 5-inch pointed metal scissors are longer, heavier, and sharper. The more-skilled cutters in kindergarten and the primary grades may prefer these.

16. Some young children have difficulty holding the scissors in the air and working both blades. Children who find scissors heavy or awkward can rest the bottom blade on the table and let only the top finger do the work.

17. Some papers are easier to cut than others. Very lightweight papers, including tissue and cellophane, are flimsy, difficult to cut, and will tear. Cardboard, posterboard, and wallpaper are too thick and resistant for most children's strength and scissors. Manila, butcher paper, newspaper, newsprint, and drawing paper are recommended for beginning cutters. Skilled cutters can move on to construction paper.

scissoring hand working together. Children do not develop this important skill without some guidance and practice.

Social Development

Infants begin life as asocial, egocentric beings with little regard for the needs of others. Through socialization they are introduced to a wider arena of family, relatives, and significant others. Their individual desires are slowly curbed in response to the needs of others. Young children are egocentric and may need assistance in learning how to share; wait patiently; take turns; listen to others; and respect the property, rights, and ideas of others. They can also express empathy in appreciating the plight of others hurt or in trouble.

According to Erikson (1963), it is important for parents and caregivers to help

- infants develop a sense of trust rather than mistrust
- toddlers develop a sense of autonomy rather than doubt or shame
- preschoolers develop a sense of initiative rather than guilt

Young children are struggling with their freedom. At times they will be independent and autonomous. At other times they will be dependent, seeking comfort, security, and reassurance. Young children are talkers and socializers. They learn language and social skills from interacting with others, observing significant models, and witnessing the effects of their behavior upon others. For example, a young child who constantly snatches toys from others may find that they refuse to include her in their play. Young children are interested in themselves: who they are, what they look like, what they know, and what they can do. Their interest also extends to their peers and the immediate community. They enjoy being part of a social group other than their family.

Art and Social Development   Art helps children learn about themselves and others. Children validate their uniqueness by making a personal statement through art. "This is my chalk mark," says Deidra. It is a part of her, an extension of her self,

and unlike others. Missy finds out that she prefers using clay to pasting. She likes to work intently alone, away from the noise and social interaction. Missy is independent. Art helps children become comfortable with themselves, learning what they like and dislike and what they can and cannot do. Yet Missy rarely has the art center all to herself. The classroom is a social setting, and she is learning how to interact positively with others. The art center has rules that protect the welfare of both the group and the equipment. In turn, children learn responsibility for cleanup and proper return of materials to their rightful place. This is difficult for Missy, who is an only child and is used to getting her own way at home. Slowly, she is learning to share materials, take turns, and wait patiently.

Clemens (1991) views art as a form of positive child guidance. She sees artwork as a preventative measure, a benign alternative to letting children express themselves in destructive ways. Art is offered because it makes survival in the classroom more likely. Controlling children is not the issue. If you give children interesting choices, your class will run more smoothly. For these reasons, Clemens believes that art should take a prominent place in one's daily program.

Emotional Development

Most young children like themselves—who they are, what their name is, what they look like, and what they can do. It is our job to help them continue to feel good about themselves. The concept of one's self is in a very formative stage during early childhood. Young children need an abundance of opportunities to experience mastery, success, and acceptance and to witness their own competence: "Look, teacher, I did it all by myself. Good for me!" Young children may transfer their parental attachment to their teacher or caregiver. They may express love and affection and be overly possessive. They may be jealous of their peers and expect or demand a caregiver's total time, interest, attention, and praise.

Art and Emotional Development   Art is an emotionally pleasurable experience. Most children express happiness, joy, and pride in their art. In turn, this results in positive mental health and an expression of feelings. Young children are emotional beings, and art allows intense involvement. Art helps children nonverbally express those objects, ideas, people, places, experiences, events, and feelings that are emotionally significant. Often, a child is unable or unwilling to verbally discuss highly emotional topics or feelings about self, family, and friends. Art, however, allows these feelings, fantasies, fears, and frustrations to surface and be expressed (see Figure 4–4). It allows children the opportunity to represent in fantasy what cannot happen in reality. Negative feelings and impulses can be released in a positive, acceptable way through art. For example, anger against another cannot be physically expressed in the classroom, but it can be portrayed and expressed through art. "Show me in your picture how angry you are right now" (see Figure 4–5).

FIGURE 4–5   Art allows children to express how they feel.

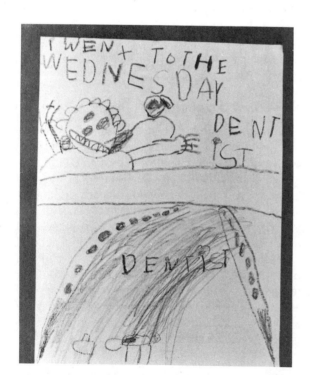

FIGURE 4–4   Through art, children can represent and master unpleasant experiences.

Art enhances a child's self-concept and feelings about self. Because art guarantees success, children experience mastery, which further enhances a positive self-concept. It is important for young children to have a positive self-concept, since it is a prerequisite to learning. Children who do not feel good about themselves do not learn. Their energy and attention are focused on fear of failure and self-doubt. It is a lot wiser to focus our attention on developing a positive self-concept in the early years as a preventive measure rather than attempting to remediate a negative self-concept in older children who may have given up on themselves, learning, and life.

Cognitive Development

The early years are a time of very rapid cognitive development. By age two, the brain has reached 75 percent of its adult weight. By age five, the brain has attained 90 percent of its adult weight. The

Art Therapy

Art, play, music, dance, literature, dramatics, and puppetry are vehicles for psychotherapy. Although therapy with adults is largely verbal, children profit from nonverbal forms.

Qualified therapists look for some of the following in art:

- An expressive use of colors. Red, bright orange, or black may be used repeatedly to symbolize objects of emotional importance. Black may be used to represent fear or death, red for rage or love.
- Personal meaning behind the repeated use of a symbol. Art therapists try to "crack the code," or discover the link between the artistic symbol and the unconscious. What meaning lies behind a child's repeated portrayal of a charging horse, a monster, a knife, or blood?
- An exaggeration, distortion, or overemphasis of objects reflecting emotional significance. Perhaps this is why young children first draw themselves as a large head with protruding arms, mounted on stick legs. They like their faces and how they look, so they draw them big. Arms and legs help them do things and get around, so they are also emphasized. Refer to the self-portrait (Figure 4–6) drawn by a four-year-old. Note the "wound" on the face. At the time she had a bruise from a fall and was very vivid in pointing it out, representing and exaggerating it in her self-portrait.
- The omission or underemphasis of objects also provides emotional clues. For example, children with low self-concepts often omit themselves or make themselves tiny by comparison with others. Children with intense sibling rivalry may simply omit that sibling when drawing the family. Art allows children to accomplish in fantasy what they cannot do in reality. For a child with sibling rivalry, it may mean the elimination of that sibling, at least on paper.
- Placement provides clues to emotional significance. Objects that are drawn large and in the center of the paper are important. Children with low self-concepts may draw themselves off in a corner or in the far background. They may also be hidden behind larger objects of emotional significance placed in the center foreground. Painful, fear-evoking content may also be reduced in size and safely "tucked away" in a far corner of the picture.
- Defense mechanisms that protect the ego appear in art. Harmful or painful thoughts and experiences that are repressed in reality may be safely uncovered and expressed through art. The child who has been abused may portray herself with unusual colors or designs on her body. Identification may be reflected in a

wound on chin

FIGURE 4–6   *Children include, distort, and exaggerate what is personally meaningful to them.*

continued

Art Therapy, continued

child's repeated use of a symbol with which to identify. The aggressive child identifies with the soldier or the marauding tiger. The fearful child becomes the scared witch on paper.

There are inherent dangers in the use of art therapy. First, it requires extensive training. Second, one needs many samples of a child's artwork over a long period of time to recognize patterns, rather than making a snap judgment or rash interpretation. For example, it would be naive to assume that a child's preoccupation with the color red indicates a fixation with blood, violence, fire, or rage. There are many possible explanations. Red may simply be the child's favorite color, the nearest color, or the only one available. Even early childhood educators who are untrained in art therapy, however, can use art to help children nonverbally express their feelings and emotions. Our aim is to provide a vehicle for emotional expression and release rather than analysis or interpretation.

early years provide an opportunity for mental stimulation and challenge. Young children are self-motivated, curious explorers who are eager to learn about themselves, others, and the world. They need concrete materials to manipulate; problems to solve; people, places, and events to experience; and a time to discuss and ask questions. Books and the media may provide important vicarious, secondhand information, but they are no substitute for direct experience.

According to Piaget, young children's thinking is action-oriented and largely nonverbal. He believed that thinking precedes the development of language. Language enhances thinking, but is not its source. Children understand and know more than they can verbalize. Likewise, what a child can say or discuss may not be an accurate indicator of intelligence. A young child's understanding and representation of the world proceed through stages.

Overview of Piaget's Stages of Development

During Piaget's *sensory motor stage* (birth to age two), infant thinking is limited to sensory impressions and motoric behaviors. A toy rattle is something to be held, shaken, dropped, stared at, listened to, smelled, and tasted. There is no thinking about the rattle apart from these sensory and motoric actions.

Toddlers attain significant cognitive achievements as they leave the sensory motor stage (birth to age two) and enter the *pre-operational stage* (ages two through seven). Representation frees toddlers from a reliance on action-based thinking. They can now form mental images, symbolize, and think about their world in the absence of direct action.

Preschoolers in Piaget's pre-operational stage (ages two through seven) are using symbols, including play, art, and language, to represent their world. They continue to construct and refine their concepts of time, space, classification, seriation, and number. Preschoolers in Piaget's pre-operational stage think in ways that are qualitatively different from adult logic or reason.

Children in the primary grades have entered Piaget's stage of *concrete operations* (ages seven through eleven). An operation is an internalized action. Older children have attained several important cognitive operations, including reversibility, conservation, classification, and seriation, as well as addition, subtraction, multiplication, and division, that

FIGURE 4–7   *Children draw what they know.*

help them think in more logical terms. Their thinking, however, is still bound to the concrete. They are unable to think abstractly.

Art and Cognitive Development   Eisner (1976) makes one of the strongest cases for the relationship between art and thinking, learning, and overall academic performance. Art reflects what a child knows about the world (see Figure 4–7). Children who have directly experienced a wide variety of people, places, and objects will have an array of things to choose from when doing art. Children who have neither been to a zoo nor been exposed to pets will probably not include animals in their art. One must know about something before one can re-create it through art (see Figure 4–8).

Translating ideas, concepts, and experiences into art involves many thinking skills. One must decide what to represent and how to execute it. "To make a dinosaur, should I use clay, markers, or paint?" thinks Nate. He must plan, organize, and make choices. Art involves concentration, staying on a task, and seeing it through to completion—all

FIGURE 4–8   *A field trip to the zoo prompted one child to make this elephant.*

important work skills and habits. "What steps are involved and how should I go about it?" ponders Nate. He decides to draw an outline with pencil, trace over it with thick marker pen, cut it out, and then paint it at the easel. Art involves problem solving. Nate needs dark paint when only the three primary colors are available. He decides to mix all three together into a muddy color that he thinks is just the right color for a "beast." Nate becomes upset when the muddy color runs into the white of the dinosaur's eye. Using too much water has thinned down the paint. Nate has learned about cause and effect. He hypothesizes and gets a crumpled paper towel to gently blot it out. It is impossible to document all the thinking that is going on in Nate's head while he is doing art. By the way, Nate is a bright four-year-old who is largely nonverbal. Art provides an opportunity for him to symbolize what he knows but cannot and will not discuss. Over time, he may. Through art, Nate can communicate with himself and others. "Yes, Nate, I see how hard you worked to get the eye just right," says his teacher. The thinking cycle moves from planning to implementing and reworking, if necessary. The author believes that the thinking side of art has been neglected in favor of identifying physical, social, emotional, and creative ends. The major benefits of art may very well be cognitive in nature.

Through art, children learn about the concepts of color, shape, size, line, texture, and other artistic elements. For example, Beth knows her basic geometric shapes. She discovers that squares combine to form a rectangle. Painting red over yellow makes orange. Lines that intersect form an X or cross shape. White added to blue lightens it and makes it the perfect color for Beth's sky. Difficult spatial concepts, including right, left, up, down, over, beside, through, next to, on top of, between, and under, are represented in art. These spatial concepts will be vital to reading comprehension at a later time.

Art serves as an index of a child's thinking. We can look at children's artwork, particularly painting and drawing, and find out what they know about their world, what they consider important, and how they choose to represent it. Detailed artwork indicates that a child knows much about that particular subject. Children who can express what they know about their world will be at an advantage later when they are expected to write and read about it. Signs (words) spoken or in print must have some referent. Art gives children the opportunity to symbolize that

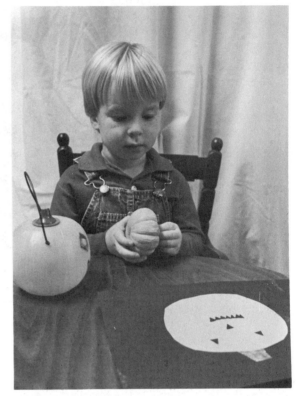

FIGURE 4–9   *Young children are concrete learners. Art helps them symbolize their experiences.*

referent and serves as a bridge between object and sign (see Figure 4–9).

Creative Development

Creativity begins during infancy as babies invent solutions to problems and engage in novel actions. According to Torrance (1965), young children are at their peak of creative functioning, which declines with age. Young children are highly imaginative. Imagination is strongly related to creativity. Rewarding a child's sense of autonomy and initiative enhances creative functioning (Erikson, 1963).

Art and Creative Development   As seen in Figure 4–10, art allows children to express their own creativity, originality, and individuality. Children's artistic expressions may be vaguely similar yet still

FIGURE 4–10   Art fosters creative expression.

significantly different from all others. Art is the perfect medium for young children, who are so highly imaginative. Their fantasy can be given form through art. Art is an open-ended activity that encourages discovery, exploration, experimentation, and invention. All of these skills are vital to creativity. Gene thinks about what will happen if he uses two paintbrushes at a time. He tries it out and is pleased with the double-stroked result. He asks his teacher to help him tie a rubber band around three paintbrushes. Through active experimentation, he invents a new way to paint.

CONTEXT: INTERACTION OF CHILD DEVELOPMENT AND ENVIRONMENTAL INFLUENCES

Our developmental profile neatly dissected the whole child for the purpose of analyzing the different aspects of development one at a time. The truth is that children are much more than the sum of their developmental parts. Physical + Social-Emotional + Cognitive + Language ≠ Whole Child. Development is not this simplistic and does not occur in isolation. Children develop within a context, and this wider setting must be studied to understand the impact it makes upon a developing child. Children's development is influenced by home, community, and environmental influences. For example, children will be influenced by family changes, poverty, and socioeconomic variables, including neighborhood crime. The influences are mutual and reciprocal—children also influence their home, community, and environment. For example, children who are under stress as a result of divorce may regress and become dependent. In turn, parents may change their parenting techniques, providing extra comfort and reassurance. The wider context of children's development is depicted in Figure 4–11.

religion/spirituality

family
composition

schooling

values & beliefs

experiences

parenting style

child rearing

ethnicity

media

gender

race

community

culture

social class

FIGURE 4–11   The Context: Interaction of child
development and environmental influences

PROCESSING WITH ART MATERIALS AND TOOLS

Very young children process with art materials long before they purposely decide to make an art product. They enjoy tearing and taping paper, smear-ing and spreading paste and glue, and using scissors and staples. Some very simple activities include

- tearing paper
- cutting with scissors
- pasting and gluing
- taping and sticking
- stapling
- punching holes in paper

Each of these is not only enjoyable by itself but is also a necessary skill for other art activities.

Scissors and Cutters

There are many different tools for cutting, including:

blade cutter—for cutting mats

blunt—steel scissors; blunt is fine, as long as they still cut

comfy or cushie grip—with rubber-coated finger holes

crinkle-cut scissors

Fiskars—cut anything! They come with comfort-molded universal ring handles for right or left hand

Fiskars Paper Edgers—can be used left- or right-handed and cut papers in six different designs.

hole punchers

Krazy Kut scissors—cut papers in little and big wave, lightning, zig-zag, scallop, and zipper patterns

lefty—designed specifically for left-handed children

paper cutter—for cutting paper into a variety of shapes and sizes, as well as paper strips

paper punchers—assorted shapes

pinking shears—jagged edge on paper and fabric adds variety

safety—lightweight plastic for right- and left-handed cutters

scissors rack—metal or wood for safely and neatly storing scissors

sharp—steel, in right- and left-hand models, for experienced and older four-year-olds and five-year-olds

snip loop or easy grip scissors—recommended for beginning cutters or for children with limited motor control

Food for Thought: Food for Art?

Opinion is divided on the use of food in art projects. Breakfast cereal and macaroni are often strung on string or yarn for necklaces. Beans and popcorn are glued on paper. Rice is used in collage. Younger children enjoy hand painting with pudding, frosting, or whipped topping. Infants and toddlers like to use applesauce. The above activities are enjoyable and may serve important developmental and sensory ends. The author, however, advises against the use of food in art for several reasons.

1. Food is expensive. If parents want to donate, they can bring in junk recyclable materials, ingredients for cooking, or other more crucial and perhaps costly supplies such as wooden blocks, books, or puzzles.
2. Food is a precious commodity that many take for granted and waste.
3. There is such a pressing need for food in Third World countries that the casual use of food in art can be questioned on moral and ethical grounds.
4. The number of homeless people has increased dramatically in recent years. In times of economic recession, some middle-class families may find themselves homeless as a result of job loss. Families with children represent a large segment of our homeless population. Some areas have a severe shortage of food targeted for the homeless. It may be difficult to justify stringing O-shaped pieces of breakfast cereal when one knows that many local children will go to bed hungry.
5. The use of food in an art activity may offend some cultural groups who use that food item for religious or ethnic celebration.
6. Foods such as frosting, pudding, and whipped topping are highly caloric and contain an abundance of sugar.
7. Adults should never use food in art activities with toddlers because they are developing self-regulatory skills and must learn to distinguish between food and other objects that are not to be eaten (Bredekamp, 1987).

In summary, there are many sound alternatives to the use of food in art. Small drinking-straw sections can replace macaroni for stringing. Sand rather than rice can be glued. Styrofoam squiggles can replace beans in a collage activity. Be creative in identifying alternatives to food in art activities.

---

teacher's straight shears—very sharp; for teacher's use only!

training—double-handled with four rubber-coated finger holes; teacher and child cut together

X-Acto knife—for cutting mats

Hint Regardless of the type selected, scissors must cut. There is nothing more frustrating to a young cutter than a pair of scissors that snag, tear, or clog up with paper but do not cut it.

Hint Mix water, white glue, and food coloring or liquid watercolor for the very young paster. Toddlers would also enjoy placing pieces of precut or pretorn papers onto a piece of construction paper with glue. Glue can be mixed with water to both extend it and eliminate its crusty appearance when dry. Mix water and white glue in equal parts, for example, ½ cup white glue to ½ cup water.

Hint Add liquid watercolor to clear glue to get a colored glue that is richer in color than colored white glue.

Hint Tap-N-Glue cap, a relatively new product, has taken the mess and waste out of gluing. Young children can easily turn the bottle upside down and gently tap. The special cap makes the glue come out in small drops. There is no opening and closing of tops and no clogs or leaks. Special caps fit bottles of white glue. Tap-N-Glue caps are inexpensive and make gluing an economical art activity that can be offered on a daily basis. Call 1-800-992-9018.

Adhesives: Glue, Paste, Tape, and Accessories

The following list suggests many different adhesives:

cloth tape—for color coding
colored tape—for taping and sticking
E-Z-up clips—held with wax to the wall; claims to stick to any surface; holds artwork; reusable
glue sticks—no drips or mess
masking tape—for taping and sticking
paste—individual containers with applicators for bonding paper
paste brush—rather than using fingers
paste cups—with lids; small margarine tubs are ideal
paste refill—pint, quart, or gallon
Plasti-Tak—reusable, no-mar adhesive for displaying art on walls
Popsicle sticks—make good paste spreaders
roll-on glue—same as glue stick, no drips or mess
School Glue Gel
Scotch or clear tape—for taping and sticking
Tap-N-Glue caps—no mess or waste
wall clips—same as E-Z-up clips; for displaying artwork on wall
white liquid glue—good all-purpose adhesive; buy individual small bottles and large refill. Good for paper, wood, Styrofoam, nature specimens, and most junk.

Hint Some young children enjoy eating paste, given its smell and touch. Provide a damp sponge or paper towel and encourage periodic wiping of fingers before the big gob of paste gets too tempting.

Hint Since paste dries out very fast, it is important to replace the lids. Children will forget. Try gluing a small piece of wet sponge to the inside lid to keep the paste moist. Use baby food jars with lids, margarine tubs, or other small, covered containers.

Hint Small bottles of white glue are easy to hold and use. Also, some children feel obligated to use up a whole bottle. A smaller bottle may satisfy this need to empty the container without wasting paste.

Hint Some teachers prefer to pour small amounts of white glue into a small plastic bowl or lid. This bypasses the use of individual bottles, which dry out very quickly because children often forget to twist the tops shut.

Hint Some children enjoy spreading the liquid glue with their fingers. Small sponges can also be used to dab the glue and apply it. A special glue stick is easy to make. Wrap a piece of netting twice around a Popsicle stick and secure it with a rubber band at one end. The weave in the netting holds the glue until the child is ready to apply it.

Paste and Glue Recipes

Please refer to the Box titled "Food for Thought: Food for Art" regarding a discussion of the use of food in art before deciding on recipes using flour, cornstarch, and other food products.

Paste (uncooked)

8 cups wallpaper paste mix
10 cups water

Slowly add water to wallpaper mix. Mix thoroughly.

Watered-Down Glue

white liquid glue
water

Slowly add water to glue. Stir thoroughly. Add more water if too thick. Use this to coat strips of paper.

Paste (for paper, cooked)

1 cup sugar
1 cup flour
1 teaspoon alum
4 cups water
oil of cloves

Mix the sugar, flour, and alum. Add water. Cook until thick. Stir constantly. Let cool. Add several drops of oil of cloves. Store in covered jar.

Flour Paste (cooked)

1 cup flour
1 teaspoon salt
2 cups water

Slowly add water to salt and flour mixture. Simmer about 5 minutes. Stir constantly.

Flour Paste (uncooked)

½ cup flour
½ cup water

Slowly add water to flour. Mix thoroughly. Add more water if too lumpy, more flour if too runny.

Cornstarch Paste (uncooked)

cornstarch
water

Slowly add water to about I cup of cornstarch. Mix thoroughly. Add more water if too lumpy, more cornstarch if too runny.

Wheat Paste (uncooked)

Wheat paste is available from hardware stores. Add wheat paste to water. Mix thoroughly until smooth.

Tearing Paper

Young children should not feel excluded from art activities just because they cannot use scissors. Very young artists can tear paper. Tearing paper is a good activity for developing the hand and finger muscles. Begin with very thin papers like newspaper, scrap tissue, or old phone directories. The individual pieces can be pasted or glued to each other or onto a piece of paper.

Torn-Paper Picture

Torn-paper pieces can be arranged and pasted or glued onto a piece of paper to form a torn-paper picture (see Figure 4–12). Older children may enjoy using construction paper. Being able to use scissors does not mean that one has outgrown the interest in tearing paper for art activities. The author observed a classroom where kindergartners were making a

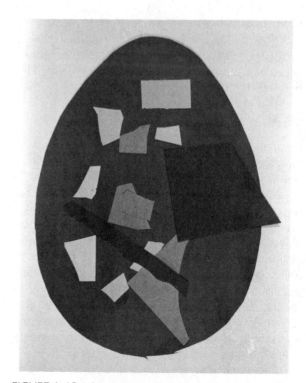

FIGURE 4–12   A torn-paper picture

Halloween mural out of torn-paper shapes. Torn shapes with rough, jagged edges are ideal for this activity. One witch's hat had a long, exaggerated point, and so did her nose!

Cutting with Scissors   P K

Recall this chapter's discussion of the developmental sequence for using scissors. Successful cutting with scissors is a developmental landmark. Some children will cut for the sheer sake of cutting, with little regard for the pieces cut. Some will want to take their individually cut pieces home in a bag. Others will enjoy pasting the pieces that they have cut onto paper. You may want to tape a paper bag to the table to catch the cut paper snips as they fall, rather than attempting to pick or sweep them off the floor later.

Folding and Cutting   K S

Children can fold a thin piece of paper and use their scissors to snip out a piece. Refold the paper in a different direction and continue cutting and snipping. Open up the paper and glue it against a colored piece of construction paper for a background. This will help the cutout design stand out.

Pasting and Gluing   T P

Very young children enjoy smearing paste or dripping glue for the sheer pleasure of it. They enjoy the smell, cold feel, stickiness, and texture of solid paste. It has a thick, crumbly feel and sticks to the fingers. Liquid white glue has a very different wet feel to it. Children enjoy squeezing glue onto paper. Bottles filled to the brim may be quickly emptied. You may want to add food coloring to your paste and glue to enhance its visual appeal for beginning pasters and gluers. Very young children may not be interested in gluing or pasting anything in particular. Older children will combine pasting and gluing with tearing and cutting. Papers that have been cut or torn or both can be pasted or glued onto an art surface.

Paste and glue serve different purposes. Paste will hold lightweight papers together, but glue is needed to bond heavier objects, including boxes

and wood. Rubber cement is meant for adhering paper but should not be used with children because of its misuse as an inhalant.

Stapling   S

Staplers and stapling fascinate young children. Stapling is more a fine motor skill than an artistic process. A hand-held stapler requires a squeezing motion with one hand, while a large stapler involves a gentle pounding, stamping, hammering, or pushing action. The miniature stapler may be too small for children to activate and control. Using a stapler is noisy, but older children thoroughly enjoy it and the activity exercises their finger and hand muscles. They will staple just to get a group of staples attached to paper. Sometimes the staples will form a design or pattern on colored paper. At other times they may use a stapler in place of paste or glue for attaching small pieces of paper, fabric, or collage material to each other or a background.

Sprinkle a Picture   P K

Children can make a picture or design with paste or glue on paper. They can carefully sprinkle

- confetti *Dimitrius*
- paper dots (from a hole punch) *Dimitrius*
- small balls of cotton (on dark paper) *Adrienne*
- small shells *try*
- seeds
- pine needles *Monika*
- pieces of broken jewelry *Monika*
- sand
- Styrofoam chips or squiggles *Monika*
- glitter *Chris*

Hint   To make colored sand, place sand in plastic bag. An adult can use an ice-cream stick to scrape colored chalk dust into bag. Shake well. Some teachers use a few drops of food coloring or liquid watercolor, but this is messier and involves drying overnight. Powdered tempera can also be used.

Hint   Children under four, however, should not use glitter, according to the Society for the

Prevention of Blindness. When it sticks to fingers and children rub their eyes, the glitter can damage the eye by actually cutting it. Older children should be closely supervised when using glitter.

Carefully slide the excess off the paper and back into the container. Some teachers use salt, sugar, popcorn, cornmeal, or rice in shakers for this activity. The author advises against the use of food in art activities for reasons previously stated.

Taping and Sticking

Very young children enjoy sticking tape. Teachers can provide plastic tape in a variety of colors, widths, and lengths. Place cut or torn pieces of tape on a nonstick surface. Children will enjoy lifting them off and placing them on paper. Pieces of torn or cut paper can also be taped onto an art surface.

Lick-and-Stick Art

Children enjoy licking and sticking the colorful labels and gummed papers available from office supply and stationery stores. Items include

- paper reinforcements
- gummed stars and labels
- stickers Dimitrius
- price tags
- colored dots
- book club stamps
- seals

These can also be licked and placed in a visual arrangement.

Hole and Paper Punch Art

Older children will have the muscular strength to work with a hole punch using either one or both hands. They seem fascinated with the process. Provide strips of paper from which to punch holes. They may want to save the punched holes. Punched holes can be used for gluing. Children can also make a design outline or picture with punched holes and paste this onto another paper. For example, a design could be punched out of white paper and glued to a piece of colored construction paper for a greeting card. New versions of hole punches come in smaller squares which provide a variety of paper shapes when punched. There is also a Dial-A-Design 6-in-1 paper punch. Simply turn the wheel to choose either a tulip, star, heart, cat, dinosaur, or musical note to punch out by pressing the button.

Stringing Art

Stringing objects is not only a good activity for improving eye-hand coordination but is also a way to creatively string together items. Use a shoelace or sturdy yarn with a plastic needle. Knot the far end of the yarn or shoelace to keep the objects from sliding off. Children will enjoy stringing

- spools
- paper reinforcements
- hole-punched paper
- tinfoil
- egg-carton cups
- sections of plastic straws
- pieces of colored paper
- sections of toilet-paper rolls
- plastic paper clips
- Styrofoam pieces
- buttons
- washers
- soda-pop rings
- pipe cleaners twisted into circular shapes

Items that have been strung can be tied into a necklace, bracelet, or belt and proudly worn. Although the author advises against the use of food in art, children can string nutritious breakfast cereal and eat it throughout the morning as breakfast or a snack.

Contact Paper Art

Provide various collage materials, including colored tissue paper, yarn, paper scraps, and other flat objects. Cut clear contact paper at least 6 inches in diameter for each child. Remove the backing and place sticky side up on art table. This eliminates the need for paste or glue. Tape four corners with masking tape to secure. Very young children will enjoy placing objects on contact paper and seeing them magically stick. When done, place a larger sheet of construction paper over the contact paper to frame.

Sand Pendulum

See Figure 4–13. Punch a small hole in the center of the bottom of the inside of a paper cup. Make three evenly spaced holes in the rim of the cup. Cut three pieces of string and run them through the three holes. Tie the three ends into a knot. Set up two matching chairs back to back and about three feet apart. Place a pole, e.g., yardstick, thick dowel rod, or broomstick between the top of both chair backs. Secure with duct tape. Cut a piece of string long enough to reach from the pole to the floor. Tie one end of this long string to the pole and the other end to the knot in the cup's string. Cover the floor with newspaper. Lay black construction paper on top of the newspaper beneath the cup. Cover the hole in the cup with one finger while filling the cup with sand. The child can gently swing the pendulum while you let go of the cup. As the sand pours from the cup, it will make a design on the black paper. Children can apply glue to their black paper first if they want to save the design. If not, simply refill the cup with the contents on the black paper.

Glue Stickers

Tacky and flexible when dry, glue stickers' transferable designs will cling to most flat plastic, glass, and metal surfaces, including windows, refrigerators, sliding glass doors, and mirrors. Place a piece of clear plastic kitchen wrap on a table. Apply

FIGURE 4–13   Sand pendulum

white or colored glue to the plastic wrap and make a design using finger, brush, or craft stick. Add food coloring or liquid watercolor to color the glue. Allow sticker to dry at least 24 hours. Check to see if child's sticker needs more drying time by carefully lifting the clear wrap off the table and looking under the sticker. Lighter color spots means sticker needs more time to dry. To remove sticker, gently peel away from clear wrap.

Rainbow Glue

Add liquid watercolor to clear (not white) glue for more brilliant colors. Place in shallow bowls or squeeze bottles. Children can also use their fingers or small brushes.

Hint A new adhesive is School Glue Gel, manufactured by the same company that makes white glue. It is less messy than white glue because it will not run or drip.

Puffy Paint

This is an economical alternative to store-bought puffy paint. In a bowl, mix equal parts (e.g., one cup each) of flour, salt, and water. Add food coloring or liquid watercolor. Mix thoroughly. Pour into condiment squeeze bottle. Make sure tip has an opening that will allow contents to exit when squeezed by children. Repeat process if more colors are desired. Experiment by varying the size of the holes in your squeeze bottles. Look for color-coded or clear squeeze bottles so contents are identifiable. Cover small cardboard squares with tinfoil. Puffy paint will squeeze out like toothpaste and sparkle. Spatulas can be provided for smearing the puffy paint. Let dry overnight and it will harden on the tinfoil in 3-D relief. Puffy paint cannot be saved and containers must be cleaned after use before contents mold or harden.

Starch and Yarn Art

Pour liquid starch into small bowls. Discuss that although starch is a pretty blue color it is not to eat or drink because it could make you sick. Cut different colors and lengths of yarn. Provide a clean Styrofoam tray or sheet of wax paper for each child. Children can dip their yarn in the starch and lay it on the surface to create a design. Closely supervise. Provide wet sponges or paper towels for children to wipe off their fingers before touching their faces.

Bleeding Art   P K

This is a good outdoor activity. Each child needs a squirt bottle filled with clear water and a large sheet of white paper. Provide scraps of tissue paper and crepe paper. Have the children place the paper scraps on the white paper in an interesting design and then squirt with water. The colored papers will begin to "bleed" and the colors will run and mix. The wet scraps can be removed and discarded. Place in the sun to dry. If done indoors, place white paper in a large box lid to contain children's squirting. You can eliminate the squirt bottles by putting the papers outside on a rainy day. This combines art and science as children discuss what happened and how it happened.

SUMMARY

We have moved from an overview of wholistic child development to links between art and a child's development. This chapter explained how art fosters a child's physical, social, emotional, cognitive, and creative development. Art was viewed as a developmentally appropriate and important activity. Knowledge of a young child's physical needs and abilities suggested strategies and materials for helping the child learn to cut with scissors. Although art is pleasurable and multisensory, potential art hazards do exist. Guidelines for identifying toxic art supplies and suggested alternatives are provided in Appendix F. Although art fosters emotional expression and release, it was not recommended that art therapy be attempted without adequate training. The relationship between creativity and art has long been recognized, but the link between art and thinking may be as strong. Although the use of food in art activities appears to be creative, objections were raised. It was recommended that the teacher seek alternatives to the use of food in art.

Suggested Activities

1. Observe a young child actively involved in an art activity. Record what the child says and does. How did this art experience help the child physically, socially, emotionally, cognitively, and creatively?

2. Observe children aged three, four, and five using scissors. Using the guidelines in this unit, what recommendations can you make for each with respect to tools, paper, activity, or teacher input?

3. Arrange to work with a difficult or troubled young child. Ask the child to draw or paint how he or she is feeling. Encourage the child to talk about the picture. Encourage emotional expression without formally attempting art therapy.

4. Plan and carry out an open-ended art experience in which children process with art materials and tools.

Review

A. List the five aspects of a child's development.

1.

2.

3.

4.

5.

B. At your midyear open house, a few parents wonder why so much time is devoted to art in your preschool program. Using the wholistic model of child development, what could you say to justify your art program?

C. A parent is alarmed because her five-year-old is always drawing ghosts and graveyards. She fears that her child is abnormal or emotionally disturbed. What are some possible explanations for this child's art?

D. Suggest a nonfood art activity for each of the following:

Activity	Alternative
1. printing with cut vegetables	
2. gluing breakfast cereal on a self-portrait for facial features	
3. sprinkling powdered gelatin over white glue for sparkling lines	
4. making ice cream for a snack and then finger painting with it	

CHAPTER 5

Children Are Unique Individuals

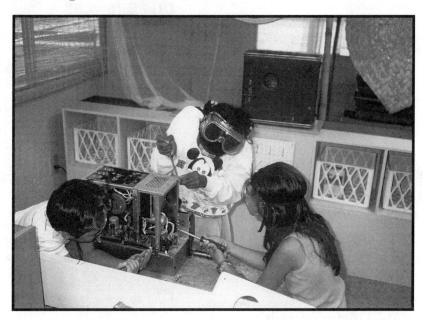

What do you see in this picture? Are you comfortable with what is going on? Is this an activity for both boys and girls?

Although school-age children are considered under the umbrella of early childhood education, they have needs and interests that separate them from younger children. After a long day at school, these three school-age children enjoy coming to the construction area and using real tools to assemble, disassemble, and reassemble a piece of broken electrical equipment. The experience is manipulative and hands-on. It involves decision making and problem solving. It is a good physical and mental activity for both boys and girls.

OBJECTIVES

After studying this chapter, the student will be able to

- Discuss how individual differences express themselves
- List five guidelines for working with young children with exceptionalities and honoring multicultural backgrounds
- Discuss how art can help exceptional children and those children from varying backgrounds
- Discuss bias, anti-bias, and diversity as they relate to the development and education of young children
- Provide multicultural art experiences

INTRODUCTION

Young children are unique individuals, and few will totally conform to our developmental norms for what is normal, typical, or average. Instead, they come to us with a variety of differences resulting from background, family, and individual factors. This may prove both fascinating and frustrating as we strive to meet their individual needs, interests, and abilities. Exceptionalities and multicultural backgrounds may be the most extreme forms of individual differences. Direct contact and knowledge can overcome any stereotypes and help set only positive expectations. Art is an excellent activity for children, who profit from nonverbal symbolic expression, social interaction, and mastery. Knowing young children, valuing individual differences, and acting on this information will help us to provide appropriate art activities that enhance the wholistic development of every child in our care.

Ⓝ GOING BEYOND NORMAL, TYPICAL, AND AVERAGE

A working knowledge of child development can be a very useful tool. Knowing the needs, interests, and abilities of young children at a given age or stage can help us design developmentally appropriate art activities. We can act on what we know. This knowledge of child development, however, will give us only a general pattern of what is "normal, typical, or average." Few children conform to the norm or can be considered typical or average. How boring life and caregiving would be if each of us were normal, typical, or average! Children are unique individuals. Their physical, social, emotional, cognitive, and creative development will reflect individual differences resulting from both heredity and environmental influences. Chronological age can be very misleading. Although our knowledge of child development tells us that children learn to skip at age five, Leslie at five and a half cannot. Her own timetable for physical development does not match the norm. In terms of skipping, she may not be typical of the average five-year-old. She need not be labeled slow, immature, or developmentally delayed.

If Leslie's overall physical profile departs radically from the norm, however, referral and remediation might be warranted.

Ⓝ VALUING INDIVIDUAL DIFFERENCES

Individual differences are the spice of life; they make teaching young children both fascinating and challenging. Within any one age group there will be a wide range of commonalities in terms of physical, social, emotional, cognitive, and creative needs, interests, and abilities. There will also be significant individual differences. Obviously, it would be much simpler to work with a group of three-, four-, or five-year-olds with similar, if not identical, developmental characteristics. But the aim of early childhood education is to foster the development of unique individuals, not to mass-produce robots.

Differences in development and learning that result from heredity or environment or their interaction are expressed in the following ways:

- background—race, culture, and social class
- family—family size, siblings, birth order, divorce and remarriage, parental educational and occupational levels, nutrition, parental teaching style, and child abuse or neglect
- individual—gender, personality and temperament, motivation, learning style, and personal interests

Identifying and discussing every factor that can potentially influence the development of individual differences is clearly beyond the scope of this section. Further, background, family, and individual influences interact and may produce different effects on different individuals.

Ⓝ PROVIDING FOR YOUNG CHILDREN WITH INDIVIDUAL DIFFERENCES

The greatest expression of individual differences will be for children with

- exceptionalities
- multicultural backgrounds

There are many terms used to refer to children with special needs. The World Health Organization offers the following definitions:

1. An impairment is an anatomic or functional abnormality or loss which may or may not result in a disability.
2. A disability is a loss or reduction of functional ability which results from an impairment.
3. A handicap is the disadvantage caused by the disability.

The last quarter of the twentieth century has witnessed legislation in support of children with special needs. The Education for All Handicapped Children Act of 1975 (PL 94-142), now known as the Individuals with Disabilities Education Act (PL 101-476 or IDEA), targeted special-needs children between the ages of five and twenty-one and established four major rights for them. These include free appropriate public education, placement in a "least restrictive environment," fair assessment procedures, and parental involvement in the educational decision-making process. Parents are actively involved in the development of an individualized family service plan (IFSP) and the individualized education program (IEP) written to meet their child's unique educational and related service needs. PL 99-457 was passed in 1986 authorizing Programs for Infants and Toddlers with Handicaps and the Preschool Grants Program, targeting special-needs children ages three through five. In 1992, the Americans with Disabilities Act (ADA) went into effect, mandating equal rights in employment and public services as well as access to child care and early childhood programs.

According to Karnes (1993), the value of art activities for children with special needs cannot be overemphasized. However, since art may be a new experience for some children with special needs, a good beginning is talking about the art media and modeling how to use the materials. As with all children, the aim is to first make them feel comfortable and successful. After this, provide time and space for them to independently explore, discover, and create. Remain a resource and consultant to them, offering assistance as needed. Karnes (1993) identi-

fies five categories of children with special needs and offers the following suggestions:

1. Children with visual disabilities need teachers to verbally describe materials and the ways they might be used. At first, finger paint may feel cold and repulsive especially if one is not prepared for the experience and has no visual cues. Go slowly and encourage children to manipulate items as you talk. Provide a tray which defines their work surface and keeps art tools at hand. Children with marginal vision can do art activities in a well-lighted area. Children who are visually impaired enjoy tactile experiences like hand painting and using play dough.
2. Children with hearing impairments will learn by having teachers or other children model the process. Demonstrate in precise ways especially if there are several steps. Communicate with children about their art using sign language, lip reading, or any methods they understand.
3. Children with physical disabilities may need to use art materials in different ways, such as lying on the floor over a bolster to color or paint. Provide adaptive art tools like fat bingo markers, chunky crayons, and large markers. Taping a group of crayons or markers together or applying nonskid tape to marking instruments will ensure a better grip. Provide double-handed ambidextrous scissors and those that are activated with a squeezing motion. Glue sticks prove less frustrating than trying to use a bottle of glue with a rotating top that easily clogs. When painting, provide no-spill paint cups. Or, cut a hole through a sponge and fit it around the bottom of a juice can. Trim the sponge to fit into the easel tray. The sponge will secure the paint container and catch paint drips. Velcro can be attached to a glove or mitten and a paintbrush. The child wears the glove or mitten, which secures the brush for painting. Replace thin-handled brushes with old knobbed shaving brushes or sponges, which are easier to grasp. Brushes, markers, and crayons can also be inserted through foam hair rollers to secure a better grip. For children with limited hand control, adults may need to guide their

hands while manipulating the tools. Offer as little assistance as possible but as much help as needed. Put the child in control by asking him or her how the marking instruments should move. A child in a wheelchair may enjoy using a small wall-paint roller (edger type) to paint on paper taped to a wall or to an easel that can be moved close to the seated painter.

4. Children with cognitive disabilities may need extra direction and close supervision when experimenting with art. As always, provide safe and success-oriented materials for creative processing rather than complex teacher-directed activities with many steps, which invite failure.

5. Children with attention deficit disorder need their own materials and space to ensure success. They enjoy making multiple products. Art accomplishes three goals for them. It sustains their attention; it allows them to express their feelings; and their artistic competence enhances their self-esteem.

Ⓝ Gifted and Talented Children

A sixth category—gifted and talented children—can be added to the list. Although it is important to discover the creative potential and talent inherent in each and every child, children who are considered gifted or talented show high performance in one or more of the following areas: general intellectual ability, academic aptitude, creative thinking or production, leadership ability, talent in visual and performing arts, and physical ability, such as athletics. Identifying gifted and talented children should include an individual intelligence test, observations, and interviews with parents. According to Safford (1989), the early identification of gifted and talented children is difficult because certain groups of children, including those from low-income families, minorities, and those with special needs, are "under identified."

Although it is difficult to characterize gifted and talented children, and development may be uneven, precociousness is a common denominator. Adults observe that these children walk, talk, and some even teach themselves to read at an early age. They are very curious, inquisitive, have a good sense of humor, and learn quickly. Difficult concepts are easily grasped and their vocabulary is extensive. They ask thought-provoking questions and have long attention spans. They may be perfectionists and intolerant of their less mature peers. The gifted and talented prodigy, however, can quickly become a problem child. They become bored in a slow-paced classroom and lockstep curriculum that offers mundane tasks that they find unchallenging and stifling. They may act up or withdraw by becoming underachievers.

How are the needs of gifted and talented children best met? According to Safford (1989), in the early years the vast majority are in the educational mainstream. This may or may not be the "least restrictive" environment, depending upon the appropriateness of what is provided to meet their needs. Programs and approaches that provide challenge, nurture diversity and divergent ways of thinking and enable children to learn at their own pace and in multiple ways provide a good match for gifted and talented children. They also need enrichment activities to supplement their mastery of the core curriculum and challenge their gifts and talents. Mixed-age grouping is recommended, since a child who exhibits one or more gifts or talents may not excel socially. The discrepancies between cognitive and other developmental areas, including physical and social, may prove frustrating. The five-year-old who thinks like an older child may lack the corresponding physical and social skills. Open-ended art activities (Chapter 11) and the art center approach (Chapter 14) provide a creative challenge for gifted and talented children.

SOME GENERAL GUIDELINES FOR WORKING WITH YOUNG CHILDREN WITH EXCEPTIONALITIES

1. Accept the child unconditionally, including disabilities, handicapping conditions, and limitations. Accept the child "as is," not as what you might like him or her to be, do, or look like.

2. Build on the child's strengths and capitalize on what he or she can do. Slowly, work on weaknesses and deficiencies.

3. Adapt the physical environment to meet the child's special needs. Rearrange classroom space and furniture. Remove any potential hazards or obstacles. See Figure 5–1.

4. Encourage independence and wean the child from overdependence on you. Expect the child to do some things independently, and reward him or her for doing them (see Figure 5–2).

5. Treat all children equally. Being disabled is no excuse for behavior that continually violates classroom rules. Children with disabilities need and want to be treated like everyone else.

6. Be informed and educate your students about specific handicapping conditions. Discuss these in an open and honest way, giving children time and space to express their feelings and fears. For example, children need to know about a seizure and what they can do for a child who is having one.

7. Provide multisensory stimulation. Incorporate an array of things for the children to visually in-

FIGURE 5–2   *I can do it!*

spect, listen to, touch, smell, and taste. Capitalize and build on sensory strengths.

8. Allow ample time, practice, and repetition for learning. Children with disabilities have developmental delays and need time and additional practice if learning is to occur.

9. Help the child with special needs to be successful and experience mastery. Systematically break down complex tasks into smaller, manageable steps.

10. Help children develop a positive self-concept by feeling good about themselves. Help them to view themselves as unique individuals with one or more individual differences that just happen to be more noticeable or extreme.

PROVIDING FOR YOUNG CHILDREN FROM VARYING BACKGROUNDS

Multicultural backgrounds are comprised of racial, ethnic, and cultural differences. Racial differences are expressed in skin color. Cultural differences are expressed in foods, dress, language, customs, values, and celebrations. Like exceptionalities, racial and cultural differences extend, enhance, and enrich society.

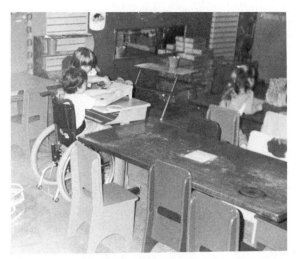

FIGURE 5–1   *All children should have access to art.*

SOME GENERAL GUIDELINES FOR WORKING WITH YOUNG CHILDREN FROM VARYING BACKGROUNDS

1. Accept the child unconditionally, including ethnicity. Accept the child "as is," not as what you might prefer in the way of looks, skin color, dress, or customs.
2. Value, accept, respect, and encourage the child's native language and ethnicity as strengths and as expressions of a unique individual difference.
3. Build on the child's strengths and what he or she can do. Provide instruction in the child's native language. Slowly work to help the child become bilingual and proficient in standard English.
4. Help the child feel comfortable in school. The sights, sounds, and surroundings may be unfamiliar and overwhelming to some children who have nothing to compare them with. See Figure 5–3.
5. Treat all children equally. Children of all backgrounds need and want to be treated fairly.

Guidelines, rules, and rewards should apply to all children.

6. Be informed about ethnic differences. Take a course on multicultural education. Eat at ethnic restaurants, sample ethnic foods, visit ethnic stores and shops, participate in ethnic celebrations, learn a second language, travel to a foreign country. See Figure 5–4.
7. Discuss and study similarities and differences among people. It is important for children to focus on human similarities as a framework for the individual differences resulting from culture and ethnicity. Some examples include:

> What are some things that all people need? We all need housing and food. Where he came from, Lin lived on a houseboat with his parents and grandparents. What do you think it would be like to live on a boat? Now he lives in an apartment. How many of you have ever lived in an apartment? I did while I was going to school. So even though Lin talks differently from us, he is still a lot like us. He has his own language and a place to live, just as we do. We are going to help Lin learn our language, and he will teach us his.

8. Involve the parents. Some immigrant parents may have great reservations about school. Some may be embarrassed about their lack of standard English. Others may be ashamed of

FIGURE 5–3   *Art helps all children make a very personal statement.*

FIGURE 5–4   *A cultural display*

their minimal level of education. Some will place great value on their child's education and may have unrealistically high expectations. All will be proud of their culture and willing to share their ethnicity if encouraged and invited. Help them feel comfortable. Let them know that they have something very special that the children would like to know more about. For example, Lin's mother was invited in to cook a rice dish with the children for a snack. Others could come dressed in native costume or bring in cultural artifacts. Their presence and participation will make their child feel good about being in school.

9. Help immigrant children to be successful and experience mastery. Many of them are experiencing *culture shock*. They are aware of their language and cultural differences. They need an abundance of things they can do successfully rather than an endless list of things they need to remediate.

10. Help ethnic children feel good about themselves just the way they are. They may be different, but differences are not only OK, they often are our strengths. See Figure 5–5. We are all different. Being different does not mean being bad or wrong. Ethnic children have a language, a culture, customs, and individual worth. They just happen to be different from the white middle-class culture and customs of many schools.

FIGURE 5–5   Let's learn about each other.

11. Give children time to observe and feel comfortable. Art activities may appear foreign and even overwhelm some children, especially if this is their first school experience in a new land. Find them a buddy who speaks their language and shares their background.

12. Understand that cultural differences may underscore a child's reluctance to do art. Children who have not been encouraged to be independent and autonomous may seek direction, instruction, and specific assistance in making art. They may want you to guide their hands or do it for them. Parents who value realistic art may see little value in open-ended processing which, to them, resembles nothing. They may conclude you are not doing your job in permitting scribbling rather than teaching their child how to draw. For other parents, the cultural issue may be neatness. Their children come to school dressed in their Sunday best. Girls in party dresses will avoid messy activities like art, having been warned to stay clean. These children have been sent cultural messages that are not bad or wrong but simply different from the culture of ECE and the values underlying developmentally appropriate practices. Two-way communication is needed. Newsletters and parent handouts can address these issues. Increase the probability that parents will read them by writing them in their home language. Talk and listen to families about their cultures. Ask about art, children, and creativity. Accept points of difference and negotiate a compromise. Since neatness is important to families, they may feel comfortable providing their own paint smock or shirt. Assure them that their child can dress up on party days or field trips. Avoid confrontations in which parents are made to feel or even told outright that "this is the way we do it here."

13. Learn key art words in the languages your children speak. Ask parents to translate the names of colors, words like art, paint, and play, and phrases like "Do you want to . . ." and "Do you like that?" in their home language. Ask them to write these down and speak them slowly as you rewrite them phonetically. Keep your language

cards posted near the art center for quick reference. You may also want to post the art center sign and labels in a second language.

14. Make your art program racially and culturally responsive. Crayola and Lakeshore have developed multicultural art products. Provide paint, crayons, markers, and paper in a range of skin tones. Provide play dough in shades of light, medium, dark brown, beige, tan and black. Few, if any, people truly have white skin. Provide yarn and a range of hair colors for making people. Display art posters depicting children and adults from around the world. Include cultural artifacts. For example, include a garlic and tortilla press with your clay and play-dough tools. Examples of multicultural arts and crafts that celebrate children's cultural roots are presented later in this chapter.

Art is recommended as a basic activity in multicultural classrooms. Because art is a form of nonverbal expression, there is no language prerequisite and no need to understand verbal directions. Children can discover on their own or observe each other. Art time is a good opportunity for children who do not speak it to hear and informally practice standard English. The setting for art is usually relaxed, and the child may feel less inhibited about speaking. Art time is also a good time for standard-English-speaking children to hear and practice other languages. Ethnic children enhance and enrich any classroom. Art is also a good vehicle for teaching about cultures. All cultures have their respective art forms (see Figure 5–6). For example, Japanese children may practice origami. Although it is difficult, most children can learn some simple paper folds.

HELPING CHILDREN GROW UP FREE OF BIAS

What do we mean by the terms *bias* and *antibias?* According to Derman-Sparks (1989), bias is any attitude, belief, or feeling that results in and helps to

FIGURE 5–6   Every culture has its own art.

justify unfair treatment of one's identity. *Anti-bias* refers to an active or activist approach to challenging prejudice, stereotyping, bias, and the "isms," including sexism, racism, and handicappism. It is necessary for each individual to intervene, challenge, and counter behaviors that perpetuate bias and oppression. The activist approach characterizes empowerment: knowing what is morally right and acting on one's convictions. To do nothing to counteract bias amounts to supporting bias by virtue of one's inaction (Derman-Sparks, Gutierrez, and Phillips, n.d.).

Because bias undermines the optimal development of children as unique individuals, anti-bias attitudes must be fostered early. According to Derman-Sparks (1989), pre-prejudice, the beginning ideas and feelings in very young children, may develop into real prejudice. Pre-prejudice takes many forms. It may be misconceptions based on young children's limited experience and developmental level, or it may consist of imitation of adults at home or in the media. More serious forms are behaviors that indicate discomfort, fear, or rejection of differences.

Research indicates that between ages two and five, children become aware of gender, race, ethnicity, and disabilities. Because some of the most basic elements of ethnic identity are established before age three, very young children thrive in a setting that is culturally diverse. Caregivers must recognize and support what is unique, and possibly culturally inspired, about each child (Bredekamp, 1987).

What else can be done? Multicultural and nonsexist experiences, materials, and equipment should be provided for children of all ages. Providing a wide variety of multicultural, nonstereotyping materials and activities helps ensure that the curriculum will be relevant for all the students. Multicultural experiences, however, should not be limited to a celebration of holidays. Such an approach characterizes a tourist curriculum that is both patronizing, emphasizing the "exotic" differences, and trivializing, dealing not with the real-life daily problems and experiences of different people, but with surface aspects of their celebrations and modes of entertainment (Derman-Sparks, 1989). Foods, music, families, shelter, and other aspects common to all cultures should be included (Bredekamp, 1987). Neugebauer (1987) would include art as another element common to all cultures.

Derman-Sparks's (1989) notion of empowerment advocates implementing an anti-bias curriculum that incorporates the best of multicultural education, but it is broader in scope. An anti-bias curriculum provides a more- inclusive education in three ways. First, it addresses more than cultural diversity by including gender and differences in physical abilities. Second, it is based on children's developmental tasks as they construct identity and attitudes. Third, it directly addresses the impact of stereotyping, bias, and discriminatory behavior in young children's development and interactions.

Derman-Sparks and the ABC Task Force (1989) identified four goals of an anti-bias curriculum. Those goals and activities to meet them are, first, to construct a knowledgeable, confident self-identity. An art activity would be to mix paints to reflect each child's skin color for painting life-size paper cutouts of each child. Provide a full-length mirror, and encourage children to note their features and value what they see. Purchase paints, crayons, and markers that come in an array of skin tone shades. One could also fill the learning environment with pictures, books, dolls, toys, media, wall decorations, and other materials showing a range of skin colors, eye shapes, and hair textures. The author would add art prints, postcards, and posters reflecting diversity. Resources for multicultural and anti-bias materials are listed at the end of this chapter.

The second goal is to develop comfortable, empathetic, and fair interactions. A regular activity would be to read stories about children from different ethnic groups and include family issues faced by young children, such as divorce, adoption, or having a sibling with special needs.

The third is to develop critical thinking about bias. An activity would be to have children contrast true, fair pictures with stereotypic ones that are untrue, unfair, and hurtful. Use magazines, books, posters, and greeting cards. Have the children identify and think critically about stereotypic images.

The fourth goal is to learn the skills for standing up for oneself and others in the face of injustice. Make it a firm rule that a person's identity is never an acceptable reason for teasing or rejection. An ongoing activity would be to set an example by your actions. Immediately step in if you hear or see discriminatory behavior. Make it clear that you disapprove of such behavior but do not make the child feel rejected. Support the child who has been hurt. Try to find out what underlies the biased behavior and work to resolve it (Derman-Sparks, Gutierrez, and Phillips, n.d.). Teachers can also empower children. Encourage children to use their words. For example: "I don't like it when you call me that, that's not my name," or "Don't say that; it hurts my feelings," or "That's not fair, girls can use the tools too," or "I need my wheelchair to get around—and that's OK."

Ⓝ MULTICULTURAL ARTS AND CRAFTS

Including multicultural arts and crafts in the early childhood curriculum is an issue that divides educators. Many believe that a commitment to cultural diversity would include exposing children to the arts and crafts of various cultures. Since the beginning of time, all people everywhere have participated in making arts and crafts characteristic of their group. For those educators who include crafts and adult-directed activities in their art program, this section will merely provide additional resources. People who have grown up in countries where crafts were taught to them as children may also be comfortable with teaching crafts to children at an early age. Others would disagree. Exposing children to cultural artifacts and crafts is one thing; teaching children how to make them raises several issues. First, most crafts are made by adults and attempts to teach children result in a teacher-directed approach which is more product than process oriented. For example, children will not discover origami or paper folding on their own without specific instruction. This raises the issues of developmental appropriate-

ness and creativity. One's intentions may be good in teaching children how to do a craft, but what has been gained if children become frustrated and unsuccessful when asked to merely copy or use skills that are beyond their developmental level? One compromise is to help children engage in making a craft while allowing for creative processing. For example, children may be instructed in how to fold a paper fan and encouraged to decorate it any way they see fit. Children's attempts at folding and all creative folds would be accepted and children would not be corrected if their finished product did not meet the teacher's standards. Again, this is a compromise which neither guarantees developmental appropriateness nor complete creative processing. Second, some crafts like tie-dye and batik are not only difficult but also dangerous for children. Third, there is a risk that the craft might not reflect the total cultural group. For example, although many Japanese children learn origami at a very early age, it cannot be concluded that all Japanese know and practice it. This would lead to a stereotype represented by the following equation: Japanese = origami. This is stereotypic and negates our efforts at accurately portraying cultures. Fourth, the study of a group of people and their representative crafts must be done in a way that is wholistic and integrated, as opposed to randomly addressed. For example, doing origami one day with a brief discussion of Japan, followed by a week's unit on Mexico, and culminating in making a piñata out of papier-mâché would reflect a "tourist approach" in which children quickly visit one culture after another, highlighting differences rather than recognizing and appreciating similarities. As a result, children may lack a wider context and stereotypically equate the whole culture with only one visible artifact, whether it be food, clothing, or craft. Our intent should be to help children construct a view of cultural similarities, including the making of arts and crafts, which includes a recognition and valuing of differences.

On paper, however, a culturally sensitive approach to arts and crafts is difficult. One traditional approach is to group people geographically by origin and identify representative artifacts, including arts and crafts. An incomplete list might include the following:

ASIAN: Japanese

Artifacts

paper folding, origami
lantern
screen making
carp kite
coolie hat
fan
doll

Activity: folding screen   K S

Japanese artists make folding screens, carved with floral designs or landscapes and painted black. They are often made in miniature to sit on the tops of tables. Children can make their own miniature screens by folding paper. Children will need a sheet of black construction paper or sturdy white paper. For an accordion fold, have the children fold their paper in half like a book. Fold the top half down toward the center fold. Turn the paper over and repeat the last step. The screen can be decorated with stickers, magazine pictures, markers, or paint. Children can also glue small nature items, including petals and leaves, onto their screens.

Activity: carp kite   K S

The carp has a special place in Japanese life. This fish represents strength, bravery, and longevity. Children can make their own carp kite using two equal lengths of tissue paper. Cut the papers into rectangular shapes measuring at least 1 foot long by 6 inches wide. Round off one narrow side and cut a "V" shape for the mouth. This will serve as the head and the opposite end will be the tail. Children can use markers or paint to decorate both papers. Because tissue paper is thin, children must use care and light pressure. They may also want to add fish scales and paper streamers to the tail. Staple or glue long sides of both decorated papers together. Leave the mouth and tail open. Use hole punch to make

hole above the mouth and thread a string through and knot securely. Outdoors, children can run while holding the string and flying their kites. Kites can also be stuffed with crumpled paper and hung on the wall or suspended from the ceiling.

Activity: Japanese paper fan   P K S

In Japan, a fan called "uchiwa" is made of split bamboo and washi, a type of Japanese paper. This type of fan is used during the Obon festival celebrated in July and dedicated to those who have died. The streets are decorated with paper lanterns and people dress in kimonos and dance with their fans, which are beautifully decorated with flowers like cherry blossoms, leaves, bamboo, or koi (Japanese carp). Children can make their own fans out of paper. They will each need a piece of white poster board which they can colorfully decorate with paint, crayons, markers, or stickers. When finished, an adult can staple the fan to a sturdy tongue depressor for the handle.

ASIAN: Chinese

Artifacts

fan
lantern
dragon
pen and ink
paper cutting and folding, paper making
masks
Lai-See (good luck money)

Activity: moon lantern

Festivals of thanksgiving for the harvest are celebrated throughout the world. In China, the Harvest Moon Festival is held in the fall during a full moon. This outdoor festival includes dancing, music, poetry, and a lantern parade. Children can make their own moon lanterns. Blow up and tie one round balloon for each child. Each child will also need approximately 20 lengths of yarn, each measuring about 18 inches. Children can dip their yarn into a small bowl of white glue or liquid starch and carefully wrap the wet yarn around their balloons. Let dry overnight. Adult can pop and remove the balloon. The stiff yarn moon form remains. Hang the moon from a stick or dowel and march in a parade.

Activity: dragon puppet   ⬛ **K S**

The dragon is a symbol of good fortune in China. Children can make their own puppets similar to the large dragons carried by men in a Chinese New Year parade. Children will need their own small milk container or paper Chinese food take-out container. Have children open their food containers. Cut off the two small side flaps which will become the ears. Turn container and two remaining flaps upside down. The bottom is now the top of the dragon's head. Adult can insert scissors into the large flap which has the slit and cut an opening for the dragon's mouth. Children can attach the ears and use markers to decorate their dragons. Provide lengths of crepe paper which children can tape to the back flap.

ASIAN: Vietnamese

Artifacts
dragon
lantern

Activity: dragon   ⬛ **K S**

The Dragon Dance, in which young men dance under a papier-mâché and cloth dragon, is an integral part of the Tet festival parade celebrating the Vietnamese New Year. Children can make their own miniature dragon using a paper cup, straw, and paper. Cutting wide V-shaped slits out of both sides of a cup forms the mouth. Children can use markers to add eyes to the top of the cup and decorate the dragon's face. Punch a hole at the bottom of the cup and run the straw into the cup head and along the bottom of the mouth. Secure with tape. Provide children with a strip of construction paper, 18 inches long by 2 inches wide and help them fold it accordion-style. They can use markers to decorate their dragon's body. When done, one end of the body can

be taped to the small circle on the bottom of the cup which has become the back of the dragon's head.

ASIAN: Korean

Artifacts
fan
dragon

ASIAN: Thai

Artifacts
kite

ASIAN: Indonesian

Artifacts
batik

AFRICAN: African-American

Artifacts
fabric art—weaving, batik, mud cloth, adinkra, kente cloth
Kufi hat
masks
Kinara candlestick
drum
doll

Activity: paper kufi   ⬛ **P K S**

To show pride in their heritage, young African-Americans and young Africans often wear a round hat called a kufi. Some are made from kente cloth. Children can make and wear a paper kufi in celebration of Black History month. Children will need a strip of dark-colored construction paper for the headband, measuring 2 feet long by 2 inches wide. They will also need 6 strips of construction paper measuring 1 foot long by 1 inch wide as follows: 2 red, 2 yellow, and 2 green. Help children fit the headbands snugly around their heads and staple ends together. Arrange the 6 strips of colored paper so they overlap to form a wheel. Staple all strips together at top of hat. To connect to headband, place one strip along the outside edge of the headband and staple. Continue stapling all strips to outside bottom edge of headband. The stapled pieces should form a dome shape.

AFRICAN: Egyptian

Artifacts
beads

Activity: paper bead making **K S**

Egyptians and African tribal groups use beads for making jewelry items like necklaces and for decorating pouches and their clothing. Children can roll strips of colorful paper to make their own beads. Gift wrap or brightly colored magazine pages can be sent through the paper cutter and cut into 1-inch strips or cut with scissors into tapering pennant shapes. The paper strips can be wound around a toothpick, chopstick, or thin brush handle. Glue the end and carefully slide off. String the beads on a length of yarn. If the yarn end is first dipped into glue and left to dry, the beads will be easier to string. Items such as buttons can also be included for variety.

HISPANIC: Mexican, Central and South American

Artifacts
ojo de Dios (God's eye)
paper flowers
papier-mâché piñata or mariachi instruments
yarn art
weaving

Activity: paper flowers **P K S**

Colorful tissue-paper flowers are a traditional craft of Mexico and Central America. Paper flowers are used in ceremonies and sold on street corners. Cut out different sizes and colors of tissue paper in round shapes with wavy edges, rather than perfect circles. Have children layer the pieces of tissue paper together, going from large on the outside of the flower to small on the inside. Have an adult use scis-

sors to carefully poke two holes in the center of each bundle of tissue paper petals. Insert a pipe cleaner up one hole and down through the second hole. Twist the two ends of the pipe cleaner together to make the stem.

EASTERN EUROPEAN: Russian

Artifacts
nesting dolls (Matryoshka)

Activity: nesting dolls **K S**

Matryoshka dolls are hollow wooden doll sets containing smaller nesting dolls inside. Matryoshka in Russian means "grandmother." If possible, bring in one or more sets of nesting dolls for the children to inspect. Items of graduated sizes including cans, tissue paper rolls, and tubes fashioned from construction paper can be used. Children can decorate each doll in the series by drawing a face and clothing.

JEWISH

Artifacts
star of David
dreidel
menorah

Activity: star of David **P K**

Make the star of David by cutting two sponges into triangle shapes, or use two triangular cookie cutters. Apply paint with a brush or dip into paint. Inverting one triangle over the other forms a six-pointed star.

Activity: clay menorah **K S**

Use real clay to make a menorah. A menorah should have spots or holes for eight candles, plus a raised spot to hold the shamash, a ninth candle used to light the others. A menorah could also be fashioned from tissue paper tubes or construction paper cut into four matching pairs of different lengths. Children can arrange their pairs in ascending order, reserving the middle spot for the tallest candle (shamash). Yellow and orange tissue paper can be applied to represent the flames. One candle is lit on the first night of Hanukkah or Festival of Lights; a second is lit on the second night, and so on, until the eighth night when all the candles are lit.

NORTH AMERICAN: Native American

Artifacts

Native American vest
totem pole
dream catcher
mask
sand painting
clay pottery
beads, necklace
drum
weaving
doll

Activity: paper bag vest

Children will need their own large brown paper bag for decorating their vests with Native American designs. Open the bag and cut up the middle of the front and around the neck area for the head. Cut a circular shape near the top of each side of the bag, large enough for the arms to fit through. Children may want to cut fringe all the way around the bottom and decorate their vest with markers or paint. Discuss how Native Americans created symbols for the sun, rain, moon, stars, clouds, and animals for decoration.

Activity: dream catcher

A dream catcher is made out of a wood hoop with a web and feathers. It hangs above the bed of a newborn baby or newly married couple. It is believed that bad dreams get caught in the web and disappear while good dreams float into the web, down the feather, and onto the sleeper. To make a dream catcher, each child will need a white paper plate. Draw a large ring inside the rim of the paper plate and cut out the larger middle leaving only the 2-inch ring. Use a hole punch to make at least a dozen holes around the remaining ring. Children can use a length of yarn and create a web by crossing the yarn to fill up all the holes around the ring. Cut a piece of yarn about 8 inches long and loop it through the bottom hole of the ring. Provide plastic beads for children to string up the yarn. Finish off by knotting the end after the last bead is strung and inserting an inverted feather into the path of strung beads.

Activity: kachina doll

The Hopi and Zuni, Native Americans of the southwest, believe that spirit kachinas bring water and help crops grow. Kachina spirits can take animal and human forms. Kachina dolls are hung by a baby's cradle. Use a toilet paper tube and foil or Styrofoam ball for making the kachina doll's body and head. Use masking tape to secure the ball onto the tube. Cover with light paper or fabric. Decorate face and body with paint. The body is streamlined so there is no need to add arms and legs. If desired, feathers can be attached to the back of the head.

NORTH AMERICAN: American (United States)

Artifacts

Hawaiian lei
Eskimo mask
Uncle Sam
bumper sticker

Activity: tissue paper lei

The lei necklace is a symbol of friendship and hospitality. Children can make their own by using a blunt tapestry needle to string tissue paper flowers onto string or yarn. Provide circular pieces of tissue paper or children can crumple larger squares of tissue paper into balls before stringing.

Activity: bumper sticker

School-age children would enjoy using markers to design their own bumper sticker, room banner, bedroom door knob hanger, or postage stamp.

This approach, however, merely illustrates the problems introduced in the opening section. This list is not comprehensive and the collection of items begins to portray a stereotypic picture. However, it also begins to show how certain crafts such as mask making or paper art transcend individual groups. A positive approach focuses on finding cultural similarities rather than only highlighting differences.

Since cultural groups celebrate holidays and celebrations throughout the year, a second approach is to work with an annual calendar. With this approach, cultural groups and their representative arts and crafts are studied in the context of holidays and celebrations, a common feature. All people celebrate holidays and they can be studied as they occur throughout the year. Children also see group similarities since different cultures celebrate the same holidays, including Independence Day and New Year's. Based on geographical and social factors, the same group may celebrate the same holiday but in different ways. There is much variation within groups and not all Christians celebrate Christmas exactly the same way. A list of all international holidays and celebrations is beyond the scope of this book. A basic but incomplete list follows, although specific dates have been omitted since many vary from year to year.

MONTH: HOLIDAY AND CELEBRATION:

January   New Year's Day
          Genjitsu (Japanese New Year's Day)
          Martin Luther King Day (U. S.)
February Presidents' Day (U. S.)
          Gung Hay Fat Choy (Chinese New Year)
          Vietnamese New Year
March   Hina Matsuri (Girls' Day in Japan)
          Purim (Jewish)
          Now Ruz (Persian New Year)
          Independence Day (Greece)
April   Earth Day
          Passover (Jewish)
          Easter
          Children's Day (Turkey)
          Pan-American Day (Southwest U. S., Central and South America)
May   May Day (U. S., Canada, Europe)
          Lei Day (Hawaii)

MONTH: HOLIDAY AND CELEBRATION:

May,   Cinco De Mayo (Mexico)
continued Tango-No-Sekku (Boys' Day in Japan)
          Mother's Day (U. S.)
          Victoria Day (Canada)
          Memorial Day (U. S.)

CINCO DE MAYO

Cinco de Mayo, or the Fifth of May, is one of Mexico's most important holidays. It commemorates the winning of a battle against the French which eventually led to Mexico's independence. Cinco de Mayo is celebrated in Mexico and in many Mexican-American communities with parades and marching bands as well as fiestas including music, dancing, and feasting. Like the Fourth of July, Cinco de Mayo is often celebrated with fireworks.

June   Father's Day (U. S.)
          Dragon Boat Festival (China)
July   Dominion Day (Canada)
          Independence Day (U. S.)
          Bastille Day (France's Independence Day)
          Egyptian National Day
          Ethiopian National Day
          Spain's National Day
August   Whai Oh! (Jamaica's Independence Day)
September Independence Day (Mexico and Central America)
          Rosh Hashanah (Jewish)
          Oktoberfest (Germany)
          Yom Kippur (Jewish)
          Native American Day
          Labor Day (U. S.)
October   Sukkot (Jewish)
          Halloween
November Thanksgiving
          El Dia de Los Muertos (Mexico)
December Hanukkah (Jewish)
          Las Posadas (Mexico and Spain)
          Kenya's National Holiday (Africa)

MONTH:	HOLIDAY AND CELEBRATION:
December, *continued*	Christmas Kwanzaa (African-American)

HANUKKAH

Hanukkah, the Festival of Lights, is an eight-day Jewish holiday to celebrate religious freedom. Many years ago the Jewish soldiers defeated the Syrians and won back their holy temple. The holy temple needed to be rededicated but there was only enough sacred oil to keep the temple's candelabrum lit for one night. Miraculously, the flame continued to burn for eight nights, which signified the strength of the Jewish faith. During this festival a candle is lit each day at sundown. Traditionally, each candle is lit by a shamash or helper candle and placed in a candleholder known as a menorah. The shamash is used to light the other candles, one each day until all are shining. During Hanukkah, children receive a small gift, usually "gelt" or coins for each day of the celebration. Children may also play with a dreidel, or square-sided top, and eat latkes (potato pancakes).

KWANZAA

Kwanzaa was created in 1966 by Maulana Karenga, a black-studies professor, as a spiritual recognition for African-Americans and others of African heritage. It is celebrated from December 26 through New Year's Day in recognition of traditional African harvest festivals. Kwanzaa means "first fruits" and the holiday stresses the unity of the family and community. During Kwanzaa, celebrants focus on the Nguzo Saba, or seven guiding principles. These include Umoja (unity), Kujichagulia (self-determination), Ujima (collective work and responsibility), Ujamaa (cooperative economics), Nia (purpose), Kuumba (creativity) and Imani (faith). Each day, one of the seven principles is recognized by the lighting of a new candle in the kinara, a seven-

MONTH:	HOLIDAY AND CELEBRATION:
December, *continued*	pronged candleholder. There are seven candles, one black, three green, and three red; a straw mat upon which the kinara rests; a unity cup; and the black, red, and green flag, colors symbolizing the African people, their blood, and the earth. The karamu or Kwanzaa feast is celebrated near the end of the holiday, incorporating foods from the Caribbean, Africa, and the African-American experience. Kwanzaa yenu iwe na heri or Happy Kwanzaa!

Time, knowledge, resources, and school policy may make it difficult to celebrate some, let alone all, holidays. Do not expect to be knowledgeable about all cultures and their celebrations. Consult with the children's families; they are an excellent resource. Ask them about their holidays and the ways they celebrate. Invite them to share their customs and be part of your celebrations. It is important to have a written policy regarding the celebration of holidays. Be sure to check with your school or center policy before planning celebrations, since they may offend some cultural and religious groups. Some Jewish families and those with certain religious beliefs may object to a lengthy celebration of Christian holidays, including Christmas and Easter. Others question Halloween and St. Patrick's Day. A decision to avoid celebrating holidays is a safe stance, in that no one is offended, yet the curriculum then does not reflect what is happening in the child's home and community. A compromise is to celebrate nonreligious holidays or those associated with the seasons. For example, fall is associated with giving thanks for the harvest, which celebrates the agrarian roots of many groups. If you decide to celebrate holidays, be sure to inform parents of upcoming celebrations and provide an alternate activity for those children who are in attendance but must refrain from participating.

A third approach identifies arts and crafts of a given group of people, but improves on the first approach by focusing on artifacts like crafts that cultures share. For example, although many Japanese practice origami there are other groups that also make objects out of paper, whether it be masks, lanterns, toys, or flowers. An incomplete list of artifacts and their representative groups follows:

ARTIFACT/CRAFT:	PEOPLE:
postage stamps	all
clothing and jewelry	all
hats	all, for example, Japanese coolie, African kufi
flag	all
art from paper	Japanese, Chinese, Korean (See section on paper art in Chapter 11.)
flowers	Hispanic, Hawaiian, Asian
fan	Asian
lantern	Asian

Activity: Paper lantern

Lanterns are used in Chinese, Japanese, and Vietnamese celebrations including New Year's. According to the Vietnamese calendar, Trung-Thu, a children's festival culminating in a lantern parade, is held on the fifteenth day of the eighth month of the year. Children can make their own paper lanterns and celebrate with a parade. Children each need a sheet of construction paper which they fold in half lengthwise. Mark lines on the paper about ½-inch apart beginning at the folded edge and stopping one inch from the top. Older children can cut along these lines. Unfold, flatten, and decorate with crayons, markers, or stickers. When decorated, bring short sides together stapling at the top and bottom allowing for cut slits to fall open when lantern stands. Finish by stapling a strip of construction paper to the top for a handle.

ARTIFACT/CRAFT:	PEOPLE:
kite	Asian
doll making	all
toys	all
puppets	all (See section on making puppets in Chapter 14.)
dragon	Chinese, Vietnamese, Korean

Activity: papier-mâché dragon's head

See section on papier mâché. This is a group project for school-age children with much adult guidance. Apply the strips of papier-mâché around a balloon or box, building up layers to resemble a dragon's head. Apply pieces of egg carton and cardboard for eyes, ears, nose, and mouth. Paint when thoroughly dry. Attach it to bedsheets for use in a dragon dance.

ARTIFACT/CRAFT:	PEOPLE:
mask making	Asian, African, Native American, Eskimo (See section on making masks in Chapter 14.)
weaving	Hispanic, African kente, Native American (See section on weaving in Chapter 16.)
batik	African, Indonesian
candlestick	African kinara, Jewish menorah
drum	African, Native American

Implementing this approach involves weaving commonalities throughout the curriculum. For example, the music center may contain samples of drums used by Africans, Native Americans, and others, and clothing from around the world may be found in the house area, along with baby dolls of color. A candle lit during storytelling would be compared to the candles and candleholder in an African kinara or a Jewish menorah. When doing a book extension activity involving mask making to accompany a favorite story, present samples of masks from different countries. For example, people of Asian, Eskimo, Native American, and African origin make masks. Help children see that many, if not all, people make masks, but in different ways and styles. There are also many different types of masks including handheld and over-the-head. Identify ways to help children make different types of masks, using paper, cardboard, grocery bags, or containers, that are within their skill level and not totally dependent on adult direction.

A fourth approach is first and foremost developmentally appropriate. It emphasizes providing art media and materials that are culturally responsive to the diversity of the children's families and community. The emphasis is on helping children creatively construct and artistically represent the world around them. Children are surrounded by artifacts celebrating human diversity. Differences are valued and celebrated, while similar characteristics are identified. Focus on helping children construct a concept that groups of people with similar characteristics get their basic needs met in different ways, not on teaching them how to make artifacts. Some guidelines for this approach in an art program include:

- Avoid presenting only white and black art media for people making. Few people have pale white skin and not all dark-skinned people identify with the color black.
- Provide art materials, including paper, markers, paint, crayons, colored pencils, fabric, and paper in a wide variety of skin colors, including flesh tones of beige, brown, and black.
- Provide a wide range of yarn in shades of yellow, red-orange, brown, black, and gray for making hair.
- Make play dough in a range of skin colors.
- Include cultural artifacts like a tortilla press at your play dough table.
- Provide diverse magazines like *Ebony* and *National Geographic* for children to use in making a collage or mural about people.

You can also expose children to multicultural arts and crafts by displaying artwork representative of cultural groups, as well as pictures of people of color engaged in art activities.

SUMMARY

Few children match the developmental norms for what might be considered normal, typical, or average at a given age or stage of development. One goal of early childhood education is to foster the development of children as unique individuals. Our aim is not to produce children who are typical or average. A child's uniqueness is expressed in individual differences resulting from the interaction of various background influences, including culture, family, and personal ability and disability. Young children who have a handicapping condition or who speak nonstandard English provide an additional challenge.

Art is a developmentally important activity for all children, regardless of developmental ability, disability, lag, or difference.

Suggested Activities

1. Observe a room of same-age children. Note the expression of individual differences within the same age range. Record your findings.

2. Observe or volunteer to work with young exceptional children who have been mainstreamed.

3. Observe or volunteer to work in an early childhood bilingual or multicultural program.

4. Spend one morning in an early childhood classroom looking for examples of diversity or bias. Examine the books, music collection, wall displays, as well as the clothing, props, dolls, and tools in the house area. Do the curriculum and room environment reflect the cultures of the children present? Explain and offer suggestions.

Review

A. List the major ways in which differences in development and learning are expressed.
  1.
  2.
  3.

B. List general guidelines for working with exceptional young children.
  1.
  2.
  3.
  4.
  5.

C. List general guidelines for working with children from varying backgrounds.
  1.
  2.
  3.
  4.
  5.

D. Critique the following holiday activities:

  It is Thanksgiving week. Mrs. Howard plans to have her preschoolers make headbands out of construction paper. They will decorate the headbands with Indian symbols. They will also learn how to make a canoe by folding newspaper. Mrs. Howard will offer face painting or war paint to those who request it. Children also will have the option of making pilgrim bonnets and collars out of paper doilies. Mrs. Howard has tried to plan activities that would appeal to the boys and girls in her room.

Resources for Multicultural and Anti-Bias Materials

Afro-American Publishing Company
819 S. Wabash Ave.
Chicago, IL 60605

American Indian Resource Center
6518 Miles Ave.
Huntington Park, CA 90255

Anti-Defamation League of B'nai B'rith
Dept. JW
823 United Nations Plaza
New York, NY 11117

Bilingual Educational Services, Inc.
2514 S. Grand Ave.
Los Angeles, CA 90007

Childcraft
20 Kilmer Rd.
P. O. Box 3081
Edison, NJ 08818

Children's Book & Music Center
2500 Santa Monica Blvd.
Santa Monica, CA 90404

Children's Book Press
1461 Ninth Ave.
San Francisco, CA 94122

Claudia's Caravan
P.O. Box 1582
Alameda, CA 94501

Clearinghouse for Immigrant Education
100 Boylston St.
Suite 737
Boston, MA 02116

Constructive Playthings
1227 East 199th St.
Grandview, MD 64030

Council for Exceptional Children
Division of Early Childhood—Diversity
    Resources
1920 Association Dr.
Reston, VA 22091

Council on Interracial Books for Children
1841 Broadway
New York, NY 10023

Educational Equity Concepts Inc.
114 East 32nd St.
New York, NY 10016

Educational Materials, Inc.
6503 Salizar St.
San Diego, CA 92111

Global Village Books & Toys
2210 Wilshire Blvd.
Box 262
Santa Monica, CA 90403

Greenhouse Corp.—Asian Books
10937 Klingerman St. South
El Monte, CA 91733

Gryphon House
P. O. Box 275
Mt. Rainier, MD 20712

The Heritage Key, Inc.
6102 East Mescal
Scottsdale, AZ 85254

Information Center on Children's Cultures
Institute for Peace and Justice
4144 Lindell
Room 122
St. Louis, MO 63108

Judy Instructo
4325 Hiawatha Ave. South
Minneapolis, MN 55406

Lakeshore
2695 E. Dominguez St.
P. O. Box 6261
Carson, CA 90749

Lerner Publications
Carolrhoda Books
241 First Ave. North
Minneapolis, MN 55401

Nasco
901 Janesville Ave.
Fort Atkinson, WI 53538

National Association for
   Bilingual Education
Union Center Plaza
810 First St. NE, 3rd Floor
Washington, DC 20002

National Association for the
   Education of Young Children
1834 Connecticut Ave. Northwest
Washington, DC 20009

National Black Child
   Development Institute
1463 Rhode Island Ave. Northwest
Washington, DC 20005

National Women's History Project
7738 Bell Rd.
Windsor, CA 95492

New England School Supply
Multi Cultural Program Materials
P. O. Box 1581
Springfield, MA 01101

New Society Publishers
P. O. Box 582
Santa Cruz, CA 95061

Ninos
5959 Triumph St.
Commerce, CA 90040

Peter Bedrick Books
2112 Broadway
Room 318
New York, NY 10023

Positive Images Children's Books
593A Macon St.
Brooklyn, NY 11233

Redleaf Press
450 N. Syndicate
Suite 5
St. Paul, MN 55104

The Red Sea Press, Inc.
African-American Books
15 Industry Court
Trenton, NJ 08638

Rising Arrow
Native American Craft Supplies and Books
265-M Sobrante Way
Sunnyvale, CA 94086

Treasure Chest Publications
Native American/Southwest
1802 W. Grant Rd., Suite 101
P. O. Box 5250
Tucson, AZ 85703

United Indians of All Tribes Foundation
Community Educational Services
Discovery Park
P. O. Box 99100
Seattle, WA 98199

United States Committee for UNICEF
331 E. 38th St.
New York, NY 10016

Women's Educational Equity Act
   Publishing Center
Education Development Center
55 Chapter St.
Suite 200
Newton, MA 02160

CHAPTER 6

Children's Artistic Development

weliswa

What can you tell about the child who painted this picture? How old might this child be? How does this piece of art compare with the human figures you have seen children make?

Children share many similarities. They all scribble before they engage in controlled drawing. They play with colors before they paint recognizable pictures. Children also draw what is familiar to them. They use what they know as the basis for their art. This is a self-portrait painted by a South African girl.

OBJECTIVES

After studying this chapter, the student will be able to

- Discuss and critique the different explanations for the development of children's art
- Match the corresponding artistic accomplishments with Kellogg's and Lowenfeld and Brittain's stages
- Overview artistic development from birth through age eight using the author's sequence
- Provide children with experiences in painting

INTRODUCTION

Children's art has a mysterious quality to it. The flow of lines, shapes, colors, and overall design may make more sense to the child artist than to the adult observer. Why do children scribble? What does their art mean? Why do they draw stick figures when they know people do not look that way? Theories and stages attempt to provide answers to these questions. This chapter surveys and critiques a physical, emotional, perceptual, cognitive, general developmental, and cognitive developmental explanation for children's art. The author has used the stages identified by Kellogg and by Lowenfeld and Brittain in proposing one general sequence to account for the development of art from birth through age eight.

EXPLAINING CHILDREN'S ART

Appreciating children's art may be easier than understanding it or attempting to explain it. Beyond the sheer enjoyment, adults have been trying to make sense out of children's art for decades. Researchers, teachers, parents, art educators, and those interested in child development are concerned with the content, motive, process, and product. Their interest focuses on the following:

- what children choose to include or represent (content)
- how children create (process)
- why children create (motive)
- what they create as a result (product)

The *content* refers to the subject matter or object being represented. This might include a pet animal, person, feeling, mood, wish, dream, or impulse. The content of children's art is often very personal or idiosyncratic. For example, a wide stroke of black paint may represent a tree trunk. On the other hand, it may represent a child's creative exploration with paint and brush and not be intended for public communication. Too often, adults are prone to search for public meaning where there is none. The *process* refers to the actions and skills involved in creating

an art product—cutting and tearing paper, rolling clay, painting, or marking with crayons. Not all art processing results in the creation of a finished art product. Many young children process for its own sake. The *motive* refers to the reason underlying a child's art. For example, adults may explore why a child filled a paper with wide strokes of black paint. Does the child's preoccupation with the color black signify some underlying emotional problem? Is the mark characteristic of a lack of maturation? Does the solitary mark represent social isolation? Or, is the child representing the concept of one? The *product* refers to the final outcome. Examples include black paint smeared across a paper, a clay dinosaur, a paper-bag puppet, or a geometric design done in watercolor. The finished product may or may not bear any resemblance to the content or subject matter.

In analyzing the what, why, and how of children's art, there is a risk of misinterpretation or of reading too much into this art. After studying children and their artwork for an extended period of time, however, trends and patterns do emerge. A skillful observer can note these trends and patterns and begin to make some generalizations about what, why, and how children create.

THEORIES OF ARTISTIC DEVELOPMENT

Theories of artistic development attempt to explain what, why, and how children create. The theories are similar yet different. All theories of artistic development attempt to do the same thing—explain a child's artistic development. Each, however, takes a different slant, perspective, or focus. Some theories do a better or more complete job of explaining than others.

Why does one need a theory of artistic development? A theory provides the overall structure or foundation for what we do with children. Different theories suggest different educational practices. For example, there is much debate about the roles of theory and practice in the preparation of early childhood educators. We all want teachers who are competent practitioners. Someone who is long on theory but short on practice would not do a good job in the classroom. Our aim is to translate theory into practice. A theory can be our blueprint or road map, steering us to sound, developmentally appropriate practice. Theory can also help us justify how, why, and what we do with children.

There are numerous theories and explanations that attempt to explain the development of child art. They can be grouped into the following six categories:

1. physical
2. emotional
3. perceptual
4. cognitive
5. general developmental
6. cognitive developmental

1. Physical Explanation for the Development of Child Art

A physical explanation for the development of child art holds that the content, process, product, and style of children's art are indicative of their limited physical development. The young child is limited in eye-hand coordination, fine motor control, small muscle development, manual dexterity, and visual acuity. Young children mark aimlessly, scribble, and draw unrecognizable shapes because they are physically incapable of anything else. Young children's drawing often appears immature and unintelligible to some adults.

It is obvious that the physical development of a young child does affect artistic expression. For example, one cannot expect a toddler to draw a detailed still life in realistic fashion. Yet, a child may simply choose to scribble or explore with the media, just as an adult may choose to doodle. Accomplished artists who have mastered the techniques of realism often opt for an impressionistic, expressionistic, or abstract style. Adult primitive art with its simplistic quality conveys purposeful intent rather than limited physical development and lack of coordination.

2. Emotional Explanation for the Development of Child Art

An emotional explanation for the development of child art holds that the content and style of children's art is indicative of their emotional makeup, personality, temperament, and affective state. Objects, emotions, people, and events of significance are often emphasized in children's drawings and paintings through an exaggerated, distorted, and expressive use of color, size, shape, line, texture, and overall treatment. For example, when a child draws her father as a "Superman" caricature with bulging muscles, a huge red heart, and a wide smile, this may signify her love, respect, admiration, and identification rather than distortion due to faulty vision or limited physical development.

3. Perceptual Explanation for the Development of Child Art

A perceptual explanation for the development of child art holds that the content and style of children's art reflects their perceptual development. A perceptual explanation is not identical to a physical one, since perception is not synonymous with vision. Vision, the mechanistic recording of reality, involves projecting images upon the retina. Perception is influenced by the neurophysiological structure, personality, and prior learning. The perceptual explanation holds that a child draws what he or she perceives rather than what he or she sees. The task of art is to create the structural equivalent of the perceived three-dimensional object on the two-dimensional canvas. This can be a monumental task for the artist, regardless of age.

The development of child art provides support for a perceptual explanation. The young child's first attempts at drawing are scribbles with a minimum of line and shape; they gradually increase in complexity and clarity. Some children, however, draw or paint less than they actually see. For example, a child may choose to paint the stripes of a tiger with wide, sweeping strokes, and ignore the head or other extremities. It is also possible that the medium can limit one's expression of the perceptual image. For example, using a wide-bristle brush dipped in watered-down paint might limit the number of details that appear in one's painting. The size of the paper also places constraints on what can be fit into the picture.

4. Cognitive Explanation for the Development of Child Art

A cognitive explanation for the development of child art holds that the content and style of children's art is indicative of general intelligence and a function of conceptualization. Children can draw or paint only what they know. One's concept of an object will determine how that object will be represented. For example, when one draws an apple, one's concept of an apple is determined by one's experiences with its color, taste, size, shape, and smell and by related experiences in picking apples, polishing apples, planting apple seeds, climbing apple trees, paring apples, bobbing for apples, mashing apples for cider, and baking and eating an apple pie. Observation of

young children involved in art supports a cognitive explanation. Young children rely on memories, images, experiences, and concepts when they draw or paint. Detailed drawings will reflect concepts with which the child has had extensive experience. For example, it would be expected that an urban child will have a less-developed concept of a silo, tractor, and barn than a child living on a farm. The differences will appear when each child draws or paints a farm scene. One would expect the child living on a farm to execute a picture with greater detail and elaboration (see Figure 6–1).

Goodenough (1975) devised the Draw-A-Man test, a nonverbal measure of intelligence. It is assumed that the child's drawing of the human figure is a reflection of that child's concept of a man. Indices of conceptual maturity include appearance of limbs and location, size, and relationship of body parts (see Figure 6–2). If a child has a well-defined concept of a man, reflected in an accurate drawing with properly located body parts, this would indicate a

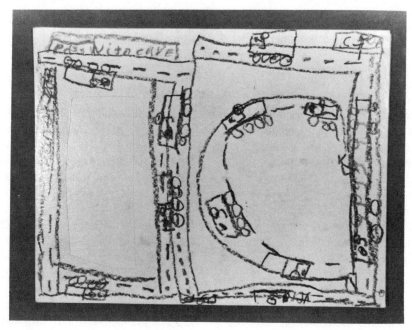

FIGURE 6–1   *Children draw the world as they know and interpret it.*

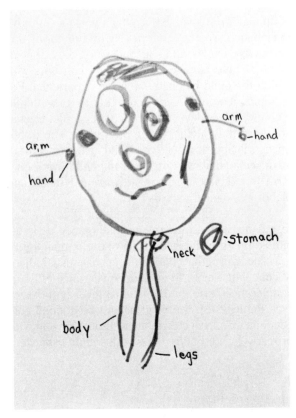

FIGURE 6–2   The young artist is not concerned with proper placement of body parts.

Concept formation and perceptual analysis are reciprocal processes. Knowledge of an object can improve one's ability to accurately observe its details. In turn, careful observation can lead to increased knowledge of the object.

5. General Developmental Explanation for Child Art

A fifth explanation for the development of child art is more global. It provides a general developmental explanation that incorporates social, cultural, personality, and environmental factors as well as elements of former explanations. General developmental explanations make use of a stage sequence approach in attempting to explain the artistic expression of the child in "wholistic" fashion.

Theories have given us ages and stages to help understand a child's artistic development. Like theories, there are many stage sequences for the development of children's art. Knowing stages will help us:

- understand where a child is developmentally
- set appropriate but flexible expectations, neither too high nor too low
- plan a developmentally appropriate art program
- serve as a framework for evaluation and for conferences with parents
- appreciate the process and products of art during the early years

Like all development, artistic expression follows a predictable sequence, shifting and changing as the child grows. Development, however, is fluid, meaning that children may move back and forth between stages. Development is also individual, and children move at their own rate and pace.

Rhoda Kellogg (1969) has amassed over a million paintings and drawings of children from the United States and thirty other countries over the past few decades. Her stages appear in Figure 6–3.

According to Kellogg, some twenty basic scribble patterns make up the first stage of development. These basic scribbles are the foundation for future graphic art, pictorial and nonpictorial. As the child proceeds from scribbling to picture making, he or

high level of intelligence on the Goodenough measure. The problem with this normative approach is its neglect of individual differences, experiences, and motivational, attitudinal, and environmental factors that can either foster or inhibit concept formation. Ears may be particularly relevant to a young girl with pierced ears. A child living in an area where both sexes sport long hair may be oblivious to ears. A related problem with the human figure drawing test is that some children choose to omit body parts out of whim rather than lack of knowledge. The human figure drawn without ears may be simply the result of creative expression and personal preference. It is also possible that the child may have run out of paint, patience, or interest.

SCRIBBLE STAGE

There are 20 basic scribbles.

1. dot ●

2. single vertical line

3. single horizontal line

4. single diagonal line

5. single curved line

6. multiple vertical lines

7. multiple horizontal lines

8. multiple diagonal lines

9. multiple curved lines

10. roving open line

11. roving enclosed line

12. zigzag/waving line

13. single loop line

14. multiple loop lines

15. spiral line

16. multiple-line overlaid circle

17. multiple-line circumference circle

18. circular line spread out

19. single crossed line

20. imperfect circle

FIGURE 6–3   Kellogg's stages

2–3 year olds: PLACEMENT STAGE

Scribbles become more controlled and the child becomes concerned with placement. There are 17 different placements.

Some include:

all over

central

bottom/top

diagonal

right/left

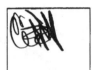

top/bottom quarter

3 year olds: SHAPE STAGE

Former scribbles drawn at 2 produce overall ''gestalts'' or forms. These gestalts or forms contain the following implicit shapes:

Later, the above implied shapes are drawn as single outline forms called DIAGRAMS.

FIGURE 6–3   (continued)

3 year olds: THE SIX DIAGRAMS include:

circle   cross   X   square   triangle   odd form
(and oval)   (and rectangle)

3–4 year olds: DESIGN STAGE

Two diagrams are united to form a COMBINE

For example:

Some COMBINES include:

Three or more diagrams are united to form an AGGREGATE

For example:

Some AGGREGATES include:

FIGURE 6–3   (continued)

4–5 year olds   **PICTORIAL STAGE**

Their structured designs begin to look like objects that
adults can recognize. The pictorial stage can be divided
into two phases:

1. early pictorial
2. later pictorial

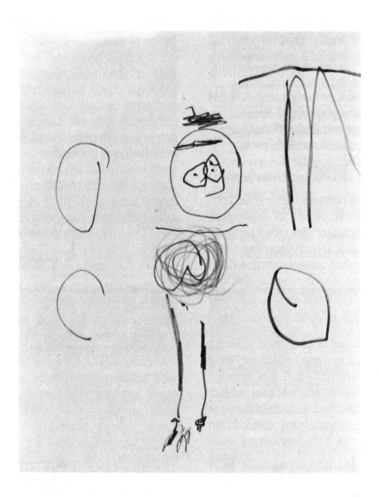

FIGURE 6–3   (continued)

she passes through stages: placement, shape, design, and pictorial. More specifically, the twenty basic scribbles are subsequently drawn according to some seventeen different placement patterns by the age of two. By the age of three, these diagrams or gestalts contain shapes, including the circle, cross, square, and rectangle. One basic diagram, the "mandala," dominates the child's visual thinking at this time and serves as a basic artistic referent in future drawing. Children use mandalas to draw people, flowers, and the sun. Gestalt psychology has shown the mandala, a crossed circle, to be a universal pattern that the brain is predisposed to utilize in all visual perception (see Figure 6–4).

FIGURE 6–5   Shapes combined into designs become mandala figures.

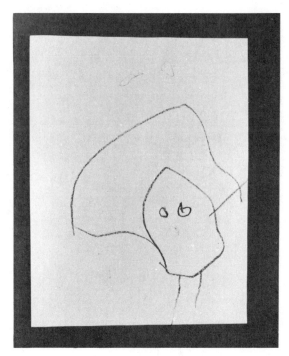

FIGURE 6–4   An early mandala figure

With the ability to draw diagrams or mandalas, the child moves into the design stage. Two diagrams are put together to make "combines," or structured designs (see Figure 6–5). Three or more united diagrams constitute an "aggregate." Between the ages of four and five, most children arrive at the pictorial stage, in which their structured designs or aggregates begin to represent objects. Kellogg likens the development of stages in child art with primitive art. Her normative approach supports the position that all children everywhere draw the same things, in the same way, at the same age. The development of artistic ability in the individual appears to recapitulate the artistic development of the human species.

Kellogg's (1979) stages in drawing a human figure are depicted in Figure 6–6.

Lowenfeld and Brittain (1987) are interested in the creative and mental growth of children. Their theory and stages of artistic development are widely recognized and accepted. Their ages, stages, and characteristics appear in Table 6–1.

1. Scribbling:

2. Drawing a single shape:

3. Combining single shapes into designs:

4. Drawing mandalas, mandaloids, and sun figures:

5. Drawing a human figure with limbs and torso:

FIGURE 6–6   Kellogg's stages in drawing a human figure

AGE:	STAGE AND CHARACTERISTICS
2–4 years:	**I Scribbling: The Beginnings of Self-Expression** Scribbling is a developmentally and artistically important kinesthetic, manipulative, and expressive behavior.
1½–2½:	**Substage IA: Disordered and Random Scribbling** • large muscle, whole arm movements • kinesthetic pleasure, pure processing • whole-hand grip on marking tool • may not look at paper while marking • accidental, random motoric mark making • haphazard lines • swing of arm coming in contact with paper results in mark • uses shoulder motion • may scribble beyond confines of paper • exploration—what can I do by moving these tools on paper? • lines made with simple movements • tight grip with rigid wrist position • minimal movement with fingers in marking
2, 2½–3:	**Substage IB: Controlled Scribbling** • smaller marks, better control and organization • marking motions are repeated • uses wrist motion with greater control • stays within drawing area of paper • variety of lines and direction appear • better visual and motoric control over where to make lines • watches intently while scribbling • more-intricate loops and swirls appear • wider range of scribbles
3, 3½–4:	**Substage IC: Named Scribbling** • spends more time mark making • gives names to scribbles • relates scribbles to things in environment • name of scribble may change in the process • holds marking tools with fingers, better fine motor control • greater variety of lines • increased concentration • more-intentional placement of marks • awareness and intentional use of empty space • scribbles do not match name or label given except to child artist • moves from sheer physical expression to making marks that stand for something else by giving them a name
4–7 years:	**II Preschematic** A schema is a generalized symbol that represents a specific concept. For example, a child's stick-figure drawing is used to represent all people. • child makes first representational attempts • symbolic representation built up from former scribbles

TABLE 6–1   *Stages of Artistic Development by Lowenfeld and Brittain*

AGE:	STAGE AND CHARACTERISTICS
4–7 years:	**II Preschematic (continued)**
	• appearance of recognizable geometric shapes
	• placement and size random and out of proportion
	• random floating spatial arrangement
	• may turn or rotate paper while drawing
	• distortion and omission of parts in human figure drawing
	• head-feet representation of human figure as in Figure 6–7
	• head-feet representation of human figure
	• over time, arms, body, fingers, toes, clothes, hair, and other details appear
	• objects drawn as isolated entities; no relationship
	• art as personal self-expression rather than for public communication
	• very personal idiosyncratic symbols
	• can copy a square at age four, triangle at five
	• relative size appears at end of stage
	• child learns that what is known or experienced can be symbolically represented by mark making
	• children draw how they feel or think about an object, leading to omission, exaggeration, and distortion
	• color used randomly, not realistically
	• schemas or symbols begin to be recognizable to others
	• children enjoy talking about their art
	• draws things that are important, relevant, or personally meaningful, e.g., family, pets, or friends
	• objects drawn facing forward
7–9 years:	**III Schematic: Achievement of a Form Concept**
	• form concept is developed and repeated
	• drawing reflects a child's concept, not perception of an object
	• bold, direct flat representation
	• two-dimensional spatial representation
	• baseline appears to portray space
	• skyline may also appear at top
	• drawing reflects what a child knows
	• subjective portrayal of space
	• x-ray drawing appears simultaneously, showing exterior and interior view
	• representation of space shows a frontal and aerial view depicted simultaneously
	• human figure made up of geometric shapes is repeated and refined
	• detailed and decorative
	• move to greater conformity or "stiffness" in drawing things the way they should be
9–12 years:	**IV Dawning Realism: The Gang Age**
	There is a greater awareness of details. Older children are more self-conscious about their art. The plane replaces the baseline. Objects are drawn smaller and less distorted.
12–14 years:	**V Pseudo-Naturalistic/Realistic Drawing**
	Young adolescents are very self-critical of their drawing. Detailed human figures with sexual characteristics appear. Cartoons, caricatures, and action figures are also popular. Depth and proportion appear. End of spontaneous art.
14–17 years:	**VI Artistic Decision: Adolescent Art**
	For some adolescents, natural artistic development does not extend beyond the former stage unless they are given further instruction. Some pursue naturalistic style, while others use art for a personal statement. They may copy an artistic style in forming their own personal style.

TABLE 6–1   (continued)

FIGURE 6–7   *Preschematic art: head-feet representation of the human figure.*

Art Moves from Manipulation to Representation

Children's art does become more realistic over time, and it appears that there is a general sequence or progression to their artistic development. Very young children are in a manipulative stage. The younger the child the greater the reliance on processing, exploring, making, doing or playing with crayon, marker, paintbrush, or play dough. Actions on objects are repeated and there is little concern for making something. For example, a child may simply squeeze play dough between her fingers without trying to use the play dough to symbolize something else. Older children, kindergartners, and school-age children, in particular, are very concerned that their art resembles something. They are in the stage of representation and work hard at

making their artistic symbols look realistic and recognizable to others. They may become disappointed and avoid art if they cannot produce realistic art.

In sum, the developmental explanations, including Kellogg and Lowenfeld, use some form of stage sequence to account for the development of child art. In viewing the child as a whole, they also recognize physical, social, emotional, perceptual, and cognitive factors that influence artistic expression. Yet a general developmental explanation must also account for cultural, religious, individual, and environmental factors in tracing the development of child art. A child's culture and religion might affect his or her drawing ability depending on whether or not the culture values art. A child with an unfulfilled need for acceptance might draw realistic pictures in order to win the praise of a teacher who dislikes abstract art. Environmental factors include home and family, who might constantly punish a child for manipulating, experimenting, exploring, and getting messy. A normative comparison might label this child uncreative or developmentally delayed in artistic expression without allowing for environmental effects.

6. Cognitive Developmental Explanation for Child Art

It would appear that an explanation that incorporates the best of cognitive and general developmental explanations would account comprehensively for the development of child art. Since early childhood educators have been educated in Piaget's theory, it would seem feasible to see whether this theory can be applied to the realm of art. A comprehensive theory that explains all sectors of child development would be more useful than separate theories that explain different behaviors.

Piaget on Child Art

What can Piaget tell us about children's art? His theory and stages of intellectual development claim to be comprehensive, encompassing, and universal. Artistic expression is, at least in part, a cognitive activity. It follows that a cognitive developmental theory such as Piaget's should explain the development of child art. The task, however, is a difficult one, since Piaget himself believed that it is more difficult to establish regular stages of artistic development than of mental functions. He notes that general development is one of progression, whereas artistic development is one of retrogression. The artwork of the young child appears more creative than that of the older child. In reviewing the theories of children's artistic development, it appears that Piaget accounts for physical, emotional, perceptual, cognitive, and individual factors within his cognitive developmental framework.

Piaget's theory is cognitive in that his interest was in how children think. It is developmental in that his focus was on how children's thinking changed over time. He believed that all children progress through four major stages of development, which proceed in invariant sequence. Cognitive development proceeds from sensory-motor, concrete activity to symbolic, higher-order conceptual functioning.

Piaget holds drawing or the graphic image to be a form of the semiotic or symbolic functions and as such a representational activity that is considered to be halfway between symbolic play and the mental image. It is like play in its functional pleasure and autotelism (assimilation) and like the mental image in its effort at imitating the real (accommodation). The first spontaneous attempts at artistic expression can be seen as a series of endeavors to reconcile the tendencies inherent in symbolic play and those that characterize adapted behavior. Through drawing, the child attempts to simultaneously satisfy the need for assimilation and to adapt himself or herself to objects and others through accommodation. According to Piaget and Inhelder (1969), the very first form of drawing does not seem imitative but is more like pure play. It is this play of exercise or scribbling that toddlers do when given a pencil, crayon, or marker. Soon, however, the young child realizes forms in these aimless scribbles and tries to repeat them from memory. There may be little or no likeness between these scribbles. As soon as this intention ex-

ists, Piaget and Inhelder believe, drawing becomes imitation and image.

Lowenfeld and Brittain's stages of artistic development appear to parallel Piaget's stages of cognitive development. A comparison of Piaget with Kellogg and Lowenfeld and Brittain is found in Table 6–2.

PAINTING

Painting is a pleasurable, messy, and creative art activity. It also allows children to plan; to make decisions about what to paint, colors, and placement; and to work on their own. Not all children will have had experience painting before coming to school. Painting will be a popular activity. For these reasons painting should be made available throughout the day every day. Some children panic when they see only one or two easels and fear that they will never get a turn if painting is allowed only once a day for a short period of time. (See Figure 6–11.)

Generally, painting involves the use of tempera or watercolor paints. Tempera paints are opaque and give a smooth, flat covering of intense color. They are water-soluble, and adding water will dilute them and dull their intensity. Tempera paints come in both liquid and powder form. The liquid form is more expensive but comes ready to use. The powder form is more economical but must be mixed with water. Also, powdered tempera paints are not recommended for children under 12 (see Appendix F). Powdered tempera colors create inhalable dusts, and some colors contain toxic pigments, preservatives, and additives. Wear a mask when preparing the powder, and do not mix in the presence of children. When your supply of powdered tempera is depleted, switch to liquid tempera for the sake of child safety.

Watercolor paints are transparent and allow for a layering of colors. Children should have experience with tempera before graduating to watercolors. Still, children never outgrow their interest in tempera painting. There are many different painting arrangements, including

• standing at an easel
  This position allows for whole-arm strokes and

Schirrmacher's Stages: A General Overview of Artistic Development

A General Overview of Artistic Development (Birth to Eight)

The author has attempted to combine the different stages of artistic development suggested by Kellogg, Lowenfeld and Brittain, and others into one workable general sequence. The levels or stages are overlapping, and ages are approximate. Schirrmacher's sequence of early childhood art follows.

I. Manipulating the Media: Scribbling and Mark Making (1–2 years)

Very young children's first art experiences are purely sensorimotor actions resulting in scribbles. They approach crayons, markers, and play dough with the intent of exploring their properties and discovering what they can make them do. What happens if the crayon is mouthed, swung, and then accidentally strikes the paper? What an interesting thing, thinks the toddler. The very young child lacks fine motor control and eye-hand coordination. Scribbles or vague marks will appear random and haphazard to the adult but wonderfully creative to the young artist who accomplished this feat. Scribbling is nonverbal self-expression. Scribbling and mark making are to drawing as babbling is to speech and crawling is to walking. Scribbling has sensory appeal in that children see the mark they make as they move the tool across the paper. So much the better if the paper tears or the crayon breaks. Look what I made happen, thinks the young artist. Toddlers move from random scribbling to making scribbles which are more controlled, deliberate, and pronounced. Circular strokes are repeated and crayons are moved horizontally or vertically back and forth, making lines which cross and intersect. Some lines and circles are repeatedly traced over. Scribbles become more purposefully placed rather than extending beyond the paper and onto the table or easel. Scribbles may be named, although there may be no connection between the verbal label and graphic symbol (see Figure 6–8).

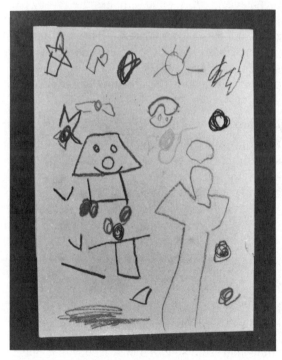

FIGURE 6–8   *Scribbling and mark making produce very personal symbols and designs.*

II. Making Shapes, Outlines, Designs, and Symbols That Have Personal Meaning (2–4) years)

Young preschoolers work at refining their circles, ovals, lines, and attempted geometric shapes. Lines cross or enclose space forming squares, triangles, and rectangles. A cross enclosed by a circle forms a

continued

Schirrmacher's Stages, continued

mandala. Children progress from mandalas to suns to stick figures. Single and repeated round and linear marks become a circle which may represent the sun. A sun with facial features, including eyes and mouth, becomes a face. A circle or sun-face with radiating lines develops into a person with arms and legs radiating out from the round face. The potato person is born. Since infants are intrigued by the human face it is no surprise that the human figure is first drawn as all face. This stick figure is a schema, a generalized symbol or form concept that will be used to represent any and all human figures, regardless of age, sex, or build. Animals develop from this human figure. They are vertically or horizontally portrayed as the human with a tail or animal ears. A square becomes a schema for any and all buildings. A circle atop a vertical line is the "lollipop" schema used to portray trees and flowers. Eisner (1976) would call these examples of pictographs, or simplified flat, two-dimensional shapes. The child adds, omits, distorts, exaggerates, or streamlines these very personal symbols. The result is an abbreviated form with little concern for actual color, shape, or size. Spatial arrangement is random, and the child may simply rotate the paper to fit objects in. The very personal symbol or design may not be recognizable to the observer. Children in this stage are still very much process-oriented. They delight in playing with colors, shapes, and forms. They enjoy talking about their creations but may walk away from or discard their products, indicating their relative love of processing.

III. Pictorial Art That Is Becoming Recognizable to Others (4–6 years)

Older preschoolers and young school-age children become concerned with creating art that looks like something. They may plan their art in advance and use details to polish their products. Their art becomes more recognizable to others although color, shape, size, placement, proportion, and perspective are arbitrary. A purple dog may dwarf a green cow, both of which appear to be floating in the sky. Color is used emotionally, reflecting their relationship to the symbols rendered. Triangles and squares mastered in the prior stage are now combined into houses which appear to float in space. Later they will rest at the bottom of the paper or on a drawn baseline. Over time, houses are decorated with geometric shapes, including a rectangular door, square windows with parted curtains, and a smoking chimney drawn parallel to the roof line, defying gravity. Facial features, body parts, and clothing are added to the human figure. Some personally important parts like the head, eyes, smile, and belly button tend to be exaggerated. If a child's father has a beard, he may be given one in the picture (see Figure 6–9). Other parts appear distorted as when a circle or claw is used to symbolize hands and feet. Some children will choose to simply eliminate body parts like the neck and shoulders. During this stage some children become interested and even obsessed with producing multiple products. They will draw a favorite subject like themselves over and over again. Their desire to simultaneously portray the inside and outside of objects, for example, the exterior of a plane in a storm and interior with pilot and passengers, leads them to make "x-ray drawings" reflecting what the child knows rather than how it appears in reality. Children in this stage lack the control, coordination, and skill necessary to realistically represent their three-dimensional world on a two-dimensional canvas.

continued

Schirrmacher's Stages, continued

FIGURE 6–9   Early attempts at representing the human figure

IV. Realistic (school-age years 5–8)

School-age children want things to look right, to draw and paint things the way they appear in reality. They strive for photographic realism (see Figure 6–10) and seem dissatisfied making abstract or nonrepresentational art. Nonrealistic art is relegated to younger children who scribble. School-age children work on size placement, shape, color, perspective, proportion, depth, shading, and the use of details to capture reality. Rather than floating in space, a house rests on a lower baseline and the sky and sun inhabit a top baseline. Things in the distance are drawn smaller and set back, giving the illusion of depth and perspective. School-age children develop, repeat, and refine symbols which can often be categorized

continued

Schirrmacher's Stages, continued

by gender. Generally, boys draw male super-heroes, race cars, vehicles, army and war scenes, and sports events. Generally, girls draw female superheroes, princesses, horses, fair maidens, and unicorns. With increasing age, children become self-critical and succumb to peer pressure, internalizing hurtful comments which focus on their artistic shortcomings. The few who receive guidance and specific instruction will continue to engage in art. Others pursue impressionistic, expressionist, and non-realistic art. Unfortunately, too many will close the door on their short-lived artistic and creative career, concluding they are uncreative and untalented in art.

FIGURE 6–10   The older artist strives for realism.

PIAGET'S STAGE	KELLOGG'S STAGE	LOWENFELD AND BRITTAIN'S STAGE
Sensory motor (0–2)	Scribbling (2)	
Preoperational: (2–7)		
• Preconceptual (2–4)	Placement (2–3)	Scribbling (2–4): • disordered and random • controlled • named
	Shape (3): • Gestalts • Diagrams Design (3–4): • Combines • Aggregates	
• Intuitive (4–7)	Pictorial (4–5) • Early • Late	Preschematic (4–7)
Concrete Operations (7–11)		Schematic (7–9) Dawning realism (9–12)
Formal operations (11–adult)		Pseudo-realism (12–14) Artistic decision (14–17)

TABLE 6–2   Stages of Art Compared with Piaget's Stages of Cognitive Development

FIGURE 6–11   The young painter at work

total body involvement. It allows for the use of long-handled brushes. Easel painting, however, does have its drawbacks. Given the slant or angle, paint tends to run and drip down. This frustrates some children who expect liquid paint to defy gravity and stay put where they place it. They expect it to act like a marker or crayon. On the positive side, easels encourage verbalization and socialization between painters, especially if the easels are placed side by side. (See Figure 6–12.)

• seated at a table

Children can also paint on a flat surface while seated at a table. This placement keeps paint from dripping and allows layers of paint to be built up. Usually a table can accommodate a few painters at one time. Children can use short-handled brushes, as in watercoloring. Paint will be more controllable, but the amount of arm and body movement will be restricted.

FIGURE 6–12   A trio of easel painters

- standing at a table
  This position allows for whole body movements while painting on a flat surface. Whereas four children can sit down and paint at the same time, only one can stand and paint at each end of the table. This position is highly recommended.

- on the floor
  Painting on the floor provides a flat surface, although this position also restricts whole body movement. It is hard to involve the bottom torso when one is kneeling. Children, including those who are physically challenged, enjoy sprawling on the floor and will find this position comfortable. Standing for a long period of time while painting tires and bores some young children.

- outdoors
  Use any of the above indoor arrangements to paint outdoors.

Although painting while standing at a table or easel is highly recommended, it is wise to give children experience painting at a variety of different angles and placements.

Paints and Painting Accessories

brushes—see Brushes

condiment bottles—squeeze ketchup and mustard bottles with pointed tips make good paint dispensers

cotton swabs—for dabbing paint

dispensers—ketchup or mustard bottles for squeezing paint

drying rack or line—to let pictures dry undisturbed

extender—a bulking powder that extends paint without losing its brilliance

finger paint—good for hand painting, given its thick, chunky texture

fluorescent, water-, or tempera colors—for the advanced child artist

food coloring—added to water makes a fast paint

funnels—to avoid waste when pouring powder paint and for printing

glass—pane of glass or sheet of Plexiglas for monoprinting

ice-cube trays—for color mixing

ink—one bottle of black is standard

kitchen gadgets—for printing with paint

liquid laundry starch—add to tempera to make finger paint

magic brush set—paint, water, and brush are combined into one magic brush tube. A cross between a marker and a paintbrush. The set is commercially available.

media mix—add to tempera to make finger paint; it claims to intensify colors

messless sign caddy paint system—a complete rainbow assortment of nontoxic water-soluble paints in squeeze bottles, used with special felt brushes. Spillproof containers available. Pretty colors and expensive.

muffin tin—for paint palette

no-spill paint cups—hold paint and resist tipping

paint pots—with lids; fit snugly in a tray

paint stirrers—Popsicle sticks, tongue depressors, or coffee stirrers will do

paint tumblers—with snap-on lids to keep paint from drying out

plastic dryer—a hanging dryer with pinch clips for holding wet pictures. Available in housewares at discount stores.

plastic spoons—for mixing paint

poster paint—brighter and more expensive than tempera. Good for making signs, posters, or banners on poster board.

pumps—fit gallon paint containers; one pump yields one ounce

spatula—to mix paints in bulk

splatter screen—for spatter printing

sponges—for printing

spoon rest—to hold brush with paint

squeeze bottles—good for dispensing tempera paint. Some companies offer liquid tempera in squeeze bottles.

sweater dryer—wire screen or net for spatter printing

syrup dispensers—good for storing mixed paint and for use with art palette method of painting

tempera cakes or color paint cakes—concentrated tempera; use like watercolor, comes in tray, refills available, no spilling or mixing involved, more expensive than liquid and powder tempera liquid—more expensive than powder but saves on measuring and mixing. Colors more brilliant than powder.

tempera powder—most economical but requires mixing

watercolor—individual sets of eight are recommended

Hint   Remember to buy and use only lead-free, non-toxic paint.

Hint   Buy red, blue, yellow, black, and white in bulk. These can be mixed to produce other colors, shades, and tints. Start beginning painters with the primary colors.

Hint   Add liquid dishwashing detergent to tempera paint. It will make it bubbly and easier to wash off hands and out of clothes. It will also help paint adhere to slick or glossy surfaces, such as glass, plastic, metal, tinfoil and waxed cartons. Detergent also keeps paint from cracking when it dries.

Hint   Add a drop or two of oil of cloves or oil of wintergreen to prevent spoilage if you mix paint days in advance.

Hint   Add glitter to paint for a shiny look.

Hint   Add coffee grounds, salt, or sand along with white glue to paint to give it a rough, coarse, gritty texture. Adding sugar will give it a sparkling appearance when dry. Adding sawdust will give it a thick, lumpy texture. Adding white glue to paint thickens it.

Hint   Finger paint can be made by
   • adding liquid laundry starch to tempera or food coloring.
   • using mud—messy, but children love it.
   • mixing wheat paste (wallpaper paste), water, and tempera paint until smooth.
   • mixing liquid starch, soap flakes, and tempera paint.
   • adding small pieces of finely ground colored chalk to paste. Add a few drops of water if too stiff.

WARNING

The reader has been previously warned about using tempera powder with young children. It is important to use up remaining bottles of tempera powder and order only liquid paint in the future.

Hint   To mix powder paints:
Pour powder through a funnel into a paint container. Mix with enough water to form a thick, creamy liquid. Aim for the consistency of yogurt. Test on paper. It should not run. Add more water if too thick, more powder if too thin and runny. A recommended ratio is 2 parts tempera powder to 1 part water. Add a few squirts of liquid dishwashing detergent to aid cleanup. Shake or mix well until smooth and creamy.

Hint   To mix liquid paints:
Place a spoonful in a container. Slowly add water. Test on paper. Add more water if still too thick, more liquid paint if too thin and runny.

Hint   Individual jars or bottles of paint can be stored in a plastic tub to keep them from tipping over. You can also make a paint holder out of a plastic egg carton. Use only the top section, and discard the individual egg holders. Trace three circles using the jars, milk cartons, or juice cans that will later hold the paint. Carefully cut out the three holes. Insert the containers and fill each with paint and one brush. A shoe box could also be used because it is deep and sturdy.

Hint   Glass baby food jars are slowly becoming obsolete. Since they are glass, they are potentially dangerous, but they have the advantage of letting the child quickly see the color of the paint inside. Tall plastic cups or see-through containers are recommended. Juice cans or small milk cartons are an ideal size but do not allow the child to see the color within. Painting the outside of the container the same color as the paint it will hold will solve the problem.

Hint   Biocolor paint is made from natural ingredients and cosmetic pigments, ensuring a completely nontoxic and environmentally safe product. Unlike other tempera paints, Biocolor will not crack, flake, or fade. It is economically priced so it can be used as everyday high-quality tempera paint. It is available from Discount School Supply. See Appendix D.

Hint   An extender like Bentonite reduces paint cost and gives the desired consistency. It also can be added to tempera to make finger paint. Other extenders can be made by mixing flour or cornstarch with water; cornmeal will produce a different texture. Extra soap or detergent powder will also thicken paint.

Hint   Liquid starch makes the paint creamy and results in a glossy finish. Too much starch causes flakiness when the paint dries.

Hint   Keep a tight lid on paint containers and store in a cool place. Refrigerate if milk is used in the recipe.

Hint   The following procedure is recommended when children paint at the art table. Place an absorbent paper towel at the bottom of a Styrofoam tray and add paint. The towel works as a blotter, absorbing the paint but providing just enough color when touched by a brush. It also facilitates cleanup.

Hint   Make your own no-spill paint containers. Trace the top of a small empty juice can onto a sponge. Cut out the inside circle. Slide juice can through sponge. Cut sponge to snugly fit inside easel tray. The sponge secures the paint container and catches paint drips.

Paint Recipes

Salt Paint

½ cup liquid starch
2 cups salt
1 cup water
tempera powder or food coloring

Thoroughly mix liquid starch, salt, and water. Slowly add food coloring or tempera powder. Use as paint. Pictures will sparkle when the salt paint dries.

Easel Paint

In a tall container, mix

1 cup liquid starch
½ cup soap
1 cup powdered tempera

Stir gently until all the powder is dissolved into the liquid. Let stand for one hour. Stir again, breaking up any large lumps—pour into empty tempera jar, cover tightly and shake. Consistency improves overnight. Shake gently before using.

Whipped Soap Paint

soap flakes
warm water
food coloring (optional)

Pour soap flakes into a bowl. Slowly add water. 1 cup soap flakes to ½ cup water is a good ratio. Beat with rotary eggbeater until frothy but not stiff. Use as paint on black construction paper. Good for making winter snow scenes. It has a thick, heavy texture that adds a three-dimensional effect. Or add food coloring and use on white or other colors of paper.

Special Paint

1 part glycerin (available at drugstore)
1 part water
1 part white glue
tempera paint (powder or liquid)

Mix to the consistency of cake icing. Add tempera slowly. Stir well. Cover with lid and let set for a few days. Use with foam-head paintbrush. See the section on special painting and special painters in the activity section in this chapter.

Brushes

There are many different types of brushes recommended for painting (see Figure 6–13). Long-handled brushes with flat bristles are called flats. They produce wide strokes. Brushes with rounded and pointed bristles are called rounds. They produce narrow lines and strokes. Be sure to include a wide array of brushes for painting, including

bath brush—for easel painting
bowl brush—new, not used, for easel painting

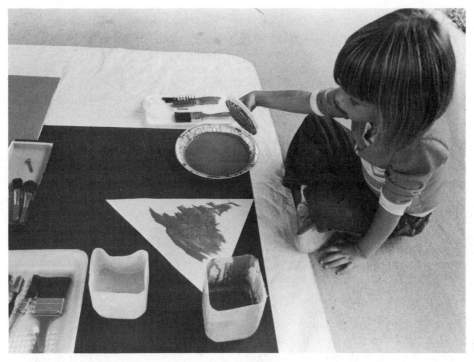

FIGURE 6–13   *Provide an array of brushes for painting.*

detergent dispenser—fill with paint and use as brush

dish pom-pom—for a novel paintbrush

easel—long-handled for painting while standing at the easel

feather duster—for interesting effects while easel painting

foam-head brush—for innovative painting

hairbrush with plastic spikes

household brushes—an array of inexpensive household and paintbrushes found at discount stores is also recommended

makeup brushes—provide nice variety for the older artist

nail brush

paste brush—for spreading paste

pastry brush—for painting while seated

scrub brush—for large, vigorous, sweeping strokes

shaving brush—stubby handle is easy to grip

short-handled brush—for painting while seated or close up at easel

silverware sorter or tray—to sort and store brushes

spoon rest—for holding wet brush while painting

stencil brush—short-handled with stiff bristles for dabbing and small strokes when making a stencil

toothbrush—for general painting, stencil, and spatter printing

varnish brush—wide, inexpensive, found at discount stores

vegetable brush—for general painting

watercolor brush—short and thin, with pointed bristles

whisk broom

Hint   Brushes come in a variety of sizes, shapes, qualities, and prices. Long-handled brushes are good for easel painting, where a child stands a short distance from the paper. Short-handled brushes are often used for painting while seated at a table, where the distance between artist and paper is minimal. Buying flats, rounds, and both short- and long-handled brushes will encourage a variety of paint strokes. Brush tips are made of red sable, camel hair, bristle, natural, or synthetic materials. A moderately expensive brush with stiff bristles is a good investment. The bristles will hold up to thick paint and will not fall out with the first washing. Never use a brush to mix paint. Instead, use a stick or spoon.

Hint Brushes need to be washed soon after each use, preferably before the paint has become dried and crusty. Rinse out excess paint. Add a small drop of liquid detergent and gently wash the bristles. Rinse thoroughly with warm but never hot water. Hot water will melt the glue that holds the bristles in place. Squeeze out excess water. Reshape bristles to their natural shape (e.g., twirl a watercolor brush into a pointed shape). Let air dry. Always store brushes with their handles down and bristles up. Tall, thin potato chip cans are ideal.

Hint Brushes can be homemade. Clamp a small sponge with a pinch-type clothespin and use as a brush. A wad of cloth tied to a pencil makes a good paintbrush. Cotton swabs can be tied with string or yarn and used for dabbing paint.

Hint Trim the edges of inexpensive foam paintbrushes into shapes and designs.

Hint Bristles on brushes will split and spread over time. Carefully use a razor blade to trim jagged edges or stray bristles.

Hint Insert a small paintbrush into a hair roller or ball of clay. This will provide a larger, graspable surface for the child with limited fine motor coordination and control.

Other Painting Tools

A brush is not the only tool for painting. Also, there is no reason to use only one brush at a time. Children can paint with a brush in each hand or with two brushes tied together. Other recommended painting tools include

- balloons
- fingers and hands
- eyedroppers
- cotton swabs or cotton balls
- straws
- sponges
- combs
- Popsicle sticks or tongue depressors
- feathers
- toothpicks
- sticks, twigs, bark, weeds, hay, straw or pine needles
- string
- rags
- assorted kitchen gadgets
- powder puffs
- spatulas
- kitchen shakers
- empty plastic razors
- wads of cloth tied to thick pencils
- small paint rollers for trim
- pipe cleaners twisted into unusual shapes
- shoe-polish applicators

Painting Surfaces

Children do most of their painting on paper. It is important to provide paper in a variety of colors, shapes, sizes, and textures (see Figure 6–14). Children can explore painting on papers that are wet as well as dry. Painting on damp paper will provide an effect similar to that of watercolors. The colors will bleed and blend. The edges will be soft, with many unplanned creative accidents where paint ran together to form unusual shapes. Allow time before adding too many colors, which may just all run together and form a dark blot. Some other things to paint on include

- glass or windows
- Formica or tabletops
- cardboard
- boxes
- wood
- wallpaper
- paper bags
- newspaper
- tinfoil (over cardboard)—add liquid detergent to paint

FIGURE 6–14   *The shape of Lauren's paper poses a challenge.*

- smooth stones
- paper plates
- plastic

Easel and Art Surfaces

art storage and easel—a long, double-sided easel with room for four children and shelves for storage. Commercially available, but fairly expensive.

chalkboard—for use with chalk

double- or triple-sided easel: self-standing with paint rack

easel clips—two clips to hold the upper corners; large paper clips or clothespins will do. Make sure children can work them.

messy tray—a plastic self-contained area for one finger painter. A large cookie sheet will also do.

see-through easel—acrylic, plastic or Plexiglas, transparent, see-through, wipe-off surface

wall easel—a board attached to the wall that swings out when in use and stores flat against the wall the rest of the time. A real space saver and a good project for a volunteer parent/grandparent/carpenter.

Hint   Easels are expensive but a good investment. Standing easels allow for whole arm sweeping strokes. Make sure the easel is at the child's height. Paper should be placed in front of the child's chest and within easy reach, neither too high nor too low. Saw off the legs of the easel if necessary. Actually, a minimum of two easels should be provided for a large group of children. Having too few easels makes children anxious and concerned that they will never get a turn.

It is also possible to construct a homemade tabletop easel out of a sturdy cardboard carton. Two pyramid-shaped tabletop easels can be made by cutting the carton diagonally. Cut two slits at the top for inserting clothespins or clips to hold the paper. Two identical hardwood panels can be hinged together to make a more durable tabletop easel. Add a small chain between the panels to keep the easel stationary when it is open.

Hint   There is another way to make a homemade tabletop easel. Find a large wallpaper sample book. Remove the pages and save the cover. One book makes a double-sided easel. Find a shallow carton lid that the book can rest on. Select your angle and cut notches on the book covers. Insert the carton into the notches. Use clothespins or clips at the top to hold paper.

Hint   Remember to use easel clips or clothespins that the children can work by themselves. Some teachers prefer to place several pieces of paper at each easel in the morning. This eliminates the continual taking down of the completed painting and hanging up of the clean sheet. Also, remember to place some form of covering under the easel. Newspaper is easy to come by and disposable. An old washable throw rug, however, will not only protect the floor but also be more attractive and comfortable to stand on.

Painting Precautions

Remember to roll sleeves up, remove sweaters, and use a smock. Provide one brush or painting tool for each color. Do not fill paint jars full. Full jars only add to the dripping and mess. Instead, fill jars less than half full and add paint as needed. Try to use a clear container so that children can easily see the color of the paint. Glass jars are clear but also potentially dangerous. Fairly large, see-through plastic cups or containers are ideal. Or paint a tin can the color of the paint it will hold. Encourage children to keep the paints and brushes to their left and paper to the right. This will reinforce the left-to-right progression so crucial to later reading and writing.

How many colors should be provided? Some believe that beginning painters need only one color until they have learned the basic processes involved in holding a brush, dipping for paint, wiping excess, positioning on paper, and making strokes. Others begin with two. The author recommends providing the three primary colors. Additional colors will appear on the canvas through accidental or purposeful mixing. They can also be mixed using the palette method. Containers of white and black will help children lighten or darken colors. There is no one right answer to the opening question. Those who stress the technical skills involved will recommend using only one color. Those who stress the importance of color mixing and creative expression would provide two or more. Five would be maximum. More is not necessarily better when providing colors of paint. The same holds true for the number of crayons in a box. Children can be as creative with the basic eight as they can with an overwhelming sixty-four.

Painting is a messy activity. Remind children to scrape the side of the brush on the inside rim of the jar before they remove it from the paint. This will help eliminate the dripping of excess paint on table, floor, smock, and paper. Encourage children to replace the brush or painting tool in the one designated container. Mistakes will happen. Be sure to rinse thoroughly to avoid unwanted mixing of paints. Children should wash their hands before taking off their smocks. This will avoid smearing of paint on skin, hair, and clothing.

Paint Palette

Children who have had some experience in color mixing can be introduced to painting with a palette. An aluminum pie plate, frozen dinner tray, or plastic lid is recommended. Children take blobs of mixed paint and mix their own colors, shades, and tints on their palette. Always have the primary colors and white and black available. Children need their own brushes for color mixing on the palette. They also need a cup of water for cleaning the brushes between color mixings.

Here are some activities for painting.

Hand Painting   T P K

Finger painting is an activity that is not usually offered in the home. Still, most young children have had some experience spreading soap on the sides of the bathtub or food on the tray of their high chair. *Finger painting* is not an accurate term. The activity, which involves much more than merely spreading paint with the fingers, should more accurately be called hand painting. Often, adults approach hand painting by neatly dabbing their forefingers with their "pinkies" gracefully up in the air. The whole hand and arm should be involved. Some teachers allow children to paint with their feet. Hand painting is messy but developmentally appropriate. The children make direct contact with the medium. There is no brush to separate the artist from the paint. Children enjoy the cool, slimy texture. It gives young children the opportunity to get messy without fear of reprimand. It is an activity that should be provided on an ongoing basis. Some children will be reluctant. They may fear that their clothes will get dirty or that their parents will be angry with them for making a mess. They will need time and gentle reassurance. Seeing the other children and their teacher engaging in hand painting may reassure them. A child should not be forced to do hand painting against his or her wishes. (See Figure 6–15.)

When hand painting, children should be encouraged to get fully involved by using the

- front or palm of the hand—for wide strokes
- back of the hand—for wide strokes
- side of the hand—for long, thin strokes and zigzags
- fingertips and joints of the fingers—for dabbing marks

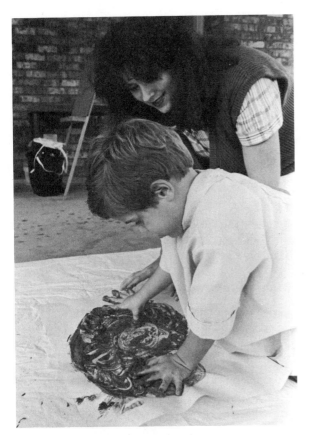

FIGURE 6–15   *The teacher guides and facilitates hand painting.*

their large arm muscles more freely, reach all over their papers, and have a better view of what they are doing. Standing up also keeps one's smock from dangling in the wet paint.

Music sets the mood for finger painting. Slow music encourages lazy, smooth strokes. Fast music encourages rapid, swirling lines.

Infants and toddlers enjoy hand painting with pudding and applesauce, although the use of food in art has already been discussed. Some would argue that there is no added expense or waste because the food will be eaten. Others fear that playing with all food is encouraged through this activity. It may be best to eliminate the use of food in art.

Shaving cream can also be used. It is thicker than most finger paints, and children enjoy the texture. Remind them that it is not whipped cream and is not edible. Squirt a glob for each child and spray water to dilute.

Hand painting should be done on paper with a glossy or glazed surface. Finger paint paper is commercially available but fairly expensive. Slick cardboard, shiny shelf paper, gift boxes, magazine covers, or a nonstick baking sheet can also be used. Add liquid detergent to the paint and do hand painting directly on a Formica tabletop. Lay a sheet of paper over the table, rub gently, and take a print of the hand painting. This will please those children who want to save what they made. Adding some vinegar to the wash water will help clean the tables.

Begin by giving each child a piece of paper. The papers can be laid out glossy side up and sponged down with water first or occasionally squirted with a pump sprayer. Begin with the primary colors. Add one glob or teaspoon of paint. Paint that is applied too heavily will crack or chip off when dry. It is difficult to manage hand painting with a large group at the same time. The first child may finish before you even give paint to the last child. It may be easier and less stressful to do hand painting in shifts with fewer children. This allows you to observe and interact rather than merely dispense.

Encourage children to use both hands in thoroughly spreading the paint. Squirt with water if the paint becomes dry. Add a second color. Over time the colors will become thoroughly mixed. Mixing

- fingers, front and back—for long marks
- thumbs—for round marks
- knuckles—for a series of marks
- fingernails—for fine lines that etch through the paint
- fists—for massive marks and round swirls
- wrists—for massive marks
- hand with fingers spread wide—for hand prints
- whole arms, toes, and feet—best done outdoors on a warm day

As with brush painting, sleeves need to be rolled up and sweaters removed to encourage freedom of movement, and smocks should be worn. Hand painting while kneeling or sitting on the floor restricts movement. Hand painting while standing at a table is recommended. It allows children to use red and blue will make purple. This may be the time to stop. You may want to add yellow or white to lighten it up if the children are still interested and want a third color. Placing the paper flat on newspaper to dry will result in a curled picture. When the picture is thoroughly dry, turn it over and press it flat with a warm iron. Or place the paper on a larger piece of newspaper before painting. Some paint will stick the paper to the newspaper, resulting in less curling when dry.

Etched Hand Painting   P K

Objects such as a comb, a paper clip, a fork, a key, or a notched piece of cardboard can be pulled and swirled through the wet hand painting. This will produce an interesting etched design. Still, these are merely accessories and do not replace the active processing with both hands.

Hand Painting Print   T P K

Children who are process oriented may not need expensive finger paint. They can finger paint directly on a tabletop, tray, or cookie sheet. If they choose to save what they have created, slowly lay a sheet of paper on top and gently lift up. A print of their finger painting results. This saves on the cost of buying expensive finger paint paper. It also cleans the table.

Hint   Provide thin disposable plastic gloves for children with sensitive skin.

Shaving Cream Hand Painting   P K

Using shaving cream is an alternative to finger paint. Please see precautions discussed in the Hint that follows. Be sure to dampen the tabletop or finger paint paper first to facilitate movement. Make sure the glossy side of the paper is facing up. The adult can squirt a mound of shaving cream and let the children first explore its tactile properties. Add a few drops of liquid watercolor. Avoid food coloring because it stains the hands in concentrated form. Children would enjoy using squirt bottles with plain water or liquid watercolor with their mound of shaving cream.

Hint   Shaving cream is not recommended for children under the age of three since it can be harmful when ingested. Only an adult should handle the can of shaving cream. Since children may confuse shaving cream with whipped topping, provide close supervision and discuss safety precautions. Always avoid mentholated shaving cream because its fumes can be harmful if inhaled. Children with skin conditions can wear clear disposable gloves.

Shaving Cream Print   P K

Follow the directions for making a hand painting print. Black paper makes a good contrast for white shaving cream.

Finger Paint Recipes

Cornstarch Finger Paint

$\frac{1}{2}$ cup cornstarch
4 cups boiling water
cold water
food coloring or tempera powder

Dissolve cornstarch in small amount of cold water. Gradually add boiling water. Stir constantly. Cook until mixture is clear. Continue stirring. Glycerine can be added to remove stickiness and provide a smooth texture. Add food coloring or tempera powder. Scents can also be added. Cool.

Detergent Finger Paint

liquid dishwashing detergent
water
food coloring or tempera

Add water slowly to detergent until you get a pasty mixture. Add coloring. Easy to clean up.

Flour and Water (Paste) Finger Paint (cooked)

$\frac{1}{2}$ cup flour
$\frac{1}{2}$ cup cold water
$1\frac{1}{2}$ cups boiling water
2 teaspoons alum
food coloring or tempera powder
extract, e.g., peppermint, lemon, or perfume
(optional)

Mix flour and cold water. Stir in boiling water and bring mixture to a boil. Stir constantly. Remove from heat. Add alum and coloring. Add extract if children are able to enjoy the smell without tasting. Finger paintings done with this recipe tend to dry flat.

Liquid Starch Finger Paint

1 cup liquid starch
1 teaspoon tempera powder

Slowly add tempera to liquid starch until you reach the color desired.

Paste Finger Paint (uncooked)

flour
water
food coloring

Mixing flour and water provides a very economical paste. Add food coloring to it and use it as finger paint. Add water to flour until you get a paste consistency, easy to spread around but not too thin or runny. Paint on tabletop or cookie tray for easy cleanup.

Starch Finger Paint

2 cups instant laundry starch
1 quart water
3 cups Ivory flakes
¾ cup talcum powder
1 teaspoon oil of cloves
food coloring

Dissolve starch in water and mix. Slowly add soap flakes. Add talcum and then oil of cloves. Continue mixing until thick and it forms peaks. Add food coloring to water before mixing.

Wheat Paste or Wallpaper Paste Finger Paint

wheat paste or wallpaper paste
lukewarm or cold water
food coloring or tempera powder
oil of wintergreen (available at drugstore)

Slowly add water to paste to get a creamy texture. Stir until smooth. Add coloring. A drop or two of wintergreen will disguise the odor if children find it

unpleasant. Check to make sure paste ingredients are nontoxic.

Easy-to-Clean Finger Paint

⅝ cup water
½ cup dry laundry starch (chips or powder)
½ cup mild soap powder
coloring (optional)

Combine all ingredients. Beat until thick. Add liquid watercolor if desired. Children use their hands to paint.

Soap Flakes Finger Paint

2 cups soap flakes (not liquid)
2 cups warm water
coloring (optional)

Add soap to water. Beat with mixer until reaching consistency of whipped egg whites. Spray with liquid watercolor if desired. Children use their hands to paint.

Flour and Salt Finger Paint

1 cup flour
1½ cups salt
¾ cup water
coloring (optional)

Mix first three ingredients. Add liquid color if desired. This paint has a grainy quality and provides a different tactile experience.

Water Painting: Where Did My Picture Go? T P

Children need something to put on their painting tools, but not necessarily paint. Most young children enjoy painting with water. They may have done it at home in the bathtub or sink or on the pavement. It is a good introduction to using a brush and is highly recommended as an outdoor art activity. Provide old household brushes and plastic pails of water. Painting caps and old painting clothes, e.g., coveralls, may help ease them into the role of painter. Children can paint cement, brick, trees, outdoor nonrusting equipment, and windows. Food coloring can be added, but it will streak the surface being washed.

Whipped Soap Painting   P K

Whipped soap is thick and good for making snow scenes on black construction paper, white hearts on red, or on wax paper. A few drops of food coloring or powder paint can also be added.

Roll a Line Design   P K S

Find a lid from a box. Cut a paper to fit in. Mix paints. Find items that roll, including

- toy cars
- marbles
- small balls
- beads

Carefully dip them in paint and place them in the box lid. Encourage the child to tilt, tip, and move the lid to get the items rolling in different directions. Dip them in more paint if needed. The result will be a criss-crossed linear effect.

The author prefers doing this with a frisbee, pie tin, or cake pan. The round frame provides a strong contrast to the linear design. Cut a circle out of paper. Make sure that it fits into the bottom ridge. Use light paints, including white, yellow, and light blue, if working on black construction paper.

Roll Painting   K S

Children can use a rolling pin or brayer to make their paintings. Use a spoon to add different globs of paint on one half of a large sheet of paper that has been folded and opened. Refold. Roll over it with the rolling pin or brayer. Roll gently from center to sides. This will distribute the paint in different directions. Carefully reopen. Add additional colors. You will have a painted design on both sides, each a mirror image of the other.

String Painting   K S

Fold a sheet of paper in half. Open it and spread it flat. Place globs of paint on one half. Place a foot-long piece of string curled up on one inside half before refolding. Make sure one end of the string is sticking out. Gently pull on the string while holding the folded paper in place with the other hand.

Straw Painting: Blow a Blot   K S

Children enjoy blowing through a straw to spread blobs of paint. Young children will need to practice holding and blowing through a straw in preparation for this activity. Perhaps they could blow bubbles for a science exploration. Paint should be fairly thin. Place paint in the middle of the paper with a small spoon. Encourage children to hold their straws close to but not touching the paint. Blow out, not in. Move the paint from the middle to the sides of the paper. Add other colors. Blow the colors into each other. Rotate the paper if necessary. The result will be an interesting design composed of mixed colors, weblike patterns, and intersecting lines.

Hint   Cut a notch near the top of the straw. If children suck in, the paint will exit the notch rather than entering their mouths. Remind children to use only their own straws.

Special Painting with Special Painters   P K S

Children enjoy using sponges and foam as painters. Sponges or foam of various widths can be cut into different shapes and inserted into pinch-type clothespins. A Popsicle stick can also be gently inserted and glued in place. Use a razor blade, X-Acto knife, or scissors to cut the top edge into a pointed, grooved, forked, notched, or wavy pattern. This will result in a different type of stroke when painting. Encourage children to use the special painters in different ways. They can make dots and dabbing motions, twirls to make circular shapes, and long strokes, either up and down or sideways. See the recipe for Special Paint included in this chapter. Remember to have the painter slightly wet before using special paints.

Squeeze and Dribble Painting   P K

Pour paint into squeeze bottles, old liquid glue bottles, meat basters, or mustard and ketchup dispensers. Children can squeeze and dribble a design on paper. Paint can also be squeezed from a small hole in a thick plastic bag.

Shake a Painting   P K

Fill kitchen shakers with different colors of powder paint. Make sure the holes in the shakers are large enough for the powder to shake out easily. Wet the paper with a sponge or squirt bottle. Shake different colors onto the wet paper. Mix with a Popsicle stick or paintbrush.

Drip Drop a Painting   P K

Children can use a medicine or eyedropper to make a painting. Provide different colors. One eyedropper can be used if the child remembers to clean it out between colors. Paint can be squeezed up into the eyedropper and slowly dropped in a design on a white paper towel, a coffee filter, or white drawing paper.

Etch a Painting   S

Place tinfoil over a piece of cardboard. Tape it on the back. Children enjoy working with tinfoil. Add Ivory flakes to the paint to help it adhere to the slick surface. Use only one color of paint to paint over the tinfoil background. Let the paint dry. Use a Popsicle stick to carefully etch or scratch a picture through the dried paint. Etching too hard will tear through the tinfoil. The result will be an outline of a picture in shiny silver.

Dot Painting   K S

Encourage children to dip the end of the paintbrush handle in paint and make a picture composed of circular dots of paint. One finger could also be used to produce the same effect.

Sensory and Texture Painting   T P K S

Vary the texture of paints you provide at the easel or painting table. Offer very thick paint one day and thin and runny the next. Try mixing one or more of the following to your paint:

- sand
- sawdust
- liquid starch
- coffee grounds
- shaving cream
- herbs or spices
- crumbled nature items, including leaves and flower petals
- powdered laundry soap
- baby powder
- baking soda
- glitter
- shaved ice

Encourage children to use words to describe what they see and feel as they paint.

Painting in a Bag   T P

An alternative to the mess (and tactile experience) of hand painting is to paint in a bag. Provide each child with a sturdy zip-lock bag filled with about 4 tablespoons of finger paint or liquid tempera. Glitter could be added. Shaving cream could also be used. Release extra air and secure with duct tape. This is a good alternative for shy children or those with sensitive skin.

Magnet Painting   K S

You will need a piece of Plexiglas, strong magnet, metal objects including washers, paper clips, nuts, bolts, and two blocks. Place Plexiglas across two blocks forming a bridge, allowing enough room underneath for a child's hand to move freely. Tape a piece of paper on top of the Plexiglas. Metal objects can be tied together using embroidery thread. Dip the metal objects into paint and place on paper. Have child hold magnet under the Plexiglas and move the magnet about. The magnetic pieces will spread paint on the paper, creating a design. Children discover a science concept while doing art.

Vehicle Tracks Painting   T P K

Locate cars, trucks, planes, and other toy vehicles with two or more wheels. Provide low but ample containers of paint. Child can roll vehicle in paint and then onto paper. Driving their vehicle creates a design. This activity reinforces a discussion on modes of transportation.

Ice-Cube Painting   T P K

Fill an ice-cube tray with colored water. Use liquid watercolor rather than food coloring. Insert a craft stick in each cube. Sticks do not need to be inserted vertically. Freeze overnight. Children enjoy rubbing their ice-cube painters across slick paper. Use finger paint or shiny freezer wrap. Children love to watch the ice melt, spreading color. This is a good activity to do outdoors on a warm day. This activity extends a discussion about the sun or seasons.

Mirror Painting   P K

Provide handheld or full-length mirrors. Children can use tempera paints and brushes to paint facial features and clothing. They could also draw with water-based markers. When done, children can wash the mirror, using warm soapy water, and towel dry for the next person.

Roll a Can Painting   P K S

Find coffee cans with lids. Measure the inside circumference and depth. Cut papers accordingly. Provide paint and items that roll, including marbles and golf balls. Curl and position paper inside can. Child places one or more rolling objects dipped in paint into can. Securely attach lid. Place on floor and gently roll. Remember to create a path that makes it safe to roll without bumping others.

Paint Pendulum   K S

This activity is similar to the sand pendulum discussed in Chapter 4. See Figure 4–3. Find a paper cup with a pointed bottom. Punch a small hole at the point. Make three evenly spaced holes in the rim of the cup. Cut three pieces of string and tie them through the three holes. Tie the three ends into a knot. Set up two low matching chairs back to back and about 3 feet apart. Place pole, thick dowel rod or broomstick between the seats or tops of the chairs. Secure with duct tape. Cut a piece of string long enough to reach from the pole to the floor. Tie one end of this string to the pole and the other to the knot in the cup's string. Cup should be 6 to 12 inches above ground. Cover large area under and around chairs with newspaper. Lay paper between chairs. Tape over hole in cup and add thinned liquid tempera. Show child how to gently swing cup. Remove tape. Paint will drip an interesting design as it swings back and forth.

Oil and Water Painting   K S

Mix one color of paint in a cup until thin and watery. Mix a second color of paint with cooking oil in another cup. Place a sheet of paper in a baking pan or small tray. Child uses an eyedropper or spoon to drip spots of the thinned paint onto the paper. Use another eyedropper or spoon to drip spots of the oily paint on top of the watery paint. Tip pan back and forth to mix. Observe and discuss what happens. Oil and water do not mix and the oily paint floats on the water to create unusual effects. Children are artists and scientists with this activity.

SUMMARY

Children's art has a fresh, spontaneous quality that is easier to appreciate than to explain. Theories have attempted to explain what, why, and how children create. Different theories have different explanations for the content, motive, process and product of children's art. A physical explanation holds that young children scribble and draw unrecognizable marks because they lack motor coordination and control. An emotional explanation states that children distort, add, omit, and exaggerate through art those things that have high emotional value to them. A perceptual explanation holds that children rely on their perceptions when drawing. Young children's perceptions lack clarity and refinement, and their artwork will reflect this. A cognitive explanation holds that children draw what they know. Children who lack experience and sensory involvement with people, places, and things will have little to include in their art. A general developmental explanation using a stage sequence approach incorporates the former explanations while addressing the whole child and individual differences. Kellogg's stages move from scribbling to placement, shape, design, and pictorial. Lowenfeld and Brittain's stages include scribbling, preschematic, schematic, dawning realism, pseudo-naturalism, and artistic decision.

Suggested Activities

1. Collect several art samples from children (later infancy to age eight). Attempt to sequence them according to Kellogg's, Lowenfeld and Brittain's, and the author's general sequence. Which system works best for you? Why?

2. Recall the physical explanation for children's art. Check out books on art history. Note the similarities and differences between children's art and adult abstract and "primitive" art.

3. Collect several samples of art from one young child over an extended period of time. Note patterns or growth over time. Attempt to explain the what, why, and how of children's art using different theories of artistic development.

4. Ask children aged two, three, four, five, and six to draw a picture of themselves using crayons or markers. Ask their permission to keep or borrow the pictures. Try to sequence them according to Kellogg's stages in the development of human figure drawing. Do your data support her stages?

Review

A. Match the artistic term with an appropriate example:
   ___ product   1. "I get so mad sometimes, and that's why I make scribbles all over my paper."
   ___ content   2. Jim looks in the mirror and smiles. He runs back to the easel and works on his self-portrait.
   ___ motive   3. Amy folds, tears, and staples a sheet of scrap paper. She crumples it up and tosses it in the wastebasket on the way to lunch.
   ___ process   4. Keely paints several lines and shapes. She says, "See my pretty, pretty design."

B. Identify the major theories or explanations for children's art.
   1.
   2.
   3.
   4.
   5.
   6.

C. Match the age range with its appropriate stage according to Lowenfeld and Brittain.
   1. 1½–2, 2½   ___ Named scribbling
   2. 2, 2½–3   ___ Schematic
   3. 3, 3½–4   ___ Pseudo-naturalistic/realistic
   4. 4–7   ___ Disordered and random scribbling
   5. 7–9   ___ Preschematic
   6. 9–12   ___ Dawning realism
   7. 12–14   ___ Controlled scribbling

D. Identify the author's general stages of artistic development:
   1–2 and up   _____
   2–4, and up   _____
   4–6   _____
   5–8 primary grades and up   _____

Art and Aesthetics

What do you see in this picture? Is this a place that young children would go to? What makes it so inviting? Do you have a quiet area in your classroom? The cushion, pillows, and stuffed animals make it a soft, small, safe environment. The dinosaurs enhance its appeal. The area is aesthetically appealing. What might you do here? It's a place to go if you want to be alone or are not feeling well. It's a place to snuggle up with a book or talk with a best friend. It can also be used as a place to renew and refresh if you need to think about what you have said or done to hurt another. Do you have a place where you go to be alone and get away from it all?

Chapter 7, The Elements of Art, identifies the building blocks that all artists use when making art. Artists use line, color, shape or form, mass or volume, design or composition, pattern, space, balance, and texture. Adult artists may strive for a particular effect by consciously using one or more of the artistic elements. Young children are less deliberate and more spontaneous as they process with the media. This does not mean, however, that their artwork lacks the artistic elements. Think of scribbling as nothing more than a series of colorful lines and shapes in space.

Chapter 8, Aesthetics, focuses on helping children experience and appreciate the beauty in their world. This photograph depicts an aesthetic environment set up by Florence Pirofski at an early childhood conference. There is beauty in the simplicity and use of natural materials. The rocking chair invites you to come rest and experience what surrounds you. The environment reflects a balance of hard and soft items. There are collections of beautiful things to look at, touch, listen to, and smell. A discussion with Aline D. Wolf should facilitate the reader's understanding of aesthetics and art appreciation in the early years.

Chapter 9, Sensory Experiences, is a resource of activities for the visual, auditory, tactile, olfactory, gustatory, chromatic, thermic, sterognostic, baric, and kinesthetic senses. Providing sensory stimulation helps children have aesthetic experiences. An aesthetically pleasing classroom environment makes good use of all available space. Objects suspended from the ceiling provide an additional source of visual stimulation and supplement objects displayed on the walls.

Is early childhood art ever more than just letting children experiment and explore? Is there something more to art than scribbling, handling play dough, smearing paint, and gluing things onto a collage? Chapter 10, The Complete Early Childhood Art Program, provides the bigger picture. A complete art program provides children with ample time, space, and materials to make art; experiences for the senses; an introduction to art, artists, and their styles; and aesthetic involvement.

CHAPTER 7

The Elements of Art

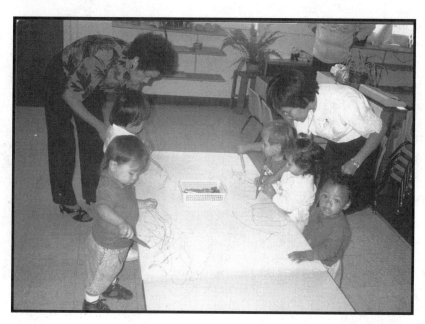

Have you ever worked with toddlers? Can toddlers do art? At what age should children be given experiences in art? What do you see happening in this picture?

Even toddlers can engage in art if given appropriate materials and close supervision. This group is making a mural. Two children are using the markers by themselves to make their own lines. Art can be made up of lines. Two other children are being assisted by their teachers. The children fail to grip the marker and do not apply pressure. The teachers are guiding them to press down while moving the marker. The youngest child is more interested in watching the photographer. Children are unique individuals with different skills and interests. Their differences should be respected.

OBJECTIVES

After studying this chapter, the student will be able to

- List and briefly explain the artistic elements
- Discuss the categories and physical properties of color
- Devise an art activity that will help children learn about the artistic elements
- Help children make prints

INTRODUCTION

Some people have difficulty separating whether a work of art is good or bad from how they feel about it. Liking a work of art does not make it good. Although artistic tastes and preferences are personal, we can use accepted criteria to talk about, analyze, and critique art. The artistic elements are one accepted criterion. They include line, color, shape, mass or volume, design or composition, pattern, space, balance, and texture. A work of art can be critiqued in terms of how successfully the artist has used one or more of the artistic elements. Art activities to help children learn about, appreciate, and use the artistic elements will be provided in this chapter.

AESTHETIC CRITERIA

What does one look for in an aesthetic experience? How does one analyze, let alone critique, a dance, musical score, or work of art? The various expressive arts have their own criteria. In dance, one might match up an individual dancer's movement with the music. Do the movements flow? Evaluating a musical score on the basis of rhythm, tempo, and one's emotional response is appropriate when listening to music. The visual arts have their own criteria or artistic elements (see Figure 7–1). These include

1. line
2. color
3. shape
4. mass or volume
5. design or composition
6. pattern
7. space
8. balance
9. texture

Each of these will be explained and illustrated with activities. Some are discussed further in Chapter 9, Sensory Experiences. Please refer to Appendix E for books on the artistic elements—line, color, and shape in particular.

FIGURE 7–1 Can you identify artistic elements in works of art?

1. Line

What is a line (see Figure 7–2)? A line

- is a visible mark made by an artistic tool, such as a crayon, moved across a surface, such as paper.
- is a continuation of a dot.
- usually suggests direction, movement, rhythm, or form.
- does not exist in nature. Nature produces edges. Artists produce lines to represent edges.
- helps the artist define shapes and contours or represent edges.
- is something we use to make letters, words, numbers, symbols, and signs.

Lines can be used in many different ways. Lines have their own dimensions, including size, direc-

FIGURE 7–2   *Art can be made using lines.*

tion, length, width, and weight. They also have their own personality. Lines can be

- long or short (length).
- tall or short (height).
- thick, fat, heavy; or thin, skinny, light (weight). Heavy lines may convey a feeling of force, weight, boldness, or strength. Thin lines may add a delicate, light, or timid touch.
- big or little (size).
- horizontal, vertical, or diagonal (direction). Horizontal lines suggest calm, quiet, and a sleeping, restful position. Vertical lines suggest stability and strength. Think of the lighthouse in the middle of the sea, an upright steel girder, or a rocket blasting off. Diagonal lines suggest tension and activity, as in climbing uphill or skiing downhill.
- up or down (direction).
- forward or backward (direction).
- to the right or to the left (direction).
- continuous; or broken, dotted.
- open or closed.
- jagged or smooth.
- patterned or irregular.

- straight or curved, zigzag or wiggly. Curved lines suggest graceful movement, as in a dance or in nature. Zigzag lines suggest energy, as in a bolt of lightning.
- controlled; or uncontrolled and spontaneous.
- dark or light.
- parallel or perpendicular, intersecting or crossed.
- fast or slow.
- plain or fancy.
- sharp or soft.

Here are some art activities that will help children learn about lines.

Line Design   K S

Children can make abstract line designs using string and a frame. Secure a wooden picture frame. Hammer small nails a few inches apart around the frame. By pulling the string taut from nail to nail, the child can create a line design. Different colors of yarn will add the element of color to the linear design. A cardboard frame can also be used. Cut 1-inch-long slits on all four sides. Encourage children to connect the slits with yarn. The result will be a line design.

Dancing Lines   T P K

This activity is a variation of drawing to music. Play a short passage of music and ask the children to respond by making a line with a marker, brush, or paint. For example, a march might suggest a forceful, patterned up-and-down line. A waterfall might suggest thick vertical lines, whereas water dripping from a faucet might suggest a vertical dotted line. What kind of a line is suggested by the following taped sounds?

- water boiling
- rocket blasting off
- siren blaring
- sawing wood
- ice skating music
- a polka

- thunder
- hopping on one foot
- jumping rope
- a creaking swing in motion

Line Art   P K

Children can make their own line art by dipping cut pieces of string into a small bowl of white glue.

Gluey string can be creatively arranged in a linear design on a black sheet of construction paper. Colored yarn can be glued onto white drawing paper. Let dry.

Squeeze and Sprinkle   K

Children can be encouraged to make a linear design using a small bottle of white glue. Before it dries, have them sprinkle sand, glitter, or crushed eggshells to highlight their line design. Let dry.

Lots of Lines   P K S

Children can cut line strips out of construction paper. Encourage them to make some thick, thin, wide, fat, short, and long. Provide cut strips of paper for very young children who lack scissoring skills. Children will enjoy arranging their cut-paper lines into a design and gluing them onto a piece of colored construction paper.

Stick Art   P K S

Children can make line designs using toothpicks, Popsicle sticks, or pipe cleaners. Each of these can be spread with glue and pressed onto cardboard or sturdy paper. The arrangement will be a linear design with angles. Children may bend the pipe cleaners into nonlinear forms. This is to be expected. Arrange and let dry.

2. Color

A world ablaze with color provides a beautiful backdrop for our daily lives. What is color? Color

- is based on the passage of light. It is the visual sensation of light caused by stimulating the cones of the retina. As the light source changes, so does the color. With no light there is no color.
- comes from the sun. We see colors because of the way certain objects reflect color rays to our eyes. For example, we see a banana as yellow because the banana absorbs all the color rays except yellow and reflects the yellow rays back to our eyes.
- makes each of us respond with feeling. Some of us have favorite colors. Children develop their color preferences and palettes early in life. These

influence the colors that we use to select articles of clothing, home furnishings, and cars, and to do art.

Colors can be categorized as

1. Primary
   Red, blue, and yellow are the three primary colors. They are called primary because they are used to produce the other colors.
2. Secondary
   Mixing two primary colors in equal amounts results in a secondary color. For example,

   red + yellow   = orange
   yellow + blue = green
   red + blue   = purple/violet

3. Intermediate
   Mixing an adjoining primary and secondary color in equal amounts results in an intermediate color. For example,

   yellow + orange   = yellow-orange
   red + orange   = red-orange
   red + violet/purple   = red-violet
   blue + violet/purple   = blue-violet
   blue + green   = blue-green
   yellow + green   = yellow-green

4. Complementary
   Complementary colors are opposite each other on the color wheel. They provide a dramatic visual contrast. Examples include red and green, yellow and purple, and blue and orange.
5. Neutral
   Neutral refers to pigments that do not have a particular color. Black and white are considered neutrals.

Please refer to the Color Wheel (on the back cover), which identifies colors as primary, secondary, and intermediate.

   Colors have recognizable physical properties, including

1. Hue
   Hue refers to the color name. Hue is color in its pure, unmixed form. For example, red and blue have different hues.

2. Value

Value refers to the relative lightness or darkness of a hue. It refers to the amount of light that a surface reflects back to the eye. For example, the value of a hue such as yellow is lighter than that of a darker hue such as purple. Red and blue can have the same value (dark) but different hues.

3. Intensity

Intensity refers to the purity of light reflected from a surface. Terms like bright and dull refer to color intensity. Pure colors are most intense or bright, and mixing a color with others dulls its intensity.

4. Tint

Adding white to any color lightens its value and results in a tint. For example, adding white to red makes pink.

5. Shade

Adding black to any color darkens its value and results in a shade. For example, adding black to red makes maroon.

Colors also have thermal qualities that have a psychological impact on the viewer. Colors make us feel. Colors can

1. Be warm

Warm colors, including red, yellow, and orange, remind us of hot or warm objects, such as the sun or fire.

2. Be cool

Cool colors, including blue, green, and purple/violet, remind us of cold or cool objects, such as water, ice, grass, and shade.

3. Give the illusion of size and space

Light colors make objects appear to be larger than they actually are. Dark colors make objects appear to be smaller than they actually are. For example, painting a room off-white will make it look larger. Painting the same room a dark tan will make it look smaller. Light colors make objects look closer. Dark colors make objects look farther away.

Adult artists are consciously concerned with how the viewer will be affected by their choice of color.

An artist might use red, yellow, and orange to convey the sense of heat in painting a Fourth of July picnic. Blues and greens could be used to paint a ship adrift at sea. Light colors would be used to paint a portrait. Dark colors might be used to hint at the presence of crowds in the far background. Color has many possibilities and personalities. Some of these are

- light or dark (value)
- bright or dull (intensity)
- warm or cool (thermal quality)
- opaque (oils, acrylics, thick tempera) or transparent (watercolors, thinned tempera)
- primary, secondary, or intermediate
- pure or mixed

Here are some activities for color. Others will be presented in the sections on the visual and chromatic sense in Chapter 9.

Color Sort   P K

Children enjoy sorting different objects by color. Provide a muffin tin or egg carton. Very young children can use only a few openings. Older children can be challenged with a dozen openings. Cut circles of different colors and place one in the bottom of each opening. Use pieces of construction paper, small yarn balls, or pom-poms for the children to sort. Children can use metal tongs to pick up the yarn balls or pom-poms and place them in the matching opening.

Wheel of Colors   P K

Use a round, clean pizza cardboard. Glue on pie-shaped wedges of different colors. Find as many pinch-type clothespins as you have color wedges. Use markers to color each clothespin a corresponding color. For example, a red pie wedge will have a clothespin marked with red. Encourage children to clip each clothespin to the matching color. Older children may enjoy using a separate set of clothespins that have color names written on them. The color names can be matched with the corresponding colors.

Color Cooking   P K

Sweet snacks should be the exception rather than the rule. When used, however, they can be turned into an educational experience. Children can learn the principles of color mixing by frosting cookies, graham crackers, or cupcakes. Begin with clear icing or vanilla frosting in three small bowls. Put blue, red, or yellow food coloring into one of the bowls. Children can frost some of the goodies with the primary colors. Mix any two of the primary colors to get purple, orange, or green frosting. This can be done in conjunction with holidays.

- red and green during Christmas
- pink, white, and red for Valentine's Day
- green for St. Patrick's Day
- purple and yellow for Easter
- orange and black for Halloween
- red, white, and blue for the Fourth of July
- orange, brown, and yellow for fall and Thanksgiving

A recipe for a drink that reinforces color:

Orange Drink

6-ounce can of concentrated orange juice
1 cup milk
½ cup water
10 to 12 ice cubes
1 teaspoon vanilla

Pour in blender. Blend until frothy.

A recipe for a snack that reinforces color:

Edible Color Blocks

1 envelope Knox gelatin
⅓ cup cold water
1 small box Jell-O (experiment with colors and flavors)
1 cup boiling water

Dissolve Knox gelatin in cold water. Dissolve Jell-O in boiling water. Mix everything together. Pour into rectangular pan. Cool. Cut into shapes.

Color Mixing   P K

Children will enjoy experimenting with mixing colors. Find six baby food jars. Six sections of a plastic egg carton can also be used. Fill three with several drops of water. Add one of the primary colors of food coloring to each. This leaves three empty for color mixing. An eyedropper can be used to mix equal parts of any two colors. What new color do you get? Repeat the process using two different colors.

A variation on this task includes additional materials. Provide a color mixing directions card as follows:

red + blue   =
blue + yellow =
red + yellow =

Provide a separate eyedropper for each of the primary colors. Label three jars red, blue, and yellow. Label three other jars red + blue, blue + yellow, and red + yellow. Young children need directions using actual color swatches rather than the color words. Older children can do the color mixing by reading the color names.

Hand Painting   T P

Finger, or more appropriately, hand painting, is a good opportunity to learn about color mixing. Provide one primary color, and encourage the children to use their entire hands in moving the paint about. Next, add a second primary color. What happens when they mix? What color did you make? This may be enough color mixing at one sitting for young children. At a different time, repeat the above process using the primary color that was not originally involved.

Color Clay   T P K

Teachers can use one of the recipes for homemade clay or play dough listed in Chapter 12. Start with three uncolored balls. Add a few drops of food coloring of one of three primary colors to each ball. Knead. Divide the primary-colored balls in half. Use half to experiment with color mixing. What happens if balls of red and blue, blue and yellow, or red and yellow are mixed together? What new color of clay do we get? The result will be different-colored clay balls.

Made in the Shade   K S

Children can learn to make tints and shades of a color. Individual finger paint sets or tempera paints can be used. Begin with the three primary colors. Add a small dab of white to each. What happens? What color did you get? Is it lighter or darker than the one you started with? Mix the three secondary colors and repeat the process. Repeat the process adding a very small dab of black. Adding white will produce tints of red, yellow, blue, and the secondary colors. Adding black will produce shades.

Color Helpers **P K**

Discuss with children how community helpers often wear a certain color. Fire fighters wear red. Police officers wear blue. Doctors, nurses, veterinarians, ambulance drivers, paramedics, and hospital workers wear white or green (in surgery). Cooks and chefs also wear white.

Color Day **P K**

Declare a day of the week to have a specific color. For example, every Friday is color day. This Friday's color will be green. Encourage children to wear something green. Activities, songs, stories, and snacks can be focused on the color green. Some color-coordinated snacks are

- red: apples, cherries, strawberries, ketchup
- yellow: bananas, scrambled eggs, mustard
- green: grapes, celery, lettuce
- orange: carrots, cheese, pumpkin bread
- purple: grape juice, grapes
- brown: whole wheat bread, peanut butter, chocolate milk or pudding
- blue: blueberry muffins
- white: cottage cheese, milk, plain yogurt, rice, mayonnaise

Color Stories **T P K**

Please see Appendix E for a list of art-related books. *Slobodkina's Caps for Sale* is an excellent one to read and act out. Children will enjoy stacking the red, blue, brown, and gray caps. They can take turns being the peddler or monkeys.

3. Shape

Shape is an appropriate criterion for critiquing two-dimensional art that has length and width (see Figure 7–3). Specifically, what is a shape? Shape

- refers to the outside form of an object.
- is the edge of an enclosed space.

FIGURE 7–3   *Michelle learns about shape by painting on round paper.*

SECTION THREE Art and Aesthetics

- is defined by a line or outline, or by contrasting color or texture in the surrounding area.
- represents positive space or figure.
- is created by connecting lines.

Shape has its own qualities and personalities. Some characteristics are

- simple or complex
- circular or angular
- geometric, including circle, square, rectangle, or triangle; or nongeometric, including irregular, freeform, organic, or amorphic
- active or quiet
- clearly defined or vaguely defined
- tall or short
- big and large; or small and little
- open or closed
- solid, heavy, massive; or open, light
- proportional or nonproportional
- concave or convex
- transparent or opaque
- hard or soft
- abstract or realistic
- symmetrical or asymmetrical
- precise or vague

Here are some activities that help children learn about shape.

Sandpaper Shapes

Geometric shapes, including circles, squares, triangles, rectangles, diamonds, and so on, can be cut out of pieces of sandpaper and mounted on sturdy cardboard. Children will enjoy using their fingers and hands to feel the shapes. Older children can progress to feeling only the outlines of shapes done in sandpaper.

Bean Bag Shapes

Children will enjoy manipulating and tossing beanbags that have been cut into geometric shapes. Shape beanbags can vary in size, shape, and color. They can be sorted and classified as well as tossed in a basket or dropped in a pail.

Puzzling Shapes

Geometric shapes can be carefully drawn with a ruler on poster board. Use a different color for each shape for younger children. Older children will not need the color clue. Cut each shape into a number of pieces. Color code the pieces on the back if necessary. Laminate the individual pieces and trim the excess. Match the number and sizes of the pieces with your age group. For example, a square cut in half diagonally may challenge a toddler but might bore a kindergartner.

Sew a Shape

Trim the raised edges off plastic foam meat trays. Cut each into a different geometric shape. Sturdy cardboard could also be used. Use a hole punch to carefully punch an inner outline of the shape. Encourage children to sew the shape by following the line of holes that outlines the shape. They can use a shoelace or thick yarn rather than thread. Use a large plastic needle or tape the beginning end to get it through the holes. Tie a large knot, button, or bead at the end so that it will not pull through. Some children will sew with an over-under, in-and-out motion as one would do with needle and thread. Others may prefer to loop or lace around the edge. Either of these is preferred to randomly connecting the holes without any notice of shape.

A piece of Peg-Board with the outline of a shape drawn through the holes could also be used. The children could use golf tees rather than yarn to complete the outline of the shape.

Safety Shapes

An awareness of shape serves many purposes beyond mere aesthetic beauty. Different shapes are used on signs that help people live, walk, and drive safely. The same is true for colors. Even if one cannot read a sign, the shape and color tell us what to do. Take a short neighborhood walk and look for safety signs, such as STOP. Safety shapes include the octagon, triangle, diamond, and circle. Children may want to make red, green, and yellow circles and paste them in proper order against a black background to make a traffic light.

Shape Stamps   P K

Children enjoy placing objects on an inked stamp pad and stamping that impression on a piece of paper. Find items that have round, square, rectangular, and triangular shapes. The round edge of a plastic hair roller is ideal for a round shape. Find hair rollers in different sizes. Encourage children to creatively combine the shapes into a design or picture.

Shape Spatter Paint   K S

Cut geometric shapes out of sturdy cardboard. Place a sheet of paper into the lid of a box. Place one shape on the paper. Place a thin screen over the top. Dip an old toothbrush in paint. Carefully brush across the screen, making sure that the paint is spattering around the edge of the shape. Remove the screen and carefully lift up the shape. The outline of the shape will appear on the paper. Repeat the process, creatively combining shapes at a different sitting as a separate activity.

There are many standard activities that are appropriate for learning about color as well as shape. Some are described below.

Signs   T P K

Signs or displays of colors and color names as well as shapes and their corresponding names help children learn these concepts. A color caterpillar can have a body made up of different-colored sections. Each circular ball of the body is a different color. A shape train can have a regular locomotive but cars of different geometric shapes. The names can be neatly printed above or below the items in each. Remember to post these at children's eye level rather than high up at adult level.

Manipulative Games   P K

Traditional games can be specifically designed and adapted to learn about shapes and color. Recommended examples include

- bingo
- lotto
- dominoes
- card games, including old maid, rummy, hearts, and fish

Browse through the aisles of a toy store or the pages of a toy catalogue, noting board games and manipulative materials. Then, creatively adapt your own version.

Match and Memory   P K

Make pairs of colors or shapes on index cards. Encourage children to match pairs. Older children enjoy turning all the color or shape cards over and trying to remember where the pairs are. If the two cards that are turned up match, the player gets another turn.

Classify   P K

Children can be challenged to find different ways to classify an array of cards. Index cards can be grouped on the basis of color, shape, and size. Older children will enjoy playing with a total deck of twelve cards per color. For example,

- Red: circle, square, rectangle, triangle; small, medium, large

If you use this formula for each of the three primary colors, you will end up with a total of thirty-six cards.

Gone Fishing   P K

Draw an outline of a fish on a series of index cards. Add a color or shape to each. Staple a paper clip at the mouth of each fish shape. Find a paper towel roll to use as a fishing rod. Tie a length of string to one end and a small magnet at the other. Spread the fish out on the floor on top of a piece of blue construction paper for the water. Encourage children to catch a fish and name the color or shape.

Partner Match   P K

This is a good activity for the entire group. Give each child an outline of a geometric shape or color to hold. Older children may enjoy working with shapes of different colors. Gather children in a circle, holding up their shapes. Have them carefully look around to find someone who is holding the same shape, then take turns finding the partner whose shape matches. Exchange and repeat.

Flip-Flop Books

Find a small book of index cards that are bound with spiral wire binding. Neatly cut each card in half. Actually, you will have too many cards, so you may want to carefully remove some. Or you can use the book to cover color, shape, and other concepts. Open up the book to any page. You will have a top and bottom section on the right and left sides, four index-card sections. For example, for the red page in the color book, find or draw something red in the upper half of the right page. Carefully print the word *red* in red marker on the bottom half of the right page. Find or draw something else that is red, but carefully divide it up between the top and bottom halves of the left side. Encourage children to flipflop through the various pages, top and bottom, until they find a match. For example, the red balloon (top right) with the word in red (lower right) matches the completed picture of a red apple on the left.

4. Mass or Volume

Mass and volume are appropriate criteria for critiquing three-dimensional art, which has height, length, and width. What a circle is to two-dimensional shape, a sphere is to three-dimensional mass or volume. What is mass or volume? These are terms that refer to a solid body. An artist such as a sculptor can portray mass or volume in many different ways. Mass or volume can be portrayed as

- open or closed
- heavy, bulky, massive; or light, delicate
- solid, impenetrable, blocklike; or open, penetrable
- opaque or transparent
- geometric or organic
- static or dynamic
- angular or curved

- hard or soft
- large or little, big or small
- stationary or moving

5. Design or Composition

Throughout this book, the term *design* has been used as a polite way to describe anything and everything young children create in art. A scribble of lines, a splash of colors, and an array of shapes have been referred to as designs. Adult artists use design in a different sense, as in overall composition. Design or composition is the overall mark of success, the standard of achievement, and the frosting on the cake. Design and composition as artistic criteria attempt to address the following questions.

- Did the artist accomplish what he or she originally set out to do? Was the artist successful?
- Do line, shape, color, texture, and form blend and work together as a unified whole? Is the arrangement of these artistic elements pleasing and satisfying?
- Does the finished work impart a sense of overall order, coherence, equilibrium, and organization?
- Did the artist strike a balance between monotony and chaos or unity and variety?
- Is there a focal point, emphasis, center of interest, or dominant spot that attracts and holds attention? Does it make the viewer want to return and admire again and again?

With a good design or composition, the answer to the above questions would be yes. Adult artists walk a fine line between unity, variety, and contrast. It is difficult to create a unified work that hangs together while adding novelty, variety, contrast, and an element of surprise to make it interesting. Child artists, who are less concerned with their finished products, may have little concern for design and composition. We can, however, use the principles of design and composition to talk about works of art and make children aware of the planning and energy that often accompany the making of art.

Overall design and composition, although less directly relevant to early childhood art than some of the other criteria, do form an arch or backdrop for the other criteria.

6. Pattern

Pattern surrounds us. Fence posts, steps, rungs of a ladder, railroad tracks, and spokes on a wheel all suggest a repetitive pattern. Patterns not only appear in art and skills in patterning also facilitate learning in the curricular areas of math and reading. Pattern

- refers to the treatment given to a surface
- suggests flow, rhythm, motion, or movement
- suggests regularity and repetition.
- can be made with forms, shapes, lines, colors, textures, or symbols that move across a surface in a recurring sequence.

Patterns have their own identity. They can be

- ornate and fancy; or plain
- regular or irregular
- symmetrical or asymmetrical
- sequenced or alternating

Here are some activities for learning about pattern.

Sponge Painting   **P K S**

Cut different geometric and abstract shapes out of household sponges. Encourage children to identify a pattern, e.g., circle-square-circle, and repeat that pattern on their paper. The pattern can be arranged in horizontal, vertical, or diagonal fashion (see Figure 7–4).

Pattern Printing   **P K S**

Provide an array of items to print with. Examples include cookie cutters, lids, corks, and bottle tops. Encourage children to identify a pattern and repeat it on their papers. Encourage them to come up with different ways to repeat their patterns horizontally, vertically, or diagonally by dipping their items in paint and making a pattern.

Pattern Picture   **K S**

Shapes cut out of wallpaper, fabric scraps, or gift wrap can be glued or pasted in a repetitive sequence. For example, a pattern could consist of scraps of

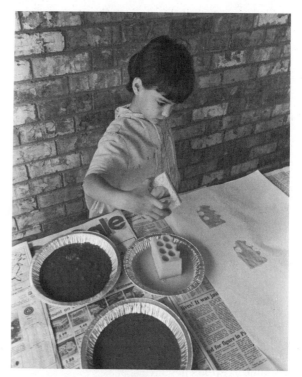

FIGURE 7–4   *Making shapes with sponges dipped in paint*

white burlap, foil, gift wrap, and white burlap glued in a row. A different pattern sequence could follow below, or the same pattern could be repeated.

String a Pattern   **P K**

Children can use wooden beads and a shoelace to create a pattern and series of repeated patterns. Children may enjoy repeating a pattern that a teacher begins. Others enjoy making a pattern as it appears on an index card. Remember to tie a large knot at one end. The lacing end should be pointed and reinforced with tape.

7. Space

An artist's ultimate space is determined by the size of the canvas, be it paper, cardboard, wood, or a shoe box. Within the overall space, the artist must deal with the problem of arranging elements. How many shapes or symbols will be used? Where will they be placed? How much room will be left? How

FIGURE 7–5   Example of positive and negative space

much blank space will remain? Basically, there are two types of space:

1. Positive space
   Positive space is the space taken up with lines, colors, shapes, and forms. Subject matter, content, and design occupy positive space.
2. Negative space
   Negative space is the space left between or surrounding subject matter, symbols, or shapes.

Positive space refers to the shape, and negative space is what is left empty. In Figure 7–5, the white star occupies positive space and the black background represents negative space.

Artists use space in different ways. Some artworks are completely filled with vibrant colors and exciting designs (positive space), with little white paper (negative space) showing. Other works may highlight one object or symbol by surrounding it with much negative space.

Some of the different ways artists can use space include

- positive or negative
- unoccupied, empty, sparse; or occupied, filled, dense
- vertical, horizontal, or diagonal
- symmetrical or asymmetrical
- ordered or random
- balanced or unbalanced

The following activity is for helping children learn about space.

Stencil

A stencil can be cut out of cardboard. Use an X-Acto knife or safety razor blade to cut out a simple shape, for example, a star. The cutout star is positive space.

The surrounding area is negative. Children can hold the star securely on a piece of paper. They can use their drawing or printing hands to mark around the star, using chalk, crayon, or paint. Chalk is preferred because of its ability to combine with other colors. Also, it does less damage to the stencil than paint. Children can also use the surrounding piece that the star was cut from. Instead of chalking away from the star stencil, they now stroke inward.

8. Balance

When the forms appear to be in proportion to each other, the picture is said to have balance, equilibrium, or harmony. Balance involves how an artist uses positive and negative space (see Figure 7–6). Basically, there are two ways of achieving balance:

1. Symmetrical or formal
   With this type of balance, the shapes are evenly or equally balanced around some point, e.g., up or down, right or left, horizontally, vertically, radially, or diagonally. Think of two children of the same weight balanced on the two ends of a seesaw. This is symmetrical or formal balance. Symmetrical balance is often evident in the artwork of children. For example, a house painted on the right side symmetrically balances a large tree on the left. This type of balance is not bad or wrong; it is merely obvious, and gets boring with repeated use.
2. Asymmetrical or informal
   With this type of balance, the objects are not evenly or equally balanced from a point. For example, a house painted near the upper left corner can be asymmetrically balanced with half of a large tree emerging from the right edge of the paper. The balance is unusual and intriguing.

There are many ways to achieve balance. A dark color may balance lighter ones. A massive shape may be balanced with a few smaller ones.

9. Texture

Texture refers to the surface quality of a work of art. How does it feel? Layers of paint, dried finger paint, and a fabric collage all have texture or a certain feel to them. Texture is a term that is appropriate to

FIGURE 7–6   *How is this painting balanced?*

discussing and critiquing collage, construction, assemblage, and other three-dimensional art activities. Texture can be actual or implied. Young children work with actual textures. Adult artists use both. Implied texture involves technical proficiency in skillfully using the medium to suggest wood grain or peeling rust that does not actually exist on the canvas.

Some terms that relate to texture in art are

- rough, bumpy; or smooth
- hard or soft
- coarse or fine
- wet, sticky, or dry
- raised or lowered
- flat or layered
- dull or shiny
- pebbled
- granular
- rubbery
- slippery, slick
- spongy
- furry, fuzzy
- sharp

The element of texture will be explored further in Chapter 9. Here are two art activities to help children learn about texture.

Texture Collage

Provide an array of textured objects. Encourage children to glue or paste an array of textured items onto a piece of sturdy paper or cardboard. See Appendix A for artistic junk to include. Since nature items have such a variety of textures, they can be included.

Texture Rubbings

Go on a texture hunt with the children. Both indoor and outdoor environments offer a wealth of textures. For example, placing a piece of white paper over the bark on a tree and rubbing with the side of a crayon will produce an impression or rubbing. The same thing will happen if you rub over cement, wood grain, coins, a license plate, corrugated cardboard, or an embossed greeting card. Encourage children to overlap and creatively combine their rubbings. Older children might enjoy sketching a very simple picture containing large objects, such as a house and a tree. Later, they can finish their picture with rubbed areas. For example, one could rub with a dark crayon over bark in the area sketched for a tree trunk.

MAKING PRINTS

Most young children have had experience making prints at home. Rubbing a food-stained mouth on a white bath towel or napkin will leave a print. Muddy shoes will leave a print on the kitchen floor, and touching a wall with dirty hands will leave fingerprints. Many children arrive in the morning with a print of Mom's lipstick on their face from a kiss.

Printing is an extension of painting. Painting involves making movements with a brush or other painter across a surface. Printing involves stamping paper with an object dipped in paint. Printing involves less whole-arm activity and greater concern for placement and overall design. Discuss and show examples of patterns in wallpaper, brick wall, windows, fabric, gift wrap, flowers, and nature when introducing printing. Tempera paints should be fairly thick for the printed impression to show up. A variety of papers can be used.

Young children may approach printing activities as an extension of painting. They may use print making tools as things to paint with. In turn, they may smear objects all over the paper, resulting in a paper covered with paint but not clear prints. This tendency reflects a process approach to making art and should not be interpreted as a lack of success at teaching print making.

Here are some printing activities.

Hint Place a thick stack of newspapers under the printing paper. The thickness will help make a good clear print.

Hint To make a print pad, place a few paper towels on a flat plate. Pour on some tempera paint. Press the printing items on the wet pad. This will cover them evenly with paint.

Monoprint

A pane of glass, sheet of Plexiglas, acrylic cutting board, or any nonporous surface, such as a Formica tabletop, can be used. Children can paint their picture or design right on the surface. Use fairly thick paints. Place a larger piece of paper over the painted area. Rub gently with brayer or hand. Carefully lift up. As the term *monoprint* suggests, you will produce one print off the painted surface. Designs can also be etched into a solid mass of paint before the print is taken. Children will also enjoy hand painting on the surface and having a monoprint taken.

Ink-Pad Print   K S

Children enjoy placing their fingers on an ink pad and making a stamped impression on a piece of paper. Ink pads come in colors other than black. What does the fingerprint impression suggest? Children may want to use fine-point markers to make their basic fingerprints into something else by adding body parts, wheels, and details.

Small objects with interesting shapes and textures include

- corks
- coins
- paper clips
- buttons
- seashells
- caps and bottle tops
- nuts and bolts
- carved wooden blocks
- eraser tops on pencils
- spools
- hair rollers
- Styrofoam pieces and squiggles
- plastic tops from milk containers
- embossed guest soaps
- erasers in different shapes

These can also be printed as described above. Re-ink with liquid ink when the print appears dull. Several thicknesses of heavy paper towels or an old washcloth soaked with tempera paint can also serve as a stamp pad.

Sponge Printing

Sponges can be creatively cut into an array of shapes and sizes. Encourage children to dip the shapes in paint and make a stamped print. Geometric shapes can be arranged to form a picture. Or children can repeat a sequence or pattern of printed shapes. Provide one or more shapes for each color. Wash out a sponge if it is accidentally dipped in a different color. (See Figure 7–7.)

Food Print

Food is generally too expensive to be used for art. However, should a parent or grocer donate surplus fruits or vegetables, they can be used in a printing activity. Vegetables and fruits that can be cut and used for printing include

- orange
- potato
- lemon
- apple
- carrot
- turnip
- radish
- green pepper
- cabbage
- cauliflower
- tomato
- onion
- avocado
- mushroom

A Corny Print   K S

Painting an ear of corn and rolling it like a rolling pin on a piece of paper makes a very good print.

Roller Printing   K S

Printing with an ear of corn is one example of roller printing. Other examples of rollers that can be used for printing include

- a hair roller—insert a pencil to hold when rolling
- a long bottle, dowel, or plastic tumbler wrapped with a yarn or string design
- a toilet paper roll with shapes cut out
- a cardboard paper towel roll with shapes cut out
- a brayer with raised shapes glued onto it
- a rolling pin with raised shapes and designs or flocked wallpaper glued onto it
- a spool with lines and designs carved or etched in—insert a pencil to hold when rolling
- a tin can with yarn or string glued to it

Roll the roller in a low dish, pan, or large plastic foam tray of paint. Roll on paper.

FIGURE 7–7   A sponge print

Kitchen Gadget Printing

An array of kitchen gadgets is listed in the section on Paints and Painting Accessories in Chapter 6. Others include

- plastic or nylon utensils
- slotted spoon and fork
- spatula
- pie slice lifter
- wire whisk
- funnel
- fly swatter
- potato masher
- pancake flipper
- cookie cutters
- plastic forks
- pie tin (bottom)
- embossed lids and bottoms of jars
- plastic scourer and scrubber with knob handle

These can be dipped in paint and printed on paper. Encourage children to creatively combine and overlap printed shapes to form designs or pictures. (See Figure 7–8.)

Recycled Junk Print

Actually, many of the items mentioned in the sections on printing with a stamp pad and with kitchen gadgets could fit in here. See Appendix A for a list of artistic junk. Look for objects with different textures and uneven surfaces. Some items that can be recycled into a printing activity include

- corks
- spools
- combs
- hairbrushes with plastic spikes
- bottle tops and jar lids
- pill bottles and vials
- Styrofoam pieces
- corrugated cardboard
- hair rollers
- keys
- toy cars

FIGURE 7–8 A print made with kitchen gadgets

FIGURE 7–9   Recycled Junk print

- crumpled paper
- bars of soap with raised letters or design
- license plates
- embossed ceramic tiles

Apply paint to the object and place it down on paper. Carefully remove. (See Figure 7–9.)

Plastic Foam Tray Print K S

Trim the raised edges off small plastic foam trays. You should have a flat piece to work with. Draw or etch a picture or design into the plastic, using a Popsicle stick. Press in without breaking through. The incised line will remain white when the tray is covered with ink or paint and printed. Ideally, a brayer is dipped in ink and spread across the tray. Paint can also be brushed on. Paint over the etched surface with a single color of paint. Press a piece of paper over the tray and gently rub with your hand over the entire surface. Carefully lift the paper to see your print. A second print can be taken immediately if paint is left on the tray. Children can make a series of prints this way. Wash the tray before changing colors.

Nature Print   P K S

Items collected from a nature walk can be inked and printed. Look for leaves, pinecones, and other nature specimens with interesting textures and surfaces.

String Printing   K S

Find small blocks of wood or small, sturdy gift boxes. Dip string in white glue and wrap it around the block or box in an interesting design. Or arrange the gluey string in a design on only one side. Let the glue dry. Dip the best side of the block in ink or paint. Place it on paper and gently push down to make an impression. Carefully remove the block to see the print. Repeat and make a continuing series or pattern. Stay with the color chosen rather than trying to wash the printer. Small wood blocks or boxes could also be stamped in an ink pad.

Pieces of dense foam in sheet or tape form can also be cut, built up into raised layers, and glued onto a printer.

Cardboard Print   K S

Secure sturdy cardboard for the background. Cut smaller pieces of cardboard or thick paper and build up a raised picture or design. Glue and let dry. Paint over the design. Press the cardboard on paper. Rub gently all over with your hands. Carefully lift the cardboard to reveal your print.

Corrugated cardboard is highly recommended for building up interesting line designs that go in different directions.

Ceramic Tile Print   K S

Roll a layer of ink or paint on a ceramic tile square. Etch a picture or design, using a cotton swab or your finger. Place a small piece of paper over the tile. Rub gently. Carefully remove the paper to reveal your print. A tile with raised or embossed surfaces will have a prepared surface ready for printing.

Game Piece Print   K S

Dominoes, checkers, game tokens, bingo markers, and magnetic letters and numbers make interesting designs when dipped in paint and used as stampers to make a print.

Bubble Print   K S

Fill a shallow container with water and tempera paint or liquid watercolor to which dishwashing detergent has been added. Two parts tempera paint to one part liquid dishwashing soap is recommended. Stir. Cut out notch near top of straw. Blow bubbles over the rim of the container using a straw. Place white paper on top of the bubbles to get a print. The result will be a print made up of circular designs that can serve as a background for collage, drawing, or other art activity.

Push-Up Stick Print   K S

Ice-cream bars and Popsicles come on a push-up stick. Save the push-up sticks. Cut a design or shape out of Styrofoam and glue it onto a push-up stick. Dip the Styrofoam in paint or on an ink pad and press it on paper.

Crayon Sandpaper Print   K S

Children can draw a picture or design with crayons on a piece of sandpaper. Encourage them to press hard and fill up the sandpaper. An adult can place a piece of white paper over the colored sandpaper and press with a warm iron. The heat will melt the wax from the colored sandpaper and transfer the design or picture to the paper.

Glue Print   K S

Use white liquid glue to draw a design or picture on a piece of cardboard. Make sure the outline or impression is fairly thick. Let the glue dry. Spread the design with ink or paint. Gently press paper on

it. The paint or ink will adhere to the raised dried glue outline. Or glue a picture cut from a magazine to your piece of cardboard. Trace the outline with white liquid glue. Repeat the steps involved in making a glue print. This time you will get a print that resembles the picture cut out of the magazine.

Berry Basket Print   P K

Collect an array of plastic produce baskets with different patterns. Children can use brushes to paint over the bottom design of the baskets or dip in print pads, then apply the baskets to paper.

Bubble Pack Print   T P

Collect an array of packing with small and large bubbles. Lay the packing bubble side up and let child paint on top of bubbles. Lay paper on top, gently rub, and carefully lift off to reveal print.

Balloon Print   K S

Adult should blow up balloons but not so full that they might pop. Encourage children to handle balloons carefully. Balloons can be dipped in paint and gently pressed onto paper. Replace after a few children have handled them, to avoid popping. This activity is recommended for older children. Provide close supervision if used with young children, making sure they do not put balloon pieces in their mouths.

Windup Toy Print   P K

Find windup or battery-operated small toys like cars and trucks. Cover a large table or floor space with butcher paper. Brush paint on wheels, activate, and release on paper. Colorful tracks will appear as the vehicle moves about.

Watercolor Tablet Print   P K

Instead of using the brush provided, children can wet their fingers with water and press them into the watercolor tablets. Gently press fingers onto paper, making oval designs or a combination of creative shapes.

CD-Case Print P K S

Collect clear compact disc cases. Child can paint on the top surface. Carefully place a piece of paper on top and gently lift off a print.

Caster Print P K

Locate round spiked caster cups used under furniture to protect carpets. Provide containers of paint. Encourage children to dip the caster into paint and gently push down on the paper. Lift to see a dotted or spiked print.

Baby Shoe and Sneaker Print P K S

Collect old, small shoes with textured soles. Ask families for donations because once painted and washed they cannot be worn again. Use a brush to apply paint to the sole rather than dipping shoe into paint. Carefully rock entire shoe from heel to toe or vice versa onto paper. Encourage children to creatively overlap and combine shoe shapes.

Make It Yourself Stamp Print K S

Foam shoe inserts are a good material for making your own stamps. The foam can be easily cut into various shapes. An adult can use a glue gun or rubber cement to mount the shapes onto a stamper such as a spool, jar lid or wood block. Use with ink pads and provide small sheets of paper. Small stamped impressions get lost on a large sheet of paper. Children can push stamps into pad and gently stamp on paper. Remind them they need not pound to get the stamp to work. Rubber inner tubing also works well as stamping material. Tempera paint can be substituted for ink pads.

Paraffin Block Print S

Paraffin blocks are sold inexpensively at grocery and craft stores. They are easy to carve, providing more than one side for printing. Children can carve in their own designs using a pointed tool like a craft stick, key, or linoleum cutter. Remind children that letters will come out backwards. Use brush or brayer to spread paint over carved block. Press

paper over the block and gently rub the surface with the hand. Then lift off the print. Paper can first be folded in half or quarters to make greeting cards or stationery.

Feet Print P K

Toy dinosaurs, dolls, and even children's feet can be used. Children will enjoy doing this with their bare feet, outdoors on a warm day. Roll out a length of butcher paper. Pour liquid tempera into shallow containers large enough to accommodate one child's foot. Encourage the children to step in the paint and then press his or her foot to leave a print. Repeat with other foot. Remind children that moving about with painted feet is dangerous. Have handy a bucket for washing feet and towels to dry. This activity is best done one-on-one.

Fold A Print P K S

Encourage children to fold their sheets of paper in half. They can use a spoon to drop one or more colors of liquid tempera onto one side of their paper. Slowly fold over and gently press down, using the hand to rub all over. Carefully open up to see the mirror-image print. Older children can paint half of their desired image near the fold but only on one side. For example, a child who paints half a yellow circle next to the crease will have a sun emerge when the paper is folded and then opened back up.

Leaf and Glue Print K S

Collect an array of leaves and ferns. Child can cover one side of the leaf with glue and press it down on paper, leaving a glue print. Carefully lift off leaf. Sprinkle glitter from shaker or small confetti onto glue print.

Scraped Print K S

Children can paint inside a plastic tray. Using a pointed tool like the handle of a paintbrush, scrape a design or picture into the paint. Before dry, put a piece of paper over the paint using hands to rub all over the surface. Carefully lift to see the scraped print. Remember that scraped letters will appear in reverse on the print.

Oil Paint Print [IMG: ruler icon] **S**

Mix tempera paint and cooking oil in a cup until creamy. Set aside. Fill a round cake pan half full with plain water. Spoon a few drops of the oil paint mixture on top of the water. Use a fork to gently swirl. Next, have child lay a piece of white paper on top of the swirl. Let the paper float for about a minute. Carefully lift the paper out holding on to two corners. Place the print elsewhere to dry. Glitter can be added by shaking from a container. Use this process to design greeting cards or stationery, by first folding white paper in half or quarters.

Salad Spinner Art [IMG: icon] **P K**

Locate one or more salad spinners which are used to rinse and dry a head of lettuce. Remove the top and measure the size of the inside round bottom. Draw a master pattern on cardboard and cut it out. The adult or child can trace individual round shapes on paper and cut out. Place paper inside salad spinner along with one or more marbles dipped in paint. Close and secure lid. Children will need some hand strength and control to rotate the knob. This turns the inside paddle, thereby moving the marbles which create a design. Ask parents for an old salad spinner or try garage sales and second-hand stores.

STENCIL, SPATTER, AND SCREEN PRINTING

Stencil, spatter, and screen printing are fairly involved activities that require some amount of instruction and special tools. It is unlikely that young children will discover on their own how to make a stencil, spatter, or screen print.

Stencil [IMG: ruler icon] **S**

A stencil can be cut from sturdy cardboard or thick paper, including tagboard or poster board. It can also be torn out of construction paper. When you cut a stencil, you actually get two. Recall our discussion of positive and negative space. The shape cut out occupies positive space and is called the positive stencil. The remaining frame or background occupies negative space and is called the negative stencil. Each type of stencil has its own process. Hold the stencil with one hand and use the other hand to stroke from the piece out when using the positive stencil. Hold the background or frame and stroke inward when using the negative stencil.

Stenciling can be done with crayons, paint, or chalk. The author prefers chalk dust dabbed on with cotton balls because of its ability to blend. It also does less damage to the stencil than paint does. Paint can be gently dabbed on with cotton balls, a small sponge, or a brush. Short, stiff-bristle brushes used with an upright gentle dabbing motion are recommended for the skilled stenciler. Whatever is chosen to stencil with, do not saturate it with paint. Be careful that the paint, chalk, or crayon does not get under the stencil, causing smears.

It may be difficult for very young children to cut their own stencil out of cardboard. Perhaps it could be drawn by them but cut out by an adult Encourage them to design a very simple picture with a minimum of fine detail. An X-Acto knife can be used to cut out a stencil. Remember not to cut through the frame to get to the inside. Very young children can tear out a vague abstract shape that will work very well in a stencil activity.

Stencils can also be painted with spray paint or sprayed from a sprayer, e.g., a bug sprayer filled with liquid tempera. This method is best done outdoors. Place the paper in the lid of a large box. Tape the back of the stencil in place. Spray with paint. Let dry. Carefully remove the stencil.

Paper Plate Stencil [IMG: ruler icon] **K S**

Put a paper plate down on a piece of thick paper and trace around it. Cut out the circle and fold it into a small wedge. Cut bits out of the folds to make a stencil. Unfold the stencil and put it back on the paper plate. Dip a sponge in tempera paint and gently blot paint on the stencil, transferring the design onto the paper plate.

Spatter Printing

You will need a large but not too deep box, a screeń or mesh wire (e.g., a window screen, kitchen grease guard, or metal strainer), and an old toothbrush. Cut or tear a stencil out of paper. Or items with interesting shapes, such as coins, a comb, cookie cutters, keys, and nature specimens, can be used as positive stencils and placed on a sheet of paper inside the box. Dip your toothbrush in paint and gently move it across the screen, releasing a mist of paint. Dark colors will show up best on white paper. The paint will spatter and outline the stencil or objects. The space taken up with the positive stencil or objects will remain white or the color of the background paper. Carefully move the stencil or objects and repeat with a different color. Switch stencils and work with the negative stencil.

Young children will need to use a large box covered with a fairly large spatter screen. Older children may be able to use a small, handheld food strainer and move it around the stencil. They can carefully rub chalk across the food strainer at the same time. A small spatter screen can also be made by carefully cutting the top and bottom off a sturdy small box. Attach wire or screen to the top. Use with small stencils. Or fasten plastic mesh or screen into an embroidery hoop. If no screen is available, scrape the bristles of the toothbrush toward you with a stick. If you scrape away from you, the spray will spatter you. The thumb can also be used to scrape bristles.

Printing

Silk-screen printing is actually a stencil method of printing. Paint is forced through a piece of stretched mesh fabric that has been prepared with a design. The paint is printed onto fabric or paper. Silk screen is a way to create several prints of the same image and therefore recommended for making greeting cards or stationery. First, a screen must be prepared.

An embroidery hoop, an old picture frame, or a frame cut from the lid of a shoe box can be used for screen printing. Use an old nylon stocking or a piece of silk, organdy, dotted swiss, or cheesecloth for the silk-screen material. Cut it larger than your frame, pull it tight, and secure it with tacks, tape, or nails. Cut a stencil and place it on paper. Put the silk-screen frame over the stencil. Use a brush, tongue depressor, or cardboard strip to gently spread thick paint on the silk screen, which will cover the stencil. Carefully lift your silk-screen frame. Thoroughly rinse the silk screen after each application of paint. Add different colors if desired. Repeat the pattern while overlapping or creatively combining pieces from different stencils.

SUMMARY

Artistic elements are the building blocks of artist expression. Artists process with line, color, and shape until these elements are successfully combined into a harmonious design or overall composition. Children go through the same steps, but on a more informal and often unplanned basis. These elements are the criteria for making, understanding, appreciating, and critiquing art. Our intent is not to turn children into art critics. That would be developmentally inappropriate. It is our intent, however, to use the vocabulary of the artistic elements so that children can learn to value and directly participate in the arts. They will come to know good art when they see it and will be able to use the artistic elements in justifying their evaluation.

Suggested Activities

1. Visit an art museum or check out books with art reproductions. Use the artistic elements in analyzing a work of art.

2. Implement an art activity involving one or more of the artistic elements.

3. Complete the Color Clock activity at the end of this unit.

4. Facilitate a printing experience with children.

Review

A. List the major artistic elements discussed in this unit:

1.   6.
2.   7.
3.   8.
4.   9.
5.

B. Complete the following color equations:

red + _____   = orange
yellow + blue   = _____
_____ + _____ = purple

C. Put the proper color term in front of each color: P   for Primary
                                                        S   for Secondary
                                                        I   for Intermediate
                                                        N   for Neutral

_____ yellow-orange   _____ blue
_____ green   _____ blue-green
_____ yellow-green   _____ orange
_____ red   _____ red-violet
_____ black   _____ yellow
_____ red-orange   _____ white
_____ blue-violet   _____ purple/violet

D. Match the following columns related to color.
   1. The colors that are used to produce all other colors.
   2. Orange, green, and purple.
   3. Mixing a primary and a secondary color results in this.
   4. These colors are opposite each other on the color wheel.
   5. Black and white are examples.
   6. A pure, unmixed color.
   7. Lightness or darkness of a color.
   8. Brightness or dullness of a color.
   9. Adding white will produce this.
   10. Adding black will produce this.
   11. Red, yellow, and orange are examples.
   12. Blue, green, and purple are examples.

   _____ neutral colors
   _____ complementary colors
   _____ secondary colors
   _____ primary colors
   _____ warm colors
   _____ hue
   _____ value
   _____ intensity
   _____ tint
   _____ shade
   _____ cool colors
   _____ intermediate colors

E. Match the following columns related to artistic elements.
   1. Has hue, value, and intensity.
   2. Can be symmetrical or asymmetrical.
   3. Can be positive or negative.
   4. A recurring, repeated sequence.
   5. Refers to the integrated whole.
   6. Refers to three-dimensional art.
   7. A visible mark made by moving an artistic tool across a surface.
   8. Refers to the surface quality of a work of art.
   9. Refers to two-dimensional art.

   _____ texture
   _____ balance
   _____ space
   _____ pattern
   _____ mass/volume
   _____ design/composition
   _____ shape/form
   _____ color
   _____ line

Color Clock

1. Get white paper.

2. Use watercolors.

3. Draw a large circle
   —black-in center
   —blob of paint

4. Fill-in (with blob of paint)
   12 = yellow (primary)
   4 = red (primary)
   8 = blue (primary)

5. Mix (secondary colors)
   12 + 4 = 2 (add blob and name of color to clock)
   4 + 8 = 6 (add blob and name of color to clock)
   8 + 12 = 10 (add blob and name of color to clock)

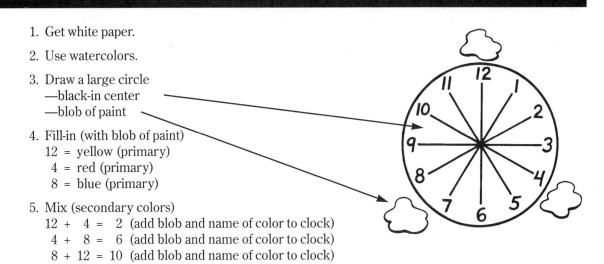

6. Mix (intermediate colors)

    12 + 2 = 1 (add blob and name of color to clock)
      2 + 4 = 3 (add blob and name of color to clock)
      4 + 6 = 5 (add blob and name of color to clock)
      6 + 8 = 7 (add blob and name of color to clock)
      8 + 10 = 9 (add blob and name of color to clock)
    10 + 12 = 11 (add blob and name of color to clock)

P. S. Mathematically incorrect!

7. Let dry.

8. Refer to back cover of this book.

9. Turn in to instructor.

CHAPTER 8

Aesthetics

Do you think children would enjoy visiting this area? What might they do here?
The area is inviting. The beanbag chairs make it soft and snuggly. The thatched roof adds a tropical touch, while the mosquito netting offers the illusion of privacy. It's a great place to visit when you want to be by yourself, listen to a story, or read a book. Because it's nonpunitive it might be a good place to go if you need a time out. Come visit when you need to get away from others. It is an aesthetically pleasing environment.

OBJECTIVES

After studying this chapter, the student will be able to

- Define and provide a rationale for aesthetics in early childhood education
- Discuss the aesthetic attitude, process, and response
- Discuss the teacher's role in aesthetics
- Provide experiences using watercolors and ink

INTRODUCTION

Think of a time when you found yourself in a beautiful place. Maybe it was inside a cathedral or atop a mountain. How did it make you feel? Full of awe and wonder? Relaxed and comfortable? These positive feelings can also happen in your classroom when you make it an awesome, beautiful place to be. Although taste is individual, adults and even children appreciate beauty and beautiful things. Working in a pleasing environment will accomplish four goals. First, being surrounded by beauty and having beautiful experiences will help children's aesthetic development and enrich their lives. Second, it will make the environment a pleasant place for you and the children to be for a large amount of the day.

Third, you will feel good about being there while reducing your stress level. Fourth, it will subtly influence children's behavior in positive ways.

What is aesthetics and why should it be addressed in early childhood? This chapter attempts to answer these two basic questions. Our concern for the young child's aesthetic development and education stems from our wider concern for the whole child. Young children are aesthetic experts. They demonstrate the aesthetic attitude in their spontaneity, wonder, and amazement at things that adults may take for granted. What is the teacher's role in aesthetics? Teachers can be aesthetic models in the way they dress, behave, and communicate. The indoor and outdoor environment can also be aesthetically pleasing and stimulating.

Early Childhood Art Education (R. S.)

The following is a discussion between the author (R. S.) and Aline D. Wolf (A. W.) who is the founder of the Pennsylvania Montessori Academy in Altoona, Pennsylvania. She is the author of *Mommy, It's a Renoir* and four volumes of accompanying art postcards entitled "Child-Size Masterpieces."

R. S.   Some critics believe that art education and aesthetics are too advanced and abstract for young children. What is your response?

A. W.   I disagree. Young children are constantly absorbing stimuli from their environment. It follows that we should put beautiful things in their environment for them to absorb. For example, pretend you are planning to use pictures of animals as part of your unit of study or theme. What do you use as resources? There are many beautiful art prints depicting animals which could be used. Examples include Durer's "Hare" and Franz Marc's "Red Horses." When studying the circus, remember that Renoir, Picasso, and Chagall have all painted pictures on this theme.

With three-year-olds my goal is for them to look and enjoy. I am not concerned with teaching them the title or artist's name. Over time they begin to note details while developing good taste. Aesthetics is not something you can schedule once a week for thirty minutes. You need to expose children to beautiful things on an ongoing basis.

R. S.   Could you clarify Montessori's views on art and aesthetics in the early years?

A. W.   Actually, Maria Montessori was a pioneer in addressing the importance of aesthetics in the environment of young children. She insisted that children's surroundings be beautiful. She suc-

continued

Early Childhood Art Education (R. S.), continued

ceeded in bringing beauty into the Children's House by insisting, first of all, on cleanliness and order. On the walls and shelves she used light-colored paint, which never clashed with the bright colors of her materials. She accented this harmonious, peaceful setting with plants, fresh flowers, a beautiful shell collection or even fragile china dishes, which she allowed the children to use. The walls were hung with attractive pictures, carefully chosen and representing simple scenes which would interest children. Since children absorb from their environment, children placed in a beautiful and aesthetically pleasing environment would absorb good taste.

For Montessori, art appreciation begins at a very early age. Materials including the metal insets, color tablets, and geometric shapes foster an indirect preparation for art in that each trains the eyes and hands. Montessori did not devise materials which would specifically foster appreciation. That's why I devised my art postcards.

R. S. Some critics believe that Montessori programs provide too little emphasis on creativity and free expression. They believe there are too few open-ended materials and too little creative messing about. What do you say?

A. W. I disagree. In my visits to Montessori classrooms across the United States I have seen easels and clay provided for free expression. This has been the norm rather than the exception. Other Montessori programs include a wider range of art activities and materials for free expression.

R. S. Aline, I visited one Montessori classroom where only one color of paint was set out at the easel. There was no opportunity for color mixing. Other children were pasting precut shapes onto a sheet of black construction paper. Is this typical?

A. W. No. Montessori never recommended that children paint with only one color. I would need to know more about the children. Perhaps this particular child would benefit from using only one color. Maybe the children were very young and being introduced to paint and painting for the very first time.

R. S. Tell us about your art postcards.

A. W. We know that children learn best by touching and handling. Montessori herself said that the hand was the child's chief teacher. Yet fine art is something we have put out of children's reach or say "Don't touch!" In doing so we deprive them. My art postcards try to reconcile this. They uphold Montessori's principles regarding the importance of visual stimulation while encouraging the use of the hands. The result is a much deeper dimension of learning.

I developed the art postcards so that all children could firsthand experience the beauty of fine art. The cards work in any classroom. One need not be a Montessori teacher to use them. They are inexpensive, small, lightweight, and ready for use individually or in small or large groups.

I also developed the art postcards to combat so much of the ugliness in our world. Offhand I think of lunch boxes, binders, and children's clothing that depict monsters and creatures. Why? We should be giving our children the best. Fine art need not be reserved for the affluent or those

continued

Early Childhood Art Education (R. S.) continued

living close to art museums. Art postcards bring the museum to the children. With them, all children can know beautiful art while holding it in their hands.

I also suspect that some teachers who do not have a background in art may be uncomfortable with this strategy. I believe that teachers and parents learn about art as they use these materials with children. That is how I learned about art. If readers want to learn more about my materials they can write: Parent Child Press, P. O. Box 675, Hollidaysburg, Pennsylvania 16648-0675.

Art postcards can also be purchased at museum gift shops. It is a good idea to include postcards of paintings in local museums so that children are familiar with the painting when they visit the museum to see the originals.

R. S.   Share some other strategies you have either used or observed.

A.W.   • Give children one or two of their favorite art postcards to keep in their own folder at school.
   • Encourage children and families to collect art postcards.
   • Encourage children to collect art postcards as souvenirs of their trips to art museums.
   • Have children mail art postcards to the school and recognize their donation by displaying their name as donor.
   • Hang lovely art prints in the classroom. For example, display one at child's eye level on the door.
   • Encourage parents to hang a child's favorite art print on their bedroom door or wall.

AESTHETICS

Aesthetics is an abstract concept that means "perception" in Greek. Although we may feel it is important that children learn something about aesthetics, we may not be quite sure what the term entails. Aesthetics is not synonymous with art. Aesthetics includes art, and the other expressive arts like music and dance, but it also goes beyond them. Just what is aesthetics? Aesthetics

• is a nondiscursive and metaphorical way of knowing and experiencing.
• involves the love and pursuit of beauty as found in art, movement, music, and life.
• is an awareness and appreciation of the natural beauty found in nature and one's surroundings.
• is a basic human response to life.
• means being a beholder of beauty and savoring beautiful things in the world around us.

• involves being connected with one's experiences.
• links knowing and feeling, the cognitive and affective.

Some examples of aesthetic experiences are

• touching the sparkling design of frost on a window.
• viewing the translucent silkiness of a spiderweb.
• watching the movements of leaves and branches on a windy day.
• seeing and touching the delicate petals of a rosebud.
• listening to and moving to the beat of an ethnic folk song.
• stopping to savor the aroma of freshly baked bread.
• sitting in wet sand and splashing in the waves on the shore.
• slowly sipping hot cider while marveling at all the different colors crackling in a campfire.

- admiring the linear design and pattern in a skyscraper.
- noticing the wood grains in a row of blocks.

The type of beauty that aesthetics pursues is the type taken for granted in our everyday lives, rather than the artificial Hollywood-type definition of beauty.

RATIONALE

Why are aesthetics and aesthetic education important in early childhood? There are five reasons. First, our humanistic concern for the whole child motivates us to provide for all aspects of child development. Second, it is our belief that children who marvel at beauty in the world around them will be able to appreciate the beauty of letters, words, numbers, stories, poems, formulas, books, symbols, and people of other cultures. Third, children with the aesthetic sense will develop into adults who know and value good design and can use this as wise consumers in choosing vehicles, clothing, home furnishings, and entertainment as well as on a wider level in planning cities, highways, and attempting to solve problems of pollution, war, poverty, and urban blight. Fourth, it is important for children to value the arts and directly participate in a variety of the arts. Fifth, aesthetic experiences foster concept development.

Aesthetics is a branch of philosophy concerned with an individual's pursuit of and response to beauty. Aesthetics involves

1. attitude
2. process
3. response

1. Aesthetic Attitude

The aesthetic attitude involves:

- openness or childlike freshness
- spontaneity
- intense focusing on the here and now
- a sense of joy, wonder, marvel, or excitement
- willingness to perceive as if experiencing something for the very first time
- commitment or willingness to "stop and smell the roses"

Young children constantly demonstrate the aesthetic attitude. They are sensory gluttons who need to look at, listen to, touch, smell, and taste everything they come in contact with. This may prove embarrassing to some adults: "Nina, please don't touch the daisies." Over time Nina may decide not to wonder at flowers. She may learn to take them for granted. Or, as her mother told her, "If you've seen one, you've seen them all." Unfortunately, Nina's mother has lost the aesthetic attitude. The author observed a preschool field trip to the library. The children were stopping to watch and listen to the sights and sounds at a construction site. The teacher was hurrying them up, urging them to walk faster to get to their destination. A rich sensory experience was lost. We live in a too-fast-paced world. We rush from home to work. In the process we may ignore rainbows in the sky, colorful patterns in rain puddles, or daisies growing alongside the freeway. The aesthetic experience takes time. It means being frozen for the moment and totally caught up in the here and now.

2. Aesthetic Process

The aesthetic process is intrinsically motivating. Children sense and perceive for the sheer joy of it. The aesthetic process involves active engagement rather than passive taking in. It means using all the senses to ravish an object or experience, getting completely lost or totally consumed. Examples of the aesthetic process include:

- listening attentively to music rather than merely hearing a song
- visually exploring or quietly contemplating a work of art rather than merely glancing at it
- manipulating and feeling a peacock's feather rather than quickly touching it

Aesthetic processing takes time and a commitment to flow with the experience. Children are more aesthetically proficient than adults. They thoroughly examine their world with all their senses. Adults can learn much more about aesthetics from watching children explore the world.

3. Aesthetic Response

The aesthetic attitude and process result in an appreciative response or reaction on many different levels. Our affective response may involve a sense of wonder, appreciation, surprise, a feeling of being moved or touched, awe, exhilaration, or being carried away. We may get lost in the aesthetic experience and totally caught up or consumed for the instant. At the physiological level, our response may result in a smile, grin, laugh, perspiration, shiver, chill, heavy sigh, or even "goose bumps."

Our reactions will also entail a mental response in the form of a decision, judgment, or evaluation. One may ask

- Was this personally enjoyable, and why?
- Is this work of art, music, or dance good, and why?
- Do I like it, and why?

Our intent is to help children apply simple criteria to discuss and critique works of art. They can learn to separate what is good or bad from what they like or dislike. For example, a young boy may not like ballet, but he can still appreciate the beauty and grace of the movements. Over time, children will slowly construct their own personal preferences and tastes. They need not follow the crowd in believing that what is popular or current must be good. They will come to identify with and value the arts. One hopes that they will grow up reading good books, listening to a variety of music, and with tolerance for different artistic styles. Life will offer them more than being passively entertained by TV.

Expose Not Impose

As early childhood educators, our task is to expose rather than impose. Expose children to a

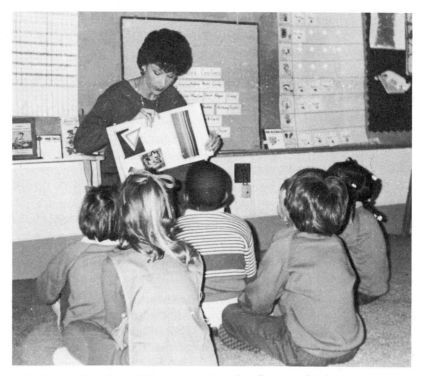

FIGURE 8–1   Exposing children to a variety of art forms and styles

wealth of sensory experiences and variety in each of the arts. Encourage them to critique, develop personal preferences, and value art, music, movement, dance, and literature. Children can use accepted criteria, including the artistic elements, as standards in developing their own preferences. Expose children to a wide variety of art forms and styles without imposing your own preferences. For example, a teacher may not like abstract art, but that does not mean that it is junk or bad, or that realistic art is better. Help children see that art can be good in terms of design or composition even though one may not like it (see Figure 8–1).

TEACHER'S ROLE IN AESTHETICS

What can early childhood educators do to foster aesthetic development? Aesthetics does not come neatly packaged in a kit, series of books, text, unit, or set of materials to purchase. Still, it is important and within our reach. There are guidelines for making the teacher, children, and classroom aesthetically alive. Some of these are discussed here.

Teacher As Aesthetic Model

It is important that the teacher personally invest the time to become aesthetically responsive. Teachers can model their own aesthetic awareness and sensitivity. The way one dresses is an aesthetic statement. One need not dress like a fashion model, however, to make this statement. First and foremost clothing should be neat, comfortable, and appropriate for stooping, moving, playing, and sitting on the floor. We can reflect an appreciation of color and color harmony in choosing articles of clothing and accessories. For example, a young girl is proudly showing off her new sweater. Her teacher asks her to identify the colors. Nikki replies, "It has red and blue." Her teacher replies, "My dress has red and blue in it, too. And I wore my white earrings. I wore the same colors that are in our flag." Or, "Jim, you mixed blue and yellow in your picture and made green. I wore blue slacks with a yellow blouse and my green belt. We match."

Teacher's Inner Beauty

The teacher's inner beauty can be demonstrated by positively relating to all children and valuing their uniqueness. Find something unique and beautiful in each child, and let that child know. Convey beautiful messages. Children appreciate being talked to in regular tones. There is no need to artificially raise the pitch of one's voice and speak in a "syrupy sweet" manner. Refer to oneself as I rather than as Miss Jones or Teacher, as in "Miss Jones doesn't like it when the children are not paying attention," or "Teacher will just have to get some more apple juice for snack, won't she?" Talk to children in a natural voice rather than in a condescending or patronizing tone. Unfortunately, the elderly are often subjected to this same vocal treatment.

Provide for a Wide Variety in the Arts

Children can be exposed to different examples within a variety of the arts. For example, different types of music can be informally introduced throughout the day: slow lullabies or waltzes during rest, classical as background music during snack, and a march or rock-and-roll during cleanup.

Aesthetic Classroom

The classroom can be an aesthetically pleasing and sensory-rich environment (see Figure 8–2). Do a beauty check of your room. Cartoon characters in bright competing colors can be removed from the walls and replaced with aesthetically pleasing artwork, wall hangings, tapestry, weavings, posters, stained glass panels, or prints. Signs on the doors of the classrooms or learning centers can be tastefully constructed, with care taken in the choice of color, material, placement, and printing. Utilize windows and take advantage of the natural light. Hang up objects that play with the light, including mobiles made of cellophane papers and children's art. Items suspended near windows create interesting patterns which move and change throughout the day. Adding mirrors gives a feeling of openness and

FIGURE 8–2   An aesthetically pleasing use of classroom space

reflects all the beauty in your room. Mirrors can be placed in different centers and even on the ceiling for an interesting perspective. Have the children grow plants indoors. An outdoor flower garden provides flowers to display throughout the room. Think quality rather than quantity. Did you ever get the feeling of clutter when visiting some antique shops, model homes, or furniture showrooms that appear to fill every inch of living space with prized objects? More is not always better when decorating with beautiful objects.

Aesthetic centers for experiencing art, music, and movement can be arranged. Aesthetically pleasing displays can be set up with

- beautiful things around a given color, shape, pattern, texture, or design theme, such as things that are square, yellow, checkered, or soft (Figure 8–3)

FIGURE 8–3   The classroom should be a beautiful environment.

FIGURE 8–4   An aesthetically pleasing display of nature items

- flowers, plants, nature specimens, or seasonal fruits and vegetables like harvest corn (Figure 8–4)
- machine and appliance parts, gears, tools, and mechanical things
- musical instruments
- postcards and souvenirs
- ethnic costumes and artifacts
- an array of artwork, including drawings, paintings, pottery, ceramics, sculpture, weaving, stitchery, batik, collages, watercolors, and prints
- art: books, postcards, prints, posters
- antique kitchen gadgets and farm tools
- special collections of postage stamps, cookie cutters, baskets, ceramic animals, stuffed animals, license plates, fans, hats, coins, music boxes, arrowheads, minerals, rocks

Szekely (1990) views children's picture books as works of art. Illustrators, like artists, use different media to visualize their thoughts and words. A precise sketch in ink or a realistic painting may work for one book, while a collage or abstract watercolor may work for another. In sharing a beautifully illustrated book with children, you can treat each picture as an artistic creation. Children can freely explore the works in books, in contrast to works in a museum, perhaps carefully running their clean fingers over interesting details. By commenting on the illustrator's use of color, shape, and other artistic elements, art teachers can use books to enhance children's art appreciation skills.

Artists who illustrate their own works are in a special position to find the visual image that best reinforces their words. The following is a list of classic author-illustrators and a sampling of their works. The list is incomplete in that neither all author-illustrators nor all of their works are represented. For example, the more contemporary work of Audrey and Don Wood is missing from the list.

Asch, Frank
Bear Shadow
Bear's Bargain
Goodbye House
Goodnight Horsey
Happy Birthday Moon
Just Like Daddy
The Last Puppy
Moon Cake
Moongame
Skyfire

Carle, Eric
Draw Me a Star
The Grouchy Ladybug
A House for Hermit Crab
Papa, Please Get the Moon for Me
The Very Busy Spider
The Very Hungry Caterpillar

de Paola, Tomie
The Art Lesson
*Nana Upstairs and
   Nana Downstairs*
Now One Foot, Now the Other
Oliver Button Is a Sissy
Sing, Pierrot, Sing (wordless book)
Strega Nona: An Old Tale

Freeman, Don
Corduroy
Dandelion
Mop Top
A Pocket for Corduroy

Keats, Ezra Jack
Goggles!
Peter's Chair
The Snowy Day
Whistle for Willie

Lionni, Leo
Alexander and the Wind-up Mouse
Frederick
Leo the Late Bloomer
Swimmy

McCloskey, (John) Robert
Blueberries for Sal
Make Way for Ducklings

Marshall, James (Edward)
The Cut-Ups (series)
George and Martha (series)
Miss Nelson (series)
The Stupids (series)

Potter, (Helen) Beatrix
The Tale of Benjamin Bunny
The Tale of Jemima Puddle-Duck
The Tale of Peter Rabbit
The Tale of Squirrel Nutkin

Sendak, Maurice (Bernard)
In the Night Kitchen
Where the Wild Things Are

Seuss, Dr. (Pseudonym for Theodor Seuss Geisel)
The Butter Battle Book
The Cat in the Hat
The Foot Book
Fox in Socks
Green Eggs and Ham
Hop on Pop
Horton (series)
How the Grinch Stole Christmas
The Lorax
Mr. Brown Can Moo! Can You?
One Fish, Two Fish, Red Fish, Blue Fish
The Sneetches and Other Stories
Yertle the Turtle and Other Stories

Slobodkina, Esphyr
Caps for Sale

Van Allsburg, Chris
*The Alphabet Theater Proudly Presents
   the Z Was Zapped*
Ben's Dream
The Garden of Abdul Gasazi
Jumanji
Just a Dream
The Polar Express
The Stranger
Two Bad Ants
The Wreck of the Zephyr

Williams, Vera B.
A Chair for My Mother
Cherries and Cherry Pits
Music, Music for Everyone
Something Special for Me

The Reggio Emilia Experience

This section is based on the writings of Malaguzzi (1993), Bredekamp (1993), Gandini (1993), Edwards, Gandini, and Forman (1993), Katz (1990), and New (1990, 1993). Recently there has been a sustained interest in the Reggio Emilia schools reminiscent of the fervor of open education and the British Infant Schools during the 1970s. In our quest for developmentally appropriate practices, an examination of the Reggio Emilia experience should provide inspiration, insight, and direction.

The Reggio Emilia school of northern Italy reflects a longstanding commitment (over 30 years) to quality education for children and support for families. Loris Malaguzzi, founder of the Reggio Emilia schools, was influenced by the works of Rousseau, Pestallozi, Froebel, Dewey, Piaget, and Vygotsky, among others. His philosophy and ideology are shared by contemporary American counterparts. Learning is viewed within an interactive-constructivist framework. It is something that children do, not something done to them. Based on Dewey's concept of progressive education, schools should promote children's natural curiosity and creativity as well as active interaction with their community. Children are active learners—exploring, inquiring, problem solving, and representing their experiences in a number of ways.

Gandini (1993) identified the following points which capture the Reggio Emilia experience.

1. A positive image portrays children as competent, curious learners with prior knowledge and much potential. This contrasts a negative image viewing the child as deficient, disadvantaged, egocentric, and needy. Bredekamp (1993) makes an interesting point. Viewing children as needy permits adults to do the very least for them, while recognizing children as competent requires that we provide them with the best environments and experiences possible. Children are trusted and respect is mutual.
2. To understand and work with children, they must be viewed within a social context or system which includes teachers, peers, parents, and the community.
3. Children, parents, and teachers form an important triad. All have needs as well as rights. Children have a right to the best education possible.
4. Parent participation is an essential component. It is an ongoing process taking many forms.
5. The school is viewed as amiable in that it is designed to foster communication and social interaction. Since children learn from their peers, activities are done in small groups. This facilitates problem solving, negotiating, and verbal give-and-take. Each child has a communication box in which letters and notes written by children are exchanged. This gives new meaning and function to cubbies.
6. Time is fluid, not rigidly set by the clock. Children stay with the same teachers and peers for three-year cycles (infancy to three and three to six). Each year the group changes environments.
7. Teachers are active partners and co-constructors in the learning process. Their role is to observe, participate, and serve as resources to children.
8. Cooperation and organization form the foundation of the educational system. Teachers work in pairs as equals. Cooperative efforts between staff and families facilitate the attainment of goals set by the Reggio Emilia schools.
9. Rather than being planned in advance, the curriculum is emergent, based on teachers' observations of children at play. Ideas for projects and possible learning experiences emerge from these observations.

continued

The Reggio Emilia Experience, continued

10. Children are encouraged to pursue themes and projects. This project method originated with Dewey and is currently advocated by Lilian Katz. Ideas for short- and long-term study originate with the children and not from curriculum how-to or idea books.
11. The "atelierista," or art teacher, operates within an atelier or art studio. See Chapter 14 for a discussion of art centers. The art studio is stocked with art materials, in transparent containers on open shelves and in bountiful supply. This enables children to autonomously pursue their interests. Children's two- and three-dimensional art is attractively displayed throughout the school.
12. Teachers take seriously their work as observers and researchers. Documenting what children do is an ongoing process taking many forms. Tape recorders are everywhere. This strategy resembles authentic assessment in which teachers assemble individual portfolios.

Two more aspects that can be added to Gandini's (1993) list include aesthetics and the use of space, and the concept of one hundred languages.

Reggio Emilia schools believe the arrangement of classroom space influences social interactions and facilitates creative expression. Aesthetically pleasing features include big windows, see-through space with glass walls, portholes, and glass partitions for easy supervision. Inside there are glassed-in courtyards; outside caves are built into playgrounds. Lofts and tiered risers provide varied spatial viewpoints. There are mirrored structures and fountains. There are tablecloths on the tables in the eating area. What a beautiful setting to spend much of one's day.

The metaphor of one hundred languages is a metaphor for the child's ability to symbolize what he or she is learning in a variety of ways. Multisymbolic representation includes drawing, painting, clay modeling, talking, using numbers, moving, singing, dramatizing, and using puppets, among others. Absent from the list are paper-and-pencil tests, which are developmentally inappropriate ways of finding out what children know and can do.

In summary, the Reggio Emilia experience does not come with a set of tricks or tips to make it happen painlessly overnight. The American school experience operates within a very different social and family structure and its own geopolitical and cultural context. Reading about, discussing, and observing the Reggio Emilia experience, however, can lead practitioners to reflect upon their own teaching and begin to improve their classroom settings.

Art Visitors

Invite professional artists, musicians, dancers, craftspeople, volunteers, and parents who have some interest and skill in one of the arts. Remember to include this when you survey parents at the beginning of the year concerning any interests and skills that they might volunteer. Get to know the artists, musicians, and dance companies in your area. Remember to provide brief training just as you would with any volunteer. Some may feel more comfortable answering questions or modeling their art or craft. Others may enjoy working directly with the children.

Art Trips

In addition to having visitors come into the classroom, it may be possible to take children on a field trip. Art abounds in nature, and a simple outdoor walk qualifies as a recommended field trip. Most communities have at least one of the following to visit:

- museum
- art gallery
- exhibit
- concert
- play
- children's theater
- ballet
- recital
- performance
- planetarium
- artist's studio
- arboretum

It is wise to first attend by yourself to make sure that your particular group will profit from this experience. Field trips involve a great deal of planning, energy, and often expense, and they need to be well thought out. In arranging the field trip, try to match what the experience has to offer with your group's developmental needs, interests and abilities. For example, most toddlers would not sit still through an hour of chamber music. See if there is someone on the staff who has experience in giving tours to young children. Some museums have special children's rooms and exhibits. Others may have collections that they loan out. Many libraries have art prints that may be rented or checked out.

Sensory Literacy

Help the children become sensory literate. This can be done in two ways. First, help them to stop, sense, and heighten their awareness of the experience at hand. For example, ask the mother of a newborn to let the children at least look and listen. Touch may come weeks later with a supervised bath. Second, stimulate their senses. An array of sensory experiences appears in the following chapter.

Figure 8–5 depicts a school corridor celebrating the beauty and sensory quality of children's art.

In a sense, the teacher and classroom quietly whisper, "Beauty, it is all around you. Together we will take the time to get involved."

WATERCOLOR AND INK

Tempera painting is a prerequisite to painting with watercolor or ink. Using watercolor and ink requires coordination and fine motor control. These media will frustrate the very young artist. They are used with smaller brushes that are harder to manage.

Watercolor **P K S**

Watercolors tend to be wet, runny, and transparent. Often, they produce very unintended results. The wet colors may bleed when the child artist is trying to make facial features. The writer recommends that children begin using watercolors to make lines, colors, shapes, and abstract designs rather than attempting realistic, detailed art. Watercolors come in their own small sets with individual semimoist cakes. Buy a medium grade. The brushes that come with the cheapest sets will have bristles that fall out after the first washing.

Watercolors can be used on either wet or dry paper. Watercolors put on wet paper will run and bleed into very interesting patterns and designs. Papers can be wet with a sponge or from a pump spray bottle. A small sponge allows children to blot up excess water or unwanted runs. Special spots can be saturated with water dropped from an eyedropper. The author observed one child doing just that in making a bull's-eye effect or rainbow of blended colors.

Since there is only one brush for several colors, it is important that children wash their brushes each time before changing colors. They will need

FIGURE 8–5 *A beautiful display of children's art*

individual water containers, which should be emptied every time they appear muddy. When they are done, excess watercolor paint in the set should be carefully blotted up. A careful rinse under the sink will remove excess paint. Be careful not to merely rinse away the unused paints. Let the set air dry. Sets that are closed when wet tend to get gummy. Children find them unappealing.

Hint   Liquid watercolors, of which one brand name is Liquid Watercolor, are nontoxic and less expensive than food coloring. They produce a range of secondary colors and shades that cannot be matched by food coloring. Liquid watercolors wash out of most fabrics. The colors are intense so they can be used in small amounts or diluted as a liquid dye. Liquid watercolor is available from Discount School Supply. See Appendix D.

Watercolor paper is very expensive if purchased separately by the sheet. Purchased in tablet form, it is still moderately expensive. White drawing paper is acceptable. The author finds that onionskin or good bond typing paper has a good texture for watercolor. An office with outdated letterhead stationery may have a surplus of this. You could easily trim off the letterhead.

Tissue Paper Water Coloring   P K

Tear tissue paper into 1-inch squares and separate by color. Fill clear containers with water. Add squares and use a brush to mix. The dye from the paper will bleed into the water. Children discover that adding more squares of the same color strengthens the intensity of that color. Children can also creatively mix colors. You may want to begin by providing the three primary colors. Children can paint with the colored water that results.

Spray Bottle Watercoloring   P K

Collect child-sized clear spray bottles with a trigger-type release. Fill each with water and add a few drops of liquid watercolor. Show the children how to pump the release while aiming only at their papers.

Provide large pieces of paper and art smocks. This is a good activity to do outdoors. Use clothespins to attach the papers to a fence or tape them to the cement.

Coffee Filter Creations   P K

Provide containers of water to which liquid watercolor has been added. Children can fold a coffee filter and dip into one color, squeeze, and select other colors if they choose. Open the coffee filter and lay out flat to dry on newspaper. Indicate child's name on masking tape near his or her filter. When dry, provide a pipe cleaner for those children who want to fashion their filters into flowers, butterflies, bows, or creative creations. Vary the activity by providing absorbent paper towels.

Crystal Watercolors   K S

Encourage children to paint with clean water on white paper. Provide construction or drawing paper. Next, children paint using liquid watercolors. Colors should spread, blend, and bleed together. Children can also use spray bottles filled with clear water to keep their designs wet and mixed. When done, give child a sheet of clear plastic wrap that is twice the size of his or her white paper. Demonstrate how to crumple and place gently down on top of wet painting. Set in safe place to dry. Pull plastic wrap off when dry. This produces a very interesting textured effect. Try tinfoil, wax paper, bubble wrap, and nature items in place of plastic wrap.

Brush and Roll   P K

Provide shallow containers of water to which liquid watercolor has been added. Children use small foam brushes and small paint rollers to make creative designs on drawing paper or watercolor paper.

Ink   S

Even young children can appreciate the beauty of Chinese pen and ink drawings that capture nature with a minimum of lines. Ink comes in colors other than black and tends to be fairly expensive. One bottle of black may suffice for use with older children. Ink can be economically used on small sheets of paper with a thin brush. It is appropriate for making linear drawings and designs with a minimum of line and ink. Ink can also be used in printing and stencil activities. It is not recommended for use at the easel or for general painting.

Ink Blots **S**

Children can drop ink on a piece of paper. Carefully fold the paper in half and open. Change colors and repeat the process. Cut around the ink blots and mount them on colored paper.

Dye (Water-Based)

Traditionally, dye activities involve the use of food colors which tend to be expensive, limited in color range, and stain hands and clothing. Liquid watercolors avoid the above pitfall and can be used whenever food colors are needed.

Dribble Dye **P K**

Provide each child with a heavyweight, white paper towel. Encourage him or her to fold it into squares. Provide small bottles of food coloring or liquid watercolor. The children can very carefully squeeze small dots or dabs of different colors on the corners, edges, or middle section. Use just enough to bleed through. Open up to reveal a colorful design. Let dry.

Dip and Dye **P K**

Provide a white, heavyweight paper towel for each child. You will also need different colors of dye. Place a few drops of food coloring or liquid watercolor in a small dish or container of water. Adding more drops will make colors darker. Different colors can be poured into the different openings in a muffin tin. Encourage children to fold their paper towels into squares. Different folds (horizontal, vertical, diagonal, and random) will produce different effects. Carefully dip the corner or edge into one color. Gently squeeze out the excess. Dip a second small area into a different color. Colors can also be mixed. For example, dip the towel in yellow and then in red. Orange will result. Dry on layers of newspaper. These can be taped over windows for a colorful effect. They can also be carefully taped together to form a quilt, banner, or backdrop for a bulletin board.

SUMMARY

Aesthetics and young children go hand in hand. Babies begin by exploring and marveling at their world. Over time, children will internalize adult "don'ts" and learn not to look, listen, touch, taste, or smell. They will take their senses and the world of lines, shapes, colors, and design for granted. Our task was identified as a multipurpose one. We need to stimulate their senses; be an aesthetic model in dress, behavior, and communication; and set up a sensory-rich and appealing learning environment. Our discussion focused on a rationale for including aesthetics in early childhood. First, it was seen as a part of a child's wholistic development. Second, it will help children see the beauty of line and shapes in the world of letters, words, and numbers they will encounter. Third, it was believed that children who grow up with the aesthetic sense will become wise consumers and concerned citizens who will advocate for beauty in the community and workplace. Fourth, it will help children understand and appreciate a wide range of arts. Fifth, sensory data fosters thinking and concept formation.

Suggested Activities

1. Reflect on your most recent or vivid aesthetic experience. Sketch it or attempt to put it into words. Describe how you felt and your reaction.

2. Critique the use of indoor classroom space for its aesthetic appeal. Make specific recommendations.

3. Set up an aesthetically pleasing display of objects that have sensory appeal.

4. Arrange an aesthetic experience through a simple field trip such as a nature walk.

5. Facilitate a watercolor or ink activity with children.

Review

A. Explain aesthetics as an
   1. attitude
   2. process
   3. response

B. List aspects of the teacher's role as it relates to aesthetics.
   1.
   2.
   3.
   4.
   5.

CHAPTER 9

Sensory Experiences

A beginning teacher was starting her internship in a private kindergarten. The master teacher asked the intern to supervise the area in the photograph. What kinds of things are on the table? What name would you give to this learning center? What might children do at this center? Would you add or change anything?

This sensory table encourages children to come over and look, touch, listen, and smell. As the intern, you could have the children talk about the colors, sizes, and shapes. You could also ask open-ended questions including, "Where do you think this came from?" or "How did it get this way?" After their active sensory exploration, children can count, compare, and classify items like shells.

OBJECTIVES

After studying this chapter, the student will be able to

- Discuss the relationship between sensing, perceiving, feeling, thinking, and concept development
- List and briefly explain the different senses
- Construct a multisensory activity
- Provide art activities based on the process called "resist"

INTRODUCTION

Young children use all their senses to process their aesthetic experiences. They are sensory gluttons who are intrinsically motivated to look, touch, listen to, taste, and smell everything they come into contact with. They respond on both affective and cognitive levels. For example, they not only experience pleasure in looking at and smelling a flower but also enhance their concept of what a flower is. One hopes that young children with the aesthetic sense will grow up to be wise consumers and planners for a better future that includes beauty and peace.

FROM PERCEPT TO CONCEPT

Perception is the ability to receive sensory impressions from one's surroundings and relate them to what one knows. Sensing, perceiving, thinking, and developing concepts are closely related. The aesthetic experience merges the cognitive with the affective response. Thinking and feeling come together. For example, when they hear bells chime in a church for the first time, young children may perceive the sound, smile with amazement, think about it, and relate it to the doorbell or clock chimes at home. The process can be depicted as:

Sense +	Perception +	Feeling +	Thinking =	Concepts
visual	look	enjoy	compare	color
auditory	listen	marvel	contrast	tone
tactile	touch	joy	analyze	texture
olfactory	smell	happy	classify	scent
gustatory	taste	amazed	describe	flavor

The world has much to offer. A child with a sensory handicap or deficit may miss stimuli. Often, such children develop strengths in other areas. For example, children who are blind often develop a strong sense of touch or hearing. A child who does not invest the time in perceptual activity or who lacks sensory stimulation is also at a disadvantage. For example, a child who has never touched, looked at, smelled, or listened to an elephant will be at a loss when asked to discuss or read about elephants.

N MORE THAN FIVE SENSES

Children use their senses to thoroughly explore their environment. Traditionally, the five senses are:

1. visual
2. auditory
3. tactile
4. olfactory
5. gustatory

To this basic list Montessori (1967) would also add the following senses:

6. chromatic
7. thermic
8. sterognostic
9. baric
10. kinesthetic

Each of the above senses will be explained and exemplified with activities. Appendix E contains an incomplete list of books on the senses.

Multisensory Experiences

Most experiences involve more than one sense (see Figure 9–1). Cooking is a good example of a multisensory experience. Making popcorn involves looking at and touching the kernels before, during,

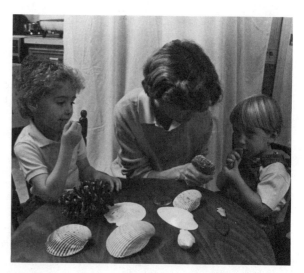

FIGURE 9–1   Many experiences are multisensory.

and after popping; listening to the sound of popcorn popping; smelling the scent of melted butter being poured over hot popcorn; and eating the popcorn in big handfuls. Children would also enjoy moving like popcorn popping, starting off as small, compact "kernels" that slowly expand and puff up as they get hotter. A coconut has a distinctive color, shape, covering, texture, and taste. Children can look at the outside of a coconut and discuss its color, size, shape, and covering. "What do you hear when you shake it? What do you think is inside? What can we do to find out? How can we open this coconut? What words describe how it looks and feels? Does it smell? I also have a bag of shredded coconut. How are the two similar? How are they different? Let's cut the coconut in half and look inside. Now what do you see and smell? Scrape off a piece of the white inside. How does it taste? Does it taste the same as the flakes of coconut in the bag?" The line of questioning, discussing, and experiencing is endless. The same process could be done with an artichoke, melon, pineapple, or when baking cookies.

1. Visual

The visual sense involves looking and seeing. Ideally, it involves a thorough visual exploration rather than a passing glance or quick look. Vision and discriminating between letters and words will be required for reading.

The indoor classroom should be a visually rich, appealing environment with nature specimens, artifacts, and objects to visually explore. Samples of children's art as well as art posters or prints can be displayed on the walls. A science center or discovery table can display a collection of seashells, antique kitchen items, or postcards to visually explore.

Some recommended materials to encourage visual exploration include:

- prism
- magnifying glasses: handheld and three-legged stool or stand
- safety mirrors: both handheld and full-length
- lenses: concave and convex (making things bigger or smaller)

- microscope and slides
- telescope
- kaleidoscope
- binoculars
- camera
- cellophane color paddles
- sunglasses
- flashlight
- viewer and round picture reels

Water play with bubbles is a simple visual activity. Provide a tub of water, liquid dishwashing soap, and rotary eggbeaters. Food coloring is optional, and children love the effect. A related activity is blowing bubbles outdoors. Children enjoy trying to catch them. Encourage them to note the transparent quality of bubbles as well as the rainbow of colors present. A simple recipe for homemade bubbles follows.

Iridescent Soap Bubbles

1 cup of water
2 tablespoons of liquid dishwashing detergent
1 tablespoon of glycerine (available from drugstore)
½ teaspoon sugar

Here are some other visual activities.

New View

Encourage children to view their indoor and outdoor environment from new perspectives. What do you see when you

- lie on the floor and look up?
- lie on the floor on your right or left side?
- lie on your back outdoors on the grass? What appears in the sky? What shapes do you see in the clouds?
- climb to the top of the jungle gym and look down or up?
- balance on your hands and stand on your head?
- are swinging on the swing? What colors and shapes appear?

SENSE:	RECOMMENDED:
Visual—to Look at	multicultural and anti-bias pictures beautifully illustrated children's books book covers displayed on walls posters displays of children's artwork art prints photographs of children and their families printed labels, words, signs, recipe cards, and charts objects with interesting visual qualities artifacts and souvenirs collections of shells, gems, and nature specimens media: check movies, filmstrips, and videotapes for quality vases of flowers potted plants classroom pets wall hangings, weavings, tapestries mobiles rebus, poem, song, chant, experience, recipe, and story charts changes in food during cooking
Auditory—to Listen to	variety of music poetry rhymes finger plays and body action rhymes storytelling with or without props books read aloud taped sounds and asking, "What could have made that sound?" stories on tape and following directions and playing "I Spy" informal conversations songs musical and rhythm instruments
Tactile—to Touch	objects and identify them without looking rough and smooth sandpaper and fabrics objects with different textures including fruits, vegetables, and nature items tubs filled with shaved ice, cold, cool, or warm water mitts covered with various textured fabrics foods during food preparation activities
Olfactory—to Smell	flowers scents aromas spices and extracts foods potpourri
Gustatory—to Taste	variety of nutritious foods from different cultures healthy snacks children helped make
Kinesthetic—to Move	in creative movement activities through obstacle courses

Ⓝ TABLE 9–1   Sensory Experiences at a Glance

Nature Walk   **P K S**

Take magnifying glasses when going on a nature walk. Look for interesting shapes and designs in nature. Stop to

- look at moss, berries, insects, fungus, mushrooms, nests, tree stumps, shadows, birds, spiderwebs, ant hills, or the pattern in rust on a building.
- listen to birds chirping, leaves rustling, wind blowing, dogs, cats, squirrels, twigs cracking, and acorns or nuts falling.
- touch tree bark, damp moss, dry leaves, sand, and cold mud.
- smell evergreen trees, pinecones, pine needles, damp earth, dry leaves, and crisp, cold air.

Collect interesting specimens to bring back to the science table. Some teachers may prefer to leave the natural environment intact and not remove bugs, leaves, or twigs.

Focus Scopes   **P K**

It is sometimes difficult to notice design and detail in an environment that is alive with color, shape, sound, and movement. Children may need help focusing their visual sense. This is why magnifying glasses, cameras, binoculars, and telescopes are recommended. An empty tissue roll makes a very good focus scope. The outside can be decorated or covered with contact paper to enhance its appeal. Encourage children to examine the indoor and outdoor environment by very slowly exploring with the focus scopes. Pay attention to small things that might be missed by just looking. Focus scopes can also be covered with cellophane at one end and used like color paddles. Children can also join their fingers to make a frame to focus their vision.

Peek Frames   **P K S**

Find an interesting picture in a magazine. Look for color and design and cut off any words. Find sheets of construction paper that are the same size or larger than the picture. Peek frames can be used in many ways. Neatly cut a 1-inch round hole out of your sheet of construction paper. Place this sheet over your picture. Ask the children, "What do you see through my little window? Let's think of many different things that the picture might be." Peek frames can have more than one opening. The hole can also be torn into and slowly peeled larger to foster continued guessing and heighten suspense. This activity forces children to focus their visual sense on a small area of design, color, or shape. The idea is not to guess the one right answer but to use the visual clues to come up with many possibilities.

Look and Match   **P K**

Children enjoy matching objects or pictures that are the same. Find pairs of some of the following:

- magazine pictures
- fabric scraps
- wallpaper samples
- tile or linoleum samples

Younger children will enjoy matching pairs that are quite distinct. Older children can be challenged with subtle variations in color or design, such as those found in wallpaper sample books.

Masterpiece Match   **P K S**

Children would enjoy matching pairs of art postcards. Art postcards are available from art museums. See Appendix C for other sources. Try to find pairs of postcards that are similar but not identical—for example, a family done in realistic and abstract styles. The subject matter may be the same, but the treatment is different. Older children may also enjoy playing a "memory" game with the postcards. You will need at least six pairs of postcards. Arrange them face up on the floor. Turn them over. Older children may not need to see them turned right side up. Next, encourage children to turn over a pair. If they match, the child gets another turn. If one child gets all the pairs correct in sequence, this might indicate that there are too few pairs.

I Spy   **P K**

This activity involves both looking and listening and can be played with a large group. Focus on an item in the room that has a distinct color or shape. "I spy something in the room that is bright red. What could it be?" Children may need additional clues. "It is bright red only on the front. The back side is white. What could it be?" Or, "I spy something on the wall that has a triangle shape. What could it be?" Children enjoy being the leader for this activity. Encourage them to use color or shape clues rather than merely saying, "I spy the round clock on the wall that ticks. What is it?"

Watch the Waves

Capture a wave in a bottle. Find a large plastic bottle. Add mineral oil and some water that has been colored with blue food coloring. Cover tightly. Tilt, tip, and watch the waves.

2. Auditory

The auditory sense involves hearing and listening, which are two very different processes. Children who hear do not always listen. Our world is a noisy one, with people talking, appliances, stereos, traffic, and televisions. Children are exposed to much auditory stimulation and learn at a very early age to tune much of it out. Casual hearing is appropriate much of the time. Music, literature, or teacher's directions warrant concentrated listening. Our aim is to help children know when to switch from passive hearing to active listening. Recommended objects that foster active listening include

- stethoscope
- tape recorder with tapes of stories, rhymes, and poems
- record player with music and story records
- rhythm instruments
- tuning fork
- music boxes
- bells
- metronome

Art Postcards

Wolf (1988, 1990) has applied the Montessori skills of matching, pairing, sorting, using control cards, and using a time line to art appreciation. The steps involved in using her art postcards are:

Step 1. Match identical paintings. The child matches three identical pairs. Pairs are gradually added until the child can match six identical pairs.

Step 2. Pair similar paintings by an artist. Children pair companion paintings, two paintings by the same artist that are not identical but are similar in subject matter and style. An example would be two paintings of birds by Audubon.

Step 3. Group paintings by an artist. Children begin grouping four paintings by each of three different artists. For example, they begin with highly contrasting subjects—four still lifes by Cezanne, four abstract works by Kandinsky, and four paintings of people by Goya.

Step 4. Children refer to control cards to match the last name of artists with their paintings. After repeating the exercise several times, the children attempt to match the name cards to the paintings without using the control cards.

Step 5. Control cards are used to learn the names of famous paintings.

Step 6. Children are introduced to paintings grouped according to schools of art.

Step 7. Children put paintings into rows corresponding to the school of art to which they belong.

Step 8. Use of the time line. A large number of paintings of one subject, children for example, are placed beside a time line according to their dates. When completed, the line graphically illustrates the development of painting through the centuries.

Some activities are described below.

Quiet Time

Quiet Time can be used as a relaxation technique after a noisy activity. It is a good routine to quiet the children. Gather children and have them sit quietly. They may giggle at first but will improve with practice. Encourage them to close their eyes and listen. "What do you hear? Think about the sounds but do not talk yet. Let's keep on listening to the noises inside our bodies and around the classroom." Wait a few seconds or minutes, depending on the group. Children may hear their heart beating, blood flowing, stomach grumbling, throat swallowing, lungs breathing, or classroom pet moving about.

Sounds Around Us

Tape-record distinct sounds, for example:

- toast popping out of a toaster
- clock ticking
- whistle blowing
- vacuum cleaner in operation
- horn honking
- bell ringing
- blender or electric mixer in operation
- running water
- toilet flushing
- water going down the drain
- animal sounds
- traffic sounds
- telephone ringing
- alarm clock ringing
- door slamming
- siren wailing
- baby crying
- ball bouncing
- someone jumping rope

Some more difficult sounds might include

- sticks or twigs cracking
- someone walking on leaves
- a match being struck
- a refrigerator door being closed
- tape pulled off a dispenser
- coins being dropped

- wind blowing
- car ignition being turned on and off

Pause between sounds. Play the sounds back and encourage the children to quietly listen (not just hear) and guess what made the sound. Children may want to close their eyes to help focus exclusively on the sounds without any distracting visual stimuli. Younger children who know but cannot verbalize may enjoy hearing the sound and pointing to a corresponding picture or sketch that you provide.

Sound Detectives

Encourage children to close their eyes and listen very quietly while you perform some action. They must actively listen and attempt to guess what you have just done. Some actions include

- clapping hands
- jumping
- snapping fingers
- rubbing hands together
- blowing a kiss
- yawning
- stamping feet
- bouncing a ball several times
- stapling papers
- dropping a pencil
- writing on the chalkboard
- whistling
- opening and closing a book
- walking on tiptoe
- shutting a door
- turning on a water faucet

Children enjoy taking turns being the leader in this game. Encourage them to think up new actions, not merely repeat what was just done.

Sound Containers

Active listening involves being able to discriminate among sounds. Auditory discrimination involves listening to sounds and deciding which ones are similar and which are different. Hearing similarities and differences will help children with speaking, phonics, and reading. Find a matched set of at least six opaque boxes or containers. Small milk cartons or soda pop cans are fine. Plastic toy eggs or egg-shaped pantyhose containers are also recommended. Cover half of the set in one color and half in another—e.g., three red and three blue. Since the cues can only be auditory, it is important that the children cannot see what is inside. Separate your set into three, four, five, or six pairs. Fill each pair with an equal amount of one of the following:

- marbles
- salt
- rice
- cotton balls
- paper clips
- wad of papers
- toothpicks
- string
- pennies
- tacks
- ribbons

First, test the items chosen to make sure each pair has identical sounds. Pairs must be significantly different from each other. For example, a pair filled with salt and a pair filled with sugar will probably sound identical. With very young children or those with auditory problems, limit the set to two or three very distinct pairs. Slowly add to your collection as the children begin to master the task. Inconspicuously mark or code the pairs on the bottom to foster a quick check.

Water Sounds   **P K S**

Children can listen to sounds and make music in containers filled with water. Find a set of at least three identical glass bottles or jars. Fill one to the top with water, another halfway, and the third a half inch from the bottom. Different amounts of water will make sounds of different pitch when the bottle is struck with a metal spoon. Practice making sounds that vary in volume (soft and loud) depending on how lightly you strike. Which makes the highest pitch? Which makes the lowest pitch? Encourage children to seriate the sounds from low to high or vice versa. The children will enjoy playing music on the bottles. They may want to incorporate their water sounds with music made on other rhythm instruments. Additional bottles with different water levels can gradually be added.

Listen Along   **P K S**

Children enjoy being read to. Reading to them is one way to encourage an interest in and love of reading. Get animated and stress words and phrasing. Encourage children to hear words that rhyme in poems. Storytelling with props, such as puppets or a flannel board, allows you to get dramatic with the story line while making continual eye contact. It also allows the children to get involved.

3. Tactile

The tactile sense involves feeling and touch. For our purposes the tactile sense may operate in conjunction with the visual sense. Activities that involve touching and feeling textures will be categorized as tactile. Those involving touching to identify, recognize, and name an object without looking will be categorized as sterognostic and covered in a later section.

Sandpaper Feel   **P K**

Different grades of sandpaper, from rough/coarse to fine/smooth, can be used in this activity. Make a pair of strips for each grade of sandpaper. Start with fine and very coarse and add in-between gradations as the children master this activity. Cut the sandpaper into 2-inch-wide strips about 4 inches long. Mount the sandpaper strips on sturdy cardboard or a piece of wood. Encourage children to trace down the strip with an index finger and feel the texture. Ask them to find another strip of sandpaper that feels the same. What word describes how it feels? Is it rough or smooth? Older children might enjoy seriating the sandpaper strips from smooth to rough or vice versa.

Fabric Feel   **P K**

Children can wear blindfolds or agree to close their eyes for this activity. Provide identical pairs of some of the following:

- burlap
- velvet
- silk
- netting
- corduroy
- denim
- cotton

- gauze
- fur
- terrycloth
- vinyl
- wool
- carpet

Remember to make the sizes the same so that the only clues will be tactile. Encourage children to discuss their matched pairs. How do they feel? What word tells us? Are they soft, smooth, rough, wrinkly, or bumpy?

How Does It Feel?

Discuss with children how different things feel hard or soft (see Figure 9–2). Encourage them to give examples. Neatly print "hard" and "soft" on separate sheets of paper. Encourage children to say the words after you. Place a picture of something hard and something soft on the corresponding papers. En-

courage children to put the following items under the proper heading:

- cotton
- velvet
- stone
- coin
- feather
- plush stuffed animal
- wet sponge
- dry sponge
- powder puff
- sandpaper
- rubber squeeze toy
- tree bark
- cactus
- yarn ball
- plastic
- emery board
- tinfoil (over cardboard)
- plastic wrap (over cardboard)
- steel wool

FIGURE 9–2   How does it feel?

Young children will enjoy sorting the actual objects. Older children will enjoy cutting pictures of hard and soft objects out of magazines and pasting them onto the corresponding sheet. They may also expand their tactile vocabulary to include rough, smooth, slick, bumpy, prickly, fuzzy, furry, porous, and coarse.

Texture Collage

Children enjoy pasting or gluing objects with varied textures into a collage. The group can also work on a thematic collage containing both pictures from magazines and actual objects that are rough, smooth, sharp, fuzzy, or furry. Provide sturdy cardboard for the background when pasting or gluing heavy objects.

4. Olfactory

Although animals rely heavily on the sense of smell, people do not. We use our sense of smell on a very limited basis, to smell food or perfume or cologne, or to react to unpleasant odors. Children use their sense of smell more than adults. For example, they enjoy scratch-and-sniff stickers. Still, they may refuse to try a food solely on the basis of its smell or color (visual cue). Green, yellow, and orange vegetables hold little olfactory or visual appeal for some children. Some activities to stimulate the olfactory sense are described below.

Scent Bottles

Find a set of identical bottles or containers with lids or tops. Pill vials, empty spice bottles, or film containers are ideal. Make two, three, four, five, or six pairs. Color-code the lids in each set, for example, six green and six orange. Place a ball of cotton in each pair if you are using liquid scents or extracts. Make air holes in the lids if solids are used. Pieces of nylon stocking can be placed over the opening and

A Sensory Table Makes Good Sense

A sensory table can be filled with items that involve more than one sense, for example, looking and touching. Fill with items that have tactile and visual appeal. Rotate the contents over time. Possibilities include the following:

- buttons and beads
- rice
- cornmeal
- beans
- sand
- dirt or mud
- water (plain or colored), with or without ice cubes, shaved ice, or snow
- wood shavings
- shaving cream
- nature specimens, e.g., grass, weeds, leaves, pinecones, flower petals
- Styrofoam pieces
- marbles
- pebbles and stones
- aquarium gravel
- counters, e.g., teddy bears
- birdseed
- pom-poms
- golf balls

Although toddlers enjoy exploring at the sensory table, small marbles may be problematic for those who insist on putting everything in their mouths. Provide close supervision and use only larger items for the very young. There is no need for an expensive sensory table. Use a wading pool, baby bathtub, or large basin. Depending on the contents, add dinosaurs, small people, vehicles, and animals, as well as kitchen utensils and a variety of containers to foster complex sensory play.

secured with rubber bands. Fill each pair with one of the following:

- cinnamon
- mustard
- garlic
- coffee
- pepper
- sawdust
- baby powder
- perfume
- bath crystals or bath salts

- vanilla
- lemon peel
- pine
- tea
- onion
- cloves
- peppermint
- talcum

Cotton balls soaked in clear liquids or extracts provide no visual clues. Scents need to be fresh and will have to be replaced from time to time. Remind children to replace the lids or tops after use. Items like coffee or tea cannot be used in clear containers, since the cue will be visual rather than olfactory. Remind children to smell without inhaling or tasting. Match up pairs that smell the same. Use a word to describe how each one smells. Is it sweet, sour, spicy?

It Smells Good Enough to Eat

The olfactory and gustatory senses work together. In general, foods that smell good taste good. This activity can be done with a small group as a lead-in to snack time. Encourage children to close their eyes while you hold a piece of food on a toothpick under their noses. Pause long enough for them to get a good sniff without making skin contact. A piece of banana is one example. Next, hold a different food, such as a pineapple chunk. Do they smell the same or different? Encourage children to match an array of fruits or vegetables on a plate in front of them with your standard. The finale to the activity is being able to eat the samples for snack.

The classroom can also be an olfactory-rich environment. Teachers can add scents and aromas. A bowl or dish of rose petals, pine needles, sachet, incense, dried orange rinds, scented soaps, or potpourri provides a lovely fragrance. Flowers such as roses, mums, and carnations, as well as scented candles and perfume samples also encourage children to stop and smell. The following recipe can be used to produce a cinnamon scent in your room.

Soak several whole cinnamon sticks in cinnamon oil. Dry. Tie together with dried flowers in a bundle. Add a pretty ribbon or lace. The fragrance of cinnamon should last for months.

To make a simmering stove-top potpourri mixture, follow this recipe:

Combine whole allspice, whole cloves, cinnamon sticks, and pieces of dried orange peel. Put a tablespoon or two in 3 cups of water and place in a pot. Bring to a boil on the stove and simmer. Add more water as needed.

Children enjoy sticking whole cloves into oranges that have been pierced with holes. Tie with pretty ribbon and hang. They can also be taken home as gifts if the children have had a good deal of input into making them.

More important, the classroom should be free of stale, musty smells. Spraying with a disinfectant spray or air freshener may eliminate or mask stale odors. Fresh air and a routine airing out are essential.

5. Gustatory

Eating and quiet time spent enjoying home-cooked meals have become a luxury in many households. Many children may never see their parents cook a meal. Meals are now quickly eaten on the run or even skipped. Convenience foods may be bland, precooked, or low in nutritional value. Eating occurs out of habit and routine rather than for its gustatory or taste appeal. Eating may be something that is done at different times by different family members, perhaps in front of television, or merely something children do before getting ready for bed. Perhaps this is why most early childhood educators value snack time and cooking as a time to talk, socialize, and share food and experiences. Here are some recommended gustatory activities.

Snacks and Cooking   **T P K**

These two activities are vital in any early childhood program. Snacks should be more than crackers and sugary juice. Although they are moderately expensive, nutritious snacks provide their own characteristic look, color, shape, texture, taste, smell, and sound when eaten. Recommended snacks include

- banana slices
- pineapple wedges
- peanut butter
- orange slices
- carrot sticks
- apple wedges
- cheese chunks
- celery stalks
- grapes
- melon balls
- pear halves
- grapefruit sections
- cauliflower
- cucumber slices
- sunflower seeds, raisins, and nuts
- strawberries

Cooking experiences using nutritious ingredients with much child input are also highly recommended. For example, children can be actively involved in making fruit salad: washing and dividing the fruit, reading the recipe, mixing, and measuring ingredients. Baking bread is another multisensory cooking activity that involves learning across many, if not all, of the early childhood curricular areas. To bake bread one must read a recipe and measure ingredients. Children are actively involved in kneading dough. Is it magic or science that makes the dough rise? Bread baking has a wonderful aroma, and the bread has an equally good taste when it is topped with homemade butter. Cooking with apples provides unlimited possibilities for learning and eating. Apples can be cut, peeled, pared, or baked, or the slices can be spread with peanut butter or dipped in melted cheese. The following recipes suggest more uses for apples.

Apple Juice

½ cup seeded apples
1 cup water
1 teaspoon sugar

Put ingredients in blender and blend thoroughly. Chill and serve. Will serve two, so vary recipe given the size of the group.

Applesauce

Cut several apples. Place in electric frying pan or covered skillet. Cover apples with cider. Put lid on pan and bring to a boil. Reduce heat and simmer until apples are soft. Let cool. Take turns grinding in a food mill. Add sugar and cinnamon to taste.

Dried Apples*

Peel and core several apples, and cut them into rings or slices. Place them in salted water for 15 minutes. Dry for 2 weeks.

* Dried grapes become raisins using this recipe.

Taste Party

Children can sample an array of foods and classify them as sweet, sour, hot, cold, or salty. Bitter, bland, and spicy may be difficult for young children. They can be added as children master the basic tastes. Each child will need his or her own spoon. Using an eyedropper, place a drop of a sweet substance, e.g., sugar water, onto each child's spoon. Encourage them to think about the taste before guessing. They should wipe their spoon and take a drink of water from their own cup between tests. Repeat the procedure using salt water. Sample tastes include

- sugar water
- salt water
- chocolate syrup
- cinnamon
- nutmeg
- brewed tea
- orange juice
- lemon juice
- honey
- vinegar water
- maple syrup

Solids can also be introduced at a taste party. Try using

- chocolate chips
- carrot cubes
- apple squares
- banana slices
- cheese chunks
- cinnamon candy
- cottage cheese
- melon balls

Remember to check for food allergies before any taste test or food experience.

6. Chromatic

Montessori views the chromatic sense as a subset of the broader sense of vision. The chromatic sense involves the ability to identify, match, and discriminate among colors. Below are some activities for the chromatic sense.

Color Matching   P K

Very young children enjoy matching colored shapes cut out of construction paper (see Figure 9–3). Begin with red, blue, and yellow and add more colors as children master this task. Or glue colored shapes in a vertical column on a sheet of cardboard or a file folder. Draw an outline of an identical shape next to each color. Cut out a second set of colored pieces. Encourage children to place the second set next to its match. Paint samples obtained from hardware or paint stores can also be used. Select bright enamels rather than pale pastels. Older children may enjoy matching color names. Later they can match a color name printed on an index card with a color cue.

Color Seriating   P K

Not all colors are created equal. Colors come in different shades, tints, tones, intensities, and values. Black added to red will turn it into a darker shade, perhaps scarlet. White added to red will turn it into a lighter tint, such as pink. To make a color game for seriation, first find color charts or paint strips that have variations in tint or shade. Begin with very obvious gradations: light green, medium green, and dark green. Glue an identical set to a piece of cardboard or a file folder and let children first match the shapes in order. Later, they can lay them out in a trainlike array from darkest to lightest. Gradually increase the number of colors or add more difficult gradations in color as children become more proficient. This seriation activity can also be made self-correcting or self-checking. For example, place each of the five shades of red on its own index card. The cards can be coded 1 through 5 or A through E in small numbers or letters on the back side. Or, a simple picture, such as a caterpillar, can be drawn on the back. When the colors are put in proper sequence, the picture will be complete when the cards are turned over. The caterpillar should appear whether the cards are seriated from darkest to lightest or lightest to darkest.

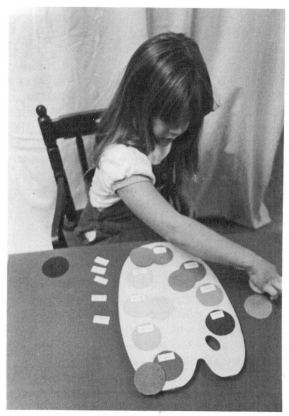

FIGURE 9–3   *Refining the sense of color*

Color Our World   P K

Viewing objects through pieces of cellophane will distort their color. Color paddles are sturdy pieces of cellophane or translucent plastic. They are commercially available, or it is easy to make a set. Individual sheets of cellophane wrapping paper or term paper covers can be mounted or framed in cardboard to form a sturdy holder. Provide at least the primary colors. Color paddles can be used individually or together. For example, viewing the room through red over blue will make it look purple.

Create Colors   P K

Provide round pieces of tissue paper in the three primary colors for each child. Tissue paper is difficult to cut, and you may have to provide precut pieces for younger children. Cut a large piece of wax paper for each child. Children can arrange any two pieces of tissue paper on the wax paper. Make sure the two primary colors have some overlap. Add the third colored circle, making sure it overlaps the other two. Carefully place a second sheet of wax paper on top. Press with a warm iron. Older children should be able to press their own provided they have direct supervision. The heat will melt the wax and seal the round shapes. Hold the picture up to the light or display it on the window. Notice how purple appears where red and blue overlap, orange where red and yellow overlap, and green where blue and yellow overlap. What color appears in the very center, where red, blue, and yellow overlap?

Color Show

You will need an overhead projector for this activity. Project on a blank wall or white sheet. Find a flat glass dish and place it on the illuminated projector. Add several drops of water. Add a few drops of food coloring. Start with one primary color. Wiggle the dish and swirl the beads of food coloring with a toothpick. Add a second primary color. Repeat the process and watch the colors mix. What has happened? Continue with your color show by adding new colors or starting over with a different combination of primary colors. A squirt of black ink will also make an interesting pattern in water. Adding a very small drop of black ink to food coloring will make shades.

As a variation on this activity, fill three Zip-Lock plastic storage bags with water. Add a different primary food color to each. Do not fill them to the top or bulging. Lock securely. Hold them up and let children view their surroundings through different colors.

7. Thermic

The thermic sense deals with one's perception of temperature. How do things feel: hot, cold, warm, lukewarm, or tepid? Our thermic sense responds when we touch a hot stove, eat frozen ice cream, or take a cold shower. Recommended materials include a thermometer and barometer. Here are some activities for the thermic sense.

Fingers Swim

Fill three shallow or low bowls with water. One bowl should contain hot water; a second cool, or room-temperature water; and a third cold, or melted ice water. The bowls of water should look the same but feel very different. Encourage children to put one or two fingers into one bowl and tell you how it feels. Is the water hot or cold? Pairs of bowls can also be used. Can you find water in another bowl that feels just the same as the water in this one? Since the bowls are open, the hot and cold water will return to room temperature very quickly. Encourage children to discuss which feels like the water they use in the bathtub, to swim in, to water the lawn, to drink on a hot day, or in soup.

Temperature Jars

This activity must be prepared fresh each time. It works best with a very small group. Locate three pairs of identical glass jars. Spice jars are ideal. Fill each pair with equal amounts of one of the following:

- hot (but not scalding) water
- cold or melted ice water
- tepid/lukewarm or room-temperature water

Begin by having children hold one of a pair in one hand. Ask them, "How does it feel? What word describes it? Is it hot, warm, cold, or cool?" Encourage them to use their other hand to find a match that feels the same. Remember that this activity must proceed fairly quickly, since the water in all the jars will quickly return to room temperature. As children master this activity, intermediate temperatures, including finer grades of warm and cool, can be added.

How Does It Feel?

Encourage children to discuss how they feel when they directly experience some of the following:

- being in snow
- being out in the rain
- being in front of an air conditioner or fan
- being near the stove or oven
- being near the fireplace
- taking a bath

- having their hair washed and rinsed
- when opening the door of the refrigerator or freezer
- walking barefoot on sand at the beach in the summer
- playing outside in summer with the sun shining
- walking barefoot in mud
- splashing in the waves at the beach
- having their hair dried with a hair dryer
- fanning a piece of paper in front of their faces
- sucking on a Popsicle
- holding an ice cube

Encourage children to use thermic terms such as hot, warm, cold, freezing, cool, and burning when discussing their reactions.

Thermic Moves

Encourage children to use their bodies to show what happens to water under different temperature conditions.

- Pretend you are a drop of water in the ocean. Someone picks you up with her shovel and carries you home in her sand pail.
- She leaves you outside, and it is getting colder and colder. Winter is coming, and soon it will snow.
- It is freezing cold, and you turn into an ice cube. Someone picks you up and rolls you in the snow. He keeps rolling you until he gets a big ball of snow. He makes two more big balls and stacks them into a snowman. You are up near the snowman's head, and you are very proud.
- Slowly, the sun starts to shine. It is getting warmer and warmer. You are beginning to melt, slowly, very slowly.
- All that's left of the snowman is a big puddle of water.
- Someone scoops you back into the sand pail and brings you inside. She pours the water into a pot and puts it on the stove. She turns the heat on. It feels good being warm inside. The water comes to a boil, and you start to jump around because it is so hot.
- She pours you into the dishpan, and you help make bubbles and clean the dishes.

Thermic Cooking

There are many simple cooking experiences that include heating or freezing ingredients. Here are two simple ones.

Popsicles

1 cup of hot water
2 cups of lemonade
1 package Jell-O (any flavor)

Mix and pour into ice cube trays. Insert a toothpick or Popsicle stick in each. Freeze. Children and adults enjoy these because the Jell-O slows down the melting process and eliminates much of the mess.

Snow Sherbert

Snow (fresh, clean, and white)
1 egg
$\frac{1}{2}$ cup sugar
1 teaspoon vanilla
1 cup milk

Mix ingredients. Slowly add snow. Stop when it reaches the consistency of sherbert.

8. Sterognostic

Being able to recognize objects through tactile-muscular exploration without the aid of vision is the sterognostic sense. Touching and feeling a pinecone involve the tactile sense. But closing one's eyes while touching and handling a pinecone to identify it involves the sterognostic sense. Whereas the tactile sense usually involves visual clues, the sterognostic sense does not. Below are activities for the sterognostic sense.

Feely Bag

Place a margarine tub at the bottom or toe of an old large sock. Children enjoy working an arm through the sock to find the object in the tub. Use objects made of wood, metal, paper, plastic, cloth, cork, glass, rubber, and leather (see Figure 9–4). Encourage children to verbally describe

- how the object feels: Is it rough, smooth, or bumpy?
- the size of the object: Is it big or little?

FIGURE 9–4   Identifying an object by touching without looking

- the shape of the object: Is it round, square, triangular, flat, or solid?
- what the object is made of: Is it made of wood, paper, rubber, glass, or metal?
- the length of the object: Is it long or short?
- the weight of the object: Is it heavy or light?

Children can also guess the object's

- color
- function or purpose: What is it used for?
- name: What is it called? What do you think it is?

As with all questioning, it is important for children to attempt to justify their answer. Asking them, "How do you know?" or "Why do you think so?" encourages them to go beyond random guessing. For example, "I think it's money 'cause it's round, small, and feels like a penny."

Young children may prefer to match the object they touch with its picture or a sample of the actual object. Toddlers will enjoy merely putting things in and out of the Feely Bag.

Blindfold Game

Children can be blindfolded or agree to keep their eyes closed. The child can be given an object—for example, a doll—to thoroughly touch and feel without the aid of vision. The child can use these sterognostic cues to guess what the object is. Young children do tend to peek or tell each other the answer. This is to be expected.

9. Baric

Recognizing objects as heavy or light and gradations in between involves the baric sense. Here is an activity for the baric sense.

Weight Jars

Find a set of six large plastic spice jars and spray paint the insides the same color or cover them with identical wrap. Separate them into pairs—for example, three brown and three yellow—and fill one of each pair with plaster of paris or some other self-hardening and weighted substance

- to the very top
- to the middle
- one-half-inch full

Encourage children to hold one jar in one hand and find another jar that weighs the same. Children should be encouraged to use both hands like a balance scale, with one jar in each hand. Put the matched pair aside. Keep going until the children have decided that the three pairs weigh the same. Subtly coding each matching pair on the bottom will aid in checking. Encourage children to talk about weight. Which pair is heavy/light? Which pair is the heaviest/lightest? Children can order or seriate from heaviest to lightest or vice versa. Older children may enjoy using a set of ten with finer gradations in weight.

10. Kinesthetic

The kinesthetic sense involves a whole-body, sensory-motor muscular response. When we talk about children learning by doing or being actively involved, we are referring to their kinesthetic sense. For example, young children learn about animals by observing, listening, smelling, touching, and using their body to act like them. Moving on all fours like a tiger will help the child form a strong concept of that animal, which is necessary for talking about, reading, or making art objects related to tigers. Some activities for the kinesthetic sense follow.

Musical Moves

Record on tape or find albums of different types of music, including

- jazz
- classical
- waltzes
- calypso
- lullabies
- reggae
- rap
- Latin rhythms
- rock-and-roll
- Irish jig
- polka
- marches
- electronic
- tango
- Broadway show tunes
- country
- soul
- Hawaiian
- African
- zither
- Mexican hat dance
- flamenco
- any and all ethnic

Each piece of music has its own characteristic mood, tempo, and rhythm. Therefore, each will suggest a certain type of bodily expression through movement. This activity combines listening with the kinesthetic sense of body movement. Play different samples of music and encourage children to move the way the music makes them feel. The teacher may want to model and move along with the group. However, encourage children to come up

with their own way of moving rather than imitating the teacher's moves. Turning the lights off may help set the tone. Moving with the aid of scarves or pieces of fabric may help some children. Other shy or insecure children may prefer to merely watch, not participate. Reassure them, but also encourage their eventual participation. Over time and with repeated practice children will become more comfortable and confident in their creative movement.

Listen and Move

Children can also move in response to taped sounds. Tape-record some of the following:

- a waterfall
- birds chirping, soaring, or flapping their wings
- feet marching
- a jet soaring
- sounds of laughter
- animals growling
- waves pounding against rocks
- popcorn popping
- a car engine trying to start on a cold day
- toast popping out of a toaster
- a chainsaw starting up
- skating on ice
- people swimming in a pool
- water coming to a boil
- teakettle whistling
- jumping off a diving board

This movement activity is more sophisticated than the former. It will take more thought on the part of older children to translate what they know about a waterfall into bodily movement.

Shapes Movement **T P K**

Young children will enjoy crawling through openings of different shapes. Find a large cardboard appliance carton. Cut a large geometric shape out of each side. Use a circle, square, triangle, and rectangle. Make sure that each shape is large enough for your biggest child to fit through easily. Mark and reinforce the edges of each cut-out shape with different-colored cloth tape. Children can take turns listening to your directions and crawling through the appropriate shape; for example, "Go in the square and come out the triangle." This activity involves listening, sequencing, shape recognition, and body movement. Make the directions longer and more difficult for older children; for example, "Go in any four-sided figure, come out a red shape (marked with colored cloth tape), and walk around all the shapes two times."

Squeeze, Mash, and Taste

Children will enjoy the movement and physical activity needed to

- squeeze oranges, lemons, limes, or grapefruits on a reamer for juice
- mash apples for cider
- mash tomatoes for juice
- mash carrots for cookies or cake
- mash strawberries for natural ice cream
- mash bananas for yogurt

The finished products can be sampled for snack. Juices that look the same do not always taste the same. Adding sugar to lemon juice changes it from sour to sweet.

Artistic Dramatic Play

Children may enjoy pretending that they are artists. Think of what an artist might wear and do. Items to include would be an old white shirt, a beret, an easel, an art supply box (perhaps an old suitcase), a palette, brushes, goggles, and a sketchbook. Place these in the dramatic play center.

Keep on Movin'   **T P K**

Find a large open space and help children locate their own personal space in which they can move without touching another child. "Today, we are going to pretend that our room is filled up with some very different things. Listening and thinking about the different things will help us move. For example, what if the room was filled from the floor to the ceiling with balloons and we had to move? How would we do it? Show me with your body how you would move. How would it feel on your body?" Ask children how they would move to get through

- Jell-O
- snow
- mashed potatoes
- sand
- ice
- water
- peanut butter
- honey
- frozen yogurt
- ice cream
- cotton candy
- syrup
- glue
- rubber tires
- pillows
- jelly beans

Gingerbread Children

Read the children's classic tale: The Gingerbread Boy. Encourage children to take turns acting out the different parts. Cooking can also be coordinated.

Gingerbread Children

1 box butterscotch pudding mix
½ cup shortening
½ cup brown sugar
1 egg
1½ cups flour
1½ teaspoons ginger
½ teaspoon cinnamon
½ teaspoon baking soda

Cream shortening and sugar. Add egg and let children take turns mixing well. Add dry pudding mix, flour, and spices. Mix well. Distribute individual balls to children. Roll thin and flat, and cut with cookie cutter. Or, mold like clay into gingerbread child. Bake on greased cookie sheet at 350°F for 10 minutes. Will make about a half dozen.

RESIST ART ACTIVITIES

A dried design or picture will resist a second liquid put on top. The process of resist is a fascinating one that intrigues children. They do one picture, put a second covering over it, and end up with a totally different effect.

Here are some resist activities.

Crayon Resist

Children can make a picture or design with crayons. It is important to press hard and color fairly dark. Although much of the paper is covered, some empty space should be left. The colored picture can be covered with

- watercolor
- ink—producing a pitch black, midnight background
- hand painting
- Magic Marker
- shoe polish
- tempera paint

Whichever of these is used for the second coating, the crayon wax will resist the liquid. The liquid will fill in the remaining white negative space. It may also bead up on the colored wax to produce an interesting textured effect.

Paste or Glue Resist

Children can paint a picture or design by making thick marks with paste or glue on white paper. Or apply adhesive to paper and fold the paper in half to get a mirror image. Quickly open up the paper. Let dry thoroughly. Later, paint over the entire paper with

- watercolor
- ink
- tempera paint

The paste or glue will resist any of these liquids. The background will fill up with color, and the dried adhesive will leave a crackled white picture. Let dry thoroughly.

Ink Resist

Children can paint a picture with tempera. Be sure to leave some space white. When the paint is dry, they can cover the entire sheet of paper with black or colored ink. The effect is striking. Black provides a good background for night scenes or Hal-

loween. Blue ink is effective for underwater or sky scenes.

Wax Paper Resist

Place a piece of wax paper over a sheet of white paper. Secure it with tape or paper clips. Use a Popsicle stick to heavily etch a thick line, design, or picture. The pressure will transfer the wax to the paper. Discard the wax paper. Paint over the entire sheet of paper with watercolor or ink. The lines drawn with the Popsicle stick will remain white. This activity takes much patience and fine motor control and is recommended for older children.

Embossed Greeting Card Rubbing

This is a good activity involving families by recycling their greeting cards. Remove fronts of cards, saving those with embossed or raised words and pictures. Remove papers from crayons and also provide chalk. Have child place card on table with embossed side facing up. Child lays thin paper on top and rubs with crayon or chalk. Onionskin paper works well and construction paper is too heavy. Remind child to use the sides of crayon or chalk rather than the tip. Card can be taped in place if it moves about. Allow child to use one card or mix and match several cards.

Masking Tape Resist

Cut different widths and lengths of masking tape and place on table or surface with one end freely unattached for easy removal. Have child pick off and place masking tape onto white paper, making a design. Some children may want to stop here and that's OK. Others may want to paint liquid watercolors or tempera over their taped designs. The watercolor will bead up on the tape, leaving an interesting effect. When dry, if children choose to carefully remove the tape, they will see the white paper underneath contrasting with their painting.

Liquid Shoe Polish Resist

Provide sponge-tip applicator bottles containing liquid shoe polish. Children can first draw a picture on white paper using crayons. Remind them to press firmly. Next they can paint over their pictures using dark shoe polish. When the bottle is empty, check to see if it can be refilled with liquid watercolor or tempera.

Puzzle Pieces Rubbing

Locate puzzles with flat pieces. Provide thin paper. Have child select a puzzle keeping the pieces in the frame. Lay a piece of thin paper on top of the puzzle. Using the side of a peeled crayon or chalk have the child gently rub all over the paper. Upon removing the paper the child will see how the outlines of the individual pieces form the puzzle.

Black Magic Pictures

The secret of these pictures is fluorescent crayons which glow brightly through a wash of black paint. Encourage children to press hard with their crayons and do thick coloring. Provide black poster or tempera paint. Dilute your paint so it is thick enough to color the paper but thin enough to let the colors show through. Have children brush their pictures using broad sweeping strokes. The fluorescent crayons resist the paint so the picture stands out brightly against the black background.

Name Savers

Write child's name in white wax crayon before he or she begins painting at the easel. Encourage child to paint over your white marks. Magically, his or her name appears.

White Crayon Resist

Remove the white from boxes of crayons and set them aside for resist activities. Provide white crayons and white paper. This may frustrate children who want to see what they are doing. Have them persevere and paint with tempera or liquid watercolors to reveal their marks.

Secret Message

Kindergartners and school-age children will enjoy writing secret messages with white crayons on white paper. They can pass their notes to a friend who then paints it with liquid watercolor or tempera to reveal the message. Remind children that secret messages must be positive and not hurtful or offensive.

White Wax Candle Resist

Provide children with white wax candles. They can be used for drawing or coloring on paper. When done, children can use liquid watercolor or tempera to wash over their marks. The wax resists the paint, leaving the marks intact. You can also do this resist activity on a piece of white cloth. Press down very hard with the white wax candle. The child can brush undiluted liquid watercolor or liquid tempera over the cloth. The fabric remains white where the candle left white marks.

Spray Bottle Resist

Provide clear child-sized spray bottles with trigger-type handles. Fill each with diluted liquid watercolor. Locate flat objects like keys, combs, craft sticks, and puzzle pieces from an incomplete set. This activity is best done outdoors. Roll out a long piece of butcher paper. Have the child choose and arrange shapes on the paper. Teach child how to use and aim the spray bottles to squirt the objects. The child can remove the objects when dry. The shapes resist the watercolor, leaving their impression. Provide a bucket of water and towels so children can wash and dry their objects for the next child.

SUMMARY

Sensory stimulation was viewed as involving more than the five senses. Experiences in sensory stimulation can begin in infancy. Montessori identified the chromatic, thermic, sterognostic, baric, and kinesthetic as vital senses. Materials and activities for each of these senses were provided. Senses, however, do not operate in isolation, and a multisensory approach was advocated. The relationship between sensing, perceiving, feeling, thinking, and concept formation was identified.

Suggested Activities

1. Select one of the sensory activities from this unit and implement it with young children.

2. Plan and implement a multisensory cooking experience.

3. Observe in a Montessori classroom. Focus on the sensory materials and how children use them.

4. Stock a sensory table and use with young children.

Review

A. Match the sense with its key descriptive terms.

_____ 1. auditory   a. touch
_____ 2. olfactory   b. smell
_____ 3. chromatic   c. weight
_____ 4. visual   d. color
_____ 5. gustatory   e. hearing
_____ 6. kinesthetic   f. looking
_____ 7. baric   g. temperature
_____ 8. thermic   h. tactile-muscular
_____ 9. tactile   i. movement
_____ 10. sterognostic   j. taste

B. Use the example of a young child eating cotton candy for the first time to explain the following equation:

Senses + Perception + Feeling + Thinking = Concept Formation

CHAPTER 10

The Complete Early Childhood Art Program

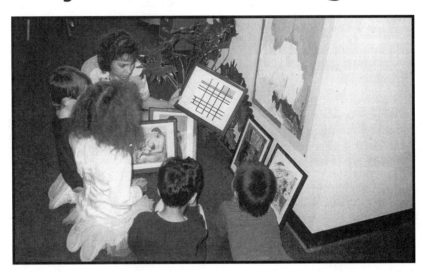

Juanita has found that some of her four-year-olds make derogatory comments about each other's art. "That's no good" or "That's dumb" or "That's not how it's supposed to look!" How would you handle this?

At times Juanita decides simply to ignore it and let her children attempt to work it out. At other times she empowers children by encouraging them to talk about how comments hurt their feelings. "I don't like it when you say my picture's ugly 'cause I worked hard." Juanita came up with a third strategy. She looked at her art program to see if something was missing. Did she set too-high standards? Did she expect realistic art that the children could not produce? Juanita decided to help her children see that art comes in a variety of forms. She did this by assembling a series of art prints. She laminated each to avoid damage. In this photo the children see that art might be nothing more than crossing lines, or it might portray a mother and her baby. Both are valid as art.

Does this strategy sound like something you could use with your children both to expose them to a wide variety of artistic styles and to validate the way they make art?

OBJECTIVES

After studying this chapter, the student will be able to

- Describe and give an example of each of the four components of a complete early childhood art program
- List and explain the three major divisions for categorizing artistic styles or movements
- Use the art critique to discuss a work of art
- Provide collage activities

INTRODUCTION

Although making art is a first priority, it is only one of the four major components of a complete early childhood art program. It is also important for young children to engage in sensory experiences; learn about art, artists, and their styles; and pursue beauty through aesthetics. This unit will focus on constructing a total or complete early childhood art program.

EARLY CHILDHOOD ART: STUDIO-ORIENTED OR DISCIPLINE-BASED?

The approach to art advocated throughout this book is mainly but not exclusively a studio-oriented approach. This approach holds that young children should be left free to experiment with creative materials. The studio-oriented approach has dominated teacher training and influences current thinking and practice with respect to early childhood art. A second approach, discipline-based art education (DBAE), is gaining hold in elementary and secondary education. This approach, advocated by the Getty Center for Education in the Arts (1985, 1989; Kaagan, 1990), recommends going beyond teaching mere technical skills. The Getty Center adopted an approach to visual arts education calling for the teaching of content and skills from four disciplines that contribute to the creation, understanding, and appreciation of art. These are art production, art history, art criticism, and aesthetics.

The author's approach has been somewhat comprehensive in that it stresses a studio approach while going beyond mere art production in building a complete early childhood art program. This complete program also includes aesthetics and learning about art, artists, and their styles. Sensing and experiencing, not included in the Getty Center's components, are included in this program. Although the Getty Center did not focus on early childhood education, the author believes these are vital components for the early years.

WHAT TO INCLUDE IN AN EARLY CHILDHOOD ART PROGRAM

It is important that children have ample opportunities to make art. However, although it is basic, processing with the media to make art is only one of four key components of any complete early childhood art program. A complete program provides

1. Sensory experiences
2. Beautiful and creative experiences
3. Time, space, and materials for making art
4. An introduction to the world of art, artists, and a variety of art forms and styles

The first three components should be emphasized during the early years, and the fourth component gradually introduced. Actually, the four components are interrelated, and the separation exists only for the present analysis. For example, making art is dependent on sensing and experiencing.

1. Sensory Experiences

Children do not magically create out of a vacuum or in isolation. Art has an origin. It originates from something personally experienced, an idea, object of importance, event, feeling, or person. A child's daily experiences provide a potential bank of things to include in art. For example, Joshua's idea for painting a farm did not just automatically happen. It was related to spending the weekend at his grandparents' farm. Field trips are crucial because they extend a child's personal range of experiences to the wider community. For example, taking a trip to the fire station provides new content for art.

Sometimes the term *disadvantaged* is used to refer to children who lack these basic environmental experiences. They may be uncomfortable discussing and being tested on things they have never directly experienced. It is dangerous to assume that all children have experienced and know about libraries, hospitals, airports, stadiums, skyscrapers, elevators, cathedrals, post offices, seashores, or museums. Encourage parents to take their children places and discuss what they have experienced (see Figure 10–1). This will help the children form concepts and

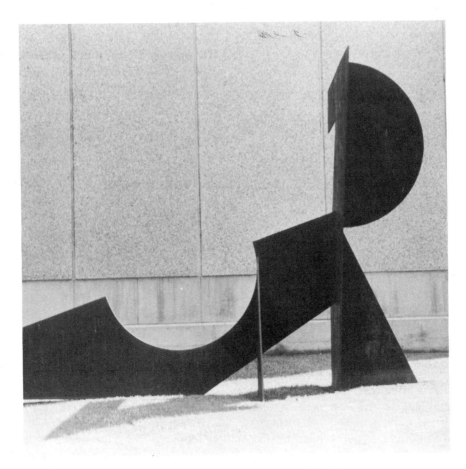

FIGURE 10–1   Young children can experience a variety of art forms.

will serve as a backdrop for future learning. For example, an informal trip to the hardware store can be a simple but sensory-rich experience filled with the sound, smell, and touch of cut wood or tools classified according to form and function.

Young children are sensory gluttons. Infants and toddlers are fascinated by pattern and detail. They will follow a bug crawling across the floor or marvel at water dripping from a melted icicle. Unfortunately, adults may take these experiences for granted and need to recapture some of this childlike wonder and awareness. Young children will need practice in keeping it alive.

According to Piaget, children come to know their world through their senses and actions. Our role is to help children note details and use all their senses to build rich object concepts. For example, smelling and tasting are appropriate when visiting a bakery, whereas looking and listening are warranted during story time in the library. Objects such as nature specimens can be brought in for focused sensory exploration. "Let's look at the empty hornet's nest. Carefully touch the sides. How does it feel? Do you hear anything when you put your ear to the opening? Let's wrap papier-mâché around a balloon and see if we can make our own hornet's nest."

2. Beautiful and Creative Experiences

Aesthetics is the study of beauty—not the Hollywood view of glamour, but beauty in color, form, and design. In a time of mass production with little concern for effort and quality craftsmanship, the quest for beauty is difficult. Still, there is a human need to make sense out of and appreciate one's self and one's environment, just as there is a basic need to create.

Beauty can be found in nature, in one's surroundings, and in everyday objects. Children can use their senses and their bodies in their pursuit of beauty. The eyes can visually explore art, and the ears can listen to sounds and music. Three-dimensional artworks can be touched, scents can be smelled, foods can be tasted, and the body can respond through movement and dance. Young children can learn to appreciate and have beautiful experiences.

Children need to take the time to perceive the beauty in their everyday environment. Classrooms or centers can be aesthetically pleasing places and models of beauty. The room should be clean, bright, and colorful without being chaotic, cluttered, and gaudy. It should appeal to the senses and have things to look at, listen to, touch, smell, and taste. Flowers, plants, animals, soft pillows, a rocking chair, and a piece of sculpture add an aesthetic touch to the room.

Displays are places that children can visit to refine their senses and build aesthetic appreciation. Aesthetic displays can include nature specimens, a postcard collection, items of different textures, art books, antique tools or gadgets, machinery parts, pottery, fabric, postage stamps, foreign currency, or items of a given size, shape, or color. Centers or areas for art, music, and movement give children opportunities to actively represent beautiful images, thoughts, feelings, and concepts through art, music, rhythm, and dance.

Aesthetics is not confined to the interior environment. Beauty abounds in nature and the community. Children can also visit exhibits of beautiful things in museums, churches, and galleries, and they can attend concerts and performances. Artists, dancers, and musicians also can be invited to perform for and work with the children.

3. Time, Space, and Materials for Making Art

Young children need to be personally expressive and creative and to experience success through art. Teachers can help children see the relationship between art and experience. For example, a child may ask, "Teacher, what should I draw?" or "I don't know what to make." A teacher can help a child refer to significant people, places, and things: "What did you watch on TV?" or "How did you celebrate this past holiday?" or "What do you remember about our story today?" Teachers can encourage children to give artistic form and substance to their ideas, urges, wishes, dreams, fears, or interests. The bulk of this book continues our discussion of making art.

4. An Introduction to the World of Art, Artists, and a Variety of Art Forms and Styles

Children may wonder: What is art? Who are artists? Why do they make art? Art is a basic human need. People make art to reflect and symbolize their existence. Children's interest in and study of community helpers can extend to artists. Children can learn that while some artists make art for a hobby, others do it as a career. Some work at home, outdoors, or in studios. Some artists exhibit and sell their works in galleries. Famous artists have their works exhibited in museums.

Children can also learn that artists work in different media. Although not all artists paint, all do have a pressing need to communicate. They use brush strokes, color, content, form, and the artistic elements to get their points across. Helping children accept and value their own artwork will enable them to appreciate and value the artwork of others. Our intent is to expose children to their rich artistic heritage rather than teach art history. Children can learn that people everywhere and from the beginning of time have made art. It is part of a culture and tells us something about people: who they were, what they looked like, how they lived, what they wore, where they lived, and what they liked to do. A discussion of the major artistic styles and movements follows.

ARTISTIC STYLES

Prehistoric or Primitive Art

Era: 25,000 years ago during the Paleolithic or Old Stone Age
10–15,000 years later during the Neolithic or New Stone Age

Artists:
Unknown cave artists

People have been doing art for many years, way back to the days of when humans first appeared. Just as we have artists' pictures hanging on our walls today, people decorated the walls of their caves with pictures. Cave artists mixed their own paints out of plants, berries, and other foods as well as earth, mud, and clay, most likely mixed with animal blood. They used sharpened sticks to draw and etch pictures. Cave artists liked to draw simple stick-figure people and animals, including leaping bison and deer, using only a few lines. Outlines were bold, and pictures were decorated with geometric patterns and designs. Proportion was correct. Cave people drew what they knew: themselves, others, and wild animals. That is what their life was about: survival, hunting, food, and safety from wild animals. Primitive people viewed art as magic. To symbolize something meant to somehow capture or control it.

An activity based on this style could be to have children paint a person or animal of their choice on a fairly large, smooth stone.

Naturalistic or Realistic Art

Era: 1700–1800s (Naturalistic)
Artists:
>   Honore Daumier
>   Francisco Goya
>   Rembrandt

Era: Nineteenth century on (United States) (Realistic)
Artists:
>   John James Audubon
>   Winslow Homer
>   Edward Hopper
>   Norman Rockwell
>   James Whistler
>   Grant Wood
>   Andrew Wyeth

Although *naturalism* and *realism* are somewhat different terms, we will use them interchangeably. Both terms emphasize the artist's attempt to make art objective and like the actual object. During the 1700s and 1800s painters attempted to portray life exactly as it was. This was a reaction against a neo-classic and romantic view of the ideal life. Naturalists chose to depict life as it was, often sordid and evil, and people as they were, overweight, ill, and less than beautiful. For example, a still life with flowers and fruit might include bugs and decaying food.

Naturalism and realism also became popular in the United States in the nineteenth century. Landscapes, birds, farms, the wilderness, and people represented the struggle and simplicity of early American life. Children can examine naturalistic or realistic art and appreciate all the time, effort, skills, and talent needed to make a photographic likeness.

An activity for older children could be to set up a very simple arrangement, for example, a stuffed animal and a doll. Encourage the children to try to draw or paint the two toys just as they are. They will need to examine them repeatedly for color, detail, and shape. This activity may prove frustrating, so it should be offered as an option.

American Folk Art

Era: 1700–1800s and currently
Artists:
>   Grandma Moses
>   Charles Wysocki

American folk artists do art with little or no formal training. They are proof that anyone and everyone is capable of making an artistic statement. As an artistic movement, American folk artists lived in New England, New York, and Pennsylvania in the late 1700s to mid-1800s. Folk artists continue to work at their art form or craft today. Folk art can be identified by its bold, simple designs, vivid colors, and simplistic handling of light, proportion, and perspective. Generally, folk art makes a social, political, or religious statement. Often common objects and events, including flowers, baking bread, going to market, or getting married, are depicted. It is this primitive, homey quality that appeals to the public. Folk artists are versatile and work in a variety of media and crafts.

An activity could be to let children make a person out of a wooden clothespin (nonclip type). Details could be added with fine markers. Yarn could be available for hair, material scraps for clothing.

Impressionism

Era: late 1800s to early 1900s
Artists:

> Mary Cassatt
> Paul Cézanne
> Edgar Degas
> Eugène Delacroix
> Raoul Dufy
> Paul Gauguin
> Édouard Manet
> Claude Monet
> Camille Pissarro
> Pierre Auguste Renoir
> Henri de Toulouse-Lautrec
> Vincent van Gogh

Impressionists were fascinated with color, sunshine, contrasts, light, reflection, and shadow. They were concerned with making only a quick sketch of an object to capture its essence. Later they rapidly filled in their crude outline with intense patches of pigment. They used color and light to represent the artist's impression. Impressionists painted what they saw rather than what they knew to be there. They preferred painting outdoors with natural light. Landscapes were popular subject matter. When viewed from up close, Impressionist paintings depict a vibrating brilliance of colors, pure and unmixed. When viewed from a distance, however, the eyes fuse these neighboring color patches, constructing form and perceiving movement.

An activity could be to make an outdoor painting by dabbing paint with an index finger. Encourage children to place separate dabs rather than mixing them. Or children could use bright fluorescent crayons in making their strokes.

Pointillism

Era: late 1800s to early 1900s
Artist:

> Georges Seurat

Pointillism, an offshoot of Impressionism, involved a concern for color and an innovative technique for representing it. Pointillists worked on large canvases, spending as much as a year or more on one canvas. Small dots or points of pure color were used instead of Impressionist dashes or strokes. Pointillists were concerned with the complementary relationship between colors. They did not mix colors, but instead required that the observer fuse neighboring colors. For example, pointillists would represent water as composed of neighboring dots or points of green and yellow. When viewed from up close, the observer would see only green and yellow dots. From a distance, however, the eyes would blend the yellow and green and perceive blue water.

An activity could be to use crayons or markers to make a picture composed entirely of different-colored dots. Encourage children to use dots rather than lines at all times. Or children can make a picture by dipping the eraser end of a pencil into red, blue, and yellow paint and making a print in the shape of dots. This activity is recommended after children have had an opportunity to do color mixing. For example, if they want to make a purple car, they can use the pointillist technique of alternating red and blue dots in printing. Dots are placed close together with white space between. Younger children who do not have a command of color mixing should be encouraged to merely make a picture or design with colored dots.

Expressionism

Era: late 1800s to 1900s
Artists:

Paul Gauguin	Emil Nolde
Wassily Kandinsky	Georgia O'Keeffe
Piet Mondrian	Diego Rivera
Edvard Munch	

Expressionists, reacting against Impressionism, searched for emotional expression in their artistic statements. Expressionists purposely altered space, form, line, and color to make an emotional statement that was expressionistic rather than realistic, naturalistic, or impressionistic. The actual subject matter was often lost in the colorful and even violent play of color, line, shape, contrast, and movement. Expressionists distorted reality to express their own view and mood. Since this movement was popular at the time of World War I, it is easy to see how the art reflected contemporary culture. Much of the artwork at this time was violent, depressing, and highly emotional.

An activity could be to let children finger paint to mood music. Music that conveys sorrow, joy, and anger could be played. Encourage children to paint how they feel.

Abstract Expressionism

Era: late 1940s
Artists:

Elaine de Kooning	Jackson Pollock
Willem de Kooning	Mark Rothko
Hans Hofmann	

Abstract expressionists were intrigued with color and the physical qualities of paint: "What can I do with paint on canvas?" Abstract expressionism began after World War II. Jackson Pollock is a good example of an abstract expressionist who practiced action or gesture painting by dripping, dribbling, spraying, pouring, throwing, and splashing paint. Design was often left to chance or accident. These painters worked on very large canvases with no concern for capturing reality or shape or for telling a story through pictures.

An activity could be to put globs of paint on paper and let children use a soda straw to blow the paint around. The straws should be held close to the paint but not make contact with it. Remind children to exhale or blow out and not inhale or suck in. Children may also like to work outdoors on a group mural. Children can take turns dripping paint, using squeeze bottles or carefully trickling paint from a paper cup.

Fauvism

Era: 1910s
Artists:

André Derain	Henri Matisse
Raoul Dufy	Amedeo Modigliani
Paul Gauguin	Georges Rouault

Fauvism is an offshoot of Expressionism. Fauvists experimented with pure, bright colors in daring and innovative ways to represent positive emotions, including joy, pleasure, comfort, love, and happiness. Often there was little concern for the naturalistic or realistic use of color. Fauvists might not be concerned with mixing the proper color for skin. Human skin could be painted pink, green, or whatever, depending on the artist's mood. In this way, Fauvists believed that they could use color to make an emotional statement. Objects were characterized with bold outlines and abstract lines. An emotional use of color was of primary concern.

An activity could be to make a picture depicting a positive emotion or feeling, such as joy, love, hope, happiness, or caring. Encourage children to select and use the crayons that they believe best capture their feeling, with little or no concern for the naturalistic or realistic use of color. What does "happy" mean to you? Let's find a "happy" colored crayon to make our happy picture. "No, Sara, your happy picture doesn't have to look like anything!"

Cubism

Era: 1900s
Artists:

Georges Braque	Fernand Léger
Paul Cézanne	Piet Mondrian
Marcel Duchamps	Pablo Picasso
Juan Gris	Georges Rouault

Cubism is the source of all twentieth-century abstract art. It seeks an intellectual conception of form and shape. Cubists attempt to break everything down into its component geometric or architectural shapes. How can three-dimensional form, including the back side and bottom, be represented on a two-dimensional flat canvas? To do this, Cubists abandoned traditional treatment of space and form and instead focused on the use of the cylinder, sphere, and cube. For example, a Cubist might represent a tree by simultaneously depicting its top, sides, back, insides, and bottom. Intellectually, we are shown the entire tree. There is little concern for color, depth, or proper perspective. Objects appear flat, with little concern for background or foreground. They may be repeated in an overlapping sequence to suggest motion and movement. Cubists introduced the art form of collage.

An activity could be to make a collage using only geometric paper shapes, either cut or torn. Since a collage often has letters embedded in it, children could search through magazines and add letters to their own collage.

Kinetic Art

Era: 1920s
Artists:

>   Alexander Calder
>   Marcel Duchamps

Why must art be flat and motionless? Kinetic art attempts to incorporate physical movement by using levers, gears, and movable parts. Kinetic art invites participation. People interacting with kinetic sculpture cause it to move or change. Wind also causes the hanging objects on a mobile to move.

An activity could be to have children make a mobile. Or older children could attempt a moving junk sculpture or assemblage. For example, a robot could be constructed using fasteners, yarn, string, wire, nuts and bolts, and rubber bands, which would facilitate movement.

Surrealism

Era: 1900s
Artists:

>   Marc Chagall   René Magritte
>   Salvador Dali   Joan Miró
>   Jean Dubuffet   Georgia O'Keeffe
>   Max Ernst   Man Ray
>   Raoul Hausmann   Henri Rousseau
>   Frida Kahlo   Ben Shahn
>   Paul Klee

Surrealism means superrealism. It attempts to create a magical, dreamlike world that is more intense than reality. Dreams, images, fantasies, and the subconscious are chosen as subject matter and portrayed either realistically or abstractly. Objects, space, symbols, size, perspective, time, and shape may be distorted, transformed, or superimposed. For example, a fish with a human head may fly through a rock-laden sky. The viewer may appear shocked and ask, What is it? What is it supposed to be? What does it mean? The artist has been successful in causing the viewer to stop, observe, and emotionally respond.

An activity could be to encourage children to represent their dreams, wishes, fantasies, nightmares, and innermost thoughts and feelings. Encourage children to make a personal statement that may not always be pleasant, pretty, or intelligible.

Pop Art

Era: 1950s
Artists:

>   Jasper Johns
>   Roy Lichtenstein
>   Andy Warhol

Pop, or popular, art makes a social statement or critique of contemporary American culture. Pop artists chose subject matter that was familiar to everyday life—soup cans, soft drink containers, movie stars, cartoons, and other examples of advertising art. The common, taken-for-granted product becomes art. Although obvious in subject matter, these objects were represented, often in repeated fashion, with painstaking, realistic detail. Again, photographic realism was attempted and attained. There was no intent to make an emotional statement beyond the satire of the commercialism of contemporary culture.

An activity could be to have older children design their own package or wrapper for a candy bar, cereal, or soft drink. Or children could attempt to draw their own or a group cartoon strip with finepoint markers. Four or five frames may be sufficient.

Op Art

Era: 1960s
Artists:

>   Frank Stella
>   Victor Vasarely

Op, or optical, art was an artistic style that developed in the psychedelic 1960s. Op artists were intrigued with the effects of black and white, color, figure-ground relations, and depth. They used the principles of optics and perception to create optical illusions with shapes, lines, and patterns. Wiggly and concentric lines and patterns suggested movement and form in the eye of the beholder.

Op art is a style that demands much in the way of technical proficiency and does not easily translate into an early childhood art activity.

Different artists use different styles. The same artist may use different styles at different times or periods. Children also have their own artistic styles. There is no one right or best way. Different styles are appropriate depending on the artist and what he or she is trying to say through art. Exposing children to the major artistic styles or movements serves two purposes (see Figure 10–2). First, it shows children that there are many possible ways to make art. Second, it shows the similarities between their own styles and the styles that artists have used in the past and continue to use today. For example, children's art resembles both prehistoric art and modern abstract art.

A very simplistic breakdown of the major artistic movements includes

- realistic or naturalistic
- abstract
- nonobjective

Realistic or naturalistic art attempts to represent people, places, and objects exactly as they appear. There is an emphasis on objectivity, detail, and photographic realism. Children who aim for photographic realism in their art will be disappointed because developmentally they lack the necessary perceptual, physical, and cognitive ability. Realism or naturalism is merely one of many styles. Many adult artists are successful and satisfied in spite of their inability to produce realistic or naturalistic art.

Abstract art bears only a partial resemblance to the object being represented. The object is somehow streamlined or distorted. An example would be a child's drawing of a box on two wheels to represent a race car.

FIGURE 10–2   Young children can be introduced to the different artistic styles.

Nonobjective art involves a creative play with color, shape, line, and design. It is abstract art pushed to the limits. What is produced bears no resemblance to any actual object. For example, a child could paint racing swirls of paint to represent the speed and exhaust fumes associated with a race car rather than abstractly capturing its overall shape.

Art Critique   Even young children can be taught to critique a work of art. First, a teacher provides some background information about the particular piece: who made it, what the artist was like, what the world was like at the time. Young children are egocentric and may be more interested in their own art than in the artwork of others. Cognitively, they will be unable to empathize fully with the lives, plights, and historical times of famous artists. Still, an introduction to the foundations of good art and our artistic heritage is warranted.

Langer (1957) wrote that in order for effective art criticism to occur, three components are necessary: a communicator, the artist; a medium, the artwork; and a receiver or viewer who accepts, interprets, and incorporates what the artist has communicated. Cole and Schaefer (1990) add a fourth component, a facilitator. A teacher who guides the encounter between artwork and child by carrying on an art critique is acting as a facilitator. The role of the teacher as facilitator or enabler will be discussed in detail in Chapter 15.

The art critique can focus on the following five points:

1. What is it?
   Is it a painting, drawing, batik, weaving, or print? What are its physical properties? Is it big, small, square, round, solid, moving, or framed? What is it made out of? Did the artist use paper, paint, metal, clay, or yarn?
2. What do you see when you look at this work of art?
   Encourage children to focus on the artist's use of line, color, shape or form, mass or volume, design, pattern, space, balance, and texture. How are these artistic elements used? What shapes do

you see? What colors were used? Can anyone find lines?
3. What is the artist trying to say?
   Try to put the artist's picture into words. What is the message? Pretend that this is a book with pictures. What words go along with the picture the artist has given? Discuss what you see: people, animals, buildings, or events.
4. How does it make you feel?
   Do you feel happy, sad, angry, scared, or funny? What does the artist do to make you feel this way?
5. Do you like it?
   Why or why not? What is it about the work of art that makes you like or dislike it? How would you change it?

Questions 4 and 5 will evoke very different responses. Our aim is to help children acquire artistic appreciation and make judgments based on accepted standards, including the artistic elements.

COLLAGE

A collage is a picture composed of different shapes or elements. A collage can be two-dimensional and composed of flat pieces of paper, or it can be three-dimensional and made with Styrofoam chips and raised layers of fabric. Pieces of paper that are torn, cut, pasted, or taped can be creatively arranged into a collage. Although the activities are listed separately, there is no reason that materials used in one activity cannot be included in another. There is an endless variety of papers that can be used in collage. Some include

- junk mail
- postage stamps
- postcards
- greeting cards
- gift wrap
- wallpaper samples
- travel brochures
- magazines
- newspapers
- coupons
- tinfoil

A collage is not limited to paper. There is an infinite supply of collage materials. The key is quality and organization. Not all junk will have artistic value or potential. Items that are dirty or damaged may hold little aesthetic appeal. A pile of unorganized junk may trigger little creative transformation. It is important to organize collage materials according to some scheme—for example, papers in one bin; ribbon, lace, and yarn in another; magazines in a neat stack on the shelf; and so forth. Children need some basic order to help them see artistic possibilities.

Geometric Shapes Collage

Younger children who lack scissoring skills may enjoy pasting precut geometric shapes into a design or picture. Provide an array of different colors, sizes, and shapes. Older children who have scissoring skills can draw and cut their own geometric shapes. Encourage children to place their shapes into some arrangement before gluing or pasting them. Or a rough sketch or outline can be drawn first and later filled in with geometric shapes.

Corrugated Cardboard Collage

Corrugated cardboard has an interesting texture and linear look. Older children can cut different shapes or pieces out of it and make a collage. Encourage them to note how the ridges can go in different directions. This is what gives a corrugated cardboard collage its visual appeal. Corrugated cardboard, with its raised ridges and neutral color, provides a striking contrast when it is used with flat or colorful papers or fabric.

Tissue Paper Collage

Colored tissue paper can be torn or cut. Because it is so thin, it may frustrate the young cutter. Provide small bowls of liquid starch and sponge squares or small brushes for spreading. Encourage children to note both the transparent quality of tissue paper and the possibilities for creating new colors by overlapping and building layers.

Or form a tissue paper collage on a piece of wax paper. Lay another piece of wax paper on top. An adult can gently press with a warm iron. The heat will melt the wax and seal the collage.

Or use thinned white glue to paste tissue papers inside the plastic lid of a coffee can. This will provide a ready-made frame. Carefully punch a hole at the top, lace with yarn, and hang.

Magazine Picture Collage

Magazines offer a wealth of letters, words, and pictures just waiting to be torn or cut out and pasted or taped to paper.

Montage

Montage refers to a collage built around a theme, such as love, friendship, family, pets, or helping. Words and pictures related to the theme can be included. A montage around the theme of vehicles might include pictures of cars, trucks, bikes, airplanes, boats, motorcycles, stop signs, and traffic lights.

Collage Mural

A collage can also be a group project correlated with a unit or concept under study. Some examples include

- color
- shape
- size
- initial consonants
- people
- community helpers
- other classes, concepts, and categories

Children can search through magazines looking for samples or examples of the concept. A collage mural can be an extended activity; it need not be completed in a short period of time. It could be set up as a center, with children adding to it from time to time over a period of a few days.

Magazine Mix-Ups

Children have a silly sense of humor. They might enjoy making a picture out of unrelated parts—for example, an animal with a human head or the front of a car with the tail of an airplane. One teacher introduced this activity by providing part of a picture for each child. The pieces, cut from a magazine, were different for each child. Examples included a cat's head, a person's body, the trunk of a tree, and a diving board with no steps. Children were encouraged to look through their magazine and find a part that would finish their mixed-up picture by adding a silly top, bottom, head, body, or side as needed. There was no need to correctly finish the picture.

A collage does not always have to be done on paper. Be creative. Provide

- cardboard
- paper plates
- box lids
- wood
- plastic foam meat trays
- egg cartons
- containers

Nor does collage entail only the use of paper. Look through your artistic junk for a variety of materials that can be pasted, glued, stapled, or taped, such as

fabric scraps	lace
felt	computer junk
feathers	including resistors,
Styrofoam scraps	wafers, carriers, etc.
and pellets	rickrack
dried grass	yarn
leaves and twigs	curling ribbon
bottle caps	stars and stickers
tinsel	cornhusks
cotton balls	paper baking cups
tongue depressors	jar lids
washers	broken toys
beads	coffee grounds
coffee filters	hair rollers
gauze	zippers
sawdust	burlap
wool	excelsior
game pieces	shoelaces
emery boards	toothpicks
sequins	beads
bias tape	wire
broken egg shells	ribbon
rubber bands	string
electronics parts	pipe cleaners
paper scraps	pinecones

wood scraps	shells
straws	flowers
foil	seeds
gravel	Q-tips
flat wooden spoons	spools
bolts	acorns
wool	fur
bones	jewelry
Easter grass	chains
berry baskets	keys
paper cups	foam rubber
checkers	nature items
cork	hardware
paint-chip samples	springs
buttons	

Nature Collage

Nature specimens can be carefully glued onto paper or sturdy cardboard. Some examples include

- leaves
- ferns
- grass
- petals
- weeds
- flowers

Other examples of nature items are listed in Appendix A. Some prefer to first press their nature specimens for about a week between layers of newspaper with heavy objects on top to get them flat. Or they can be arranged on wax paper with a second sheet on top and pressed with a warm iron. (See Figure 10–3.)

Fabric, Felt, or Material Collage

Children enjoy using materials other than paper in their collage. Provide small scraps of fabric, felt, or material for the young child to paste or glue. Older children with fairly sharp scissors and good cutting skills may be able to cut out or tear their own pieces. (See Figure 10–4.)

String or Yarn Collage

A collage can be composed of string or yarn. Each can be dipped in glue and creatively arranged on an art surface. Remind the children to squeeze the excess glue out before placing the string. Obviously,

FIGURE 10–3 Nature collage

string or yarn should be incorporated with other collage material.

Texture Collage

Most of the collage activities mentioned involve textures. A collage can also specifically focus on textured papers, including

- sandpaper
- flocked wallpaper
- tissue paper
- newspaper
- magazine pages

or a variety of textured fabrics and materials, including

- wool
- cotton
- velvet
- burlap
- netting
- foam rubber

A variety of textured nature specimens, listed under Nature Collage, above, and in Appendix A, can be included. (See Figure 10–5.)

FIGURE 10–4 Fabric collage

FIGURE 10–5   Texture collage

SUMMARY

This unit focused on building a comprehensive early childhood art program. Recommended program components included experiences in sensing; beautiful experiences; making art; and learning about art, artists, and their styles. Although young children need not become art historians, it was recommended that they be introduced to the major artistic movements. These were identified as realistic or naturalistic, abstract, and nonobjective. Individual styles and artists within each general category were identified. A format for conducting an art critique was also provided.

Suggested Activities

1. Arrange to visit an art gallery, exhibit, or museum. Try to identify works of art that belong in each of the three major artistic movements or styles.

2. Use the art critique to analyze and discuss a work of art. Research the artist and era.

3. Begin a collection of art postcards, photographs, prints, posters, or books. Visit thrift shops, used book stores, and library sales.

4. Arrange to accompany a group of young children on an informal field trip to a local art museum, gallery, or artist's studio. Visit in advance to know what is available.

5. Arrange for an artist to come in, model art processing, and informally work with the children.

6. Set up a collage center and help children create.

Review

A. List the components of a complete early childhood art program.
   1.
   2.
   3.
   4.

B. Identify and briefly explain the major artistic movements.
   1.
   2.
   3.

C. List the major points or questions for conducting an art critique.
   1.
   2.
   3.
   4.
   5.

Providing Art Experiences

*I*t is time to translate what you have learned about art, creativity, and child development into curriculum. What is curriculum? A simple definition is that curriculum is what happens in the classroom—both the planned and unplanned. Our focus will be on planning art activities and turning the unexpected and unplanned into meaningful learning experiences. Chapter 11, Child-Centered Art vs. Teacher-Directed Projects, provides criteria or guidelines for selecting activities which have artistic merit as opposed to non-art activities which rely on patterns and much adult input. Chapter 12, Planning, Implementing, and Evaluating Art, focuses on the role of the teacher as curriculum developer. The chapter also offers different approaches to curriculum development. Chapter 13, Integrating Art Across the Early Childhood Curriculum, makes a connection between art and the curricular areas. Activities are provided to show how art can support academic learning by being part of experiences in mathematics, science, literacy, social studies, and the expressive arts. Chapter 14 provides criteria for setting up an art center.

Byron, nearly five, is painting at the easel. What has he painted? Byron has used paint and brush to practice making letters that he knows. He has taken creative liberty with some, but there is no need for concern. Most likely, he will correct himself. Byron has used art to practice printscript. The lines and circles that once formed his earlier scribbles are now coordinated and form letters of the alphabet.

J. T., an older toddler, is standing at the art table. What do you see happening? What kind of art activity has the teacher planned? Which materials appear to be J. T.'s favorite? Why did he use only the toy cars and ignore the lids and small plastic rake? What does this tell you? In planning, did the teacher put out too many items? Were some of the items placed out of J. T.'s reach? Would you plan this art activity differently? Would this same activity work better for younger or older children? How might you change it for school-age children?

It is late afternoon in a High/Scope program for school-age children. What do you see happening? The director is looking over the shoulder of his head teacher, who sits with her group of younger school-age children for an art activity. Can you tell from the materials on the table what she has planned? What is the nature of this art activity? What will the children do? What will the result be? How does creativity fit into this picture?

CHAPTER 11

Child-Centered Art vs. Teacher-Directed Projects

W hat do you see in this photograph? What does Adam's face tell you? Does he appear to be a bit unsure about art?

Adam has not had a lot of experience using paint, crayons, or markers. He watches what other children do with the media. At times, art can be messy. This confuses Adam because his family expects him to stay clean at school. Adam's parents also expect him to create beautiful pictures that look like something recognizable. His family values art. As Adam's teacher, however, you sense that Adam is not ready to create realistic art. You want to let Adam observe and creatively process and explore. You also feel pressure from his parents to teach Adam how to make art that looks like something they know.

What should you do? What kinds of art experiences are appropriate for young children like Adam?

OBJECTIVES

After studying this chapter, the student will be able to

- State the criteria or guidelines for early childhood art activities
- Apply the criteria or guidelines for early childhood art activities in critiquing photocopied or mimeographed sheets; coloring books; crafts; holiday gifts
- Identify alternatives to activities masquerading as creative art
- Distinguish child-directed art from teacher-directed projects
- Provide art activities using paper

INTRODUCTION

Children's art fascinates adults. Although they may not understand it, parents are proud of their children's art. Early childhood educators also value children's art and allow ample time for it in the daily schedule. Although most young children are neither interested in nor ready for formal academics such as reading, virtually all young children are interested in and ready for art.

Most of us recognize the importance of early childhood art, but not everyone would agree about what it entails. Is scribbling art? Can coloring in a coloring book be considered art? This unit provides criteria or guidelines for determining the creative merits of an activity or approach to art. Traditional teacher-directed and product-oriented art activities will be critiqued. Activities masquerading as creative art will be identified, and alternatives will be suggested.

What is art? The great philosopher Susanne Langer believed that humans are born with an urgent biological need to create art. Art helps us put our life experiences into symbolic form. We are then able to stand back and clarify, critically examine, and share our experiences. But how is this done? There are many ways to express one's experiences artistically. Some of these are

- literature
- drama
- music
- visual arts: plastic and graphic

For our purposes, we will focus on how young children use the visual arts to represent their life experiences. The plastic, or three-dimensional, arts include sculpture, ceramics, and architecture. The graphic, or two-dimensional, arts include painting, printmaking, and drawing.

HOW TO CHOOSE ART ACTIVITIES

What should be included in an early childhood art program? Mrs. Mills has baked cookies, and her toddlers will soon spread frosting on them for an art activity. Across the hall, kindergartners are neatly coloring in a butterfly photocopy as part of their unit on spring. Their teacher reminds them that they have only a few minutes left for art. What can one say about these activities? Which have artistic merit? Do they represent the essence of what early childhood art should be? The author would respond negatively to these questions. Although spreading frosting may be an enjoyable tactile, perceptual-motor, and edible activity, it is not art. Simply coloring in a butterfly photocopy may strengthen eye-hand coordination and figure-ground relations, but it offers little or no opportunity for creativity. A more creative version would be to let the children draw their own butterflies with little concern for realistic rendering.

Child-Directed Art or Teacher-Directed Projects

Arts and crafts are terms that are often viewed as opposite. In terms of approach, art activities are viewed as developmentally appropriate while crafts are often teacher-directed, product-oriented, and lacking artistic merit. The term "project" is presently used in place of "craft." Although some would refer to teacher-directed activities as crafts, the terms are not interchangeable. Crafts have artistic merit and craftspeople work long and hard to produce products, many of which reflect their culture. Crafts may also be functional as with candles, jewelry, clothing, or windchimes. Therefore, it would not be fair to use crafts in the same sense of teacher-directed art projects. Instead, teacher-directed projects, rather than crafts are the opposite of child-centered art. Substituting teacher projects for art does children a disservice for it robs them of the opportunity to make self-expressive, self-initiated art. See Table 11–1 for a comparison and contrast of these two approaches.

Is There A Place for Teacher Projects?

Although teacher projects should not dominate your art program, they do have a place and are to your art program as spices are to cooking. Some people avoid spices while others use them sparingly

ART ACTIVITIES	TEACHER PROJECTS
are creative, unique, original	are uncreative and resemble each other, appear mass-produced and very similar if not identical to each other
are diverse and individual like the children who create them	are uniform and resemble each other or the teacher standard or model
are open-ended and unstructured	are closed-ended and structured
are child-centered and child-directed	are teacher-centered and teacher-directed
come from within the child	are imposed from without by the teacher
involve much child input	involve much teacher input
empower children who say, "Look what I made all by myself."	empower teachers who think, "Look what I got the children to do. Won't the parents be pleased?"
involve self-expression	involve copying and imitating
foster autonomy	foster compliance and following directions
are process oriented	are product oriented
may not be recognizable	are recognizable
may not appeal to adults since the finished product may not be recognizable	usually appeal to adults since the finished product is recognizable
may not be useful or practical	may be useful and practical
are success-oriented, no fear of failure	may be unsuccessful if child is unable to approximate teacher's model or standard
child decides content	idea related to holiday, season, theme, unit of study, decided by teacher
please the child	please adults
need open blocks of time	may involve time constraints in giving everyone a chance to make one; child may be rushed to complete
involve legitimate artistic media	may involve consumable and expensive supplies like glitter, feathers, wiggly eyes, and fur

TABLE 11–1   Child-Directed Art Activities or Teacher-Directed Projects

to enhance but not overpower or dominate the taste of food. When should teacher projects be used? They can be used occasionally

- with older children who have a solid foundation in processing and are interested in learning how to make art products.
- when children tire of visiting the art center and appear to run out of ideas for processing. They appear stuck or out of ideas. It appears the art center is not being used.
- to introduce children to new cultures by directly experiencing representative crafts. The process involved in making crafts must be tailored to

meet the developmental needs of your group. Refer to Chapter 5 for a discussion of multicultural arts and crafts.

- while allowing for individual expression, as in the choice of color or type of decoration added. For example, children can be taught how to make a piñata without specifying what it should look like when finished.

WHAT EARLY CHILDHOOD ART SHOULD BE

Often it is easy to recognize negative examples or instances of uncreative art. Just what should one look for in planning an early childhood art activity? Early childhood art should

1. allow children to be personally expressive
2. subtly balance artistic process and product
3. be open-ended, allowing children to be creative
4. allow for discovery and experimentation
5. allow for active engagement and sustained involvement
6. be intrinsically motivating
7. be success-oriented
8. be developmentally appropriate
9. involve legitimate artistic media
10. be available to all children

1. Allow Children to Be Personally Expressive

Young children need to express themselves personally with a variety of artistic media. The expression should be personal because individual children will approach art in unique ways. After visiting the zoo, several three-year-olds were encouraged to make or do something related to what they had just experienced. At the easel, Jean painted a caged black bear. Three children headed for the clay table. Jim squeezed a ball of clay and called it a seal. Tam rolled tiny clay snakes to make the rays of the hot shining sun. Kaley cut an outline of an elephant into a slab of clay using an ice cream stick. Personal choice was reflected in the use of paint or clay. Furthermore, the children at the clay table found three

different ways to express what was personally meaningful to them.

2. Subtly Balance Artistic Process and Product

The art activities provided should subtly balance artistic processing and the making of art products. A good art program understands and accepts the fact that individual children can be oriented toward process, product, or both in their approach to art. Art processing includes the skills involved in a given art activity. For example, paper work involves tearing, cutting, folding, pasting, stapling, braiding, and weaving. The product refers to the result. For example, processing with paper may result in a paper collage, paper weaving, or paper sculpture. Young children are process-oriented (see Figure 11–1). They enjoy art for the sake of doing and making, often with little concern for how it turns out. Perhaps this is why some children fail to claim their finished art products. They forget which one they did or merely toss it into the wastebasket as they depart. One carpool mother complained about how the backseat of her van was strewn with children's art. For these children the joy was in the actual doing or process rather than in what resulted, the finished product. Older children, however, become product-oriented. They are very concerned about size, shape, color, placement, detail, and realism. They are quick to put their name on their art and may become upset when papers tear or curl, or when paint smears. It may be important for these children to take one or several art products home each day.

The author once observed a boy in a transitional kindergarten diligently working on a clay dinosaur. When the teacher announced, "Cleanup time; everybody clean up," he was devastated. He pleaded to take it home or at least keep it out for display. He was near tears when he was directed to roll it back into a ball and return it to the clay tub. Clearly, he was product-oriented in his approach to art. Art is dependent on both process and product. Artistic processing is necessary to arrive at a finished product. Elaborating or refining a product involves processing.

FIGURE 11-1   *Processing with art media is as important as making a finished product.*

3. Be Open-Ended, Allowing Children to Be Creative

Early childhood art programs should also encourage young children to be creative. They can encourage children to represent their world creatively by allowing them to choose

- what they want to make (content)
- how to go about making it (process)
- what it will end up looking like (product)

In general, planned activities that are loosely structured set the stage for creative expression. For example, paints, brushes, and paper at the easel may be enough for some children. All they need is to invest time and pursue an idea. Others may need a teacher's subtle guidance. "Try to think of something that happened over the weekend, maybe involving someplace or someone special. This could give you something to paint." We rob children of the opportunity for creative artistic expression when we specify what the finished product should be or look

like and exactly how to do it. For example, coloring, cutting out, and correctly pasting together a train does not involve much creativity.

Still, creative expression must abide by general rules, guidelines, and limits. Pretend-fighting with scissors is dangerous and not creative. Children need to be taught the proper way to handle scissors and all other artistic media, equipment, and supplies. Rules need to be discussed and posted. "Chris, bring me your scissors. They are only for cutting paper."

4. Allow for Discovery and Experimentation

Children can arrive at artistic products through discovery and experimentation. For example, teaching sponge painting or printing directly may not be necessary. It is possible to provide paints and an array of sponges, cookie cutters, and Styrofoam shapes, and encourage children to see what they can do with these "painters" and the paint (see Figure 11–2.) They may experiment by spreading paint with sponges or using the sponges in a stamping

FIGURE 11–2   Different brushes help Lauren discover and experiment.

motion. Either way, they have discovered for themselves a new artistic technique through their own active experimentation. Planning each art activity with a predetermined product and step-by-step procedure robs children of the opportunity to explore, discover, invent, and creatively experiment on their own.

5. Allow for Active Engagement and Sustained Involvement

Art should actively engage your children. They are active physical beings, and their artistic expression should reflect this. They need upright easels to encourage sweeping whole-arm movements while standing. Clay needs to be torn, punched, pulled, rolled, flattened, pinched, and pounded. Recommended early childhood art activities will encourage and capitalize on the young child's need for sensory-motor exploration and movement. Ample blocks of time are needed to foster sustained involvement. Not all children are able to complete an art activity in a predetermined block of time. Some will want to continue working later or even the following day. Other children will impulsively finish their art in a matter of minutes. "Look, teacher, I'm done! What can I do now?" Teachers may want to encourage such children to continue their involvement. Obviously, few young children will work for hours at the same art activity. Still, they can be encouraged to examine and extend their art. "Tara, I see you finished your painting. Is there anything else you want to add?" "Yes, I see. It is a turtle. Have you thought about where it lives or what it might like to eat? You have a lot of time and more paper, so keep working on your turtle." The teacher did not tell Tara her turtle was wrong or bad. She encouraged Tara to refine her art and continue her involvement. In this case, Tara chose to ignore the teacher's suggestions and announced that her turtle picture was finished. Over time, Tara may begin to see that additional time and effort spent working usually produce a more elaborate and detailed picture.

6. Be Intrinsically Motivating

Art—like music, movement, and play—is an intrinsically motivating activity. Children will engage in art for the sheer pleasure and reward inherent in painting, coloring, working with clay, or making a collage. The author believes that one of the major joys of being an early childhood educator is working with young children who are so internally motivated to learn and to make sense out of their world. They manipulate, explore with all their senses, and ask endless questions. Although praise and rewards are effective, they are not always needed in art. The author observed a teacher praising a child's finished art product. "Oh, look how pretty Marla's painting of a house turned out!" Later, several children copied Marla's idea and style to win this teacher's praise. Their motivation for doing art had moved from internal to external. Instead, Marla's teacher might have praised her efforts and involvement. "Maria, you are working so long and hard" or "I see a lot of action at the clay table. Sam will keep working until he gets it just the way he wants." Research by Lepper and Greene (1975) has shown that external motivation and techniques of behavior modification actually decrease a child's intrinsic motivation. Praising preschoolers' use of felt-tip markers actually decreased their interest in using them. Anderson, Manoogian, and Reznick (1976) studied the effects of different rewards on four- and five-year-olds' intrinsic interest in drawing. They found that monetary and symbolic rewards—for example, money and stickers—decreased children's interest in drawing. A teacher's verbal praise, however, actually increased it. Still, it is recommended that the praise be aimed at the process and involvement rather than at the outcome.

7. Be Success-Oriented

Early childhood art activities should be planned to be success-oriented. Choosing art activities that are developmentally appropriate and moderately challenging will ensure a child's success. In turn, feelings of success and mastery foster a child's positive self-concept. A major goal of early childhood education is to help children become competent and feel good about themselves. Activities that are too difficult or detailed may frustrate children and lead to failure. The danger is that young children may generalize their failure at a task to failure as a person. For example, a group of four-year-olds at summer day camp were given a group of cardboard insects to trace, cut, and paste. The objects were small, with many details, including thin legs and feelers. The cardboard was flimsy, and the scissors were dull. Papers were torn, and insect heads and tails were missing. Few, if any, of the children could match the teacher's standard, which was hanging overhead. The children became restless and frustrated. The camp counselor meant well but did not translate the developmental abilities of four-year-olds into a success-oriented art activity.

8. Be Developmentally Appropriate

What could be an alternative to the activity described above? A good art activity can foster success by taking into account a child's developmental abilities. For example, the camp counselor, after reading a book on insects and taking a nature walk to collect specimens, could have encouraged the children to draw a favorite bug or create a new one. What might a "butter-quito" or "spider-hopper" look like? There is no one right answer; there are many possibilities. Art activities that require excessive cutting, fine detailing, pasting of small pieces, or precise folding are not developmentally appropriate for young children with limited fine motor control and coordination. The author recalls a first attempt at origami, a precise Japanese paper-folding activity. Although the teacher produced an intricate, correctly folded swan, the author's looked like a lopsided beast. Anyone who has felt discouraged and unsuccessful can easily empathize with young children who do not experience success through art.

The National Association for the Education of Young Children (NAEYC) has drafted a position statement on developmentally appropriate practice in early childhood programs serving children from birth through age eight (Bredekamp, 1987). (See inside front cover.) A major determinant of program quality is the extent to which knowledge of child development is applied in educational practice. The concept of developmental appropriateness has two dimensions: age appropriateness and individual appropriateness. Knowledge of typical development of children within the age span served by one's program provides a framework from which teachers prepare the learning environment and plan activities deemed age-appropriate. Because each child is unique, materials and activities must also be individually appropriate. For example, cutting with scissors may be age-appropriate for four-year-olds but individually inappropriate for Lashonda, a four-year-old in your group who lacks fine motor skills and is more interested in tearing paper. Cutting with scissors would not be a good instructional match, given what we know about Lashonda.

9. Involve Legitimate Artistic Media

A variety of art media, such as easels, finger paints, and clay, should be available for creative expression. Toddlers are able to explore and manipulate art materials, but they cannot be expected to produce finished art. Although older children's scribbles are more controlled than those of toddlers, and three-year-olds will create and even give names to designs with horizontal and vertical strokes, adults should not expect representational products from this age group.

The NAEYC guidelines suggest that children be given developmentally appropriate art materials. This means that toddlers should be given such art materials as large crayons, watercolor markers, and large sheets of paper. It also means that four- and five-year-olds should have daily opportunities for aesthetic expression and appreciation of art and music. In the primary grades, art and other expressive activities should be integrated as relevant to the curriculum and as needed for children to express themselves aesthetically and physically. Children can also use art to express ideas and feelings. It is sometimes appropriate to call in specialists to work with classroom teachers and children.

A recommended early childhood art program will involve legitimate artistic media. Children work with paint, watercolor, collage, paper, clay, printing, design, resist, and sculpture—the same media that adult artists use. Providing legitimate artistic media tells children, "You are creative artists, and you can be trusted with the appropriate tools and media." The materials, equipment, and supplies related to these media are basic, moderately expensive, and good investments. Paint brushes, easels, and watercolor sets of good quality will last if given proper care. Generally, buying in advance and in bulk gets the major art expense for the year out of the way. Expense, however, does not guarantee creative art. For example, one teacher distributed a precut doll shape to a small group of three-, four-, and five-year-old children. The children were instructed to glue on button eyes and precut fur for hair, sprinkle glitter, and to attach an ice cream stick base. The activity was costly and short-lived, and it involved little artistic processing. The doll puppets all looked identical. Creative input from the children was absent. Many parents and local businesses would be willing to donate extra fabric, trim, magazines, and papers to supplement the basic artistic media and hold down expenses. See Appendices A and B for a list and sources of artistic junk.

10. Be Available to All Children

Art should be available to all children. Older infants who can hold a nontoxic marker or crayon can be subtly guided to make marks on paper. They can scribble while seated in a high chair or sprawled atop a long roll of paper. Toddlers enjoy painting and using markers, crayons, and clay. The preschooler can be provided with an even wider array of legitimate artistic media. Art is neither masculine nor feminine; both boys and girls should be encouraged to engage in art. If the easels or art center become monopolized by one sex, a teacher may need to do some social engineering. For example, girls in one kindergarten were drawing pictures of food to take to the housekeeping center. The boys avoided both the art and housekeeping centers and concentrated in the block area. After two days of this sex-segregated play, the teacher took action. She suggested that the boys work together with the girls in building a restaurant. One boy designed his own play money from scrap construction paper. Another painted a store sign.

All children should have access to art. Because art can foster a child's feelings of esteem and success, it is vital for children who have special needs, exceptionalities, or multicultural backgrounds. Art gives them the vehicle to validate themselves by making a personal statement: "I am unique, and my art proves it!"

Some teachers report that they use art as a reward for work completed. The good students get to visit the art center or engage in art. Others may be denied art. Although misbehavior and incomplete work cannot be tolerated, the punishment does not fit the crime. The children in question may be those who need art the most. Academic deficiencies or behavior problems leave them with few routes for success in school. Success in art may generalize to success in academics. Art can also be used as a springboard to academics. For example, eight-year-old Dusty is a poor reader who draws detailed hot rods. Perhaps his hot rod drawings could be used as a way to help him talk, read, and write about his interests.

ACTIVITIES MASQUERADING AS CREATIVE ART

Merely labeling an activity "art" is no guarantee that the activity will have artistic merit. Likewise, uncreative activities are often mistakenly called "creative." Too many activities masquerade as creative art. Some of these include

- photocopied or mimeographed sheets
- cut-and-paste activities
- tracing patterns
- coloring book pages
- dot-to-dot sheets
- crafts
- holiday gifts
- seatwork or busywork

Although these activities may have some merit for developing fine motor control or eye-hand coordination, they lack artistic and creative merit. Activities that masquerade as creative art share the following three criteria:

1. an emphasis on teacher input and direction
2. a high degree of structure
3. a specified product

Workbooks, worksheets, coloring books, and teacher-made models of art products for children to copy are not appropriate for young children, especially those younger than six (Bredekamp, 1987).

Lowenfeld and Brittain (1987) warn against the use of photocopies, coloring books, and patterns by citing the research of Russell and Waugaman (1952), who found that children who had originally been interested in spontaneously drawing birds lost their creativity when exposed to workbook drawings. They quickly changed their once-creative pictures to resemble the common stereotype. Photocopies, cut-and-paste activities, and tracing patterns (Figure 11–3) have a high degree of teacher input and direction, with the responsibility for making art shifted from child to teacher. For example, Miss Sally drew a teddy bear and ran off copies for the children to color. They were encouraged to take their time, color neatly, and stay within the lines. The teacher imposed her concept of what a teddy bear should look like. A photocopy can easily become a cut-and-paste activity. Miss Sally could have asked the children to cut out their teddy bears along with a predrawn hat and cane and paste them on construction paper. Or she could have provided cardboard patterns for the children to trace. These activities, however, lack artistic merit because the focus is on the teacher's concept of a teddy bear, not the child's. Instead, Miss Sally could have encouraged each child to represent a personally

FIGURE 11–3   *This activity is masquerading as art.*

meaningful symbol of a teddy bear without concern for realistic use of color, shape, size, body parts, placement, or detail.

Teacher-directed art activities usually entail a high degree of structure, reflected in specific directions and step-by-step progression. The teddy bears in Miss Sally's room looked alike and appeared mass-produced.

Other examples of highly structured activities include coloring book pages and dot-to-dot sheets. Pages from coloring books reflect the artist's concept and representation of an object. A steady provision of coloring books frustrates young artists and leads them to question their own creative ability. Further, it denies them practice in making personally meaningful art. Instead, they merely complete someone else's art. This may be why some older children are at a loss when asked to draw anything they want. They have become too dependent upon coloring books and cannot create for themselves.

An anticipated response in defense of coloring books is that children like them. Children, however, are not the best judges of what is good or bad for them. For example, children like candy and some would eat it to the exclusion of vegetables, but adults would not allow this to happen. The same holds true for coloring books and creativity. A steady diet of coloring books inhibits a child's creative expression.

Dot-to-dot pages add an element of math to the coloring book page. Connecting the dots in proper numerical sequence results in closure by completing the picture.

Highly structured, teacher-directed art activities often focus on making a finished product, like Miss Sally's teddy bears. Sometimes teachers display their own finished products as standards or models. Although well-intended, this practice will frustrate young artists who cannot trace, color, cut, or paste as well. Although a teacher quickly adds, "Do your

FIGURE 11–4   The perfect gift for a child to give

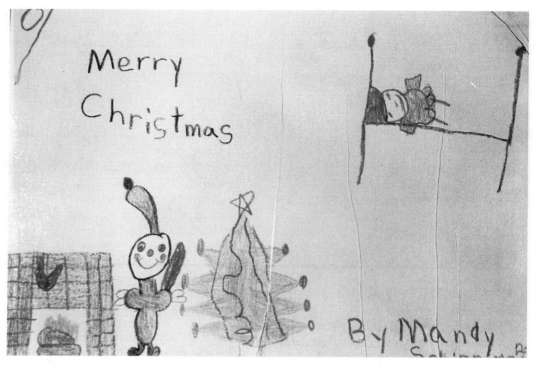

FIGURE 11–5   *The artist has been personally expressive.*

best," children know that their products will never come close to looking like their teacher's.

So-called "crafts" and holiday gifts are examples of finished products that masquerade as creative art. Two small stones glued to a larger stone can be painted to resemble a frog. It looks like something, and it is useful in that it can be used as a paperweight. However, creative art may not look like anything and may not have any use beyond the initial joy of self-expression.

Moyer (1990) has identified practices that do not challenge children to grow artistically. These include providing children with premarked papers to fill with specific colors, giving them patterns to produce an identifiable product and expecting them to replicate the teacher's model step by step. Children become dependent on patterns; they learn very early that their ideas and artistic expressions are not valued by the teacher and therefore are unacceptable. When the emphasis is on the end product rather than on the process, undesirable competition

results. Displaying only the "best" artwork, or the products that most nearly meet the teacher's example, discourages individual expression. Moreover, it is difficult, if not impossible, to discuss individual art if all the children have produced identical work.

"Crafts" are often given as holiday gifts. Most parents would be delighted to receive a paperweight or pencil holder constructed by their child. Although it is important to please parents, it is equally important to meet the creative needs of children. Providing for child input, planning, decision making, and creative processing guarantees that each finished product will be as unique and individual as the child who produced it. Gifts need not involve time or expense. A completed finger painting could also be ironed flat, framed, wrapped, and presented to parents as a gift (see Figure 11–4). Taking the time to talk with parents about the nature of children's art will help them appreciate the finger painting for the unique gift it is. See Figure 11–5 for a Christmas card Mandy made for her family.

FIGURE 11–6   What can I make the paint and brush do?

- torn
- cut
- glued or pasted
- taped
- stapled
- folded
- slit
- curled
- pleated
- twisted
- braided
- fringed
- looped
- scored (made to curl by pulling it against the blade of scissors)
- chained (rings or loops made into a continuous chain)
- punched with a hole punch
- pricked with a toothpick (and placed against a contrasting-color background)
- made into a cone or cylinder
- ringed (a strip made into a crown, headband, or bracelet)

Alternatives to activities that masquerade as art take a commitment of time and planning. Art should not be used merely to fill in extra time before lunch or dismissal. Coloring in the figures on a math, phonics, or reading-readiness workbook sheet is not art. Generally, the figures are small, blurred, and drawn by someone other than the child. This is seatwork or busywork, not art. Art is more like turning your finished work over and drawing whatever you want.

In Figure 11–6, Samantha is totally involved and caught up in making art her way.

PAPER ART

Children have many experiences with paper long before they enter school. Some papers are scrap, whereas the pages in books are not to be written on, cut, or torn. Children see their parents handle paper money and write checks. Greeting cards and mail are made out of paper. Paper serves many purposes. Art activities dealing with paper will be introduced in this section. Instructions for making paper are also provided.

Processing with Paper   P K S

What can an artist do with paper? Many different things can be done to and with paper (see Figure 11–7). As children experiment and explore with paper, they find that it can be

Cones and Cylinders   K S

Children will discover that paper can be folded into three-dimensional forms, including cubes, cones, and cylinders. Cones and cylinders are easy to make. Rolling paper into a tube shape makes a cylinder. Cylinders can be creatively combined to make people, animals, buildings, castles, towers, tunnels, spyglasses, and vehicles. A round piece of paper can be cut to its center and gently turned to form a cone. Cones suggest heads, bodies, animal beaks, hats, ice-cream cones, horns, teepees, and mountains.

Monofold Creation   K S

Fold a piece of paper in half once (monofold). Keep the creased edge at the top. Children can draw an object and carefully cut through both thicknesses of paper. The object, however, must remain joined at the top. When the paper is opened, the vehicle, animal, or object will be joined at the top and able to stand up. It will be symmetrical.

Stars and Snowflakes   K S

Round or square paper of thin weight, such as tissue paper or origami paper, can be used. Construction paper is too thick to fold and cut through.

FIGURE 11–7   *Children enjoy processing with paper.*

Coffee filters are an ideal size, shape, and thickness. Encourage children to fold their paper into quarters (in half and half again). Older children with good scissoring skills can continue folding. The more folds there are, the thicker the paper will be to cut through but the more intricate the design. Encourage children to cut out small snips or to make angular cuts into the folded paper without cutting through or cutting any off. Carefully open. Refold and continue cutting if not satisfied with the star or snowflake. Finished products can be taped over windows for the light to shine through. Or an adult can seal them between two pieces of wax paper using a warm iron.

Paper Weaving

The teacher may need to provide most if not all of the paper for this activity. Fold a 9 × 12 sheet of construction paper in half either way. Cut slits from the folded edge out, stopping about 1 inch from the opposite end. The slits can be even or randomly spaced. They can be cut straight, curved, or jagged. Open the paper. Measure how long a strip of paper must be to be woven through the slits from one end to the other. Make several strips. Again, the paper strips can be cut straight, curved, or jagged. Children can weave with the paper strips, using an over-under motion. The next row will necessitate an opposite under-over motion. The ends of the woven paper strips can be secured with a dab of paste or glue. Trim paper strips that extend beyond the edge of the paper.

Cutting the paper and strips straight produces a neat, uniform checkerboard effect. Cutting strips of different widths or angles produces an optical illusion-type design. Try to provide a variety of papers to weave with. Adding strips of wallpaper provides a dramatic touch. Paper weaving is like finger painting, a basic early childhood art activity with many possibilities. Try adding ribbon, lace, yarn, and pipe cleaners along with your paper strips.

Magazine Picture Weaving

Children can find a large picture in a magazine that they find interesting. National Geographic, with its vivid animal pictures, is highly recommended. Carefully remove the page or cut the picture into a large square or rectangle. Cut the picture into strips. Use the guidelines given in the paper-weaving activity to make a larger slit frame. Weave the magazine picture strips. The result will be a slightly distorted but visually pleasing rearrangement of the selected picture. Or weave the strips in incorrect order for a visually unexpected effect. Or interchange strips from different pictures—for example, an animal head with a child's body.

Stuffed Paper Pillow

Each child will need one large grocery bag for this activity. Cut through the three joined edges until only the flat front and back remains. Encourage children to draw a simple but large object that fills up most of the paper bag. Animals, vehicles, or shapes with a minimum of fine detailing are recommended. Carefully cut through all layers. Separate the layers into a top and a bottom. Children can decorate the front and back sides with crayons, markers, or paint. Later, they can use a stapler to carefully staple the outer edge shut while slowly stuffing the bag with small pieces of wadded newspaper. Continue to staple and stuff.

I'm Stuffed

Children will need a length of mural or butcher paper that is slightly more than twice their length. Fold the paper in half for double layers and have the child lie on top. Trace around the child with a thick pencil, crayon, or marker. Cut out the outline. Encourage children to decorate with crayons, markers, or paint. Provide a mirror for them to note the color and placement of facial features and clothing. Use a stapler to carefully staple shut the outer edge while slowly stuffing with small pieces of wadded newspaper. Continue to staple and stuff. Children will enjoy taking their "twin" home.

Paper Strip Critters

Strips of paper ½ inch and wider can be formed into three-dimensional characters or animals. Three strips on top of one another form a snowman. An accordion-pleated strip of paper becomes a snake. The possibilities are endless. Try to suggest possibilities without telling children what to make. Encourage them to play around with the paper and see what results.

Paper Mosaic

A mosaic is a design made by placing pieces of tile, stone, glass, or other material very close together. Children can do a mosaic using paper. Begin by drawing a fairly simple large picture on a piece of drawing paper. Cut out small squares of colored paper. Here is where scrap pieces of construction paper that have been saved come in handy. Squares can range from ½ to 1 inch square, depending on the age of the child. A teacher may decide to use the paper cutter to cut up squares for young children. Squares can be sorted by color and placed in an egg carton for easy access. Encourage children to paste them inside their sketched picture. Mosaic squares should be close but not touching. A paper mosaic takes much time, planning, and patience. It need not be completed in one sitting and is recommended for older children.

Paper Relief

Relief refers to a raised or three-dimensional effect. One way to get this is to build up layers of paper. Begin with a cardboard base. Use additional cardboard or thick paper to cut out designs or pieces of a picture. Continue building up layers. Cut additional shapes, but make them smaller than the previous ones. Continue to cut and glue smaller pieces until a design or picture with different levels results. This activity takes much time and patience and is recommended for older children.

Grocery Bag Top Hat

Children enjoy decorating and wearing their grocery bag top hats. Each child will need a large grocery bag. Open bag and stand on its open side. Help the child gather one side and begin rolling up. This forms the brim. To make it child-sized, gather the paper as you roll. Rotate bag and roll up all four sides until you get a top hat shape that fits the child's head. Remove and let child decorate with paint or trims.

Paper Making   K S

This activity involves making decorative papers from recycled papers. There are many variations. It is a multistep process but not difficult. It does take much advanced preparation and one-on-one assistance. Try the process out yourself first before doing it with children.

Preparation:

1. Collect the following:
   - any nonplastic and nonmetallic papers that will easily break down when soaked in water: toilet paper, facial tissue, grocery bags, paper towels, paper napkins, bond paper, newspaper, construction paper, junk mail, computer paper, tissue paper, egg cartons, gift wrap, glossy magazines, old yellow- and white-page phone books
   - one or more kitchen blenders
   - measuring cup
   - sponges
   - flat tool like a blunt plastic knife (use with adult supervision)
   - old cloth towels for blotting
   - embroidery hoops (can be shared)
   - mesh window screen (fine), one piece per child
   - tubs or dish pans (at least two)
   - additions to the paper: dryer lint, rose petals, metallic confetti, potpourri, dried flowers, scents, spices like cinnamon, perfume, Easter grass, glitter, coffee grounds, tea leaves, small seeds, thread

2. Fill tubs about 6 inches full with water. Cover tables with layers of newspaper. Place tubs on newspaper.

3. Make screen frames by placing the mesh screen inside the two pieces of the embroidery hoop and tighten the screw. Hoops can be shared, but children each need their own piece of mesh screen. Measure size of the hoop and allow extra screen to extend beyond the edge for a tight fit.

Process:

1. Choose your paper and tear into approximately twenty 1- or 2-inch squares. Place in kitchen blender and add 4 cups of water. Put on lid and grind at lowest speed for a few seconds or until paper has turned into pulp. Add more water and repeat at high speed. Paper makers call this pulp a "slurry."

2. Pour pulp into another tub filled half full with water. Mix pulp with hand. Add any of the desired additions listed earlier. Use sparingly, for example, a spoonful of scent.

3. Put screen frame into tub vertically. Slide screen frame on bottom of tub to reach pulp and additions that have sunk to the bottom.

4. Gently stir pulp with one hand while lifting screen to catch pulp and any additions. You want pulp and any additions to float and evenly settle on top of screen. Use both hands to lift screen out, allowing excess water to drain through screen. Gently blot with sponge. You should have a thin layer of pulp with no holes or thin spots. If not, turn screen upside down and lightly tap it in water to remove pulp. Repeat steps.

5. When satisfied with layer of pulp, remove screen from the frame (hoop) without disturbing the pulp on top. Lay pulp-covered screen on a flat surface and use cloth towels to gently blot. Let thoroughly air dry by placing the screen out in the sun.

6. When dry, run finger around bottom edge to lightly lift edge of paper from screen. If necessary, use a flat tool to separate the dried paper from the screen and carefully peel.

Hint The color of your homemade paper depends on the color of your original paper. Newspaper ink runs and muddies the pulp. Sort and use similar colors with construction or tissue paper.

Hint   Add a small amount of food coloring or liquid watercolor to your pulp while it is in the blender, if color is desired.

Hint   Coarse paper like grocery bags may need to soak overnight to break down.

Hint   Coarse additives like flower petals and seeds can be added to the ground pulp in the blender and blended for a few seconds if you want them to blend in rather than stand out. Dryer lint must be blended or it will produce large lumps.

Hint   If there is no blender available, children can use rotary egg beaters. Or put pulp in a jar with a lid and shake.

Hint   Although young children need the sturdy hoop frame, school-age children can use berry baskets for retrieving pulp. Follow the above steps. You can also use old coffee cans. Use a can opener to remove the top and bottom lids. Hold screen over one end of can and use as you would the hoop in above steps.

Hint   This variation uses a kitchen whisk and adds cornstarch for a creamy consistency. Let watery paper mixture sit overnight. Use a wire whisk and beat the watery paper mixture into a pulp in tub. Dissolve 3 tablespoons of cornstarch in one cup of water. Add the dissolved cornstarch to the pulp in tub and stir thoroughly. Submerge the screen into the creamy mixture and remove the pulp following the above steps.

Molded Paper

Follow the above steps but mold pulp into fancy ice-cube trays or candy molds rather than drying flat. Make sure excess water is completely drained. Molded paper can be carefully removed by gently tapping the tray. Given their thickness, allow ample time to thoroughly dry. Molded paper can be used as beads on a necklace or for holiday decorations. It can also be used in collage or glued onto folded paper for a greeting card.

Hint   Lightly spraying the mold with cooking oil makes the molded paper easy to remove.

SUMMARY

Sometimes activities that lack artistic or creative merit masquerade as art. Perhaps teachers merely forget to examine critically what they do with children. This unit provided some criteria or guidelines to help determine what early childhood art should be. Art activities that allow all children to be actively engaged, personally expressive, and creative were recommended. Art should also be success-oriented and intrinsically motivating. It should allow for both process and product, be developmentally appropriate, allow for experimentation and discovery, and involve legitimate artistic media. Not all those criteria apply to any one activity. They can, however, be used as guidelines for planning appropriate art experiences.

Suggested Activities

1. Recall your earliest experiences with art. What did you do? Did you enjoy art? Why? How did your parents or teachers respond to your art? How do you feel at present about your artistic development? What, if anything, has happened since your childhood to influence your feelings and abilities in art? Write your impressions, feelings, and thoughts in a brief one-page diary entry.

2. Observe an experienced teacher conducting an art activity with a group of young children. Does the activity require the children to be creative? List specific suggestions for making the activity more creative.

3. Visit an early childhood center during art time. Critique the ongoing art activity using our ten-point criteria or guidelines for recommended art activities. Does the activity masquerade as art?

4. Ms. Wilton, a kindergarten teacher, has made sturdy cardboard stencils of a cornucopia and harvest food as a tracing and coloring activity for her unit on fall. Critique this art activity. Suggest an alternative if necessary.

5. Facilitate paper art activities with children.

Review

A. Place a T (True) or F (False) in front of the following:
   ____ Art should allow children to be creative.
   ____ Art should always result in something to take home.
   ____ Children should be externally motivated to do art.
   ____ Art activities should be planned according to a child's development.
   ____ Discovering and experimenting through art are a waste of precious time.
   ____ Art activities for young children should take no longer than eight to ten minutes to complete.
   ____ Art activities should be planned to ensure a child's success.
   ____ The finished art product is more important than the steps leading up to it.
   ____ Art is best used as a reward for children who do their work or behave.
   ____ It is important for children's art to resemble very closely what the teacher had in mind when developing the activity.

B. A teacher has run off a bunny pattern for a unit on spring. Children will color, cut, and paste bunnies on egg-shaped pieces of purple construction paper. Critique the creative merits of this activity. Is this an example of child-directed art or a teacher-directed project? Justify your position. Offer specific suggestions for making it more creative. How might you plan a spring art activity without using any patterns?

C. Put an X in front of each activity that is masquerading as creative art.

____ Staying within the lines and neatly coloring in the pages in a holiday coloring book.

____ Cutting and pasting a picture of a seal carefully drawn by the teacher.

____ Using watercolors to paint a picture that shows what each child liked best about a recent field trip.

____ Coloring in a picture of a rocket ship, using red for all the areas marked 1, yellow for 2, and blue for 3.

D. Circle the correct term within each statement. Recommended early childhood art activities should have

1. an emphasis on (teacher/child) input and direction.
2. a (high/low) degree of structure.
3. a(n) (specified/unspecified) product.

CHAPTER 12

Planning, Implementing, and Evaluating Art

*A*re you able to take your art program outdoors? Adding art to outdoor play extends the range of choices for children. It also gives you an opportunity to provide art activities that entail a high level of noise and excessive mess. Making prints by standing in paint and carefully stepping on paper comes to mind.

What do you see in this photograph? How have the teachers planned for art? What have they done to get the easels ready? Do the shapes of the papers give you a clue as to what the children are studying? The papers are cut into large dinosaur shapes to integrate the theme of dinosaurs. The children take creative liberty in painting them as they see fit. Who says dinosaurs can't sport speckled spots?

OBJECTIVES

After studying this chapter, the student will be able to

- Describe the PIE cycle in curriculum development
- Identify the major developmental goals in early childhood education
- Compare and contrast strategies for integrating art into the early childhood curriculum
- Distinguish planned from spontaneous or emergent approaches to curriculum
- Make and use clay and play dough with children

INTRODUCTION

It is time to move beyond our knowledge of child development and translate it into curriculum. Actually, it is as easy as PIE—Plan, Implement, and Evaluate. Goals will give direction to our long-range planning; objectives are useful for our daily work with children. Our values and beliefs will influence our goals and the experiences chosen to meet these goals. Our wholistic model of child development will serve as a framework to ensure that our program is child-centered and developmentally focused. Taking into account management concerns and devising effective procedures will help us implement our activity. Evaluation helps us check on our effectiveness as teachers and providers. Different teachers use different strategies in teaching. Four strategies for planning and providing art experiences will be portrayed.

TEACHER AS PLANNER AND CURRICULUM DEVELOPER

All teachers are planners and curriculum developers. Some build their own curriculum; others follow a prescribed one. Curriculum development involves planning what to teach and how to teach it. A unit on dinosaurs may send the beginning teacher to the library to do some research. Learning activities must be organized. Centers must be stocked with materials, equipment, and supplies that are relevant to the curricular theme. Teaching without a curriculum or plan is like traveling cross-country without a map. It does a disservice to the children and hinders professional development. Without a curriculum, the teacher operates in a random, disorganized way. Quality teaching requires planning and curriculum development.

One way of planning and developing a curriculum is to ask oneself a series of questions. These might include

- WHO?
  Who am I as a teacher? What types of things do I know about and do well? What special interests or skills do I have? What do I value and believe about early childhood? Who are my children—ages, needs, interests, abilities, likes, dislikes, family, culture, background?

- WHAT?
  What do I want my children to learn, know, or be able to do?

- WHY?
  Why am I planning this activity? Why should my children know, learn, or be able to do it? Why is this important or relevant?

- HOW?
  How will I carry out this activity? How will I present it? How will I motivate the children or capture their interest? How will I know if I have been successful? How will I know if the children have learned anything? How many children can do this activity at one time? How will it be done—individually or in small groups on a rotating basis?

- WHERE?
  Where will this activity take place?

- WHEN?
  When will this activity take place? How long will it take?

We need to act on what we know about children and their development in developing curriculum and planning activities. We need to translate theory into practice. How do we begin? Basically, planning is as easy as PIE. The three key components of early childhood curriculum development are

- P lanning
- I   mplementing
- E valuating

Developing an early childhood curriculum is a lot like taking a trip. Planning helps us decide where we want to go. Do we want to take the fastest or the scenic route? What do we need to take along? All of these concerns are taken into account during our planning. Implementing is similar to actually taking the trip. We think we have done a good job of planning and now are ready to depart. Implementing our trip involves reading the map, stopping as planned, and allowing for unexpected diversions. Was the trip worth it? Did it cost too much or take too long? Were the benefits appropriate to the expense? Would you do it again? How could you improve on the trip? All of these questions attempt to evaluate the trip.

Teachers follow the same steps in developing curriculum. Planning involves deciding what we want children to learn and be able to do. Planning is a continuous, ongoing process. It involves acting on what we know about children and their development in setting appropriate goals and objectives. All planning is influenced by the values and beliefs one holds about children and education.

Implementing involves two major processes. First, management concerns must be considered. Second, effective procedures for carrying out one's activity must be established.

Evaluation attempts to assess the effectiveness of what was done. It attempts to answer the following question: How do I know if what I set out to do was ever accomplished?

The three PIE components can be illustrated with the following example. A teacher could devise an art activity that would help children discover that different types of brushes can be used in painting (planning); see Figure 12–1. Different brushes are located, identified, introduced, labeled, and displayed at the art center (implementing). Evaluation could entail observing the different ways children use the brushes and their ability to use many different brushes for painting. The PIE model for planning and curriculum development is depicted in Figure 12–2.

FIGURE 12–1   What happens when different brushes are introduced?

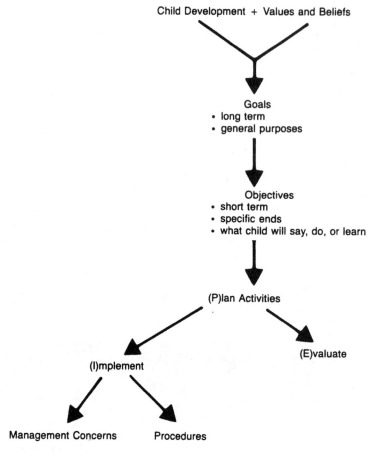

FIGURE 12–2   PIE model for planning and curriculum development

GOALS

A goal is something to strive for. For example, being creative is a lifelong pursuit and goal. Few reach their creative potential. A goal is like the brass ring on the merry-go-round. We reach out for it but rarely capture it. Still, goals give direction or focus to what we do with children on a monthly or yearly basis. Translating goals into more manageable objectives helps us plan for the week, day, and hour. Try as one may, however, one can never plan completely. At times, plans will change because of unexpected or unforeseen events. The relationship between long-term and short-term planning and between goals and objectives is depicted in Figure 12–3.

The Goals of Early Childhood Education

What are some of the goals of early childhood education? Our wholistic model of child development can help us further identify goals for early childhood. These might include:

1. PHYSICALLY (to develop):
- large-muscle or gross motor coordination
- small-muscle or fine motor coordination
- perceptual-motor or eye-hand coordination
- sensory awareness
- self-care

2. SOCIALLY (to develop):
- self-understanding and acceptance

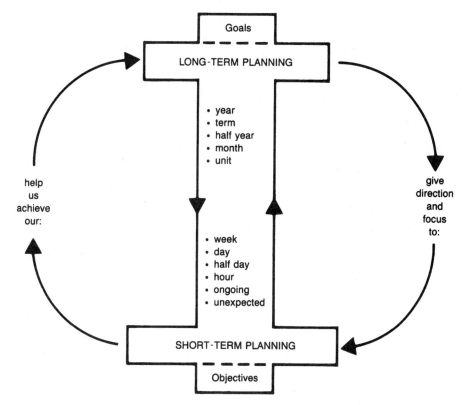

FIGURE 12–3   Planning cycle

- positive relations with others
- positive self-concept

3. EMOTIONALLY (to develop):

- a positive self-concept
- positive and appropriate emotional expression
- self-control

4. COGNITIVELY (to develop):

- a wide range of thinking skills, including problem solving and discovery
- concepts, skills, and learning in the curricular areas
- language

5. CREATIVELY (to develop):

- original thinking
- imagination
- verbal and nonverbal expression

If these are important developmental indicators, and if our program is child-centered, it follows that these can serve as goals or aims that can influence what we do with the children in our care. For example, creative expression, both verbal and nonverbal, is an important aspect of creative development. Art is one way to nonverbally express one's creativity. Art activities help us reach our goals for creative development.

VALUES AND BELIEFS

Goals also reflect our values and beliefs about children—how they develop and learn, what they should know, and the purpose of schooling and life. Teachers who value early academic performance and competition may view early childhood as a time to push children ahead by filling their heads with facts. They will set goals that stress competition and early academic accomplishment and will select activities in reading, writing, and counting to meet those goals. Teachers who view early childhood as a time for discovery and social interaction will set goals for developing curiosity and will provide socializing experiences in play to meet those goals. Different values and beliefs lead us to set different goals and activities. There are no right or wrong, good or bad beliefs. Some values and beliefs may, however, suggest educational practices that are not in line with what we know about young children. The key is to consistently match what we value and believe about children and schooling with an appropriate curriculum, one that is firmly grounded in child development. Although one may value and believe in the formal teaching of reading in the early years, our working knowledge of child development suggests that this practice is developmentally inappropriate.

OBJECTIVES

Objectives are the bridge between goals and activities. They are specific and short-term intended outcomes. As a result of a given activity, we expect children to be able to say, do, or demonstrate what they have learned. Objectives can be worded loosely or in precise behavioral terms. Regardless of the wording, teachers need to be able to set objectives and develop activities to meet them. For example, Karen Thomas wants her four-year-olds to interact with others, to be creative, to be successful at what they do, and to develop fine motor control. These are some of her goals. Her objective is for children to creatively experiment with different ways of painting. She plans to bring in an old toothbrush and shaving brush for her proposed art activity.

Referring to Figure 12–2, Ms. Thomas must still address how she will implement and evaluate this proposed activity. She must consider some concerns related to classroom management.

- Where should this activity take place—indoors, outdoors, at the easel, on the floor, or at a table? These are space considerations.

- When will this activity take place—before or after snack, in the morning or afternoon? Will it be offered as an additional free-choice activity, or will it be added to the ongoing art center? How much time will be allotted? These are time considerations.

- What is needed? Ms. Thomas has already found two different types of brushes. She will also need to think about paints, paper, and smocks.

- How many children can do this activity at one time? Will everyone get a chance in one session, or will it continue throughout the week? Will children self-select to do this activity, or will she need to systematically rotate them through? These are considerations related to grouping.

- How will this activity be supervised? Will it need the constant supervision of an adult? Probably not.

Ms. Thomas will also need to think through her procedures.

How will she introduce the activity? Would a story, book, or picture be appropriate? How can she capture the children's interest and get them motivated? She chooses to introduce her activity with questions during morning circle time. "Children, today I brought in two things to show you" (holding up a toothbrush and a shaving brush). "Yes, they are both brushes. Each has a special name and use." "Yes, this one is a toothbrush. How many of you have one and use it? Good. What about the other one?" Jamie says his grandfather has one, but he doesn't know its name. "Jamie, what does he use it for?" "Yes, for shaving. It's called a shaving brush. You use it to mix shaving soap and water and put it over your whiskers and beard before you shave." The children giggle. "Well, I have a different idea. I wonder if we could use them in our art center?" Children gasp and groan. "Let's quietly think of how we could use these new brushes to paint." Stephanie says, "You could use the toothbrush to paint up and down just like when brushing your teeth." Lacey says, "You could just make touches of paint on your paper." "That's very good thinking. I bet there are many, many different ways to use them as we paint. Remember to try out some different ways when you get your turn."

Actually, there is no definite teacher-directed procedure, since this is a creative discovery lesson. Ms. Thomas also reminded them to creatively explore while upholding the rules.

Evaluation was ongoing. Ms. Thomas checked to see whether the brushes were being used in different ways. They were. Some children used a pulling, pushing, swirling, dabbing, dotting, stamping, or circular motion. The finished products also revealed differences. From this she concluded that her activity was a success. She had met her objective. This activity helped children become more creative and versatile in their painting. As a follow-up activity she planned to bring in two additional types of brushes from home to increase the possibilities. As a recommendation, she noted that she should bring in two of each, since it was very difficult for the children to wait their turn. Also, the child with the brushes was very engrossed and spent more time than she had planned. Even though her activity was successful as planned, she knew it could be improved upon.

Karen Thomas is an experienced preschool teacher for whom planning and curriculum development now come easily. She relies on brief plans that work for her. That was not always the case. She began teaching by writing extremely detailed plans. She was afraid of leaving something out. She believes that her prior experience in writing out lesson plans, although it was time-consuming at the time, has helped her become the professional early childhood educator she is today.

A lesson plan format that closely follows our model for planning and curriculum development is given here.

STRATEGIES FOR INCLUDING ART IN THE EARLY CHILDHOOD CURRICULUM

Although we have introduced goals, values, and beliefs, we have yet to systematically deal with the nuts and bolts of daily planning and curriculum development. Let us continue by studying general ways to include art in the early childhood curriculum. The examples that follow illustrate the following five strategies:

1. art as a separate activity
2. art used to extend or reinforce learning in another curricular area
3. art as a superactivity integrating several curricular areas
4. art as an integrated part of an extended unit of study
5. art as a child-directed pursuit

1. Art As a Separate Activity

A teacher may find, hear about, or read about something that sounds like a good art activity that the children would enjoy. For example, Mr. Kent was glancing through a magazine in the director's office when he got the idea for painting or printing with sponges of different geometric shapes. The children had not done this activity before. He felt it would encourage creative processing with different shapes to make new forms. The activity would also help his four-year-olds and young five-year-olds with their fine motor skills. The activity was developmentally appropriate and sounded enjoyable. He planned to do the activity the following morning, since he had not yet planned an art activity. Further, he planned separate activities for the morning, but did not try to integrate or relate them. His daily lesson plan is found below.

TEACHER: Mr. Kent
CLASS: four- and five-year-olds
DATE: Monday

Areas/Activities:

ART—painting and printing with sponges cut into
     different geometric shapes
MUSIC—sing a "silly song"
     I know an old man who had a black dog . . .
MOVEMENT—alphabet march in a circle
CONCEPT—Science (for Monday)
     Sort and discuss attributes of nature specimens.
     Bring in pinecones, leaves, grass, twigs, stones,
     acorns, and so on.
GROUP—discuss weekend activities
     Encourage Ariel to discuss her hospital stay.

Lesson Plan

Activity:

PLANNING

    Goals:

    Objectives:

IMPLEMENTATION

    Management concerns:

    Procedures:

EVALUATION/REFLECTION

EXTENSION/VARIATION

SNACK—vegetable slices and cottage cheese dip
  Double-check for allergies to milk products.
PLAY—continue work on airport (block corner); restock shelves in grocery store (housekeeping)

Mr. Kent wished he had discovered this art activity last week, when they were studying geometric shapes in concept time. He did not think to find a song or movement activity that would tie in. Mr. Kent's approach is not bad or wrong. It is fragmented, with the different learning experiences left without integration or relation to each other.

2. Art Used to Extend or Reinforce Learning in Another Curricular Area

Mrs. Gomez's four-year-old pre-k group had also been studying geometric shapes during math concept time. She tried to find an art activity that would tie in. She cut sponges into geometric shapes and encouraged the children to print with them. During group or circle time, the children had a "show-and-tell" session during which they discussed the different shapes they invented and also named the shapes used. Art extended and reinforced what the children were learning in math. Her lesson plan for the day is found below. The arrows indicate integration between the different activities. Group time and art extended or reinforced the concept of geometric shapes discussed during math concept time.

DAILY LESSON
Mrs. Gomez
four-year-olds
Monday

Welcome:
  • do calendar
  • sing good morning song
  • read Little Red Hen
Blocks:
  • take large hollow blocks outside (with Mrs. Raines) if nice day
Dramatic Play:
  • introduce doctors and nurses, tools, careers
  • encourage hospital play
Table Toys:
  • put out Legos, new puzzles, flannel boards

Concept Time: • math (Monday)—discuss geometric shapes
  ↕
Creative Arts: • sponge painting with geometric shapes
  ↕
Group Time: • show-and-tell with geometric shape pictures

3. Art As a Superactivity Integrating Several Curricular Areas

Ms. Lansky's kindergartners were reviewing geometric shapes. She planned to devote Monday to this review. She included the following activities in her superactivity. Note the curricular areas in parentheses, indicating integration.

• Children counted and classified the different sponge shapes on the basis of color, shape, and size (math).
• They observed a dry sponge being submerged in water. They noted differences between wet and dry sponges. They put the wet sponge in the sun and predicted and observed what would happen (science).
• They took a field trip outdoors to identify geometric shapes in nature (science).
• They played shape bingo (visual discrimination, pre-reading).
• They discussed things that are hard and soft and the many uses of sponges (speaking, creative thinking).
• They listened to a story on shapes (listening).
• They printed their name or initials with rectangular shapes dipped in paint (pre-writing).
• They created their own geometric shape pictures (art).
• They listened to a march and participated in a shapes dance (music and movement).
• They moved like dry stiff sponges, sponges in a bubble bath, sponges being squeezed dry, wet sponges lying in the sun on a beach (movement).
• They discussed diving for sponges and people who dive for a living (social studies).

Ms. Lansky's approach to planning helped children integrate and coordinate all experiences related to learning about geometric shapes, as well as

A Time and a Place for Teaching Art

There is a time and place for teaching art. Use direct instruction sparingly. The criterion is if children might better discover a process on their own. For example, collage need not be taught. Simply laying out an array of collage items along with paper and glue is all that most children need. They will take it from there. Other activities introduced throughout the text, however, might never be discovered and therefore should be introduced in unobtrusive ways that still allow room for individual creativity. For example, some children might never discover the artistic process called resist, as discussed in Chapter 9. Introducing children to the process and how to do a resist is very different from specifying what they should make or what their finished product should look like. Art activities can also be informally introduced at times when children appear restless with processing on their own. They appear ready and motivated to move on and learn something new. The following guidelines will help you decide when and how to teach art.

1. Practice the activity by yourself. Make sure you have mastered it and it works. Think of the interests and abilities of the children in your group. How might you adapt the activity for a child with special needs or one who does not speak any English?
2. Plan and be prepared in advance. Have all the materials at hand. Waiting is stressful to children, as is having to share one art tool with several children.
3. Limit the number of children. The smaller the group, the easier to supervise and give individual assistance. Adjust the number according to their age level, complexity of the activity, and amount of art supplies available.
4. Cover table with newspapers and drape smocks over chairs. Locate a space for messy art activities to dry as well as to display.
5. Decide on a system—either group or individualized. If group, arrange materials in baskets, trays, or clear containers in center of table along with items to be shared, including tape or glue. If individualized, arrange individual setups with each child receiving a tray holding portions of all the materials needed to complete the activity. This avoids problems with sharing, waiting, and taking turns. It allows children to work at their own pace. When a child is finished, his or her tray is restocked for the next child. Involve children in the cleanup.
6. Build in choices and options by providing construction paper and paper plates, masking tape and glue, crayons and markers.
7. Reassure children waiting for a turn that they will get one. Neatly print their names and cross them off as children get their turns. This helps anxious children who fear you will forget that they were next to have a turn. It also becomes a literacy event as children read names.
8. Briefly introduce your activity. Model the process without making and displaying a finished product. Again, your aim is to help children learn a new way of doing art, rather than making art that resembles yours.
9. Allow children to go about the activity in their own ways, as long as health and safety safeguards are upheld. If they choose to ignore your invitation to do resist and want to simply color, that's OK. It doesn't mean you failed; it means they are simply not interested in doing it at this time. Allow them to pursue their own creative route or even leave without finishing. Serve as a resource or consultant offering minimal help and only when needed.
10. Talk with children. Focus on what they are doing. Describe colors and effort while avoiding remarks that judge their products as wonderful or beautiful.

incidental learning about sponges. See Figure 12–4. Ms. Lansky's only objection was that she felt the children's enthusiasm for and interest in studying shapes and sponges were more than she had expected and planned for in one day's flow of activities. Chapter 13 continues our discussion of integrating art across the early childhood curriculum.

4. Art As an Integrated Part of an Extended Unit of Study

Miss Susan enjoys teaching four-year-olds through the use of units. Her units are organized around a theme, such as geometric shapes. Her units are planned for days and even weeks at a time, depending

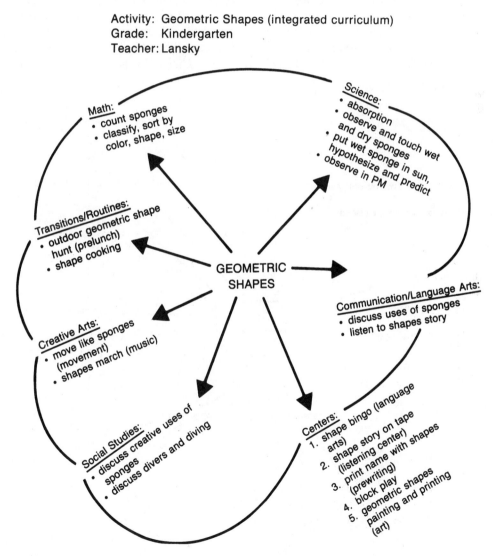

Activity: Geometric Shapes (integrated curriculum)
Grade: Kindergarten
Teacher: Lansky

Math:
• count sponges
• classify, sort by color, shape, size

Science:
• absorption
• observe and touch wet and dry sponges
• put wet sponge in sun, hypothesize and predict
• observe in PM

Transitions/Routines:
• outdoor geometric shape hunt (prelunch)
• shape cooking

GEOMETRIC SHAPES

Communication/Language Arts:
• discuss uses of sponges
• listen to shapes story

Creative Arts:
• move like sponges (movement)
• shapes march (music)

Social Studies:
• discuss creative uses of sponges
• discuss divers and diving

Centers:
1. shape bingo (language arts)
2. shape story on tape (listening center)
3. print name with shapes (prewriting)
4. block play
5. geometric shapes painting and printing (art)

FIGURE 12–4

on the level of interest and involvement of her particular group. She believes that a unit approach provides a focus for all of her planning. Each activity relates to her theme. In turn, everything children experience during the unit is somehow related to the theme under study.

Miss Susan begins by sketching out a flowchart. See Figure 12–5. She writes her theme of shapes in the center and merely writes in anything and everything related. At this point she is more concerned with terms, concepts, and understandings than with actual activities. Items on her flowchart will suggest activities. Miss Susan brainstorms with her fellow teachers sometimes, using a blackboard in working and reworking her flowchart. She may have more on her flowchart than will appear on her plan. Some concepts may be too difficult or may not translate into a specific early childhood activity.

The second step is moving from a flowchart to a general plan of activities. Miss Susan decides to allow one week for the study of shapes. She bases this decision on the interests of her particular group and her experience with teaching this theme in the past. Although she does not teach shapes exactly the same way every year, she does use her flowchart and plans as a general guide. Slowly, she is accumulating a wealth of flowcharts and thematic plans. Her weekly plan for shapes is found in Figure 12–6.

FIGURE 12–5   Flowchart on shapes

THEME: SHAPES

	MONDAY	TUESDAY	WEDNESDAY	THURSDAY	FRIDAY
EXPRESSIVE ARTS	Making shapes out of clay	Making shapes using self and others	Sing shapes song: I'm a little circle . . .	Sponge painting and printing with sponges cut into shapes	Make, bake, and frost shape cookies
LANGUAGE ARTS	Read and discuss story on shapes	Locate shapes in our ABCs	Match word with its shape	Play shape bingo and dominoes	Dictate story: "If I were a ○, □, △, ▭, I would . . ."
MATH	Count number of square shapes on flannel board	One-to-one correspondence with: ○, □, △, ▭	Classify items by shape	Seriate circles	Conservation game: more, less, same ○, □, △, ▭ shapes
SCIENCE	Outdoor shapes hunt Shapes in nature	Indoor shapes hunt: I spy . . .	Sink and float: does an item's shape make a difference?	Test out: Can all shapes roll? fall? slide?	Blow up balloon Discuss shape deflated and inflated
SOCIAL STUDIES	Discuss facial features as shapes	Draw self using geometric shapes	Show filmstrip on housing. Discuss shapes of igloos, pyramids teepees	Discuss shapes in foods: round pizza, square sandwich, triangular half-sandwich	Identify shapes in safety signs

FIGURE 12–6

Let us compare the four strategies. Mr. Kent taught art and all other areas as separate activities. There was no integration or tie-in. Mrs. Gomez used art and group time to extend and reinforce what children were learning during math concept time. Ms. Lansky planned a superactivity, focusing on geometric shapes and sponges that integrated the day's activities. Miss Susan planned for a week around the theme of shapes. Separate activities throughout her day were all related to a study of shapes (see Figure 12–7).

The first four strategies place the responsibility for curriculum development with the teacher. The problem is that the curriculum can become overly teacher-directed. What he or she plans may not be what the children want to do. There may be a mismatch between planned activities and children's interests. A well-planned unit on whales may not

work for a group of children who have little interest or a pressing need to learn about whales. A good curriculum aims for a balance between the teacher-planned and the spontaneous. This should not be equated with abdicating one's role as planner and curriculum developer. Children cannot plan curriculum. This is not about replacing all organization with unplanned chaos. Children do, however, provide cues as to what interests them. A skilled observer who watches and listens as children play is privy to a host of cues. Rather than dismissing them as unimportant, seize them as indicators of what children are about. Use them as avenues for high-interest learning. In turn, the curriculum organically emerges. Based on Kristeller (1994), the comparison and contrast between a planned versus a spontaneous or emergent curriculum is depicted in Table 12–1.

FIGURE 12–7   These children discover what they can do to and with clay.

5. Art As a Child-Directed Pursuit

There is a fifth strategy. Child-directed art is the type that children discover, invent, construct, and create on their own. It empowers them to be autonomous and in control. It may not look like something but children take great pride in their individual accomplishments. Child-directed art is deceivingly simple but it does not just happen. It occurs when teachers plan and subtly set the stage. Herein lies the delicate balance between teacher-directed art and child-directed art. Let's try a food analogy. You may appreciate the opportunity to build your own salad since only you know your food preferences. You are grateful for a well-stocked salad bar that offers many items from which to choose. And so it is with art and young children. Provide easy access to a wide variety of art supplies and let children create on their own. Children are motivated indefinitely to pursue this type of art. When they temporarily run out of interest or ideas, supplement by teaching one of the activities listed throughout this book. As always, model the process without specifying the finished product. Chapter 14 continues the discussion of viewing art as a child-directed pursuit by offering guidelines for setting up and maintaining an art center.

CLAY AND PLAY DOUGH

Many children will have had experience at home with commercially available Play-Doh or the homemade type. They will find the look, smell, and feel very pleasurable. It may remind them of cookie dough. They will approach clay with active processing in mind: "What can I do with clay?" By manipulating and handling it they will discover that clay can be pulled, torn, cut, rolled, and so forth. Older children may have a product in mind when they approach the clay table: "What can I make out of my lump of clay?" Three seriated balls of clay on top of each other will make a snowman. Often, there is much verbalizing and socializing at the clay table. "My clay is so hard." "Keep rollin' it till it gets soft." "Can I use the roller when you're done?" Verbal exchange and social skills are demonstrated at the

PLANNED CURRICULUM	SPONTANEOUS OR EMERGENT CURRICULUM
is teacher-centered	is child-centered
focuses on teacher's product	focuses on child's processing
stresses program goals and objectives	stresses children's interests and choices
provides security and familiarity	offers challenge and risks
meets needs of the group	meets individual needs
is predictable and routine	is flexible and open
may not match children's needs and interests	matches children's needs and interests
solitary venture	joint venture between teacher and child
empowers teacher	empowers child

TABLE 12–1   Planned vs. Spontaneous or Emergent Curriculum

clay table. Children make direct physical contact with clay. There is no brush, scissors, or marker between them and the medium.

Working with clay fosters large muscle and fine motor control. Clay is fairly resistant and will need to be kneaded and worked to make it pliable. Children can stand or sit while using clay. Standing provides the advantage of a whole body muscular reaction to the clay. Hard clay provides a solid resistance that the child must overcome. This will involve using muscles in the shoulders, arms, hands, and fingers if the child is seated. Slowly, the child gains control over the medium, making it do or become what he or she wants it to.

Children enjoy working with clay for many reasons. For one, it is a natural material and has the same appeal that water, sand, and wood hold for young children. As a preferred art form, it allows them to change or undo what they have begun. For example, a snowman can be disassembled, flattened, and transformed into a pizza. This is not always possible with crayons, markers, or paint. It also gives them control over a medium. The snowman's head will stay on top of the body if the two are joined together. The painted outline of a snowman might run or mix with other colors. If the clay head falls off, it can always be put back on. It is more difficult to correct a painting, especially if it has dried.

Working with clay is a multisensory experience. Clay has a distinct texture, temperature, color, and smell. Involving children in making homemade play dough provides a learning opportunity to read a recipe, measure, and mix ingredients. Children enjoy the feel of clay. It allows them to get dirty and messy. It might remind them of infantile pleasures attained during earlier, toilet training days. Because of this, some children will find clay appealing, while others may find it repulsive. Playing with clay should be an option. Over time and with subtle encouragement, the reluctant child may become an active participant at the clay table. Seeing that clay can be washed off hands and from under fingernails may also add reassurance.

Using real mud provides an earthy experience in which children are brought in close touch with nature. Working with clay provides an opportunity to release feelings in a socially acceptable way. A child may not display aggression against a peer but is free to pound on a clay person. Clay has a therapeutic effect. It allows the working through of emotions and creating of model situations. A child who is upset by a recent divorce may be unable to verbally express how he or she feels. Clay, however, provides this child with the opportunity to work through his or her feelings by talking to and dramatizing with a family made out of clay.

Children need lots and lots of clay. A grapefruit-sized ball for each sculptor is recommended. Play dough and clay, in particular, will require a lot of kneading to become pliable. Clay must be kept in a sealed container, such as a plastic tub with a snap-on lid. Over time, certain types of clay (earth) washed from hands will clog up the sink. Some teachers prefer that children rinse their hands in a bucket and flush the muddy water down the toilet.

Types of Clay

Different types of clay let children process in different ways. Below, three major types are described.

Real Clay   Different parts of the country have their own characteristic clays. Many types can be used in the classroom. Soak the clay in a bucket and pour it through a screen to remove sticks and stones. This treatment will help make the clay more pliable. Real clay is dug up from the earth and can be purchased in art supply stores. Water-based or potters clay products can be fired and preserved. It is the type of clay that adult sculptors work with. Make sure the brand is nontoxic. It can be bought in a ready-to-mix powder or premixed form. Premixed is more expensive. However, extra time will be needed if you are using a ready-to-mix powder that also needs to set. Real clay is less expensive, messier, but more pliable than plasticene. Its dull gray or brown color may not be visually appealing, but its cool feel and inviting texture will attract participation. Since it is water-based, it will dry out when exposed to air.

Provide a small pan of water and encourage children to wet their fingers and moisten real clay to keep it pliable. This clay will also dry unfired or can be reused by forming it into 4-inch balls and putting it back in the storage container wrapped in a wet paper towel. Poke a hole in each clay ball and fill it with water to further preserve pliability. Check your clay from time to time. If it is too wet, it will get moldy and smell. If it is too dry, it will harden. Add or remove moisture as needed. Real clay is messy and is best suited for outdoor use. Simply hose down the area when you are finished. Products made from real clay can be glazed and fired in a kiln for the beautiful shiny finish that you see on ceramic pieces. Most centers and schools for young children will not have access to a kiln. This is no problem. Finished pieces can also be left to dry on their own; this will take several days. Of course, most young sculptors will be happy returning their mass of clay to its original ball shape for the next clay session.

Plasticene   Plasticene is a type of clay with an oil base. It is fairly inexpensive, does not stick to surfaces, and will not dry out if kept covered when not in use. It is fairly solid and requires a good deal of kneading and heat from the hands to become pliable. It is reusable and cannot be fired or painted. It may frustrate the toddler or young preschooler who lacks muscular strength in the fingers and hands. Not all children like the smell of plasticene.

Play Dough   Play-Doh is commercially available. It comes in bright colors and is fairly inexpensive. It is also very fragrant and may tempt the young sculptor into tasting it. Its major disadvantage is that it tends to crumble and flake, with tiny pieces spreading all over the table and floor. Even in its lidded can, Play-Doh will dry up, harden, or mold over time. Try placing the Play-Doh in a sandwich bag sealed with a twist tie before storing it in the container to make it last longer.

Play dough can also be homemade. Children enjoy making and using play dough because it is soft and pliable. It also combines cooking with art. One major ingredient is flour, making this type of clay fairly inexpensive and able to be baked and preserved. Place it in a covered container and store it in the refrigerator. Recipes are provided later in this chapter. Different recipes provide different textures. Be sure to vary the color and scent added.

Very young children will find play dough more appealing and easier to work with than plasticene. Inhibited children may prefer play dough or plasticene to real clay. Still, young children should be exposed to a wide variety of clays and play doughs.

Processing with Clay

Young children can discover that there are many, many different ways to work with clay (see Figure 12–8). Processing with clay may, but need

FIGURE 12–8   *An activity to help children learn about shapes*

not, result in a finished clay product. Some ways to process with clay include

- fingering and squeezing clay
- rolling clay into round balls, eggs, eyeballs, marbles, peas, or meatballs
- coiling, stretching, and lengthening clay into long snakes, worms, rope, hot dogs, spaghetti, noodles, or sausage; smaller coils often become a ring, bracelet, or necklace
- patting, flattening, hammering, squashing, or pounding clay into a pancake, pie, hamburger, cookie, pizza, or face
- pinching off pieces of clay to make facial features, bugs, or bits of candy
- cutting clay with blunt scissors to make french fries

- poking holes or openings into clay to make a donut or facial features in a face or head
- tearing or pulling apart as well as joining pieces of clay
- stamping or imprinting clay with cookie cutters, bottle caps, buttons, pinecones, seashells, and so forth
- twisting or braiding lengths of clay
- forming or molding clay into nests, bowls, or birthday cakes
- squeezing or sculpting clay into a solid three-dimensional, self-standing form, such as a snowman, animal, or human figure
- incising or cutting into clay with a plastic knife, fork, Popsicle stick, toothpick, fingernails, and so forth
- processing with clay and a variety of clay tools and accessories
- folding or bending clay into a taco, flower, or boat

Stages of Working with Clay

More has been written about stages of children's drawing and painting than about working with clay. The author has synthesized the research on the child's developmental progression in the use of clay (Brittain, 1979; Golomb, 1974; and Hartley, Frank, and Goldenson, 1952) in proposing the following stages:

Stage 1: What Is Clay?   In this first stage, two-year-olds experiment with and explore the properties of clay. They use their senses to visually explore, touch, smell (and often stick up their noses), lick and taste, and listen to clay being worked with their hands. They will drop it, step on it, throw or try to bounce it, and stick it to their skin. They are not interested in making something out of clay. Their talk will be limited to words related to their sensory experiences with clay, for example, "yucky," "gooey," "mushy," or "mmmmmm."

Stage 2: What Can I Do with Clay?   The first stage quickly builds into the second. Three-year-olds are more systematic in their attempts at processing with the clay. As scientists, they put clay to a series of tests by rolling, pinching, tearing, pulling, and poking it. By physically acting on clay they discover its properties. Clay can roll, but it cannot bounce or pour. The child does not deliberately set out to make something at this stage. By chance and through active manipulation, simple forms such as small balls, patted cakes, or snakes may result. These actions will be repeated, with the child making several products.

Stage 3: Look What I Made! Four-year-olds will creatively combine clay forms and actions performed on them. One clay ball is put on top of another. Flattening and rolling a piece of clay produces a new shape. Openings will be pushed into the mass of clay, and pieces will be pulled out. There is more labeling and talking about what they are making. For example, while a stage-2 child might simply poke a hole through a thin sheet of clay, the older stage-3 sculptor might make a total of three pokes and call it a face. The finished product may be crude and simple. Balls of clay can be added to a coiled snake, with the child saying, "My snake can see you." Children in this stage often dramatize with their clay products. The clay snake slithers around the table, hissing and biting the children. Clay products are becoming more complex at this stage. Still, many clay creations are more the accidental result of processing than the result of systematic planning in advance or intention. Clay creations are idiosyncratic and personal, and others may not recognize the finished product.

Stage 4: I Know What I'm Going to Make out of My Clay! Five-year-olds approach the clay table knowing what they want to make out of clay and announce this in advance. They have an idea, a name, and a finished product in mind. They need to find a process or technique that is suitable. There is more discussion while processing and about the finished clay product. Products evidence fairly realistic representation and can be recognized by others. Children in this stage know that their clay food or snake is only a symbol or model and not the actual object itself. They will not try to eat the food as a younger child in stage 3 might. Five-year-olds enjoy adding details using clay tools and accessories, as well as artistic junk such as buttons and toothpicks.

The stages of clay appear to parallel stages of the child's artistic development in painting or mark making. Scribbles come to be named just as children give names to their clay creations. Still, clay is a three-dimensional art form, whereas painting and mark making are two-dimensional. Since children live in a three-dimensional world, it may be easier for them to use clay to represent their world. Putting the three-dimensional world on a flat two-dimensional surface with paint, crayons, or markers involves abstraction and may be more difficult. Does this mean that children should be given clay before other art media? Brittain (1979) conducted a study to determine whether clay would facilitate a more advanced type of representation than drawing. In carefully examining the artwork of seventeen preschoolers, he found no superiority of clay over drawing when judging the accuracy of representation. A child who is having difficulty drawing a person would have similar difficulties making one out of clay. Young children need experience with a wide variety of artistic media, and no strict order of presentation is supported by the research. Still, our working knowledge of children and their development tells us that batik is inappropriate for most two- and three-year-olds, whereas play dough is recommended.

Clay Techniques

Above and beyond processing with clay, there are specific techniques for making clay products that the older child might enjoy learning. Often, they are discovered. Here are some of those techniques.

Pinch Using the pinch method will result in a clay bowl or pot. Begin with a clay ball. Stick both thumbs into the center of the clay ball with the fingers holding the outside. Gently press the thumbs against the sides while pinching and rotating the clay ball. Continue pinching and pulling the sides upward and out into a pot or bowl.

Coil The coil method builds on the child's experiences with rolling long clay snakes. A pot or bowl can also be formed with this method. Native

Americans made pottery using the coil method over a pinch pot. Begin by wrapping coils of clay over the basic pinch pot or into any shape or form desired.

Slab   Begin with a slab of clay. Roll it flat with a rolling pin until it is about ½-inch thick. Use a plastic knife or other clay tool to cut out the outline of the desired object. Smooth out the cut edges.

Adding Clay   Start with a ball or lump of clay and slowly add parts and details. For example, one child made a horse from a solid mass of clay. A head, legs, and a tail were carefully added. Clay pieces made this way tend to be fragile, and the added parts do not always stay attached. The child was very frustrated because her horse's legs kept breaking under the weight of its heavy body.

Pulling Out Clay   This method will avoid the problems associated with adding clay. Start with a fairly large mass of clay. Think of the total object as a solid piece rather than as made up of connected parts. Slowly pull out the parts you need. For example, by molding and carefully pulling out legs, arms, and a head, one child made a person out of clay. It was fairly sturdy and stable, since it was an intact mass without added-on parts and pieces.

Taking Clay Away   Start with a fairly large mass of clay. Take away the excess or unwanted pieces of clay, using fingers or clay tools and accessories. For example, one child used a plastic knife to carve her irregularly shaped clay ball into a round jack-o'-lantern. Facial features were cut out.

Outlining with Clay   Some children use strips of flattened clay as if they were strokes of paint or lines drawn with pencil, crayons, or markers. They approach clay as if it were a two-dimensional medium and overlook its three-dimensional possibilities. This is to be expected, and for most it will be a temporary stage. Objects can be outlined in clay rather than represented with a solid mass of clay. Since the object is outlined flat and stationary on the clay board, there is no need to worry about it moving, falling over, or coming apart. This technique allows children to add small details.

Clay and Accessories

alphabet clay cutters—commercial set makes miniature ABCs
apple divider—for slicing clay
cheese slicer—for slicing clay
clay board—with nonstick surface
clay cutters—plastic knives and spoons
clay hammers—for pounding and flattening clay
cookie cutters—for making shapes out of clay
dough press—for making decorations out of clay
dowel rods—for rolling, poking, and designing clay
egg slicer—for slicing clay balls
Formica—for clay boards
funnels—for making circular impressions in clay
linoleum—for clay boards
meat baller—for scooping and making clay balls
meat tenderizer mallet—for flattening and making impressions in clay
melon baller—for scooping and making clay balls
modeling clay
natural or real clay
pastry blender—for kneading and working clay
pastry tube—for making decorations out of clay
pie crimper—for incising clay
pizza cutter—for cutting through clay
plasticene
Play-Doh
play dough
potato masher—for mashing clay
rolling pins—for rolling clay
scoop—for scooping and making clay balls
self-hardening clay
storage container with tight lid to keep clay from drying out

Hint   Remember that clay tools are mere accessories and are not intended to replace manipulative processing with the fingers and hands. Do not begin with the tools, but slowly add them as a variation to working clay with the hands.

Hint   Floor tiles, Formica, and linoleum make good individual clay boards. Some have interesting colors, lines, and designs. Cut into 1-foot squares if they come in a large sheet or roll.

Hint   Add a few drops of perfume, bath oil, or peppermint oil to homemade play dough to keep it sweet-smelling and to prevent spoiling.

Hint   Add a few tablespoons of vegetable oil to play dough to make it easier to sculpt.

Hint   Add a tablespoon of powdered alum when making homemade play dough to keep it from getting moldy.

Clay Activities

Clay Creations   **P K S**

Children may enjoy decorating their clay creations with recycled junk materials. Some items that go well with clay include

- toothpicks
- pipe cleaners
- nuts and bolts
- screws and nails
- keys
- buttons
- straws
- Popsicle sticks
- paper clips
- acorns
- seashells
- small sticks and twigs
- golf tees
- short pencils

Baked Ornaments   **P K S**

Check the recipe section in this chapter for play dough recipes that allow you to paint, bake, and preserve the finished product. Remember to poke a hole in the product before baking if you want it to hang.

Plasticene Print   **K S**

Children can use clay tools and accessories, such as a plastic knife, to carve designs into a thin slab of plasticene. Carefully dip the carved piece of plasticene in paint or press it on a stamp pad. Press on a piece of paper. Repeat the impression to make a pattern.

Clay Numbers and Letters   **K S**

Young children who are interested in the world of letters and numbers may enjoy using magnetic letters and numbers to make clay impressions. Remove the small magnet piece from each. Children can also use plastic knives, Popsicle sticks or toothpicks to carve their name, their initials, the alphabet, words, their address, or their phone number

out of clay. These could also be formed by combining small coils of clay.

Clay Overs   **K S**

Children may enjoy sculpting clay pieces or parts and attaching them to a larger base. For example, a small juice can or box can be decorated with coils and balls of clay.

Clay and Play Dough Recipes

Bread-Dough Clay (inedible)

4 slices bread
3 tablespoons white glue
2 drops lemon juice
plastic bag

Remove crusts from bread. Tear bread into small pieces. Mix pieces of bread with glue and lemon juice. Knead. Do not eat. Sculpt. Allow to dry for a couple of days before decorating. Place unused bread-dough clay in a plastic bag and store in the refrigerator.

Edible Candy Clay

⅓ cup margarine
⅓ cup light corn syrup
¼ teaspoon salt
1 teaspoon vanilla or peppermint extract
1-pound box powdered sugar
food coloring

Mix all other ingredients, then add powdered sugar. Knead until smooth. Add more powdered sugar if necessary to make nonstick, pliable clay. Sculpt and eat.

Edible Dough Clay

1 package of dry yeast
1½ cups very warm water
1 egg
¼ cup honey
¼ cup shortening
1 teaspoon salt
5 cups flour

Mix yeast with water. Add egg, honey, shortening, and salt. Slowly add flour until a ball of dough forms.

Add more flour if too sticky. Knead dough. Sculpt. Make only flat figures, since dough will rise. Cover the sculptures with a towel. Let rise in a warm place for about a half hour. Let it rise longer if you want it fatter. Bake at 350°F for 20 minutes or until golden brown. Sculptures can be eaten or painted and coated with shellac to preserve.

Decorating Dough

4 cups self-rising flour
1 cup salt
1½ cups water
food coloring or powdered tempera (optional)

Mix flour and salt in large bowl. Slowly add water. Mix thoroughly. Add food coloring. Knead for 5 to 10 minutes. Add more water if dough is too stiff, more flour if too sticky. Food coloring is optional. Sculpt or cut with cookie cutters. Sprinkle board with flour to keep from sticking. Press in hairpin holder if hanging is desired. Dry at room temperature for several days, or bake at 300°F for 1½ hours. Refrigerated dough will last for 5 days.

Goop

2 cups salt
water
1 cup cornstarch

Mix salt and ⅔ cup water. Heat in pot for 3 to 4 minutes. Remove from heat and quickly add a mixture of the following:

1 cup cornstarch
½ cup cold water

Stir quickly. Return to the heat if too "goopy."

Play Dough (cooked)

2 cups flour
1 cup salt
2 cups water
2 tablespoons cooking oil
4 teaspoons cream of tartar
food coloring (optional)

Mix the flour, salt, and cream of tartar together. Add the water, oil, and food coloring (if desired).

Cook the mixture over low to medium heat for 3 to 5 minutes. Keep stirring until the mixture forms a solid ball. Cool. Items made can be baked at low heat for 20 to 25 minutes, depending on their thickness.

Play Dough (uncooked)

2½ cups flour
½ cup salt
1 tablespoon alum
3 tablespoons cooking oil
1½ cups hot water
food coloring

Combine oil, water, and food coloring. Combine dry ingredients. Pour liquid into dry ingredients. Mix thoroughly. Knead.

Soap and Sawdust Clay

1½ cups soap flakes
1½ cups sawdust
water

Slowly add water to soap flakes. Make a thick, creamy mixture. Whip soap until it is stiff and fluffy. Slowly mix in sawdust. Sculpt. Let figures dry for several days.

Soda and Cornstarch Clay

1 cup cornstarch
2 cups baking soda
1¼ cups water
food coloring

Combine cornstarch, baking soda, and water in pan. Cook over medium heat. Stir constantly. Stop when mixture thickens like dough. Knead and add food coloring when cool.

Mud Dough

2 cups mud
2 cups sand
½ cup salt
water

Slowly add water until pliable. Children enjoy the texture.

Peanut Butter Clay (edible)

4 tablespoons peanut butter
1 tablespoon honey
1 tablespoon wheat germ
2½ tablespoons powdered milk

Mix. Sculpt. Eat!

Peanut Butter Play Dough (edible)

1 cup peanut butter
1 cup honey
1 cup powdered milk
1 cup oatmeal
food coloring (optional)

Mix thoroughly. Adding food coloring is optional. Sculpt as if it were clay. Eat!

Pretzel Clay I (edible)

1 package dry yeast, dissolved in cold water
3 cups flour
1 teaspoon sugar
1 teaspoon salt
water

Mix yeast mixture and flour. Slowly add about 1 more cup of flour until the mixture can be kneaded. Let children take turns kneading it on a floured countertop. Sculpt as clay. Sprinkle with kosher salt. Bake at 350°F for about 20 minutes. Makes approximately 20 small pretzels.

Pretzel Clay II (edible)

1 cup warm water
1 package yeast
1 tablespoon salt
2½ cups whole wheat pastry flour

Mix water and yeast. Let sit for a few minutes. Add salt and flour. Mix and knead. Roll into shapes. Place on lightly greased cookie sheet. Bake in preheated oven at 425°F for 12 minutes or until brown. Beat an egg and brush on your creations if want a glazed look.

Silly Putty

white liquid glue
liquid starch
food coloring

Mix equal parts of white liquid glue and liquid starch. Stir immediately. Add a few drops of food coloring. Knead until silly putty is soft and smooth. Store in container with lid.

Frosting Dough (edible)

1 can frosting mix
1½ half cup of powdered sugar
1 cup peanut butter

Use large spoon to mix all ingredients in a bowl. Knead into workable mixture. Provide small ball for each child. Model as with any dough. Eat if desired.

Kool-Aid Play Dough

2½ cups flour
½ cup salt
2 13-oz packages of Kool-Aid
3 tablespoons vegetable oil
2 cups boiling water

Mix flour, salt, and Kool-Aid. Add vegetable oil and boiling water in a large bowl. Knead until a good consistency is attained. Store in an airtight container or in locking plastic bags. Play dough smells good but should not be eaten.

Soft Cloud-Like Play Dough

6 cups flour
1½ cups vegetable oil
1 cup water

If color is desired, add food coloring or tempera to large bowl with flour. Add oil and water to flour and knead well. If needed, add small amounts of water until dough is soft and fluffy. Add more flour if dough is too sticky. Store dough in a covered container and refrigerate.

Vinegar Dough

3 cups flour
1 cup salt
1 cup water
¼ cup vegetable oil
2 tablespoons vinegar

Mix all ingredients together in a large bowl. Add more water if too dry. Knead. This soft play dough keeps well when stored in a plastic bag and refrigerated. Knead water into dough to refresh.

Ooey-Gooey: Cornstarch and Water

1-pound box cornstarch
1½ cups water
food coloring or liquid watercolor (optional)

Mix all ingredients together into large container like a shallow dishpan where children can experiment together. Or mix individual portions of ooey-gooey in small plastic food savers. Adding more water or cornstarch changes the consistency. Encourage children to discover what happens when they handle the ooey-gooey by grasping, squeezing, and pouring.

Borax Putty

1 cup water
1 cup white glue
food coloring or liquid watercolor (optional)

Mix water and glue together, color if desired. Set aside.

1 teaspoon Borax powdered laundry detergent
hot water

Dissolve Borax in 2 tablespoons of hot water. Add Borax mixture by stirring it into the glue mixture. Pull out gooey mixture. Knead. Repeat pulling-out step. May need to add more glue or Borax depending on consistency of putty. Store in plastic bag and refrigerate.

Rainbow Stew

1 cup cornstarch
¾ cup sugar

4 cups water
2 different primary colors (food colors or liquid watercolors)
Ziplock freezer bags
sturdy tape, e.g., duct

Mix first three ingredients in a pot. Place on medium heat, stirring constantly, until thickened. Remove from heat and let cool. Divide into two bowls and add one color to each bowl. Place one or two heaping tablespoons full of each colored mixture into each child's freezer bag. Use sturdy tape for extra security. Encourage the children to mash and mix the colors together and discuss what they see happening. Repeat on another day using two different primary colors and note resulting combinations. Hold bags up to light, or tape them on window.

SUMMARY

This chapter focused on curriculum development by presenting a PIE model for planning, implementing, and evaluating. Figure 12–9 shows how a theme can be woven into many art activities. Goals, based on what we know about children and their development as well as our values, give direction to our planning. Breaking goals down into short-term objectives assists in daily planning. Implementing raises management and procedural concerns about carrying out activities. Evaluation addresses the match between what we set out to do and what actually happened. The chapter also compared and contrasted different strategies for integrating art into the early childhood curriculum.

FIGURE 12–9 (A) A tasting party for sampling some of the foods dinosaurs may have eaten; (B) Dinosaur dictation and graphing; (C) Dinosaurs in the water activity table; (D) Dinosaurs at the sensory table

Suggested Activities

1. As a group, brainstorm your goals for early childhood education. Are they developmental in focus? Do you agree? How do they reflect different values and beliefs? Can you reach consensus? What might this indicate about the state of early childhood education?

2. Observe how different teachers use planning, implementing, and evaluating in their programs.

3. Use the lesson plan format to write and implement an art activity.

4. Divide the class into four groups. Each group is responsible for very general daily planning for teaching the concept of primary colors, using one of the five strategies discussed in this chapter.

5. Facilitate an activity with play dough or clay.

Review

A. Complete the cycle of curriculum and development.

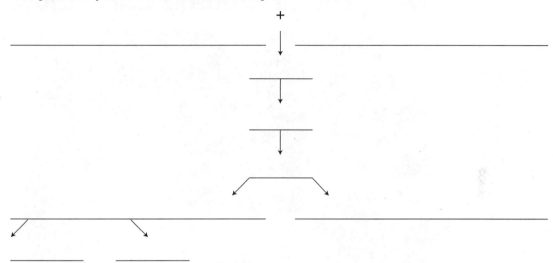

B. Identify the components of the PIE approach to curriculum development.
1. P _____
2. I _____
3. E _____

C. List strategies for including art in the early childhood curriculum.
1.
2.
3.
4.

D. Provide examples that distinguish a planned approach from a spontaneous or emergent approach to curriculum.

CHAPTER 13

Integrating Art Across the Early Childhood Curriculum

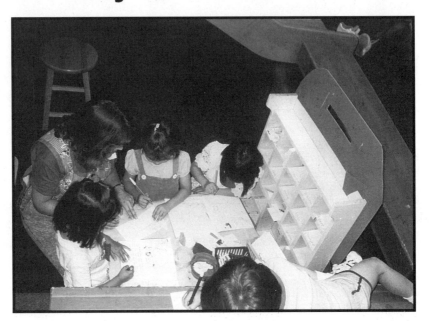

What do you see going on in this picture? Is this something you would do with children?

The children are producing stories. Some are making only pictures to tell their story. Others are dictating their stories to their teacher, who carefully and neatly prints it as spoken. Another child attempts to make letters and words. The teacher is careful to accept all attempts without concern for how letters are made or words are formed. Her intent is to get children to express themselves. Although art is a nonverbal means of expression, many children are motivated to talk about their pictures. Art can lead to speaking, which in turn can be written down and read. Art and literacy go hand in hand.

OBJECTIVES

After studying this chapter, the student will be able to

- Compare and contrast different ways of viewing the early childhood curriculum
- Identify the major early childhood curricular areas
- Discuss how art fosters learning in other early childhood curricular areas
- Provide three-dimensional art activities

INTRODUCTION

Curriculum means different things to different people. Two major ways of viewing the curriculum are as an overall program or as subject areas. Each view will be discussed in this chapter. Art is merely one of many curricular areas. How can art reinforce and extend learning in the other curricular areas? Integrating art throughout the early childhood curriculum will be the focus of this chapter. Refer also to the color insert.

ART AND THE EARLY CHILDHOOD CURRICULUM

The word *curriculum* is used to refer to an educational program, activity, or set of activities, and to guidelines set by a school district office, state, corporation, or professional organization. In its widest sense, curriculum refers to what happens in schools or centers. Two major ways of viewing the early childhood curriculum are

- curriculum as program
- curriculum as subject matter, content, or academic area

Curriculum As Program

To some, curriculum means the total program, such as an infant, toddler, preschool, Montessori, Head Start, or kindergarten program. In this view, curriculum refers to all the things children learn in school or center. This is a very broad view of curriculum. It would include learning how to wait one's turn, sit in a circle for group time, and share toys, as well as learning about colors and shapes. In this view, children learn through specifically planned learning experiences as well as through incidental learnings. For example, Mel's parents are pleased that he enjoys his child-care program and is making friends. However, they are concerned that he has become more verbally and socially aggressive, behaviors that they had never observed before he attended child care. Children who are in groups for long periods of time learn these behaviors as ways

to cope and protect themselves. Children learn much more than is planned and intended in any curriculum or program.

Curriculum As Subject Matter, Content, or Academic Area

A second way to look at curriculum is to view it as a separate subject, content, or academic area of study. The present text focuses on art in the early childhood curriculum. Traditionally, the school curriculum has centered around the following curricular areas:

1. math
2. science
3. language arts/communication arts/literacy:
   - speaking
   - listening
   - reading
   - writing
4. social studies
5. expressive arts
   - art
   - music
   - movement

See Figure 13–1 for a visual portrayal of this model of the early childhood curriculum.

Just as child development cannot be dissected into neat divisions, the curricular areas are not separate entities. The model indicates that the curricular areas interact and influence each other. Children do not simply "switch channels" or "change gears" to move from mathematical to scientific thinking. Knowledge and skills are not neatly compartmentalized according to subject area. This is why math and science, communication and language arts, and the expressive arts are depicted with overlapping circles. Experiences such as cooking and play are highly recommended because they cut across and involve learning in many, if not all, of the curricular areas. Although the separation will work for our present analysis, children are wholistic individuals who learn in wholistic ways. For example, they engage in creative thinking and problem solving that

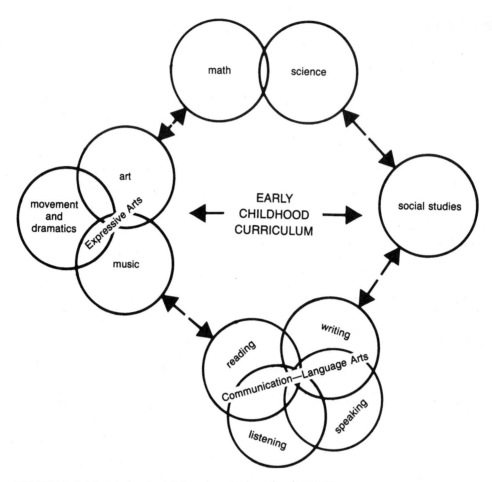

FIGURE 13–1 Model of early childhood curriculum development

may cut across the areas of math and science, art, and social studies.

ART AND MATH

Children naturally quantify art materials, equipment, and supplies. "There are four jars of paint out, but only three brushes. There are more jars than brushes." The teacher asks, "How many more brushes do we need to make them equal?" Some paintbrushes have longer handles and wider bristles than others. "My red crayon is longer than your blue one." "Yes, but mine is fatter and wider than yours." "This paste cup has less than the others," states Evie. Her teacher asks, "What can you do to make them the same?" Evie gets the large paste container and adds more.

Children quantify as they create. "There, now my bug has six legs, just enough," announces Ty as he coils a final leg out of clay. Marcy adds a second eye to her self-portrait. She carefully counts fingers and toes as she paints them on one by one. Some children use geometric shapes in composing their picture. "A tall brown rectangle with a green circle on top. Now, I'll color in my tree," announces Tess.

Some activities that incorporate art with math follow.

Geometric Shape Picture

Older children can cut an array of circles, squares, triangles, and rectangles of different sizes. These can be creatively arranged and pasted to form a picture. Teachers may want to cut out the geometric shapes for younger children. Precutting for children is warranted in this activity. Children see how common objects, people, vehicles, and animals are made up of geometric shapes and can be constructed from them.

There are two ways to vary this activity. Teachers can cut shapes out of flannel, including circles, squares, triangles, and rectangles that vary in color and size. Children can creatively arrange these shapes on a larger piece of flannel that forms the background. Some teachers pin or tape pieces of flannel to a bulletin board or chalkboard. Others cover a large piece of cardboard with flannel. A second variation is to use magnetic tape. Wide strips of magnetic tape can be cut into geometric shapes, or small pieces of magnetic tape can be glued to the back of poster board or cardboard shapes. In turn, these shapes can be creatively arranged on a cookie sheet.

Cube Art

Older children may enjoy making a picture or design using graph paper. Graph paper with large squares is recommended. This activity will take time and patience and is not recommended for very young children. The paper may need to be cut in half or quarters if children become overwhelmed by all the squares on the paper.

Lines, Arcs, and Circles

Young children enjoy using the tools of the mathematician: ruler, compass, and protractor. Specific instruction in the proper care and use of these instruments should be given. Model different ways of using a ruler, compass, protractor, and pencil to produce interesting designs and patterns. Children may want to color in the spaces between or connect forms with thin markers.

Variety of Paper Shapes

Art can be done on round, square, triangular, diagonal, rectangular, and odd-shaped pieces of paper. Each unique shape poses a new challenge to the child artist. Wide, sweeping strokes are appropriate on a big rectangular sheet of paper. A smaller, detailed picture may fit better on a smaller six-sided sheet.

Teachers can point out and discuss the different shapes of the paper provided. For example, "I put out some different paper today. What shape could we call it?" (holding up a piece of round paper). Since it is round with a hole cut out of the center, the children decide that circle, wheel, and doughnut are appropriate terms.

Teachers can also discuss how a large square sheet can be cut into smaller square pieces of paper. Four small squares make one larger square. Cutting the large diamond-shaped sheet of paper in half makes two triangular pieces of paper. In this way, children are slowly introduced to fractions through an integrated art activity.

Geoboard

Children can practice making geometric shapes with rubber bands on a geoboard. See Figure 13–2 for a geoboard pattern. Find a piece of wood. Carefully hammer in rows of evenly spaced nails.

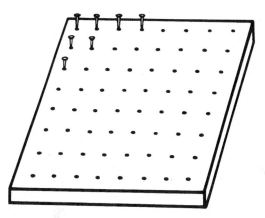

FIGURE 13–2 Geoboard

Use short nails with wide heads or upholstery tacks. A 1-inch space between rows and columns of nails is recommended. The total number of rows and columns will depend on the size of the board. Eight rows and eight columns are recommended.

Encourage the children to answer

- How many nails can you fit under just one rubber band?
- How many nails do you need to include to make a circle (square, rectangle, diamond, triangle, and so on)?
- Does it take more or fewer nails to make a square, triangle, circle, or rectangle?
- How many different shapes can you make using ten nails?

String Design K

Children can make abstract linear designs with string on a wooden frame. Find an old picture frame. Lay the frame down flat and hammer in a row of nails on each of the four upright sides. Encourage children to connect the nails using string, rope, or yarn. The result will be a creative linear design. Children can note the designs, patterns, shapes, and angles produced.

Tangram P K

The tangram is an old Chinese puzzle consisting of seven angular shapes that can fit together to make a square. (See Figure 13–3 for a tangram pattern.) The shapes can also be creatively combined to make pictures and designs. You may want to reproduce, cut out, mount on poster board, and laminate the individual pieces to ensure durability. Time invested in protecting the pieces will pay off in the long run. When laminating, remember to cut out the individual pieces first, then laminate them to avoid frayed ends. Covering the pieces with clear contact paper is also recommended.

Crayon Patterns P K

Empty several boxes of crayons onto a table. Allow children to create patterns, for example, red-blue-red-blue, etc. They may enjoy making patterns

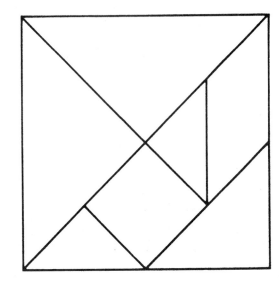

FIGURE 13–3   *Tangram*

for their friends to copy. Start a pattern, for example, one red–two blue–three yellow–one red–two blue–? and have the child complete the pattern.

Numerals Rubbing K

Find a puzzle with numerals. Lay a thin sheet of paper like onionskin (rather than thick construction paper) over the puzzle. Unwrap some crayons and also provide chalk. Encourage the child to rub with the side of the crayon or chalk on the paper. The numerals will appear. Read the numerals together. Children may want to try making their own numerals or finding sets of objects that correspond with the numerals. You can also provide old license plates and wooden blocks with numerals.

Dominoes Rubbing K

Lay a thin sheet of paper over a domino. Encourage children to rub with the side of the crayon or chalk on the paper. The numerals will appear. Resulting dots can be counted, matched with numeral, added together, or used in subtraction.

Numeral Sponges P K

Do sponge painting with sponges in numeral shapes. Fill low plates with liquid paint. Provide brushes so child can paint on bottom side of numeral. Gently press onto paper. Children can print their age, address, phone number, numerals in sequence or just make a collage by combining and overlapping numeral shapes. Numeral sponges can also be used at the water table.

Seriation Art K

Provide corks in a variety of widths. Children can seriate them from smallest to largest. Provide ink pads and paper for them to print their own designs made up of different-sized circular shapes. Encourage children to use comparative words when talking about their picture. For example, "Let's find the biggest shape." A variation of this activity is to provide round lids in a variety of sizes. Children can trace around the lids creating their own circular designs.

Addition Prints S

Children can use their hands and/or feet to make prints. Think of the number of possibilities. One hand, five fingers; two hands, ten fingers; etc. Hands, feet, fingers, and toes can be added. Hand prints can be made indoors, whereas foot printing is best done outdoors on a warm day. Children can also compare their prints, noting size differences.

Math Cards K

Children can use markers, crayons, or colored pencils to draw sets of objects which match numerals or number words. Separate pages or individual math cards can be bound into group books.

ART AND SCIENCE

Art activities help children discover scientific principles. Adding water to watercolor cakes produces a liquid. Over time, wet paint dries. Placing wet paintings in the sun will hasten the drying process. Clay remains moist if it is kept wrapped. On Monday morning Ms. Carlson announces, "Someone left their clay work out on the table over the weekend. What has happened to it?" "It turned

hard," answers Juan. "Yes, it got hard and brittle when exposed to the air for three days," explains his teacher. "Also, someone left a wax crayon on the radiator. What has happened to it?" "Yes, it melted. Why?" "Yes, the heat from the radiator melted the wax. What would happen if we left our crayons out in the sun on a hot summer day?" The possibilities of scientific thinking, hypothesizing, predicting, observing, questioning, discussing, and explaining are endless.

Too much water makes paint runny and uncontrollable. Little or no water produces a thicker, intense stroke. Pressing hard or lightly produces different effects. Children are learning about force. Children learn about resistance when they discover that they can cut paper but not cardboard with their scissors.

Some activities that incorporate art with science follow.

Food Groups Collage   P K

After studying the major food groups, children can be encouraged to find pictures of foods in magazines. These can be cut and pasted onto poster board sheets, one for each of the major food groups.

Nature Art P K

Young children and nature go hand in hand. Children enjoy taking short nature walks and collecting nature specimens. These can be creatively arranged and glued onto a paper plate, cardboard, or construction paper.

Children also enjoy making nature rubbings. Thin white paper can be placed over leaves, flowers, bark, stones, or other objects. Children can gently rub one side of an unwrapped crayon over the specimen. The texture and outline of the item will leave an impression. Children can also take their crayon and paper outdoors and make rubbings as they find them. Overlapping produces a different, more complex impression.

Children can also make nature prints. Paint can be brushed on a leaf, or an acorn can be lightly dipped in paint. The items can then be carefully pressed onto white paper. Gently lifting the item results in a print. Repeated prints result in a pattern. Separate prints can be creatively combined into a new design.

Color Mixing   **P K**

Children can discover the principles and joys of color mixing. Provide paint and a separate brush and container for each of the primary colors: red, blue, and yellow. Encourage children to mix any two colors in equal parts or dabs and see what happens. What color did you make? What happens if three colors are mixed together? This activity can also be done using food coloring, a plastic egg carton, and an eye dropper.

After this tempera paint activity has been successfully completed, white paint can also be provided. What happens if white is mixed with red, blue, or yellow? What happens if white is added to your mixture of red and yellow, red and blue, or blue and yellow? Let's find out.

Mobile   **K S**

Mobiles help children learn about balance, motion, and the effects of air and wind. A tree branch makes an excellent support or base for a mobile. (See Figure 13–4.) Acceptable nature items include shells, pinecones, feathers, leaves, and anything else that can be hung with thread, string, or fishing line. Items for a mobile can also be suspended from a coat hanger, yardstick, dowel rod, or broom handle.

FIGURE 13–5 Coat hanger mobile

Advanced mobile makers can experiment with different levels or planes. This provides an opportunity to experiment with weight, placement, space, and balance. A coat hanger mobile with several levels is shown in Figure 13–5.

Ecology Construction   **P K S**

Children can assist in the cleanup of litter, both indoors and outdoors. Recycled items can also be brought from home. Children can discuss the importance of avoiding needless waste, not littering, and recycling. Such items as scrap paper, boxes, containers, and plastic packaging can be recycled into a construction activity. For example, boxes and bottle tops inspired one preschooler to construct a robot.

FIGURE 13–4 Mobile

Color Magic P K

Provide three clear cups or containers and three brushes or plastic spoons per child. Tear red, yellow, and blue tissue paper into 1-inch squares. Have child dip several like-colored papers into container and use brush or spoon to mix. Observe what results. The primary colors can also be mixed to produce orange, purple, and green. What happens when three of the primary colors are mixed together? How can we make our colors light or intense? Does it matter how much water is used or the amount of tissue paper in a container? Experiment and find out. Provide eyedroppers and coffee filters or paper towels for dripping and further color mixing.

Color Overlays P K

Children can also mix colors using cellophane or acetate book-report covers. Each child will need small squares of cellophane in each of the three primary colors. Distribute one color, such as red, and have children look through it and discuss its transparent quality. Hold up to natural light and place on skin and clothing. Tape extra piece to the window. Discuss how you can see through it but it makes everything look red. Distribute the yellow pieces. Repeat the above step. Have children place their two pieces together. They can discuss their observations. What happened when we put red and yellow together? Repeat with the combinations of red and blue and yellow and blue. Children can save their pieces in a bag to take home or have the option of making a picture or collage with them.

Colors in a Bag T P

This no-mess activity helps children discover that two colors can produce a third. Give each child a ziplock bag. Write child's name on masking tape and place on bag. Provide liquid paint in red, blue, and yellow. Ask them to pick any two colors and put a spoonful of each into their bags. Securely seal. Encourage the child to gently squeeze and mix the colors. Discuss what is happening and what results. Child can make a second bag using two different

colors or the activity can continue on another day. Bags can be taped to a window.

Pet Rock P K S

Take a nature walk and allow children to find a rock or stone that appeals to them. It should be large enough to paint or decorate but small and light enough to fit in a child's hand. The teacher may want to collect a few extras. Upon returning, talk about how the stones and rocks look and feel. Use descriptive words and open-ended prompts like, "Use words to tell me all about your special rock." Provide paint, brushes and collage trims. Let children personalize their own rocks.

Dental Art P K

To incorporate art into your health program, use toothbrushes to paint with. Use dental floss for stringing or in string art activities. Coordinate with dental health week.

Mushroom Spore Prints K S

Each child needs a fresh mushroom, preferably one picked outdoors. Look for a mushroom that is old enough to have gills showing. Gills are the thin, radiating blades on the underside of the mushroom. Provide a sheet of construction paper and a clean plastic cup or jar big enough to cover the mushroom without touching it. Carefully cut the stem off the mushroom cap. Set the mushroom cap on the construction paper, gill side down. Cover the mushroom cap with cup to keep out air. Leave the cup alone for at least 24 hours. Carefully remove the cup and the mushroom. You will have a beautiful spore print that looks like a flower. Remember that mushrooms can have spores that are black, brown, white, pink or yellow, so try using different kinds of mushrooms and different colors of paper. Remind children that since wild mushrooms can be poisonous they should not be eaten.

Erupting Colors K S

Pour milk into a cake pan until the bottom is covered. Sprinkle several large drops of food coloring on the milk. Add a few drops of liquid dishwashing detergent into the rings of color. Observe what happens. Colors will erupt. If erupting stops, add more food coloring and then more detergent. If no results, begin again with new ingredients.

ART AND THE LANGUAGE/COMMUNICATION ARTS AND LITERACY

Art gives children the opportunity to represent what they know nonverbally or graphically. With encouragement, they may also choose to talk about what they have created (see Figure 13–6). Children read their artwork just as adults read words from a book. At times children enjoy having their titles or story lines printed on their pictures. They can be encouraged to read along with the teacher. Older children may attempt to print their own words as a story line. They may invent letters and misspell. This is to be expected; it is an important step that children go through as they become writers and readers. Scrib-

bling, mark making, and painting strokes are important steps in the development of printing and writing.

Art gives children an opportunity to include art vocabulary in their discussions with peers and adults. Teachers can introduce and model the use of these terms as they talk with children about their art. Children recognize colors, shapes, textures, lines, and movement in their own art and that of others. Lines can be thick, intersecting, crisscrossed, wavy, horizontal, vertical, diagonal, curved, or broken. Paint can be dry, wet, dripping, sticky, tacky, runny, slick, or crackled.

Anne Haas Dyson (1982, 1985, 1986, 1988, 1989, 1990) has studied the link between children's play, pictures, and print. She emphasizes the critical role of art and play in children's growth as symbol makers, particularly as makers of written symbols. Drawing is viewed as a literacy activity, because both drawing and language provide children with opportunities to reflect upon, organize, and share their experiences. When children draw, they are not simply communicating about their experiences; they are also solving visual problems. The problems they

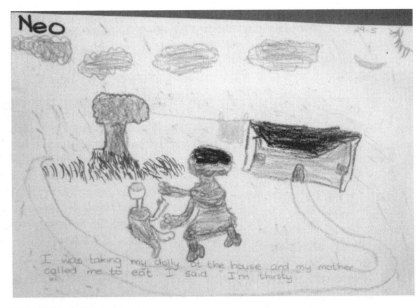

FIGURE 13–6 Neo's story

solve influence the nature of the texts they create. Although children need opportunities to give dictation and have their words written down for them, they also should engage in their own writing. They need to take marker or pencil in hand and explore the connection between meaning and print.

Some activities that incorporate art with the language/communication arts or literacy follow.

Art Talk   **T P K**

Encourage children to talk about their art, but do not require that art be followed by verbalization: "What would you like to tell me about your picture?" or, "Your colors and shapes make an interesting design; what words could you use to tell about it?" Labels, titles, and story lines can be recorded. For example, Marie asks a parent volunteer, "Can I tell you about my bunny picture?" Marie's words are carefully printed across the top of her paper. The parent points to each word as she reads the story back to Marie. She encourages Marie to read along. Marie says she's done for now but will trace over the letters with a pencil tomorrow. Ned prefers to talk his story into the tape recorder. His teacher will listen to it, transcribe it, and read it back to him.

Puppets   **P K**

Making a puppet is an art activity that can evolve into a speaking activity. For example, Tami, a shy four-year-old, makes an animal puppet out of a folded paper plate. She hides behind a bookshelf and lets her animal speak to and answer questions from two other children. Tami's puppet is a prop that gives her the psychological boost to speak in a group. After all, it is the puppet, not Tami, who is speaking.

Consonant Collage   **K**

One kindergarten class had been studying words that begin with the letter sounds. They practiced these sounds at concept time. They hunted through magazines for pictures of things that start with these sounds. The "b" page had pictures of a book, bicycle, bird, boy, Big Bird, bag, and Band-Aid. Pictures of a dog, duck, doll, doughnut, dishes, and dancers were pasted on the "d" page. By the end of the year, the children hoped to complete a collage page for each of their sounds.

Art Words   **P K**

Children at the clay table were trying to think of something new to make. Their teacher suggested that they form the letters in their names. Some also made their initials, ABCs, and simple words out of rolled clay.

As a variation, children could finger paint their names or letters of the alphabet. Getting the actual feel and direction of making a "b" and "d" may help some older children who are learning to print and who tend to reverse these letters.

Children also enjoy using squirt bottles to paint their names, letters, or words. Find a bottle with a pointed tip and a fairly small opening so that the paint will not merely run out. Bottles that hold white glue are a recommended size and shape for young hands.

Listen and Draw   **K S**

Mrs. Banks enjoys reading books to children. She wants children to listen attentively, appreciate literature, and get the main idea. She knows how important these skills will be when they learn to read. She often asks her children to draw a picture about the story she has just read. Sometimes she stops short of the ending and asks them to draw how they think the story will end. The pictures clearly reveal which children were listening and which might need additional practice in this area.

The creative teacher will invent many variations on this activity. For example, children can be encouraged to listen and then draw what the teacher requests. For example, "Please draw three cats of any color with long tails sitting by a tree." Children need to listen, remember, and represent. The details requested must be minimal and within the memory range and drawing ability of young children. Details such as "inside," "behind," "checkered," or "star-shaped" may be too difficult to represent.

Alphabet Letter Collage

Use stencils or die-cut press to create precut lower-case letters of the alphabet. Children can find and name letters they recognize. Some may want to make their names or simple words; others may want to make creative designs by combining and overlapping letters.

Alphabet Letter Rubbing

Find a puzzle with the alphabet. Lay a thin sheet of paper (like onionskin) over the puzzle. Encourage the child to rub with the side of unwrapped crayon or chalk on the paper. The alphabet will appear. Read the letters together. Children may want to try making their own letters.

Alphabet Letter Print

Provide alphabet sponges, wooden alphabet blocks, and alphabet magnetic letters which can be painted and pressed on paper for a print. Children can make their names or familiar words. Smaller items, like the magnetic letters, can be pressed into ink pads and stamped on paper. Rubber stamps featuring the alphabet are also commercially available.

I Can Make My Name

Provide finger paint and encourage children to make their names and other familiar words on glossy paper. You may want to keep their nametags close for reference. Provide craft sticks and have children scrape out their names in paint or shaving cream. Children can also form their names out of play dough.

Personalized Placemat

Provide each child with a large sheet of white paper. Ask where they would like you to put their names. Print them neatly in large letters, capitalizing the first letter of their names. Provide crayons and markers and encourage children to decorate the space around their name. For each mat, cut two sheets of contact paper about an inch or two larger than the placemat. Peel off backings and cover both sides of the mat. Trim edges and round off corners. Use at snack or small group time.

Please refer to color insert for more language activities that incorporate art. These include Alphabet Pop-up Mural, Pattern Books, Story Extensions, Sequence Story, Card Making, and Bedtime Stories. A child-illustrated Recipe Chart appears on the cover.

ART AND SOCIAL STUDIES

Art helps children get in touch with themselves and others. Representing oneself through self-portraits and human figure drawings increases one's awareness of self, body parts, and others. Through art, one takes on and identifies with the role of artist. A study of artists can be part of a lesson on community helpers. Children can visit a museum or gallery. An artist can come in and model artistic processing and work with the children. This can also be a brief introduction to history and culture, because artists and their different styles have been around since prehistoric times. Different cultural groups have their own art forms (see Chapter 5). Some activities that incorporate art and social studies follow.

"Me" Book

Children can illustrate pages of their "All About Me" book. Sample activities include drawing one's face, body, senses, likes, dislikes, house, family, and friends.

My Twin

After learning about "me," children can lie down on a long sheet of butcher paper. Encourage children to slightly spread out their arms and legs. The teacher can carefully trace around the outline of each child. Children can cut and color their twin, paying attention to color of hair, eyes, and clothing. A full-length mirror should be handy. Do not, however, expect a mirror image or realistic likeness.

My 3-D Twin

Using two sheets of butcher paper, follow the directions for the previous activity. Children can color or paint in the front and back. Slowly staple both sides together while gently stuffing with crumpled newspaper. As with the previous activity, expect children to take creative liberty. Since this tends to be a long activity, you may want to split it into several sequences. For example, separate sessions to trace, cut, color, stuff, and staple may be warranted. Art projects or activities need not be hurriedly completed in one session.

Family Flag   K S

Briefly discuss how flags are symbols for countries. In our country, the United States, we use stars and stripes and the colors red, white, and blue. Let children carefully examine the flag. Encourage them to make their own flag for their family. "What can you put on your flag that tells us about you and your family?" Family members and things that remind them of their families can be included.

Murals   P K S

Making a mural is a good activity to wrap up or synthesize something. It is an activity that can be repeated with different areas or concepts being studied. For example, after a field trip to the bakery, children can draw a mural to represent what they experienced—people baking, decorating baked goods, rolling and kneading dough, selling bakery products, stocking shelves, and so on. After studying a unit on the farm, children can represent what they have learned about the farm in a mural. If a farm mural does not contain animals, vehicles, and buildings related to the farm theme, the teacher might conclude that perhaps the children did not learn much about the farm. The teacher might want to review key concepts in discussing the farm mural. Or, it might simply be that the bus ride over and the picnic lunch were more meaningful.

Feelings Puppet   P K

Use group time to discuss different feelings. Label feelings and discuss events that make us feel this way. Make a face and pass around a hand mirror so children can see how a certain feeling makes

them look. Discuss how feelings are always good although the behavior that accompanies them might not be acceptable. For example, it is OK to feel angry and everyone does; it is not OK, however, to hit someone because you are angry. Make a two-sided puppet. Begin a feelings discussion by introducing and comparing feeling happy and sad. A child can make a happy face on one side of the plate and a sad face on another. Discuss what makes each child feel happy or sad. Attach a craft stick for a handle. Children can turn their puppet to either happy or sad as you discuss specific situations, such as not having a friend to play with.

Group Mobile   K S

This activity provides a sense of group belonging and is recommended for the beginning of the year. Some teachers use photographs while others ask children to draw their own pictures. Names can be added. Provide a forked tree branch or dowel rods and let each child hang his or her own picture. Mobiles are versatile and children can make their own. Pictures cut from magazines symbolizing children's feelings, interests, and so forth can also be hung from a smaller base, such as a pencil or single branch.

"Me" Prints   T P K

Children can use their fingers, hands, or feet to leave marks which represent who they are. Fingers can be pressed on water-soluble ink pads and printed onto paper. Hands and/or feet can be painted and printed onto paper. The shapes suggest possible designs and children may want to combine and customize their body prints.

Holiday Art   P K S

Before Thanksgiving, use group time to engage children in a discussion of things they are thankful for and ways to give thanks. Lay out a long piece of butcher or mural paper. Provide markers and crayons and let children represent the people, events, and things in their lives for which they give thanks. In the spring, around Easter time, make a collage using eggshells. Make hard-boiled eggs for snack and save the shells to make a collage. Place large shell pieces in bag and carefully crush. Provide colored construction paper and encourage children to glue pieces into a design. Dying or decorating eggs prior to eating them is another option.

Holiday Sentiments P K S

Art, child-directed and initiated, is the perfect gift for a child to give. It may be nonverbal, but it conveys personal meaning and love. After studying any of the major holidays, children can be encouraged to plan and implement an artistic representation of the joy, hope, love, and fellowship associated with that particular holiday. A simple but personalized greeting card or collage may result (see Figure 13–7).

ART AND THE EXPRESSIVE ARTS

Art is merely one mode of creative expression. Music and movement are two other expressive arts that are vital to early childhood. Both art and movement involve nonverbal expression. What children represent in art can also be represented through movement. Liz is fascinated with unicorns. She attempted to make one out of clay. Its long horn was prominent. During a "Guess what I am" movement session, she pretended to be a unicorn, moving on all fours while indicating something sticking out of her forehead. Just as music can foster artistic expression through a certain mood, tone, tempo, or beat, it can also trigger spontaneous movement.

Some activities that incorporate art with the other expressive arts follow.

Musical Painting T P K

Encourage children to hand paint or color to different types of music. These might include slower classical, pop show tunes, and rock music. Discuss how paint strokes, movement, and design are related to the tempo of the music.

Costumes and Props K S

Children can design, paint, or color masks, costumes, scenery, and props related to a play or movement activity. For example, children can design paper-plate masks for the different characters in "The Gingerbread Boy." A mural can be decorated and used as scenery.

Musical Instruments P K

Children can make and play their own homemade musical instruments. There are many possibilities. We will focus on making a guitar. Children will need their own shoe box which can be deco-

FIGURE 13–7 Children can make their own unique holiday greeting cards.

rated with paint, crayons, markers, and stickers. The teacher needs to cut a large oval hole in the lid. Cover box and tape the edges of the lid to the box. Wrap four strong rubber bands around the box lengthwise. Children can strum their guitars.

Streamers   P K

Children can make their own streamers to accompany their creative movement and dance activities. Provide small paper plates which the children can decorate. Assist them in attaching lengths of crepe paper. These can be stapled on or threaded through punched holes and knotted. Turn on the music and watch children run outdoors or move creatively indoors while holding their streamers. Variations for streamer holders include wooden paint-mixing sticks and cardboard tubes from toilet paper or paper towels.

THREE-DIMENSIONAL ART

Assemblage refers to a three-dimensional collage in which children creatively assemble an array of objects. *Construction* and *sculpture* are similar terms referring to three-dimensional art that may or may not resemble anything. Technically, children can also sculpt with clay; this was discussed in Chapter 12. Our present discussion of sculpture will address forms other than clay. Even young children are aware that objects are composed of parts and pieces. A table needs a top supported by legs. People have a trunk that supports their head and rests on limbs. Cars have a body supported by a frame on wheels. "How can I make my own three-dimensional model of the things that are important to me?" asks the young sculptor.

Fixatives and Fasteners

Most three-dimensional creations will require some sort of fixative or fastener. Some common types include:

brads
clothespins—pinch-type
glue sticks
metal fasteners
paper clips
paper fasteners
pipe cleaners
rubber bands
stapler—small, but not miniature, and staples
string
tape—cellophane, masking, and colored
twist ties
white glue
wire
yarn

Here are some three-dimensional art activities recommended for young children.

Container Creations   K S

The shapes of containers suggest the shapes of people, animals, vehicles, buildings, machines, and objects. Children enjoy using tape, glue, and staples to hold together an array of boxes, bottles, and cartons. Encourage children to think of something—an animal, a vehicle, or an object—that the containers suggest. For example, square boxes stacked together might suggest a robot. A row or strip of egg cups from an egg carton might suggest a caterpillar, snake, or train. A plastic milk container might suggest a head if yarn is added for hair. Look for boxes, bottles, and cartons that have an unusual shape. As always, container creations need not resemble anything at all. Some recommended containers include

- oatmeal boxes
- salt boxes
- small gift boxes
- cereal boxes
- pill bottles
- milk cartons, cardboard and plastic
- coffee tins
- detergent bottles
- toilet tissue rolls and cardboard tubes
- egg cartons
- film containers
- food containers

- berry baskets
- cigar boxes
- round pizza plates
- deli containers

Containers can be glued or taped together. Decorate them with bottle caps, lids, ribbon, paper cups, paper scraps, straws, and other small pieces. Creations can be painted, with detergent added to paint to help it adhere. (See Figure 13–8.)

Egg Carton Art

Individual egg cups from egg cartons or groups of cups can be creatively combined on a piece of cardboard. Children will enjoy varying the color,

placement, shapes, and sizes. The raised, patterned three-dimensional effect is visually pleasing.

Wooden Wonders

Children can use liquid white glue to affix small wooden scraps together. A hammer and nails can also be used. The resulting construction may represent something or merely be an assemblage of wood pieces. Check with local lumberyards, carpenters, or high school shop teachers for small wood scraps. Request wood scraps with interesting shapes and angles. Creations can also be decorated with trim or nature specimens and painted if the child decides it is necessary. One teacher suggested

A

B

FIGURE 13–8   (A) Processing with containers results in (B) a creative construction.

that children think up their very own machines and then try to make it out of wood scraps. Some children decided to make candy, toy, and fun machines. Pieces of string (for fan belts), wire, nuts and bolts, and small machinery parts were added for decoration. Others decided to merely glue together their wooden scraps. All products were accepted and valued.

Tinfoil Treasures

Children can glue an array of small objects onto a piece of sturdy cardboard. Recommended three-dimensional items include

- golf tees
- rubber bands
- paper clips
- buttons
- nuts, bolts, washers, and screws
- small nature specimens
- beads
- cotton swabs
- pieces of yarn, string, or cord

Use an old brush to paint white liquid glue over the entire surface. Arrange the items on the gluey cardboard. Carefully place a larger sheet of tinfoil over the raised surface. Very carefully, press, wrinkle, and mold the tinfoil around the raised objects to reveal their characteristic shape. Be careful that the embedded objects do not tear through the tinfoil. Fold the excess tinfoil under the cardboard and secure it with tape or glue. The result will be an interesting raised effect or relief, done in silver. Thoroughly wash the glue out of the paintbrush before it gets a chance to harden.

Tinfoil Sculpture

Children will enjoy working with tinfoil as the medium for sculpture. For example, tinfoil can be rolled to form an elephant's trunk and wadded to form its head. Individual parts can be taped together or stuck together with straight pins. Or children can form their sculpture out of one piece of tinfoil. For example, the elephant's legs can be carefully pulled, pinched, molded, and rolled out from the body. Re-

member to start with a fairly large piece of tinfoil—about 12 inches × 16 inches. Remind children that since they are starting with a large, flat sheet, they can expect their finished three-dimensional product to be much smaller.

Plastic Foam and Toothpick Sculpture

Children enjoy sticking toothpicks into plastic foam. An upside-down foam tray or thicker solid piece can form the base. Smaller pieces of plastic foam—chips, squiggles, or egg carton sections—can be stuck on toothpicks and inserted into the base. Individual plastic foam pieces can also be connected with toothpicks to add height and a three-dimensional effect. The sculpture can also be decorated with paper, ribbon, lace, and other scraps. These sculptures will be very fragile and may not make it home intact. They can be proudly displayed in the classroom art gallery.

Hanger Head

You will need old stockings or pantyhose and coat hangers for this activity. Stretch the hanger out into a fairly round face shape. Cover it with pantyhose or a stocking and tie to secure. This will form the head. Encourage children to complete the face by adding yarn, felt, fabric scraps, or paper. Leaving the hook on top will allow it to hang. Keeping the hook on the bottom allows it to be held and used as a mask.

Spool Sculpture

Wooden spools are getting harder to find. Children love to stack them and glue them together. Spools can be added to a basic wood construction. Spool shapes may suggest people, animals, or vehicle forms.

Paper Sculpture

As discussed in Chapter 11, paper can be rolled, folded, coiled, and made into three-dimensional cones, cubes, and tubes. These might suggest legs or body forms and the base for further paper sculpting.

Paper Strip Sculpture K S

Strips of construction paper are ideal for making sculpture. Start with a plastic foam tray for a base. Children can secure one end of a paper strip to the base. The balance of the strip can be pleated, folded, or connected to other strips. Continue processing with paper in sculpting a three-dimensional form. Remind children that the result can be an interesting intersection of paper strips and need not look like anything.

Stuffed Newspaper Sculpture K S

This activity is similar to "My 3-D Twin," presented earlier in this chapter. The present activity extends beyond a self-portrait. Each child will need four large sheets of newspaper. Older children may want to draw their outlines first and then cut them out. For example, a large dinosaur can be sketched. Avoid adding fine details and small parts. Carefully cut out the outline through all four layers of newspaper. Two layers will form the front and two the back. Slowly, stuff with small wads of crumpled newspaper while stapling shut. Use paint, crayons, or markers to decorate.

Totem Pole Sculpture K S

Ice cream parlors might save round gallon-size ice-cream cartons for you. The shape and size are ideal for making masks. Individual cartons can be decorated and stacked on top of each other like a totem pole. Secure with tape between cartons.

Soap Sculpture S

Older children who know use a knife properly can be trusted to do this activity with supervision. They will need their own bar of soap and a small but fairly sharp knife for carving. Encourage them to draw the outline of an object on their bar of soap and to use their knife to sculpt. Advise them to select a fairly simple shape, without intricate parts or details. Rough edges or cut sides can be smoothed by rubbing with a wet finger.

Soap Suds Sculpture P K S

Children enjoy sculpting and molding this white clay substance. To make, pour ¾ cup of soap powder and 1 tablespoon of warm water into a mixing bowl. Beat with electric beater to clay-like consistency. This will make about 1 cup. Have children sculpt and mold as they would clay or play dough. Items can be decorated with trims. Allow to harden. The clay dries with a permanently hard finish.

Ice Sculpture P K

Making an ice sculpture is a good outdoor activity on a hot day. Freeze water in a large container, such as a plastic mixing bowl, the day before. Place the ice chunk in a dish tub or large baking pan. Provide plastic spray bottles. Fill some with clear water and others with water to which you have added liquid watercolor. Provide colors that mix and complement rather than turn muddy when mixed. Also provide shakers of salt and glitter. Set the bottles for "stream," not "spray." Encourage children to "mist" the ice with water and observe. What happens when salt is sprinkled on the ice? Shaved ice and ice cubes can also be added and compared. Do some melt faster than others? You can also provide eyedroppers or plastic meat basters, along with containers of warm water. Does water temperature make a difference in the time it takes for the ice to melt?

Wire Wonders S

Use a fairly sturdy but flexible grade of wire for sculpting. Thin copper, florist's, aluminum, baling, insulated telephone (in a rainbow of colors), or No. 19 stovepipe wire are recommended. Children will enjoy twisting and turning the wire into unusual shapes. They may also try to represent something. The wire sculpture can be glued or nailed to a small piece of wood for a sturdy, supportive base.

Scene in a Box S

Children will need their own shoe box for this activity, which is also called a diorama. This activity takes much time, planning, and patience in positioning smaller items and is recommended for older children. The shoe box becomes the overall three-dimensional frame or stage. Children can choose a theme—for example, family or a favorite story. The inside of the box can be decorated like one's house, with family members added. Remember, the internal space is deep, allowing for three-dimensional placement. Objects can be placed in several rows to suggest depth. Items such as fish could be suspended from the inside top with string for an underwater scene. One young girl did just that, basing her Scene in a Box on the book *Swimmy* by Leo Lionni. (See Appendix E for a list of art-related books.)

Salt Sculpture

Children will need their own clear glass bottles or jars with lids. You will need several different colors of salt. Salt can be colored by rubbing it with colored chalk. Place one color in each section of a muffin tin or in a paper cup. Gently pour one color into the bottle or jar. Use a small spoon or paper cup, or let it slide in from the fold of a creased paper. Make the layer any height. Add a second color by carefully directing the flow and position as you pour. There is no need to shake or tip the bottle or jar. Each layer will form its own uneven shape. Use a pencil to carefully poke along the sides and through layers for an interesting effect. Add different-colored layers until the jar is full. Let it sit overnight to settle. You may need to add an additional color the next day to get it completely full. Cover the jar tightly with the lid. This makes an excellent gift, especially if the children did most of the work by themselves. Very young children may need to use a fairly small container with a wide top.

Glue Overs

Each child will need a piece of plastic foam cut from a meat tray. Encourage them to use markers to make a picture or design. Use a wide variety of colors, and leave little empty space. Let dry. Use an old paintbrush to paint liquid white glue over the entire surface. Let dry thoroughly. This will produce a sealed, slick surface that enhances the colors underneath. These make attractive ornaments or items to hang from a mobile.

Papier-Mâché

Papier-mâché means "chewed paper" in French and refers to the process of building up layers of paper that has been torn, wadded, and molded (although not chewed) to make a three-dimensional form. The paper is dipped in an adhesive mixture. Newspaper that has been torn in strips and soaked overnight will be more pliable. Squeeze excess water. Some of the many ways to do papier-mâché that are appropriate for young children are described below.

Paper Strip Method   Strips of newspaper or paper towels, about ½ to 1 inch wide, are dipped in a mixture of white glue and water or other papier-mâché medium. (See recipe.) Strips cut from paper bags are also recommended because of their thickness and texture. Carefully squeeze out the excess liquid between your fingers. Layers that are too thick with glue or paste will mold when drying. Begin to form your object. The strips should be smooth and overlapping. The layers should go in different directions to provide strength. Remove wrinkles or bubbles by smoothing with the hand. Apply only two or three layers at a time. Let dry. Details can be added to transform the basic shape. Or add additional layers. For example, a wadded ball of newspaper can be added to the top of a jar or bottle to form a head. Secure with masking tape. Let dry thoroughly before adding additional layers. Add a final layer of paper towels to give a clean top surface for painting or final decorating. Set on wax paper to dry thoroughly before painting. An adult can seal tempera paint by spraying with a fixative or cheap hair spray. This activity should be conducted over a series of days. It may prove frustrating for the very young child who wants the project completed in one short session.

It is recommended that young children do their papier-mâché over some solid base or form such as a

- blown-up balloon: carefully cut finished product in half to get two bowls or two face masks.
- bottle or jar.

- gift box.
- tissue roll.
- container.
- crushed or rolled newspaper.
- plastic milk or detergent bottle.
- light bulb: to make a sound shaker or music maker similar to a maraca. When it is decorated and dry, gently hit it on the floor to break the inside bulb without damaging the exterior papier-mâché shell. Patch if necessary.

Papier-Mâché Paste (cooked)

3 cups water
1½ cups flour
oil of peppermint

Stir flour into cold water. Cook over low heat until mixture thickens and resembles creamy paste. Add more water if too thick. Cool. Add a few drops of peppermint oil. Use this paste to coat strips of paper.

Hanger Objects   K S

The Hanger Head activity can also be used with papier-mâché. Stretch a coat hanger into a desired shape or form. Add long strips of newspaper dipped in papier-mâché mixture to form a solid base. Decorate as a face or whatever the shape suggests. For a self-portrait, add yarn for hair and buttons for eyes.

Stuffed Bag   K S

A paper bag can be filled with wads of newspaper and shaped into a general form. This can be the base. Strips of newspaper dipped into a papier-mâché mixture can be wrapped around the base and used to form details, such as arms, legs, head, tail, and so forth.

Papier-Mâché Relief   S

The older child who is experienced in papier-mâché might like this variation. A piece of cardboard is needed for the base. A simple picture or design should be sketched in pencil. The picture or design will be continued in relief by building it up with strips or small pieces of paper that have been dipped in a papier-mâché mixture. The paper can be twisted, rolled, coiled, or formed into the needed shape. For example, a round, flat mass could be used for the sun, and thin, rolled paper snakes could be the rays. Keep building up additional layers to give the three-dimensional or relief effect.

Piñata   K S

A blown-up balloon can be used as the base for a Mexican piñata. Wrap papier-mâché over the balloon. Follow the directions for papier-mâché. Poke the balloon with a needle when you are finished. Cut open a small hole and fill the piñata with stickers, candy, tokens, or small treats. Cover the hole with additional strips of papier-mâché. Hang it overhead or from a tree limb outdoors. Blindfolded children will enjoy swinging a stick at the piñata. Breaking the piñata will result in a shower of goodies and shrieks of excitement.

Casting Capers   S

See the recipe for making plaster. You will also need some damp sand to form the mold for casting with plaster. Line a box, grocery bag, or old dishpan with a plastic trash bag or tinfoil and fill it with 4 inches of sand. Make an impression by carefully scooping out the sand. Wiggle your fingers for an interesting effect. Do not scoop down to the bottom of the container. Add nature specimens and small pieces of artistic junk. This will form the front of your cast sculpture and will become your mold. Remember, the casting will be the opposite of the impression you make. For example, holes dug into the sand will be cast as bumps protruding out of your sculpture.

Always add water to powder and mix plaster to a milkshake consistency. Keep stirring and work quickly. Carefully pour plaster into the mold. Add food coloring or tempera if coloring is desired. Gently shake or tap the container to help settle the mixture. Insert a hairpin, paper clip, or bent wire at the surface (which will really be the back side) if you want the sculpture to hang. Or simply insert both hands to cast a hand print. The top will now be your front side. Let the plaster set, and when it is thoroughly dry, gently brush away the sand. Casting is a time-consuming activity that only one child can do at a time, given this setup. It may be easier to do this outside in the sandbox, or ideally at the beach!

Plaster (for molds)

8 cups patch plaster
5 cups water

Mix thoroughly. Recipe will make enough for four molds. This recipe can be used in place of plaster of paris, which dries very fast. Patch plaster is inexpensive and takes at least 30 minutes to dry.

Squeeze a Sculpture

   For this activity, simply pour plaster into a small, sturdy, ziplock, plastic bag. Fill it 3 inches full, squeeze out excess air, and add nature specimens, artistic junk, or coloring. Seal bag securely. Wait several minutes for the plaster to thicken. Encourage children to squeeze and manipulate the filled bag into an interesting shape. Hold it in place for a few minutes until it feels warm and it begins to harden. Let the plaster dry overnight. Tear away the plastic bag and paint or decorate the sculpture with markers. The result will be a piece of sculpture with an interesting shape that would also make a good paperweight or gift for parents.

Balloon Creatures

Using an old bowl, adult stirs and mixes plaster of paris until creamy. Pour into an empty balloon using a funnel with a large opening. This takes teamwork involving at least two. Set plaster-filled balloon on table, gently molding until it starts to harden. This will take several minutes and may exceed the patience of the very young. Stop handling. Let go and allow to completely dry for at least 30 minutes. Gently tear off balloon. Decorate and paint if desired. Disposable kitchen gloves can also be used as the mold. Remember to work quickly, for once mixed the plaster begins to harden. Do not pour excess plaster down the drain for it may harden in the pipes, causing a plumbing problem.

SUMMARY

   Curriculum means different things to different people; it can mean the overall program or a particular subject area. In this second view, art is merely one curricular area. A discussion and suggested activities emphasized the relationship between art and math, science, communication/language arts or literacy, social studies, and the other expressive arts.

Suggested Activities

1. Interview two teachers regarding their views and definitions of curriculum. Do they agree or disagree? Do their views match those in the unit?

2. Devise an activity that integrates art with one or more of the early childhood curricular areas.

3. Implement one of the integrated art activities with an individual or small group.

4. Facilitate a three-dimensional art activity with children.

Review

A. Identify the two major ways of viewing the early childhood curriculum.
   1.
   2.

B. List the major early childhood curricular areas.
   1.
   2.
   3.
   4.
   5.

C. Match each art-related activity with a curricular area that it attempts to incorporate or integrate.

_____ 1. counting the number of children at the art center to see if there are too many

a. speaking

_____ 2. explaining to another child the steps involved in making a print of one's finger painting

b. writing

_____ 3. doing a Thanksgiving collage of people and things we are thankful for

c. science

_____ 4. Zak painting XZo across his picture for his name

d. social studies

_____ 5. Larry finding that quickly stirring water into powder tempera makes colorful bubbles

e. math

CHAPTER 14

The Art Center

Think of a young child faced with the opportunity to engage in art. There are many decisions to make. The child asks, "What should I make?" and "What should I use to make it?" What message does this art center convey to the child? Would you like to have this art center in your classroom? Why or why not?

The materials appear to be arranged, organized, and grouped together. For example, all the pipe cleaners go together in one tub. The tubs are constructed of clear plastic so that the contents are visible. Clear containers help not only in locating materials but also in cleanup. There are several, but not too many, choices. Materials are rotated weekly to sustain children's interest in returning to the art center.

OBJECTIVES

After studying this chapter, the student will be able to

- List and discuss the five criteria for setting up an early childhood art center
- Compare and contrast two- and three-dimensional art media
- Identify potential rules and limits for successfully operating an early childhood art center
- Evaluate the effectiveness of an art center/program
- Make puppets and masks

INTRODUCTION

Have you ever attended a buffet dinner? Salads were grouped together. Dishes, silverware, and napkins were arranged at the ends of the table. Desserts were clustered near the end of the table. Special arrangements were made for keeping certain dishes warm. This logic and organization can be applied to setting up an art center.

Examine the art center depicted in Figure 14–1. What do you see? What message does this art center convey? In this High/Scope classroom, similar materials are grouped together. Opaque containers are labeled with a piece of their contents glued to the outside. An outline and drawing of the contents of each container appear on a label adhered to the shelf on which the container rests. Art centers will vary depending on available space, resources, and individual teacher's style.

The pair of pictures (Figures 14–2 and 14–3) feature a self-standing art center photographed from two different positions. In this High/Scope Pre-K classroom, items are organized and labeled with a sketch and printed word.

The art center will take care of itself most of the time. Many children will be able to make choices, decisions, and see connections between media and materials. Others will process until they tire or until they create a product that pleases them. Some will have an idea of what they want to make beforehand. Rotating materials will keep the children returning.

FIGURE 14–2

FIGURE 14–3

FIGURE 14–1

Offering new activities will also extend the array of possibilities.

The rationale for setting up the art program around a center format is that this allows for discovery, choice, responsibility, and independent activity. The early childhood art center should be an artist's studio, conveniently located and easily accessible, well stocked, orderly and organized, with rules and limits. These criteria or guidelines will be explained in this chapter.

THE ART CENTER

The classroom art center is an area where children can go to do art. Most programs already have centers set up for manipulatives, table toys, blocks, books, and dramatic play. Others have centers for science, water play, and sand play. Although space is always at a premium, an early childhood art center is warranted. Just what is an art center, and how does one go about starting it and maintaining it? (See Figure 14–4.) The criteria for an art center would include the following. An art center is

1. an artist's studio
2. conveniently located and easily accessible
3. well stocked with developmentally appropriate materials
4. orderly and organized
5. a place with rules and limits

Each of these five points will be examined in detail.

1. An Artist's Studio

An artist's studio should be visually appealing and inviting. By its appearance it conveys a message that this is a place where creative art happens. Children need a well-thought-out space where they can explore, not just a table from which the teacher conducts adult-directed projects. An artist's studio is a place to make connections and choices from an array of materials conducive to making two- and

FIGURE 14–4   Art centers come in a variety of styles.

three-dimensional art. An artist's studio is an inviting spot that reflects creative clutter and often some noise rather than an emphasis on excessive quiet and neatness. It is a place to go and discover, process, experiment, and explore. The art center resembles a workshop where participants engage in maximum effort with some mess. Artists enjoy visual stimulation and like to see the work of artists depicted in posters, prints, or calendars, as well as their own work, displayed at their eye level. Reserve adjacent wall and counter space for displaying children's creations. Be sure to include books about art and artists, thereby connecting your art and literacy program.

The child should be exposed to a variety of stimulating activities and experiences with legitimate artistic media. These will complement, broaden, and balance self-directed free expression. They will

FIGURE 14–6   Mixed media—construction paper and coloring

FIGURE 14–5   *Children experiment and explore at the art center.*

depend, in part, upon the individual child's developmental level, coordination, ability, and interest level. A balance between process and product can be built into one's art center. The creative process of painting and exploring visual symbols is as important as the finished product, perhaps a painted picture. Pounding, rolling, pinching, and stretching clay are as important as the aesthetic quality of the finished clay piece. (See Figure 14–5.)

Art Activities As Suggestions, Not Prescriptions There is danger in merely listing or prescribing a set of art activities. These are included merely as suggestions or possibilities, not as a set of activities to fill the pages of one's lesson plans on a day-to-day basis. Teaching them directly as specific activities would negate everything we have discussed about art as a creative discovery process. Instead, encourage children to discover many of these extensions or possibilities on their own. The activities are based on a few media (see Figure 14–6).

(N)   *Mixing Media*   Mixing media results in the discovery of new artistic possibilities. For example, let us assume that children have worked with crayons at the table and paints at the easel. Ask children, "What would happen if we used them together? Can you paint over your coloring? Or can you use markers along with colored pencils? Have you ever tried to do a collage over your dried hand painting?" The possibilities for creative mixing are endless. One need not suggest specific combinations but merely reinforce experimenting with and joining different artistic media.

(N)   *Varying the Tool, Method, and Media*   Varying the tool will help children discover new artistic possibilities. For example, they have painted with an array of paintbrushes, flat and round. Ask them, "Can we paint with a toothbrush? Is there a brush in your house or garage that could be used for painting? Let's think of things other than brushes that we could use for painting."

Varying the method will also lead to new possibilities. Paint can be spread with a brush to make long, sweeping lines. There are also many other ways to apply paint. It can be dabbed, swirled, sprayed, dripped, and dribbled.

Varying the medium also increases the range of possibilities. Children can paint with water, colored water, transparent watercolors, thick opaque tempera, or tempera to which sand, salt, or sugar has been added.

Incorporate Both Two- and Three-Dimensional Art Media   Similarly, there should be a balance between two-dimensional and three-dimensional art media. Two-dimensional activities involve a relatively flat artistic surface with height and width portrayed. Three-dimensional art activities also portray depth. Some activities, including work with paper, allow for both two- and three-dimensional expression.

2. Conveniently Located and Easily Accessible

An art center should be conveniently located and easily accessible, not cramped into a crowded corner. It should be located near a sink and removed from the main stream of classroom traffic. The location of the sink and of neighboring centers will determine where the art area is placed. For example, an art center should not be placed in the middle of the room, where children will walk through it while visiting other centers. Since different activities or centers have their own noise levels, it would be wise to locate the art center near other noisy activities. For example, the art center could be located near the block area, since both centers encourage children to move, talk, socialize, and be active. It is not recommended that the art center be located adjacent to the book corner or quiet area. If your room does not have a sink, pails of water can be stored in the art area. Paper towels should also be provided.

An art center need not be restricted to the indoors (see Figure 14–7). Art can be offered as an activity during outdoor free play. An easel or art cart on wheels can be easily rolled in and out as needed. When identifying the best spot for your art center, try to select a spot that is easy to view and supervise, both up close and from a distance. The tabletops should be easy to clean. A plastic-laminated tabletop can be easily wiped clean with a damp sponge. Try to avoid placing the art center in a carpeted area. If necessary, cover the flooring under the easel and art table with newspaper or an old shower curtain. An old washable throw rug placed under the easel would be both practical and attractive. Ideally, children will clean up after themselves. Try to reserve adjacent wall space to display children's artwork. Samples of artists' work reflecting different artistic styles can also be displayed. Our intent is not to encourage children to copy but to expose and educate them to the different ways in which people have done and continue to do art. If space permits, art books, laminated prints, and art postcards can also be kept close, but at a sufficient distance from water, paint, and other media that

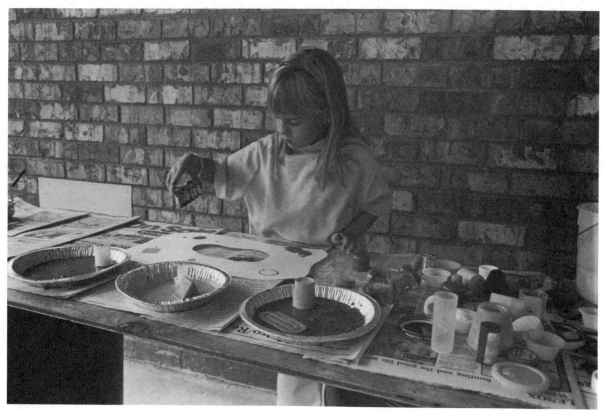

FIGURE 14–7   An outdoor art center

might soil them. Adjacent counter space can be reserved for displaying three-dimensional artwork, including clay, sculpture, construction, assemblage, and papier-mâché. Adjacent floor space can be reserved for drying paintings, or a commercial drying rack can be used.

3. Well Stocked With Developmentally Appropriate Materials

The art center should be well stocked with developmentally appropriate basic art media, tools, equipment, accessories, and artistic junk. An art center need not entail great expense and can operate on a modest budget if planning and economical purchasing are involved. Plan with other teachers to order in bulk.

Buy high-quality nonconsumable items like brushes, which will last. Much of your art budget

will go for purchasing consumable items such as paint and paper, which will be used up in time and will need to be reordered. Frills like glitter, fur, feathers, sequins, and wiggly eyes are not necessary. They are expensive and can be quickly used up. Supplement purchased items with things you can recycle. Thrift shops, garage or yard sales, and rummage sales are good sources of inexpensive items which can be recycled into art activities. Families are an excellent source of contributions. Send home a list that specifically lists what you need. Mom may be able to bring computer paper or outdated office forms from work. Grandma may respond to your request for buttons and fabric by donating the contents of her old sewing box. Donating benefits everyone. The family feels involved and your art center becomes well-stocked.

What should be on the shelves of your art center?

There are at least six basic categories of art materials, including:

- tools for mark making, e.g., crayons, pencils, markers, chalk
- papers in a variety of shapes, sizes, and textures (specific examples to follow)
- modeling and molding materials, e.g., clay and play dough, and tools.
- items for cutting, fastening, and attaching, e.g., scissors, glue, paste, tape, hole punches, staplers and staples, string, pipe cleaners
- items for painting and making prints, e.g., paint, brushes, and related tools
- collage items, e.g., nature specimens, fabric, old jewelry, wallpaper, yarn, gift wrap

Papers

The number of different types of paper that children can use in their artwork is practically infinite; for example, they can use

adding machine tape—for paper sculpture and paper chains

adhesive-backed—solicit scraps for paper art activities

blotter—for soaking up excess water with watercolors

boxes—for painting and marking on

brown wrapping paper—for murals, puppets, papier-mâché, paper sculpture, and paper art activities requiring sturdy paper

butcher paper—a long roll for making murals; good for finger painting

calendars

carbon paper—for transferring designs

cardboard—flat, corrugated, tubes for a variety of art activities

catalogues—for paper tearing, cutting, pasting, and collage

cellophane—for color paddles, collage, and paper art activities

colored plastic wrap

coffee filters—for use with mark making, melted crayons, or dip and dye with food coloring

computer paper scraps—use the clean side for paper art activities

construction paper—good for crayons, chalk, and paint but not watercolor; difficult to fold in different directions; will fade over time; buy large sheets in assorted colors and cut down

contact paper

crepe paper—optional; buy other basic art papers first

doilies—for collage and other paper activities

egg cartons—cardboard and plastic

envelopes—good for mark making and artistically addressing

fadeless art paper—easier to fold and cut than construction paper but more expensive; only one side is colored and will not fade

finger paint paper—glazed surface; buy the largest size!

gift wrap or wrapping paper—for collage and other paper activities

graph paper—large squares; you can easily make your own

greeting cards—recycled, for cutting, pasting, mobiles, and collage

grocery bags—all sizes and colors, heavy weight for painting and paper work activities

gummed stars, stickers, and labels—for licking and sticking on paper

kraft paper—3 feet wide to make murals, trace around children, and use for bulletin boards

magazines—for collage and montage

manila paper—a better grade than newsprint: rough surface, cream color, heavier weight; more expensive than newsprint but less expensive than white drawing paper. Manila paper is good for collage, gluing, coloring, painting, and pasting activities. Buy big and cut down.

manila file folders—old, used, sturdy

matboard—for making mats in picture frames; expensive

metallic paper—too expensive to put out on a daily basis

newspaper—for painting, stuffing, and cleanup

newsprint—least expensive paper for marking, scribbling, drawing, and coloring. Thick or heavy paint will bleed and soak through. Easy to fold, but tears with pressure. Comes in a variety of sizes. Buy big and cut down.

oak tag—comparable to manila paper in use and cost

oatmeal paper—textured paper for crayons, chalk, and prints

onionskin paper—nice texture for watercolor

origami paper—special paper for Japanese art form of paper folding

paper bags—in all sizes, for puppets, masks, and so forth

paper plates—plain white for masks and a round art surface

paper reinforcements—for stringing and making eyes, Os, and buttons

paper scrap saver—empty box or container

paper towels—for painting, dyeing, papier-mâché, and cleanup

picture story—to draw a picture and dictate a story

place mats—a good background for paper and other art activities

poster board—cheaper than matboard for making mats and frames

rice paper—fairly expensive; good surface for ink and watercolor

sandpaper—for resist, collage, and melted crayon wax

shelf paper—for making murals; good for hand painting if surface is glazed

shopping bags—cut open and lay flat for painting

tinfoil—for sculpture and special paper activities

tissue paper—comes in a variety of colors. Buy big and cut down.

tracing paper

typing paper—good for ink and watercolor

velour paper—nice velvety texture but expensive; use sparingly

wallpaper scraps, samples, and books—for matting, framing, collage. Also, most wallpaper will hold up to painting.

watercolor paper—expensive if bought by the sheet; also comes in tablet form

wax paper—for sealing paper shapes, resist activities

white drawing paper—a very good grade, heavy and fairly expensive. Good for all art projects, including painting. It looks clean and stands up to erasing. 60-pound weight is recommended. Buy big and cut down.

wrappers—from gum and candy, for pasting and collage

Hint The larger the paper, the more expensive it will be. Still, large sheets can be used sparingly in their entirety and creatively cut down into smaller sizes and shapes. This will avoid boredom and needless waste and will be more economical in the long run.

Hint Try butchers, carpet stores, print shops, and newspaper plants for newsprint, end rolls of paper, and brown wrap. These are good for making murals.

Hint Use different types of paper, and be sure to include newspaper, grocery bags, and cardboard. The want ads make a good backdrop for a painting or collage. The colored comics section makes a good background for linear designs in black. Different surfaces pose a new problem and challenge for the painter. A torn-paper collage would work on the colored advertisement section. Grocery bags are heavy and can stand up to the repeated strokes of heavy paint from the very young painter.

Hint Provide papers that pose a challenge. For example, cut papers into flag, diamond, rhombus, or amorphic shapes. Cut circles, squares, rectangles, and triangles from the inside of papers. This will force the artist to modify or adapt his or her processing to fit the paper. For example, one cannot merely sweep paint, crayons, or markers across a figure-eight-shaped paper. The curves will suggest a different swirling or circular type of arm movement and stroke.

Tools/Accessories/Miscellaneous

Accessories for children to use in their artwork are limited only by the imagination. Some items the author has used with success include:

brayer—for painting and making prints
cookie sheets—as an art surface
cutting board—acrylic, undecorated for monoprints and clay

eggbeater, rotary—for art recipes, water play

Formica—as an art surface

hangers—for making mobiles, weaving, puppets, and so forth

hot plate—for melting crayons

kitchen tools—for mixing ingredients, painting, and printing

linoleum—as an art surface

measuring cups and spoons—for recipes

mixing bowls—for mixing ingredients in recipes

paper punch—for mark making

pencil compass—for mark making

protractor—for mark making

rolling pin—for clay, painting, and printing

rubber stamps—for printing

ruler—for making marks with a pencil

screen—for spatter screen prints

spatula—for mixing paint and ingredients, work with clay, and printing

sponges—for painting and printing

spray bottle—for adding water to paint, as during hand painting and for wet watercolor

stamp pad—for printing

trays—for art surfaces

wax—for resist

wire—florist's, telephone, electronics—for construction, assemblage, weaving, sculpture, mobiles, and stabiles

Hint Formica and linoleum make good art surfaces for painting with brushes, hand painting, sculpting with clay, or monoprinting. They define the individual artist's space, are easy to obtain, and easy to clean. Old trays or cookie sheets are also recommended.

4. Orderly and Organized

The art center is orderly and organized to maximize efficiency. Although surplus junk may have creative potential, it remains useless junk unless it is somehow organized and attractively displayed. Children do not know where to begin with a box of fabric, ribbon, yarn, and gift wrap all thrown together. Too many items, fostering too many possibilities, overwhelm young children. Materials that are similar should be grouped together on low, open shelves.

Therefore, basic tools like crayons, markers, and pencils should be placed next to each other. A second shelf can hold an array of papers grouped by size and shape. Ideally, containers should be clear so the contents are clearly visible. If not, add labels. Use a glue gun to affix an actual sample of the contents to the front of the container. For example, glue a twig and pinecone to the front of the box housing nature items. You may also want to neatly print the words "nature items." Labeling surrounds children with functional print that enhances their emerging literacy. Some teachers prefer to stock their shelves with activities set up on individual trays. For example, the tray for doing watercolor holds all the equipment one needs, including watercolor set, brush, sponge, and water container. Teach children the find-use-return cycle. Every item has a special place where it can be found. Use it safely and remember to return it when finished. This teaches personal responsibility and frees the teacher from total responsibility for maintaining the art center.

Shelves that are well-stocked with materials, equipment, and supplies provide options from which to select. Start by putting out a limited number from which to choose. If you feel compelled to put out everything, children will feel obligated to use it all. Remember the three Rs: replenish, rotate, and renew. Some items like markers and crayons will stay out all the time. Other items like collage materials will be rotated over time. For example, replace the nature specimens with fabric scraps. Initially, take children on a walking tour of the art center explaining the items, what they are called, how they are used, and where to find and return them. Continue to add items and enrich your art center over time as children display their ability to handle additional options. New items should be introduced during group time. For example, when placing sponges or twigs at the easel say "Today I replaced the brushes at our two easels with twigs. Think of how you might use a twig to paint and see what happens."

Through this subtle structuring, regularity, and predictability, the ordered environment of the art center serves as a model for children, who are often confused by disorder in their life and surroundings. In the art center, everything has its rightful place,

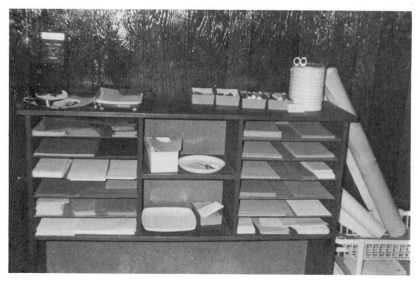

FIGURE 14–8   The art center should be orderly and organized.

and the child artists are responsible for daily maintenance and operation (see Figure 14–8).

Storage and Containers

art carryall—plastic divided carrier with handle. Good for storing art supplies. Available at discount stores in housewares. Recommended for artist at home.

art cart—a two- and three-tiered cart on wheels. Lets you take your art program around the room and outdoors.

baskets—for storing ribbons, lace, trims, crayons

beverage carriers—cardboard with individual compartments to hold jars of paint

bleach bottles—for holding water or paint

bookcase—with deep shelves for storage

boxes—to organize art supplies

bureau—old, for storing art supplies

cabinet—with doors removed and shelves for storage

cake pans

cardboard cartons

cigar boxes—for crayons, markers, lace, ribbon, and trims

classroom materials organizer—good for cubbies or for organizing different types of paper

coffee cans—with lids, to store clay

commercial ice-cream containers—fasten together and stack pyramid-style with open end visible; use for storage or art cubbies

corrugated cardboard cartons—sturdy, for storage

crates—stackable, for storage

cutlery tray—plastic, with compartments for organizing art supplies that go together, such as brushes

desk organizer—with compartments for small art supplies

dishpans—to hold papers, paste, glue, jars of paint, and brushes

easel and art storage—expensive but ideal! A large easel allows two painters at each side. Below are shelves for ample storage. Commercially available.

egg cartons—cardboard or plastic foam for storing small art supplies, such as buttons and beads

file cabinet—metal or cardboard; can hold art supplies. The problem is that the contents are not visible.

food keepers—see-through, good for storage

frozen dinner tray—with dividers, for holding small items

fruit basket—plastic, for holding ribbon, lace, spools, and so forth

hardware organizer—small plastic drawers for holding nails; good for organizing very small art items like buttons and jewelry pieces

ice-cream tubs—commercial, to hold paper and fabric scraps

juice cans—large, for storing paint, pencils, rulers, brushes, and other tall items

lazy Susan—good for organizing small items; rotate to bring close the items you need

loaf pans

margarine tubs—for storing paint, clay, and small art supplies

mini bins—stackable; good for storing art supplies

muffin tins—for melting crayons and sorting small art supplies like buttons and beads for collage

pie tins—to hold paint when making prints

pizza pans

plastic—pail, tubs, containers, squeeze bottles, pump sprayers, lidded food savers, cups, housewares

plastic foam—produce, meat, and fruit trays

shelving—sturdy, wood planks stacked on cinder blocks

shoe boxes—several the same size could be uniformly stacked and labeled with the word and picture of contents

shoe file—cardboard organizer with individual compartments, good for cubbies; available at discount stores

shoe organizers—with pockets to hang on wall; can hold rolled paper and other art supplies

storage bins—stackable in different sizes and colors

storage boxes—large plastic boxes with lids. Select clear so that you can see at a glance what is inside.

storage crates or cubes—plastic milk-type crates to stack; great for storing; found at discount stores; some can bolt together for stability

storage pails or buckets—with lid and handle; good for clay

storage unit—with shelves

sweater boxes—plastic with lids for storage

tin boxes—for holding crayons, chalk, and markers

trays—to define individual art space, hold paper, and so forth

utility cart—plastic pullout drawers in stand with wheels. Carts with solid frames are durable and stand up to constant pushing and pulling. Available in housewares at discount stores.

utility pans

Hint   Shelving can be made using sturdy lumber, thick and wide, stacked on cement blocks. Boards should be sanded free of splinters or covered with fabric or adhesive-backed paper. Position the blocks in a safe way so that young walkers will not bump into or trip over them.

Hint   A Peg-Board with hooks by the art center is very useful. Smocks can be hung up on hooks. A sign system to indicate the number of people allowed at the art center at any one time can be displayed—for example, four palettes, one per hook, in the top row. Some art accessories can be hung from the hooks. For example, clear plastic or vinyl bags containing ribbon, fabric, and trims can be hung.

Hint   Regardless of the storage facility, make sure all containers are clearly labeled in print as well as with a picture. For example, a cigar box filled with markers would have the word *markers* and a sketch or picture of markers on the side facing the room.

Hint   Display paper on flat shelves. Put paint and brushes on a plastic-lined shelf. This will stand up to water and drops of wet paint.

5. A Place with Rules and Limits

An art center provides the child with unlimited opportunities for attaining self-responsibility. Children abide by reasonable rules and limits. These rules and limits should be verbally discussed in advance, with the reasons for each rule clearly explained. Children need to know both the rules and the reasons behind them. For example, children discuss the proper use of materials. Paintbrushes are for painting. Waving paintbrushes in the air could either splash paint or hurt someone. Rules can also be posted in writing and pictures near the art center for easy reference. Rules and limits need to be discussed, posted, and enforced. Children who break a rule can be removed from the art center. When they have had time to reflect and believe that they are ready to abide by the rule, they can return.

Rules and limits will vary from teacher to teacher, center to center, classroom to classroom, program to program, and age group to age group. The following is a comprehensive list of guidelines from which you can select those that work best for you and your group.

Limit on the Number of Children at the Center at Any One Time   This number will depend on the number and size of tables, floor space, and easels. For example, Mrs. Tull displays four Art signs on clothespins at her art center. When all have been removed, children know the art center is full. Ms. Valdez allows eight children in her larger art center. Four children can work at the tables, two at the easel, and two on the floor. When children ask if they can do art, she asks them to count the number of children or see if there is an open or vacant spot for them.

Use a Smock During Art Activities   Children whose parents warn them about staying clean and avoiding messy activities may be apprehensive about doing art. Teachers can strongly recommend that parents provide "work" or "play" clothes rather than party attire. Young children need to dress appropriately for an active day at school, and art activities will involve getting dirty. Adding liquid detergent to paint will also make the paint easier to wash out when doing the laundry. Children should be reminded to let their paintings dry thoroughly before moving them or attempting to take them home. This will minimize smudging and smearing of paint onto clothing.

Slightly oversized children's shirts make good smocks. Cut off the sleeves, put them on backwards, and have someone button up the back. Daddy's old shirts are often too long, bulky, and

FIGURE 14–9   A smock

awkward. The sleeves constantly need to be rolled up and often dangle in the paint. Smocks are vital during painting. They also protect clothing when children are using glue, paste, and markers. It is a good idea to wear a smock for any and all art activities. Shirt sleeves should be rolled or pushed up above the elbows. Removing sweaters is a good idea, since this will allow greater freedom of movement and eliminates the possibility of their getting stained with paint. Attractive smocks can also be made from oilcloth or vinyl cut into a large square with a head opening and worn as a poncho. Velcro or elastic can hold the sides. See Figure 14–9. Or, a child-sized apron can be made, with elastic at the waist and neck. Allow about 18 inches for the neck and about 20 inches for the waist. Adjust according to specific needs and sizes within your group (see Figure 14–10).

A painting smock could be made out of an old large bath towel. Fold it in half and cut a large opening for the head. Sew up the sides, leaving ample room for the arms. Young children do not like clothing that fits snugly over their heads, so make sure

FIGURE 14–10   An apron

FIGURE 14–11   Art sleeves

you use a large towel and leave plenty of extra room for it to slide on easily.

Some companies make special art sleeves that give good protection for the arms, although not the chest. Basically, they consist of elastic sewn to both the cuff and upper arm of a shirt sleeve. Make them out of durable material that will hold up to repeated washing (see Figure 14–11).

The author saw one teacher effectively use a plastic trash bag as a makeshift smock. Holes for the head and arms were quickly cut at the closed end. The children enjoyed wearing their artist's costume.

Use Art Tools Properly   This is not to suggest that there is only one way to paint or draw. It does mean that brushes are for painting and scissors are for cutting paper. Teachers should discuss and model the proper care and use of all art media in advance.

Use Only What You Need   Discuss the economical use of paper, glue, paste, and so forth, and the avoidance of needless waste. Have a variety of paper sizes available. Not all children need or want to work on a large sheet of paper. Some children have a small idea that fits nicely onto a smaller paper square. Avoid putting too much paper out at any one time. Children may feel obligated to deplete the pile or believe that there is an endless supply.

Complete Your Art Activity   The writer has seen children go through a pile of papers by making a series of aimless, quick marks. Quality rather than sheer quantity should be the goal. Teachers can encourage children to take their time and finish each picture. "Jill, you have started a picture that has a lot of action and movement. But there is so much more room on your paper. Maybe you would like to keep working on it." Jill is free to accept or reject her teacher's suggestion.

Share Supplies   Items at the art center need to be shared. There may not be enough glue or staplers to go around. Children learn that the items belong to the school or center and are available for all children to use. Some children will have difficulty following this rule. They may become possessive and clutch the sharpest pair of scissors or the prettiest roll of ribbon.

Respect Others   Children learn to respect and value the ideas, styles, and work of others, just as they have come to value their own. Children cannot ridicule or criticize the ideas and work of others: "That's a dumb picture," or "That's no good; it don't look like no train!" Children's statements may be well intended, but the message hurts. It also hampers creative expression. Teachers can discuss how children can draw, color, or paint anything in any way they want. It is their decision and their rendering, not someone else's, that matters. "I'm sure James knows the sun is yellow, but he chose to paint it purple. It's his picture, and he can paint it any way he wants." Perhaps children who receive criticism or correction for their own artwork also become overly critical of others.

Children may also get possessive of available space. They may try to occupy the majority of the table. Young children who are used to having their own way and having one of everything at home will need guidance. Young children who have little space and no toys may also squander and require intervention. "The art center is for everyone, but only four at a time. This means we each have this much space [marking off with fingers] and we must share our things. Anyone who cannot share will have to leave the art center."

Return Everything to Its Place When Finished   Small paper scraps are thrown in the wastebasket. Larger scraps of construction paper can be saved in a scrap paper box for collage. Smocks are hung up on a hook.

Clean Up When Done   Brushes need to be washed. Spilled glue needs to be wiped up with a wet sponge. Remind children to leave their space clean for the next artist to use. Children know that they need to wash their hands and clean up the space they occupied. They should also check the floor before they leave. In short, children learn that the art center is primarily their responsibility, with the teacher playing only a minor role in its subtle guidance, maintenance, and supervision. See Figure 14–12.

Some important cleanup supplies include

bar soap
brooms—child-sized and whisk
dustpan with rubber edge and small broom
liquid dishwashing soap
mop
paper towels

plastic pail, bucket, dishpan; utility organizer with
    compartments and handle for cleanup supplies
rags
scrub brush
shower curtain—to protect floor or carpeting
smocks
sponges
table covering, e.g., newspaper, oilcloth, vinyl, plastic
throw rug—old, washable, to put under easel
wastebasket

EVALUATING AN ART CENTER/PROGRAM

You can evaluate the effectiveness of your art center/program by asking yourself the following questions:

FIGURE 14–12   Activities are labeled at this art center.

1. Is your art program comprehensive? Does it include provisions for sensory experiences; time, space and materials for making art; aesthetics; and introducing children to the world of art, artists, and a variety of art forms and styles?
2. When providing art experiences is your approach more child-centered than teacher-directed? Do you let children discover, invent, and process with the media as opposed to "teaching" art?
3. Do you engage children in creative experiences that extend beyond art? Do children's thinking, language, music, movement, and play activities reflect creativity?
4. Do you integrate art across your curriculum?
5. Do you capitalize on the language/literacy potential in art by providing labeled supplies, taking dictation, and viewing scribbling and mark making as beginning attempts at writing?
6. Do children have ample time and equal access to an art center on a daily basis?
7. Do you follow the three Rs—replenishing, rotating, and renewing the items in your art center?
8. Do you provide art experiences outdoors on a regular basis?
9. Do you include multicultural arts as a way to help children learn about their similarities to other cultures?
10. Do you encourage children by commenting on the artistic elements found in their art as opposed to simply praising them?
11. Do you facilitate children's artistic development by supervising and offering yourself as a resource? Are you careful not to impose your suggestions and solutions?
12. Do you value developmental appropriateness in art and thereby provide multisensory, messy activities which involve more processing than the making of a predetermined product? Do you supplement by occasionally teaching children a new art technique.

The ideal would be to answer affirmatively to all of the above. This may not always be possible or practical, given individual situations and constraints. The purpose of answering the questions is to assess where you stand in terms of your art program and to suggest some next steps to take to make your program comprehensive, developmentally appropriate, integrated, and child-centered. It is a process that takes time, commitment, and faith in children's innate capacity to be creative and make art.

PUPPETS AND MASKS

Puppets and masks serve many developmental ends. They are psychological props. They give young children something to hold and hide behind when speaking. After all, if a child makes a mistake or speaks incorrectly, it is the puppet or mask rather than the child who is to blame. Puppets and masks allow children to hide their identity and become someone or something else for a period of time. Children also have a way of telling us emotionally important events through their play with puppets and masks, often things they would never say or do without the props.

Young children enjoy making puppets and masks as much as they enjoy dramatizing and verbalizing with them. They also provide the opportunity for problem solving. Puppets can help children decide how disagreements can be resolved. A teacher can use a puppet to play the part of an imaginary young child who refuses to share. Children can use other puppets to discuss and act out this scenario and possible solutions.

There is an infinite number of ways to make puppets and masks. Here are some that are recommended for use with young children.

Puppets from Paper

Papier-Mâché Puppet

A puppet head can be slowly built up by draping gluey paper over a crushed ball of newspaper and a tissue paper roll. Refer to the section on papier-mâché in Chapter 13. Begin winding paper around the roll to form a neck and continue to build up a head over the crushed newspaper ball. Paint with tempera when thoroughly dry. Attach a piece of fabric for a body.

Or the papier-mâché can be made over a clay base. Children can use clay to make their puppet head. Next, wind strips of papier-mâché over the form. Make the layers go in different directions for strength. Let dry thoroughly. Carefully cut the head in half with a sharp knife and remove the clay. Use additional papier-mâché to seal the two halves together. Reinforce the neck with additional strips. Carefully smooth rough spots with sandpaper. Paint or decorate with trims. Seal with cheap hair spray if it is painted with tempera. Add a puppet body following the directions given here.

Puppet Body A very simple puppet body or clothing can be made from a 12-inch-square piece of scrap fabric. Fold it in half and cut three small openings along the center fold. The middle opening will be for the index finger, which also supports the puppet head. The two side openings are for the thumb and middle fingers, which serve as hands. Measure the children's hand span before cutting to ensure that the openings are neither too close nor too far apart.

Paper Bag Puppet **P K**

Provide each child with a lunch-size paper bag, neither too big nor too small for their hand to fit in and grasp. Paper bags are recommended because their construction provides a built-in movable mouth. Children will enjoy using paint, crayons, markers, and trims to decorate their puppet. Clear, undecorated sandwich bags provide a small, snug-fitting, see-through puppet that can be used as a last resort.

Stuffed Paper Bag Puppet **K**

Stuff a large paper bag with crumpled newspaper. Insert a stick, ruler, or dowel. Make sure the end of the handle is sticking out for a handle. Continue stuffing. Gather the bag and tie it securely at the handle with string to form a neck. Decorate the stuffed paper bag head with paint, crayons, or markers. Add paper scraps, yarn, and trims.

Paper Plate Puppet **P K**

An easy puppet can be made by decorating a paper plate and attaching it to a handle, such as a stick or ruler. Or, paper plates can be folded to make a talking puppet. Each child will need two paper plates. Fold one in half. Cut the other in half. Staple one half to the top and the other half to the under side of the folded paper plate. This will allow four fingers to be inserted into the top jaw and the thumb in the lower jaw. This will help the child move his or her fingers and get the puppet to talk. Although a frog readily comes to mind, a folded paper plate puppet can be used to make a variety of animals, people, and objects. Decorate with crayons, markers, paper scraps, and trims. A cloth sleeve can be placed on the child's arm for an added effect. For example, one child wore a sleeve made out of green printed fabric, which worked well with his dragon puppet made from a paper plate.

Cardboard Tissue Tube Puppet **P K**

Children will enjoy using paint, crayons, or markers to decorate their cylindrical puppet. A roll or tube is an ideal size for small hands. Nothing else is needed. A smaller section can also be used as the head with a puppet body made from fabric. Place the puppet's cloth body over the fingers and insert the puppet head over the index and middle fingers.

Puppets from Wood

Wooden Stick Puppet **P K**

Tongue depressors and Popsicle sticks can be used and decorated as the puppet itself. They can also be used as the base or handle to which a paper plate, magazine picture, cardboard, poster board, or other type of puppet is attached. Dowel rods or straws can also be used as handles for puppets.

Wooden Block Puppet **P K**

A small rectangular piece of scrap wood that can be held in a young child's hand can be fashioned into a puppet. Features can be added with paints, crayons, markers, small wood scraps, or trims. Make sure the edges are sanded smooth and free of splinters.

Wooden Spoon Puppet **P K**

An old, large wooden cooking spoon can be turned into a puppet. Decorate with fine markers. A piece of scrap material can be tied at the neck of the spoon to add the element of clothing and conceal the stick handle. Add yarn for hair. Children can hold onto the stick handle while working their puppets.

Puppets from Fabric

Sock Puppet

Find an old sock. Cut a slit across the toe, halfway to the heel, for the puppet's mouth. Cut a piece of felt or material to fit inside the mouth. Fold it in half, position it in place, and sew it on. See Figure 14–13. Four fingers will fit into the upper jaw. Glue a piece of cardboard under the lower jaw. This will help the thumb. Add trims: buttons and beads for eyes, yarn for hair, and so forth.

Glove Puppet

Old garden, work, utility, driving, dress, or plastic gloves can be made into puppets. Encourage the child to put on the glove and think of decorative possibilities. Small trims—buttons, yarn, and so forth—can be sewn or glued on. Or single fingers can be cut off to make one puppet, which will nicely fit on one or two child-sized fingers.

Puppets from Containers

Plastic Foam Cup Puppet

Cut one hole into a plastic foam cup. Encourage the child to put one finger through. Does it remind you of anything? It could be an elephant with the finger for a trunk. Or could it be a head, tail, leg, or tongue? Try cutting two holes at opposite sides. Encourage children to put one finger into each hole. What does it remind you of? Could these be arms or legs? Do

four holes allow fingers to represent arms and legs or wheels on a vehicle? Or the cup could be decorated with markers without cutting holes and snugly positioned on a toddler's clenched fist or raised fingers.

Tin Can Puppet

A juice can that is tall and slim can be transformed into a puppet. Discard any with rough or sharp inner rims and edges. Cans can be covered with paper and decorated. Add yarn, pipe cleaners, buttons, and other trims.

Container Puppet

Plastic and cardboard containers for holding milk, detergent, shampoo, toothpaste, or bleach have their own characteristic shapes and will suggest vehicle, person, or animal puppets to make. Skinny necks on containers make good handles to hold when using the puppet. Other containers come with built-in handles. Decorate the containers with paper and other trims.

Box Puppet

Boxes with interesting shapes, including toothpaste and fast-food boxes, may suggest puppet possibilities. Decorate them with paper and other trims. Add dishwashing detergent to tempera paint to make it stick if the surface is slick. A small milk carton is an ideal size for a fist puppet.

Coat Hanger Puppet

Bend a wire coat hanger into a geometric or abstract shape of a puppet. Keep the hook at the bottom for a handle. Place a nylon stocking or pantyhose over

FIGURE 14–13   Sock puppet

the coat hanger and fasten it with string or a rubber band. Decorate the puppet with fabric scraps, yarn, ribbon, trims, and paper.

Puppet Stage

There is no need to spend a lot of money on a commercially made puppet stage. Children will enjoy making, painting, and decorating their own. Find a very large appliance box, such as a refrigerator carton. Carefully remove the back side and cut a window opening in the front panel for the puppets. The opening or window should be placed such that when the children are sitting or kneeling behind the screen it is above their heads, but within arm's length. Children might enjoy a window in their puppet stage that opens and closes by folding the cardboard back. Curtains can also be hung. To provide a backdrop, hang scenery that the children create from a dowel rod, curtain rod, or broomstick. Make sure that the pole fits across the top. Make a small notch in each side panel of the carton in which the scenery hanger can securely rest. Allow ample room for the puppets to move about freely in front of the scenery. One foot from the front is recommended. The puppet stage can be painted and decorated as the children see fit. It should be a project inviting group participation and planning. The result may not be as pretty as a commercially available puppet stage, but the children will be proud of their accomplishment and will likely use it as a result.

Masks

Making masks is an ancient art form that is presently practiced in many cultures. Often, the masks also have utilitarian value in religious and cultural celebrations. Presently, masks are used in the celebration of Halloween. Many children are frightened by masks. Some will refuse to put something over their heads or against their faces. They may fear suffocation or loss of identity. Their wishes should be respected. Others enjoy losing their identity, at least for the time being, by putting on a mask and becoming someone or something else.

There are many different ways to make a mask. Basically, there are two ways to wear a mask: by putting it over the head or by attaching it to the face. Here are some examples that are appropriate for use with young children.

Over-the-Head Masks

Grocery Bag Mask **P K S**

Find a grocery bag that will easily slip over the child's head. Place it over the child's head and use pencil to indicate where the eyes should be placed. Take the bag off and cut out eye holes for the child. Cutting additional openings for the nose and mouth will help the child breathe better. Slit the four sides so that the bag easily slips over the child's shoulders and stays in place. Encourage the child to use paint, crayons, or markers as well as trims to decorate the mask.

Cardboard Box Mask **P K S**

Find a cardboard box that will fit easily over a child's head. Place it over the child's head and use pencil to indicate where the eyes should be placed. Take the box off and cut out eye holes for the child. Add openings for the nose and mouth if needed. Encourage the child to use paint, crayons, or markers as well as trims to decorate the mask.

Ice-Cream Carton Mask **P K S**

Ask ice cream parlors to save the drum-shaped commercial ice cream tubs for you. They are good for making a stacked totem pole as well as individual masks. Place the tub over the child's head and use pencil to indicate where the eyes should be placed. Take the carton off and cut out eye holes for the child. Encourage the child to use paint, crayons, or markers, as well as trims, to decorate the mask.

Face Masks

Paper Plate Mask **P K**

Hold a paper plate over the child's face and indicate where the eyes should be placed. Cut out eye holes for the child. Encourage the child to use paint,

FIGURE 14–14   *Paper plate mask*

crayons, or markers, as well as trims, to decorate the mask. When the mask is completed, attach a string to each side and tie in back. (See Figure 14–14.)

Pie Plate Mask   **P K**

Hold a pie plate over the child's face and indicate where the eyes should be placed. Cut out eye holes for the child. Make sure the cut metal leaves no sharp edges. The mask can be painted with paint to which dishwashing detergent has been added. Trims can also be glued on. When the mask is completed, attach a string to each side and tie in back. Children like the slick, shiny metal surface, which often suggests robots or superheroes.

SUMMARY

This unit focused on setting up an art program around a center format. By definition, an art center is an artist's studio, conveniently located and easily accessible, well stocked, orderly and organized, with rules and limits. It was recommended that the art center provide for an array of two- and three-dimensional art media and that children be encouraged to creatively mix media and invent their own activities.

Suggested Activities

1. Observe a successfully run art center. Note the teacher's role.

2. Use the criteria for an art center to informally evaluate an early childhood art center.

3. Set up an informal art center. Observe its operation for a period of several days. Play an indirect role as guide or facilitator. Document your findings in a journal or diary.

4. Evaluate an early childhood art center program. Make recommendations if necessary.

5. Facilitate a puppet- or mask-making activity with children.

Review

A. List the criteria or guidelines for an early childhood art center.
   1.
   2.
   3.
   4.
   5.

B. List major rules for successfully operating an early childhood art center.
   1.
   2.
   3.
   4.
   5.

C. List any five questions that address the effectiveness of an early childhood art center/program.
   1.
   2.
   3.
   4.
   5.

SECTION FIVE

Roles and Strategies

Planning is but one of the many things a teacher will do in providing art experiences. Chapter 15, Roles That Facilitate Children's Artistic Expression, views the role as a multifaceted one. This means not only that the job is important, but also that there are many tasks that need to be done. Examine the photograph of a teacher and her children at the long art table.

What do you see? The head teacher has planned a group construction activity. Materials are available, and the children are engaged in much creative processing. The teacher's job is far from over. She may need to model a way to keep the Styrofoam pieces from falling off. She may choose to participate in the activity and add her own creative contribution to the structure. In the photograph, she appears to be doing some observation and supervision. As a facilitator, she knows when to stand back and let children work things out and when to step in and offer support or assistance to a child in need.

Examine the photograph of the student intern reading a book about snails. The children have observed and carefully handled snails. The book provides background information. Her plan was to heighten an interest in snails and nature that would spill over into their art. Perhaps the children will draw or paint snails or make them out of play dough.

Chapter 16, Responding to Children's Art, focuses on how teachers respond, both verbally and nonverbally, to children's art.

The teacher took art dictation by carefully listening to what the child artist said and writing the words across the picture. The teacher can also use the artistic elements to comment on what is represented. She might say, "I see your people dressed in such bright colorful clothes. And that's an interesting cone shape to the right." And the child is free to reply, "No, that's a road."

Chapter 17, Strategies For Enhancing Children's Artistic Development, provides ideas for both sparking the production of art and ways to celebrate children's art.

How do you know how children are doing in art or if they're progressing? Chapter 18, Art Assessment, focuses on children's artistic development, stressing the importance of observation coupled with art samples as a way of gathering valuable developmental information. The Instrument for Artistic Evaluation, based on the whole child, attempts to informally evaluate children's artistic development.

CHAPTER 15

Roles That Facilitate Children's Artistic Expression

*T*his photograph, taken from a balcony overlooking a classroom for three-year-olds, depicts a head teacher and her student teacher at the art area during free-choice time. What do you see happening?

Adults need to set the stage for art. They set out the media and materials. This may be all the assistance some children need. Other children will need more. Some will request adult participation. "Teacher, do one with me." Some children will need to have directions or a technique modeled. "Here, watch how I dip the fork in paint and then move it on my paper." And still others want caring adults to remain close and talk with them as they engage in art activities. What might the teachers in this photograph be saying to the children?

OBJECTIVES

After studying this chapter, the student will be able to

- Use the continuum of approaches to identify three different ways to teach art
- Discuss the teacher's role as a facilitator, model, and participator in early childhood art
- Identify ways in which a teacher can be a creative individual and art specialist in the center or classroom
- Help school-age children make mobiles and stabiles

INTRODUCTION

There are many different ways to approach the teaching of art. This chapter will identify and critique teacher-directed, guided, and child-directed approaches. What is the teacher's role in children's art? Adults can stimulate children to make art by being a model and participant. Adults can model creativity in their daily lives and actively participate in art activities themselves. Although it is important to be an art specialist and to know about art, an adult does not need to be a talented artist to provide creative art experiences for children.

The different approaches to working with young children reside along a continuum. Teacher direction and child direction are two opposite points along the continuum. See Figure 15–1. Both points are valid at certain times for certain children and certain activities. The role of facilitator or guide is a compromise and midpoint position between these two opposite roles.

A facilitator or guide is readily available without directly monopolizing the activity, as is the case with direct instruction. A facilitator or guide is a keen observer who knows when to subtly step in, intervene, ask a question, or pose a problem. Children who need assistance know that their teacher is a resource person who is available to share facts, knowledge, skills, abilities, time, and attention.

APPROACHES TO TEACHING ART

The major approaches to teaching are also applicable to teaching art. The three approaches are:

- Teacher-directed
- Child-directed
- Teacher-guided

Some art projects are structured and teacher-directed. The teacher has an idea of what to make and how to go about it. Specific directions are given to ensure a recognizable product. Often, there is little input from the children. For example, a teacher distributes a piece of paper with an outline of a tree. The children are instructed to use a dark color, such as black or brown, to color in the trunk and green for the top. They also cut or tear small circles from red construction paper. These are pasted onto the green top. The completed apple trees look nearly identical. Generally, this approach is used when art is approached with the entire group or small groups of children. Most craft projects are teacher-directed, as seen in Figure 15–2, where two older girls are being taught how to use a silkscreen.

An opposite approach is to be unstructured and completely child-directed. A teacher may distribute, pieces of paper and encourage children to make whatever they want or encourage them to visit the easel or art center. In this approach, children have much input and choice. There is very little structure. For example, in Figure 15–3, the teacher has merely set the stage at the clay table in an inviting way. Some children do very well with this approach. They may have a bank of ideas to represent through art. They may also see endless artistic possibilities at the easel or art center. Many children, however, are uncomfortable with this approach. It may be too loosely structured. Some children quickly tire of

	X	
Teacher-directed	Guided	Child-directed
• direct instruction	• facilitation	• complete freedom
• teacher intervention		• nonintervention
• structured		• unstructured

FIGURE 15–1   Continuum of approaches

FIGURE 15–2   Let me show you how to use a silk screen.

FIGURE 15–3   Teacher has prepared the clay table.

inventing their own daily art program. They look to the teacher for some structure, guidance, or possibilities.

Teacher As Facilitator

A teacher-guided approach offers the best of the two former approaches: subtle structure with much child direction and input (see Figure 15–4). For example:

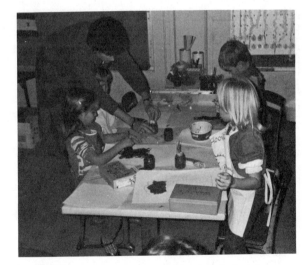

FIGURE 15–4   A facilitator or guide gives help when needed.

• A teacher supplies the theme.
  "Children, it's getting very close to summer. Today, we will make a picture that reminds us of this season." Although the theme is given, there is no specified product. Children are free to use paint, crayons, markers, or clay to make their own versions of what summer means to them.

• A teacher introduces new materials at the art center.
  "Today I put some spools and buttons near the easels and art table. I want you to look at them and think of how they might be used in art. Try out different ways of using them." Children are free to use them as brushes, make a stamped impression, or paste them to a collage, as long as the rules for the art center are upheld.

• A teacher extends or builds upon an existing activity or suggests a new technique.

Children's Drawing: Free Expression or Skill to Be Taught?

Controversy surrounds the issue of how children learn to draw. Can young children be taught to draw? Some people believe they can. A more important question is, Should they be?

Emberley (1991) views drawing as a skill that can be taught. His series of drawing books, developed for the K–3 population, consists of simple, step-by-step instructions using a collection of shapes to draw imaginary creatures, faces, and buildings. Brookes (1986), author of *Drawing with Children,* claims to be able to teach three-year-olds to go beyond stick figure drawing to make representational and realistic drawings. Her method is based on teaching five basic elements of shape: the dot, circle, straight line, curved line, and angle line. These five groups of form constitute basic visual building blocks that lie at the heart of all other shapes. She encourages children to notice these elements in everyday life and to use them to build their own artistic creations. Students begin by copying simple illustrations, moving on to more-complex pictures, and finally drawing from real life.

Johnson's (1990) *Teach Your Child to Draw* is aimed at parents. Her method features learning from what real artists have done. At the heart of each lesson are examples drawn from both old and new masters. Johnson believes that over time readers will begin to see their surroundings with an artist's eye and will be able to break down objects and scenery into the following components: line, pattern, texture, light and dark, shading, negative and positive shapes, proportion, point of view, movement, and distance.

These three authors advocate an approach that is teacher-directed, according to Figure 15–1. A set of artistic elements is at the heart of each of these approaches. The author believes that although artistic elements are the building blocks of art, there is no need to directly teach young children how to make them just to get them to draw realistically. The artistic elements can be used for analyzing art (Chapter 7) and in responding to children about what they have created (Chapter 16).

How do you feel about Emberley, Brookes, and Johnson's approaches to teaching young children to draw? Lowenfeld and Brittain (1987) and most early childhood educators, including the author, advocate an opposing position that views drawing as free expression. This child-directed position would lie at the opposite end of the continuum depicted in Figure 12–1. If children must be taught to draw something, they are not developmentally ready. Teaching them how to draw will not enhance their drawing ability. Teaching young children to draw emphasizes the product over the process.

Edwards' (1979) *Drawing on the Right Side of the Brain* assumes a middle position and compromise. Although she believes that older children need to be taught how to draw, she does not believe that they need a visual symbol system or group of shapes to help them to draw more effectively. She does not advocate that young children be taught to draw but instead believes that age ten is a good time to start. By age ten many preadolescents are frustrated with their own crude attempts and are motivated to learn how to draw realistically. Her visual exercises include copying upside-down pictures, drawing a common object such as a stuffed animal without taking one's eyes off it, and paying attention to empty or negative space. The author has noted the popularity of Edwards' methods in elementary and secondary art education programs. Her approach has also been successfully used with adults who claim they could never draw.

"I've noticed how much we enjoy easel painting with our long-handled brushes. I found these small tree branches outside and am leaving them at the easels. Let's see if we could use them to paint with." Or, "Let me show you another way of doing watercolor by first wetting your paper." Or, "I see how much you enjoy your paper-bag puppet. If you like, I could show you how to sew one out of cloth." Or, "Did you enjoy your paper weaving? Would you like to learn how to weave on a loom with yarn?"

- A teacher poses a problem.
  "Let's see how many different shapes we can cut out of paper for pasting." Or, "How could we use these empty boxes and ribbon?" Or, "What will happen if we try painting on newspaper or the colored pages in this magazine?"
- A teacher extends art into other curricular areas.
  "There seems to be a lot of excitement in your picture. Would you like to share it by telling me a story?" Or, "The dog you painted looks so happy, let's work together and write a poem about it." Or, "Perhaps you would like to plan a play for your ferocious dinosaur."

Different approaches may work for certain activities and certain children. Young children will not automatically discover how to use a watercolor set. They will need some direction and instruction in its use and care. They need not, however, be told what to make or what it should look like. For example, Emily is having difficulty deciding what to include in her summer picture. Her teacher senses her frustration and asks her to name things that remind her of summer. Emily answers, "Sun and swimming." Her teacher further structures the task by asking Emily to choose one. With the teacher's subtle guidance, Emily chooses the sun and now must decide if she should use paints, watercolor, crayons, markers, or clay to represent it.

Teacher As Model

Children learn in different ways. Some profit best by listening to a teacher. Others may learn by simply observing what a teacher does. For example, it would be more beneficial for a teacher to simply demonstrate how to sew or weave than to verbally tell children all the steps involved. Rather than telling children to "walk quietly," showing them how to walk quietly is more effective. In these cases, the teacher serves as a model or demonstrator. Simply modeling or demonstrating a new activity will draw a small group of curious observers who can be eased into participating. For example, a teacher who models different ways to work with clay and clay tools will soon find the clay table filled with willing sculptors (see Figure 15–4). One way of learning how to be a good teacher is to observe others modeling good teaching.

Teacher As Participator

Children enjoy playing, both by themselves and with other children. They also enjoy an adult's participation in their activities. There are times when a teacher would be most welcome as a participator or player in one of the centers.

Do art with children but be careful not to do art for them. Doing art for children sets them up for disappointment. Inevitably they will try to copy you and end up frustrated and discouraged. Announce that sometimes you don't like what you do on the first try and you simply try again. Share your frustration with trying to get it just the way you want when the paint runs and colors bleed in ways you don't like. Children will welcome your participation, especially if they appear stuck or frustrated. Work along with them but focus on just doing, rather than overwhelming them with your adult products. For example, the play dough table is one of the author's favorite spots. Sit with the children and observe what is or is not happening. If children appear "stuck," participate by modeling options. Say, "I think I'll try squeezing and flattening my play dough. Let's see what happens." Children may join in by squeezing and flattening their play dough which provides them with a new option and opens the door to discussion. Children may begin talking about their "pancake" shapes. They can also choose not to follow your suggestions.

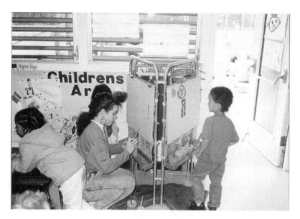

FIGURE 15–5   Enabling children to engage in art

In Figure 15–5, a parent engages in art alongside a child. At other times, children will not welcome a teacher's presence and may even ask him or her to leave. "No big people, just kids!" states a group of block builders. Their wishes should be respected. It is important that all children sometimes have a teacher's participation in their activity. The close contact is valuable, especially since the children are being met on their terms. This stands in opposition to a teacher-directed activity, where children are simply assimilated into the existing activity.

Although the author recommends taking on the role of participator, some may feel that it is intrusive and robs children of the opportunity to discover techniques on their own, for example, squeezing and flattening play dough. Where do you stand on the adult's role as participator in children's art activities?

Teacher As Creative Individual

A teacher must also be a creative, unique individual. Creative teachers encourage creativity in their children. They model creativity. "I don't have a paper cutter. What else can I use to make paper strips for our weaving?" "We don't have an easel to take outdoors. How else can we have art outside?" Children come to see that problem solving and cre-

ative solutions are necessary and vital parts of daily living.

The creative teacher develops

FROM	TO
1. viewing children in terms of groups on the basis of sex, age, or ability	1. viewing children as unique individuals
2. viewing highly creative children as a threat, nuisance, or menace	2. seeing creativity as an asset
3. stressing conformity in thinking and behavior	3. encouraging creative thinking and different ways to do things
4. looking for children to give the one right answer or best idea	4. considering many possible solutions and ideas
5. viewing self as uncreative	5. seeing how all people have the potential to be creative
6. a teacher-centered program	6. a child-centered program that values child input and decision making
7. a structured program, planned in detail	7. subtle planning that allows for diversion and sudden twists and turns
8. equating creativity with art, music, and movement	8. seeing creativity as a skill that cuts across the program
9. adding creative activities here and there	9. weaving creativity throughout the entire program
10. confining creativity to a certain day, time, or slot	10. including creativity throughout the entire day

Creativity is something we strive for. We may not be very creative during our internship, student teaching, or first year of actual teaching. We hope, however, to be successful and slowly move toward our lofty goal of becoming creative early childhood educators.

TEACHER AS ART SPECIALIST

It is also important for us to be art specialists. We need to know about art, artists, artistic elements, and developmentally appropriate art activities. Just as one need not be a hockey player to enjoy viewing a game or be a musician to appreciate a concert, one need not be a gifted or talented artist to provide art experiences for children. It is more important that teachers display artistic sensitivity, awareness, and discovery, than that they develop an endless list of art activities. Encouraging children to use all their senses, to experiment, to explore, and to represent what they know about the world does make one an art specialist.

MOBILES AND STABILES

Mobiles and stabiles are three-dimensional works of art consisting of separate parts joined together by thin connectors, usually wire or string.

Mobile

A mobile is a hanging sculpture that moves. Generally, it has pieces that are suspended and are free to move about (see Figure 15–6). Wind or movement will activate a mobile. Wind chimes and hanging infant toys suspended over the crib are good examples of mobiles. Mobiles contain at least one level from which items are suspended. A mobile can be suspended from a ceiling or doorway using string and a thumbtack. Advanced mobile makers are faced with the problem of balance when they work with more than one level. To start, one must find a sturdy overhead base from which the items will be suspended, using string, rope, yarn, thread, or fishing line. Some recommended supports from which heavy items can be suspended include

- driftwood
- dowel rod
- broom handle
- thick tree branch
- pencil
- stick
- yardstick
- coat hanger
- three coat hangers wired together at their hooks
- wood ruler

FIGURE 15–6   Mobile

Supports from which light objects can be suspended include

- straws
- tongue depressors
- ice-cream sticks

These smaller supports can be creatively combined with the items previously listed. Here are some mobile activities recommended for use with young children.

Group Nature Mobile

You will need a fairly sturdy tree branch. Look for one that has an interesting branched-out shape. This will provide a number of different levels from which items can be suspended. Rest or prop up the branch as it will later be hung, but closer to the children's level. They need to be able to reach the branches to attach nature items. Nature items can be collected on a nature walk or brought from home. Encourage children to look for nature specimens that have fallen to the ground. Not all items will be able to be tied or secured. Seashells, feathers, acorns, mushrooms, twigs, leaves, and pinecones are well suited. Attach them with string or yarn and suspend them from a branch. Nature specimens should be suspended at different lengths rather than in a neat row. Lengths of string can have more than one item suspended from them. When the mobile is completed, place it near a window or doorway where a breeze will activate it. This is a good multisession activity. Items on the mobile can be continually added to or changed.

Group mobile projects need not be restricted to the use of nature items. Include any of the recycled junk items listed in Appendix A, as well as

- paper scraps, cut and torn pieces
- pictures from magazines
- tissue paper shapes sealed in wax paper
- plastic tops and caps
- anything interesting that can be suspended; be creative!

Remember to decorate the front and back of items, since both sides will be visible. Mobiles can be made around the above-mentioned nature theme or

- main characters in a favorite story, book, or song
- weather and seasons
- holidays
- animals
- community helpers
- traffic signs and safety
- food groups
- transportation

Yarn Shapes Mobile

Begin with a papier-mâché mixture. (See recipes in Chapter 13.) Children will each need their own piece of wax paper to work on. Take lengths of rug yarn and dip them into the papier-mâché mixture.

Squeeze out the excess between your fingers. Arrange the yarn lengths into a shape or object. Be sure to crisscross and overlap the yarn. Let dry thoroughly. Carefully peel off the wax paper. Hang the yarn shape from a mobile.

Multilevel Mobile

Advanced mobile makers can make a mobile that has more than one level. For example, begin with a dowel rod and suspend pencils attached to string of different lengths. Do not worry if the mobile does not balance at this point. Start to suspend items and glue string or yarn in place. Slowly work toward balance. One object on a very short line may balance a much lighter object suspended from a long line. More than one object can be placed on any one line, which will also influence balance. Older children may enjoy the challenge presented by this activity.

Baked Clay Mobile

Check Chapter 12 for a clay recipe that involves baking the finished product. This will provide a nice tinkling sound when the items rustle in the wind. Children can use cookie cutters or clay tools when making their items. Remember to make a hole through each item to allow for hanging.

Picture Parts Mobile

Discuss with children how objects can be cut up into parts. For example, a person could be divided into a head, a body, and legs. Each could be connected separately on a line, with a small space left in between. This will provide a comical effect when the wind moves the cut-up parts about. This same process can be done with animals, vehicles, or whatever. Magazine pictures are a good source, or children may want to draw their own pictures. A clown, a rocket ship blasting off, and a Christmas tree are just a few that the author has seen.

Stabile

A stabile is nothing more than a self-standing, stationary mobile. Whereas a mobile is suspended, a stabile, with one or more arched wire arms, rests on a fixed base. Although it is fairly similar to a mobile, a stabile is more difficult to make. You will need at least one length of fairly sturdy wire attached to a wood base. The base must be large and heavy enough to support the wires and suspended items without tipping over. Basically, any of the activities recommended for the mobile apply to the stabile. Suspended items that are too big or heavy will pull down the wire. Also, it will be much more difficult to get several layers hanging from a wire that is bent close toward its base than from a mobile hanging overhead.

Simple Stabile **S**

Provide each child with a drinking-cup lid, pipe cleaners, and play dough or plasticene, as well as an array of greeting cards, postcards, or magazine pictures. Children can glue or tape their cutout pictures onto one end of a pipe cleaner. A piece of play dough is molded either inside or on top of the cup lid. Children gently push their pipe cleaners into the play dough. Pipe cleaners can be creatively twisted and arranged at different heights and positions. Stabiles can complement a holiday theme by using relevant pictures. Children might also enjoy making a stabile titled "me" or "my family."

SUMMARY

This unit focused on the teacher's multifaceted role with respect to children's art. A teacher can model and participate in art activities. Knowing about art will help one become an art specialist and provide creative experiences for children. It was recommended that the teacher be a creative individual who demonstrates creative thinking and expression on a daily basis. Different approaches to teaching art were also identified. Teacher-directed and child-directed were opposite positions. Being a guide or facilitator was recommended as providing a good balance between child input and subtle teacher direction.

Suggested Activities

1. Observe a teacher involved in an art activity. Use the continuum of teaching approaches to decide whether the activity was teacher-directed, teacher-guided, or child-directed.

2. Use the continuum of teaching approaches to plan a single art activity in three different ways:
   • structured and teacher-directed
   • unstructured and child-directed
   • teacher-guided

3. Practice using a guided approach in working with children during art. Be a facilitator as you respond to children.

4. Practice being a model and participator as you interact with children making art. Record your reactions.

5. Facilitate a mobile or stabile activity with school-age children.

Review

A. Fill in the indicated three points along a continuum of approaches to teaching.

X _____   X _____   X _____

1. _____   2. _____   3. _____

B. Fill in the approach to teaching next to its corresponding activity:

1. _____   The children are free to explore at the art tables or easels.

2. _____   The teacher encourages children to design their own Valentine's Day cards for their parents. She provides paint and paper.

3. _____   Children cut out the outline of a heart traced by their teacher. The teacher writes, "I Love You Mom and Dad" across the front.

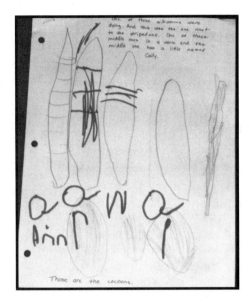

CHAPTER 16

Responding to Children's Art

A study of silkworms prompted this piece of art. What would you say to the child who showed you this picture and said, "Look!" The child's teacher sensed his excitement and asked if he would like to tell a story about it. The teacher wrote as the child dictated the following:

> One of these silkworms were dying. And this was the one next to the striped one. One of these middle ones is a worm and the middle one has a little named Cally.

The child returned to his drawing and added some letters of his own near the cocoons.

What did the teacher accomplish? By investing the time to listen and write down the child's words, the teacher conveyed her sincere interest in his art. She did not dismiss the child with a curt response such as "Oh, that's great," or "I love it." Nor did she correct the child's grammar. She helped the child artist see that ideas and experiences can be represented through art. The visual image can be talked about. Words can be written down and read back. Thinking, artistic representation, and literacy go hand in hand.

OBJECTIVES

After studying this chapter, the student will be able to

- Critique different approaches to talking with children about their art
- Use the artistic elements to analyze and discuss children's art
- Discuss the teacher's role as troubleshooter in children's art
- Assist children with sewing and weaving

INTRODUCTION

Adults can respond both verbally and nonverbally to children's art. What should one say to a child artist? Should a teacher praise, judge, question, or correct? This chapter will overview and critique different strategies. Art Dialogue, a strategy using the artistic elements, will be presented as a preferred approach. Although the art program will run smoothly most of the time, individual children may have difficulty on occasion and will need direct intervention. The role of the teacher as trouble shooter will be portrayed.

TEACHER AS RESPONDER

Teachers can respond and react to children's art both nonverbally and verbally. Often, we are unaware of our nonverbal communication. A smile conveys approval, while a frown or puzzled look conveys disapproval. For example, a teacher may verbally say that she likes a child's abstract artwork, but her wrinkled forehead and squint convey quite the opposite. Posture and overall body language also communicate a message. Giving a cold stare to a child who is making a creative mess communicates one's preference for order and neatness. Hands on hips or crossed arms while staring down at a child conveys a cold, aloof message. Stooping down to eye level or sitting close to a child conveys warmth, respect, and acceptance. Young children are physical beings who use their bodies to express what they feel. In turn, they are sensitive to the nonverbal messages conveyed by adults. One goal for early childhood educators is to develop positive nonverbal communication and establish congruence between our nonverbal and verbal messages to children.

ART DIALOGUE*

Verbal comments that teachers traditionally make concerning children's art take the following six approaches:

---
* This section has been adapted from the original work by Robert Schirrmacher, "Talking with Young Children About Their Art," *Young Children* 41 (1986):3–7.

- complimentary
- judgmental
- valuing
- questioning
- probing
- correcting

The impact of each of these on the child artist will be analyzed, and an alternative to the six traditional approaches will be presented.

With the complimentary approach, teachers tell children that their art is nice, pretty, lovely, super, or beautiful. Specific comments include, "That's a beautiful painting," "Oh, how lovely," "Pretty, a very pretty picture," or "Yes, very nice." In turn, the child will often smile, say "thank-you," and walk away. The opportunities for rich verbal dialogue are limited. A second limitation is that these terms become vague and overworked platitudes. For example, the term "nice" is used so freely, as in "Have a nice day!" that it conveys very little meaning or sincerity. What are the criteria for a "nice" picture? Is an abstract picture "not nice"? The term "pretty" is another example. Not all children's art is pretty. A solid mass of black paint may be dark, massive, thick, layered, or rectangular, but it is not pretty. The terms *nice* and *pretty* are empty ones and should be replaced with terms that provide specific feedback to the child.

With the judgmental approach, the teacher tells children that their art is good or great. Specific comments include, "Very good" and "That's great work." Since most teachers do not want to judge and rank children's art as good, better, or best, they may simply tell all children that any and all of their art is good. In turn, these judgmental terms become overworked and meaningless. A teacher may lose credibility with the judgmental approach. How can one child's impulsive scribble and another's detailed portrait both be good? Is the teacher not telling the truth? Or could it be that the teacher is not really looking, but merely rubber-stamping them in production-line fashion with the same empty judgment?

With the valuing approach, the teacher tells children that she likes or even loves their art. Specific comments include, "I like that a lot" and "Oh, I just love it." Obviously, it is important to tell children that you recognize all the time and effort they have spent processing with the medium. You can appreciate how hard a child worked to get a clay dinosaur to stand up. Rewarding and encouraging the child for processing, however, is different from putting the teacher's seal of approval on the finished product. Children create to express themselves. They should not make art to please a teacher. Unfortunately, many children create art that is personal and therefore devalued by adults. Stereotypic, impersonal art is often the type valued by adults. A classic example is the square house flanked by trees with a triangle roof and a smoking chimney. Often there are two windows with parted curtains and a smiling sun in the sky. Adults understand and may even encourage the making of stereotypic art. This type of picture gets praised and displayed at home on the door of the refrigerator. The stereotypic symbols or schema convey public meaning. Although they may reflect a developmental landmark in attaining realism, they are not better than children's abstract art.

With the questioning approach, a teacher directly and bluntly asks children, "What is it?" or "What is that supposed to be?" An older or very verbal child may answer. Some children may not be able to verbalize what they have represented on a very personal level. It may be difficult for a child to respond, "I just painted how I feel inside when I'm mad." Young children may not know why or what they have painted. In response, they may shrug their shoulders, cast their eyes downward, say, "I don't know," or walk away. Some teachers continue their questioning. "Well, is it a _____ or is it a _____?" A child may verbally play along just to end the interrogation.

Much of young children's art is private, egocentric, and not intended to look like something. According to Smith (1983), it is unwise and even harmful to ask, "What is it?" of a child who is making nonrepresentational art. According to Kamii and DeVries (1978), for young children who engage in nonrepresentational art, art may have primary value as a physical knowledge activity. Motoric hand and arm movements result in brushing, dabbing, swirling, and smearing paint. The finished product or end result is of no consequence. Other children may be hurt or insulted that their teacher did not immediately recognize their splash of thick blue paint as the ocean.

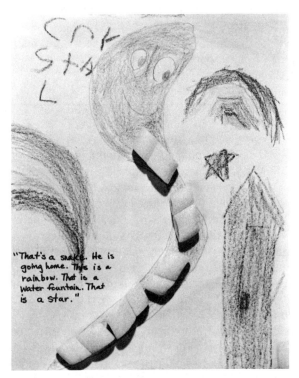 With the probing approach, the teacher attempts to draw from children some hint, title, or verbal statement about their art. Typical comments include, "Please tell me all about it" or "What can you say about this?" This approach is less forward and abrasive than the previous one. It is supported by an integrated approach to curriculum development (Chapter 13) in which children's art is used as a lead-in to other curricular areas. This probing approach has merit, but it should be used sparingly. Children cannot and need not always verbalize, dictate a story, or write about their art. Also, there is a tendency for this approach to grow stale with repeated use. A young boy once told his peers not to show their artwork to the new student teacher because "she will make you tell a real long story about it and then you have to wait while she writes it across your picture." Encouraging but not mandating that children talk about their art is sound practice (see Figure 16–1).

FIGURE 16–1   *Children enjoy inventing their own spelling. Teachers can also record children's talk about*

Art Dictation

Many children will want to talk about their art. Some will provide a title, labels, or sentence to accompany it (see Figure 16–2). Some teachers elect to very neatly print these words across the picture. The author, however, recommends using a separate piece of paper for two reasons. First, adult artists rarely have words written across their canvas. Second, often there is little blank space, and the words have to be written too small or squeezed in. Using a separate piece of paper has a few advantages. It allows a separate story to be stapled or taped to the bottom. A blank sheet allows you to print in fairly large letters. Therefore, it will be easier for the child to see and read back. Last, it allows room for the child to trace over the letters and words. Leaving blank space between lines provides room for the child to attempt to copy the letters, words, and sentences.

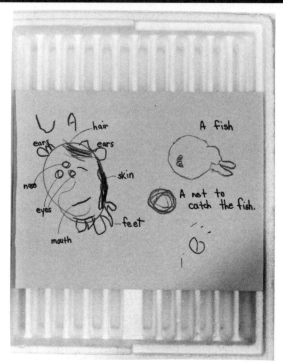

FIGURE 16–2   A teacher can label as a child dictates.

The correcting approach attempts to provide children with specific feedback that will enable them to improve their art or make it "better" by more closely approximating reality. For example, a child shows her teacher a drawing of a green spider. The teacher replies, "Very good, but remember to draw legs on your spider. Spiders have many legs. And remember when you color that most spiders are black." This teacher's intentions were good but misdirected. Art, and child art in particular, is not a copy of the real world. Photography, not art, copies reality. Instead, the child artist freely chooses to creatively improvise. For example, children know what their faces look like. Still, their self-portraits may reflect faces that lack ears or eyebrows. Lowenfeld (1968) warns that a teacher's corrections or criticism only discourage children and do not foster their artistic growth (see Figure 16–3).

So what is a teacher to say or do? Nothing? Smile or nod approvingly? Eisner (1976, 1982) recommends that teachers shift from searching for representation in child art and focus on the abstract, design qualities or "syntax," such as shape and form. Children's art is related to the work of adult artists in the use of these artistic fundamentals. Discussing the formal elements of the visual arts is vital to the development of aesthetic awareness and aesthetic potential. Even very young children can understand artistic terms such as shape, pattern, line, design, and color.

Merely knowing about the artistic elements will not suffice. Teachers can use the aesthetic elements

FIGURE 16–3   This artist has taken creative liberty. There is no need to correct.

FIGURE 16–4   "You have been working hard. I see colorful lines that cross, circles, and squares."

of art as a framework for verbally responding to children's art. One need not be an artist to understand and implement this approach. There are different ways of identifying and organizing the artistic elements. Consensus is lacking on the one best list or approach. Hardiman and Zernich (1981) emphasize the following seven artistic elements:

- color
- line
- mass or volume
- pattern
- shape
- space
- texture

Balance, overall design or composition, and time and effort can be added to the above list.

This expanded list is both manageable and developmentally appropriate for talking with young children about their art (see Figure 16–4). It will serve as the framework for the alternative approach advocated in this section.

Keep three principles in mind when talking with young children about their art. First, consider children's developmental levels. For toddlers and young preschoolers, keep your comments short and to the point. Talk about physical movement, saying, "Look how fast your arm is moving the crayon." Or, "I see thick dots where you pressed hard." Second, relate comments to the artistic elements the child has used in picture making. Say, "Look at all the colors;

let's name them—red, blue, and purple." Or, "Big squares that make rectangles are up at the top of your paper." Third, use encouragement rather than praise. Say, "I know you feel proud when you get the scissors to cut all by yourself." This conveys a very different message than saying, "Good girl" or "Great job." Saying, "The smiling sun in the sky matches your happy face" conveys your interest and appreciation. Words of encouragement help children feel good about their art. Children can easily get addicted to praise and end up doing art to please adults and get the verbal rewards.

Develop an Art Vocabulary Based on the Artistic Elements

Let's match specific comments to each of the above ten artistic elements listed previously.

color—
I see bright colors. Here (pointing) are the three primary colors—red, blue, and yellow.
You made purple on your paper. Do you know how you did that? Yes, you mixed red and blue together.
line—
So many lines are on your paper. Some are straight up and down; others are curvy. These two lines formed a cross and here you made an X.

mass or volume—
Your clay animal is heavy and solid.
Let me see what you have put on your Styrofoam. You used toothpicks, yarn, and sticks deep in the back. What a massive piece of art.
pattern—
I see a pattern of painted shapes. It goes: tree, then a house, and then another tree.
shape—
Look at all the different shapes you made. Help me name them. Yes, there's a circle and here's a rectangle. And over here? Yes, your square house has a triangle roof.
space—
Your hand painting fills up all of your paper. There is no empty space left.
texture—
Thank-you for showing me your collage. The shiny metallic paper feels so smooth. But over here the dried glue with sand feels bumpy and rough. You have two different textures.
balance—
Do you know your picture is balanced? What do you think that means? On the left side (pointing) you drew yourself and over here on the right (pointing) you drew your bunny.
overall design or composition—
You used many different lines and shapes to make your picture. Here they fit into each other like puzzle pieces. You placed them all over your paper. It makes a very interesting design.
time and effort—
I can tell you worked very long and hard at this picture. You must be very proud of yourself (encouraging remark).
I bet you're glad you didn't give up. You finally got the play dough to work so your animal can stand up.

Teachers can also say, "I like the way you . . .

- are working so hard."
- are being so creative."
- are trying to come up with your very own idea."
- are not giving up."
- are trying new ways."
- are putting things away."
- are sharing at the art center."

Teachers can also verbally reflect the way a piece of art makes them feel. For example, "Robbie, your bright colors make me feel so happy." Or, "The big bright yellow sun makes me feel so warm all over." Or, "All those lines racing around your paper make me feel like moving around."

Teachers are being responsive when they carefully examine children's art and provide a rich dialogue in which the artistic elements are pointed out and discussed. No one piece of children's art will contain all of the artistic elements. Texture is useful in describing collage or painting, where surfaces are rough, smooth, nubby, or layered. Mass or volume in three-dimensional art is a useful term in describing a child's clay work, sculpture, construction, or assemblage.

A teacher may want to comment on other qualities that are not formally considered artistic elements. It is also important to comment on the handling of the materials and media. A child's unsuccessful attempts or disappointments with the media should be discussed. For example, a child tries to paint a rainbow with watercolors, but the colors run together. A teacher could say, "I know you worked hard at trying to keep your colors separate. Watercolors get very wet, and colors sometimes run. What could you do differently next time?" Or, "Try using less water next time."

A teacher may want to relate art to life. "You have drawn so many colorful flowers they remind me of my backyard flower garden." Or, "I see so many squares and rectangles in your picture. Remember when we went on our field trip downtown and saw all those tall buildings that looked like squares and rectangles." Or, "How is your robot like the ones you see on TV?"

At times it may be wise to wait and say nothing. This serves two purposes. First, it gives the teacher time to study the child's art and reflect on the artistic elements evidenced before speaking. This will eliminate an impulsive, curt response like, "That's nice." Second, it will give the child an opportunity to talk first if he or she so chooses. This provides a lead-in and agenda for a teacher's comments. It may be difficult to break the habit of immediately responding with words like good, great, nice, wonderful, or beautiful when children share their art with you. Learn the ten elements and practice using them as you would in learning a second language. Add them to your art vocabulary. Do not feel compelled to give an immediate response. Saying, "That's interesting" or "Let me look for a minute" allows you to buy time, think, and structure a meaningful comment.

It is also important to help parents respect and encourage their children's artistic processing and production. Perhaps a letter similar to the one below will help.

Dear Parents,

This is one of many pieces of artwork your child will be bringing home this year. Please consider it a personal gift from your child and thank him/her. Use magnets to proudly display it on the refrigerator door where all can see it.

Do not worry if you cannot figure it out. Its beauty may reside in your child's use of colors, lines, and shapes. Do not ask, "What is it?" Consider it a design. Encourage your child to discuss it if he or she chooses.

Your child would probably enjoy doing art at home. Art supplies make good gifts. Keep a small box filled with the following: scissors, glue, paste, tape, crayons, markers, ruler, stapler, watercolor set, clay or Play-Doh, and paper in a variety of sizes, shapes, colors, and textures.

Your child will also enjoy doing art with you. Enjoy art together!

Your Child's Teacher

TEACHER AS TROUBLESHOOTER

Not all young artists will trust their own creative urges and impulses. Some have learned to doubt their own ability or personal worth. Others are frustrated by their inability to meet a standard of realism held by others. From time to time, all children will need a teacher's subtle guidance and direction in making art. They may need verbal and nonverbal encouragement to accept, trust, and act on their creative impulses. A teacher can act as a troubleshooter, identifying children who are artistically or creatively "blocked" and use an appropriate inter-

vention strategy. Below are some examples of how to recognize blocked children and intervention strategies.

Children Who Criticize Another's Art

One child at an easel tells another at the other side, "Your picture is dumb; it doesn't look like nothing!" The second child gets upset and begins to cry. Children need to know that they cannot criticize another's art idea or work. "Tyrone has worked very hard at painting his colorful picture. Remember, pictures can be made up of bright colors without looking like anything." Or, "It is Tyrone's picture, and he can paint anything he wants. If he doesn't want it to look like something, that's okay too."

Children Who Copy and Imitate

Although imitation and copying are forms of flattery, children do not see it that way. "Teddy has spent a lot of time making his picture. Let's all come up with our own ideas." "Remember, it's yours—your idea, your way, and your very own picture."

Children Who Are Not Progressing Artistically

Artists, whether young or old, sometimes get stuck in a rut. They continue to make the same things in the same way. A teacher can help by suggesting a new activity. "Les, try watercolor today. You have been painting at the easel for days, and it is time for a change." Or, "Les, I see how much you enjoy painting houses at the easel. What other kinds of buildings could you paint? Let's try to paint something different today."

Children Who Refuse to Try

Some children will totally avoid involvement in art. They will stand close by but refuse to try. They may need a teacher's subtle prompting, guidance, and guarantee of success. "Here, Susan, I'll stay with you and get you started. I'll dip the brush in the paint. Now you take over. I know you can finish on your own."

Children Who Do Not Like to Get Dirty or Messy

For some young children, staying neat, clean, poised, compliant, quiet, and obedient reflect cultural values. In turn, they will avoid messy art activities. There is a cultural difference because the school may operate valuing messy art activities. The issue is not who is right or wrong but how to diplomatically resolve the issue. Other children grow up in homes where they are discouraged from getting messy or dirty. They may have been punished for playing with their food, soiling their clothes, or walking in mud. Others will come to school inappropriately dressed in expensive outfits with a warning to "stay clean." Young children do get messy and dirty. This is a fact of childhood. Smocks, however, can protect clothing, and hands can be washed. Children need to be reassured that they will not get in trouble for getting dirty or messy. "Your parents know we paint at school and want you to enjoy it. You can wear a smock and clean up afterwards." It is also important to inform parents of the importance of art and that making a mess and getting dirty are part of the process. Encourage parents to send their children appropriately dressed for dirty, messy work.

A child may be repulsed by messy art activities. Allow time for the child to see that others enjoy the activity and the paint does wash off. Offer activities that use brushes rather than hand painting, or perhaps plastic gloves may be acceptable to the child. Go slowly. Putting only one finger in the paint may be the first step. Keep paper towels nearby for a quick cleanup if the child appears uncomfortable.

Children Who Avoid Art

Some children will completely avoid the art area. Given the choice, they will choose other areas. It is like the child who, if given a choice, eats only meat and refuses any vegetables. Occasionally, this may be acceptable. However, the author believes that over time all children need to participate at all centers. One solution is to rotate children through the centers. "Joey, I know you like to go to blocks every day, but there are many other things to do at school.

Today, I want you to spend some time at the art area and try at least one activity. Let me know when you are finished so we can talk."

Children Who Do Not Know What to Make

"Teacher, what should I make?" "I don't know what to paint." Some children say this hoping that someone else will give them an idea. Usually this is the case for a child who has been pampered, spoiled, or catered to at home. Try diverting the question back to the child. "Fay, that's a good question. What should you make? Since you are the artist, you need to think and come up with an idea. Try to get a picture in your head. Look around the room, outside, or in our books. There are many, many things just waiting for you to make in art." A list of books on color, shape, senses, and art, which may also be a stimulus for making art, is found in Appendix E.

Children Who Dislike Their Own Art

Some children are overly critical of their own artwork. They may tear up picture after picture because it does not turn out just right. Sometimes they are frustrated with their childlike results. Others have poor self-concepts and doubt their own ability. These children will need heavy doses of praise, support, and encouragement. "Oh, Todd, please let me have that picture. Don't throw it away. I would like to add it to my collection of children's art." Or, "I don't think it looks like a dumb giraffe. I see a tall yellow animal. You did a very good job of painting and worked very hard."

Children Who Set Unreasonable Expectations

Some children may set themselves up for disappointment. They expect photographic realism that they are developmentally incapable of producing. They may want perfect pictures without smudges, smears, runs, or tears. Perhaps their parents hold unreasonably high expectations and expect and will accept only the best. These children become their own worst critics. They need to be accepted for what they are—young artists. "Cammy, I enjoy seeing all the bright colors in your picture. It doesn't matter that the colors have run together; it helped mix new ones." Or, "Remember you are making your idea of a rainbow, not taking a picture with a camera. I think your rainbow is just as colorful as the ones I see in the sky."

Children Who Want an Adult to Do Art for Them

"Teacher, make one for me. I can't do it." Or, "Teacher, I can't draw a pig. Please make one for me." Adults should not do art for children, regardless of how much they plead. It makes them dependent on others and teaches them to distrust their own ability. "Sean, I have difficulty drawing animals too. Just try and do your best." Or, "Sean, everyone has to do his own work. I make my own pictures, and you need to make your own too. I can help you in many other ways, but I cannot make art for you. I know you are an artist, and artists just have to keep trying and practicing."

SEWING AND WEAVING

Sewing, stitchery, appliqué, and weaving are activities that allow both creative expression and practice in eye-hand coordination and fine motor control. They are recommended for both boys and girls. Unfortunately, they are often overlooked when developing an art program for young children. Some simplified ways of approaching these activities are provided in the following experiences.

Sewing

Sewing involves little more than painting with needle and thread or yarn. Young children can invent their own simple in-and-out or over-and-under way to sew and need not learn fancy stitches like the French knot. Here are some simple sewing activities.

Yarn Picture

This is a presewing activity that is recommended for young children who are not able to use a needle and yarn. You will need a piece of wood. Sand the edges to remove sharp edges or splinters. Hammer nails in randomly. One-inch round-head brass brads are recommended. Nail them halfway in. Encourage children to take a length of yarn and wrap it around the nails to make a picture or design. Rug yarn is recommended because it is heavy and sturdy and will not tear easily if pulled tightly. It is also possible to make an outline of a specific object, such as a house, with nails, but that would severely restrict the range of artistic possibilities.

Sandpaper Designs

Each child needs a sheet of fine sandpaper. Cut pieces of colored yarn, lace, or embroidery floss. Arrange in a basket or clear container. Encourage children to arrange their yarn pieces onto the sandpaper. The yarn will stick to the sandpaper much like Velcro. The design is nonpermanent and children can repeat the process.

Simple Sewing

We can reduce some of the steps and frustration involved in sewing by providing a sewing surface that is already perforated with holes. Such a surface is similar to the commercially available sewing cards, although we need not provide a specific outline to complete. Carefully poke or punch out smooth holes. All the child needs to do is guide a needle and yarn in and out of the holes. Select a fairly sturdy surface. Some recommended sewing surfaces include

- plastic foam tray
- cardboard shape with holes punched out around the edges
- berry basket
- poster board
- mesh hardware cloth (¼ inch), cut into squares with tin snips
- plastic screen
- paper plate

Flimsy sewing surfaces, such as burlap and other open-weave fabrics or the mesh bags that onions or grapefruit come in, should be secured in an embroidery hoop. Beginning sewers have a tendency to sew over the hoop. This poses no problem, since the stitches can later be cut to provide a fringed effect. Provide a large, blunt plastic needle and yarn. Or use a bobby pin as a needle. Enclose the yarn and wrap the open ends shut with tape. There is no need to even use a needle. Merely dip the sewing end of the yarn into white glue. Form the yarn into a point and let it dry. The end can also be wrapped with clear tape and shaped into a point. Tie a knot at the opposite end. The older child with experience in sewing can move on to using a smaller needle with embroidery or sewing thread.

Paper Stitchery   K S

The older child with experience in sewing might enjoy making stitches in heavy paper. This will be good preparation for sewing on fabric. Paper has the advantages of being easier to get and providing a sturdy surface. A large plastic needle with yarn will tear the paper. Provide a large metal needle and embroidery or sewing thread. A picture can also be drawn in advance. This same activity could also be done on a plastic foam meat tray.

Mixed Media Why not encourage children to creatively combine art media that usually do not go together? For example, they could stitch a frame around their drawing. Or they could use needle and thread to highlight lines in their painting. Or they might enjoy stitching fabric to a paper collage. What are some other creative ways to combine art media?

Fabric Stitchery   K S

The older child with experience in sewing would enjoy using cloth as the background for his or her stitchery. Any loosely woven fabric will do. A piece of old sheet can be secured in an embroidery hoop as a preparation for fabric stitchery.

Appliqué   S

Appliqué involves sewing pieces of fabric onto one another. The result might be a stitched fabric collage. Burlap, with its open weave, makes an excellent background. Try to find material scraps with interesting colors, patterns, sizes, shapes, and textures. Some recommended ones include

- gold lamé
- silver brocade
- velvet
- felt
- fur

Items other than fabric scraps to appliqué include

- lace
- buttons
- ribbon
- rickrack
- beads
- shells
- small straw sections
- jingle bells

Encourage children to glue their fabric scraps in place first before sewing. This will help them sew without the scraps moving around.

Stuffed Pillow   K S

Children will need to draw the outline of an object, such as an animal, on a piece of folded fabric, perhaps an old white sheet. Carefully cut through both pieces of material. Begin to sew the two together while stuffing with small pieces of crushed newspaper, cotton, or stuffing. Continue to sew and stuff. Decorate the pillow with fabric markers when it is completed. Children enjoy making stuffed people pillows by adding yarn for hair and buttons for eyes after the sewing and stuffing is completed.

Weaving

Weaving is another art activity that is often overlooked in early childhood programs. This may be so because weaving is a detailed activity, involving much patience, eye-hand coordination, and fine motor control. The paper weaving activities discussed in Chapter 11 provide a good introduction. Once children have mastered the alternating over-under and under-over movement with paper, they may

FIGURE 16–5   *Items are creatively combined in this weaving.*

want to continue by weaving with yarn or other items. (See Figure 16–5.) Weavers use their own terminology.

- The loom is the structure you weave on.
- The warp is the lengthwise yarn or string that is strung on your loom.
- The weft is the yarn that is woven over-under and under-over the warp.

Here are some simplified weaving activities recommended for use with young children.

Twig Weaving

Provide each child with a Y-shaped or forked twig for a loom. Try to find one that has fallen to the ground or has been carefully removed from a dead tree. Wrap the twig with parallel rows of yarn stretching between the two branches. This will form the warp. Do not pull too tightly or the branches will snap. Weave lengths of yarn (weft) with an alternating over-under, under-over movement, starting from the notch and moving to the top of the Y shape. Encourage children to push their rows fairly close together. Alternate colors. Since no two twigs will be exactly the same, the finished products will be unique. Older children who are experienced weavers may enjoy weaving on a larger twig with three or more forked branches.

God's Eye Weaving

Ojo de Dios means "eye of God" in Spanish. Mexican tribes made these for good luck. They are visually attractive and culturally meaningful. You will need two crossed sticks for the base. Some recommended sticks include a pair of

- pencils
- dowel rods
- plastic straws
- ice-cream sticks
- cotton swabs
- sticks
- plastic stirrers
- chopsticks
- pickup sticks
- Tinker Toys

Form a cross with the two sticks and tie yarn in a knot around the sticks where they cross. Add a dab of glue to secure. Encourage the children to use their over-under and under-over motions. With a length of yarn, weave over one stick and under the next, back over and under again to where you started. Continue this pattern without crossing over previous rows. Each successive layer will build the diamond-shaped pattern, or God's eye. Change colors of yarn often if you want a multicolored effect. Also, vary the thickness of the yarn. Lengths of yarn can also be twisted before wrapping to provide a different visual effect.

Burlap Weaving

Burlap, with its loose, open weave, is recommended for sewing and weaving projects. Cut small, individual, square or rectangular pieces. Pull out ten to twenty threads every few inches to allow open space for objects to be woven into the burlap. Objects to weave in include

- feathers
- yarn
- lace
- ribbon
- old jewelry
- paper strips
- tinfoil
- leaves, stems, twigs, and other nature specimens
- fabric strips
- plastic straws
- rickrack
- sewing tape
- bias tape

Nature specimens are especially attractive when woven into a natural fabric like tan-colored burlap.

Mixed Media

Sewing and weaving go well together. Experienced weavers may enjoy sewing or stitching onto their weaving. Individual lengths or widths of burlap can be gathered and tied with thread, ribbons, or lace to break the monotonous solid appearance.

Loom Weaving

Professionals use a large commercial loom to do their weaving. Child-sized looms are commercially available but costly. It is very easy to provide a child-sized substitute. Objects that make good improvised looms include the following:

- wooden picture frame
  Place the picture frame flat and hammer a row of evenly spaced nails across the top and bottom. Wrap string or yarn from the top nail to the matching bottom nail. Continue until the warp is completed. Children can weave from right to left and left to right using their alternating over-under, under-over motion. Weave with yarn, but feel free to add lace, ribbon, nature specimens, fabric, paper, and other recycled junk.

- berry basket
  Small plastic berry baskets come with the warp completed. Children will enjoy weaving yarn, fabric, or paper strips in and out of the openings. This is a good starting point for the young, inexperienced weaver. (See Figure 16–6.)
- plastic foam tray, flat cardboard, or cardboard box
  Carefully cut ¼-inch slits into the top and bottom edges. Wind string or yarn from top to bottom. Your warp will cover the front and back. Children can weave with yarn with an over-and-under alternating motion. The raised edges of the tray and cardboard box will allow room for the child's hand when weaving under.
- wire coat hanger
  Carefully spread the hanger into a round, square, or diamond-shaped loom. Wrap string around one end and pull it to the other side. Continue until the open section is filled with parallel lines. The warp

FIGURE 16–6   Weaving with a berry basket

is then completed. Encourage children to use lengths of yarn to weave in and out of their loom.

• two hanging sticks

You will need two sticks for this loom. Lay them out on a table, about 1 foot apart; one will be the top, and the second will be the bottom. Begin to fashion a warp by wrapping yarn around the top stick, down to the bottom, around the bottom, and then back up to the top. Continue this process until the warp is completed. Tie the yarn to the top stick and hang it on the wall where children can weave with yarn and other nature specimens. This loom is flimsy and is recommended for the more experienced weaver.

• big looms strung from tree branches

These work well outdoors where children can weave in vines, sticks, long grasses, branches, ferns, husks, stems, twine, and natural fabrics like lengths of burlap.

• paper plate or round cardboard or poster board

Cut an uneven number of slits, such as seven, on the outer edge. Make each slit ¼ inch deep. Cut a 1-inch circle out of the center. Your loom is ready. To prepare the warp, wrap yarn or string from the center hole over the notch, around the back, through the center hole, and up to the next notch. Continue until all spokes and notches are filled. Start at the center and weave in and out or over and under the spokes with a length of yarn. Tie a different color to the end and continue weaving. The back side can also be woven. When finished, cut through the yarn covering the notches. The result will be a colorful, round, woven, fringed plate or decorative piece.

Or cut an uneven number of slits from the outer edge in. Stop about 1 inch from the center. Weave lengths of yarn over and under the wedges, starting from the center and working out. Change colors of yarn often.

• soda straws

You will need four or five plastic straws to make this loom. The straws become the warp and are held in place with the hand. Tape the ends together. You may want to start this weaving for the child. Hold the straws in a spread fan position.

Begin with the ends that are held close together in your hand and slowly wrap them with yarn in an over-under motion. When they are fairly secure, let the child take over. Continue weaving to the top of the straws.

Sewing and Weaving Accessories

Some common sewing and weaving accessories include:

Easy Weaver loom—commercially available and suited for young weavers

plastic screen—for sewing, weaving

standard-weight yarn—double-weight rug yarn is too thick

string—for a variety of art activities

thin crochet yarn—for sewing, stitchery, weaving, and appliqué

thread—colored, for sewing, stitchery, weaving, and appliqué

yarn needles—large, plastic, blunt, with big eye for threading

Hint Yarn cones can be purchased in special containers that keep the yarns from tangling or getting unwound. You could stand each yarn cone in a box slightly larger than the cone itself, for example, an oatmeal box. Cut a small hole in the lid, pull the yarn through, and use the box as a yarn dispenser.

SUMMARY

This unit identified the different ways to talk with children about their art. Complimentary, judgmental, valuing, questioning, probing, and correcting approaches were critiqued. Art Dialogue, a strategy incorporating the artistic elements, was provided as an alternative to saying "pretty," "nice," "good," or "What is it?" Art Dictation was proposed for children who might want their art talk put into written form. It was recommended that teachers become troubleshooters when individual children have difficulty or appear to be artistically stuck.

Suggested Activities

1. Listen to a teacher talking with a child about his or her art. Which approach was used? If necessary, think of some alternatives that would be more effective.

2. Encourage one child to show you his or her artwork. Use the artistic elements as a framework for your Art Dialogue. If possible, tape-record your session. Did you use any of the traditional approaches or remarks? If so, suggest alternative statements.

3. Encourage but do not demand that a child talk about his or her art. Conduct Art Dictation.

4. Identify a child who is having difficulty or who is artistically stuck. Act as a troubleshooter.

5. Facilitate a sewing or weaving experience with children.

Review

A. Match the comment with the approach to talking with children about their art.
   1. correcting   _____ "I love it!"
   2. probing   _____ "I think you left something out."
   3. questioning   _____ "That's just wonderful."
   4. valuing   _____ "What is it supposed to be?"
   5. judging   _____ "Explain it to me, please."
   6. complimenting   _____ "Yes, very, very good."

B. Fill in the artistic element that matches each comment.
   1. _____ "I see red, blue, yellow, and green all over your paper."
   2. _____ "Here your dry paint feels so smooth, but over here where they mixed it feels rough."
   3. _____ "So many lines—straight, crossing, and swirly."
   4. _____ "Your picture fills the entire sheet of paper."
   5. _____ "Your clay elephant is thick and solid and can stand on its own."
   6. _____ "I see rows of circles, squares, and triangles."
   7. _____ "You repeated these trees across the bottom of your paper. What an interesting effect."
   8. _____ "Just look at how all the animals fit into your big circle. Yes. I can see how they are all performing in the circus ring."
   9. _____ "You have spent most of the morning painting at the easel. I can see how hard you have worked to get your painting just the way you want it."
   10. _____ "You have drawn a house in the middle of your paper with two tall trees, one on each side."

CHAPTER 17

Strategies For Enhancing Children's Artistic Development

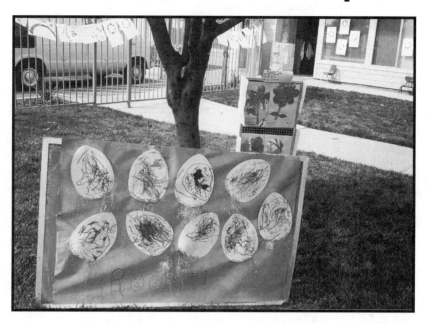

W hat can a teacher do to celebrate children's art? Often, teachers display children's art on the walls of the classroom. That is not always possible. Some children insist on taking every piece of artwork home. Some centers have little vacant wall space. One center solved these two problems by celebrating children's art outdoors in conjunction with an open house. Is this something you have participated in or would like to try? How does an art open house benefit the children, parents, and center?

OBJECTIVES

After studying this chapter, the student will be able to

- Identify specific strategies for enhancing children's artistic expression
- Compare and contrast art group time with show-and-tell
- Discuss different ways to frame and display children's art

INTRODUCTION

This chapter identifies strategies for enhancing children's artistic expression. An Art Idea Book uses pictures to provide potential ideas of things to make in art. Even young artists can be encouraged to sign or mark their artwork. Matting and framing children's art communicates our interest in what they have created. Displaying their art provides an opportunity for all to share in the child's creation. Hosting an Art Party lets parents join in the celebration of children's creative expression through art.

ART IDEA BOOK

Teachers can browse through magazines for large and interesting pictures of people, places, objects, and animals. Look for vivid colors and interesting designs. Mount one or more pictures on each page of a scrapbook or photo album. Children can be encouraged to browse through the Art Idea Book when they are at a loss as to what to color, draw, paint, or make. For example, Fay's teacher directed her to the Art Idea Book. She was intrigued by a picture of circus animals and decided to make performing animals out of clay. The book need not be taken to the art center as a model to copy. The pictures are merely stimuli and suggestions.

ART GROUP TIME

Large group time is a popular routine in early childhood programs. The author prefers group time to show-and-tell because it encourages language, social development, and synthesis, without the use of toys and possessions from home. The focus can be on what children do during art.

Some guidelines for art group time include

1. Set aside a specific time each day. The end of the day is an excellent time to summarize and synthesize the day's events and plan for tomorrow. "Let's show and talk about what we did today. Who would like to share their art with us?"
2. If possible, split the large group into smaller groups. Or offer group time as an option during free play time. With fewer children, the time spent waiting and listening will be compatible with their developmental level.
3. The time should initially be kept brief and slowly increased as the year progresses.
4. The teacher should remain seated with the group. Smiling, making eye contact, and nodding will nonverbally communicate your interest in the activity. The teacher may also want to encourage or gently prod the child who is shy or reluctant or who offers only minimal utterances. Always reinforce the child's verbalizations. Saying, "Thank-you for sharing that" or "You did a good job of telling us about your picture" will make the child want to verbalize in the future. Always accept what the child says, whether it is grammatically correct or incorrect. For example, three-year-old Tab says, "Sees what I did." Don't attempt to correct the child or point out the error. Instead, simply mirror the essence of what the child has said, using correct grammar. For example, "Yes, Tab, I see what you did at the art table. It's a very colorful picture." In this example, the teacher not only accepted the child's speech and modeled grammatically correct feedback, but also expanded on the child's natural language.
5. It is important to begin on time. Do not wait for everyone to be seated, quiet, and ready to begin. This wastes too much time. Instead, begin slowly. The other children will slowly join your group, especially if they sense they will miss out on something important.
6. Do not let the older, brighter, or more verbal children dominate the discussion. All children have the right to speak during group time. It is the teacher's responsibility to encourage each child to exercise that right. We can also respect the child's right not to participate.
7. You are a model. If you appear bored, restless, or preoccupied, so will the children. Do not expect a quality group time if you plan to file papers or hang a bulletin board at the same time. If by your actions you show children that group time is important, they will respond accordingly. You may also want to model and share some-

thing important that you were successful at during the day. "Children, I am so pleased that we got our winter bulletin board up before the first snowfall. I worked hard cutting out my letters, and I like how they look."

8. Focus on artwork rather than on toys or possessions brought from home. Our goal is to make children so proud of their daily school accomplishments that they will want to verbally share them with their peers each day. Obviously, this is a long-range goal that takes a great deal of time, patience, practice, and encouragement.

9. Talk about beauty. Read books with beautiful words and illustrations or share art postcards. Encourage children to verbally share or show something they think is beautiful. Focus on the qualities that make something beautiful. It may be color, texture, or shape. Help children see that a rainbow or the quietness of night are beautiful things. Conduct group time outdoors where children are surrounded by the beauty in nature.

10. Ask children to bring in things that they find beautiful. It may be a rose from their garden or a cultural artifact. Focus the discussion on why we believe things are beautiful and how they make us feel. Help children see that taste is individual and it is OK to disagree. Respect others' rights to voice their own opinions.

MATTING AND FRAMING CHILDREN'S ART

Matting and framing children's art tells them that you value what they have done. You have invested the time and effort to finish their artwork. Matting and framing "finish" a picture by adding the final touches. This does not make a picture better; it simply further enhances its aesthetic quality. It is a nonverbal way of showing children that their work is important and deserving of special care. (See Figures 17–1 and 17–2.)

There are many possible ways to frame art. Rickrack, fabric, yarn, or strips of construction paper or wallpaper make attractive borders, giving the

FIGURE 17–1   Mandy draws herself as her favorite food— a pickle!

FIGURE 17–2   Mandy mats and frames her own art.

appearance of a frame. Use a large group hand painting or collage as a backdrop to frame smaller pictures. Here are some more suggestions appropriate to early childhood.

Framing Art In . . .

A variety of lids, containers, and boxes make ideal frames (see Figure 17–3). Match a picture to the size and shape of a container. Ask the child's permission to "crop," or trim, excess white area to get a better fit between the picture and the frame. Be creative. Whoever said picture frames had to be square or rectangular? Circular swirls of paint show up very well in a round frame. Children's art can be framed in a

- shoe box
- lid of a box
- gift box

- large Styrofoam packing container
- pie tin
- plastic meat tray
- metal ham container
- coffee can lid
- plastic storage container
- plastic berry basket
- precut mat board frame

Framing Art On . . .

Children's artwork can also be glued or pasted directly onto

- construction paper
- poster board
- cardboard
- gift wrap (over cardboard)
- wallpaper
- newspaper

FIGURE 17–3   Be creative when framing children's art.

Try to pick out a color in the picture when you select a frame. In this way the two will complement, not fight, each other. For example, a painting composed of large red, blue, and black shapes with smaller yellow swirls would look good framed in yellow. Black would also set off the primary colors. A finger painting composed largely of browns and greens would not be set off properly with a purple frame. Be creative and experiment with double and even triple frames. Combine wallpaper and construction paper together as multiple frames. Over time, children can select and frame their own artwork. Ideally, this will involve planning and searching at home and school for just the right frame.

Art Framed in a File Folder or Envelope

Cut a picture-sized square or other shape out of one side of a colored file folder or large mailing envelope. The size of the opening should be about 1 inch smaller than the picture being framed. Insert the picture. Strips of construction paper can be glued to the four outside edges of the opening, if square or rectangular, to enhance the frame. These frames can be used and reused.

Art in a Picture Frame

Having artwork professionally framed involves great expense for both labor and materials. Garage sales and thrift shops are excellent sources of inexpensive plastic, metal, and even wooden frames.

Frames Hung in Different Positions

Framed pictures can also be hung diagonally or in a diamond position if the picture allows. However, a picture of a street scene painted horizontally would not look good hung diagonally or at an angle.

ARTIST'S SIGNATURE

Even young artists can be encouraged to sign their art. The result may be a printed name, a letter, or a configuration of lines and shapes. It does not matter. Avoid printing a child's name across a picture without first asking the child's permission.

Many children do not want their names plastered across their canvas. Many prefer to have their names printed on the back. If the child has no preference, print the name in the upper left-hand corner of the paper. This encourages the top-down, left-to-right progression used in reading and writing. Print clearly and neatly. Avoid printing with all upper-case letters. Capitalize only the first letter of the name. Keep a list of the proper spellings of the children's names near the art center for easy reference. Parents may get upset when their child Lauren brings home art with her name spelled Lorin.

DISPLAYING CHILDREN'S ART

Space is at a premium in most early childhood classrooms. Although guidelines mandate square footage per child, there is rarely enough wall space to go around. Available wall space is taken up with windows, doors, restrooms, sinks, counters, and so forth. The remaining wall space holds children's names, their birthdays, the schedule, first-aid procedures, notes from parents, reminders, lesson plans, a calendar, bulletin boards, chalkboards, a weather chart, a helper's chart, classroom rules, and current events. Usually, some wall space is reserved for children's work. There are many ways to provide space for displaying children's art. (See Figure 17–4.)

Children's Art Gallery

If space allows, devote one area to a classroom art exhibit. Pictures that are matted and framed can be displayed in aesthetically pleasing ways. A table, shelf, or ledge allows three-dimensional products in clay or construction to be exhibited. A bookshelf could hold art books or sample prints for children to examine but not copy. The intent is to expose children to a variety of styles, not to encourage imitation. They can wonder and marvel at the beauty in nature and their surroundings and see how different artists have represented them. The classroom art exhibit or gallery is a good place to quietly escape to and reflect. It is important that children's artwork be displayed at their eye level. Since this is a children's art gallery, it is important that they

FIGURE 17–4   There are many ways to display art.

share some responsibility for displaying. The pictures may not be hung in straight or well-spaced rows, but they do reflect the children's input and will be a source of pride. It is also important to respect a shy child's wishes not to have his or her art publicly displayed. Be sure to display a wide range of artwork, and not just the more realistic ones or the types you happen to prefer.

Art Kiosk

An art kiosk is a workable solution to limited wall space. A kiosk is a self-standing display with three or more sides. It can be constructed of panels of sturdy cardboard, wood, or stacked cartons. It is space-efficient in that many pictures can be simultaneously displayed on a number of sides in a few feet of floor space. A set of folding screens may serve the same purpose.

My Own Space

It is possible to divide up the available wall space among the children. Each child can decide what he or she would like displayed. One teacher follows this practice and rotates displayed work on a weekly basis. Children keep their work in folders stored in their cubbies. Every Friday they select the work they want displayed for the upcoming week, then they hang it up as they enter on Monday morning.

ART PARTY

Parents can be invited to a classroom art party. (See Figure 17–5.) Children can design and decorate the invitations. Samples of artwork from each child can be collected, framed, and displayed. The art party can be held in conjunction with an open house or as a separate annual event. Children can accompany their parents and proudly point out their artwork. Perhaps the art center could be open, with parents and children rotating through it. This could be a good lead-in to a discussion of children's art, creativity, and child development. Although parents may find an excuse not to attend a regular night meeting, most will show up if their child is somehow directly involved. Serving simple refreshments and snacks made by the children may also boost attendance. The art party should remain just that—a celebration of children's art. It is not a contest or competition. All children win

FIGURE 17–5   Teachers, parents, and children celebrate with art.

through art. Prizes, awards, trophies, and ribbons have no place at an art party.

SUMMARY

This chapter provided an array of strategies for enhancing children's artistic expression. For example, an Art Idea Book provides artistic possibilities without encouraging copying and imitation. Art circle time provides children with the opportunity to show and tell about their art. Even young artists should be encouraged to sign or mark their art. Strategies for matting, framing, and displaying children's art were discussed. An art party was recommended as a strategy for encouraging family participation in the celebration of children's artistic expression.

Suggested Activities

1. Make an Art Idea Book for use with young children.

2. Ask a teacher's permission to conduct art group time at the end of an art session. Encourage children to talk about their art using the artistic elements. Model the process for them.

3. Ask a child's permission to mat, frame, and display his or her piece of art.

4. Ask a teacher's permission to help plan, organize, and implement an art party.

Review

A. List different strategies that foster a child's artistic expression.
   1.
   2.
   3.
   4.
   5.

B. List guidelines for art group time.
   1.
   2.
   3.
   4.
   5.

CHAPTER 18

Art Assessment

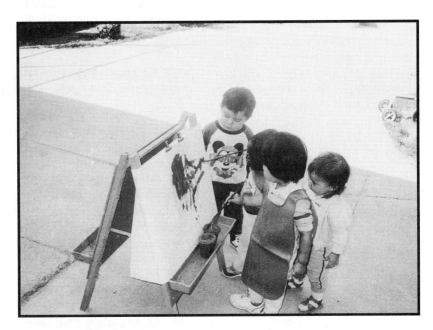

What are the children in this picture doing? One is painting. Take a close look at his painting. What do you see? Is it recognizable? Do you see lines and shapes? Another child, although uninvited, begins to help out. Two children are standing back and observing.

Which of your children enjoys art? Who is reluctant to get dirty? Who is willing to take creative risks? Who is more comfortable watching and copying others? Observing children as they engage in art activities provides opportunities to gather and record valuable information about them and their artistic development. Over time, these recorded observations, supplemented with actual samples of children's work, provide a developmental record.

OBJECTIVES

After studying this chapter, the student will be able to

- Discuss the teacher's role as observer, recorder, and evaluator, and discuss how observational data assist in artistic assessment
- Discuss the role of assessment in art
- Identify strategies for collecting and storing children's art
- Distinguish standardized testing from authentic assessment
- Discuss portfolio assessment, including guidelines for assembling, maintaining, and reviewing portfolios

INTRODUCTION

Terms like testing, evaluation, and assessment may elicit a negative reaction. Some parents, teachers, and administrators may be suspicious of attempts at evaluating young children at all, let alone in the areas of creativity and art. This chapter adds observer, recorder, and evaluator to our list of teacher roles. Being a keen observer of children and an objective recorder of their behavior will help in assembling individual portfolios. Observational data is essential in evaluating children's artistic development in authentic ways. Actual samples of children's work and performance can also be included in a portfolio to provide a comprehensive developmental portrayal. In turn, the portfolio serves as a basis for noting strengths and documenting progress, matching weaknesses with recommendations, individualizing curriculum and communicating with parents. The chapter outlines procedures for collecting and storing artwork so it can then be used as an instrument for evaluating children's artistic progress.

Consider This:

Mrs. Pati has returned to teaching after raising her own children. She has been assigned to a K–1 combination classroom in a progressive school district. She is eager yet anxious. She has spent the last few weeks of summer arranging her room and planning curriculum with her colleagues. As she prepares for a full-day workshop on Authentic Assessment, she begins to feel inadequate. She asks herself many questions. What is the role of testing and evaluation in a K–1 classroom? Are they developmentally appropriate? How are they conducted? How does one manage to do them given a full schedule? Her list of questions seems endless. By lunch, most of her questions were addressed but she still felt overwhelmed. The afternoon session stressed how authentic assessment is an ongoing process which can be integrated into the curriculum. It is not an additional requirement requiring an extra period. It is also a process which empowers children, in that they are actively involved. She was also given helpful strategies for building, maintaining,

and using children's individual portfolios. Upon returning home, Mrs. Pati began making individual file folders and storage boxes for her group. She was convinced that what she had learned would help her know her group better and enhance her ability to work with families.

Ⓝ TEACHER AS OBSERVER, RECORDER, AND EVALUATOR

This chapter adds three new roles to our list of roles that teachers play. These include observer, recorder, and evaluator. Observation allows us to witness development and learning in progress. Recording helps capture the moments by putting our observations down in writing. Recorded observations can be later analyzed and used to informally evaluate children. Evaluation tells us how children are progressing and is useful in our work with parents and in curriculum development.

The Importance of Systematically Observing and Recording Children's Behavior

Why study children? Studying children and their development provides a working knowledge of children at different ages and stages. Studying individual children helps you apply what you have learned about how they grow, learn, and develop. Reasons for studying individual children include the following:

1. to understand children
2. to document a problem or concern
3. to develop a comprehensive assessment including strengths, weaknesses, and recommendations
4. to plan a program that is developmentally appropriate and individualized
5. to communicate with families

1. To Understand Children

It is enjoyable and often amusing to watch children at play. One cannot help but notice their zest for life and energy. Random watching, viewing, and looking, however, may provide enjoyment but do not enhance our understanding of children. A careful study of children does. Observing a child provides valuable baseline data about what the child knows and can do. Ongoing observation can be documented and included in a child's file or portfolio. Strengths, weaknesses, and recommendations across developmental areas should be included.

Just as photographs of children tell us much about what children look like on the outside, their artwork reveals what they look like on the inside. Children use art to tell us many things about themselves. Learn to read their pictures. Observing children engaged in art and collecting samples of their artwork over time provide a wealth of information. Collecting and analyzing children's art will help us understand:

Who They Are   Children include themselves, the most important person in the world, in their artwork. They begin drawing themselves resembling large "O"s or potatolike shapes, balanced on stick legs with arms protruding where ears are usually found. This is a normal stage in artistic development. Children are learning about themselves and their bodies. Although they can look in a mirror and know what body part goes where, they are physically and mentally unable to represent it in realistic fashion. It serves no purpose to correct children's artwork. It will only erode their self-confidence and destroy their creative spirit.

Who and What Is Important to Them   Children live in a family context and they will introduce you to their family through art. Grandpa may automatically appear in a child's art, announcing that he has come to stay with the family. Dad may suddenly disappear after a separation or divorce. Pets will be included as valued family members. Children choose as subject matter those things that make them happy. If they have just learned to use in-line skates there is a good chance that they will depict themselves skating in their artwork.

What Is Going On in Their Lives and What They Know About Their World   Children will use art to communicate how they feel about themselves, others, and their world. If happy with themselves and their lives, they may paint themselves large and grinning from ear to ear. If feeling unimportant, they might make themselves small or even missing from a family portrait. The way children use color, shape, size, and placement to portray themselves and significant others are valuable cues to how that child feels about self and others. Look for patterns but do not jump to conclusions. Children may draw themselves without facial features for reasons other than low self-esteem. It's when children repeat an upsetting image that one becomes concerned and looks beyond the canvas for other cues. Children will share both pleasant and unpleasant experiences. Art helps them celebrate the pleasant and deal with the painful and unpleasant. The content of children's art reflects things they have strong feelings about. For example, if they love their pets then these animals will be depicted. If they are afraid of monsters they may use art as a way to express, work through, and eventually master that fear. Their art may also reflect feelings of anger, hate, rage, rejection, and despair. An intense scribbling of color may be all that the child artist can express. The result may be unrecognizable but the content and underlying emotion are very real. The content of children's art reflects what they know. If they watch TV, there is a good chance that they will include what they view in their art. A child who has not been to a circus will not draw or paint it. Children's art reflects what is important to them—what matters. Some children draw horses, princesses, castles, and butterflies; others draw superheroes, vehicles, and villains.

2. To Document a Problem or Concern

When a problem is suspected or a concern arises, it is wise to collect observational data to substantiate your educated guess. For example, when reporting suspected child abuse or neglect, you are required to back up your suspicions with written proof or evidence based on what you have seen and heard. This forms the basis for making a referral or requesting special services. Likewise, you may be concerned about a child who does art to the exclusion of all other activities or one who never approaches the art center. Your observational data helps you decide on a plan for helping the child in question.

3. To Develop a Comprehensive Assessment, including Strengths, Weaknesses, and Recommendations

Since children grow, learn, and develop at a rapid rate, it is important to celebrate their achievements. The Instrument for Artistic Evaluation at the end of this chapter serves as one framework for informally assessing artistic development. Children who can only scribble in September may be able to make recognizable shapes by summer. Collecting samples of children's art documents this developmental progression. Art samples can be dated and placed in the child's portfolio. When laid out chronologically and carefully examined, the child's progress becomes apparent. Artistic and creative achievement is not only documented but also shared with parents. A child's concept of the body is reflected in the inclusion and spatial arrangement of body parts. Weaknesses can also be noted through observation or collection of performance samples. For example, children's involvement at the play dough table can be photographed at regular intervals. The photos can be dated and arranged in chronological sequence. Over time, the child may move from random processing to making flat pancake shapes. Moving on to making detailed three-dimensional human figures signifies a developmental advancement in the child's perceptual and spatial awareness. The child has moved beyond working in a flat, two-dimensional plane.

4. To Plan a Program That Is Developmentally Appropriate and Individualized

Observing what interests children and what activities attract their sustained involvement should provide a basis for curriculum development. For example, observing that a theme of dinosaurs permeates the block area could lead you to provide small plastic dinosaurs for making feet prints, or to offer children an opportunity to make dinosaur masks. If children are frustrated using scissors, you can plan art activities that involve tearing paper. You may also want to plan activities involving fine motor and eye-hand control to help prepare children for using scissors.

Or, it may simply be that children need your individualized instruction and guidance in how to hold and use scissors.

5. To Communicate with Families

The observational data you collect from studying individual children will help parents better understand their child. Information collected from various child study techniques will form the basis for your ongoing communication and conferencing with parents. It is widely accepted that children may act one way at home but act very differently in a school setting. Although parents need to see the "bigger picture," do not be surprised if they deny information that runs counter to what they have experienced or choose to believe. They may say, "I just can't believe what you are saying" or "That doesn't sound like my child." You will need to provide evidence and documentation. This is meant to support your views and assessment rather than proving the parents wrong. For example, observational notes based on a child's frequent aggressive use of art tools might help parents see the need for family counseling or a parenting course. Remember that communication is an ongoing two-way process. Parents may be wary of your attempts to communicate if you only seek them out to report problems. Daily, ongoing communication builds a relationship in which parents feel comfortable talking about their child and receiving feedback which not only celebrates their child's strengths but addresses problem areas. Families can provide a wealth of information, including a child's play interests and creative pursuits. A child who has no exposure to art materials at home and has been advised to stay clean at school may not approach the art center. Ask parents open-ended questions or prompts like, "Tell me about your child at home." Listen actively, attentively, and without judgment. Reassure parents that some behaviors are typical of children at certain ages. For example, many children prefer painting their hands rather than applying paint to paper. Others enjoy mixing several colors together until a dark, unrecognizable, thick mass results. First-time parents in particular may not know what to expect of their child at a given age. Empower parents by helping them become part of the solution. Brainstorm how you might work together to help their child trust and act on his or her creative impulses, instead of always asking others to make him or her a picture. Solicit their input and offer specific suggestions. Verbalize and restate a mutually agreed-upon plan. Record what transpired after the conference and plan a follow-up meeting to review progress, or rework a plan, if warranted.

Ⓝ Observing and Recording

Knowing and understanding children involves two major strategies: observing and recording. Although you may have excellent vision, you may lack the ability to observe. Observation is a learned skill that improves with practice. Observation requires time, a focus, an objective attitude, and patience. One must commit time to carefully study one or more children. Observation must also have a focus, such as children's art. An adult observer is unlike a mechanical video camera and cannot objectively observe and write for endless periods of time. Observation alone will not suffice. Observation and recording are complementary processes. Recording guarantees that what you have observed will not be forgotten. Observations must be objectively recorded, with subjective impressions or an analysis kept separate. Be factual, using words that are specific and descriptive. Imitate a video camera and tape recorder, documenting what you observe and hear. Later, become a commentator, adding your analysis, interpretation, or inferences.

Guidelines for Observing and Recording

There are five guidelines for effective observing and recording.

1. Be Prepared to Observe and Record.

Develop a system that works for you. Some teachers wear a pen or pencil around their necks and carry clipboards with blank, lined paper. Other observers prefer to use index cards. Punch a hole through a small stack of index cards and attach them to a large key ring or shower curtain ring. This can be carried around your thumb. File individual index cards into a file box with dividers for each child. Still other observers wear an apron with small note pads in the pockets. You may want to use the larger sticky notes or peel-off adhesive labels that can be posted on the child's folder and later transferred into a permanent record. A tape recorder is useful when recording children's conversation, especially if you write slowly or your children talk fast. It also helps capture rich descriptive language that is sometimes lost. A video camera can capture the words and actions of one child or of children in small groups. This provides the advantage of repeated playbacks at a later time. Set a realistic schedule for observing. It is humanly impossible to observe and record the behaviors of all the children in your care in one sitting. Supervision is always your first priority. One suggestion is to plan on observing four children per day, so that the entire group is observed on a weekly basis. The main point is to be ready to observe and record at all times.

2. Be Unobtrusive.

Maintain a distance and do not become involved with the child or children you are trying to observe. Avoid talking or interacting with the child or children observed. If they approach you, redirect them back to what they are doing. Tell them you are just writing notes about what different children say and do at school. You want children to act natural, talking and behaving as they would without noticing your presence. When children know they are being observed and that someone is writing down what they say and do, their behavior changes and your data is contaminated. Children may end up performing. What you observe and record may not be indicative of what they normally say and do.

3. Get a Focus and Be Selective About What You Observe.

Know what you are looking for and observe and record when it happens. If you are interested in a child's artistic development, then observe during art time and at the art center. If you are interested in creative expression, it makes good sense to select art time. Be flexible and spontaneous enough to capture through observation those unplanned moments that may hold a wealth of developmental data.

4. Be Objective, Impartial, and Non-biased in Recording.

Record what the child says and does. Include non-verbal cues like facial expression, body posture, and gestures. Add child's name, date, time, and overall setting, such as at the art center, as well as who else is involved. Develop a shorthand system using abbreviations that work for you. For example J = Julia or rgu = argue. Observe frequently. Observe the same child in different settings and at different times. Avoid comments like good, bad, nice, or naughty, for two reasons. First, they cannot be directly observed. Second, they are evaluative rather than descriptive. What is labeled bad behavior by one observer may not be considered bad by another. Be sensitive about using words which stereotype children on the basis of gender, race, culture, ethnicity, social class, or special needs.

5. Separate Your Observation from Your Analysis and Interpretation.

Observation is descriptive and based on fact; analysis and interpretation are based on inference. For example, hitting and kicking behaviors can be directly observed while "being aggressive" is a global interpretation, not directly observable. What does it mean to be aggressive? Does it mean swearing, talking back, punching, or shouting? The term is unclear. Some observers choose to add their interpretations at the end of their observations or at a later point in time. This allows time for reflection through a careful rereading and insightful analysis, rather than jumping to a quick conclusion. Others record observations down the left half of the paper, leaving the right column blank, where an analysis is later added. A one-time observation will provide little if any significant data from which to draw conclusions. Patterns will emerge over time with ongoing observation. Patterns provide support for your analysis and interpretations.

Fact or Inference? Good observation is based on what is heard and seen rather than what is inferred. Decide which of the following statements are based on descriptive observation and which rely on inference:

1. Child is out of sorts and in a bad mood today.
2. Child used her fists to flatten the play dough.
3. Obviously, this child woke up on the wrong side of the bed and is having a bad day.
4. Child quickly ate two halves of toast and asked for seconds.
5. This child finally got a taste of his own medicine.
6. Child carefully turned the pages of the book while retelling the story in her own words.
7. Child appears distracted or detached today.
8. Child successfully reached the pedals of the tricycle and rode for three minutes without asking for help.
9. Once again, child is fussing to get his own way.
10. Child asks friend to paint with her at the easel. Her friend says, "No," and child frowns while painting alone.

Which are fact and which are inference? The odd-numbered items are based on inference, while the even-numbered items are based on fact.

6. Match a Strategy to Your Purpose in Observing.

There is an array of child study techniques from which to choose. Some are quick to administer; others take much time and writing. Some must be constructed; others require only paper and pencil. Individual techniques provide different pieces of information necessary to understand the whole child. The more time invested in child study and the more strategies employed, the more complete and thorough your understanding of the child. Strategies include narratives, time and event sampling, and checklists and rating scales.

A. Narratives Narratives are records of what the observer sees children do and hears them say. Narratives are conducted in natural settings in which the observer tries to remain unobtrusive. Diaries and anecdotes are forms of narratives.

A diary, as its name implies, is a journal or ongoing account. One observes and records what a child says and does in wide blocks of time. The diary is made up of a series of entries over a period of time. Compare it to writing your diary on a daily basis. At the end of the week, you can reflect on the preceding events, analyze and evaluate your week, and make plans for next week. Diary accounts provide a wealth of valuable data but require an investment of time in observation. Over time, the diary shows patterns or trends which help the observer make interpretations. Students of child development often do a child study which reflects heavily on a diary.

An anecdote is a shortened and more focused version of the diary. Although the diary attempts to capture anything and everything happening, the anecdote attempts to capture a specific event or behavior, including how it begins, evolves, and concludes. An anecdote might be the child's use of language or how frustration is handled and expressed. Given its broader scope, a diary may house or frame several anecdotes and therefore provides a bigger picture. The observer begins recording an anecdote when the specified behavior begins and stops recording when the child stops engaging in the behavior under study. For example, Martika's teacher has decided to use an anecdote to better understand the child's attitude toward art. She plans to carefully observe Martika's involvement at the art center. On Tuesday afternoon, Martika, age four, enters the art area and the teacher records the following:

> It's 2:15 and Martika is standing in the art area. She twists her hair with her fingers while silently watching one girl paint at the easel and one boy play with play dough at the table. The girl asks Martika if she would like to paint with her. Martika does not answer. The girl hands Martika a paint smock but Martika does not put it on. She sits next to the boy at the play dough table. There are several large pieces of play dough available but Martika sits with her hands in her pockets. She says something that resembles, "It's yucky," and leaves the art area. Ending time is 2:22.

What, if anything, does this descriptive anecdote tell you about Martika and her behavior in the art area? It is too soon to draw any conclusions based on this limited data, and further observation is clearly warranted.

B. Time and Event Sampling   Sampling observations use time intervals or categories of behavior as their focus. Time sampling provides a way of measuring the frequency of a behavior within a given period of time. With time sampling, the observer specifies the behavior under study and then counts how often it occurs within a stated block of time. For example, Martika's mother complains that Martika never brings any artwork home and questions her level of involvement throughout the day. She claims Martika has always been a watcher rather than a doer. Ultimately, she fears Martika will not be ready for kindergarten. At school, Martika does spend a lot of time by herself merely watching others. The teacher chooses to do a time sampling to study the extent of Martika's lack of engagement at school. The teacher will count the number of times Martika is engaged at a learning center for five consecutive days. She is sampling time by selecting the first ten minutes on each hour to observe. An assumption is made that what Martika does within this ten minute block of time is representative of her behavior throughout the hour. A tally indicates the number of minutes that Martika was engaged in play. The teacher's findings for one week are depicted in Table 18–1.

What does the data tell you? Are there days of the week or times of the day when Martika is more engaged and involved than others? Do you see a pattern emerging? What might account for this? It is difficult and dangerous to generalize from this limited data. Based on the limited information provided, however, one can see how Martika's involvement increases and decreases, although the pattern is fairly consistent across the days, except Monday. What might explain the low level of involvement on Monday? Her teacher notices how Martika needs much time to wake up and face the day. Does the data in Table 18–1 support this hypothesis? Why does her participation drop off before lunch and before going home? Are there any questions you might formulate to ask Martika's mother to help you better understand the pattern observed in this time sampling?

The next step is to act on the information in the anecdote and time sampling. The teacher plans to question the mother regarding Martika's sleeping and eating habits. Perhaps she is coming to school tired and without eating breakfast. She will also

	MONDAY	TUESDAY	WEDNESDAY	THURSDAY	FRIDAY
8:00–8:10					
9:00–9:10	/	//	//	//	//
10:00–10:10		//	//	///	
11:00–11:10					
12:00–12:10					
1:00–1:10					
2:00–2:10		///	///	////	//
3:00–3:10		/	/	/	
4:00–4:10		/	//	/	
5:00–5:10					

TABLE 18–1   Time Sampling: Martika's Engagement in Play

discuss how Martika spends her weekends to better understand her lower level of involvement on Mondays.

With event sampling, the observer specifies the behaviors under study and then notes when it happens. Its occurrence is indicated with a tally. Martika's teacher has been observing the activity choices of her four-year-olds. She is concerned that Martika spends much of her day being idle, rather than engaged, although she spends more time at the art area than elsewhere. By using event sampling, she hopes to learn which art activities engage Martika. The child's initial, M, appears under the art activity at a specified time. Times with no initial indicate lack of engagement. (See Table 18–2)

What does the event sampling indicate? It appears that Martika's engagement in art is limited to drawing and coloring. Could it be that drawing and coloring are less risky and less messy than the other art options? Do the three observational tools work together to advance our understanding of Martika? Her teacher wonders if Martika is bringing her artwork home to share with her mother. Her teacher is also planning to slowly encourage Martika's participation in other art activities.

C. Checklists and Rating Scales   Although commercially available, many checklists or rating scales are created by teachers. They take some time to develop but less time to complete than a narrative. In a checklist, the items are identified and the observer merely indicates which items are present or absent. For example, a checklist for art might include the following developmental indicators:

_____ scribbles and makes unrecognizable marks
_____ makes geometric shapes
_____ draws mandalas
_____ draws self as face
_____ draws human figure
_____ enjoys using finger paint
_____ creates 2- and 3-D forms with play dough
_____ art is rich with details
_____ child relies on own creativity rather than copying

The observer could place a check mark or write yes/no in front of those items that apply. Checklists may be administered more than once and some forms provide for multiple observations, documenting progress or change over time.

	EASEL PAINTING	COLLAGE	PLAY DOUGH	DRAWING & COLORING
8:30–8:40	art center closed			
9:30–9:40				M
10:30–10:40	outdoors			
11:30–11:40	lunch			
12:30–12:40	rest			
1:30–1:40	rest			
2:30–2:40				M
3:30–3:40	outdoors			
4:30–4:40				M
5:30–5:40				

TABLE 18–2   Event Sampling: Martika's Art Choices

A rating scale is a second timesaving observational tool. In a rating scale, items are identified and the observer makes a judgment regarding the degree to which the item is observed in the child. For example, the items in the art checklist on the previous page could be rated along a continuum of high-medium-low, usually-sometimes-rarely or always-sometimes-never. The rating scale provides for more accurate judgment than a checklist. What the checklist and rating scale share in simplicity, however, they lose in terms of judgment. How would you rate the following observed anecdote using a checklist or rating scale?

> Kea (who is three) shares toys but not art supplies or food at the snack table. She easily shares with adults and younger children but not with those her age or older.

A judgment must be made. Do you indicate yes or no for sharing? Actually, it may be easier to use a rating scale and rate Kea as "sometimes" or a midmark indicating a moderate or some degree of sharing. While being observed, Kea did not ask to be included in the play of others. What does this mean? Does she lack social skills? Does she not know how to ask to be included? Or, did it simply not happen this month? To avoid this problem, many rating scales include a "not observed" column.

CHILDREN'S ART FILES AND FOLDERS

Keeping samples of children's artwork is a good way to collect evaluative data. Ask the child's permission to enter his or her name and the date on the back of the piece. Try to collect a sample at least once a week. Tell children you are saving pieces for their art files or folders. Encourage their participation in making artwork they want included. Honor their requests for pieces they prefer to take home. Encourage them to make both "take home" and "folder" pieces. Use a large colored file folder or folded piece of poster board to hold the artwork. Periodically lay the pieces out in chronological order. Look for development, progression, and mastery in the use of media and materials and in the expression of ideas, concepts, objects, and feelings. Match what is artistically rendered with a particular child's artistic and overall level of development. Use these data in reporting to parents and planning future art experiences. (See Figure 18–1.)

FIGURE 18–1   A girl's concept and drawing of herself develops over time.

Formal Standardized Testing

Wouldn't it be easier to simply test children? Find a test that is quick to administer and easy to score? Wouldn't it provide the same information? According to Lessen-Firestone (1995) standardized achievement testing of young children is often inappropriate and may actually be detrimental to school success. Test results are often unreliable and invalid, influenced more by children's test-taking skills, cultural backgrounds, and stress levels than by what they know. Also, as teachers tend to teach with the test in mind, curriculum narrows and isolated, low-level, testable concepts and skills are stressed. Further, testing situations can be artificial, contrived, stressful, and intrusive, because they do not take place during children's regular activities. Standardized tests provide a formal, less authentic way to assess what young children know and can do. Young children are not good test takers, but they are good at revealing what they know and can do through their play and daily activities. Children can and should be assessed in less formal and more authentic ways.

Ⓝ Informally Assess Young Children in Authentic Ways

Assessment for young children should not and need not take the form of testing. View assessment as an ongoing process of documenting and recording a child's development. According to the NAEYC (1991) guidelines for appropriate assessment, assessment serves the following purposes: to plan instruction and communicate with parents; to identify children with special needs; and to evaluate programs. Assessment should be informal and authentic. It should not disrupt the daily program, but should happen naturally as children are engaged in playful pursuits. Observing and recording children's behavior are key components of authentic assessment. Any assessment that is authentic involves the person being assessed in the process. The professional artist's mentor does not assemble the portfolio; nor does the professional model's agent. Involvement fosters responsibility and ownership. Children can analyze and assess their developmental progress and learning over time. Authentic assessment offers a much more natural, sensitive, and realistic look at development than any set of standardized tests. Authentic assessment of children relies on observation and recording, along with samples of a child's performance and work assembled in a portfolio.

Ⓝ Portfolio Approach to Authentic Assessment

You might associate the portfolio concept with professional artists and models. Artists assemble a collection of their artwork in a large folder. It represents what they can do with different art media. Artists may supplement actual art samples with photos, slides, or videotape of their larger pieces. They may include pieces done at different times to demonstrate their versatility, style, or professional development. Models do the same. They pore through an array of photos and select those that best capture their look. These are assembled in a binder and shown to potential agents. The same process holds for young children. They are building a portfolio based on what they have learned at school. A portfolio is comprehensive and contains multiple sources of information, including:

- samples of children's work, such as art, stories, writing samples
- writing drafts and revisions
- observational data of physical, social, emotional, cognitive, and creative anecdotes
- photographs of blocks or 3-D construction
- audio recordings of language, storytelling, reading, dramatic play episodes
- video recordings of child doing art, moving to music, social interactions, dramatic play themes
- systematic records of children's activities
- health records
- parent input, such as completed questionnaires, conference notes
- notes forwarded from former teachers
- special items selected by the child

A portfolio, however, is more than a mere collection of information. According to Martin (1994), it is an attitude and a process. As an attitude, it reflects an ongoing openness and commitment to learning more about each child. As a process, it involves using multiple sources, including teacher, child, and family to provide valuable developmental data.

Guidelines for Assembling, Maintaining, and Reviewing a Portfolio

There are five basic guidelines for portfolio assessment:

1. Devise a System.

Use large colored folders or boxes. Locate a spot where the portfolios will be kept. Decide on how the content will be organized. Provide one container for each child that he or she can decorate. This begins the process of ownership. Portfolio contents must be respected and confidentiality is important.

2. Add Entries Regularly.

Date each sample you include. Provide background information. Arrange the items chronologically. Earliest work samples will appear in the front followed by more recent entries. Adding to portfolios should be an ongoing process. You may be overwhelmed if you add only a few times a year. Develop a schedule so that samples are added on a daily or weekly basis.

3. Focus on the Whole Child.

Portfolios should be comprehensive. Remember to address all developmental areas, including entries

---

Art Portfolios

Genishi (1993) believes that children's artistic progress may be documented and saved in portfolios which contain not necessarily the best of children's art, but instead samples that indicate children's abilities and preferences at specific points in time. These signed and dated pieces comprise the child's personal art museum.

---

and observations that reflect a child's physical, social, emotional, cognitive, and creative accomplishments.

4. View the Portfolio as a Collaborative Effort.

No one person is responsible for the portfolio. All adults who know and either presently work or have worked with the child can have their entries included. Resource people and specialists can also have their notes included. The same holds for the child. Empower the child to be an active participant in the portfolio process. Let them decide which samples to include and which to display or take home. This also promotes responsibility and gives them a feeling of control over their education. Include parent questionnaires and/or notes from parent conferences. Ideally, portfolios can follow children throughout their educational career. An end-of-the-year summary sheet with a dated record of the child's progress goes on to the next year's teacher. All other samples are bound and sent home in the form of a memory book.

Genishi (1993) recommends involving the child in the art portfolio process by asking questions like the following:

- Do you like this piece of artwork? What do you like about it?
- Which is your favorite piece? Why do you like it best?
- What art media do you like the best and why?
- Why did you choose to include this particular piece?
- Explain how you got this special effect (pointing to textured area).

Or, ask the child to complete the following sentences:

- This is my favorite piece because . . .
- I want this included in my portfolio because . . .
- What I remember most about doing this is . . .

Record the child's comment on an index card and attach it to the corresponding work.

5. Review Periodically.

The aim is not to compare children or portfolios but to look for and document individual growth, development, and learning over time. Plan a schedule to periodically review each child's portfolio, for example, two per evening. This is especially important before progress reports are due or to prepare for parent conferences.

INSTRUMENT FOR ARTISTIC EVALUATION

Our wholistic model of child development has served many purposes throughout the book: to understand child development, to plan appropriate experiences, to report to parents, and to justify our programs. We can also use it as a framework, or instrument, for evaluating children's artistic development.

Physical

In using artistic tools, the child demonstrates

1. _____ large-muscle or gross motor control.
2. _____ small-muscle or fine motor control.
3. Proper use of the following artistic tools:
   _____ scissors.
   _____ glue.
   _____ brushes.
   _____ crayons.
   _____ markers.
   _____ clay tools.
   _____ watercolor set.
4. Concentration and sustained involvement in art.
5. Completion of the art activity.

Social

1. Ability to work alone at art.
2. Demonstrating self-responsibility
   _____ in getting and returning art materials.
   _____ in cleanup.
   _____ in following the rules of the art center.
3. Self-direction in using own ideas in art rather than copying others.
4. Ability to work cooperatively with others at the easel, art table, or art center. See Figure 18–2.
5. Tolerance of others' art ideas, styles, and products.

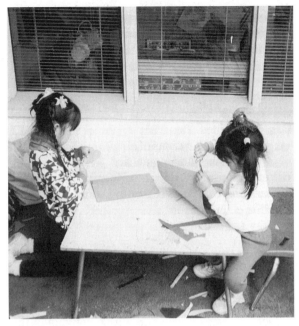

FIGURE 18–2   *Can you evaluate their cutting skills?*

Emotional

1. Acceptance of own mistakes, errors, and unsuccessful attempts at art.
2. Self-assurance and confidence in art rather than an inhibited, fearful, overly cautious attitude.
3. Expresses feelings, moods, emotions, and personality through artwork.
4. Enjoyment and pride in own art.
5. Addition, omission, distortion, and/or exaggeration of things that are emotionally significant.

Cognitive

1. Understands art and why people have made art in the past and continue to do so.
2. Interested in talking about own art and dictating labels, titles, sentences, or stories.
3. Knows and uses art vocabulary.
4. Evidences
   _____ very personal representation.
   _____ public representation with subject matter recognizable to others.

5. Demonstrates a knowledge of colors and color mixing.
6. Reflects a knowledge of shapes, including:
    _____ circle.
    _____ square.
    _____ triangle.
    _____ rectangle.
    _____ lines.
    _____ combinations of above.
    _____ other nongeometric.
7. Reflects a knowledge of people, places, objects, experiences, and events of personal importance in the environment.
8. Draws human figures.

Creative

1. Demonstrates a willingness to discover, experiment, and explore with a variety of media.
2. Demonstrates ways of creatively combining media, materials, and artistic junk.
3. Uses detail, decoration, and elaboration.
4. Reflects originality, imagination, and creativity.
5. Makes individual and personally unique artistic statements.

Aesthetic

1. Enjoys
    _____ processing with the media.
    _____ making artistic products.
2. Uses a variety of
    _____ two-dimensional artistic media.
    _____ three-dimensional artistic media.
3. Demonstrates awareness and sensitivity through
    _____ looking.
    _____ touching.
    _____ listening.
    _____ smelling.
    _____ tasting.
4. Demonstrates awareness and sensitivity to immediate
    _____ surroundings.
    _____ nature.
    _____ environment.
5. Sees similarities and differences in artistic styles.

6. Appreciates work of artists encompassing a wide range of styles.
7. Knows the following artistic elements:
    _____ color.
    _____ line.
    _____ mass or volume.
    _____ pattern.
    _____ shape.
    _____ space.
    _____ texture.
8. Uses artistic elements to discuss and appreciate
    _____ nature.
    _____ immediate surroundings.
    _____ environment.
    _____ own artwork.
    _____ artwork of others.

Personal

Number the child's favorite choices 1, 2, and 3.

Two-dimensional	Three-dimensional
_____ mark making	_____ sculpture
_____ painting	_____ clay
_____ printing	_____ papier-mâché
_____ watercolor	_____ construction or
_____ resist	assemblage
_____ stencil	_____ mask making
_____ paper work	_____ mobile
_____ collage	_____ stabile
	_____ weaving
	_____ stitchery

SUMMARY

The roles of observer, recorder, and evaluator were added to our list of teacher roles. There are many tools for observation. Guidelines for objective observing and recording were discussed. The developmental hazards of testing young children were also examined. Ways of assessing children that are more authentic, performance-based, and natural were offered as alternatives to standardized testing. The portfolio was identified as a key feature in authentic assessment. Guidelines for assembling and using portfolio information were discussed.

Suggested Activities

1. Working in teams, interview teachers about their views on assessment in early childhood, how they evaluate young children, and what they use to evaluate children's artistic progress.

2. Collect samples of one child's art over an extended period of time. Lay the artwork out in chronological order. Use the Instrument for Artistic Evaluation presented in this chapter to make some statements about this child's artistic development. Can you make any recommendations?

3. Ask a teacher's permission to review children's portfolios for the purpose of learning how to devise a portfolio system.

4. Devise your own early-childhood-style portfolio documenting what you have learned and can do as a result of teacher education.

Review

A. Discuss the teacher's role as observer, recorder, and evaluator of a child's artistic development.

B. Identify a major strategy for collecting and storing children's art.

C. Critique the developmental appropriateness of standardized testing for use with young children.

D. Discuss portfolio assessment as an authentic way to informally assess young children.

E. Identify the five steps in portfolio assessment.
   1.
   2.
   3.
   4.
   5.

Artistic Junk

Dear Parents,

We need your help! In our daily art program we use all kinds of creative junk. Our slogan is, "Don't throw it away! Recycle it by sending it along with your child."

If you have any of the following objects, please send them along with your child. We also encourage donations of creative junk from your office, business, workplace, or other sources in the community. Thank-you!

A adhesive-backed paper
   apple divider
   appliances (small, broken—good for parts)
   artificial flowers
B bakeware
   baking cups
   baskets (plastic)
   bath brush
   beads
   berry baskets
   blocks (wooden)
   bolts
   bottle caps and tops
   bottles—plastic pump-type, squeeze, and roll-on
      deodorant
   bowl brush (new)
   bowls (plastic mixing)
   boxes (gift)
   braiding
   brayer
   burlap
   butter tubs
   buttons
C calendars
   canceled stamps
   candles
   carbon paper

cardboard fabric bolts
cardboard sheets and tubes
cards (old greeting)
catalogues
cellophane (colored)
checkers
cheese slicer
Christmas cards
cigar boxes
clock parts
cloth
clothespins
coat hangers
coffee filters
combs (cleaned)
computer paper
confetti
cookie baking tray
cookie cutters
cord
corks
corrugated cardboard
cosmetic brushes, sponges, and applicators
costume jewelry
costumes
cotton balls, puffs, and swabs
crayons (old, broken)
cupcake liners
cupcake tins
curtain rings
cutting board
D deodorant bottle (roll-on)
   detergent bottles (squeeze-type with lids)
   dice
   dominoes
   dowels
E egg cartons: cardboard and plastic
   egg slicer

electronic parts
embroidery hoops and thread
envelopes
excelsior
eyedropper
F   fabric scraps
feather duster
feathers
felt
film spools
flannel
floor-length mirror
florist's foil, foam, and Styrofoam
foam rubber
foil
food grater
food savers (Rubbermaid, Tupperware)
fruit trays
funnels
fur
G   game pieces
gears
gift boxes
gift wrap
glass beads
glass pane (small)
glitter
grater (metal, food)
greeting cards
grocery bags
gummed labels
gummed paper and stickers
H   hair rollers (cleaned)
hairbrushes (cleaned)
hangers
hat boxes
hats (old)
holiday decorations
hot plate
housewares
I   ice-cream cartons (large, commercial)
ice-cube trays
iron (electric, in working order)
J   jar tops
jars

jewelry
junk (any and all!)
junk mail
K   keys
kitchen gadgets and utensils
kitchen shakers and containers
L   lace
leather
lids
linoleum tiles
M   machine parts (small)
magazines
magnets
maps
marbles
margarine tubs
material remnants
measuring cups and spoons
meatballer
melon baller/scoop
mesh—potato, onion, grapefruit bags
milk carton plastic tops
mirror (handheld, full-length)
mosaic tile
muffin tins
muslin
N   nail brush
nails
necklaces
needles and thread
netting
newspaper
newsprint rolls
nuts
nylons and pantyhose (old, clean)
P   packing material
pails (plastic)
paint charts
pans (old)
pantyhose plastic egg containers
paper bags
paper doilies
paper plates
paper reinforcements
paper scraps and tubes

pastry blender/brush
pastry tube
picture frames
pie slice lifter
pie tins
pill bottles and vials
pipe cleaners
pizza cardboards
place mats
plastic containers
plastic foam trays
plastic fruit baskets
plastic pieces and parts
poker chips
polyfiberfill
pom-pom dish scrubber
Popsicle sticks
pot scrubber with knobbed handle
pots
puzzle pieces
Q quilts, quilt scraps
R razors (empty, plastic)
rhinestones, rhinestone jewelry
ribbon
ribbon rolls
rickrack
rolling pin
S sandpaper
scraper spatula
screening—plastic and wire
seals (holiday)
sequins
sheets (old white)
shoe boxes
shoelaces
shoe-polish applicator
shopping bags
sieves
socks
spice bottles (empty)
splatter screen (for catching cooking grease)
sponges (household)
spools
spray paint can lids

sprayers
springs
squeeze bottles
stamps (canceled domestic and foreign)
stationery
stationery boxes
stickers
stockings (old)
straws
string
Styrofoam balls, bits, packing, and pieces
T telephone wire
thread
tiles
tinfoil
tissue paper
tongue depressors
toothbrushes (old)
toothpicks
towels (old)
tracing paper
travel brochures and posters
trays
trinkets
tubes—toilet paper, paper towel, mailing
tubs (margarine with lids)
twine
U upholstery fabric and stuffing
utensils (old, cooking)
V vegetables (if donated)
velvet
vitamin bottles
W wallpaper sample books and scraps
wax paper
weaving loom
wire (thin)
wire mesh
wire screen
wire whisk/whip (kitchen)
wood scraps
wooden beads
wooden blocks
wrapping paper
Y yarn

Nature Specimens

acorns
bark
corn husks
cornstalks
dried flowers and plants
driftwood
feathers
fossils
gems
gourds
hives
leaves
minerals
moss
natural clay

nests
nuts
pebbles
pinecones
pods
pressed flowers
reeds
sand
sawdust
seed pods
seeds
shells
smooth stones
straw
twigs
wood shavings

Where to Go in Your Local Community for Artistic Junk

The following list is by no means complete. The number and variety of possible sources will vary depending on the size and location of your community. Feel free to add, delete, and personalize depending on where you live and work. Please request more than is listed below. Individual sources may have a vast supply of colorful parts and pieces just waiting to be claimed. Most sources will be very willing to save, as long as you provide a prompt pickup. Specifically stating your purpose and suggesting some sample activities may help them identify artistic junk that is not contained on the list. Happy hunting!

Architectural firm
blueprint paper
outdated tools
surplus paper

Art supply store
damaged supplies
surplus stock
used goods

Attic sale
anything and everything reasonably priced!

Builder's supply and contractors
carpeting
Formica
linoleum
tile
wallpaper samples
wood scraps, trim, and molding

Building site
discarded hardware
Styrofoam packing
wood scraps, shavings, trim, and molding

Carpentry and woodworking shop
sawdust
wood scraps, shavings, molding, and trim

Church sale
anything and everything reasonably priced!

Computerized office
outdated forms
scrap computer papers and forms

Container and packaging companies
boxes
cardboard

Craft and hobby shop
damaged goods
packing
small boxes

Dentist's office
see Hospital/medical

Department store
gift wrap scraps
hosiery boxes
outdated forms
small boxes
store displays
Styrofoam packing

Doctor's office
see Hospital/medical

Dressmaking and alteration shop
bobbins
buttons
fabric
spools
thread
trims

Drugstore and pharmacy
pill bottles
plastic containers
store displays
vials

Electric power company
    packing materials
    wire
Electronics firm
    circuit boards
    components
    metal parts
    pieces
    plastic parts
    wire
Estate sale
    anything and everything reasonably priced!
Flea market or swap meet
    anything and everything reasonably priced!
Florist shop
    dried flowers
    ribbon
    scrap Styrofoam
    surplus nature items
Frame shop
    frame scraps
    mat board scraps
Furniture showroom
    cartons
    packing materials
Garage sale
    anything and everything reasonably priced!
Garment manufacturer
    buttons
    empty spools
    fabric scraps
    trim
General office and small business
    envelopes
    general supplies
    old rubber stamps
    outdated business forms
    surplus or outdated business machines
    surplus paper
Gift shop
    boxes
    ribbon
    spools
    Styrofoam packing
    tissue paper

Gift wrap service
    cardboard rolls
    damaged gift boxes
    ribbon
    scrap wrapping paper
    tissue paper
Hardware store
    linoleum
    spare parts and pieces
    tile
Hospital/medical
    boxes
    containers
    pill bottles
    plastic parts and pieces
    trays
    vials
    x-rays
Ice-cream shop
    cardboard packing
    commercial drum-shaped ice-cream
        cartons
Interior design studio
    boxes
    displays
    fabric packing
    sample books
Lumberyard
    dowels
    molding
    sandpaper
    sawdust
    wood scraps and shavings
Machine shop or small plant
    small specialized pieces and parts
Moving and storage company
    cardboard
    cartons
    wrapping paper
Nature and outdoors
    nature specimens
Newspaper plant
    newsprint
    paper roll ends
    scrap papers

Office supply
- cardboard
- damaged goods
- packing
- small boxes

Paint store
- linoleum
- paint charts
- surplus water-based paint
- tile

Photography shop
- containers
- scrap papers

Plastic company
- parts
- plastic pieces
- Plexiglas
- tubing
- wire

Plumbing supply
- plastic pipes and pieces

Print shop
- cardboard pieces and tubes
- heavyweight papers
- paper "seconds" and scraps
- tickets

Rug store
- rug scraps
- samples

Rummage sale
- anything and everything reasonably priced!

Stationery store
- "as is" papers
- paper scraps
- small boxes

Supermarket and grocery store
- baskets
- cardboard lining and packing
- old price stampers
- small boxes
- store displays
- Styrofoam
- thin tissue paper

Tag sale
- anything and everything reasonably priced!

Telephone company
- large spools
- thin colored wire

Textile and fabric shop
- cardboard bolts
- fabric scraps
- material remnants
- spools
- yarn cones

Thrift shop
- anything and everything reasonably priced!

Tile and ceramic shop
- linoleum
- tile

Travel agency
- displays
- old posters
- outdated forms
- surplus brochures
- tickets

Upholstery shop
- buttons
- fabric
- spools
- trims

Wallpaper store
- drapery samples
- wallpaper books and scraps

White elephant sale
- anything and everything reasonably priced!

Wine and liquor store
- cartons
- displays
- fancy boxes
- gift paper
- ribbons
- wooden boxes

Yard sale
- anything and everything reasonably priced!

APPENDIX C

Art Resources

The following is a partial list of art resources: post-cards, prints, reproductions, slides, posters, books, films, and videotapes related to art. If possible, use school letterhead stationery in requesting cata-logues. Remember to also check local bookstores, museums, and art galleries.

American Federation of Arts
41 East 65th Street
New York, New York 10021

Art Education, Inc.
28 East Erie Street
Blauvelt, New York 10913

Art Extension Press
Box 389
Westport, Connecticut 06881

Art Institute of Chicago
The Museum Store
Michigan Avenue at Adams Street
Chicago, Illinois 60603

Art Smart!
Prentice Hall
Englewood Cliffs, NJ 07632

Guggenheim Museum
Mail Order Department
1071 Fifth Avenue
New York, New York 10128

Metropolitan Museum of Art
Fifth Avenue at 82nd Street
New York, New York 10028

Nasco West Inc.
P. O. Box 3837
Modesto, California 95352

National Gallery of Art
Department of Extension Programs
Washington, D.C. 20565

New York Graphics Society
P. O. Box 1469
Greenwich, Connecticut 06836

Print Finders
15 Roosevelt Place
Scarsdale, New York 10583

Dayle Seymour Publications
P. O. Box 10888
Palo Alto, CA 94303

Shorewood Fine Arts Reproductions, Inc.
27 Glen Road
Sandy Hook, Connecticut 06482

Smithsonian Institution Information
   and Reception Center
Washington, D.C. 20560

University Prints
21 East Street
P. O. Box 485
Winchester, Massachusetts 01890

Catalogues

The following is a partial list of companies that carry art-related toys and basic art supplies. Generally they will send catalogues upon request. If possible, use school letterhead stationery. Shop around and compare prices, handling and shipping charges, discounts, and return policies.

A+ Discount Distributors, Inc.
300 Airport Executive Park
Spring Valley, New York 10977
1-800-443-7900

ABC School Supply Inc.
6500 Peachtree Industrial Blvd.
P. O. Box 4750
Norcross, Georgia 30091
(404) 447-5000

Arthur Brown & Bro., Inc.
2 West 46th Street
New York, New York 10036

Beckley-Cardy
7111 Perimeter Park Drive
Houston, Texas 77041
1-800-231-4620
1-800-392-2813 (Texas)

Chaselle, Inc.
9645 Gerwig Lane
Columbia, Maryland 21046
1-800-CHASELL

Child Guidance Toys
Questor Education Products Co.
200 Fifth Avenue
New York, New York 10010

Childcraft Education Corp.
20 Kilmore Road
Edison, New Jersey 08817
1-800-631-5657

Community Playthings
Rifton, New York 12471

Constructive Playthings
Main Business Office
1227 East 119th Street
Grandview, Missouri 64030
(816) 761-5900 (Missouri)
1-800-255-6124

Crayola Educational Products
Binney & Smith
P. O. Box 431
1100 Church Lane
Easton, Pennsylvania 18042
(215) 253-6271

Creative Education Supply House, Inc.
4416 York Street
Metairie, Louisiana 70001
(504) 885-6700

Creative Playthings
Princeton, New Jersey 08540

DIDAX Inc.
6 Doulton Place
Peabody, Massachusetts 01960
(617) 535-4757/4758

Discount School Supply
Capitola, California
1-800-627-2829

DLM Teaching Resources
P. O. Box 4000
One DLM Park
Allen, Texas 75002
1-800-527-4747
1-800-442-4711 (Texas)

Economy Handicrafts
50-21 69th Street
Woodside, New York 11377

Educational Teaching Aids
159 West Kinzie Street
Chicago, Illinois 60610
(312) 559-1400

Fisher-Price Toys
East Aurora, New York 14052

Galt Toys
1-800-448-GALT

Hammett
Box 545
Dept. DM
Braintree, Massachusetts 02184
1-800-225-5467

Kaplan
P. O. Box 25408
Winston-Salem, North Carolina 27114-5408
1-800-334-2014
1-800-642-0610 (North Carolina)

Knowledge Unlimited
P. O. Box 52
Madison, Wisconsin 53701-0052
1-800-356-2303

Lakeshore Curriculum Materials Co.
2695 East Dominguez Street
P. O. Box 6261
Carson, California 90749
1-800-262-1777 (California)
1-800-421-5354 (outside California)

Nasco Arts & Crafts
901 Janesville Avenue
Fort Atkinson, Wisconsin 53538
1-800-558-9595

Nasco West
P. O. Box 3837
Modesto, California 95352
1-800-558-9595

Playskool, Inc.
4501 West Augusta Blvd.
Chicago, Illinois 60651

S & S Arts and Crafts
Colchester, Connecticut 06415
(203) 537-3451

Art-Related Books

The following list contains books that focus on the artistic elements, including color, shape, and line, and the five senses, artists, and art in general.

Adams, A. *Easter Egg Artists*. New York: Charles Scribner's Sons, 1976.
   A family of bunnies design and paint beautiful Easter eggs as well as their surroundings.

Bang, M. *Tye May and the Magic Brush*. New York: Greenwillow Books, 1981.
   Tye May is a poor orphan who is mysteriously given a magical paintbrush. Whatever she paints comes alive. She gives what she paints as gifts to the poor. The greedy emperor discovers this and makes her paint only for him. Tye May, however, wins in the end when she sends him off sailing in the ocean on a painted ship.

Baylor, B. *When Clay Sings*. New York: Charles Scribner's Sons, 1972.
   A book for older children on the use of clay in prehistoric and primitive art. The book relies on a long narrative and explores symbols on Indian pottery. Highly recommended for multicultural education.

Blizzard, G. S. *Come Look with Me, Enjoying Art with Children*. Charlottesville, VA: Thomasson-Grant, 1991.
   Presents color reproductions of paintings of children done by artists ranging from Holbein to Picasso. Background information on artists and their paintings as well as questions are included to stimulate discussion. Recommended for older children.

Brandenberg, A. *My Five Senses*. New York: Thomas Y. Crowell Company, 1962.
   Overviews the five senses. The choice of colors is limited and restricted to black, white, green, and blue.

Brandenburg, F. *What Can You Make of It?* New York: Greenwillow Books, 1977.
   Fieldmouse family moves to a new home. They collect all sorts of junk, including milk cartons, toilet paper tubes, yarn, spools, egg cartons, and old magazines. In their new home they find wonderful uses for all this valuable junk.

Brenner, B. *Faces*. New York: E. P. Dutton & Co., 1970.
   Tells how we learn about the world through our senses. Four of the standard five senses are covered, with touch left out. The book is illustrated with black-and-white photographs.

Carle, E. *I See a Song*. New York: Thomas Y. Crowell Company, 1973.
   A collage of colors and shapes without words. A violin player plays colorful music that forms designs and suggests realistic objects. The book will help children visualize, imagine, and come up with creative possibilities.

Chase, A. E. *Famous Paintings—An Introduction to Art*. New York: Platt & Monk, 1962.
   The author presents approximately two hundred large pictures of famous artworks. The pictures are organized around themes, for example, children and their pets, playing games, and mother and child.

Cohen, M. *No Good in Art*. New York: Greenwillow Books, 1980.
   Jim's art teacher in kindergarten did not approve of his work. Jim did not feel very creative during that year. Now, in first grade, he has a teacher who helps him see how creative and artistic he can be. Recommended for children who do not see themselves as skilled or creative in art.

Crews, D. *Carousel*. New York: Greenwillow Books, 1982.
   Children climb atop a carousel animal. The music begins and the animals circle round and round, faster and faster. What results is a blur of color. The music stops, and the horses slow down. The original colors return. Illustrated with full-color collages and special photographic techniques.

———. *Freight Train*. New York: Greenwillow Books, 1978.
   The story of the journey of a colorful train as it goes through tunnels, by cities, and over trestles. The book is very well illustrated. The bright, colorful cars of the train bear their color name. The colors of the cars blend to suggest speed and movement and also depict color mixing.

Cumming, R. *Just Look . . . A Book about Paintings*. New York: Charles Scribner's Sons, 1979.

Contains over fifty full-color reproductions of famous paintings. Discusses how artists have used the artistic elements, including line, shape, and color, in their work. Contains some difficult vocabulary and may be most appropriate at the kindergarten or primary level.

de Paola, T. *Bonjour, Mr. Satie*. New York: Putnam Publishers, 1991.

Two talented Parisian artists end their feud with the help of Uncle Satie.

Emberley, E. *Green Says Go*. Boston: Little, Brown and Company, 1968.

A story about colors and color mixing. The author suggests that colors remind us of many different things, like holidays. Unfortunately, he stereotypically equates pink with girls and blue with boys.

———. *Wing on a Flea: A Book about Shapes*. Boston: Little, Brown and Company, 1961.

The author uses rhymes and lively drawings to help children recognize rectangles, circles, and triangles in everyday objects.

Engel, D. *The Little Lump of Clay*. New York: Morrow Jr. Books, 1989.

A little lump of clay that desperately wants to become something has its wish granted.

Fisher, L. E. *Boxes! Boxes!* New York: The Viking Press, 1984.

As the name implies, the book shows many possible uses for a box. The book has beautiful color illustrations. The words in the simplified text are set to rhyme. The book focuses on squares and rectangles.

Freeman, D. *Chalk Box Story*. New York: Lippincott, 1976.

When the lid of a chalk box opens, each colored stick helps tell the story of a little boy stranded on a deserted island and the little turtle who comes to his rescue.

Friskey, M. *What Is the Color of the Wide, Wide World?* Chicago: Children's Press, 1973.

Different animals each claim that the world is their color. Each appears on a separate page telling about things that are their color. A beautiful white bird corrects them by saying that colors change with light and seasons. The world is full of many beautiful colors. A good book for older children.

Hawkinson, J. *Pat, Swish, Twist and the Story of Patty Swish*. Chicago: Albert Whitman & Co., 1978.

The book has beautiful watercolor illustrations and is divided into two major parts. First, there is a word-less picture story of Patty Swish, a horselike animal. Second, there is a discussion of tools and techniques for watercolor.

Hoban, T. *A, B, See!* New York: Greenwillow Books, 1982.

This is one of many highly recommended books by this author. Hoban is a talented photographer. In this book, black-and-white photograms of familiar objects from A to Z are portrayed. Photograms reveal the form or shape in white against a black background. This book shows how there is beauty and design all around us.

———. *I Read Symbols*. New York: Greenwillow Books, 1983.

Colorful photographs are used to introduce the child to signs and symbols frequently seen along streets and highways.

———. *Is It Red? Is It Yellow? Is It Blue?* New York: Greenwillow Books, 1978.

There is no text, but the book is illustrated with beautiful photographs in vibrant colors. The author focuses on colors and concepts of shape, quantity, and direction. The author has creatively chosen what to include for the colors. For example, rather than apple for red, the author chooses a girl with a red raincoat and red umbrella. Each page is coded with color bubbles representing the colors stressed.

———. *Is It Rough? Is It Smooth? Is It Shiny?* New York: Greenwillow Books, 1984.

There is no text, but the book is illustrated with beautiful photographs in vibrant colors. The author focuses on textures and surfaces. The author has creatively chosen items such as a squashed soft drink can, caramel apples, and bales of hay. The photographs confirm the aesthetic belief that beauty is all around us.

———. *Look Again*. New York: Macmillan, 1971.

Excellent black-and-white photography. The sequence begins with a square cutout of a page with a photograph underneath. Guess what it is? Turn the window and see if you were right. Look again for a different view of the same object by turning the page, which brings you to the next sequence.

———. *Round and Round and Round*. New York: Greenwillow Books, 1983.

There is no text, but the book is illustrated with beautiful photographs in vibrant colors. The choice of examples is creative and unusual. For example, round holes in a Swiss cheese sandwich on a round bun and round ripples in water are but two of her clever examples.

————. *Shapes and Things*. New York: Macmillan, 1970.
There are no words, but beautiful photograph-type white impressions of common objects appear against a black background. This book will help children see the beauty in shape, outline, and form.

Hughes, S. *Noisy*. New York: Lothrop, Lee & Shepard Books, 1985.
Part of a series on concepts. The story of a little girl who describes the many noises that can be heard inside and outside her house. The illustrations are charming and depict family members as real people. Children will be able to relate to these characters. The parents appear frazzled, and baby sibling always seems to have food spilled on the floor.

Hutchins, P. *Changes, Changes*. New York: Macmillan, 1971.
There is no text, and illustrations tell the creative adventures of two wooden toys and their building blocks. The blocks catch on fire, convert into a fire truck, and float in the water. Children will enjoy guessing what is going to happen next. What else could they do with blocks?

Johnson, C. *Harold and the Purple Crayon*. New York: Harper & Row, 1955.
The story of Harold and his adventures with a purple crayon. Harold goes out for a walk and sketches some adventures. The book is small, compact, and made for small hands. The illustrations are simple, and the purple line is bold. The story resolves itself with Harold falling asleep and dropping his purple crayon.

————. *A Picture for Harold's Room*. New York: Harper & Row, 1960.
One of a series on the adventures of Harold and his purple crayon. This one has been made into an I Can Read Book with simple words for the beginning reader. Harold thinks his room needs a picture and decides to draw one with his purple crayon. Before finishing his picture, however, Harold takes you on a journey with his purple crayon. This particular adventure includes attention to perspective when Harold draws railroad tracks that recede into the background.

Kampmann, L. *The Children's Book of Painting*. New York: Van Nostrand Reinhold, 1971.
This story was originally written in German, and the story line gets a little wordy at times. It is the story of the painting adventures of two puppets, Alexander and Katinka. They experiment with watercolor, crayons, and markers. Beautiful samples of real children's art are included.

Keats, E. J. *The Trip*. New York: Greenwillow Books, 1978.
The story of a boy, Louie, who is having trouble adjusting to his new move. Louie's new neighborhood is portrayed with vibrant-colored collage, paint, and pastels. Homesick, Louie makes a shoe box diorama and imagines that he flies back to see his old friends, who are dressed for Halloween. A quick fantasy flight and Louie returns to his new home just in time to go trick-or-treating with his new neighbors. A good ethnic mix of characters.

Kellogg, S. *Mystery of the Stolen Blue Paint*. New York: Dial, 1982.
Belinda plans to paint a special blue picture but is interrupted by her cousin and his friends. She gives up and decides to pack away her art supplies. Where is the blue paint? The others do not have it. The mystery is solved when Belinda's dog Homer gives everyone a blue kiss.

Kessler, E., and Kessler, L. *Are You Square?* Garden City, N.Y.: Doubleday, 1966.
Square and round are emphasized, with other shapes introduced. The illustrations are fair, and the book relies on a strong story line.

Krauss, R. *I Want to Paint My Bathroom Blue*. New York: Harper & Row, 1956.
A boy's fantasy adventure with painting people and things different colors. Illustrated by Sendak, one of his earliest.

Kunhardt, D. *Pat the Bunny*. New York: Golden Book, 1962.
A multisensory experience for very young children. Look at the pictures, listen to the words, pat the bunny, and smell the scented illustration.

Lamorisse, A. *The Red Balloon*. Garden City, NY: Doubleday, 1956.
A classic that still appears on television. It is the tale of a young boy, Pascal, who lives in Paris and his encounters with his magical red balloon. There are many black-and-white photographs, with only a few color ones emphasizing red.

Lionni, L. *Colors to Talk About*. New York: Pantheon, 1985.
A small, sturdy book with cardboard pages and rounded edges. It is highly recommended for older infants, toddlers, and young preschoolers. There are no words. The book relies on attractive illustrations to show the antics of colorful mice.

————. *Little Blue and Little Yellow*. New York: Ivan Obolensky, Inc., 1979.
Depicts the adventures of torn colored paper shapes: Mama, Papa, and Child Blue. The book shows color

mixing. Little Blue hugged a friend named Little Yellow and they became as one—green. The story may be a bit contrived, but it is a good introduction to color mixing and will encourage readers to use their imagination and creativity.

———. *Matthew's Dream.* New York: Knopf, 1991.

An enchanting fable about a mouse who wants to become a painter. Explores the role of art and artist in shaping our vision and expanding our dreams.

———. *Swimmy.* New York: Pantheon Books, 1968.

Young children love Swimmy, a small, black orphan fish who comes to save the day. Just as important are the beautiful watercolor illustrations of sea creatures and seascapes. The words have been carefully chosen and are equally beautiful.

Lobel, A. *On Market Street.* New York: Greenwillow Books, 1981.

An A-to-Z picture book of old-fashioned sellers at market. Each seller is composed of the wares that he or she sells. For example, L is made up solely of lollipops. The book is colorful and a creative way to discuss shapes and composition, as well as the alphabet.

Loss, J. *What Is It? A Book of Photographic Puzzles.* Garden City, NY: Doubleday, 1974.

A series of puzzles. Each one starts with a photographic close-up. Can you guess what it is? Turn the page and see it as it usually appears at normal range. Clear black-and-white photography. Challenging for both young and older children.

Lund, D. H. *The Paint-Box Sea.* New York: McGraw-Hill, 1973.

The story of a brother and sister who explore the seashore to discover the real color of the ocean. Beautiful illustrations. Older children may be better able to relate to the older characters. Words are set in rhyme.

MacAgy, D., and MacAgy, E. *Going for a Walk with a Line—A Step into the World of Modern Art.* Garden City, NY: Doubleday, 1959.

Samples of the artwork of different artists are included to show different ways that the line has been used in art.

Martin, B., Jr., *Brown Bear, Brown Bear, What Do You See?* New York: Holt, Rinehart and Winston, 1967.

Children see a variety of animals, each one a different color, looking at them. Big, bold, colorful illustrations. Children will enjoy the repetitive, catchy rhyme.

O'Neill, M. *Hailstones and Halibut Bones.* Garden City, NY: Doubleday, 1961.

A very highly recommended book of poetry for all the different colors. Excellent and very appropriate for young children. This book is a must for any early childhood book collection.

Phillips, R. S., ed. *The Great Artists.* New York: Funk & Wagnalls, 1978.

A series of large paperback books on twenty-five artists. Each book in the series is composed of full-page reproductions with vital information concerning the artwork on the back of each. Information on each artist is in the introductory section. Prints can be removed, framed, and displayed.

Raboff, E. *Art for Children.* New York: Harper Collins Children's Books, 1987–1988.

A series. Each book focuses on one artist. The books on Picasso and Chagall provide beautiful color reproductions combined with simple text.

Reiss, J. J. *Colors.* Scarsdale, NY: Bradbury Press, 1969.

Different pages focus on different colors. The pictures are large, glossy, colorful, and done with a concern for good design. Young children will enjoy the colorful shapes.

———. *Shapes.* Scarsdale, NY: Bradbury Press, 1974.

Focuses on geometric shapes in the environment. Very well illustrated. Shapes are creatively combined to make different ones. Shapes are all around us.

Samton, S. W. *The World from My Window.* New York: Crown Publishers, 1985.

Can serve many purposes. Focuses on numbers, colors, and poetry. The book is beautifully illustrated in vibrant colors. The numbers one through ten and corresponding objects appear as seen from one window. The story line is set in rhyme.

Sazer, N. *What Do You Think I Saw? A Nonsense Number Book.* New York: Pantheon Books, 1976.

Introduces the numbers one to ten while describing in rhyme the unusual things a young rhino sees on the way to the train. The book is illustrated with animals done in watercolors.

Shapur, F. *Round and Round and Square.* London: Abelard-Schuman, 1972.

Illustrated with basic shapes in bright colors. Shows how common objects like sailboats and kites are composed of simple shapes. Identifying shapes in the night and city scenes will be more difficult, since they tend to be busy.

Shaw, C. G. *It Looked Like Spilt Milk*. New York: Harper & Row, 1947.

A classic. The story of a white blob that is searching for an identity. What can it be? The book shows how it can be many things, including spilt milk. It is hoped that children will see that their own drawn or painted shapes can also be many things. Still, the author ends on a close-ended note by stating that it was a cloud rather than spilt milk. Why couldn't it be all or none of the above?

Slobodkina, E. *Caps for Sale*. Reading, MA: Addison-Wesley, 1968.

A classic tale of a peddler, some monkeys, and their monkey business. Children love the suspense and antics. They also learn their colors from the peddler's checkered, gray, brown, blue, and red stacked caps.

Tudor, T. *Five Senses*. New York: Platt & Munk, 1978.

Tells the adventures of a little girl who uses all her senses on a farm. Set in the recent past. The illustrations are quite pretty, and the story may hold more appeal for girls than for boys.

Ventura, P. *Great Painters*. New York: G. P. Putnam's Sons, 1984.

A resource book rather than a storybook. There is no story, but rather an explanation of artistic styles. Children may enjoy looking through this book. Not all the pictures are large enough to show to the whole class during story time.

Weisgard, L. *Treasures to See*. New York: Harcourt, Brace & World, 1956.

Depicts a trip through an art museum. The pictures are illustrations rather than photographs. The book is dated, and the children appear as they did in the 1950s. Still, for the child who has never been to an art museum, it is a good start.

Wildsmith, B. *Fishes*. London: Oxford University Press, 1984.

A close-up look at a variety of fish illustrated in a rainbow of bright colors and set against an equally colorful background. You can see the artist's initial sketches and how the paint is washed over.

Wolff, R. J. *Feeling Blue*. New York: Charles Scribner's Sons, 1968.

A focus on the color blue. How do we make blue? How does blue make us feel? Where do we see blue in our world? What are the shades and tints of blue? The book is a good introduction to one primary color. The author has also written *Hello Yellow* and *Seeing Red* with an identical format.

Yenawine, P. *Stories; Colors; Lines; Shapes*. New York: Delacorte, 1991.

A series of four books on modern art created to help teach the basic vocabulary, including lines, colors, and shapes. Each book ends with brief background information that adults will find useful when talking with children about the paintings and sculptures reproduced in this series.

A Young Painter: The Life and Paintings of Wang Yani—China's Extraordinary Young Artist. New York: Scholastic, 1991.

Examines the life and works of Wang Yani, a Chinese girl who has received worldwide acclaim for her art. Yani began painting animals at age three.

Art Safety

MEAT TRAY MENACE?

Recycled meat trays serve many uses in early childhood programs. They can hold collage items or become the background for a junk collage. They can be used as paint containers if lined with paper towels for a print-making activity. They also make great frames.

It is now believed that plastic foam trays that once held any kind of raw meat or fish may carry bacteria that cause illness. Plastic foam meat trays are very porous and hold more bacteria and juices than clear plastic trays.

Why put the children at risk? What should be done? You can eliminate most of the bacteria by cleaning the trays antiseptically. The trays should be washed with soap and hot water, rinsed in a solution of two teaspoons of chlorine bleach per quart of water, and then rinsed again in warm water to remove the bleach residue. Or it might be simpler to use trays that held fruit, vegetables, or baked goods.

ART POISONING?

Many art supplies used by young children can be toxic. Examples include rubber cement, permanent felt-tip markers, pottery glazes, enamels, spray paints, lead-based supplies, and wheat wallpaper paste, among others. These toxic materials can be inhaled, ingested, or absorbed through the skin. Young children are at high risk for many reasons.

1. They are still growing and have a very rapid metabolic rate. They will absorb toxic materials into their bodies more readily than an adult.
2. Their brain, lungs, and nervous system are still forming and thus are at risk.
3. Young children have lowered body defenses.

4. Their lower body weight puts them at high risk, since a given quantity of a toxic material will be more concentrated in their bodies.
5. Young children may be impulsive, engage in thumb sucking and nail biting, have frequent hand-to-mouth contacts, and neither understand nor follow the necessary precautions.

ART SAFETY

Art can be a safe and pleasurable experience if guidelines are established and followed. Suggested guidelines for teachers follow.

1. Use judgment in providing staplers, staples, sharp scissors, tin cans, glitter, spray paint, toothpicks, hot plate, needles, pins, knives, and so on. Some young children are responsible and can be trusted to use these items at an early age with some supervision. Others may be too young (in developmental age or maturity) to understand the need for proper handling.
2. Take the time to discuss any potential hazards and dangers. Be honest and positive without dwelling on all the fatal possibilities. Focus on educating rather than frightening children.
3. Try out the art activity in advance. Is it safe? Can your particular group of children properly use the tools involved?
4. Demonstrate and model the proper way to use the tools. "This is the way to use a hole puncher. Sally now you show me how to use it." "Good, you used it the right way."
5. Supervise all art activities. Aides and parent volunteers can assist in supervision. Some activities will require closer and more direct supervision than others. Remember to anticipate the level of supervision needed when planning.

6. A table of art products to avoid and possible substitutes is found in Table 1.

7. The Art and Crafts Materials Institute has developed a voluntary program designed to promote safety in children's art materials. Look for and purchase those art products bearing their labels: AP for Approved Product or CP for Certified Product. The list of products with AP and CP label ratings is found in Table 2.

8. The label "nontoxic" is very misleading. According to present criteria, only materials that are acutely toxic merit being labeled toxic. Therefore "nontoxic" embraces a wide range of dangers from minimally to acutely toxic. Tests to determine toxicity are done on adult animals. A product considered nontoxic when tested on an adult rat may provoke a very different reaction in a young child.

9. Refuse donated art supplies unless the ingredients are known.

10. Do not use old art supplies. Older materials may be highly toxic. They may have been produced when ingredients were not listed on the label and criteria for toxicity were absent.

11. Insist that children clean up and wash their hands after doing art.

12. Food and drinks remain at the snack table or kitchen area and are not taken to the art center.

13. Children with open cuts, sores, or wounds that are not properly covered should not do art activities that involve potentially toxic supplies.

14. Parents of children with allergies, asthma, and other medical problems should consult their pediatrician regarding any limits on their child's use of art supplies.

15. Post the number of your local or state poison control center. Call your local hospital for the number. Have the product in hand when you dial so that you can quickly read off the ingredients from the label and take prompt action.

For further information contact:

Art Hazards Information Center
Center for Occupational Hazards
5 Beekman Street
New York, New York 10038
(212) 227-6220

Do Not Use	Substitutes
Dusts and Powders	
1. Clay in dry form. Powdered clay, which is easily inhaled, contains free silica and possible asbestos. Do not sand dry clay pieces or do other dust-producing activities.	1. Order talc-free, premixed clay. Wet mop or sponge surfaces thoroughly after using clay.
2. Ceramic glazes or copper enamels.	2. Use water-based paints instead of glazes. Teachers may water-proof pieces with shellac or varnish.
3. Cold water, fiber-reactive dyes or other commercial dyes.	3. Use vegetable and plant dyes (e.g., onion skins, tea, flowers) and food dyes.
4. Instant papier-mâchés (create inhalable dust and some may contain asbestos fibers, lead from pigments in colored printing inks, etc.).	4. Make papier-mâchés from black and white newspaper and library or white paste.
5. Powdered tempera colors (create inhalable dusts and some tempera colors contain toxic pigments, preservatives, etc.).	5. Use liquid paints or paints the teacher pre-mixes.
6. Pastels, chalks or dry markers that create dust.	6. Use crayons, oil pastels or dustless chalks.
Solvents	
1. Solvents (e.g., turpentine, toluene, rubber cement thinner) and solvent-containing materials (solvent-based inks, alkyd paints, rubber cement)	1. Use water-based products only.
2. Solvent-based silk screen and other printing inks.	2. Use water-based silk screen inks, block printing or stencil inks containing safe pigments.
3. Aerosol sprays.	3. Use water-based paints with brushes or spatter techniques.
4. Epoxy, instant glue, airplane glue or other solvent-based adhesives.	4. Use white glue or school paste.
5. Permanent felt tip markers which may contain toluene or other toxic solvents.	5. Use only watercolor markers.
Toxic Metals	
1. Stained glass projects using lead came, solder, flux, etc.	1. Use colored cellophane and black paper to simulate lead.
2. Arsenic, cadmium, chrome, mercury, lead, manganese, or other toxic metals which may occur in pigments, metal filings, metal enamels, glazes, metal casting, etc.	2. Get ingredient information or Material Safety Data Sheets on products which are uncertified to be certain they are free of toxic metals.
Miscellaneous	
1. Photographic chemicals.	1. Use blueprint paper and make sun grams.
2. Casting plaster. Creates dust and casting hands and body parts has resulted in serious burns.	2. Teacher can mix plaster in ventilated area or outdoors for sand casting and other safe projects.
3. Acid etches and pickling baths.	3. Should not use techniques employing these chemicals.

TABLE 1   Art Materials: Recommendations for Children Under 12   (Courtesy of Center for Occupational Hazards, *Children's Art Supplies Can Be Toxic,* Peltz and Rossol, 1986.)

PRODUCTS AUTHORIZED TO BEAR THE CP CERTIFIED PRODUCT SEAL,
THE AP APPROVED PRODUCT SEAL,
AND THE HL/NT HEALTH LABEL (NON-TOXIC) SEAL OF
THE CERTIFIED PRODUCTS AND CERTIFIED LABELING BUREAU OF
THE ART & CREATIVE MATERIALS INSTITUTE, INC. © 1997
100 Boylston Street, Suite 1050, Boston, MA 02116 617/426-6400

NON-TOXIC
OR
NO HEALTH LABELING REQUIRED

APRIL 1997

Products bearing the CP Certified Product Seal, the AP Approved Product Seal or the Health Label (Non-Toxic) Seal (HL/NT) of The Art & Creative Materials Institute, Inc. (ACMI) are certified in a program of toxicological evaluation by a medical expert to contain no materials in sufficient quantities to be toxic or injurious to humans or to cause acute or chronic health problems. This program is reviewed by ACMI's Toxicological Advisory Board. These products are certified by ACMI to be labeled in accordance with the chronic hazard labeling standard, ASTM D-4236, and Federal law, P.L. 100-695. In addition, products bearing the CP Seal meet specific requirements of material, workmanship, working qualities and color described in appropriate product standards issued by ACMI or other recognized standards organizations. Be sure to purchase products that bear the ACMI Seals!

PRODUCTS AND MANUFACTURERS	BRAND NAMES	CP SEAL	AP SEAL	HL/NT SEAL
ADHESIVES				
Glues				
Activa Products	MIGHTY TACKY			*
American Tombow	TOMBOW GLUE STICK	*		
American Tombow	TOMBOW MONO AQUA			*
American Tombow	TOMBOW MONO MULTI			*
Avery Dennison	GLUE STIC PERMANENT			*
Back Street, Inc.	ANITA'S DECOUPAGE GLUE			*
Binney & Smith	CRAYOLA			*
Binney & Smith	CRAYOLA WASHABLE GLITTER GLUE			*
Binney & Smith	JAZZY			*
Coats & Clark	J & P COATS CROCHET THREAD STIFFENER			*
Conros Corporation	KANGA ALL PURPOSE			*
Conros Corporation	KANGA CRAFT			*
Conros Corporation	KANGA OFFICE			*
Conros Corporation	KANGA STIFFY FABRIC STIFFENER	*		
Conros Corporation	KANGA WHITE			*
Conros Corporation	ROSS ALL PURPOSE			*
Conros Corporation	ROSS CRAFT			*
Conros Corporation	ROSS CRAFT STIFFY FABRIC STIFFENER			*
Conros Corporation	ROSS OFFICE			*
Conros Corporation	ROSS STIFFY FABRIC STIFFENER	*		
Conros Corporation	ROSS WHITE			*
Conros Corporation	ROSS-CONROS COLOURED PLAYTIME GLUE			*
Conros Corporation	ROSS-CONROS DURAFIX WHITE			*
Conros Corporation	ROSS-CONROS GLUE STICK			*
Conros Corporation	ROSS-CONROS KIDS GLUE			*
Conros Corporation	ROSS-CONROS MR. NATURAL SCHOOL GLUE			*
Conros Corporation	ROSS-CONROS KIDS' NATURAL SCHOOL GLUE			*
Conros Corporation	ROSS PURPLE GLUE STICK/KIDSTIK			*
Conros Corporation	SHOPRITE ALL PURPOSE			*
CVS	CVS ART & CRAFT GLUE			*
CVS	CVS CLEAR GLUE			*
CVS	CVS COLOR GLUE			*
CVS	CVS GLUE STICK			*
CVS	CVS SCHOOL GLUE			*
CVS	CVS WHITE GLUE			*
Daler-Rowney	ROWNEY RABBIT SKIN		*	
Delta Tech. Coatings	DECORATIVE STIFFENER			*
Delta Tech. Coatings	DELTA PAPER APPLIQUE			*
Delta Tech. Coatings	FLORAL GLUE			*
Delta Tech. Coatings	JEWEL GLUE			*
Delta Tech. Coatings	PHOTO TO FABRIC GLUE			*
Delta Tech. Coatings	QUICK 'N TACKY			*
Delta Tech. Coatings	RENAISSANCE FOIL ADHESIVE			*
Delta Tech. Coatings	SOBO			*
Delta Tech. Coatings	STENCIL MAGIC ADHESIVE			*
Delta Tech. Coatings	STITCHLESS			*
Delta Tech. Coatings	VELVERETTE			*
Delta Tech. Coatings	WOODWIZ			*
Dixon Ticonderoga	DIXON GLUE STICK	*		
Dixon Ticonderoga	PRANG GLUE PEN	*		
Dixon Ticonderoga	PRANG GLUE STICK	*		
Dixon Ticonderoga	PRANG ROLL-ON	*		
Dixon Ticonderoga	HOLDTU			*

PRODUCTS AND MANUFACTURERS	BRAND NAMES	CP SEAL	AP SEAL	HL/NT SEAL
ADHESIVES (continued)				
Glues (continued)				
D.O.T. Adventures	DOTS GLUE PEN			*
Elmer's Products/Borden	ELMER'S ADVANCED FORMULA OFFICE GLUE			*
Elmer's Products/Borden	ELMER'S ALL-PURPOSE GLUE STICK			*
Elmer's Products/Borden	ELMER'S BRAIN STUFF GOOEY GLUE GEL			*
Elmer's Products/Borden	ELMER'S CHINA/GLASS CEMENT			*
Elmer's Products/Borden	ELMER'S CRAFT BOND I			*
Elmer's Products/Borden	ELMER'S CRAFT BOND EXTRA STRENGTH GLUE STICK			*
Elmer's Products/Borden	ELMER'S CRAFT BOND FABRIC GLUE			*
Elmer's Products/Borden	ELMER'S CRAFT BOND PAPER CRAFT GLUE GEL			*
Elmer's Products/Borden	ELMER'S CRAFT BOND TACKY GLUE			*
Elmer's Products/Borden	ELMER'S CRAFT BOND WREATH & WOOD GLUE			*
Elmer's Products/Borden	ELMER'S EXTRA STRENGTH ALL-PURPOSE GLUE STICK			*
Elmer's Products/Borden	ELMER'S EXTRA STRENGTH OFFICE GLUE STICK			*
Elmer's Products/Borden	ELMER'S FASHION COLOR GLUE STICK			*
Elmer's Products/Borden	ELMER'S FUN DIMENSIONS FUNK-A-DELIC			*
Elmer's Products/Borden	ELMER'S FUN DIMENSIONS GLITTER GEL			*
Elmer's Products/Borden	ELMER'S FUN DIMENSIONS ICE-A-DELIC			*
Elmer's Products/Borden	ELMER'S GLITTER GLUE			*
Elmer's Products/Borden	ELMER'S GLUCOLOR			*
Elmer's Products/Borden	ELMER'S GLUE-ALL			*
Elmer's Products/Borden	ELMER'S MUCILAGE			*
Elmer's Products/Borden	ELMER'S NO-RUN SCHOOL GLUE			*
Elmer's Products/Borden	ELMER'S PROF. CARPENTER'S WOOD FILLER			*
Elmer's Products/Borden	ELMER'S PROF. CARPENTER'S WOOD GLUE			*
Elmer's Products/Borden	ELMER'S PROF. CARPENTER'S GLUE FOR DARKER WOOD			*
Elmer's Products/Borden	ELMER'S SAF-T CONTACT CEMENT			*
Elmer's Products/Borden	ELMER'S SCHOOL GLUE			*
Elmer's Products/Borden	ELMER'S SCHOOL GLUE GEL			*
Elmer's Products/Borden	ELMER'S SCHOOL GLUE STICK			*
Elmer's Products/Borden	ELMER'S TACK ADHESIVE PUTTY			*
Elmer's Products/Borden	ELMER'S WASHABLE SCHOOL GLUE			*
Elmer's Products/Borden	ELMER'S WEATHER-TITE WOOD GLUE			*
Embossing Arts Co.	EMBOSSING ARTS PEN-O-GLUE			*
Fiesta Colors	JEWELING GLUE			*
M. Grumbacher, Inc.	ACCENT TACKY			*
Hero Arts Rubber Stamp	HERO ARTS GLUE STICK			*
Hunt Manufacturing	QUICK-STICK PERMANENT			*
Hunt Manufacturing	QUICK-STICK REPOSITIONABLE			*
Itoya of America, Ltd.	O'GLUE			*
Kinko's	KINKO'S GLUE STICK	*		
Kuretake Co., Ltd.	KURETAKE OYATTO-NORI MB			*
Kuretake Co., Ltd.	KURETAKE OYATTO-NORI SB	*		
Kuretake Co., Ltd.	ZIG 2WAY GLUE B			*
Kuretake Co., Ltd.	ZIG 2WAY GLUE B&B			*
Kuretake Co., Ltd.	ZIG 2WAY GLUE MB			*
Kuretake Co., Ltd.	ZIG 2WAY GLUE MSB-15			*
Kuretake Co., Ltd.	ZIG 2WAY GLUE MSB-30			*

 # Some products in this line do not bear the CP, AP or Health Label (Non-Toxic) Seal.

TABLE 2   (Courtesy of The Art and Creative Materials Institute, Inc.)

PRODUCTS AND MANUFACTURERS	BRAND NAMES	CP SEAL	AP SEAL	HL/NT SEAL
ADHESIVES (continued)				
Glues (continued)				
Kuretake Co., Ltd.	ZIG 2WAY GLUE SB		*	
Kuretake Co., Ltd.	ZIG CHANGIN' GLUE MB		*	
Kuretake Co., Ltd.	ZIG CHANGIN' GLUE SB		*	
Kuretake Co., Ltd.	ZIG DECO-ART STICK F		*	
Kuretake Co., Ltd.	ZIG MEMO-STICK B		*	
Kuretake Co., Ltd.	ZIG MEMO-STICK B&B		*	
Kuretake Co., Ltd.	ZIG MEMO-STICK MB		*	
Kuretake Co., Ltd.	ZIG MEMO-STICK SB		*	
Leech Products, Inc.	TAP-N-GLUE COLORS		*	
LePage's Incorporated	LEPAGE'S ARTS & CRAFTS		*	
LePage's Incorporated	LEPAGE'S CLEAR GLUE		*	
LePage's Incorporated	LEPAGE'S COLOR GLUE		*	
LePage's Incorporated	LEPAGE'S GLUE STICK		*	
LePage's Incorporated	LEPAGE'S SCHOOL GLUE		*	
LePage's Incorporated	LEPAGE'S WHITE GLUE		*	
Lindow Mfg.	LINDCO SCHOOL	*		
Lindow Mfg.	LINDCO WHITE		*	
Omega Chalk Factory	OMEGA WHITE	*		
Panline USA/Alex	ALEX WHITE	*		
PDM Adhesives Corp.	LEEHO 2 IN 1 GLUE		*	
PDM Adhesives Corp.	LEEHO 2 IN 1 GLUE - BLUE		*	
PDM Adhesives Corp.	LEEHO EASY PAPER GLUE		*	
PDM Adhesives Corp.	LEEHO GLUE STICK		*	
PDM Adhesives Corp.	LEEHO MULTI-PURPOSE WHITE		*	
Pentel of America	ER101 ROLL 'N GLUE		*	
Personal Stamp Exchg.	PSX 2-WAY GLUE PEN		*	
Plaid Enterprises	FABRIC STIFFENER		*	
Plaid Enterprises	FOUNDER'S CRAFT ADHESIVE		*	
Plaid Enterprises	PETAL PORCELAIN		*	
Plaid Enterprises	STIFFY		*	
Portage	ARTWAX		*	
Portage	SUPERTACKY ARTWAX		*	
Prod. Quimicos Servis	ARTS & CRAFTS		*	
Prod. Quimicos Servis	CLEAR GLUE		*	
Prod. Quimicos Servis	COLOR GLUE		*	
Prod. Quimicos Servis	GLUE STICK		*	
Prod. Quimicos Servis	JUNIOR COLOR GLUE		*	
Prod. Quimicos Servis	JUNIOR SCHOOL GLUE		*	
Prod. Quimicos Servis	KIDS GLUE		*	
Prod. Quimicos Servis	SCHOOL GLUE		*	
Prod. Quimicos Servis	WHITE GLUE		*	
Pumpkin Masters Inc.	PUMPKIN PAINTING KIT GLUE		*	
Rose Art Industries	GOLD & SILVER JEWELRY MAKER GLUE		*	
Rose Art Industries	ROSE ART DISAPPEARING GLUE STICK		*	
Rose Art Industries	ROSE ART GLITTER GLUE PEN		*	
Rose Art Industries	ROSE ART GLITTER MAGIC		*	
Rose Art Industries	ROSE ART GLUE STICK		*	
Rose Art Industries	ROSE ART JUMBO WASHABLE GLUE STICK		*	
Rose Art Industries	ROSE ART SAVE-A-PUZZLE		*	
Rose Art Industries	ROSE ART WASHABLE GLITTER GLUE PEN		*	
Rose Art Industries	ROSE ART WASHABLE GLUE STICK	*		
Rose Art Industries	XUXA GLITTER MAGIC	*		
Sax Arts & Crafts	TRUE TACK SUPER THICK WHITE		*	
Daniel Smith, Inc.	DANIEL SMITH RABBIT SKIN GLUE		*	
Daniel Smith, Inc.	DANIEL SMITH WHEAT PASTE		*	
Tolin' Station	METAL SCULPT MEDIUM		*	
Tonka Corporation	EZ-2-DO IMAGE MAKER		*	
Union Rubber, Inc.	BEST-TEST GRADE SCHOOL		*	
Yasutomo & Co.	Y&C GLUE-IT		*	
Z-Barten Productions	JIMMY JEM'S STICKY GLUE PEN		*	
Polymer				
Binney & Smith	CRAYOLA ART & CRAFT GLUE	*		
Ceramichrome, Inc.	ED'S GLUE		*	
Conros Corporation	AQUA RUBBER CEMENT GLUE		*	
Conros Corporation	ART/GRAPHIC RUBBER CEMENT GLUE		*	
Conros Corporation	KANGA RUBBER CEMENT GLUE		*	
Conros Corporation	OFFICE RUBBER CEMENT GLUE		*	
Conros Corporation	ROSS MAGIC SCHOOL GLUE		*	
Conros Corporation	ROSS MAGIC SCHOOL GLUE GEL		*	
Conros Corporation	ROSS MUCILAGE		*	
Conros Corporation	ROSS-CONROS RUBBER CEMENT GLUE		*	
Conros Corporation	SAFE-T RUBBER CEMENT GLUE		*	
ADHESIVES (continued)				
Polymer (continued)				
Conros Corporation	SCHOOL RUBBER CEMENT GLUE		*	
Lakeside Plastics, Inc.	TRI-TIX RUBBER GLUE		*	
Paper Conversions	GEL-TAC		*	
Plaid Enterprises	MOD PODGE GLOSS		*	
Plaid Enterprises	MOD PODGE MATTE		*	
Plaid Enterprises	MOD PODGE PUZZLE SAVER		*	
Rich Art Color Co.	RICH GLU WHITE GLUE		*	
School Paste				
Binney & Smith	CRAYOLA WASHABLE WHITE		*	
Binney & Smith	CRAYOLA WHITE	*		
Binney & Smith	CRAYOLA WHITE (TUBE)	*		
Conros Corporation	ROSS-CONROS KIDS PASTE		*	
Elmer's Products/Borden	ELMER'S SNO-DRIFT PASTE		*	
Lindow Mfg.	LINDCO	*		
Rich Art Color Co.	RICH ART		*	
AIRBRUSH COLORS, MEDIUMS & ACCESSORIES				
Badger Airbrush	AIR OPAQUE		*	
Badger Airbrush	AIR OPAQUE CLEANER		*	
Badger Airbrush	AIR OPAQUE GLOSSY VARNISH		*	
Badger Airbrush	AIR OPAQUE MATTE VARNISH		*	
Badger Airbrush	AIR OPAQUE PEARLS		*	
Badger Airbrush	AIR-TEX CLEANER		*	
Badger Airbrush	AIR-TEX FABRIC		*	
Badger Airbrush	MODELFLEX CLEANER		*	
Binney & Smith	LIQUITEX AIRBRUSH MEDIUM		*	
Binney & Smith	PRO MODELER AIRBRUSH THINNER	*		
Binney & Smith	REVELL AIRBRUSH THINNER			*
Creative Art Products	STROKEMASTER WATERCOLOR		*	
Golden Artist Colors	GOLDEN AIRBRUSH COLORS			*
Golden Artist Colors	GOLDEN AIRBRUSH MEDIUM		*	
Hansa-Technik GmbH	HANSA AEROPRO		*	
Holbein Works Ltd.	AEROFLASH			*
Maimeri USA	AIR PRO		*	
Maimeri USA	AIR PRO CLEANER		*	
Maimeri USA	AIR PRO MEDIUM -GLOSS FINISH		*	
Maimeri USA	AIR PRO MEDIUM -MATTE FINISH		*	
Rose Art Industries	POWER RANGERS AIRBRUSH COLORS		*	
Royal Sovereign	MAGIC COLOR			*
Salis International	DR. PH. MARTIN'S FLUORESCENT ACRYLIC TEXTILE COLORS		*	
Salis International	DR. PH. MARTIN'S IRIDESCENT		*	
Salis International	DR. PH. MARTIN'S READY-TEX TEXTILE COLORS		*	
Salis International	DR. PH. MARTIN'S SPECTRALITE		*	
Salis International	DR. PH. MARTIN'S SPECTRALITE CLEANER		*	
Salis International	DR. PH. MARTIN'S SPECTRALITE METALLIC		*	
Salis International	DR. PH. MARTIN'S SYNCHROMATIC TRANSPARENTS		*	
Salis International	DR. PH. MARTIN'S TWILIGHT GLOW	*		
H. Schmincke & Co.	AERO COLOR SERIES 28 AIRBRUSH COLORS		*	
Winsor & Newton	DESIGNERS BRILLIANT WATER COLOURS #	*		
Winsor & Newton	DESIGNERS LIQUID ACRYLIC COLOURS		*	
BLOCK PRINTING INKS & MEDIUMS				
Oil Base				
Creative Art Products	SHIVA		*	
Hunt Manufacturing	SPEEDBALL		*	
Daniel Smith, Inc.	DANIEL SMITH RELIEF INKS		*	
Water Soluble				
Cardinal School Sply.	CARDINAL		*	
Creative Art Products	DICK BLICK		*	
Creative Art Products	SHIVA		*	
Daler-Rowney	ROWNEY BLOCK PRINTING COLOUR DRIER	*		
Demco Manufacturing	DEMCO BLOCKPRINT		*	
Graphic Chemical & Ink	GRAPHIC		*	
Hunt Manufacturing	SPEEDBALL		*	
NASCO International	NASCO BULK-INK		*	

Some products in this line do not bear the CP, AP or Health Label (Non-Toxic) Seal.

TABLE 2   (continued)

BLOCK PRINTING INKS & MEDIUMS (continued)

Water Soluble (continued)

PRODUCTS AND MANUFACTURERS	BRAND NAMES	CP SEAL	AP SEAL	HL/NT SEAL
Pyramid Art Supply	PYRA-PRINT WATER BASE		*	
Rock Paint Distrib'g	HANDY ART		*	
Rock Paint Distrib'g	HANDY ART FLUORESCENT		*	
Sax Arts & Crafts	TRUE COLOR		*	
Sax Arts & Crafts	VERSABLOCK		*	
Sax Arts & Crafts	VERSABLOCK FLUORESCENT		*	
Triarco Arts & Crafts	TRI-INK		*	

BRUSH CARE PRODUCTS

PRODUCTS AND MANUFACTURERS	BRAND NAMES	CP SEAL	AP SEAL	HL/NT SEAL
Ceramichrome, Inc.	DECO MAGIC	*		
Delta Tech. Coatings	STENCIL MAGIC BRUSH CLEANER	*		
General Pencil Co.	THE MASTERS ARTIST BRUSH CLEANER B&J ORIGINAL FORMULA	*		
M. Grumbacher, Inc.	GRUMBACHER BRUSH SOAP	*		
Hendrix Enterprises	ARTIST BRUSH CLEANER & CONDITIONER			
J. W. Etc.	FORMULA II	*		
Loew-Cornell	BETTER WAY BRUSH CLEANING FLUID FOR ACRYLIC PAINTS			
Loew-Cornell	BETTER WAY ONE-STEP FOR OILS	*		
Loew-Cornell	BRUSH CLEANER FOR ACRYLIC PAINTS	*		
Martin/F. Weber Co.	JENKINS FLORAL BRUSH CONDITIONER	*		
Martin/F. Weber Co.	PRISCILLA'S BRUSH CREME	*		

BRUSHES

PRODUCTS AND MANUFACTURERS	BRAND NAMES	CP SEAL	AP SEAL	HL/NT SEAL
Lion Pencil Co., Ltd.	CRAYON FACTORY		*	
Lion Pencil Co., Ltd.	LION		*	
Oasis Art & Craft Prod.	HOBBYBRUSH		*	
Oasis Art & Craft Prod.	SINHEUNG PAINT BRUSH		*	
Palmer Paint Products	PALMER'S #2		*	
Sargent Art	SARGENT		*	

CANVAS

PRODUCTS AND MANUFACTURERS	BRAND NAMES	CP SEAL	AP SEAL	HL/NT SEAL
Fostport, Inc.	YARKA TRIPLE-PRIMED CANVAS		*	

CERAMICS, SPECIALTY PRODUCTS

PRODUCTS AND MANUFACTURERS	BRAND NAMES	CP SEAL	AP SEAL	HL/NT SEAL
American Art Clay	AMACO AMACOTE	*		
American Art Clay	AMACO CASTING COMPOUND	*		
American Art Clay	AMACO GUM SOLUTION	*		
American Art Clay	AMACO KILN WASH	*		
American Art Clay	AMACO SP-MAGIC MENDER	*		
American Art Clay	AMACO POTTERY PLASTER	*		
American Art Clay	AMACO RUBBER LATEX	*		
American Art Clay	AMACO SETSTONE	*		
American Art Clay	AMACO SP-SNOW FLUFF	*		
American Art Clay	AMACO SP/TL 1 TEXTURIZER	*		
American Art Clay	AMACO WAX RESIST	*		
Caldex Enterprises	BON ARTISTE GLITTER GALORE	*		
Caldex Enterprises	BON ARTISTE SNOW-TEX	*		
Caldex Enterprises	BON ARTISTE STONE-TEX	*		
Caldex Enterprises	#801 OLD WORLD ART RED BASECOAT	*		
Caldex Enterprises	#802 OLD WORLD ART ADHESIVE SIZE	*		
Ceramichrome, Inc.	BRUSH 'N BLEND	*		
Ceramichrome, Inc.	CLAY CARVE	*		
Ceramichrome, Inc.	DECOART AMERICANA BRUSH-ON SEALER	*		
Ceramichrome, Inc.	FABRIC PAINTING MEDIUM	*		
Ceramichrome, Inc.	GLAZE CONDITIONER	*		
Ceramichrome, Inc.	GLO-IT	*		
Ceramichrome, Inc.	LIQUID KILN WASH	*		
Ceramichrome, Inc.	LIQUID MENDER	*		
Ceramichrome, Inc.	MEDIA	*		
Ceramichrome, Inc.	NON-FIRED SNOW	*		
Ceramichrome, Inc.	PLASTICIZER	*		
Ceramichrome, Inc.	SCULPTURE PASTE	*		
Ceramichrome, Inc.	SNOW TEX	*		
Ceramichrome, Inc.	THIXENER	*		
Ceramichrome, Inc.	WAX-TEX	*		
Ceramichrome, Inc.	WEATHERED WOOD	*		
Fiesta Colors	IRIS STARDUST	*		
Fiesta Colors	JET GLEAM	*		

CERAMICS, SPECIALTY PRODUCTS (continued)

PRODUCTS AND MANUFACTURERS	BRAND NAMES	CP SEAL	AP SEAL	HL/NT SEAL
Gare, Inc.	FINGER MINI-METALLICS		*	
Gare, Inc.	FIXALL		*	
Gare, Inc.	GLITTER-IT		*	
Gare, Inc.	HI-LO		*	
Gare, Inc.	MASQUE ALL		*	
Gare, Inc.	MIXIT		*	
Gare, Inc.	NO FIRE SNOW		*	
Gare, Inc.	RUB N GLO KIT #1		*	
Gare, Inc.	RUB N GLO KIT #2		*	
Gare, Inc.	SHADE-IT		*	
Gare, Inc.	SOFT TOUCH PASTELS		*	
Gare, Inc.	SPECIALTY GLAZE		*	
Gare, Inc.	SY-KRAKKLE IT		*	
Gare, Inc.	TEXTURE POWDER		*	
Gare, Inc.	WAX RESIST		*	
Minn/Midwest Clay	CHOXILS		*	
Minn/Midwest Clay	KILN WASH (POWDER)		*	
Minn/Midwest Clay	POTTER'S PAD		*	
Minn/Midwest Clay	POTTER'S PAD REFILLS		*	
Minn/Midwest Clay	WAX POTTER'S PENS		*	
Minn/Midwest Clay	WAX RESIST		*	

CHALKS

Charcoal

PRODUCTS AND MANUFACTURERS	BRAND NAMES	CP SEAL	AP SEAL	HL/NT SEAL
ColArt International	CONTE-A-PARIS COMPRESSED			*
Creative Art Products	DICK BLICK		*	
Empire Berol USA	BEROL CHARCOAL PENCIL		*	
Fostport, Inc.	YARKA		*	
Fostport, Inc.	YARKA NATURAL CHARCOAL		*	
Holbein Works Ltd.	HOLBEIN CARBON			*
Jack Richeson & Co.	DANIELLE ARTISTS		*	
School Mate, Inc.	CHARCOAL SQUARE PASTELS		*	

Extruded Colored (For Chalkboard)

PRODUCTS AND MANUFACTURERS	BRAND NAMES	CP SEAL	AP SEAL	HL/NT SEAL
Binney & Smith (Canada)	CRAYOLA SANIGENE		*	
Dixon Ticonderoga	HYGA-COLOR		*	
Dixon Ticonderoga	LOONEY TUNES ASSORTED	*	*	
J. L. Hammett Co.	HAMMETT'S		*	
Omega Chalk Factory	OMEGA		*	
Omyacolor, Inc.	ARTACOLOR		*	
Omyacolor, Inc.	3B BLACKBOARD BEST		*	
Omyacolor, Inc.	OMYACOLOR		*	
Omyacolor, Inc.	ROBERCOLOR		*	
Panline USA/Alex	ALEX DUSTLESS		*	
Quartet Manufacturing	OMEGA		*	
Rose Art Industries	ROSE ART DUSTLESS		*	
Sargent Art	SARGENT		*	
School Mate, Inc.	SCHOOL MATE		*	
Standard Stationery	STANDARD'S DUSTLESS		*	

Extruded Sightsaving (For Chalkboard)

PRODUCTS AND MANUFACTURERS	BRAND NAMES	CP SEAL	AP SEAL	HL/NT SEAL
Binney & Smith	CRAYOLA ANTI-DUST		*	
Binney & Smith	CRAYOLA E-Z-SYTE		*	
Binney & Smith (Canada)	CRAYOLA SANIGENE		*	
Dixon Ticonderoga	PRANG HYGIEIA FORSYTE	*	*	
Dixon Ticonderoga	PRANG HYGIEIA VELVETEX	*	*	
J. L. Hammett Co.	HAMMETT'S		*	
Omyacolor, Inc.	ARTACOLOR		*	
Omyacolor, Inc.	3B BLACKBOARD BEST		*	
Omyacolor, Inc.	OMYACOLOR		*	
Omyacolor, Inc.	ROBERCOLOR		*	
Quartet Manufacturing	ALPHASITE		*	
S. P. Richard Co.	SPARCO		*	
Sargent Art	SARGENT		*	
School Mate, Inc.	SCHOOL MATE		*	

Extruded White (For Chalkboard)

PRODUCTS AND MANUFACTURERS	BRAND NAMES	CP SEAL	AP SEAL	HL/NT SEAL
Binney & Smith	CRAYOLA-AN-DU-SEPTIC			*
Binney & Smith	CRAYOLA ANTI-DUST		*	
Binney & Smith (Canada)	CRAYOLA SANIGENE		*	
Binney & Smith (Canada)	CRAYOLA SWAN		*	
Dixon Ticonderoga	DOVERCLIFF		*	
Dixon Ticonderoga	LOONEY TUNES		*	
Dixon Ticonderoga	PRANG HYGIEIA		*	
J. L. Hammett Co.	HAMMETT'S		*	
Omega Chalk Factory	OMEGA		*	

Some products in this line do not bear the CP, AP or Health Label (Non-Toxic) Seal.

TABLE 2 (continued)

CHALKS (continued)

Extruded White (For Chalkboard) (continued)

PRODUCTS AND MANUFACTURERS	BRAND NAMES	CP SEAL	AP SEAL	HL/NT SEAL
Omyacolor, Inc.	ARTACOLOR	*		
Omyacolor, Inc.	3B BLACKBOARDBEST	*		
Omyacolor, Inc.	OMYACOLOR	*		
Omyacolor, Inc.	ROBERCOLOR	*		
Panline USA/Alex	ALEX DUSTLESS	*		
Quartet Manufacturing	ALPHA	*		
S. P. Richard Co.	SPARCO	*		
Rose Art Industries	ROSE ART DUSTLESS	*		
Sargent Art	SARGENT	*		
School Mate, Inc.	SCHOOLMATE	*		
Standard Stationery	STANDARD'S DUSTLESS	*		

Extruded Colored (For Paper and Crafts)

PRODUCTS AND MANUFACTURERS	BRAND NAMES	CP SEAL	AP SEAL	HL/NT SEAL
Binney & Smith	CRAYOLA COLORED ART	*		
Binney & Smith (Canada)	CRAYOLA COLOREX	*		
Dixon Ticonderoga	PRANG FLUORESCENT PASTELLO	*		
Dixon Ticonderoga	PRANG FLUORESCENT POSTER PASTELLO	*		
Dixon Ticonderoga	PRANG PASTELLO	*		
Dixon Ticonderoga	PRANG POSTER PASTELLO	*		

Molded Colored (For Chalkboard)

PRODUCTS AND MANUFACTURERS	BRAND NAMES	CP SEAL	AP SEAL	HL/NT SEAL
Binney & Smith	CRAYOLA		*	
Binney & Smith	CRAYOLA FLUORESCENT SIDEWALK		*	
Chemitron USA Corp.	COLORUP	*		
Dixon Ticonderoga	LOONEY TUNES WASHABLE SIDEWALK	*		
Dixon Ticonderoga	LOONEY TUNES BUCKET OF SIDEWALK	*		
Dixon Ticonderoga	MR. CHALKY	*		
Dixon Ticonderoga	PRANG GLOW IN THE DARK		*	
Dixon Ticonderoga	PRANG SIDEWALK	*		
Dixon Ticonderoga	PRANG WASHABLE SIDEWALK	*		
Milton Bradley	PACK 'N GO CHALK	*		
NES Arnold Inc.	SCOLA CHUNKI CHALKS		*	
Rose Art Industries	COLORON	*		
Rose Art Industries	KODAK	*		
Rose Art Industries	ROSE ART	*		
Rose Art Industries	ROSE ART BUCKET-FULLA WASHABLE SIDEWALK	*		
Rose Art Industries	ROSE ART GLITTER CHALK		*	
Rose Art Industries	ROSE ART GLOW	*		
Rose Art Industries	ROSE ART WASHABLE SIDEWALK	*		
Rose Art Industries	TUB FULLA CHALK, MARBLE CHALK		*	
Walbuck Crayon Co.	WALBUCK CHALKY CHUNKS		*	
Walbuck Crayon Co.	WALBUCK SIDEWALK CHALK		*	
Western Publishing	COLOR EXPRESS WASHABLE SIDEWALK	*		
Western Publishing	MERRIGOLD WASHABLE SIDEWALK	*		

Molded White (For Chalkboard)

PRODUCTS AND MANUFACTURERS	BRAND NAMES	CP SEAL	AP SEAL	HL/NT SEAL
Binney & Smith	CRAYOLA	*		
Chemitron USA Corp.	COLORUP	*		
Dixon Ticonderoga	PRANG SIDEWALK	*		
Dixon Ticonderoga	WALTHAM	*		
Rose Art Industries	NU-CHALK		*	
Rose Art Industries	ROSE ART	*		

Molded Colored (For Paper and Crafts)

PRODUCTS AND MANUFACTURERS	BRAND NAMES	CP SEAL	AP SEAL	HL/NT SEAL
Binney & Smith	CRAYOLA DRAWING	*		
Binney & Smith	CRAYOLA POSTER	*		
Binney & Smith	CRAYOLA SIDEWALK		*	
Dixon Ticonderoga	AMBRITE	*		
Dixon Ticonderoga	FREART	*		
Dixon Ticonderoga	LECTURERS	*		
Dixon Ticonderoga	PRANG COLOR		*	
Dixon Ticonderoga	PRANG FLUORESCENT LECTURES	*		
Rose Art Industries	NU-CHALK		*	
School Mate, Inc.	SCHOOL MATE COLORED DRAWING CHALK	*		

CLAYS

Modeling (Permanently Plastic, Non-Hardening)

PRODUCTS AND MANUFACTURERS	BRAND NAMES	CP SEAL	AP SEAL	HL/NT SEAL
American Art Clay	AMACO FLORAL			*
American Art Clay	AMACO PLAST-I-CLAY			*
American Art Clay	ARTONE VENUS A-18			*
American Art Clay	HBX-2 INDUSTRIAL STYLING			*
American Art Clay	PERMOPLAST		*	
Art Chemical Products	KLEAN KLAY		*	
Binney & Smith	CHANGEABLE SILLY PUTTY			*
Binney & Smith	CLAYOLA		*	
Binney & Smith	CRAYOLA CLAYTIME CLAY			*
Binney & Smith	CRYSTAL PUTTY			*
Binney & Smith	FLUORESCENT SILLY PUTTY			*
Binney & Smith	GLITTER SILLY PUTTY			*
Binney & Smith	GLOW IN THE DARK SILLY PUTTY			*
Binney & Smith	SILLY PUTTY			*
Binney & Smith (Canada)	GLOW IN THE DARK SILLY PUTTY			*
Binney & Smith (Canada)	SILLY PUTTY			*
Chavant, Inc.	CHAVANT LE BEAU TOUCHE		*	
Chavant, Inc.	CHAVANT NSP		*	
Chavant, Inc.	CHAVANT PROF. PLASTELINE		*	
Colorantes Importados	COLORITOS	*		
Dixon Ticonderoga	PRANG		*	
J.L. Hammett Co.	HAMMETT'S		*	
Jovi, S.A.	PLASTILINA			*
The Nature Company	THE NATURE COMPANY	*		
Omyacolor, Inc.	ARTACOLOR	*		
Omyacolor, Inc.	BIONATURA	*		
Omyacolor, Inc.	PLASTICOLOR	*		
Panline USA/Alex	ALEX	*		
Rose Art Industries	COLORON	*		
Rose Art Industries	PLASTICINE	*		
Rose Art Industries	ROSE ART	*		
Rose Art Industries	ROSE ART 8 COLOR MODELING SET		*	
Rose Art Industries	ROSE ART FLUORESCENT			*
Rose Art Industries	ROSE ART SOLID COLORS		*	
Sargent Art	SARGENT	*		
School Mate, Inc.	PYRAMID	*		
School Mate, Inc.	SCHOOL MATE	*		
Van Aken Internat'l	PLASTELENE	*		
Vinci de Mexico	MODELINA			*
Will Vinton Prod.	CLAYMATION CLAY	*		

Modeling (Self-Hardening)

PRODUCTS AND MANUFACTURERS	BRAND NAMES	CP SEAL	AP SEAL	HL/NT SEAL
A & K Universal Mktg.	CREATUS			*
Activa Products, Inc.	INCREDIBLE WORKABLE WAX			*
American Art Clay	AMACO MARBLEX			*
American Art Clay	AMACO MEXICAN POTTERY			*
American Art Clay	AMACO POTPOURRI MELTS			*
Binney & Smith	CRAYOLA WETSET			*
Creative Paperclay Co.	CREATIVE PAPERCLAY			*
Creative Paperclay Co.	PEARL PAPERCLAY			*
Eberhard Faber GmbH	EFAPLAST			*
Eberhard Faber GmbH	HOLZY			*
G.O.T. Trading Co.	KNEAD-O			*
Jovi, S.A.	ENDURECIBLE			*
Minn/Midwest Clay	AIR FIRE			*
Minn/Midwest Clay	AIR FIRE PREMIUM			*
Minn/Midwest Clay	RAINBOW			*
Minn/Midwest Clay	RAINBOW AIR-DRY			*
Minn/Midwest Clay	RAINBOW GRAY WITH FIBER			*
Minn/Midwest Clay	RAINBOW SELF-HARDENING			*
Oasis Art & Craft Prod.	WEATHER HOUSE/FRAME MOULDING SET			*
Omyacolor, Inc.	CRAZY DOUGH!			*
Omyacolor, Inc.	PLASTIBO			*
Omyacolor, Inc.	PLASTIROC			*
Padico Co., Ltd.	CRAFTY			*
Padico Co., Ltd.	FORMO			*
Padico Co., Ltd.	LA DOLL			*
Padico Co., Ltd.	PREMIER			*
Reeves & Poole Group	SELF-SET			*
Rose Art Industries	ALPHABET FACTORY SUPER STUFF		*	
Rose Art Industries	BEADTASTIC BEAD DESIGNER SUPER STUFF		*	
Rose Art Industries	BEAUTIFUL BIRDS SUPER STUFF		*	

Some products in this line do not bear the CP, AP or Health Label (Non-Toxic) Seal.

TABLE 2   (continued)

CLAYS (continued)

PRODUCTS AND MANUFACTURERS	BRAND NAMES	CP SEAL	AP SEAL	HL/NT SEAL
Modeling (Self-Hardening) (continued)				
Rose Art Industries	GARGOYLES FIGURE MAKER SUPER STUFF			*
Rose Art Industries	GODZILLA FIGURE MAKER SUPER STUFF			*
Rose Art Industries	GLOW BUG MAKER SUPER STUFF			*
Rose Art Industries	GOLD JEWELRY MAKER SUPER STUFF			*
Rose Art Industries	HUNCHBACK POTTERY WHEEL GRAY SUPER STUFF			*
Rose Art Industries	JEWELRY MAKER SUPER STUFF			*
Rose Art Industries	POCAHONTAS FIGURE MAKER SUPER STUFF			*
Rose Art Industries	POLLY POCKET FIGURE MAKER SUPER STUFF			*
Rose Art Industries	POWER RANGERS SUPER STUFF			*
Rose Art Industries	PREHISTORIC FIGURE MAKER SUPER STUFF			*
Rose Art Industries	SEA TREASURES MAGNET MAKER SUPER STUFF			*
Rose Art Industries	SUPER STUFF - 2 PACK			*
Rose Art Industries	SUPER STUFF - 4 PACK			*
Rose Art Industries	TROPICAL PARADISE SUPER STUFF			*
Hans Stockmar GmbH	DECORATING WAX		*	
Hans Stockmar GmbH	MODELING BEESWAX		*	
Hans Stockmar GmbH	MODELING WAX		*	
Modeling (Oven Hardening)				
American Art Clay	FRIENDLY CLAY		*	
Eberhard Faber GmbH	FIMO		*	
Polyform Products Co.	GRANITEX		*	
Polyform Products Co.	POLYFORM		*	
Polyform Products Co.	PRO-MAT		*	
Polyform Products Co.	SCULPEY		*	
Polyform Products Co.	SCULPEY III		*	
Polyform Products Co.	SUPER ELASTICLAY		*	
Polyform Products Co.	SUPER SCULPEY		*	
T & F Kunststoffe	CERNIT NO. 1		*	
T & F Kunststoffe	CERNIT CHRISTMAS SET		*	
T & F Kunststoffe	CERNIT GLAMOUR		*	
T & F Kunststoffe	CERNIT NEON-LIGHT		*	
T & F Kunststoffe	CERNIT STARTER SET		*	
Vinci de Mexico	MODELINA		*	
Modeling Dough				
American Art Clay	SUPER DOUGH	*		
Binney & Smith	CRAYOLA COLORED MODEL MAGIC	*		
Binney & Smith	CRAYOLA DOUGH	*		
Binney & Smith	CRAYOLA FLUFF	*		
Binney & Smith	CRAYOLA FLUFF STUFF	*		
Binney & Smith	CRAYOLA MODEL MAGIC	*		
Binney & Smith	POOH COLORED MODEL MAGIC	*		
Binney & Smith (Canada)	CRAYOLA CREATIVE SETS DOUGH	*		
Binney & Smith (Canada)	CRAYOLA DOUGH	*		
Binney & Smith (Canada)	CRAYOLA PRESCHOOL DOUGH	*		
Binney & Smith (Canada)	SOFT STUFF/MELI-MELLO	*		
Comet-Montrose Ltd.	COMET			
F.I.L.A. S.p.A.	AIR LITE CLAY	*		
F.I.L.A. S.p.A.	PAT MAX	*		
James Industries	SLINKY DABBLIN' DOUGH	*		
Omega Chalk Factory	OMEGA MODELING DOUGH	*		
Omyacolor, Inc.	BIONATURA	*		
Omyacolor, Inc.	MODELING PAL	*		
Omyacolor, Inc.	PAT PLUME	*		
Panline USA/Alex	ALEX	*		
Rose Art Industries	101 DALMATIONS PUPPY PARLOR FUN DOUGH	*		
Rose Art Industries	DINO-DOUGH FUN DOUGH	*		
Rose Art Industries	JEWELTASTIC SPARKLING DOUGH	*		
Rose Art Industries	ROSE ART FUN DOUGH	*		
Rose Art Industries	ROSE ART FUN DOUGH - HOT COLORS	*		

CLAYS (continued)

PRODUCTS AND MANUFACTURERS	BRAND NAMES	CP SEAL	AP SEAL	HL/NT SEAL
Modeling Dough (continued)				
Rose Art Industries	ROSE ART GLITTER FUN DOUGH	*		
Rose Art Industries	SNACK-N-GO FUN DOUGH	*		
Papier Mache				
Activa Products	ACTIVA AIR DRY			*
Activa Products	CELLUCLAY			*.
American Art Clay	CLAYCRETE		*	
Creative Art Products	BLICK'S MIX		*	
Omyacolor, Inc.	ARTMACHE			*
Powdered Sculpting & Modeling Mediums				
American Art Clay	SCULPTAMOLD	*		
Binney & Smith	CRAYOLA CAST OF CHARACTERS			*
Creative Art Products	DICK BLICK CARVE & CAST			*
Fiesta Colors	PATE			*
Jiffy Foam, Inc.	BALSA FOAM			*
Jiffy Foam, Inc.	LEXATHANE MFP-5			*
Palmer Paint	JEWELRY PIN			*
Palmer Paint	MAGIC MIX			*
Thermo Plastic				
American Art Clay	FRIENDLY PLASTIC COMPOUND PELLETS		*	
American Art Clay	FRIENDLY PLASTIC COMPOUND STICKS		*	
American Art Clay	FRIENDLY PLASTIC DESIGNER STICKS		*	
American Art Clay	FRIENDLY PLASTIC EAR EXPRESSIONS			*
Ceramic				
American Art Clay	AMACO BUFF FIRING #46		*	
American Art Clay	AMACO CLAY FLOUR		*	
American Art Clay	AMACO INDIAN RED #67 (MOIST & DRY)			*
American Art Clay	AMACO PORCELAIN #65			*
American Art Clay	AMACO STONEWARE W/GROG #48 (MOIST)			*
American Art Clay	AMACO STONEWARE BODY W/OUT GROG #480 (MOIST)			*
American Art Clay	AMACO TERRA COTTA #77 (MOIST)		*	
American Art Clay	AMACO VERSA #20		*	
American Art Clay	AMACO WARM BROWN STONEWARE #58			*
American Art Clay	AMACO WHITE ART #25 MOIST			*
American Art Clay	AMACO WHITE SCULPTURE #27			*
American Art Clay	AMACO WHITE STONEWARE #38 (MOIST)			*
A.R.T. Studio Clay	A.R.T. PORCELAIN I #134			*
A.R.T. Studio Clay	A.R.T. PORCELAIN II #135			*
A.R.T. Studio Clay	A.R.T. PORCELAIN III #136			*
A.R.T. Studio Clay	A.R.T. PORCELAIN IV #137			*
A.R.T. Studio Clay	BROWNSTONE 1 #107			*
A.R.T. Studio Clay	BROWNSTONE 2 #108			*
A.R.T. Studio Clay	BUFF 1 #103			*
A.R.T. Studio Clay	BUFF 11 #104			*
A.R.T. Studio Clay	BUFF III #132			*
A.R.T. Studio Clay	CINNAMONSTONE #129			*
A.R.T. Studio Clay	CINNAMONSTONE II #139			*
A.R.T. Studio Clay	DOMESTIC PORCELAIN #115			*
A.R.T. Studio Clay	GOLDSTONE I #111			*
A.R.T. Studio Clay	GRAYSTONE 1 #109			*
A.R.T. Studio Clay	GRAYSTONE II #110			*
A.R.T. Studio Clay	GROLLEG PORCELAIN I #127			*
A.R.T. Studio Clay	GROLLEG PORCELAIN II #128			*
A.R.T. Studio Clay	INDIAN RED #122			*
A.R.T. Studio Clay	NON-TALC WHITE #133			*
A.R.T. Studio Clay	ORANGESTONE #118			*
A.R.T. Studio Clay	PORCELAIN/CHINA #120			*
A.R.T. Studio Clay	RED RAKU #116			*
A.R.T. Studio Clay	SPECKLE BROWNSTONE #125			*
A.R.T. Studio Clay	SPECKLESTONE #117			*
A.R.T. Studio Clay	SPECKLE TANSTONE #124			*
A.R.T. Studio Clay	TERRA COTTA I #101			*
A.R.T. Studio Clay	TERRA COTTA II #102			*
A.R.T. Studio Clay	TERRA COTTA III #131			*

Some products in this line do not bear the CP, AP or Health Label (Non-Toxic) Seal.

-5-

TABLE 2   (continued)

CLAYS (continued)

Ceramic (continued)

PRODUCTS AND MANUFACTURERS	BRAND NAMES	CP SEAL	AP SEAL	HL/NT SEAL
A.R.T. Studio Clay	WHITE RAKU I #126		*	
A.R.T. Studio Clay	WHITE RAKU II #146		*	
A.R.T. Studio Clay	WHITE TALC I #105		*	
A.R.T. Studio Clay	WHITE TALC II #106		*	
A.R.T. Studio Clay	WHITE TALC III #130		*	
A.R.T. Studio Clay	WHITESTONE #119		*	
A.R.T. Studio Clay	YELLOWSTONE #123		*	
Axner Co., Inc.	AXNER EARTHENWARES		*	
Axner Co., Inc.	AXNER PORCELAINS		*	
Axner Co., Inc.	AXNER STONEWARES		*	
Bennett Pottery	APACHE RED (MOIST & DRY)		*	
Bennett Pottery	CORAL REEF		*	
Ceramic Sply. NY/NJ	#100 BUFF		*	
Ceramic Sply. NY/NJ	#109 RED		*	
Ceramic Sply. NY/NJ	#106 WHITE		*	
Chaselle, Inc.	CHASELLE 25		*	
Chaselle, Inc.	CHASELLE 46		*	
Chaselle, Inc.	CHASELLE DARK BROWN 58		*	
Chaselle, Inc.	CHASELLE GRAY 20		*	
Chaselle, Inc.	CHASELLE LT. BROWN 48 (DRY)		*	
Chaselle, Inc.	CHASELLE LT. BROWN 48 (MOIST)		*	
Columbus Clay Co.	COLUMBUS RED (MOIST & DRY)		*	
Columbus Clay Co.	COLUMBUS WHITE		*	
Continental Clay	CLFOX		*	
Continental Clay	CLPW		*	
Ex-Cel, Inc.	EXCEL STONEWARE (MOIST & DRY)		*	
Ex-Cel, Inc.	EXCEL TERRA COTTA (MOIST)		*	
Ex-Cel, Inc.	EXCEL WHITE		*	
FSC Educational	1920-1125 RED		*	
FSC Educational	1920-1115 STONEWARE		*	
FSC Educational	1920-1135 WHITE		*	
Great Lakes Clay	GREAT LAKES CLAY		*	
Highwater Clays	EARTHENWARE		*	
Highwater Clays	PORCELAIN		*	
Highwater Clays	STONEWARE		*	
Minn/Midwest Clay	COLORED PORCELAIN #		*	
Minn/Midwest Clay	DF STONEWARE		*	
Minn/Midwest Clay	DOMESTIC PORCELAIN		*	
Minn/Midwest Clay	GROLLEG PORCELAIN		*	
Minn/Midwest Clay	GROLLEG PORCELAIN WITH NYLON FIBER		*	
Minn/Midwest Clay	M SERIES COLORED CLAYS #		*	
Minn/Midwest Clay	MB STONEWARE		*	
Minn/Midwest Clay	MINNESOTA INDIGENOUS		*	
Minn/Midwest Clay	NO. 1 STONEWARE		*	
Minn/Midwest Clay	NO. 1 STONEWARE WITH GROG		*	
Minn/Midwest Clay	NO. 1 STONEWARE WITH MANGANESE		*	
Minn/Midwest Clay	NO. 2 STONEWARE		*	
Minn/Midwest Clay	NO. 3 WHITE STONEWARE #		*	
Minn/Midwest Clay	NO. 7 WHITE BUFF		*	
Minn/Midwest Clay	NORTHERN LIGHT STONEWARE		*	
Minn/Midwest Clay	NORTHERN LIGHT STONEWARE WITH IRON		*	
Minn/Midwest Clay	POLAR PORCELAIN		*	
Minn/Midwest Clay	RAKU		*	
Minn/Midwest Clay	RAINY LAKE STONEWARE		*	
Minn/Midwest Clay	RED EARTHENWARE		*	
Minn/Midwest Clay	RED SCULPTURE		*	
Minn/Midwest Clay	S SERIES COLORED #		*	
Minn/Midwest Clay	WHITE EARTHENWARE (SWT)		*	
Minn/Midwest Clay	WHITE EARTHENWARE - NO TALC (WNT)		*	
Minn/Midwest Clay	WHITE RAKU		*	
Minn/Midwest Clay	WHITE SCULPTURE		*	
NASCO International	NORTHERN LIGHT STONEWARE		*	
NASCO International	RED EARTHENWARE		*	
NASCO International	WHITE BUFF		*	
NASCO International	WHITE EARTHENWARE		*	
Runyan Pottery	SC 125 WHITE		*	
Runyan Pottery	SC 146 STONEWARE		*	
Runyan Pottery	SC 148		*	
Runyan Pottery	SC 167 RED		*	
Sax Arts & Crafts	SAX BROWN STONE SPECKLE		*	
Sax Arts & Crafts	SAX BUFF STONE SPECKLE		*	
Sax Arts & Crafts	SAX SPECKLED INDIAN RED		*	
Sax Arts & Crafts	SAX WHITE TALC		*	
Seattle Pottery	ALPINE WHITE-SP655		*	
Seattle Pottery	AWAJI-SP690		*	
Seattle Pottery	COLUMBIA RED 412-SP721		*	
Seattle Pottery	COLUMBIA WHITE-SP750		*	
Seattle Pottery	CRYSTAL STONE-SP652		*	
Seattle Pottery	CRYSTAL WHITE PORCELAIN-SP650	*		
Seattle Pottery	DOVE PORCELAIN-SP660		*	
Seattle Pottery	GOLDBAR BROWN-SP620		*	
Seattle Pottery	KENZAN PORCELAIN-SP800		*	
Seattle Pottery	KLAMATH BROWN "CCB"-SP634		*	
Seattle Pottery	KLAMATH BUFF "LLM"-SP633		*	
Seattle Pottery	KLAMATH RED "LLR"-SP637		*	
Seattle Pottery	KLAMATH WHITE "LLW"-SP632		*	
Seattle Pottery	MAPLE VALLEY RED-SP625		*	
Seattle Pottery	MIDNIGHT BLACK SP605		*	
Seattle Pottery	RAKU-SP525		*	
Seattle Pottery	REDART TERRA COTTA-SP530		*	
Seattle Pottery	SHASTA WHITE-SP505		*	
Seattle Pottery	TERRA COTTA-06-SP520		*	
Seattle Pottery	VASHON BROWN-SP611		*	
Seattle Pottery	VASHON BROWN W/GROG-SP611G		*	
Seattle Pottery	VASHON BUFF-SP609		*	
Seattle Pottery	VASHON BUFF W/GROG-SP609G		*	
Seattle Pottery	VASHON GRAY-SP612		*	
Seattle Pottery	VASHON ORANGE-SP615		*	
Seattle Pottery	VASHON RED-SP610		*	
Seattle Pottery	VASHON RED W/GROG-SP610G		*	
Seattle Pottery	VASHON WHITE-SP608		*	
Seattle Pottery	VASHON WHITE W/GROG-SP608G		*	
Seattle Pottery	WHITE-LF-06		*	
Seattle Pottery	WOLF CREEK WHITE-SP570		*	
Standard Ceramic	BROWN STONEWARE		*	
Standard Ceramic	BROWN STONEWARE MOIST		*	
Standard Ceramic	BROWN STONEWARE MOIST #225		*	
Standard Ceramic	BUFF MOIST		*	
Standard Ceramic	EARTHENWARE #417		*	
Standard Ceramic	LOW FIRE RED MOIST		*	
Standard Ceramic	LOW FIRE WHITE MOIST		*	
Standard Ceramic	LOW FIRE WHITE MOIST W/GROG		*	
Standard Ceramic	MOIST STONEWARE #119		*	
Standard Ceramic	MOIST STONEWARE #200		*	
Standard Ceramic	MOIST STONEWARE #205		*	
Standard Ceramic	MOIST STONEWARE #259		*	
Standard Ceramic	MOIST STONEWARE #264		*	
Standard Ceramic	PORCELAIN #365		*	
Standard Ceramic	PORCELAIN MOIST		*	
Standard Ceramic	PORCELAIN MOIST #213		*	
Standard Ceramic	RAKU #295		*	
Standard Ceramic	RAKU MOIST		*	
Standard Ceramic	RED MOIST		*	
Standard Ceramic	STANDARD 910		*	
Standard Ceramic	STANDARD 911 SELF-HARDENING		*	
Standard Ceramic	STANDARD SCULPTURE #420		*	
Standard Ceramic	STANDARD MOIST		*	
Standard Ceramic	STONEWARE MOIST		*	
Standard Ceramic	WHITE STONEWARE #181		*	
Standard Ceramic	WHITE STONEWARE MOIST		*	
Stewart's Clay of CA	STEWART'S CLAY 2000		*	
Stewart's Clay of CA	STEWART'S CLAY 2000 W/SAND		*	
Stewart's Clay of CA	STEWART'S CLAY 2300		*	
Stewart's Clay of CA	STEWART'S CLAY 3000		*	
Stewart's Clay of CA	STEWART'S CLAY 8000		*	
Stewart's Clay of CA	STEWART'S CLAY 8000 W/GROG		*	

Ceramic Casting Slip

PRODUCTS AND MANUFACTURERS	BRAND NAMES	CP SEAL	AP SEAL	HL/NT SEAL
American Art Clay	AMACO 46 S (MOIST)		*	
American Art Clay	AMACO SLIP #15		*	
A.R.T. Studio Clay	SPECKLESTONE #515		*	
A.R.T. Studio Clay	STONEWARE BUFF #513		*	
A.R.T. Studio Clay	WHITE TALC #710		*	
Ceramichrome, Inc.	PORCELAIN CASTING SLIP		*	
Ex-Cel, Inc.	EX-CEL SLIP		*	
Gare, Inc.	SLIP		*	
Minn/Midwest Clay	LOW FIRE (LIQUID)		*	
Minn/Midwest Clay	MC LIGHTONE (LIQUID)		*	
Minn/Midwest Clay	MC #3 (LIQUID)		*	
Minn/Midwest Clay	MC #5 CASTING (LIQUID)		*	
Minn/Midwest Clay	MC#5 (LIQUID)		*	
Minn/Midwest Clay	WHITE EARTHENWARE (LIQUID)		*	
NASCO International	WHITE EARTHENWARE		*	

Some products in this line do not bear the CP, AP or Health Label (Non-Toxic) Seal.

TABLE 2   (continued)

CLAYS (continued)

Ceramic Casting Slip (continued)

PRODUCTS AND MANUFACTURERS	BRAND NAMES	CP SEAL	AP SEAL	HL/NT SEAL
Ohio Ceramic Supply	JOHN'S SLIP		*	
Rockwell Ceramics Ltd.	ROCKWELL WHITE CASTING SLIP		*	
Zeiter's Ceramic Sply.	BUCKEYE SLIP		*	
Zeiter's Ceramic Sply.	MARY ANN PORCELAIN		*	
Zeiter's Ceramic Sply.	Z RED SLIP		*	

CRAFT MATERIALS, MISCELLANEOUS

Colored Sand

PRODUCTS AND MANUFACTURERS	BRAND NAMES	CP SEAL	AP SEAL	HL/NT SEAL
Activa Products	DECOROCK		*	
Activa Products	SCENIC SAND		*	
Binney & Smith	CRAYOLA COLORED SAND		*	
Binney & Smith	MICKEY'S STUFF COLORED SAND		*	
Conros Corporation	KANGA COLORED SAND		*	
Conros Corporation	KANGA FUN SAND		*	
Conros Corporation	ROSS ART SAND		*	
Conros Corporation	ROSS COLOR 'N SAND		*	
Conros Corporation	ROSS FUN SAND		*	
Conros Corporation	ROSS MAGIC SAND		*	
Conros Corporation	ROSS PLAYTIME SAND		*	
Conros Corporation	ROSS ULTRA SAND		*	
Sandtastik Inc.	SANDTASTIK COLORED SAND		*	
Specialty Mineral Prods.	COLORED SAND		*	

Foils

PRODUCTS AND MANUFACTURERS	BRAND NAMES	CP SEAL	AP SEAL	HL/NT SEAL
Oasis Art & Craft Prod.	COPPERFOIL		*	
Oasis Art & Craft Prod.	SCRAPERFOIL		*	

Miscellaneous

PRODUCTS AND MANUFACTURERS	BRAND NAMES	CP SEAL	AP SEAL	HL/NT SEAL
J. W. Etc.	PROFESSIONAL WOOD FILLER		*	
Palmer Paint Products	SIDEWALK CHALK MIX		*	
Rose Art Industries	ROSE ART CANDLE FACTORY		*	
Rose Art Industries	ROSE ART CHRISTMAS CANDLE FACTORY		*	
Rose Art Industries	ROSE ART DELUXE CANDLE FACTORY		*	

CRAYONS

Hard Molded

PRODUCTS AND MANUFACTURERS	BRAND NAMES	CP SEAL	AP SEAL	HL/NT SEAL
Binney & Smith	ARISTA II	*		
Binney & Smith	CRAYOLA	*		
Binney & Smith	CRAYOLA CHANGEABLES	*		
Binney & Smith	CRAYOLA FLUORESCENT	*		
Binney & Smith	CRAYOLA SO-BIG	*		
Binney & Smith	CRAYOLA WIPE-OFF		*	
Binney & Smith	LIQUITEX BASIC ART STICKS		*	
Binney & Smith	MICKEY'S STUFF	*		
Binney & Smith (Canada)	CRAYOLA FABRIC		*	
Conros Corporation	CANADA KRAYON		*	
Conros Corporation	GR8 KRAYON		*	
Conros Corporation	KID'S KRAYON		*	
Conros Corporation	MCKRAYON		*	
Conros Corporation	ROOSTIK CRAYON		*	
Conros Corporation	ROSS-CONROS KANGA KRAYON		*	
Double T Trading	TOP KOALA		*	
Globe Chemical Ind.	COLORS-IN-MOTION		*	
Lion Pencil Co., Ltd.	LION PLASTIC CRAYONS		*	
NES Arnold Inc.	SCOLAPLASTIX		*	
Playstation Inc.	COLOR CHANGES CRAYONS		*	
Playstation Inc.	GLITTER AND GLOW CRAYONS		*	
Playstation Inc.	LUMBER CRAYON		*	
Quartet Manufacturing	ALPHACOLOR LUMBER CRAYON		*	
Rose Art Industries	ROSE ART	*		
Rose Art Industries	ROSE ART HOT 'N BRITE	*		
Sakura of America	SAKURA BOLD HARD HY16	*		

Molded

PRODUCTS AND MANUFACTURERS	BRAND NAMES	CP SEAL	AP SEAL	HL/NT SEAL
Binney & Smith	CRAYOLA COLOR-N-SMELL	*		
Binney & Smith	CRAYOLA FABRIC		*	
Binney & Smith	CRAYOLA GEMTONES	*		
Binney & Smith	CRAYOLA GLITTER	*		
Binney & Smith	CRAYOLA GLOW IN THE DARK	*		
Binney & Smith	CRAYOLA KID'S FIRST BRIGHT COLORS	*		
Binney & Smith	CRAYOLA MAGIC SCENT	*		
Binney & Smith	CRAYOLA NEONS	*		
Binney & Smith	CRAYOLA POWER BRUSH		*	

CRAYONS (continued)

Molded (continued)

PRODUCTS AND MANUFACTURERS	BRAND NAMES	CP SEAL	AP SEAL	HL/NT SEAL
Binney & Smith	CRAYOLA SCENTED	*		
Binney & Smith	CRAYOLA STAR BRITES	*		
Binney & Smith	CRAYOLA WASHABLE BATHTUB		*	
Binney & Smith	CRAYOLA WASHABLE FLUORESCENT	*		
Binney & Smith (Canada)	CRAYOLA METALLIC		*	
Buncho Corp.	BUNCHO		*	
Buncho Corp.	MARBLES			*
Caran D'Ache of Switz.	NEOCOLOR I		*	
Caran D'Ache of Switz.	NEOCOLOR II AQUARELLE		*	
Chartpak	CHARTPAK CRAYONS		*	
Chemitron USA Corp.	COLORUP	*		
Comet-Montrose Ltd.	COMET	*		
CVS	CVS CRAYONS	*		
DeMoulas/Market Basket	DEMOULAS/MARKET BASKET CRAYONS	*		
Dixon Ticonderoga	IDEAL PLASTIC MARK		*	
Dixon Ticonderoga	LOONEY TUNES	*		
Dixon Ticonderoga	LOONEY TUNES BUCKET OF CRAYONS			
Dixon Ticonderoga	LOONEY TUNES BUCKET OF FUN			
Dixon Ticonderoga	LOONEY TUNES BUCKET OF GIANT WASHABLE	*		
Dixon Ticonderoga	LOONEY TUNES WASHABLE	*		
Dixon Ticonderoga	MY FIRST CRAYON	*		
Dixon Ticonderoga	PLASTIC MARK		*	
Dixon Ticonderoga	PRANG	*		
Dixon Ticonderoga	PRANG FUN PRO	*		
Dixon Ticonderoga	PRANG GLITTER	*		
Dixon Ticonderoga	PRANG GLOW IN THE DARK		*	
Dixon Ticonderoga	PRANG WASHABLE	*		
Dixon Ticonderoga	PRANG WIPE-OFF		*	
Dixon Ticonderoga	TREND		*	
Empire Berol USA	HAND HUGGER CRAYONS	*		
Fostport, Inc.	YARKA SAUCE		*	
J. L. Hammett Co.	LIVING COLORS	*		
Hasbro, Inc.	SPIROGRAPH	*		
Holbein Works, Ltd.	MAJELLE			*
Kinney Drugs	KINNEY DRUGS CRAYONS	*		
Lakeshore Learning Materials	PEOPLE COLOR	*		
Lakeshore Learning Materials	LAKESHORE RAINBOW		*	
Lion Pencil Co., Ltd.	CRAYON FACTORY WASHABLE		*	
Lion Pencil Co., Ltd.	LION WASHABLE		*	
NES Arnold Inc.	SCOLA CHUBBI STUMPS		*	
NES Arnold Inc.	SCOLA CHUBLETS		*	
NES Arnold Inc.	SCOLA FLUORESCENT		*	
NES Arnold Inc.	SCOLA GIANTS		*	
NES Arnold Inc.	SCOLA STRIPEY		*	
Omyacolor, Inc.	OMYACOLOR		*	
Omyacolor, Inc.	OMYACOLOR JUMBO		*	
Omyacolor, Inc.	OMYAWAX JUMBO		*	
Peoples Drug	PEOPLES DRUG CRAYONS	*		
Pentech International	DISNEY HUNCHBACK OF NOTRE DAME	*		
Pentech International	FISHER PRICE	*		
Playskool, Inc.	PLAYSKOOL	*		
Playstation Inc.	BLOCKSTER		*	
Plymouth, Inc.	FISHER-PRICE	*		
Rose Art Industries	101 DALMATIONS CRAYON-BY-NUMBER	*		
Rose Art Industries	COLOR CRAFT	*		
Rose Art Industries	COLORON	*		
Rose Art Industries	CRAY TUFF	*		
Rose Art Industries	GARGOYLE CRAYON BY NUMBER	*		
Rose Art Industries	GARGOYLE DESIGNER DESK		*	
Rose Art Industries	HUNCHBACK DESIGNERS DESK	*		
Rose Art Industries	HUNCHBACK OF NOTRE DAME CRAYON-BY-NUMBER	*		
Rose Art Industries	KODAK 72-CRAYON CASE	*		
Rose Art Industries	POCAHONTAS CRAYON BY NUMBER	*		

Some products in this line do not bear the CP, AP or Health Label (Non-Toxic) Seal.

TABLE 2   (continued)

PRODUCTS AND MANUFACTURERS	BRAND NAMES	CP SEAL	AP SEAL	HL/NT SEAL
CRAYONS (continued)				
Molded (continued)				
Rose Art Industries	POCAHONTAS CRAYONS FOR LAP DESK	*		
Rose Art Industries	POCAHONTAS DESIGNER DESK	*		
Rose Art Industries	ROSE ART	*		
Rose Art Industries	ROSE ART 48-CRAYON CAN	*		
Rose Art Industries	ROSE ART 64-CRAYON CAROUSAL	*		
Rose Art Industries	ROSE ART 100 CRAYONS IN A CAN	*		
Rose Art Industries	ROSE ART CRAYONS IN CLEAR CASE	*		
Rose Art Industries	ROSE ART ERASEABLE	*		
Rose Art Industries	ROSE ART GLITTER	*		
Rose Art Industries	ROSE ART GLOW	*		
Rose Art Industries	ROSE ART GOLD	*		
Rose Art Industries	ROSE ART JUMBO	*		
Rose Art Industries	ROSE ART JUMBO FLUORESCENT	*		
Rose Art Industries	ROSE ART JUMBO GLITTER	*		
Rose Art Industries	ROSE ART JUMBO GOLD	*		
Rose Art Industries	ROSE ART JUMBO SCENTED		*	
Rose Art Industries	ROSE ART PINKS & PURPLES*	*		
Rose Art Industries	ROSE ART SUPER SCENTED		*	
Rose Art Industries	WILD COLORS	*		
Sakura of America	SAKURA LY25	*		
Sargent Art	GOTHIC		*	
Sargent Art	SARGENT	*		
Sargent Art	SARGENT WASHABLE	*		
Hans Stockmar GmbH	STOCKMAR WACHSFARBEN		*	
The Straight Edge, Inc.	STRAIGHT EDGE		*	
Western Publishing	COLOR EXPRESS	*		
Pressed				
Dixon Ticonderoga	COLOR CLASSICS	*		
Dixon Ticonderoga	CRAYOGRAPH	*		
Dixon Ticonderoga	KANTROLL	*		
Dixon Ticonderoga	KINDOGRAPH	*		
Hasbro, Inc.	FASHION PLATES		*	
Hasbro, Inc.	TRAVEL PLATES		*	
Lyra-Bleistift-Fabrik	LYRA REMBRANDT WAX GIANTS		*	
Lyra-Bleistift-Fabrik	WACHSRIESEN WAX GIANTS		*	
Sakura of America	COUPY	*		
Sargent Art	SARGENT	*		
Water Color				
Binney & Smith	CRAYOLA	*		
Binney & Smith	CRAYOLA PRINT MACHINE WATER COLOR CRAYON		*	
Binney & Smith	CRAYOLA WASHABLE	*		
Binney & Smith	CRAYOLA WASHABLE SO-BIG	*		
Binney & Smith	MICKEY'S STUFF	*		
Binney & Smith	MICKEY'S STUFF WASHABLE*	*		
Binney & Smith	POOH WASHABLE	*		
Buncho Corp.	ACCENT TWIST		*	
Dixon Ticonderoga	PRANG PAYONS	*		
Holbein Works, Ltd.	HOLBEIN WATER SOLUBLE			*
Quartet Mfg. Co.	ALPHACOLOR	*		
Rose Art Industries	COLORON WIPE OFF	*		
Rose Art Industries	KODAK WASHABLE JUMBO		*	
Rose Art Industries	KODAK WASHABLE SUPER JUMBO		*	
Rose Art Industries	ROSE ART WASHABLE		*	
Rose Art Industries	ROSE ART 101 WASHABLE		*	
Rose Art Industries	ROSE ART JUMBO WASHABLE		*	
Rose Art Industries	ROSE ART SUPER JUMBO WASHABLE		*	
Sakura of America	SAKURA RAKUGAKI FWY12	*		
DETERGENT CLEANERS				
Dixon Ticonderoga	HYGIEIA LIQUID CHALKBOARD CLEANER		*	
General Pencil Co.	B&J-THE MASTERS ARTIST HAND SOAP		*	
Hunt Manufacturing	SPEEDBALL PEN CLEANER		*	
J. W. Etc.	CITRIC CLEAN HAND & FABRIC CLEANER		*	
Martin/F. Weber Co.	BOB ROSS PAINTERS GLOVE		*	

PRODUCTS AND MANUFACTURERS	BRAND NAMES	CP SEAL	AP SEAL	HL/NT SEAL
DETERGENT CLEANERS (continued)				
Winsor & Newton	ART GEL			*
Winsor & Newton	ARTGUARD			*
Winsor & Newton	ART WIPES			*
DRAWING & WRITING INSTRUMENTS & ACCESSORIES				
Colored Pencils				
Binney & Smith	CRAYOLA		*	
Binney & Smith	CRAYOLA FLUORESCENT		*	
Binney & Smith	CRAYOLA SO BIG		*	
Binney & Smith	CRAYOLA STANDARD		*	
Binney & Smith	CRAYOLA WRITE START		*	
Binney & Smith	JAZZY PENCILS		*	
Binney & Smith	LIQUITEX BASIC ARTIST		*	
Binney & Smith	MICKEY'S STUFF		*	
Binney & Smith (Canada)	CRAYOLA STANDARD		*	
ColArt International	CONTE-A-PARIS AQUARELLE		*	
ColArt International	CONTE-A-PARIS ARTISTS'		*	
ColArt International	CONTE-A-PARIS PASTEL		*	
ColArt International	CONTE-A-PARIS PIERRE NOIRE		*	
Martin Coudeau	PAX CLASSICO		*	
Martin Coudeau	PAX CROMOCOLOR		*	
Dixon Ticonderoga	COLORART		*	
Dixon Ticonderoga	LOONEY TUNES BUCKET OF FUN		*	
Dixon Ticonderoga	LOONEY TUNES SET		*	
Dixon Ticonderoga	PRANG		*	
Dixon Ticonderoga	PRANG PROFESSIONAL		*	
Dixon Ticonderoga	TASMANIAN DEVIL DOUBLE COLOR		*	
Dixon Ticonderoga	TICONDEROGA ERASABLES		*	
Empire Berol USA	CHINAMARKER		*	
A. W. Faber-Castell	FABER-CASTELL PASTELS		*	
F.I.L.A. SpA	F.I.L.A.		*	
General Pencil Co.	GENERAL'S COLORING		*	
J. L. Hammett Co.	J. L. HAMMETT		*	
J. L. Hammett Co.	LIVING COLORS		*	
Lakeshore Learning Materials	PEOPLE COLORS JUMBO		*	
Lion Pencil Co., Ltd.	CRAYON FACTORY		*	
Lion Pencil Co., Ltd.	CRAYON FACTORY JUMBO		*	
Lion Pencil Co., Ltd.	LION		*	
Lion Pencil Co., Ltd.	LION JUMBO		*	
Lyra-Bleistift-Fabrik	FARB-RIESEN		*	
Lyra-Bleistift-Fabrik	FERBY		*	
Lyra-Bleistift-Fabrik	LYRA COLOR GIANTS		*	
Lyra-Bleistift-Fabrik	LYRA REMBRANDT AQUARELL		*	
Lyra-Bleistift-Fabrik	LYRA REMBRANDT POLYCOLOR		*	
Lyra-Bleistift-Fabrik	MEGALINER		*	
Lyra-Bleistift-Fabrik	ORLOW COLORIDA		*	
Lyra-Bleistift-Fabrik	OSIRIS		*	
Lyra-Bleistift-Fabrik	PRO NATURA		*	
Lyra-Bleistift-Fabrik	PRO NATURA FARB-RIESEN		*	
Lyra-Bleistift-Fabrik	REMBRANDT SPLENDER		*	
Lyra-Bleistift-Fabrik	YOUNGSTER		*	
Omyacolor, Inc.	BIONATURA COLORING PENCILS		*	
Omyacolor, Inc.	BIONATURA JUMBO COLORING		*	
Omyacolor, Inc.	OMYACOLOR COLORING		*	
Omyacolor, Inc.	OMYACOLOR JUMBO COLORING		*	
Omyacolor, Inc.	REBO JUMBO COLORING		*	
Playtime Products	TYCO PLAYTIME		*	
Rose Art Industries	KODAK		*	
Rose Art Industries	ROSE ART		*	
Rose Art Industries	ROSE ART BICOLOR		*	
Rose Art Industries	ROSE ART LARGE		*	
Rose Art Industries	ROSE ART SMALL		*	
Sargent Art	SARGENT ART		*	
Sargent Art	SARGENT COLORING		*	
Pencils				
Binney & Smith	CRAYOLA PENCILS		*	
Dixon Ticonderoga	TICONDEROGA CHECKING PENCIL	*		
Lion Pencil Co., Ltd.	CRAYON FACTORY NO. 2 PENCIL	*		
Lion Pencil Co., Ltd.	HB NO. 2 PENCIL	*		
Omyacolor, Inc.	OMYACOLOR #2 LEAD PENCIL	*		
Omyacolor, Inc.	REBO #2 LEAD PENCIL	*		
Professional Drawing Pencils				
ColArt International	CONTE-A-PARIS ARTISTS' GRAPHITE PENCILS			*
ColArt International	CONTE-A-PARIS CARBON PENCILS			*

Some products in this line do not bear the CP, AP or Health Label (Non-Toxic) Seal.

-8-

TABLE 2   (continued)

PRODUCTS AND MANUFACTURERS	BRAND NAMES	CP SEAL	AP SEAL	HL/NT SEAL

DRAWING & WRITING INSTRUMENTS & ACCESSORIES (continued)

Professional Drawing Pencils (continued)

Manufacturer	Brand	CP	AP	HL/NT
ColArt International	CONTE-A-PARIS CHARCOAL PENCILS			*
ColArt International	CONTE-A-PARIS DRAWING PENCILS			*
M. Grumbacher, Inc.	GAMMA V675 GRAPHITE PENCIL		*	
Lyra-Bleistift-Fabrik	BISTRO WIRTEBLEISTIFT GRAPHITE PENCIL		*	
NES Arnold, Inc.	SCOLA VELVAWAX #		*	
Winsor & Newton	DERWENT ARTISTS PENCILS			*
Winsor & Newton	DERWENT DRAWING PENCILS			*
Winsor & Newton	DERWENT STUDIO PENCILS			*

Pens

| Binney & Smith | CRAYOLA COLORWORKS ERASABLE COLORED PENS | | * | |
| Sakura of America | GELLY ROLL FLUORESCENT | | * | |

Watercolor Pencils

Binney & Smith	CRAYOLA WATERCOLOR PENCILS		*	
A. W. Faber-Castell	FABER-CASTELL		*	
Winsor & Newton	DERWENT WATERCOLOUR PENCILS			*

Erasers, Rulers & Sharpeners

Binney & Smith	CRAYOLA ERASER		*	
Binney & Smith	JAZZY ERASER		*	
Lion Pencil Co., Ltd.	CRAYON FACTORY COMPOUNDING ERASER		*	
Lion Pencil Co., Ltd.	LION COMPOUNDING ERASER		*	
Lion Pencil Co., Ltd.	CRAYON FACTORY RULER		*	
Lion Pencil Co., Ltd.	LION RULER		*	
Lion Pencil Co., Ltd.	CRAYON FACTORY PENCIL SHARPENER		*	
Lion Pencil Co., Ltd.	LION PENCIL SHARPENER		*	
Sakura of America	SAKURA KNEADED ERASER		*	

DRAWING & LETTERING INKS & MEDIUMS

Non-Waterproof Drawing Ink

Berol UK	OSMIROID BOTTLED INKS	*		
Empire Berol USA	OSMIROID	*		
Hunt Manufacturing	PANACHE FOUNTAIN PEN	*		
Hunt Manufacturing	SPEEDBALL	*		
Hunt Manufacturing	SPEEDBALL PIGMENTED OPAQUE	*		
NES Arnold	MARBLING INKS	*		
Pentel of America	CHP CERAMICRON	*		
Pentel of America	CXP CERAMICRON	*		
Pentel of America	SR10 CERAMICRON	*		
Pentel of America	SR51 CERAMICRON	*		
Pentel of America	SR51-01A CERAMICRON	*		
Pentel of America	SRM01 CERAMICRON	*		
Pentel of America	SRM01-A CERAMICRON	*		
Pentel of America	SRM02 CERAMICRON	*		
Pentel of America	SRM03 CERAMICRON	*		
Pentel of America	SRM04 CERAMICRON	*		
Pentel of America	SRM2PP CERAMICRON	*		
Pentel of America	SRM3PP CERAMICRON	*		
Pentel of America	SRM4PP CERAMICRON	*		
Royal Talens	ECOLINE #			*

Technical Drawing Ink

Creative Art Products	DICK BLICK BLACK CAT INDIA	*		
Daler-Rowney	FW WHITE TECHNICAL	*		
Daler-Rowney	PEN-OPAKE TECHNICAL WHITE	*		
Hunt Manufacturing	SPEEDBALL TECHNICAL BLACK	*		
Pebeo of America	COLOREX TECHNIC			*
Pebeo of America	GRAPHIC INDIA INK			*
Pelikan USA	PELIKAN DRAWING INK A #	*		
Pelikan USA	PELIKAN DRAWING INK A-BLACK	*		
Pelikan USA	PELIKAN DRAWING INK A-WHITE	*		
Salis International	DR. PH. MARTIN'S TECH	*		
Sax Arts & Crafts	TRUE FLOW INDIA	*		

Waterproof Drawing Ink

Certified Color Corp.	CERTIFIED ARTIST	*		
Chroma Acrylics	BLACK DRAWING INK	*		
Daler-Rowney	CALLI BLACK	*		
Daler-Rowney	CALLI COLORED	*		
Daler-Rowney	F.W. ARTISTS #			*

DRAWING & LETTERING INKS & MEDIUMS (continued)

Waterproof Drawing Ink (continued)

Daler-Rowney	F.W. INDIA	*		
Daler-Rowney	F.W. WATERPROOF	*		
Daler-Rowney	LUMA PEARLESCENT	*		
Daler-Rowney	RE-WHITE CORRECTION FLUID	*		
Duro Art Industries	DURO INDIA	*		
J.L. Hammett Co.	LIVING COLORS BLACK DRAWING INK*			*
Holbein Works Ltd.	HOLBEIN #	*		
Hunt Manufacturing	SPEEDBALL	*		
Hunt Manufacturing	SPEEDBALL BLACK	*		
Hunt Manufacturing	SPEEDBALL SUPER BLACK INDIA	*		
Koh-I-Noor	ARTIST PEN INK	*		
Koh-I-Noor	ROTRING ARTISTCOLOR OPAQUE	*		
Koh-I-Noor	ROTRING ARTISTCOLOR RETARDER *			
Koh-I-Noor	ROTRING ARTISTCOLOR TRANSPARENT	*		
Kuretake Co., Ltd.	IROIRO WATO KURETAKE EKI	*		
Kuretake Co., Ltd.	KIRI KURETAKE	*		
Kuretake Co., Ltd.	KOUKABOKU MITSUMARU	*		
Kuretake Co., Ltd.	KOUKABOKU YOTSUMARU	*		
Kuretake Co., Ltd.	KURETAKE BOKUJU	*		
Kuretake Co., Ltd.	KURETAKE BOKUTEKI	*		
Kuretake Co., Ltd.	KURETAKE CHO-NOUBOKU BOKUTEKI	*		
Kuretake Co., Ltd.	KURETAKE CHU-NOUBOKU BOKUTEKI	*		
Kuretake Co., Ltd.	KURETAKE FUDE-OMOINA BOKUTEKI*			
Kuretake Co., Ltd.	KURETAKE FUKYUYO BOKUTEKI	*		
Kuretake Co., Ltd.	KURETAKE IROIRO BOKUTEKI	*		
Kuretake Co., Ltd.	KURETAKE FUKYUYO SHONOTOMO *			
Kuretake Co., Ltd.	KURETAKE NOUBOKU BOKUTEKI	*		
Kuretake Co., Ltd.	KURETAKE TOKUSEN SUMINOKAORI *			
Kuretake Co., Ltd.	WATO KURETAKE EKI	*		
NASCO International	NASCO BLACK SATIN	*		
Pelikan USA	PELIKAN FOUNT INDIA	*		
Rock Paint Distrib'g	BLACK VELVET	*		
Royal Talens	INDIA INK			*
Sakura of America	GELLY ROLL FLUORESCENT	*		
Salis International	DR. PH. MARTIN'S BLACK STAR HICARB	*		
Salis International	DR. PH. MARTIN'S BLACK STAR MATTE	*		
Salis International	DR. PH. MARTIN'S IRIDESCENT CALLIGRAHPY COLORS	*		
Salis International	DR. PH. MARTIN'S PERMADRAFT	*		
Winsor & Newton	ARTISTS' DRAWING #			*
Yasutomo & Co.	SUMI INK		*	

Stamp Pads

Avery Dennison	CARTER'S WASHABLE FELT AND FOAM STAMP PAD INKS	*		
Binney & Smith	CRAYOLA WASHABLE	*		
Binney & Smith (Canada)	CRAYOLA STAMPING STATION	*		

Mediums

Koh-I-Noor	ROTRING ARTISTCOLOR EFFECT	*		
Koh-I-Noor	ROTRING ARTISTCOLOR STANDARD *			
Koh-I-Noor	ROTRING ARTISTCOLOR UNIVERSAL*			
Sennelier Beaux Arts	SHELLAC LIQUID GUM			*

ETCHING INKS & MEDIUMS

Grounds

Graphic Chemical & Ink	GRAPHIC EXTRA SOFT OPAQUE	*		
Graphic Chemical & Ink	GRAPHIC HARD OPAQUE	*		
Graphic Chemical & Ink	GRAPHIC HARD TRANSPARENT	*		
Graphic Chemical & Ink	GRAPHIC SOFT OPAQUE	*		
Graphic Chemical & Ink	GRAPHIC SOFT TRANSPARENT	*		
H-B Products Inc.	Z*ACRYL HARDGROUND EMULSION *			
H-B Products Inc.	Z*ACRYL STOP OUT RESIST	*		

Inks

| Graphic Chemical & Ink | GRAPHIC | | | * |
| Daniel Smith, Inc. | DANIEL SMITH ETCHING INKS # | * | | |

 # Some products in this line do not bear the CP, AP or Health Label (Non-Toxic) Seal.

-9-

TABLE 2 (continued)

PRODUCTS AND MANUFACTURERS	BRAND NAMES	CP SEAL	AP SEAL	HL/NT SEAL
ETCHING INKS & MEDIUMS (continued)				
Mediums				
Graphic Chemical & Ink	GRAPHIC SURESET		*	
Daniel Smith, Inc.	DANIEL SMITH BURNT PLATE OILS		*	
Daniel Smith, Inc.	DANIEL SMITH CONVERTING MED.		*	
Daniel Smith, Inc.	DANIEL SMITH ETCHING BLACKS		*	
Daniel Smith, Inc.	DANIEL SMITH LUMP ROSIN		*	
Daniel Smith, Inc.	DANIEL SMITH PROCESS ETCHING INKS #		*	
FIXATIVES				
Back Street, Inc.	COULEE SILK FIX		*	
GESSOS & PAINTING GROUNDS				
Binney & Smith	LIQUITEX GESSO		*	
Binney & Smith	LIQUITEX BASICS GESSO		*	
Certified Color Corp.	ARTIST GESSO		*	
Chroma Acrylics	ATELIER GESSO		*	
Chroma Acrylics	JO SONJA'S ACRYLIC GESSO		*	
Creative Art Products	DICK BLICK ARTIST ACRYLIC GESSO*			
Creative Art Products	SHIVA ACRYLIC LIQUID GESSO		*	
Custom Paint & Chem.	MODERN MASTERS GESSO		*	
Custom Paint & Chem.	MODERN MASTERS PAINTING GROUND		*	
Daler-Rowney	ROWNEY CRYLA GESSO PRIMER			*
Daler-Rowney	ROWNEY GESSO POWDER			*
Delta Tech. Coatings	DELTA GESSO		*	
Demco Industries, Inc.	DEMCO NEW & IMPROVED GESSO		*	
Duro Art Industries	DURO GESSO		*	
Golden Artist Colors	GOLDEN BLACK GESSO		*	
Golden Artist Colors	GOLDEN GESSO		*	
Golden Artist Colors	SANDABLE GESSO		*	
M. Grumbacher, Inc.	ARTISTS' ACRYLIC GESSO		*	
M. Grumbacher, Inc.	ARTISTS' ACRYLIC MODELING PASTE		*	
M. Grumbacher, Inc.	ECONOMY OIL & ACRYLIC GESSO		*	
M. Grumbacher, Inc.	GRUMBACHER GESSO		*	
Holbein Works Ltd.	ACRYLA GESSO			*
Hunt Manufacturing	SPEEDBALL ACRYLIC ARTISTS GESSO		*	
Martin/F. Weber Co.	BOB ROSS BLACK GESSO		*	
Martin/F. Weber Co.	BOB ROSS GRAY GESSO		*	
Martin/F. Weber Co.	BOB ROSS LIQUID BASECOAT		*	
Martin/F. Weber Co.	BOB ROSS WHITE GESSO		*	
Martin/F. Weber Co.	CREATIVE MARK GESSO		*	
Martin/F. Weber Co.	JENKINS BROWN BASECOAT		*	
Martin/F. Weber Co.	MARTIN/F. WEBER ECONOMY GESSO		*	
Martin/F. Weber Co.	PERMALBA GESSO		*	
Palmer Paint	PALMER BLACK GESSO		*	
Palmer Paint	PALMER GESSO		*	
Pebeo of America	GESSO			*
Royal Talens	GESSO			*
Royal Talens	PREPARING SIZE			*
Sax Arts & Crafts	R. B. WALTERS TRUE FLOW ACRYLIC GESSO		*	
Sax Arts & Crafts	SAX TRUE FLOW ACRYLIC GESSO		*	
Sennelier Beaux Arts	SENNELIER UNIVERSAL GESSO		*	
Sennelier Beaux Arts	SENNELIER UNIVERSAL MODELING PASTE		*	
Daniel Smith, Inc.	WORLD'S BEST GESSO		*	
Winsor & Newton	ACRYLIC GESSO PRIMER		*	
GLAZES (CERAMIC)				
Glazes				
American Art Clay	AMACO ALLIGATOR #		*	
American Art Clay	AMACO ARROYA		*	
American Art Clay	AMACO CRYSTALTEX #		*	
American Art Clay	AMACO ENGOBES #		*	
American Art Clay	AMACO F SERIES #		*	
American Art Clay	AMACO LOW FIRE CRACKLE #		*	
American Art Clay	AMACO MAJOLICA GLOSS #		*	
American Art Clay	AMACO MAJOLICA GLOSS DECORATING COLORS (GDC SERIES)		*	
American Art Clay	AMACO MATT (LM SERIES) #		*	
American Art Clay	AMACO OLD WORLD CRACKLE		*	
American Art Clay	AMACO OPALESCENT #		*	
American Art Clay	AMACO SAHARA HIGH FIRE DRY # (HF SERIES)		*	

PRODUCTS AND MANUFACTURERS	BRAND NAMES	CP SEAL	AP SEAL	HL/NT SEAL
GLAZES (CERAMIC) (continued)				
Glazes (continued)				
American Art Clay	AMACO SAHARA HIGH FIRE LIQUID # (HF SERIES)			*
American Art Clay	AMACO UNIQUE TEXTURE			*
American Art Clay	TH-1 TEXTURIZER			*
American Art Clay	TH-2 TEXTURIZER			*
A.R.T. Studio Clay	FIREWARE - FW 2000 SERIES #			*
A.R.T. Studio Clay	GLAZEWERKS LEADFREE LOW-FIRE GLOSS - FW 2000 SERIES #			*
A.R.T. Studio Clay	GLAZEWERKS LEADFREE MAJOLICA - MK2900 SERIES #			*
A.R.T. Studio Clay	NERO (CONE 5) #			*
A.R.T. Studio Clay	NERO (CONE 6) #			*
Ceramichrome, Inc.	AR I			*
Ceramichrome, Inc.	GALAXY			*
Ceramichrome, Inc.	GLOSS #			*
Ceramichrome, Inc.	LAVA FOAM			*
Ceramichrome, Inc.	OK DINNERWARE MATT			*
Ceramichrome, Inc.	SATIN MATT			*
Ceramichrome, Inc.	SPECIALTY #			*
Ceramichrome, Inc.	SPECKLED #			*
Ceramichrome, Inc.	STONEWARE-LIKE			*
Gare, Inc.	CLEAR GLOSS			*
Gare, Inc.	GEMSTONES			*
Gare, Inc.	MAGIC FLOW			*
Gare, Inc.	NON-TOXIC			*
Gare, Inc.	POLISHED STONE #			*
Gare, Inc.	SAHARA STONE			*
Gare, Inc.	SATIN SHEEN			*
Gare, Inc.	SIMPLICITY GLAZES			*
Gare, Inc.	STARLIGHT COLORS #			*
Gare, Inc.	STONEWASHED			*
Mid-South Ceramic Sply.	OPULENCE (LIQUID)			*
Minn/Midwest Clay	LOW FIRE MATT #			*
Minn/Midwest Clay	MATT EARTHENWARE/ M SERIES (LIQUID) #		*	
Minn/Midwest Clay	MED-RANGE STONEWARE MATT/ HM SERIES (LIQUID) #			*
Minn/Midwest Clay	MED-RANGE STONEWARE TRANSPARENT/HT SERIES (LIQ.)		*	
Minn/Midwest Clay	OPAQUE GLOSS EARTHENWARE/ G SERIES (LIQUID) #			*
Minn/Midwest Clay	OPAQUE GLOSS MID-RANGE STONEWARE/ HG SERIES (LIQUID) #			*
Minn/Midwest Clay	OPAQUE GLOSS MID-RANGE STONEWARE HG SERIES (POWDER) #		*	
Minn/Midwest Clay	SLIP GLAZE (POWDERED) #		*	
Minn/Midwest Clay	TRANSPARENT EARTHENWARE/ T SERIES (LIQUID) #			*
Seattle Pottery	BASIC WHITE-SP 1			*
Seattle Pottery	BLACK STAIN-SP 13			*
Seattle Pottery	BROWN MOTTLED-SP 6			*
Seattle Pottery	BROWN STAIN-SP 14			*
Seattle Pottery	BURNT ORANGE-SP 17			*
Seattle Pottery	CHROME GREEN-SP 22			*
Seattle Pottery	DARK BLUE MOTTLED-SP 25			*
Seattle Pottery	GRAY BLUE MOTTLED-SP 10			*
Seattle Pottery	IRON TAN-SP 16			*
Seattle Pottery	MILKY BROWN-SP 21			*
Seattle Pottery	MOLASSES-SP 12			*
Seattle Pottery	OCHRE-SP 11			*
Seattle Pottery	OPAQUE-SP 8			*
Seattle Pottery	RUTILE TAN-SP 23			*
Seattle Pottery	SAND-SP 2			*
Seattle Pottery	SAND OPAQUE-SP 3			*
Seattle Pottery	STORMY GRAY-SP 19			*
Seattle Pottery	TURQUOISE-SP 15			*
Seattle Pottery	YELLOW STAIN-SP 7			*
Sherry's Western	CRACKLE			*
Sherry's Western	WESTERN CLEAR #2000			*
Sherry's Western	WESTERN OPAQUE GLOSS (MAJOLICA)		*	
Sherry's Western	WESTERN SATIN MATT		*	
Spectrum Glazes	CRACKLE			*
Spectrum Glazes	GREEN LINE #			*
Spectrum Glazes	HIGH FIRE 1100 SERIES (LIQUID)#	*		*
Spectrum Glazes	HIGH FIRE 1200 SERIES (LIQUID)#	*		*
Spectrum Glazes	SATIN #			*
Spectrum Glazes	TEXTURE#			*

Some products in this line do not bear the CP, AP or Health Label (Non-Toxic) Seal.

TABLE 2   (continued)

PRODUCTS AND MANUFACTURERS	BRAND NAMES	CP SEAL	AP SEAL	HL/NT SEAL
GLAZES (CERAMIC) (continued)				
Underglazes				
American Art Clay	AMACO DECORATING CRAYONS #	*		
American Art Clay	AMACO DESIGNER VELVETS	*		
American Art Clay	AMACO LIQUID UNDERGLAZES #	*		
American Art Clay	AMACO SEMI-MOIST DECORATING COLORS #	*		
American Art Clay	AMACO SEMI-MOIST DECORATING TUBE COLORS	*		
American Art Clay	AMACO VELVET-1-STROKE #	*		
American Art Clay	AMACO VELVETS #	*		
Ceramichrome, Inc.	ANTIQUE	*		
Ceramichrome, Inc.	BEAUTY FLO OPAQUE #	*		
Ceramichrome, Inc.	DETAIL ONE-STROKE	*		
Ceramichrome, Inc.	TRANZ ONE-STROKE	*		
Gare, Inc.	GARE #	*		
Gare, Inc.	GARE FUN STROKES	*		
Gare, Inc.	GARE-TIQUES	*		
Gare, Inc.	ONE STROKES #	*		
Minn/Midwest Clay	MINNESOTA #	*		
Minn/Midwest Clay	MINNESOTA/MIDWEST #	*		
Minn/Midwest Clay	POTTER'S PENS	*		
Minn/Midwest Clay	POTTER'S PEN REFILLS #	*		
Minn/Midwest Clay	POTTER'S SLIP	*		
Pebeo of America	FILLER UNDERCOAT			*
Pebeo of America	FILLER UNDERCOAT FOR PORCELAINE 150			*
Sherry's Western	WESTERN ENGOBES	*		
Sherry's Western	WESTERN LIQUID #	*		
Spectrum Glazes	ONE-STROKES #	*		
Spectrum Glazes	SPECTRUM #	*		
Overglazes				
American Art Clay	AMACO WATER BASED VERSA COLORS #	*		
GLITTER				
Binney & Smith	JAZZY	*		
Elmer's Products/Borden	ELMER'S GLITTER	*		
Conros Corporation	GLITTER K.	*		
Conros Corporation	KANGA GLITTER	*		
Conros Corporation	ROSS GLITTER	*		
Conros Corporation	ROSS ULTRA GLITTER	*		
Glitterex Corporation	ALU*FLAKE	*		
Glitterex Corporation	DISCO DUST GHT	*		
Glitterex Corporation	POLY*FLAKE	*		
Glitterex Corporation	ROCHEUX	*		
Omega Chalk Factory	OMEGA GLITTER GEL	*		
Rose Art Industries	ROSE ART GLITTER MAGIC	*		
GRAPHIC MASKING LIQUIDS				
Creative Art Products	SHIVA LIQUID MASQUE	*		
M. Grumbacher, Inc.	MISKET LIQUID FRISKET	*		
M. Grumbacher, Inc.	SPEED-O-PAQUE	*		
Martin/F. Weber Co.	SCHEEWE BLUE MASKING FLUID	*		
Pebeo of America	DRAWING GUM			*
Royal Talens	LIQUID MASKING FILM			*
Sennelier Beaux Arts	LIQUID DRAWING GUM			*
LITHO INKS & MEDIUMS				
American Art Clay	LITHO SKETCH INKS	*		
American Art Clay	LITHO SKETCH LITHO GUM	*		
American Art Clay	LITHO SKETCH LITHO PLATE SOLUTION	*		
American Art Clay	LITHO SKETCH TUSCHE	*		
Graphic Chemical & Ink	GRAPHIC	*		
Daniel Smith, Inc.	DANIEL SMITH 14 DEGREE BAUME GUM ARABIC	*		
Daniel Smith, Inc.	DANIEL SMITH BLACK LITHOGRAPHIC INKS	*		
Daniel Smith, Inc.	DANIEL SMITH CARBORUNDUM GRITS	*		
Stones Crayons	STONES LITHOGRAPHIC CRAYONS	*		

PRODUCTS AND MANUFACTURERS	BRAND NAMES	CP SEAL	AP SEAL	HL/NT SEAL
MARKERS				
Audio Visual				
Chartpak	AVP AUDIO VISUAL #			*
Chartpak	AVW AUDIO VISUAL			*
Dixon Ticonderoga	VISAID			*
Dri Mark Products	PROJECTORITE OVERHEAD			*
Empire Berol USA	BEROL TRANSPARENCY			*
Kuretake Co., Ltd.	ZIG PROJECTION TWIN			*
Pentel of America	PENTEL PM2 FOR FILM			*
Sakura of America	VISUAL POWER			*
Sanford Corporation	VIS-A-VIS OVERHEAD PROJECTOR PEN (CHISEL TIP, EXTRA FINE POINT & FINE POINT)			*
Brush Tip				
American Tombow	ABT DUAL BRUSH PENS			*
Dixon Ticonderoga	LOONEY TUNES BUCKET OF BRUSHPENS			*
Dixon Ticonderoga	PRANG BRUSH PENS			*
Dri Mark Products	BUFFALO COLORGRAPHICS DELUXE BRUSH MARKERS		*	
Dri Mark Products	MR. DOODLER BRUSH		*	
Empire Berol USA	COLORING BRUSH MARKER			*
Empire Berol USA	PRISMACOLOR SCHOLAR BRUSH MARKERS			*
Kuretake Co., Ltd.	KURETAKE MANNEN-MOUHITSU			*
Kuretake Co., Ltd.	KURETAKE MANNEN-MOUHITSU MARKER INK			*
Kuretake Co., Ltd.	ZIG MEMORY SYSTEM SCROLL & BRUSH			*
Kuretake Co., Ltd.	ZIG SCROLL & BRUSH TC-5000			*
Pentel of America	PENTEL FR-T101 COLOR BRUSH PEN*			
Pentel of America	PENTEL GFL-T101 COLOR BRUSH PEN*			
Rose Art Industries	KODAK BRILLIANT BRUSH MARKERS-FINELINE			*
Rose Art Industries	POWER RANGERS COLOR BRUSH BROADLINE			*
Sakura of America	PIGMA BRUSH			*
Sakura of America	PIGMA SUMI BRUSH			*
Yasutomo & Co.	Y&C KAIMEI FOUNTAIN BRUSH PEN REFILL CARTRIDGE			*
Yasutomo & Co.	Y&C INSTABRUSH			*
Calligraphy				
Dri Mark Products	BUFFALO COLORGRAPHICS CALLIGRAPHY 1900 SERIES*			
Empire Berol USA	COLORIFIC STATIONERY KIT ITALIC MARKER			*
Hunt Manufacturing	SPEEDBALL ELEGANT WRITER			*
Hunt Manufacturing	SPEEDBALL PERMANENT ELEGANT WRITER			*
Kuretake Co., Ltd.	ZIG CALLIGRAPHY TC-3000			*
Kuretake Co., Ltd.	ZIG CALLIGRAPHY TC-3100			*
Kuretake Co., Ltd.	ZIG CALLIGRAPHY EXTRA TC-3300			*
Kuretake Co., Ltd.	ZIG CALLIGRAPHY EXTRA II TC-3400 *			
Kuretake Co., Ltd.	ZIG CALLIGRAPHY PAINT PEN			*
Kuretake Co., Ltd.	ZIG MEMORY SYSTEM			*
Kuretake Co., Ltd.	ZIG POSTERMAN CALLIGRAPHY			*
Pentel of America	JM20W FOUNTAIN PENTEL			*
Pentel of America	JM208Z ITALIC FOUNTAIN PENTEL			*
Pentel of America	JM213Z ITALIC FOUNTAIN PENTEL			*
Sakura of America	PEN-TOUCH CALLIGRAPHER			*
Sakura of America	PEN-TOUCH CALLIGRAPHER FINE POINT			*
Sakura of America	PEN-TOUCH CALLIGRAPHER MEDIUM POINT			*
Sakura of America	PIGMA CALLIPEN			*
Sanford Corporation	SANFORD CALLIGRAPHIC PEN			*
Staedtler, Inc.	CALLIGRAPH DUO 3002			*
Yasutomo & Co.	Y&C CALLIGRAPHY			*
Coloring/Drawing				
Binney & Smith	CRAYOLA			*
Binney & Smith	CRAYOLA BOLD		*	
Binney & Smith	CRAYOLA BOLDER REGULAR		*	
Binney & Smith	CRAYOLA CHANGEABLES			*
Binney & Smith	CRAYOLA COLOR OVERS			*
Binney & Smith	CRAYOLA COLORFUL WRITERS			*

 # Some products in this line do not bear the CP, AP or Health Label (Non-Toxic) Seal.

TABLE 2   (continued)

MARKERS (continued)

Coloring/Drawing (continued)

PRODUCTS AND MANUFACTURERS	BRAND NAMES	CP SEAL	AP SEAL	HL/NT SEAL
Binney & Smith	CRAYOLA COLORING	*		
Binney & Smith	CRAYOLA DECORATING	*		
Binney & Smith	CRAYOLA DRAWING	*		
Binney & Smith	CRAYOLA GLASSWRITERS		*	
Binney & Smith	CRAYOLA MINI STAMPERS	*		
Binney & Smith	CRAYOLA OVERWRITERS		*	
Binney & Smith	CRAYOLA SECRET WRITER		*	
Binney & Smith	CRAYOLA SUNSPLASHED REGULAR	*		
Binney & Smith	CRAYOLA SUPER TIPS		*	
Binney & Smith	MAGIC MARKER PRESENTATION PLUS	*		
Dinney & Smith	MICKEY COLORTOPPERS	*		
Binney & Smith	PEACOCK SNAP STICKS		*	
Bio-Kingdom	BIO-KINGDOM BIO-BIRDHOUSE MARKERS		*	
Bio-Kingdom	BIO-KINGDOM BIO-WINDOWFEEDER MARKERS		*	
Buncho Corp.	BUNCHO		*	
Dallas Lighthouse	ART MARKERS 5100		*	
Dallas Lighthouse	WRITEWELL		*	
Dixon Ticonderoga	LOONEY TUNES BUCKET OF FUN	*		
Dixon Ticonderoga	LOONEY TUNES MINI STAMPERS		*	
Dixon Ticonderoga	PRANG PROFESSIONAL WATER COLOR		*	
Dixon Ticonderoga	WONDER WANDS	*		
Do-A-Dot Art	DO-A-DOT ART	*		
Dri Mark Products	BLEND-A-DOODLER	*		
Dri Mark Products	COLOR MARKS	*		
Dri Mark Products	MR. DOODLER	*		
Dri Mark Products	MR. DOODLER RECHARGEABLES	*		
Empire Berol USA	BEROL 5000		*	
Empire Berol USA	BEROL 5100		*	
Empire Berol USA	BEROL 8800 SERIES ART		*	
Empire Berol USA	COLORIFIC		*	
Empire Berol USA	COLORIFIC 8500		*	
Empire Berol USA	COLORING MARKER 10 CT., 18 CT., & 30 CT.	*		
Empire Berol USA	HANDHUGGER MARKERS		*	
Empire Berol USA	PRISMACOLOR ART		*	
J. L. Hammett Co.	LIVING COLOR WATERBASE		*	
Hasbro, Inc.	COLORBLASTER		*	
Kuretake Co., Ltd.	ZIG CLEAN COLOR TC-6000		*	
Kuretake Co., Ltd.	ZIG CLEAN COLOR II TC-6600		*	
Kuretake Co., Ltd.	ZIG CLEAN COLOR SUPER TC-7000		*	
Kuretake Co., Ltd.	ZIG MEMORY SYSTEM		*	
Kuretake Co., Ltd.	ZIG MEMORY SYSTEM OPAQUE WRITER		*	
Kuretake Co., Ltd.	ZIG POSTERMAN B		*	
Kuretake Co., Ltd.	ZIG POSTERMAN B & B		*	
Kuretake Co., Ltd.	ZIG POSTERMAN BIGGIE 50		*	
Kuretake Co., Ltd.	ZIG POSTERMAN EF		*	
Kuretake Co., Ltd.	ZIG POSTERMAN F		*	
Kuretake Co., Ltd.	ZIG POSTERMAN M		*	
Kuretake Co., Ltd.	ZIG WOODCRAFT BIG & BROAD		*	
Kuretake Co., Ltd.	ZIG WOODCRAFT CHISEL		*	
Kuretake Co., Ltd.	ZIG WOODCRAFT EXTRA FINE		*	
Kuretake Co., Ltd.	ZIG WOODCRAFT FINE		*	
Lion Pencil Co., Ltd.	CRAYON FACTORY		*	
Lion Pencil Co., Ltd.	LION		*	
Liqui-Mark	LIQUI-MARK BROADLINE WATERBASE	*		
Liqui-Mark	LIQUI-MARK WACKY TIPS	*		
Liqui-Mark	LIQUI-MARK WATERBASE L-800 SERIES	*		
Liqui-Mark	LIQUI-MARK WATERBASE L-810 SERIES	*		
Liqui-Mark	LIQUI-MARK WATERBASE SCHOOL PACK	*		
Liqui-Mark	LIQUI-MARK WATERCOLOR	*		
Liqui-Mark	SWITCHABLES		*	
Pentech International	SPARKLERS		*	
Pentech International	SUPER COLORS		*	
Pentech International	SUPER WASHABLES		*	
Pentel of America	PENTEL COLOR PENS-S360J		*	
Pentel of America	PENTEL COLOR PENS-S360T		*	
Plaid Enterprises	FASTER PLASTER MARKERS		*	
Plaid Enterprises	FASTER PLASTER PAINT PENS		*	

MARKERS (continued)

Coloring/Drawing (continued)

PRODUCTS AND MANUFACTURERS	BRAND NAMES	CP SEAL	AP SEAL	HL/NT SEAL
Rose Art Industries	GARGOYLES FUN WITH STICKERS		*	
Rose Art Industries	GARGOYLES POSTER ART FINELINE		*	
Rose Art Industries	HUNCHBACK OF NOTRE DAME MAGICOLOR CHANGERS			*
Rose Art Industries	ROSE ART	*		
Rose Art Industries	ROSE ART 24 COLORS IN CARRY CASE		*	
Rose Art Industries	ROSE ART 45 MARKERS IN A BUCKET		*	
Rose Art Industries	ROSE ART A-Z STAMPER MARKER BOX		*	
Rose Art Industries	ROSE ART CLASSIC FINELINE		*	
Rose Art Industries	ROSE ART MAGICOLOR CHANGERS	*		
Sakura of America	COLORING PEN			*
Sakura of America	OUTLINER EXTRA FINE POINT			*
Sanford Corporation	McMARKER MIXABLES			*
Sanford Corporation	MR. SKETCH UNSCENTED			*
Sax Arts and Crafts	SAX BUDGET BROAD TIP		*	
Sax Arts and Crafts	SAX BUDGET BULLET TIP		*	
Sax Arts and Crafts	SAX VANGUARD MARKER			*
Staedtler, Inc.	POLYCOLOR 326			*
Western Graphics	CREATIVE COLORING			*
Yasutomo & Co.	Y&C ARTIST-O-CRAT			*
Yasutomo & Co.	Y&C ONECAP			*
Yasutomo & Co.	Y&C ONECAP JUNIOR			*

Dry Erase/Whiteboard

PRODUCTS AND MANUFACTURERS	BRAND NAMES	CP SEAL	AP SEAL	HL/NT SEAL
Avery Dennison	MARKS-A-LOT DRY ERASE			*
Binney & Smith	MAGIC MARKER WHITEBOARD			*
Dallas Lighthouse	DRY ERASE 5430			*
Dallas Lighthouse	SKILCRAFT DRY ERASE #5420			*
Dixon Ticonderoga	QUILL DRY ERASE			*
Dixon Ticonderoga	TICONDEROGA DRY ERASE			*
Dixon Ticonderoga	TICONDEROGA WET ERASE			*
Dri Mark Products	DRI MARK CHISEL TIP DRY ERASE			*
Dri Mark Products	DRI MARK DRY MARKS MEMO BRD.			*
Dri Mark Products	DRI MARK WATER BASED DRY ERASE - BULLET & CHISEL TIP			*
Dri Mark Products	FLUORESCENT WATER BASED DRY ERASE			*
Empire Berol USA	BEROL DRY ERASE			*
Kuretake Co., Ltd.	ZIG WHITEBOARD			*
Kuretake Co., Ltd.	ZIG WHITEBOARD MARKER INK			*
Pentel of America	PENTEL DRY ERASE (MW5, 5S, 6)			*
Rose Art Industries	KODAK DRY ERASE-ASST. COLORS			*
Rose Art Industries	MIRACLE MARKER DRY ERASE			*
Rose Art Industries	MIRACLE MARKER FLUORESCENT DRY ERASE			*
Rose Art Industries	ROSE ART DRY ERASE-ASST. COLORS			*
Rose Art Industries	ROSE ART DRY ERASE BULLET TIP			*
Rose Art Industries	ROSE ART DRY ERASE KIT			*
Rose Art Industries	ROSE ART DRY ERASE 6-PACK ASSORTED COLORS			*
Rose Art Industries	ROSE ART DRY ERASE WEDGE TIP			*
Rose Art Industries	ROSE ART FINELINE DRY ERASE			*
Rose Art Industries	ROSE ART FLUORESCENT DRY ERASE			*
Sakura of America	AQUAWIPE			*
Sakura of America	BLACK LIGHTNING			*
Sakura of America	GENESIS AQUARIUS			*
Sanford Corporation	EXPO DRY ERASE (BULLET TIP, CHISEL TIP, FINE & ULTRA FINE POINT)			*
Sanford Corporation	EXPO 2 LOW ODOR DRY ERASE (BULLET TIP, CHISEL TIP, & FINE POINT)			*
Sanford Corporation	EXPO 2 LOW ODOR DRY ERASE ULTRA FINE POINT			*
The Straight Edge, Inc.	STRAIGHT EDGE			*

Dual Tip

PRODUCTS AND MANUFACTURERS	BRAND NAMES	CP SEAL	AP SEAL	HL/NT SEAL
American Tombow	TOMBOW DUAL TIP PEN			*
Dri Mark Products	BUFFALO COLORGRAPHICS VERSATIP 1300 SERIES		*	
Hunt Manufacturing	SPEEDBALL ELEGANT WRITER TWIN TIP			*

\# Some products in this line do not bear the CP, AP or Health Label (Non-Toxic) Seal.

TABLE 2 (continued)

MARKERS (continued)

Fabric

PRODUCTS AND MANUFACTURERS	BRAND NAMES	CP SEAL	AP SEAL	HL/NT SEAL
Back Street, Inc.	COULEE DETAILER			*
Dri Mark Products	BUFFALO LAUNDRY MARKER			*
Dri Mark Products	FABRIC FUN			*
Dri Mark Products	SCRUBBY PERM. LAUNDRY MARKER*			
Hunt Manufacturing	SPEEDBALL FABRIC PAINTERS			*
Kuretake Co., Ltd.	ZIG TEXTILE MARKER			*
Yasutomo & Co.	Y&C DUAL SHADER			*
Yasutomo & Co.	Y&C FABRICMATE			*
Yasutomo & Co.	Y&C FABRICMATE BLENDER			*
Yasutomo & Co.	Y&C FABRICMATE CHISEL POINT			*

Fluorescent

PRODUCTS AND MANUFACTURERS	BRAND NAMES	CP SEAL	AP SEAL	HL/NT SEAL
Binney & Smith	CRAYOLA FLUORESCENT	*		
Dallas Lighthouse	SKILCRAFT 379 SERIES		*	
Dallas Lighthouse	SKILCRAFT 385 SERIES		*	
Dallas Lighthouse	TOUCHCRAFT 379 SERIES		*	
Dallas Lighthouse	TOUCHCRAFT 385 SERIES		*	
Kuretake Co., Ltd.	ZIG ILLUMIGRAPH B		*	
Kuretake Co., Ltd.	ZIG ILLUMIGRAPH B & B		*	
Kuretake Co., Ltd.	ZIG ILLUMIGRAPH BIGGIE 50		*	
Liqui-Mark	LIQUI-MARK HARD COPY PLUS FLUORESCENT WATERBASE FINELINE		*	
Pentech International	HOTZ-WATERBASE FLUORESCENT	*		
Rose Art Industries	HOT & BRITE		*	
Rose Art Industries	KODAK BOLD		*	
Rose Art Industries	KODAK BRILLIANT		*	
Rose Art Industries	KODAK FLUORESCENT		*	
Rose Art Industries	KODAK FLUORESCENT WASHABLE BROADLINE		*	
Rose Art Industries	KODAK FLUORESCENT WASHABLE FINELINE		*	
Rose Art Industries	ROSE ART BRILLIANT BROADLINE		*	
Rose Art Industries	ROSE ART BRILLIANT BROADLINE-SOLID COLORS*			
Rose Art Industries	ROSE ART BRILLIANT FINELINE		*	
Rose Art Industries	ROSE ART BRILLIANT WASHABLE BROADLINE		*	
Rose Art Industries	ROSE ART BRILLIANT WEDGE TIP		*	
Rose Art Industries	ROSE ART BRILLIANT WEDGE TIP SOLID COLORS		*	
Sanford Corporation	BRIGHT STICKS		*	
Western Publishing	COLOR EXPRESS FLUORESCENT		*	

Graphic Art

PRODUCTS AND MANUFACTURERS	BRAND NAMES	CP SEAL	AP SEAL	HL/NT SEAL
Chartpak	AD		*	
Dri Mark Products	BUFFALO COLORGRAPHICS BROADLINE 1800 SERIES	*		
Dri Mark Products	BUFFALO COLORGRAPHICS FINELINE 1400 SERIES	*		
Fluorographic Services	COL-TEC		*	
Fluorographic Services	COL-TEC REMOVER, EXTRA FINELINE*			
Fluorographic Services	COL-TEC REMOVER, FINE LINE	*		
Fluorographic Services	FLUORO MASKING	*		
Kuretake Co., Ltd.	ZIG KURECOLOR TWIN	*		
Sakura of America	MARKER SG7	*		
Sakura of America	PIGMA GRAPHIC	*		
Sakura of America	PIGMA SKETCH PEN	*		
Sakura of America	PIGMAX	*		
Staedtler, Inc.	MARSGRAPHIC 3000 DUO	*		

Highlighters

PRODUCTS AND MANUFACTURERS	BRAND NAMES	CP SEAL	AP SEAL	HL/NT SEAL
Avery Dennison	HI-LITER GLIDESTIK	*		
Binney & Smith	MAGIC MARKER HIGHLIGHTERS		*	
Chartpak	NRBP		*	
Dallas Lighthouse	FLUORESCENT HIGHLIGHTER 5300	*		
Dallas Lighthouse	SKILCRAFT	*		
Dallas Lighthouse	SKILCRAFT 109 SERIES	*		
Dallas Lighthouse	TOUCHCRAFT	*		
Dallas Lighthouse	TOUCHCRAFT 109 SERIES	*		
Dixon Ticonderoga	LOONEY TUNES FLUORESCENT HIGHLIGHTERS	*		
Dixon Ticonderoga	STAND OUT	*		
Dri Mark Products	COLOR CODER HIGHLIGHTERS		*	*
Dri Mark Products	COMMUNICATOR HIGHLIGHTERS		*	

MARKERS (continued)

Highlighters (continued)

PRODUCTS AND MANUFACTURERS	BRAND NAMES	CP SEAL	AP SEAL	HL/NT SEAL
Dri Mark Products	DRI MARK FLUORESCENT HIGHLIGHTERS		*	
Dri Mark Products	FUNLIGHTERS FLUORESCENT HIGHLIGHTERS			*
Fibro Source USA	UNISON HIGHLIGHTERS			*
Liqui-Mark	LIQUI-MARK HIGHLIGHTER		*	
Liqui-Mark	LIQUI-MARK HIGHLIGHTER L-500 SERIES			*
Liqui-Mark	LIQUI-MARK HIGHLIGHTER L-510 SERIES			*
Pentel of America	PENTEL SL25 DATA CHECKER	*		
Pentel of America	PENTEL S16 SNAPPERS	*		
Pentel of America	PENTEL SFL16 SNAPPERS	*		
Rose Art Industries	KODAK FLUORESCENT HIGHLIGHTER BROADLINE			*
Rose Art Industries	ROSE ART HIGHLIGHTER & HIGHLIGHTER 3-PACK			*
Rose Art Industries	ROSE ART HIGHLIGHTER - SOLID COLORS			*
Sakura of America	FLUORESCENT PIGMENT			*
Sakura of America	LINE MARKER OA TWIN			*
Sanford Corporation	MAJOR ACCENT			*
Sanford Corporation	POCKET ACCENT			*
Schwan-STABILO	STABILO BOSS			*
Schwan-STABILO	STABILO FLASHLIGHTER			*
Schwan-STABILO	STABILO POCKETFLASHER			*
Staedtler, Inc.	COLORSTAR 366			*
Staedtler, Inc.	TOPIC 304			*
Staedtler, Inc.	TOPSTAR 364			*

Memo Board

PRODUCTS AND MANUFACTURERS	BRAND NAMES	CP SEAL	AP SEAL	HL/NT SEAL
Dallas Lighthouse	CHART MARKERS 5120			*
Dri Mark Products	DRI MARK EASEL PAD			*
Dri Mark Products	DRI MARK MEMO BOARD			*
Rose Art Industries	ROSE ART MEMO BOARD		*	

Metallic

PRODUCTS AND MANUFACTURERS	BRAND NAMES	CP SEAL	AP SEAL	HL/NT SEAL
Empire Berol USA	PRISMACOLOR METALLIC			*
Hunt Manufacturing	SPEEDBALL METALLIC PAINTERS			*
Kuretake Co., Ltd.	ZIG PAINTY GOLD & SILVER			*
Kuretake Co., Ltd.	ZIG PAINTY METALLIC			*
Sanford Corporation	GOLD COAT EXTRA FINE POINT			*
Sanford Corporation	GOLD COAT SLIM TIP			*
Sanford Corporation	GOLD DISKRIBE			*
Sanford Corporation	SILVER COAT EXTRA FINE POINT			*
Sanford Corporation	SILVER COAT SLIM TIP			*
Sanford Corporation	SILVER DISKRIBE			*
Yasutomo & Co.	Y&C METALLIC MARKER (BROAD, FINE & EXTRA FINE NIBS)			*

Permanent

PRODUCTS AND MANUFACTURERS	BRAND NAMES	CP SEAL	AP SEAL	HL/NT SEAL
Avery Dennison	MARKS-A-LOT DUALSHARP			*
Avery Dennison	MARKS-A-LOT STAYSHARP			*
Binney & Smith	LIQUITEX			*
Binney & Smith	MAGIC MARKER			*
Binney & Smith	MAGIC MARKER EVERLAST			*
Binney & Smith	MAGIC MARKER PERMANENT			*
Binney & Smith	MAGIC MARKER SUPERFINE			*
Dallas Lighthouse	SKILCRAFT ATL SERIES			*
Dallas Lighthouse	SKILCRAFT ATL 100 SERIES			*
Dallas Lighthouse	SKILCRAFT 575/585 SERIES			*
Dallas Lighthouse	TOUCHCRAFT ATL SERIES			*
Dallas Lighthouse	TOUCHCRAFT ATL 100 SERIES			*
Dallas Lighthouse	TOUCHCRAFT 575/585 SERIES			*
Dallas Lighthouse	WRITEWELL PERMANENT			*
Dixon Ticonderoga	QUILL PERMANENT			*
Dixon Ticonderoga	REDIMARK			*
Dixon Ticonderoga	REDIMARK PERMANENT			*
Dixon Ticonderoga	REDISHARP PERMANENT			*
Dixon Ticonderoga	REDISHARP PLUS			*
Dri Mark Products	DRI MARK PERMA SHARP			*
Dri Mark Products	DRI MARK PERMANENT BROADLINE *			
Dri Mark Products	DRI MARK PERMANENT BULLET TIP			*
Dri Mark Products	DRI MARK THE BRUTE 600 PERM.			*
Fibro Source USA	UNISON THIN LINE PERMANENT			*
Fluorographic Services	FLUORO GRAY			*
Hunt Manufacturing	SPEEDBALL PAINTERS			*

\# Some products in this line do not bear the CP, AP or Health Label (Non-Toxic) Seal.

-13-

TABLE 2 (continued)

PRODUCTS AND MANUFACTURERS	BRAND NAMES	CP SEAL	AP SEAL	HL/NT SEAL
MARKERS (continued)				
Permanent (continued)				
Pentel of America	PENTEL SUPER FINE POINT PERMANENT MF50		*	
Pentel of America	PENTEL 100W WHITE		*	
Polychem Corporation	PAINT IT PRETTY			
Rose Art Industries	ROSE ART PERMANENT BULLET TIP		*	
Rose Art Industries	ROSE ART PERMANENT WEDGE TIP		*	
Rose Art Industries	ROSE ART SUPERMARK PERMANENT		*	
Sakura of America	MICROPERM		*	
Sakura of America	PERMAPAQUE		*	
Sakura of America	PIGMA MICRON		*	
Sanford Corporation	SHARPIE FINE POINT PERMANENT		*	
Sanford Corporation	SHARPIE EXTRA FINE POINT PERM.		*	
Sanford Corporation	SHARPIE ULTRA FINE POINT PERM.		*	
Sanford Corporation	SUPER SHARPIE		*	
Staedtler, Inc.	LUMOCOLOR PERMANENT 357		*	
Staedtler, Inc.	PERMANENT 350, 352		*	
Yasutomo & Co.	Y&C PERMAWRITER II		*	
Scented				
Binney & Smith	CRAYOLA GREAT OUTDOORS SCENTS		*	
Binney & Smith	CRAYOLA SCENTED		*	
Binney & Smith	POOH SCENTED		*	
Binney & Smith (Canada)	CRAYOLA SCENTSATIONS	*		
Dixon Ticonderoga	LOONEY TUNES SCENTED		*	
Dixon Ticonderoga	PRANG SCENTED		*	
Pentech International	SUPER SCENTS		*	
Rose Art Industries	ROSE ART BROADLINE SCENTED		*	
Rose Art Industries	ROSE ART SCENTED STAMPERS		*	
Sanford Corporation	FIDDLE STICKS SCENTED FINE POINT PENS		*	
Sanford Corporation	McMARKERS SCENTED		*	
Sanford Corporation	MR. SKETCH SCENTED INSTANT		*	
Washable				
Avery Dennison	MARKS-A-LOT WASHABLE		*	
Avery Dennison	MARKS-A-LOT WASHABLE JUMBO		*	
Binney & Smith	CRAYOLA BOLDER WASHABLE		*	
Binney & Smith	CRAYOLA SUNSPLASHED WASHABLE		*	
Binney & Smith	CRAYOLA WASHABLE		*	
Binney & Smith	CRAYOLA WASHABLE BOLD	*		
Binney & Smith	CRAYOLA WASHABLE CRAZY TIPS		*	
Binney & Smith	CRAYOLA WASHABLE FLUORESCENT		*	
Binney & Smith	CRAYOLA WASHABLE HIGHLIGHTER		*	
Binney & Smith	CRAYOLA WASHABLE POSTER		*	
Binney & Smith	CRAYOLA WASHABLE WEDGE-TIP		*	
Binney & Smith	MICKEY'S STUFF WASHABLE	*		
Binney & Smith	POOH WASHABLE		*	
Dixon Ticonderoga	LOONEY TUNES FLUORESCENT WASHABLE		*	
Dixon Ticonderoga	LOONEY TUNES WASHABLE	*		
Dixon Ticonderoga	PRANG FUN PRO WASHABLE		*	
Dixon Ticonderoga	PRANG WASHABLE		*	
Dixon Ticonderoga	PRANG WASHABLE BRUSH PEN		*	
Dixon Ticonderoga	PRANG WASHABLE FLUORESCENT		*	
Dixon Ticonderoga	PRANG WASHABLE SKINTONES OF THE WORLD		*	
Dri Mark Products	DRI MARK WASHABLE BULLET TIP		*	
Dri Mark Products	DRI MARK WASHABLE CHISEL TIP		*	
Dri Mark Products	MR. DOODLER BUCKET OF WASHABLE		*	
Dri Mark Products	MR. DOODLER WASHABLE	*		
Empire Berol USA	COLORIFIC WASHABLES		*	
Fibro Source USA	UNISON WASHABLE		*	
J. L. Hammett Co.	LIVING COLOR WASHABLE	*		
Hasbro, Inc.	COLORBLASTER WASHABLE	*		
Hasbro, Inc.	PRO-DOH	*		
Liqui-Mark	LIQUI-MARK BROADLINE WASHABLE		*	

PRODUCTS AND MANUFACTURERS	BRAND NAMES	CP SEAL	AP SEAL	HL/NT SEAL
MARKERS (continued)				
Washable (continued)				
Liqui-Mark	LIQUI-MARK BROADLINE WASHABLE PASTELS		*	
Liqui-Mark	LIQUI-MARK WASHABLE L-200 SERIES		*	
Liqui-Mark	LIQUI-MARK WASHABLE L-210 SERIES		*	
Liqui-Mark	LIQUI-MARK WASHABLE SCHOOL PACK		*	
Liqui-Mark	LIQUI-MARK WASHABLES		*	
Pentech International	SUPER WASHABLES			*
Rose Art Industries	GARGOYLES ACTIVITY CASE FINELINE		*	
Rose Art Industries	GARGOYLES DESIGNER DESK BROADLINE		*	
Rose Art Industries	KODAK BRILLIANT WASHABLE BROADLINE & FINELINE		*	
Rose Art Industries	KODAK WASHABLE BOLD		*	
Rose Art Industries	KODAK WASHABLE BOLD BROADLINE		*	
Rose Art Industries	KODAK WASHABLE CLASSIC		*	
Rose Art Industries	KODAK WASHABLE FLUORESCENT		*	
Rose Art Industries	KODAK WASHABLE MARKER CUBE		*	
Rose Art Industries	LION KING DESIGNER DESK BROADLINE		*	
Rose Art Industries	LION KING MAKE YOUR OWN STICKERS		*	
Rose Art Industries	LION KING POSTER ART FINELINE		*	
Rose Art Industries	LION KING SPONGE & STENCIL CASE		*	
Rose Art Industries	POCAHONTAS ACTIVITY CASE FINELINE		*	
Rose Art Industries	POCAHONTAS DESIGNER DESK BROADLINE		*	
Rose Art Industries	POCAHONTAS FUN WITH STICKERS FINELINE		*	
Rose Art Industries	POCAHONTAS POSTER ART FINELINE		*	
Rose Art Industries	POWER RANGERS COLOR BRUSH BROADLINE		*	
Rose Art Industries	POWER RANGERS DESIGNER DESK FINE & BROADLINE		*	
Rose Art Industries	ROSE ART FUN TIP		*	
Rose Art Industries	ROSE ART PASTEL BROADLINE		*	
Rose Art Industries	ROSE ART PASTEL FINELINE		*	
Rose Art Industries	ROSE ART WASHABLE BOLD		*	
Rose Art Industries	ROSE ART WASHABLE BOLD BROADLINE		*	
Rose Art Industries	ROSE ART WASHABLE BROADLINE		*	
Rose Art Industries	ROSE ART WASHABLE BROADLINE SOLID COLORS		*	
Rose Art Industries	ROSE ART WASHABLE FINELINE		*	
Rose Art Industries	ROSE ART WASHABLE SCHOOL ROOM KIT		*	
Rose Art Industries	ROSE ART WASHABLE STAMPER BROADLINE		*	
Rose Art Industries	ROSE ART WASHABLE SUPER STAMPERS		*	
Rose Art Industries	ROSE ART WASHABLE SUPER TIP		*	
Rose Art Industries	ROSE ART WASHABLE WEDGE TIP		*	
Rose Art Industries	ROSE ART WASHABLE WEDGE TIP SOLID COLORS		*	
Rose Art Industries	SEVEN DWARFS STICKERS FINELINE		*	
Rose Art Industries	STAR WARS SUPER STAMPERS		*	
Rose Art Industries	STAR WARS WASHABLE		*	
Sanford Corporation	McMARKERS WASHABLE			*
Sanford Corporation	MR. SKETCH WASHABLE			*

Some products in this line do not bear the CP, AP or Health Label (Non-Toxic) Seal.

-14-

TABLE 2   (continued)

PRODUCTS AND MANUFACTURERS	BRAND NAMES	CP SEAL	AP SEAL	HL/NT SEAL
MARKERS (continued)				
Washable (continued)				
Sargent Art	SARGENT BROADLINE & FINELINE WASHABLE	*		
Western Publishing	COLOR EXPRESS WASHABLE	*		
Writing				
Dixon Ticonderoga	LOONEY TUNES PENS		*	
Dixon Ticonderoga	TREND		*	
Dri Mark Products	BALLOON MARKER		*	
Kuretake Co., Ltd.	ZIG EMBOSSING PEN		*	
Kuretake Co., Ltd.	ZIG MEMORY SYSTEM 005		*	
Kuretake Co., Ltd.	ZIG MEMORY SYSTEM MILLENNIUM (01, 03, 05 & 08)		*	
Kuretake Co., Ltd.	ZIG NEOTONE B		*	
Kuretake Co., Ltd.	ZIG NEOTONE M		*	
Kuretake Co., Ltd.	ZIG PAINTY		*	
Liqui-Mark	LIQUI-MARK HARD COPY FINELINE	*		
Liqui-Mark	LIQUI-MARK NOTE WRITER FINELINE	*		
Liqui-Mark	LIQUI-MARK NOTE WRITER FINELINE 1000 SERIES	*		
Pentel of America	PENTEL NS167 SIGN PENS		*	
Pentel of America	PENTEL S520 SIGN PENS		*	
Sakura of America	BALLSIGN		*	
Sakura of America	GELLY ROLL		*	
Sakura of America	OUTLINER		*	
Sakura of America	PEN-TOUCH EXTRA-FINE POINT		*	
Sakura of America	PEN-TOUCH FINE POINT		*	
Sakura of America	PEN-TOUCH MEDIUM POINT		*	
Sakura of America	PEN-TOUCH SUPER		*	
Sakura of America	PIGMA CARD WRITING PEN		*	
Sakura of America	PIGMA SIGN		*	
Sakura of America	VISUAL POWER		*	
Sanford Corporation	CELEBRITY AUTOGRAPH PEN		*	
Sanford Corporation	POWER MARK		*	
Sanford Corporation	POWER MARK PLUS		*	
Yasutomo & Co.	Y&C STYLIST		*	
MEDIUMS & VARNISHES, ACRYLIC/POLYMER				
Mediums				
Accents Unlimited	WEE CRAFTS PLASTERCRAFT GLAZE		*	
American Art Clay	AMACO FRIENDLY LACQUER		*	
Balitono	PAINT THE WILD		*	
Binney & Smith	LIQUITEX ACRYLIC OPAQUE GEL		*	
Binney & Smith	LIQUITEX ACRYLIC RETARDER		*	
Binney & Smith	LIQUITEX ACRYLIC SLOW-DRI		*	
Binney & Smith	LIQUITEX BASECOATS		*	
Binney & Smith	LIQUITEX BLENDING & PAINTING		*	
Binney & Smith	LIQUITEX EXTENDER		*	
Binney & Smith	LIQUITEX FABRIC		*	
Binney & Smith	LIQUITEX FLOW-AID FLOW RELEASE		*	
Binney & Smith	LIQUITEX GEL		*	
Binney & Smith	LIQUITEX GLOSSIES		*	
Binney & Smith	LIQUITEX GOUACHE		*	
Binney & Smith	LIQUITEX HEAVY GEL		*	
Binney & Smith	LIQUITEX IRIDESCENT		*	
Binney & Smith	LIQUITEX JAPANESE JAR COLOR EXTENDER		*	
Binney & Smith	LIQUITEX JARPAGUE		*	
Binney & Smith	LIQUITEX LIQUITHICK THICKENER		*	
Binney & Smith	LIQUITEX MATTE		*	
Binney & Smith	LIQUITEX MATTE GEL		*	
Binney & Smith	LIQUITEX MODELING PASTE		*	
Binney & Smith	LIQUITEX PAINTER'S PEARL		*	
Binney & Smith	LIQUITEX POLYMER		*	
Binney & Smith	LIQUITEX TEXTURE GEL-BLACK LAVA		*	
Binney & Smith	LIQUITEX TEXTURE GEL - BLENDED FIBERS		*	
Binney & Smith	LIQUITEX TEXTURE GEL - GLASS BEADS		*	
Binney & Smith	LIQUITEX TEXTURE GEL - GROUND CERAMIC		*	
Binney & Smith	LIQUITEX TEXTURE GEL - LIGHT MODELING PASTE		*	
Binney & Smith	LIQUITEX TEXTURE GEL - NATURAL SAND		*	

PRODUCTS AND MANUFACTURERS	BRAND NAMES	CP SEAL	AP SEAL	HL/NT SEAL
MEDIUMS & VARNISHES, ACRYLIC/POLYMER (continued)				
Mediums (continued)				
Binney & Smith	LIQUITEX TEXTURE GEL-RESIN SAND		*	
Binney & Smith	LIQUITEX TEXTURE GEL - WHITE RANDOM		*	
Cardinal School Sply.	CARDINAL ACRYLIC GEL		*	
Cardinal School Sply.	CARDINAL ACRYLIC POLYMER		*	
Cardinal School Sply.	CARDINAL ACRYLIC RETARDER		*	
Ceramichrome, Inc.	CERAM DECOR PERMENAMEL CLEANER		*	
Ceramichrome, Inc.	DECO ART EXTENDER		*	
Ceramichrome, Inc.	PERMENAMEL RETARDER		*	
Ceramichrome, Inc.	TRANSPARENT		*	
Certified Color Corp.	BEMTEMP LIQUID STARCH		*	
Certified Color Corp.	BESTEMP TEMPERA EXTENDER		*	
Chroma Acrylics	ATELIER BINDER		*	
Chroma Acrylics	ATELIER FLOW CONTROL		*	
Chroma Acrylics	ATELIER GLOSS MEDIUM/VARNISH		*	
Chroma Acrylics	ATELIER IMPASTO GEL		*	
Chroma Acrylics	ATELIER RETARDER		*	
Chroma Acrylics	ATELIER MODELING COMPOUND		*	
Chroma Acrylics	CHROMACRYL BINDER		*	
Chroma Acrylics	CHROMACRYL CLEAR GEL		*	
Chroma Acrylics	CHROMACRYL IMPASTO GEL		*	
Chroma Acrylics	CHROMACRYL TEXTILE		*	
Chroma Acrylics	JO SONJA ALL PURPOSE SEALER		*	
Chroma Acrylics	JO SONJA CLEAR GLAZING		*	
Chroma Acrylics	JO SONJA CRACKLE		*	
Chroma Acrylics	JO SONJA FLOW		*	
Chroma Acrylics	JO SONJA KLEISTER		*	
Chroma Acrylics	JO SONJA RETARDER		*	
Chroma Acrylics	JO SONJA TANNIN BLOCKING SEALER		*	
Chroma Acrylics	JO SONJA TEXTILE		*	
Chroma Acrylics	JO SONJA TEXTURE PASTE		*	
Chroma Acrylics	JO SONJA WOODSTAIN GLAZES		*	
Clay Art	CREATE YOUR OWN TRADE NAME		*	
Creative Art Products	BLICKRYLIC GEL		*	
Creative Art Products	BLICKRYLIC POLYMER		*	
Creative Art Products	BLICKRYLIC RETARDER		*	
Creative Art Products	DICK BLICK ARTIST ACRYLIC GLOSS		*	
Creative Art Products	DICK BLICK ARTIST ACRYLIC GEL		*	
Creative Art Products	DICK BLICK ARTIST ACRYLIC MATTE		*	
Creative Art Products	DICK BLICK ARTIST ACRYLIC MODELING PASTE		*	
Creative Art Products	DICK BLICK ARTIST ACRYLIC RETARDER		*	
Creative Art Products	SHIVA ACRYLIC MATTE		*	
Creative Art Products	SHIVA ACRYLIC RETARDER		*	
Creative Art Products	SHIVA GEL		*	
Creative Art Products	SHIVA ACRYLIC GLOSS		*	
Creative Art Products	SHIVA ACRYLIC MODELING PASTE		*	
Custom Paint & Chem.	MODERN MASTERS ART GEL GLOSS		*	
Custom Paint & Chem.	MODERN MASTERS ART GEL MATTE		*	
Custom Paint & Chem.	MODERN MASTERS GLOSS		*	
Custom Paint & Chem.	MODERN MASTERS MATTE		*	
Daler-Rowney	ROWNEY CRYLA GEL RETARDER			*
Daler-Rowney	ROWNEY CRYLA GLOSS			*
Daler-Rowney	ROWNEY CRYLA MATT			*
Daler-Rowney	ROWNEY CRYLA TEXTURE PASTE			*
Delta Tech. Coatings	CERAMCOAT WOOD SEALER		*	
Delta Tech. Coatings	DELTA ACRYBLEND		*	
Delta Tech. Coatings	DELTA ARTIST GEL		*	
Delta Tech. Coatings	DELTA COLOR FLOAT		*	
Delta Tech. Coatings	DELTA COLOR RESIST		*	
Delta Tech. Coatings	DELTA CRACKLE		*	
Delta Tech. Coatings	DELTA FABRIC CRACKLE		*	
Delta Tech. Coatings	DELTA FABRIC GEL		*	
Delta Tech. Coatings	DELTA SPARKLE GLAZE		*	
Delta Tech. Coatings	HOME DECOR NEUTRAL GEL		*	
Delta Tech. Coatings	HOME DECOR STAIN RESIST		*	
Delta Tech. Coatings	HOME DECOR WOOD SEALER		*	
Delta Tech. Coatings	RENAISSANCE FOIL CRACKLE		*	
Delta Tech. Coatings	RENAISSANCE FOIL SEALER		*	
Delta Tech. Coatings	SOFT TINTS SEALER & MATTE		*	
Pamela Drake Imports	PAINT-A-DIPLO-DINO GLOSS		*	
Pamela Drake Imports	PAINT-A-FISH GLAZE		*	
Pamela Drake Imports	PAINT-A-LIZARD GLAZE		*	

Some products in this line do not bear the CP, AP or Health Label (Non-Toxic) Seal.

TABLE 2   (continued)

MEDIUMS & VARNISHES, ACRYLIC/POLYMER (continued)

Mediums (continued)

PRODUCTS AND MANUFACTURERS	BRAND NAMES	CP SEAL	AP SEAL	HL/NT SEAL
Pamela Drake Imports	PAINT-A-SNAKE GLAZE		*	
Pamela Drake Imports	PAINT-A-TIPI GLOSS		*	
Pamela Drake Imports	PAINT-A-TYRA-DINO GLOSS		*	
Duro Art Industries	MATTE		*	
Duro Art Industries	POLYMER GEL		*	
Duro Art Industries	POLYMER GLOSS		*	
Fiesta Colors	KLEERKOTE		*	
Fiesta Colors	PEARLSHEEN		*	
First Preference Prods.	LINIT LIQUID STARCH		*	
Golden Artist Colors	ACRYLIC MODIFIER FOR PLASTER		*	
Golden Artist Colors	ACRYLIC RETARDER		*	
Golden Artist Colors	FILM MODIFIER		*	
Golden Artist Colors	FLUID MATTE		*	
Golden Artist Colors	GELS		*	
Golden Artist Colors	GLAZE EXTENDER (GLOSS & SATIN)		*	
Golden Artist Colors	MATTE		*	
Golden Artist Colors	MC CLOSKEY CLEAR GLAZE		*	
Golden Artist Colors	MOLDING PASTE		*	
Golden Artist Colors	POLYMER 100, 200, 500, 700, 800		*	
Golden Artist Colors	RETARDER		*	
Golden Artist Colors	VALSPAR CLEAR GLAZE		*	
M. Grumbacher, Inc.	ACCENT CLEAR SEALER		*	
M. Grumbacher, Inc.	ACCENT CRACKLE MEDIUM		*	
M. Grumbacher, Inc.	ACCENT CRAFT PROTECTOR CLEAR GLOSS		*	
M. Grumbacher, Inc.	ACCENT CRYSTAL CLEAR GLAZE		*	
M. Grumbacher, Inc.	ACCENT EXTENDER/RETARDER		*	
M. Grumbacher, Inc.	ACCENT FABRIC PAINTING		*	
M. Grumbacher, Inc.	ACCENT PAPER LAYERS GLAZE		*	
M. Grumbacher, Inc.	ACRYLIC GEL GLOSS		*	
M. Grumbacher, Inc.	ACRYLIC GEL MATTE		*	
M. Grumbacher, Inc.	ACRYLIC HEAVY GEL GLOSS		*	
M. Grumbacher, Inc.	ACRYLIC HEAVY GEL MATTE		*	
M. Grumbacher, Inc.	ARTISTS' ACRYLIC FLOW ENHANCER		*	
M. Grumbacher, Inc.	ARTISTS' ACRYLIC CLEAR BLEND		*	
M. Grumbacher, Inc.	ARTISTS' ACRYLIC GLOSS MEDIUM & VARNISH		*	
M. Grumbacher, Inc.	ARTISTS' ACRYLIC MATTE MEDIUM & VARNISH		*	
M. Grumbacher, Inc.	ARTISTS' ACRYLIC SLOW BLEND		*	
M. Grumbacher, Inc.	ARTISTS' ACRYLIC WHITE BLEND		*	
M. Grumbacher, Inc.	HYSLO		*	
Holbein Works Ltd.	ACRYLA GEL			*
Holbein Works Ltd.	ACRYLA GLOSS			*
Holbein Works Ltd.	ACRYLA MAT			*
Holbein Works Ltd.	ACRYLA MODELLING PASTE			*
Hunt Manufacturing	SPEEDBALL GEL		*	
Hunt Manufacturing	SPEEDBALL GLOSS		*	
Hunt Manufacturing	SPEEDBALL MATTE		*	
Hunt Manufacturing	SPEEDBALL MODELING PASTE		*	
J. W. Etc.	FIRST-STEP WOOD SEALER		*	
L & L Monn Productions	APPLICATING GEL & SEALANT		*	
Lakeshore Learning Materials	BEST-BUY TEMPERA EXTENDER		*	
Lefranc & Bourgeois	FLASHE			*
Lefranc & Bourgeois	POLYFLASHE GEL			*
Lefranc & Bourgeois	POLYFLASHE GESSO			*
Lefranc & Bourgeois	POLYFLASHE MODELING PASTE			*
Lefranc & Bourgeois	POLYFLASHE OPAQUE			*
Lefranc & Bourgeois	POLYFLASHE RETARDER			*
Martin/F. Weber Co.	PERMALBA GEL		*	
Martin/F. Weber Co.	PERMALBA GLOSS		*	
Martin/F. Weber Co.	PERMALBA MATTE		*	
Martin/F. Weber Co.	PERMALBA MODELING PASTE		*	
Martin/F. Weber Co.	PERMALBA RETARDER		*	
Martin/F. Weber Co.	SCHEEWE TEXTURING MEDIUM		*	
NASCO International	BULKRYLIC GEL		*	
NASCO International	BULKRYLIC POLYMER		*	
NASCO International	BULKRYLIC RETARDER		*	
Palmer Paint Products	CREATIVE TOUCH LIQUID DRAPE		*	
Palmer Paint Products	CREATIVE TOUCH OVERGLAZES		*	
Palmer Paint Products	LIQUID PODGE		*	
Palmer Paint Products	PRISM PEARLY GLAZE		*	
Palmer Paint Products	TRANSPARENT PAINT		*	
Pebeo of America	BINDEX			*
Pebeo of America	BLACK MICA MORTAR			*
Pebeo of America	CRYSTAL MORTAR			*
Pebeo of America	GLOSS			*
Pebeo of America	GLOSS GEL			*

MEDIUMS & VARNISHES, ACRYLIC/POLYMER (continued)

Mediums (continued)

PRODUCTS AND MANUFACTURERS	BRAND NAMES	CP SEAL	AP SEAL	HL/NT SEAL
Pebeo of America	HEAVY GEL			*
Pebeo of America	IRIDESCENT GEL			*
Pebeo of America	MATTE			*
Pebeo of America	MATTE GEL			*
Pebeo of America	MODELING PASTE			*
Pebeo of America	PUMICE STONE MORTAR			*
Pebeo of America	SAND MORTAR			*
Pebeo of America	STRUCTURE GEL			*
Plaid Enterprises	DECAL-IT	*		
Plaid Enterprises	DIMENSIONAL MAGIC	*		
Plaid Enterprises	EUROBISQUE SPRAY FINISH	*		
Plaid Enterprises	FASHION SHOW LIQUID BEAD FOIL BOND	*		
Plaid Enterprises	LIQUID LEADING	*		
Plaid Enterprises	ROYAL COAT DECOUPAGE FINISH	*		
Plaid Enterprises	VOLAIR	*		
Pyramid Art Supply	PYRA-CRYLIC GEL	*		
Pyramid Art Supply	PYRA-CRYLIC POLYMER	*		
Pyramid Art Supply	PYRA-CRYLIC RETARDER	*		
Rock Paint Distrib'g	HANDY ART GEL	*		
Rock Paint Distrib'g	HANDY ART POLYMER	*		
Rock Paint Distrib'g	HANDY ART RETARDER	*		
Royal Talens	HEAVY GEL MEDIUM			*
Royal Talens	REMBRANDT GLOSSY			*
Royal Talens	REMBRANDT MAT			*
Royal Talens	REMBRANDT RETARDER			*
Royal Talens	TALENS GEL			*
Salis International	DR. PH. MARTIN'S SPECTRALITE COLOR EXTENDER	*		
Sennelier Beaux Arts	ACRYLIC MEDIUM			*
Sennelier Beaux Arts	PEINTEX EPAISSISSANT			*
Daniel Smith, Inc.	DANIEL SMITH ACRYLIC GLOSS	*		
Daniel Smith, Inc.	DANIEL SMITH ACRYLIC MATTE	*		
Triarco Arts & Crafts	TRI-CRYLIC GEL	*		
Triarco Arts & Crafts	TRI-CRYLIC POLYMER	*		
Triarco Arts & Crafts	TRI-CRYLIC RETARDER	*		
Turner Colour Works	ACRYL COLOUR FOUNDATION WHITE			*
Turner Colour Works	ACRYL COLOUR GEL			*
Turner Colour Works	ACRYL COLOUR GLOSS			*
Turner Colour Works	ACRYL COLOUR GRADATION			*
Turner Colour Works	ACRYL COLOUR PRIMER			*
Turner Colour Works	ACRYL COLOUR RETARDER			*
Turner Colour Works	ACRYL GOUACHE GEL			*
Turner Colour Works	ACRYL GOUACHE PRIMER			*
Turner Colour Works	ACRYL GOUACHE RETARDER			*
Turner Colour Works	NEO COLOUR PROCESS			*
Utrecht Mfg. Co.	ACRYLIC GEL	*		
Utrecht Mfg. Co.	ACRYLIC MATTE	*		
Winsor & Newton	FLOW IMPROVER			*
Winsor & Newton	GEL			*
Winsor & Newton	GLOSS			*
Winsor & Newton	MATT			*
Winsor & Newton	RETARDER			*

Varnishes

PRODUCTS AND MANUFACTURERS	BRAND NAMES	CP SEAL	AP SEAL	HL/NT SEAL
Back Street, Inc.	ANITA'S POLYURETHANE	*		
Binney & Smith	LIQUITEX HIGH GLOSS	*		
Binney & Smith	LIQUITEX JAPANESE FAST DRY	*		
Binney & Smith	LIQUITEX MATTE	*		
Binney & Smith	LIQUITEX SATIN	*		
Ceramichrome, Inc.	MATT BRUSH-ON SEALER	*		
Chroma Acrylics	CHROMACRYL WATER BASED FINISHING	*		
Chroma Acrylics	JO SONJA POLYURETHANE	*		
Creative Art Products	DICK BLICK ARTIST MATTE	*		
Delta Tech. Coatings	CERAMCOAT WATER BASED EXTERIOR SATIN	*		
Delta Tech. Coatings	CERAMCOAT WATER BASED GLOSS	*		
Delta Tech. Coatings	CERAMCOAT WATER BASED MATTE	*		
Delta Tech. Coatings	CERAMCOAT WATER BASED SATIN	*		
Delta Tech. Coatings	EXTERIOR	*		
Delta Tech. Coatings	HOME DECOR WATER BASED EXTERIOR SATIN	*		
Delta Tech. Coatings	HOME DECOR WATER BASE GLOSS	*		
Delta Tech. Coatings	HOME DECOR WATER BASE MATTE	*		
Delta Tech. Coatings	HOME DECOR WATER BASE SATIN	*		

Some products in this line do not bear the CP, AP or Health Label (Non-Toxic) Seal.

TABLE 2   (continued)

MEDIUMS & VARNISHES, ACRYLIC/POLYMER (continued)

Varnishes (continued)

PRODUCTS AND MANUFACTURERS	BRAND NAMES	CP SEAL	AP SEAL	HL/NT SEAL
M. Grumbacher, Inc.	ACCENT CLEAR GLOSS		*	
M. Grumbacher, Inc.	ACCENT CLEAR MATTE		*	
M. Grumbacher, Inc.	ACCENT WATERBASED		*	
Holbein Works Ltd.	ACRYLA CRYSTAL			*
J. W. Etc.	POLYURETHANE GLOSS	*		
J. W. Etc.	POLYURETHANE MATTE	*		
J. W. Etc.	RIGHT STEP GLOSS	*		
J. W. Etc.	RIGHT STEP MATTE	*		
J. W. Etc.	RIGHT STEP SATIN	*		
Maple Ridge Paint Co.	1837 LEGACY STAIN	*		
Palmer Paint Products	PRISM VARNISH, GLOSS & SATIN	*		
Pebeo of America	GLOSS			*
Pebeo of America	MATTE			*
Plaid Enterprises	APPLE BARREL WATER-BASED	*		
Plaid Enterprises	DECORATOR GLAZE, GLOSS	*		
Plaid Enterprises	DECORATOR GLAZE, MATTE	*		
Plaid Enterprises	FASHION SHOW LIQUID BEAD FOIL SEALER	*		
Plaid Enterprises	FASTER PLASTER	*		
Plaid Enterprises	FOLK ART GLOW	*		
Plaid Enterprises	FOLK ART WATER-BASED	*		
Plaid Enterprises	LIQUID BEAD FOIL SEALER	*		
Turner Colour Works	ACRYL COLOUR GLOSS		*	
Turner Colour Works	ACRYL COLOUR MATTE		*	
Turner Colour Works	ACRYL GOUACHE GLOSS		*	
Winsor & Newton	GLOSS		*	
Winsor & Newton	MATT		*	

MEDIUMS & VARNISHES, ALKYD & OIL

Oils

PRODUCTS AND MANUFACTURERS	BRAND NAMES	CP SEAL	AP SEAL	HL/NT SEAL
Binney & Smith	LIQUITEX ARTIST GENUINE STAND, HEAVY		*	
Binney & Smith	LIQUITEX ARTIST GENUINE STAND, LIGHT		*	
Binney & Smith	LIQUITEX ARTIST LINSEED		*	
Creative Art Products	BLICK'S LARD		*	
Creative Art Products	SHIVA LINSEED		*	
Creative Art Products	SHIVA SUN-THICKENED STAND		*	
Daler-Rowney	ROWNEY LINSEED			*
Daler-Rowney	ROWNEY LINSEED STAND			*
Daler-Rowney	ROWNEY POPPY			*
Dhanes Company	LINSEED OIL		*	
Dhanes Company	PALE DRYING LINSEED OIL		*	
Dhanes Company	POPPYSEED OIL		*	
Dhanes Company	STAND OIL		*	
Dhanes Company	SUN THICKENED LINSEED OIL		*	
Duro Art Industries	LINSEED		*	
M. Grumbacher, Inc.	LINSEED		*	
M. Grumbacher, Inc.	PALE DRYING		*	
M. Grumbacher, Inc.	POPPYSEED		*	
M. Grumbacher, Inc.	STAND		*	
M. Grumbacher, Inc.	SUN-THICKENED LINSEED		*	
Holbein Works Ltd.	LINSEED			*
Holbein Works Ltd.	POPPY			*
Holbein Works Ltd.	STAND LINSEED			*
Holbein Works Ltd.	SUN THICKENED LINSEED			*
Holbein Works Ltd.	SUN THICKENED POPPY			*
Martin/F. Weber Co.	WEBER LINSEED		*	
Martin/F. Weber Co.	WEBER PROCESS THICKENED LINSEED		*	
Martin/F. Weber Co.	WEBER STAND		*	
Pebeo of America	CLARIFIED POPPYSEED			*
Pebeo of America	LINSEED			*
Royal Talens	TALENS PURIFIED LINSEED			*
Royal Talens	TALENS STAND			*
Sennelier Beaux Arts	BLEACHED LINSEED OIL			*
Sennelier Beaux Arts	CLARIFIED LINSEED OIL			*
Sennelier Beaux Arts	CLARIFIED POPPY OIL			*
Sennelier Beaux Arts	COLD PRESSED LINSEED OIL			*
Sennelier Beaux Arts	SAFFLOWER OIL			*
Daniel Smith, Inc.	DANIEL SMITH POPPYSEED	*		
Daniel Smith, Inc.	DANIEL SMITH REFINED LINSEED	*		
Daniel Smith, Inc.	DANIEL SMITH STAND	*		
Winsor & Newton	LINSEED - COLD PRESSED			*
Winsor & Newton	LINSEED - DRYING			*
Winsor & Newton	LINSEED - REFINED			*
Winsor & Newton	LINSEED - SUN BLEACHED			*
Winsor & Newton	POPPY - SUNBLEACHED			*
Winsor & Newton	STAND LINSEED			*
Winsor & Newton	SUN-THICKENED LINSEED			*

MEDIUMS & VARNISHES, ALKYD & OIL (continued)

Painting Mediums - Gels

PRODUCTS AND MANUFACTURERS	BRAND NAMES	CP SEAL	AP SEAL	HL/NT SEAL
Fiesta Colors	TONER MEDIUM		*	
M. Grumbacher, Inc.	M.G. GEL		*	
Royal Talens	REMBRANDT CASEIN TEMPERA BINDER			*
Daniel Smith, Inc.	DANIEL SMITH TRANSPARENT BLENDER		*	
Winsor & Newton	OLEOPASTO			*
Winsor & Newton	WIN-GEL			*

Painting Mediums - Liquids

PRODUCTS AND MANUFACTURERS	BRAND NAMES	CP SEAL	AP SEAL	HL/NT SEAL
Creative Art Products	SHIVA CASEIN EMULSION		*	
Sennelier Beaux Arts	STANDOLIE			*

Varnishes

PRODUCTS AND MANUFACTURERS	BRAND NAMES	CP SEAL	AP SEAL	HL/NT SEAL
Lefranc & Bourgeois	BALL OF BLACK			*
Lefranc & Bourgeois	SOFT BLACK			*

MEDIUMS & VARNISHES, MULTI-PURPOSE

PRODUCTS AND MANUFACTURERS	BRAND NAMES	CP SEAL	AP SEAL	HL/NT SEAL
Back Street, Inc.	COULEE SILK RESIST		*	
Ceramichrome, Inc.	CONTROL MEDIUM		*	
Creative Art Products	DICK BLICK MULTI-GEL		*	
Delta Tech. Coatings	DELTA JEWELRY GLAZE		*	
Delta Tech. Coatings	SOFT TINTS GLOSS GLAZE		*	
Pebeo of America	ANTI-DIFFUSER PEBEO SILK			*
Pebeo of America	DILUENT SETASILK			*
Pebeo of America	THICKENER MARBLING			*
Pebeo of America	THICKENER PEBEO SILK			*
Pebeo of America	WATER BASED GUTTA			*
Plaid Enterprises	COLOR STEPS REPAIR MEDIUM		*	
Plaid Enterprises	FASTER PLASTER GLUE		*	
Plaid Enterprises	FOLK ART ANTIQUING MEDIUM		*	
Plaid Enterprises	FOLK ART CRACKLE		*	
Plaid Enterprises	FRENCH WASH		*	
Plaid Enterprises	GLU 'N WASH		*	
Plaid Enterprises	PICKLING		*	
Plaid Enterprises	PICTURE THIS		*	
Plaid Enterprises	TREASURE GOLD MEDIUM		*	
Plaid Enterprises	WATERBASED ANTIQUING		*	
Salis International	DR. PH. MARTIN'S PHOTO-ACE		*	
Sennelier Beaux Arts	FISH GLUE			*
Sennelier Beaux Arts	STOP FLOW			*
Sennelier Beaux Arts	WATER BASED GUTTA			*
Daniel Smith, Inc.	DANIEL SMITH BEESWAX PASTILLES	*		
Daniel Smith, Inc.	DANIEL SMITH CARRAGEENAN	*		
Daniel Smith, Inc.	DANIEL SMITH GLASS BEADS	*		
Daniel Smith, Inc.	DANIEL SMITH GUM DAMAR CRYSTALS	*		
Daniel Smith, Inc.	DANIEL SMITH GUM TRAGACANTH	*		

MEDIUMS & VARNISHES, WATER COLOR

PRODUCTS AND MANUFACTURERS	BRAND NAMES	CP SEAL	AP SEAL	HL/NT SEAL
Chroma Acrylics	ATELIER WATER COLOR MEDIUM		*	
Daler-Rowney	COLORFLEX		*	
Daler-Rowney	GUM ARABIC SOLUTION		*	
Daler-Rowney	LUMA LIQUID MASK		*	
Daler-Rowney	OX GALL SOLUTION		*	
Daler-Rowney	WATERCOLOUR IMPASTO GEL		*	
Daler-Rowney	WAX-GRIP		*	
Eberhard Faber GmbH	FIMO SPECIAL GLOSS VARNISH		*	
Eberhard Faber GmbH	FIMO SPECIAL MATT VARNISH		*	
Pebeo of America	OX GALL			*
Salis International	DR. PH. MARTIN'S COLOR-OUT		*	
Salis International	DR. PH. MARTIN'S FRISKET MASK LIQUID		*	
Sennelier Beaux Arts	WATERCOLOR BINDING MEDIUM			*
Daniel Smith, Inc.	DANIEL SMITH OXGALL LIQUID		*	
Daniel Smith, Inc.	DANIEL SMITH PREMIUM GUM ARABIC		*	
Daniel Smith, Inc.	DANIAL SMITH STANDARD GUM ARABIC		*	
Winsor & Newton	AQUAPASTO			*
Winsor & Newton	ART MASKING FLUID			*
Winsor & Newton	ART MASKING FLUID COLOURLESS			*
Winsor & Newton	PREPARED SIZE			*
Winsor & Newton	WATERCOLOUR MEDIUM			*

Some products in this line do not bear the CP, AP or Health Label (Non-Toxic) Seal.

TABLE 2   (continued)

PRODUCTS AND MANUFACTURERS	BRAND NAMES	CP SEAL	AP SEAL	HL/NT SEAL
PAINTS				
Acrylic, Artists				
A & W Products	A & W GLOW IN THE DARK		*	
Accents Unlimited	WEE CRAFTS PLASTERCRAFT PAINTS		*	
Advancing Play	COLOUR BLAST		*	
American Art Clay	REWARD SUNBURST A TOUCH OF GLITTER		*	
Balitono	PAINT THE WILD		*	
Binney & Smith	CRAYOLA	*		
Binney & Smith	CRAYOLA CRAFT		*	
Binney & Smith	CRAYOLA PERMANENT	*		
Binney & Smith	LIQUITEX	*		
Binney & Smith	LIQUITEX ACRYLIC GOUACHE*	*		
Binney & Smith	LIQUITEX BASECOATS		*	
Binney & Smith	LIQUITEX BASICS	*		
Binney & Smith	LIQUITEX CONCENTRATED ARTIST COLORS #	*	*	
Binney & Smith	LIQUITEX CONCENTRATED DECORATIVE		*	
Binney & Smith	LIQUITEX CONCENTRATED OPALESCENTS		*	
Binney & Smith	LIQUITEX FLUORESCENT JAR COLORS		*	
Binney & Smith	LIQUITEX GLOSSIES		*	
Binney & Smith	LIQUITEX INTERFERENCE		*	
Binney & Smith	LIQUITEX IRIDESCENT		*	
Binney & Smith	LIQUITEX JAR COLORS	*	*	*
Binney & Smith	LIQUITEX JAR DECORATIVE METALLICS		*	
Binney & Smith	LIQUITEX LIQUID GEMS		*	
Binney & Smith	LIQUITEX STRUCTURAL PAINT		*	
Binney & Smith	LIQUITEX TUBE COLORS #	*	*	
Binney & Smith	LIQUITEX WOOD STAINS		*	
Binney & Smith	MICKEY'S STUFF		*	
Binney & Smith	PRO MODELER BY MONOGRAM		*	
Binney & Smith	PRO MODELER BY MONOGRAM GLOSS		*	
Binney & Smith	REVELL FLAT MODEL PAINT		*	
Binney & Smith	REVELL GLOSS MODEL PAINT		*	
Caldex Enterprises	BON ARTISTE MATTE ACRYLIC		*	
Caldex Enterprises	BON ARTISTE PEARL & METALLIC #		*	
Cardinal School Sply.	CARDINAL		*	
Carnival Arts	HAUTE COLOURS		*	
Carnival Arts	ULTRA HAUTE RADIANCE		*	
Carnival Arts	VILLAGE CLASSICS AMERICAN		*	
Carnival Arts	VILLAGE CLASSICS PASTEL		*	
Carnival Arts	VILLAGE CLASSICS PRIMARY		*	
Carnival Arts	VILLAGE INTERNATIONAL		*	
Ceramichrome, Inc.	DECOART AMERICANA		*	
Chroma Acrylics	ATELIER #			*
Chroma Acrylics	CHROMACRYL		*	
Chroma Acrylics	CHROMACRYL JUNIOR		*	
Chroma Acrylics	JO SONJA		*	
Chroma Acrylics	JO SONJA'S BACKGROUND COLORS	*		
Clay Art	CREATE YOUR OWN TRADE NAME #		*	
ColArt Fine Art/Graphics	REEVES ACRYLIC COLOURS		*	
Color Craft Ltd.	CREATEX POSTER/FABRIC COLORS		*	
Conros Corporation	ROSS-CONROS GLITTER PAINT		*	
Creative Art Products	BLICKRYLIC		*	
Creative Art Products	DICK BLICK ARTISTS		*	
Creative Art Products	SHIVA SIGNA-TEX		*	
Custom Paint & Chem.	MODERN MASTERS #		*	
Da Vinci Paint Co.	DA VINCI ARTISTS'		*	
Daler-Rowney	ROWNEY CRYLA ARTISTS #			*
Daler-Rowney	ROWNEY CRYLA FLOW #			*
Daler-Rowney	ROWNEY SYSTEM 3			*
Delta Tech. Coatings	CERAMCOAT		*	
Delta Tech. Coatings	CERAMCOAT GLAZING COLORS		*	
Delta Tech. Coatings	CERAMCOAT WATER BASED ANTIQUE COLORS		*	
Delta Tech. Coatings	DECORATIVE SNOW		*	
Delta Tech. Coatings	DELTA ANTIQUE GEL		*	
Delta Tech. Coatings	DELTA FLORAL ACCENTS		*	
Delta Tech. Coatings	DELTA GLASS STAIN		*	
Delta Tech. Coatings	DELTA SOFT TINTS		*	
Delta Tech. Coatings	FANTASY SNOW		*	
Delta Tech. Coatings	HI-GLOSS CERAMCOAT		*	
Delta Tech. Coatings	HOME DECOR GEL STAINS		*	
Delta Tech. Coatings	HOME DECOR PEARL GLAZE		*	
Delta Tech. Coatings	HOME DECOR WOOD STAIN		*	
PAINTS (continued)				
Acrylic, Artists (continued)				
Delta Tech. Coatings	PERMENAMEL CLEAR GLOSS GLAZE	*		
Delta Tech. Coatings	PERMENAMEL SATIN GLAZE		*	
Delta Tech. Coatings	RENAISSANCE FOIL ANTIQUING COLORS		*	
Delta Tech. Coatings	RENAISSANCE FOIL BASE COATS		*	
Demco Manufacturing	DEMCRYL		*	
Derivan of Canada	DERIVAN STUDENT GRADE		*	
Pamela Drake Imports	PAINT-A-DIPLO-DINO		*	
Pamela Drake Imports	PAINT-A-FISH		*	
Pamela Drake Imports	PAINT-A-LIZARD		*	
Pamela Drake Imports	PAINT-A-SNAKE		*	
Pamela Drake Imports	PAINT-A-TIPI		*	
Pamela Drake Imports	PAINT-A-TYRA-DINO		*	
Duro Art Industries	DURO		*	
Golden Artist Colors	DECORATIVE FINISHES		*	
Golden Artist Colors	FLUID #		*	
Golden Artist Colors	FLUORESCENT COLORS		*	
Golden Artist Colors	GAC HEAVY		*	
Golden Artist Colors	GOLDEN #		*	
Golden Artist Colors	HIGH LOAD		*	
Golden Artist Colors	INTERFERENCE COLORS		*	
Golden Artist Colors	MATTE		*	
Golden Artist Colors	MC CLOSKY SPECIAL EFFECTS		*	
Golden Artist Colors	PASTE		*	
Golden Artist Colors	VALSPAR DECORATIVE EFFECTS		*	
M. Grumbacher, Inc.	ACCENT		*	
M. Grumbacher, Inc.	ACCENT COUNTRY COLORS		*	
M. Grumbacher, Inc.	ACCENT CROWN JEWELS METALLIC		*	
M. Grumbacher, Inc.	ACCENT PRIMER		*	
M. Grumbacher, Inc.	ACCENT STAINING GLAZE		*	
M. Grumbacher, Inc.	BASECOATS - MATTE FINISH		*	
M. Grumbacher, Inc.	ARTISTS' ACRYLIC JAR COLORS #	*	*	
M. Grumbacher, Inc.	FINEST ACRYLIC COLORS #		*	
M. Grumbacher, Inc.	GRUMBACHER #		*	
M. Grumbacher, Inc.	HOBBYCRAFT FLUORESCENTS		*	
M. Grumbacher, Inc.	HOBBYCRAFT HIGH GLOSS ENAMEL		*	
M. Grumbacher, Inc.	HOBBYCRAFT METALLIC ENAMEL		*	
M. Grumbacher, Inc.	HOBBYCRAFT SATIN ENAMEL		*	
Harstrup Assoc./NorArt	EDVARD MUNCH ACRYL		*	
Holbein Works Ltd.	HOLBEIN ACRYLA #			*
Hunt Manufacturing	SPEEDBALL			
J. W. Etc.	ACRYLIC WOOD STAIN		*	
J. W. Etc.	WHITE LIGHTNING		*	
Lefranc & Bourgeois	FLASHE VASARELY			*
Lefranc & Bourgeois	LOUVRE ACRYLIC COLOURS		*	
Lefranc & Bourgeois	POLYFLASHE			*
Maimeri USA	MAIMERI BRERA #	*		*
Maple Ridge Paint Co.	1837 LEGACY ACRYLIC PAINTS		*	
Martin/F. Weber Co.	ART STORE		*	
Martin/F. Weber Co.	PERMALBA		*	
Martin/F. Weber Co.	PRIMA ACRYLIC COLORS		*	
Martin/F. Weber Co.	WEBER ACRYLIC BASE		*	
NASCO International	BULKRYLIC		*	
NES Arnold Inc.	SCOLA PEARL		*	
Oasis Art & Craft Prod.	OASIS PAINT BY NUMBERS		*	
Paint Effects, Inc.	PAINT EFFECTS GLAZING LIQUID		*	
Palmer Paint Products	CREATIVE TOUCH BASIC COLORS	*		
Palmer Paint Products	CREATIVE TOUCH CHRISTMAS COLORS		*	
Palmer Paint Products	CREATIVE TOUCH COLONIAL COLORS		*	
Palmer Paint Products	CREATIVE TOUCH EASTER		*	
Palmer Paint Products	CREATIVE TOUCH GLASS STAIN		*	
Palmer Paint Products	CREATIVE TOUCH HALLOWEEN		*	
Palmer Paint Products	CREATIVE TOUCH LUMINOUS		*	
Palmer Paint Products	CREATIVE TOUCH METALLICS		*	
Palmer Paint Products	CREATIVE TOUCH PEARLESCENT		*	
Palmer Paint Products	CREATIVE TOUCH STENCIL SET		*	
Palmer Paint Products	CREATIVE TOUCH TOLE		*	
Palmer Paint Products	CREATIVE TOUCH VIBRA CRYLIC		*	
Palmer Paint Products	DOLL FACE		*	
Palmer Paint Products	FLAT MODEL PAINT		*	
Palmer Paint Products	FLUORESCENT LUMINOUS		*	
Palmer Paint Products	GLITTER GLAZE CLEAR		*	
Palmer Paint Products	GLITTER PAINT		*	
Palmer Paint Products	PAX MODEL PAINT		*	
Palmer Paint Products	PRISM ACRYLICS		*	

Some products in this line do not bear the CP, AP or Health Label (Non-Toxic) Seal.

-18-

TABLE 2   (continued)

PRODUCTS AND MANUFACTURERS	BRAND NAMES	CP SEAL	AP SEAL	HL/NT SEAL
PAINTS (continued)				
Acrylic, Artists (continued)				
Palmer Paint Products	PRISM METALS		*	
Palmer Paint Products	PRISM PEARLS		*	
Palmer Paint Products	SHADED TRANSFER PAINT		*	
Palmer Paint Products	SOUTHWEST COLORS		*	
Palmer Paint Products	SPUMCO PAINT-BY-NUMBER		*	
Palmer Paint Products	VICTORIAN COLORS		*	
Palmer Paint Products	WOOD STAINS		*	
Pebeo of America	EXTRA FINE ACRYLIC #			*
Pebeo of America	GLOSSCOLOR/SOLUBRILLE	*		
Pebeo of America	INTERFERENCE GOLD			*
Pebeo of America	STUDIO ACRYLIC			*
Plaid Enterprises	800 SERIES BASE COATS		*	
Plaid Enterprises	900 SERIES BASE COATS		*	
Plaid Enterprises	APPLE BARREL		*	
Plaid Enterprises	APPLE BARREL SHINY'S		*	
Plaid Enterprises	DECORATOR GLAZE		*	
Plaid Enterprises	ELEGANT HOME COLORS STENCIL PAINT		*	
Plaid Enterprises	FASTER PLASTER PAINTS		*	
Plaid Enterprises	FOLK ART		*	
Plaid Enterprises	FOLK ART BASE COATS		*	
Plaid Enterprises	FOLK ART BASICS		*	
Plaid Enterprises	FOLK ART DESIGNER COLORS		*	
Plaid Enterprises	FOLK ART MARBLEIZING COLORS		*	
Plaid Enterprises	FOLK ART MARBLEIZING MEDIUM		*	
Plaid Enterprises	FOLK ART METALLICS		*	
Plaid Enterprises	FOLK ART PURE PIGMENTS		*	
Plaid Enterprises	FOLK ART STANDARD		*	
Plaid Enterprises	HOMEFRONT SATIN		*	
Plaid Enterprises	MOSAIC MAGIC		*	
Pottery Barn	IVY STAMPING KIT PAINTS		*	
Pumpkin Masters Inc.	PUMPKIN PAINT KIT		*	
Pyramid Art Supply	PYRA-CRYLIC		*	
Rich Art Color Co.	PEEL OFF PAINT		*	
Rich Art Color Co.	SCHOOL & CAMP ACRYLIC PAINT		*	
Rock Paint Distrib'g	HANDY ART		*	
Rose Art Industries	101 DALMATIONS PAINT-BY-NUMBER		*	
Rose Art Industries	ALADDIN LIGHT CATCHER		*	
Rose Art Industries	ALADDIN PAINT BY NUMBER		*	
Rose Art Industries	BEAUTY & THE BEAST LIGHT CATCHER		*	
Rose Art Industries	BEAUTY & THE BEAST PAINT BY NUMBER		*	
Rose Art Industries	CINDERELLA PAINT BY NUMBER		*	
Rose Art Industries	GARGOYLE 3D PAINT-BY-NUMBER		*	
Rose Art Industries	HUNCHBACK OF NOTRE DAME PAINT-BY-NUMBER		*	
Rose Art Industries	LION KING LIGHT CATCHER		*	
Rose Art Industries	LION KING LIGHT CATCHER & FRAME		*	
Rose Art Industries	LION KING LIGHT CATCHER MOBILE		*	
Rose Art Industries	LITTLE MERMAID LIGHT CATCHER		*	
Rose Art Industries	POCAHONTAS LIGHT CATCHERS ON BLISTER CARD		*	
Rose Art Industries	POCAHONTAS PAINT BY NUMBER		*	
Rose Art Industries	POWER RANGERS ACRYLIC		*	
Rose Art Industries	ROSE ART PAINT BY NUMBER		*	
Rose Art Industries	SNOW WHITE LIGHT CATCHER		*	
Rose Art Industries	SNOW WHITE PAINT BY NUMBER		*	
Rose Art Industries	STAR WARS PAINT-BY-NUMBER		*	
Royal Talens	DECORFIN			*
Royal Talens	REMBRANDT			*
Royal Talens	TALENS RELIEF			*
Royal Talens	VAN GOGH			*
S & S Worldwide	S & S GUILDCRAFT		*	
S & S Worldwide	S & S GUILDCRAFT LIGHT WOOD STAINS		*	
S & S Worldwide	S & S GUILDCRAFT WOOD STAINS		*	
Sargent Art	SARGENT	*		
Sax Arts and Crafts	TRUE COLOR			*
Sax Arts and Crafts	VERSACRYLIC	*		
Schoenfeld & Co.	LUKAS ACRYLIC		*	
Schoenfeld & Co.	LUKASCRYL			*
Schoenfeld & Co.	LUKASCRYL LIQUID		*	
Schoenfeld & Co.	LUKASCRYL METALLICS		*	
Schoenfeld & Co.	LUKASCRYL PASTOS		*	
Sennelier Beaux Arts	PEINTEX			*
ShinHan Art Materials	SHINHAN ACRYLIC COLOR #			*
Daniel Smith, Inc.	DANIEL SMITH LUMINESCENT ACRYLIC COLORS		*	

PRODUCTS AND MANUFACTURERS	BRAND NAMES	CP SEAL	AP SEAL	HL/NT SEAL
PAINTS (continued)				
Acrylic, Artists (continued)				
Tonka Corporation	EZ 2 DO GLITTER PAINT		*	
Tonka Corporation	EZ 2 DO PEARL PAINT		*	
Triarco Arts & Crafts	TRI-CRYLIC		*	
Turner Colour Works	ACRYL COLOR #			*
Turner Colour Works	ACRYL GOUACHE #			*
Turner Colour Works	NEO COLOUR BRIGHT			*
Turner Colour Works	NEO COLOUR PEARL			*
Utrecht Mfg. Co.	UTRECHT	*		
Winsor & Newton	ARTISTS COLOURS #			*
Winsor & Newton	GALERIA STUDIO ACRYLICS			*
Acrylic, Washable				
Rich Art Color Co.	RICH CRYL		*	
Alkyds				
Royal Talens	TALENS HOBBY COLOR FOR GLASS			*
Winsor & Newton	GRIFFIN #			*
Caseins				
Creative Art Products	SHIVA COLORS	*		
Pelikan USA	PELIKAN PLAKA FLUORESCENT #		*	
Ceramic Stains, Water Base				
American Art Clay	AMACO BRUSH 'N LEAF GOLD	*		
American Art Clay	AMACO BRUSH 'N LEAF SILVER	*		
Ceramichrome, Inc.	BISK-CHROME OPAQUE	*		
Ceramichrome, Inc.	BISK-CHROME PEARL FINISHES	*		
Ceramichrome, Inc.	DAZZLING METALLICS	*		
Ceramichrome, Inc.	DECOART WOOD & RESIN GEL	*		
Ceramichrome, Inc.	PEARLS	*		
Ceramichrome, Inc.	SOFTEE PICKLES	*		
Ceramichrome, Inc.	SOFTEE TRANSLUCENT	*		
Fiesta Colors	BASE COAT	*		
Fiesta Colors	RADIANT AK'SCENT	*		
Gare, Inc.	ACRYLIC TEXTURE PAINT	*		
Gare, Inc.	COLOR WASH	*		
Gare, Inc.	CULTURED PEARL	*		
Gare, Inc.	FOILZ	*		
Gare, Inc.	GOLDEN CULTURED PEARLS	*		
Gare, Inc.	LIQUID FAIRY DUST	*		
Gare, Inc.	MEGAMETALS	*		
Gare, Inc.	METALLIC	*		
Gare, Inc.	OPAQUE ACRYLIC	*		
Gare, Inc.	PEARL RUFF STUFF	*		
Gare, Inc.	RUFF STUFF	*		
Gare, Inc.	SHIMMERS	*		
Gare, Inc.	STONE RUFF STUFF	*		
Gare, Inc.	WATER BASE TRANSLUCENT*			
Pebeo of America	CERNE RELIEF			*
Pebeo of America	CLOISONNE			*
Pebeo of America	GLOSS MEDIUM FOR PORCELAINE 150			*
Pebeo of America	PORCELAINE 150			*
Designer Colors (Gouache)				
Creative Art Products	DICK BLICK	*		
Da Vinci Paint Co.	DA VINCI FIRST QUALITY ARTISTS'		*	
Daler-Rowney	ROWNEY DESIGNER'S #			*
Daler-Rowney	ROWNEY POSTER COLOURS #			*
Fostport, Inc.	YARKA ARTIST GOUACHE		*	
Holbein Works Ltd.	DESIGNERS' COLORS #			*
Holbein Works Ltd.	HOLBEIN ACRYLA #			*
Holbein Works Ltd.	HOLBEIN ANTIQUE GOUACHE			*
Lefranc & Bourgeois	LINEL 35GT #			*
Lefranc & Bourgeois	LINEL 650 #			*
Nicker Colour Co., Ltd.	NICKER #			*
Nicker Colour Co., Ltd.	NICKER ACRYLIC GOUACHE #			*
Pebeo of America	DESIGNERS' GOUACHE T7 #			*
Pebeo of America	PRIMACOLOR		*	
Pebeo of America	STUDIO GOUACHE			*
Pebeo of America	SUPER MAQUETTE GOUACHE			*
Royal Talens	EXTRA FINE #			*
Sakura of America	SAKURA ACRYL GOUACHE	*		
Schoenfeld & Co.	LUKAS DESIGNER GOUACHE #	*	*	
Turner Colour Works	DESIGN COLOUR #			*
Turner Colour Works	POSTER COLOUR #			*
Turner Colour Works	TURNER DESIGN #			*
Winsor & Newton	DESIGNERS #			*

Some products in this line do not bear the CP, AP or Health Label (Non-Toxic) Seal.

TABLE 2   (continued)

PAINTS (continued)

Dyes

PRODUCTS AND MANUFACTURERS	BRAND NAMES	CP SEAL	AP SEAL	HL/NT SEAL
American Art Clay	BATIKIT COLDPRINT DYE THICKENER		*	
Fine Art Supplies Ltd.	FAS WATER SOLUBLE (POWDER)		*	
Rose Art Industries	LION KING COLOR BLOOM		*	
Rose Art Industries	POWER RANGERS COLOR BLOOM		*	

Enamels

PRODUCTS AND MANUFACTURERS	BRAND NAMES	CP SEAL	AP SEAL	HL/NT SEAL
Plaid Enterprises	COLOR STEPS		*	
Plaid Enterprises	GALLERY GLASS		*	
Plaid Enterprises	GALLERY GLASS TEXTURE		*	
Thompson Enamel	HOT GLASS COLORS #		*	
Thompson Enamel	LEAD FREE OPAQUES		*	
Thompson Enamel	LEAD FREE TRANSPARENTS		*	
Thompson Enamel	T4 VITREARC ENAMELS FOR GLASS #		*	
Thompson Enamel	T13 ENAMELS FOR STAINED GLASS #		*	
Van Aken International	JAZZ WINDOW PREP		*	

Fabric

PRODUCTS AND MANUFACTURERS	BRAND NAMES	CP SEAL	AP SEAL	HL/NT SEAL
Binney & Smith	LIQUITEX DIMENSIONAL		*	
Carnival Arts, Inc.	HAUTE 4U		*	
Ceramichrome, Inc.	DECOART DIMENSIONS		*	
Ceramichrome, Inc.	DECOART HEAVY METALS		*	
Ceramichrome, Inc.	DECOART HEAVY METALS LIGHT		*	
Ceramichrome, Inc.	DECOART HOT SHOTS		*	
Ceramichrome, Inc.	DECOART LIQUID SEQUINS		*	
Ceramichrome, Inc.	DECOART PASTEL LIQUID SEQUINS		*	
Ceramichrome, Inc.	DECOART SHIMMERING PEARLS		*	
Ceramichrome, Inc.	DECOART SO SOFT		*	
Ceramichrome, Inc.	DECOART SO SOFT METALLICS		*	
Colortex/Tri-Chem	DIZZLE DIZZLE BRIGHTS		*	
Colortex/Tri-Chem	DIZZLE DIZZLE IRIDESCENT		*	
Colortex/Tri-Chem	DIZZLE DIZZLE PUFF		*	
Colortex/Tri-Chem	DIZZLE DIZZLE SLICK/GLITTER		*	
Colortex/Tri-Chem	DIZZLE DIZZLE SOFT		*	
Colortex/Tri-Chem	DIZZLE DIZZLE TINT		*	
Delta Tech. Coatings	DELTA FABRIC PERMANENT DYE		*	
Delta Tech. Coatings	DELTA GLITTER LINER		*	
Delta Tech. Coatings	DELTA MARBLE THIX		*	
Delta Tech. Coatings	DELTA STARLITE #		*	
Delta Tech. Coatings	DELTA TEXTILE MEDIUM		*	
Delta Tech. Coatings	LIQUID HEARTS		*	
Delta Tech. Coatings	LIQUID STARS		*	
Delta Tech. Coatings	SHINY LINER		*	
Delta Tech. Coatings	TEXTILE MEDIUM		*	
Golden Artist Colors	PHOSPHORESCENT MEDIUM		*	
M. Grumbacher, Inc.	ACCENT ELEGANCE PAINTING DYE		*	
NASCO International	FABRI-PAINT #		*	
Palmer Paint Products	CREATIVE TOUCH FABRI-CRYLIC		*	
Palmer Paint Products	PRINT PAKS SUPER IRON-ONS GLOW IN THE DARK		*	
Pebeo of America	BROD'EXPRESS			*
Pebeo of America	CREALOOK			*
Pebeo of America	MARBLING			*
Pebeo of America	PEBEO LINE			*
Pebeo of America	PEARL SETACOLOR			*
Pebeo of America	SETASILK			*
Plaid Enterprises	APPLE BARREL TEXTILE MEDIUM		*	
Plaid Enterprises	FASHION SHOW DIMENSIONAL GLITTER SERIES		*	
Plaid Enterprises	FASHION SHOW DIMENSIONAL JEWELS		*	
Plaid Enterprises	FASHION SHOW DIMENSIONAL METALLICS		*	
Plaid Enterprises	FASHION SHOW DIMENSIONAL NEON SERIES		*	
Plaid Enterprises	FASHION SHOW DIMENSIONAL PEARLS		*	
Plaid Enterprises	FASHION SHOW DIMENSIONAL SHEER SERIES		*	
Plaid Enterprises	FASHION SHOW DIMENSIONAL SHINY SERIES		*	
Plaid Enterprises	FASHION SHOW DIMENSIONAL SPARKLES		*	
Plaid Enterprises	FASHION SHOW SOFT BASICS		*	
Plaid Enterprises	FASHION SHOW SOFT GLITTERS		*	
Plaid Enterprises	FASHION SHOW SOFT JEWELS		*	
Plaid Enterprises	FOLK ART TEXTILE MEDIUM		*	
Plaid Enterprises	LIQUID BEAD GLITTERS		*	

PAINTS (continued)

Fabric (continued)

PRODUCTS AND MANUFACTURERS	BRAND NAMES	CP SEAL	AP SEAL	HL/NT SEAL
Plaid Enterprises	SHIMMERS		*	
Plaid Enterprises	SPARKLES		*	
Rich Art Color Co.	RICH ART DIMENSIONAL PAINT		*	
Rich Art Color Co.	SNEAKER PAINT		*	
Rich Art Color Co.	T-SHIRT PAINT		*	
Rich Art Color Co.	WET-LOOK FABRIC PAINT		*	
Rock Paint Distrib'g	HANDY ART #		*	
Salis International	DR. PH. MARTIN'S TWILIGHT GLOW		*	
Schoenfeld & Co.	LUKAS FABRIC PAINT	*		*
Sennelier Beaux Arts	SUPER TINFIX DYES			*
Tonka Corporation	EZ 2 DO FLUORESCENT		*	
Triarco Arts & Crafts	TRI-FAB #		*	

Finger Paint, Liquid

PRODUCTS AND MANUFACTURERS	BRAND NAMES	CP SEAL	AP SEAL	HL/NT SEAL
ABC School Supply	ABC SCHOOL SUPPLY	*		
ABC School Supply	ABC SCHOOL SUPPLY WASHABLE	*		
Advancing Play	COLOUR BLAST		*	
Binney & Smith	CRAYOLA WASHABLE	*		
Binney & Smith	CRAYOLA WASHABLE GLITTER	*		
Binney & Smith	POOH WASHABLE	*		
Chroma Acrylics	CHROMATEMP	*		
Colorations, Inc.	COLORATIONS		*	
Comet-Montrose Ltd.	COMET	*		
Conros Corporation	KANGA		*	
Conros Corporation	ROSS		*	
Conros Corporation	ROSS FUN TIME		*	
Conros Corporation	ROSS KID'S		*	
Creative Art Products	DICK BLICK	*		
Creative Works	PAINT WORKS		*	
Demco Industries	DEMCO	*		
Derivan of Canada	DERIVAN		*	
Derivan of Canada	DERIVAN KINDERGARTEN		*	
Dixon Ticonderoga	LOONEY TUNES WASHABLE	*		
Dixon Ticonderoga	PRANG MEDIA MIXER		*	
Dixon Ticonderoga	PRANG WASHABLE		*	
J. L. Hammett Co.	ART UTILITY		*	
International Playthings	CREATIVE YEARS		*	
Jovi, S.A.	PINTURA DEDOS		*	
Kaplan School Supply	KAPLAN		*	
Lakeshore Learning Materials	BEST BUY	*		
Michigan Products	MICHIGAN PRODUCTS	*		
Mounsey & Corbett	MOON PRINCE	*		
Mounsey & Corbett	MOON PRINTS	*		
NES Arnold Inc.	SCOLA		*	
Omega Chalk Factory	OMEGA	*		
Palmer Paint Products	PALMER	*		
Palmer Paint Products	PALMER WASHABLE		*	
Panline USA/Alex	ALEX	*		
Reeves & Poole Group	POOLE		*	
Reeves & Poole Group	ROYAL		*	
Rich Art Color Co.	CHILDCRAFT WASHABLE	*		
Rich Art Color Co.	CLEAN COLORS WASHABLE	*		
Rich Art Color Co.	CLEAN COLORS WASHABLE - GLITTER		*	
Rich Art Color Co.	CLEAN COLORS WASHABLE - NEON	*		
Rich Art Color Co.	RICH ART	*		
Rich Art Color Co.	RICH ART FLUORESCENT	*		
Rich Art Color Co.	RICH ART NEON	*		
Rock Paint Distrib'g	HANDY ART		*	
Rose Art Industries	KODAK	*		
Rose Art Industries	KODAK FLUORESCENT 4 JAR SET	*		
Rose Art Industries	KODAK 4 JAR SET	*		
Rose Art Industries	POOH SPONGE BUCKET FINGER PAINT		*	
Rose Art Industries	ROSE ART	*		
Rose Art Industries	ROSE ART 4 PAINTS IN SLEEVE	*		
Rose Art Industries	ROSE ART FLUORESCENT	*		
Rose Art Industries	ROSE ART FLUORESCENT IN SLEEVE	*		
Rose Art Industries	ROSE ART GLITTER MAGIC WASH.		*	
Rose Art Industries	ROSE ART SPARKLE		*	
Rose Art Industries	ROSE ART WASHABLE	*		

Some products in this line do not bear the CP, AP or Health Label (Non-Toxic) Seal.

TABLE 2   (continued)

PRODUCTS AND MANUFACTURERS	BRAND NAMES	CP SEAL	AP SEAL	HL/NT SEAL
PAINTS (continued)				
Finger Paint, Liquid (continued)				
Sargent Art	SARGENT		*	
Sargent Art	SARGENT WASHABLE		*	
Sargent Art	SARGENT WASHABLE FLUORESCENT		*	
Sax Arts and Crafts	SAX VERSA-TEMP ACTIVITY PAINT		*	
Sax Arts and Crafts	TRUE COLOR		*	
Sax Arts and Crafts	R. B. WALTERS		*	
Oils				
Binney & Smith	LIQUITEX ARTIST #	*		
Camlin Limited	CAMEL ARTISTS' OIL COLOURS #	*		
Creative Art Products	SHIVA ARTISTS PAINTSTIKS	*		
Creative Art Products	SHIVA PERMASOL	*		
Creative Art Products	SHIVA SIGNATURE	*		
Da Vinci Paint Co.	DA VINCI FIRST QUALITY ARTISTS' #	*	*	
Daler-Rowney	GEORGIAN #			*
Daler-Rowney	ROWNEY ARTISTS #			*
Delta Tech. Coatings	DELTA PAINT CREAM	*		
Duro Art Industries	DURO	*		
Fiesta Colors	ULTRA TONER	*		
Fostport, Inc.	YARKA DECORATIVE OIL-BASED	*		
Fostport, Inc.	YARKA FINE #	*		
M. Grumbacher, Inc.	GAINSBOROUGH #	*		
M. Grumbacher, Inc.	MAX GRUMBACHER ARTISTS' OIL COLOR	*		
M. Grumbacher, Inc.	PRE-TESTED ARTISTS' #	*		
Harstrup Assoc./NorArt	EDVARD MUNCH AQUAOIL	*		
Holbein Works Ltd.	ECOLSE		*	
Holbein Works Ltd.	HOC #		*	
Holbein Works Ltd.	STUDENTS'		*	
Lefranc & Bourgeois	401 EXTRA-FINE ARTIST'S #		*	
Lefranc & Bourgeois	104 FINE #		*	
Lefranc & Bourgeois	MASTER OF ART		*	
Maimeri S.p.A.	BRERA		*	
Maimeri USA	MAIMERI ARTISTI EXTRAFINE OIL COLOURS #	*		
Maimeri USA	MAIMERI CLASSICO FINE OIL COLOURS #	*		
Maimeri USA	MAIMERI PURO SUPERIOR OIL COLOURS #	*		
Martin/F. Weber Co.	ART STORE	*		
Martin/F. Weber Co.	BOB ROSS	*		
Martin/F. Weber Co.	BOB ROSS SOFT COLORS	*		
Martin/F. Weber Co.	JENKINS FLORAL	*		
Martin/F. Weber Co.	MISTY COLOR	*		
Martin/F. Weber Co.	PERMALBA #	*		
Martin/F. Weber Co.	PRIMA OIL COLORS	*		
Pebeo of America	FRAGONARD OIL COLORS #		*	
Pebeo of America	STUDIO OIL COLOURS #		*	
Plaid Enterprises	HOME DECOR STENCIL	*		
Plaid Enterprises	STENCIL DECOR DRY BRUSH STENCIL	*		
Plaid Enterprises	STENCIL DECOR PAINT STICKS	*		
Royal Talens	AMSTERDAM		*	
Royal Talens	H2OIL		*	
Royal Talens	REMBRANDT #		*	
Royal Talens	VAN GOGH #		*	
H. Schmincke & Co.	MUSSINI RESIN-IN-OIL COLOURS, SERIES 10 #		*	
Schoenfeld & Co.	LUKAS SORTE 1 #		*	
Schoenfeld & Co.	LUKAS STUDIO OIL COLORS		*	
Sennelier Beaux Arts	SENNELIER EXTRA FINE OIL COLORS #		*	
Sennelier Beaux Arts	SENNELIER OIL STICKS	*		
Daniel Smith, Inc.	DANIEL SMITH AUTOGRAPH SERIES OIL COLORS #	*		
Daniel Smith, Inc.	DANIEL SMITH LUMINESCENT OIL COLORS #	*		
Daniel Smith, Inc.	DANIEL SMITH ORIGINAL OIL COLORS #	*		
Turner Colour Works	ARTIST'S COLOURS		*	
Utrecht Mfg. Co.	UTRECHT	*		
Winsor & Newton	ARTISTS #		*	
Winsor & Newton	ARTISTS UNDERPAINTING WHITE		*	
Winsor & Newton	WINTON #		*	
Pigments, Dry Ground				
M. Grumbacher, Inc.	GRUMBACHER ARTISTS' #	*		
Holbein Works Ltd.	HOLBEIN ARTISTS' #		*	
Kremer Pigments	KREMER GREEN PIGMENTS #	*		

PRODUCTS AND MANUFACTURERS	BRAND NAMES	CP SEAL	AP SEAL	HL/NT SEAL
PAINTS (continued)				
Pigments, Dry Ground (continued)				
Sennelier Beaux Arts	SENNELIER DRY PIGMENTS #			*
Daniel Smith, Inc.	DANIEL SMITH DRY PIGMENTS #		*	
Daniel Smith, Inc.	DANIEL SMITH EXTENDERS & MISC. PIGMENTS #		*	
Daniel Smith, Inc.	DANIEL SMITH INTERFERENCE AND PEARL PIGMENTS		*	
Winsor & Newton	ARTISTS #			*
Spray				
C2F, Inc.	PRO ART WASHABLE SIGN & WINDOW PAINT		*	
Plaid Enterprises	ANTIQUING WASH		*	
Tempera, Cake				
Activa Products	ACTIVA		*	
Dixon Ticonderoga	PRANG	*		
Lion Pencil Co., Ltd.	CRAYON FACTORY		*	
Lion Pencil Co., Ltd.	LION		*	
NES Arnold Inc.	NES ARNOLD COLOR CAKES		*	
NES Arnold Inc.	NES ARNOLD FLUORESCENT		*	
NES Arnold Inc.	NES ARNOLD PALETTE PACK		*	
NES Arnold Inc.	SCOLA COLOR BLOCKS		*	
Oasis Art & Craft Prod.	BADGE MAKER		*	
Oasis Art & Craft Prod.	LITTLE PICTURE FACTORY		*	
Oasis Art & Craft Prod.	POSTER PAINTING SET		*	
Oasis Art & Craft Prod.	PRINT & PAINT		*	
Quartet Manufacturing	ALPHACOLOR	*		
Jack Richeson & Co.	OCALDO		*	
Sax Arts & Crafts	SAX CAKE TEMPERA COLORS		*	
Sax Arts & Crafts	SAX CAKE TEMPERA FLUORESCENT COLORS		*	
Winsor & Newton	REEVES TEMPERABLOCK	*		
Tempera, Egg				
Daler-Rowney	ROWNEY #			*
Tempera, Liquid				
A & W Products	A & W NEON FLUORESCENT POSTER		*	
A & W Products	A & W POSTER		*	
ABC School Supply	ABC SCHOOL SUPPLY		*	
ABC School Supply	ABC SCHOOL SUPPLY WASHABLE		*	
Advancing Play	COLOUR BLAST		*	
Advancing Play	COLOUR BLAST FLUORESCENT		*	
Advancing Play	COLOUR BLAST GLITTER PAINT		*	
Binney & Smith	ARTISTA II		*	
Binney & Smith	CRAYOLA		*	
Binney & Smith	CRAYOLA BUBBLE ART WASHABLE		*	
Binney & Smith	CRAYOLA FLUORESCENT		*	
Binney & Smith	CRAYOLA NEON WASHABLE POSTER		*	
Binney & Smith	CRAYOLA POSTER		*	
Binney & Smith	CRAYOLA WASHABLE		*	
Binney & Smith	CRAYOLA WASHABLE GLITTER POSTER		*	
Binney & Smith	CRAYOLA WASHABLE GLOW IN THE DARK POSTER		*	
Binney & Smith	KAYLOR		*	
Binney & Smith	KROMATONE		*	
Binney & Smith	MICKEY'S STUFF WASHABLE		*	
Binney & Smith	MICKEY'S STUFF WASHABLE GLITTER POSTER		*	
Binney & Smith	POOH WASHABLE		*	
Binney & Smith	TEMPRATONE CONCENTRATED		*	
Binney & Smith	TEMPRATONE ECONOMY			*
Binney & Smith (Canada)	CRAYOLA			*
BioColor America	BIOCOLOR		*	
C2F, Inc.	PRO ART		*	
Cardinal School Sply.	CARDINAL SCHOOL			*
Certified Color Corp.	BESTEMP		*	
Certified Color Corp.	BESTEMP FLUORESCENT		*	
Certified Color Corp.	BESTEMP WASHABLE		*	
Child Craft	CHILD CRAFT		*	
Chroma Acrylics	CHROMATEMP		*	
Chroma Acrylics	CHROMATEMP LIQUID TEMPERA DABBERS		*	

Some products in this line do not bear the CP, AP or Health Label (Non-Toxic) Seal.

TABLE 2   (continued)

PAINTS (continued)

Tempera, Liquid (continued)

PRODUCTS AND MANUFACTURERS	BRAND NAMES	CP SEAL	AP SEAL	HL/NT SEAL
Colorations, Inc.	COLORATIONS			*
Comet-Montrose, Ltd.	COMET	*	*	
Comet-Montrose, Ltd.	FUTURA	*		
Conros Corporation	KANGA POSTER	*		
Conros Corporation	ROSS-CONROS		*	
Conros Corporation	ROSS FLUORESCENT		*	
Conros Corporation	ROSS KID'S TEMPERA POSTER	*		
Conros Corporation	ROSS TEMPERA POSTER	*		
Creative Art Products	DICK BLICK BUDGET TEMPERA		*	
Creative Art Products	DICK BLICK PREMIUM	*		
Creative Art Products	DICK BLICK STUDENT	*		
H. S. Crocker Co.	SIERRA	*		
Demco Manufacturing	DEMCO		*	
Derivan of Canada	DERIVAN	*		
Derivan of Canada	DERIVAN GLITTER PAINT		*	
Derivan of Canada	DERIVAN FLUORESCENT		*	
Dixon Ticonderoga	COLORART	*		
Dixon Ticonderoga	LOONEY TUNES FLUORESCENT PAINT SET	*		
Dixon Ticonderoga	LOONEY TUNES WASHABLE	*		
Dixon Ticonderoga	PRANG	*		
Dixon Ticonderoga	PRANG FLUORESCENT	*		
Dixon Ticonderoga	PRANG READY-TO-USE	*		
Dixon Ticonderoga	PRANG SKINTONES WASHABLE	*		
Dixon Ticonderoga	PRANG WASHABLE	*		
Duro Art Industries	DURO		*	
FSC Educational Inc.	PYRATEMP	*		
J. L. Hammett Co.	ART UTILITY	*		
J. L. Hammett Co.	LIVING COLORS	*		
J. L. Hammett Co.	LIVING COLORS MULTICULTURAL TEMPERA	*		
International Playthings	CREATIVE YEARS		*	
Kaplan School Supply	GREAT KIDS		*	
Kaplan School Supply	KAPLAN KOLORS	*		
Krazy Colors, Inc.	KRAZY COLORS		*	
Lakeshore Learning Materials	BEST-BUY	*		
Lakeshore Learning Materials	BEST-BUY FLUORESCENT	*		
Lakeshore Learning Materials	BEST-BUY WASHABLE	*		
Lakeshore Learning Materials	LAKESHORE PEOPLE COLORS	*		
Lakeshore Learning Materials	LAKESHORE TEMPERA MARKER	*		
Michigan Products Inc.	MPI BEST BUY	*		
Michigan Products Inc.	MPI BEST BUY MULTICULTURAL TEMPERA	*		
NASCO International	NASCO COUNTRY SCHOOL	*		
NES Arnold Inc.	SCOLA ARTMIX		*	
Omega Chalk Factory	OMEGA	*		
Omega Chalk Factory	OMEGA FLUORESCENT	*		
Omyacolor, Inc.	OMYACOLOR	*		
Palmer Paint Products	FLUORESCENT GLITTER POSTER		*	
Palmer Paint Products	FLUORESCENT GLOW IN THE DARK		*	
Palmer Paint Products	GLOW IN THE DARK POSTER		*	
Palmer Paint Products	LIQUID TEMPERA	*		
Palmer Paint Products	PALMER WASHABLE	*		
Palmer Paint Products	PALMER WASHABLE PEARLESCENTS		*	
Palmer Paint Products	PRISM	*		
Palmer Paint Products	PRISM FLUORESCENT	*		
Palmer Paint Products	SPUMCO ATOMIC BLAST FLUORESCENT GLOW-IN-THE-DARK POSTER		*	
Palmer Paint Products	SPUMCO MAGIC FAIRY DUST WASHABLE GLITTER POSTER		*	
Palmer Paint Products	SPUMCO PEARLY PAINTS		*	
Palmer Paint Products	SPUMCO PSYCHEDELIC HIPPIE PAINT FLUORESCENT POSTER		*	
Palmer Paint Products	SPUMCO TV CARTOON WASHABLE POSTER	*		
Palmer Paint Products	ULTRA	*		
Palmer Paint Products	WASHABLE GLITTER POSTER		*	
Panline USA/Alex	ALEX POSTER	*		
Panline USA/Alex	ALEX WASHABLE POSTER	*		
Pearl Paint Co.	PEARL	*		
Pebeo of America	SOLUGOUACHE		*	
Pyramid Art Supply	PYRAMID PPC			*
QTL Corporation	BIOCOLOR		*	
QTL Corporation	FLEXITEMP WASHABLE		*	
Reeves & Poole Group	REGAL		*	
Reeves & Poole Group	ROYAL		*	
Rich Art Color Co.	CLEAN-COLOR		*	
Rich Art Color Co.	CLEAN COLORS WASHABLE GLITTER PAINT			*
Rich Art Color Co.	CLEAN COLORS WASHABLE PAINT MARKERS		*	
Rich Art Color Co.	CLEAN COLORS WASHABLE PAINT MARKERS - NEON		*	
Rich Art Color Co.	DAYKARE		*	
Rich Art Color Co.	EXTRA BRIGHT NEON FLUORESCENT			*
Rich Art Color Co.	FLUORESCENT TEMPRA MARKERS		*	
Rich Art Color Co.	FUN PAINTER		*	
Rich Art Color Co.	FUN PAINTS		*	
Rich Art Color Co.	LIQUID FRESCO		*	
Rich Art Color Co.	MULTICULTURAL CLEAN COLORS		*	
Rich Art Color Co.	NEON PAINT MARKERS		*	
Rich Art Color Co.	QUICK PAINTER		*	
Rich Art Color Co.	RICH ART GLOSSY		*	
Rich Art Color Co.	RICH ART PREMIUM		*	
Rich Art Color Co.	RICH ART SCHOOL		*	
Rich Art Color Co.	RICH GEL		*	
Rich Art Color Co.	RICH TEMP		*	
Rich Art Color Co.	RICH TONE		*	
Rich Art Color Co.	ROLL-N-PAINT		*	
Rich Art Color Co.	ROLL-R-PAINT (AEROSOL)	*		
Rich Art Color Co.	SIDEWALK PAINT			*
Rich Art Color Co.	SUNBURST		*	
Rich Art Color Co.	TURBO (AEROSOL)		*	
Rich Art Color Co.	TEMPRA MARKER		*	
Rich Art Color Co.	WASHABLE GLITTER PAINT FOR KIDS		*	
Rich Art Color Co.	WASHABLE PAINT FOR KIDS			*
Rock Paint Distrib'g	HANDY ART		*	
Rose Art Industries	101 DALMATIONS FIGURE MAKER PAINT			*
Rose Art Industries	101 DALMATIONS MAGNET & PIN PAINT			*
Rose Art Industries	GARGOYLES FIGURE MAKER POSTER PAINT		*	
Rose Art Industries	GODZILLA FIGURE MAKER POSTER PAINTS		*	
Rose Art Industries	GOLD JEWELRY MAKER			*
Rose Art Industries	GOLD JEWELRY MAKER WASHABLE POSTER PAINTS		*	
Rose Art Industries	GOLD & SILVER JEWELRY MAKER PAINTS		*	
Rose Art Industries	HUNCHBACK OF NOTRE DAME POTTERY WHEEL PAINT			*
Rose Art Industries	HUNCHBACK MAGNET & PIN CASE PAINT			*
Rose Art Industries	HUNCHBACK WOODWORKING CASE PAINT			*
Rose Art Industries	I LOVE SCULPTURE WASHABLE POSTER PAINTS		*	
Rose Art Industries	KODAK		*	
Rose Art Industries	KODAK POSTER		*	
Rose Art Industries	KODAK WASHABLE POSTER		*	
Rose Art Industries	POCAHONTAS FIGURE MAKER POSTER PAINT		*	
Rose Art Industries	POCAHONTAS POTTERY WHEEL			*
Rose Art Industries	POLLY POCKET WASHABLE POSTER PAINT		*	
Rose Art Industries	ROSE ART		*	
Rose Art Industries	ROSE ART ACTIVITY PAINT 6 PACK		*	
Rose Art Industries	ROSE ART ALPHABET FACTORY POSTER PAINT			*
Rose Art Industries	ROSE ART FLUORESCENT POSTER 6 JAR SET		*	
Rose Art Industries	ROSE ART GLITTER			*

\# Some products in this line do not bear the CP, AP or Health Label (Non-Toxic) Seal.

TABLE 2   (continued)

PRODUCTS AND MANUFACTURERS	BRAND NAMES	CP SEAL	AP SEAL	HL/NT SEAL
PAINTS (continued)				
Tempera, Liquid (continued)				
Rose Art Industries	ROSE ART GLITTER MAGIC WASHABLE GLITTER PAINT		*	
Rose Art Industries	ROSE ART GLITTER WASH. POSTER		*	
Rose Art Industries	ROSE ART GLOW IN THE DARK POSTER	*		
Rose Art Industries	ROSE ART POSTER	*		
Rose Art Industries	ROSE ART VELVET POSTER		*	
Rose Art Industries	ROSE ART WASHABLE POSTER	*	*	
Rose Art Industries	ROSE ART WASHABLE POSTER COLORS	*		
Rose Art Industries	ROSE ART WASHABLE POSTER PAINT IN KIT	*		
Rose Art Industries	ROSE ART WASHABLE POSTER - SPILL-PROOF	*		
Rose Art Industries	ROSE ART WATERCOLOR WAND		*	
Rose Art Industries	ROSE ART WATERCOLOR WAND FOR PAINT DOODLER	*		
Rose Art Industries	THE PAINT DOODLER	*		
Sargent Art	GOTHIC	*		
Sargent Art	GOTHIC WASHABLE	*		
Sargent Art	PEARLESCENT POSTER		*	
Sargent Art	SARGENT	*		
Sargent Art	SARGENT FLUORESCENT WASHABLE	*		
Sargent Art	SARGENT WASHABLE	*		
Sargent Art	SARGENT WASHABLE GLITTER		*	
Sargent Art	VALUTEMP	*		
Sax Arts & Crafts	TRUE COLOR	*		
Sax Arts & Crafts	VERSATEMP	*		
Sax Arts & Crafts	VERSATEMP FLUORESCENT	*		
Sax Arts & Crafts	VERSATEMP METALLIC	*		
Sax Arts & Crafts	VERSATEMP MULTICULTURAL TEMPERA	*		
Sax Arts & Crafts	VERSATEMP PEARLESCENT	*		
Sax Arts & Crafts	R. B. WALTERS	*		
Schoenfeld & Co.	LUKAS POSTER COLORS		*	
ShinHan Art Materials	SHINHAN POSTER PAINT #		*	
Southwest School Sply	COLORBRITE	*		
Southwest School Sply	SUNBURST	*		
Staedtler, Inc.	DESIGNABLES DABBERS FOR KIDS	*		
Strathmore Paper Co.	STRATHMORE KIDS SERIES	*		
Technoquimica S.A.	TEMPERAS ARTISTICAS		*	
Triarco Arts & Crafts	TRIARCO	*		
Van Aken International	JAZZ	*		
Van Aken International	JAZZ GLOSS	*		
Van Aken International	JAZZ TEMPERA MARKER	*		
Van Aken International	JR. JAZZ WASHABLE	*		
Van Aken International	LEISURE TONE	*		
Western Publishing	BARBIE GLITTER POSTER		*	
Western Publishing	COLOR EXPRESS	*		
Tempera, Powder				
ABC School Supply	ABC SCHOOL SUPPLY	*		
Binney & Smith	ARTISTA II	*		
Binney & Smith	CRAYOLA	*		
Creative Art Products	DICK BLICK	*		
Demco Industries	DEMCO	*		
Dixon Ticonderoga	COLORART	*		
Dixon Ticonderoga	PRANG	*		
J. L. Hammett Co.	ART UTILITY	*		
Lakeshore Learning Materials	BEST BUY	*		
Lakeshore Learning Materials	LAKESHORE	*		
Palmer Paint Products	DRY TEMPERA	*		
Palmer Paint Products	PALMER FLUORESCENT DRY	*		
Palmer Paint Products	PALMER WASHABLE DRY		*	
Reeves & Poole Group	POOLE		*	
Reeves & Poole Group	ROYAL		*	
Rich Art Color Co.	CLEAN COLORS WASHABLE DUST FREE	*		
Rich Art Color Co.	FRESCO	*		
Rich Art Color Co.	RICH ART DRY TEMPERA	*		
Rich Art Color Co.	RICH ART DUST FREE	*		
Rich Art Color Co.	RICH ART DUST FREE POWDER PAINT	*		

PRODUCTS AND MANUFACTURERS	BRAND NAMES	CP SEAL	AP SEAL	HL/NT SEAL
PAINTS (continued)				
Tempera, Powder (continued)				
Sargent Art	GOTHIC	*		
Sargent Art	SARGENT	*		
Sax Arts & Crafts	TRUE COLOR	*		
Sax Arts & Crafts	R. B. WALTERS	*		
Textile				
Carnival Arts	HAUTE COLOURS		*	
Delta Tech. Coatings	SHINY STUFF		*	
Palmer Paint Products	FLUORESCENT ACRYLICS		*	
Palmer Paint Products	TROPICAL COLORS		*	
Pebeo of America	PUFF BASE SETACOLOR			*
Vinyls				
Ceramichrome, Inc.	DECOART SPARKLING SANDSTONES		*	
Ceramichrome, Inc.	SPARKLING SANDSTONES		*	
Lefranc & Bourgeois	FLASHE #			*
Omega Chalk Factory	OMEGA GLOSS PAINT		*	
Turner Colour Works	NEO COLOUR #			*
Water Colors, Dry Pan				
Empire Berol USA	BEROL WATER COLOR PAINT SET	*		
M. Grumbacher, Inc.	SEE FOR YOURSELF			*
Holbein Works Ltd.	HOLBEIN ARTISTS' TRANSPARENT			*
Koh-I-Noor	KOH-I-NOOR OPAQUE	*		
Kuretake Co., Ltd.	KURETAKE GANSAI SHINBI	*		
Kuretake Co., Ltd.	KURETAKE PHYS GANSAI ART PALETTE	*		
Kuretake Co., Ltd.	KURETAKE TEPPATHI SHINBI	*		
Kuretake Co., Ltd.	ZIG WATER COLOUR PAN	*		
Kuretake Co., Ltd.	ZIG WATER COLOUR SET	*		
A. Liebetruth & Co.	ANGORA	*		
A. Liebetruth & Co.	LICO NOVA	*		
A. Liebetruth & Co.	LICOLETTE	*		
A. Liebetruth & Co.	LIEBETRUTH	*		
Loew-Cornell	LOEW-CORNELL	*		
Oasis Art & Craft Prod.	WATER COLOUR BY NUMBERS	*		
Pelikan USA	PELIKAN OPAQUE	*		
Pelikan USA	PELIKAN OPAQUE SUPER SERIES	*		
Pelikan USA	PELIKAN TRANSPARENT	*		
Jack Richeson & Co.	MOROCOLOR WATERCOLORS	*		
Royal Talens	TALENS OPAQUE WATERCOLOURS			*
Sax Arts & Crafts	AURORA WATER COLORS	*		
Winsor & Newton	REEVES WATER COLOUR TABLETS		*	
Winsor & Newton	SKETCHERS			*
Yasutomo & Co.	SUMI #		*	
Water Colors, Liquid				
Carchalk, Inc.	CARCHALK	*		
Carchalk, Inc.	GLASSCHALK	*		
Carchalk, Inc.	SPONGE MARKER	*		
QTL Corporation	LIQUID WATERCOLORS	*		
Water Colors, Powder				
Walbuck Crayon Co.	WALBUCK	*		
Water Colors, Semi-Moist				
Binney & Smith	ARTISTA II/PEACOCK	*		
Binney & Smith	CRAYOLA	*		
Binney & Smith	CRAYOLA SO-BIG WASHABLE	*		
Binney & Smith	CRAYOLA WASHABLE	*		
Binney & Smith	CRAYOLA WASHABLE WATERCOLOR WAND	*		
Binney & Smith	LIQUITEX BASICS	*		
Binney & Smith	MICKEY'S STUFF WASHABLE	*		
Binney & Smith	POOH WASHABLE	*		
Binney&Smith(Canada)	CRAYOLA		*	
Comet-Montrose Ltd.	COMET	*		
Daler-Rowney	GEORGIAN			*
Daler-Rowney	INKABLE WHITE		*	
Daler-Rowney	LUMA BRILLIANT CONCENTRATED		*	
Daler-Rowney	LUMA WHITE HIGH OPACITY		*	
Daler-Rowney	PRO BLACK		*	
Daler-Rowney	PRO WHITE RETOUCH WHITE		*	
Daler-Rowney	Q WHITE RETOUCH WHITE		*	

Some products in this line do not bear the CP, AP or Health Label (Non-Toxic) Seal.

TABLE 2 (continued)

PRODUCTS AND MANUFACTURERS	BRAND NAMES	CP SEAL	AP SEAL	HL/NT SEAL
PAINTS (continued)				
Water Colors, Semi-Moist (continued)				
Daler-Rowney	ROWNEY ARTISTS #			*
Daler-Rowney	STEIG WHITE		*	
Dixon Ticonderoga	COLORART	*		
Dixon Ticonderoga	LOONEY TUNES FLUORESCENT	*		
Dixon Ticonderoga	LOONEY TUNES WASHABLE	*		
Dixon Ticonderoga	MY FIRST WASHABLE	*		
Dixon Ticonderoga	PRANG	*		
Dixon Ticonderoga	PRANG FLUORESCENT	*		
Dixon Ticonderoga	PRANG WASHABLE	*		
Duro Art Industries	DURO DAN JUNIOR	*		
Fostport, Inc.	YARKA		*	
Fostport, Inc.	YARKA PROFESSIONAL #		*	
J. L. Hammett Co.	ART UTILITY	*		
Playtime Products	TYCO PLAYTIME WASHABLE	*		
Rose Art Industries	101 DALMATIONS PAINTS		*	
Rose Art Industries	GARGOYLES ACTIVITY CASE WASHABLES	*		
Rose Art Industries	HUNCHBACK OF NOTRE DAME		*	
Rose Art Industries	KODAK DEEP TONES	*		
Rose Art Industries	KODAK FLUORESCENT	*		
Rose Art Industries	KODAK WASHABLE	*		
Rose Art Industries	LION KING WATERCOLORS		*	
Rose Art Industries	MY FIRST WASHABLE WATER COLORS	*		
Rose Art Industries	POCAHONTAS ACTIVITY CASE WASHABLES	*		
Rose Art Industries	ROSE ART DEEP TONES	*		
Rose Art Industries	ROSE ART FLUORESCENT	*		
Rose Art Industries	ROSE ART GLITTER		*	
Rose Art Industries	ROSE ART GLOW	*		
Rose Art Industries	ROSE ART WASHABLE	*		
Rose Art Industries	ROSE ART WASHABLE SUPER COLOR SYSTEM WATERCOLORS	*		
Royal Talens	REMBRANDT #			*
Royal Talens	VAN GOGH			*
Salis International	DR. PH. MARTIN'S		*	
Salis International	DR. PH. MARTIN'S BLEED PROOF WHITE		*	
Salis International	DR. PH. MARTIN'S FLO-2 WHITE		*	
Salis International	DR. PH. MARTIN'S GRAPH-X WHITE		*	
Salis International	DR. PH. MARTIN'S RADIANT CONCENTRATED		*	
Salis International	HYDRUS FINE ART		*	
Sargent Art	SARGENT	*		
Sargent Art	SARGENT (22 SERIES)	*		
Sargent Art	SARGENT (66 SERIES)	*		
Sargent Art	SARGENT FLUORESCENT	*		
Sargent Art	SARGENT WASHABLE	*		
Schoenfeld & Co.	LUKAS #			*
Schoenfeld & Co.	LUKAS FEINE STUDIO-AQUARELLFARBE		*	
Hans Stockmar GmbH	AQUARELLFARBEN (JAR)		*	
Western Publishing	COLOR EXPRESS FLUORESCENT	*		
Western Publishing	COLOR EXPRESS WASHABLE	*		
Winsor & Newton	ARTISTS #			*
Water Colors, Tube				
Binney & Smith	LIQUITEX #		*	
Buncho Corp.	BUNCHO		*	
Buncho Corp.	BUNCHO POSTER		*	
ColArt Fine Art/Graphics	REEVES WATER COLOURS		*	
Creative Art Products	SHIVA ARTISTS' #		*	
Da Vinci Paint Co.	DA VINCI ARTISTS' #		*	
Daler-Rowney	GEORGIAN			*
Daler-Rowney	ROWNEY ARTISTS #			*
M. Grumbacher, Inc.	ACADEMY #		*	
M. Grumbacher, Inc.	FINEST #		*	
Holbein Works Ltd.	HOLBEIN #			*
Hunt Manufacturing	SPEEDBALL PROFESSIONAL		*	
Lefranc & Bourgeois	AQUARELLE 600 #			*
Lion Pencil Co., Ltd.	CRAYON FACTORY		*	
Lion Pencil Co., Ltd.	LION		*	
Loew-Cornell	LOEW-CORNELL		*	
Martin/F. Weber Co.	SUSAN SCHEEWE		*	
Martin/F. Weber Co.	WEBER PERMALBA		*	
Pentel of America	PENTEL WFP		*	
Royal Talens	REMBRANDT #			*

PRODUCTS AND MANUFACTURERS	BRAND NAMES	CP SEAL	AP SEAL	HL/NT SEAL
PAINTS (continued)				
Water Colors, Tube (continued)				
Royal Talens	TALENS			*
Royal Talens	VAN GOGH			*
Sakura of America	FANTASIA		*	
Sakura of America	IMPELLIST WATER COLOR		*	
Sakura of America	KOI		*	
Sakura of America	SAKURA MAT		*	
Schoenfeld & Co.	LUKAS MOIST ARTISTS' #			*
Sennelier Beaux Arts	SENNELIER EXTRA FINE #			*
ShinHan Art Materials	SHINHAN WATER PAINT #		*	
Daniel Smith, Inc.	DANIEL SMITH EXTRA FINE #		*	
Daniel Smith, Inc.	DANIEL SMITH EXTRA FINE LUMINESCENT		*	
Daniel Smith, Inc.	DANIEL SMITH FLUORESCENT AQUACOLORS		*	
Utrecht Mfg. Co.	UTRECHT		*	
Winsor & Newton	ARTISTS #			*
Winsor & Newton	COTMAN #			*
Yasutomo & Co.	NIJI		*	
PAPER				
American Art Clay	AMACO HANDCAST PAPER		*	
American Art Clay	AMACO HANDCAST PAPER ADDITIVE		*	
Binney & Smith	LIQUITEX ARTBOARD		*	
Hunt Mfg. Co.	PAPER KRAZE PAPER MAKING KIT		*	
Saral Paper Co., Inc.	SALLY'S ARTISTS GRAPHITE PAPER		*	
Saral Paper Co., Inc.	SARAL TRANSFER PAPER		*	
Daniel Smith, Inc.	DANIEL SMITH DRY PAPER SIZING		*	
Daniel Smith, Inc.	DANIEL SMITH METHYLCELLULOSE		*	
PASTELS				
Hard Pastels				
Quartet Manufacturing	ALPHACOLOR		*	
Quartet Manufacturing	ALPHACOLOR TRIANGULAR		*	
Oil Pastels				
Caran D'Ache of Switz.	NEOPASTEL		*	
ColArt International	CONTE			*
Dixon Ticonderoga	SKETCHO	*		
Dong-A Teaching Mat.	DONG-A		*	
Dong-A Teaching Mat.	DONG-A DREAMLAND		*	
M. Grumbacher, Inc.	GRUMBACHER		*	
Holbein Works Ltd.	HOLBEIN ARTISTS			*
Lion Pencil Co., Ltd.	LION		*	
Loew-Cornell	LOEW-CORNELL		*	
Mon Ami America	MON AMI OIL PASTELS		*	
Mungyo Kyojai Co.	GALLERY OIL PASTELS	*		
Pentel of America	PENTEL PTS-15 FABRIC FUN DYE STICKS		*	
Pentel of America	PENTEL PHN-36		*	
Sakura of America	CHUBBIES	*		
Sakura of America	CRAY-PAS FUTO FUTO	*		
Sakura of America	CRAY-PAS ORIGINAL	*		
Sakura of America	CRAY-PAS V.S.O.P.		*	
Sakura of America	HI CRAYPAS ARTISTS' STICKS (XAP)	*		
Sakura of America	JUMBO	*		
Sakura of America	SOLID MARKER		*	
Sakura of America	SQUARE STICKS	*		
Sakura of America	STANDARD	*		
Sanford Corporation	JUMBO		*	
Sanford Corporation	REGULAR		*	
Sennelier Beaux Arts	SENNELIER		*	
Yasutomo & Co.	NIJI		*	
Soft Pastels				
Colart International	CONTE			*
Daler-Rowney	ROWNEY ARTISTS'			*
Daler-Rowney	ROWNEY ARTISTS' SQUARE			*
Duro Art Industries	DURO	*		
Empire Berol USA	PRISMACOLOR ARTSTIX		*	
Fostport, Inc.	YARKA		*	
M. Grumbacher	GRUMBACHER SOFT		*	

Some products in this line do not bear the CP, AP or Health Label (Non-Toxic) Seal.

TABLE 2   (continued)

PRODUCTS AND MANUFACTURERS	BRAND NAMES	CP SEAL	AP SEAL	HL/NT SEAL
PASTELS (continued)				
Soft Pastels (continued)				
Holbein Works Ltd.	HOLBEIN			*
Holbein Works Ltd.	HOLBEIN ARTIST 1570 SOFT			*
Mungyo Kyojai Co.	GALLERY ROUND ARTIST			*
Mungyo Kyojai Co.	MUNGYO ASST. SQUARE	*		
Mungyo Kyojai Co.	MUNGYO CHARCOAL SQUARE	*		
Mungyo Kyojai Co.	MUNGYO EARTHTONE SQUARE	*		
Mungyo Kyojai Co.	MUNGYO GRAYTONE SQUARE	*		
Quartet Manufacturing	ALPHACOLOR FLUORESCENT	*		
Quartet Manufacturing	ALPHACOLOR POSTER CHALK	*		
Quartet Manufacturing	ALPHACOLOR SQUARE	*		
Jack Richeson & Co.	RICHESON ARTIST		*	
Jack Richeson & Co.	RICHESON OCALDO SKETCH STICKS*			
Royal Talens	REMBRANDT			*
Royal Talens	REMBRANDT CARRE PASTEL		*	
Royal Talens	VAN GOGH			*
Sakura of America	NOUVEL CARRE		*	
Sakura of America	SAKURA CONTE		*	
H. Schmincke & Co.	PASTELL SERIES 17		*	
School Mate, Inc.	SCHOOL MATE SQUARE	*		
Sennelier Beaux Arts	EXTRA SOFT A L'ECU		*	
Sennelier Beaux Arts	GIANT A L'ECU		*	
PHOTO EMULSIONS				
Creative Art Products	DICK BLICK		*	
Fluorographic Services	GUIDE-LINE DEVELOPER		*	
Fluorographic Services	GUIDE-LINE SENSITIZER		*	
Hunt Manufacturing	SPEEDBALL PHOTO EMULSION		*	
Hunt Manufacturing	SPEEDBALL (BLUE) PHOTO EMULSION		*	
Hunt Manufacturing	SPEEDBALL DIAZO PHOTO EMULSION		*	
Winsor & Newton	PHOTOGRAPHIC OPAQUE			*
PHOTOGRAPHIC ACCESSORY				
Fluorographic Services	FLUORO SOLVENT		*	
RESTORATION/CONSERVATION PRODUCTS				
American Art Clay	AMACO NAIL HOLE FILLER		*	
Martin/F. Weber Co.	WEBER ADHESIVE PREPARATION		*	
Sennelier Beaux Arts	BEESWAX			*
Sennelier Beaux Arts	BONE GLUE			*
Sennelier Beaux Arts	CASE ALBA			*
Sennelier Beaux Arts	COLORLESS GENUINE LAKE GUM			*
Sennelier Beaux Arts	DAMMAR GUM			*
Sennelier Beaux Arts	DEXTRIN			*
Sennelier Beaux Arts	GELATINE			*
Sennelier Beaux Arts	JUDAIC BITUME			*
Sennelier Beaux Arts	LACTIC CASEIN IN POWDER			*
Sennelier Beaux Arts	METHYL-CELLULOSE MEDIUM			*
Sennelier Beaux Arts	PUTTY RESIN (DROPS)			*
Sennelier Beaux Arts	RABBIT SKIN GLUE			*
Sennelier Beaux Arts	YOLK			*
Winsor & Newton	WINTON PICTURE CLEANER			*
SCREEN PRINTING INKS & MEDIUMS				
Acrylic				
Hunt Manufacturing	SPEEDBALL GLOSS OVERPRINT VARNISH	*		
Hunt Manufacturing	SPEEDBALL PERMANENT	*		
Hunt Manufacturing	SPEEDBALL EXTENDER BASE	*		
Hunt Manufacturing	SPEEDBALL RETARDER BASE	*		
Textile				
Creative Art Products	DICK BLICK'S TEXTILE INK	*		
Hunt Manufacturing	SPEEDBALL FLUORESCENT	*		
Hunt Manufacturing	SPEEDBALL NIGHT GLO TEXTILE	*		
Hunt Manufacturing	SPEEDBALL PIZZAZZ	*		
Hunt Manufacturing	SPEEDBALL TEXTILE	*		
NASCO International	AQUA BULK	*		
NASCO International	BULK-TEX	*		
Sennelier Beaux Arts	THICKENER			*

PRODUCTS AND MANUFACTURERS	BRAND NAMES	CP SEAL	AP SEAL	HL/NT SEAL
SCREEN PRINTING INKS & MEDIUMS (continued)				
Water Soluble				
Holbein Works Ltd.	MITSUWA MASKET			*
Hunt Manufacturing	SPEEDBALL		*	
Accessories, Water Base				
Holbein Works Ltd.	MITSUWA AQUA MASK			*
Hunt Manufacturing	SPEEDBALL DRAWING FLUID (BLUE)		*	
Hunt Manufacturing	SPEEDBALL SCREEN FILLER		*	
Hunt Manufacturing	SPEEDBALL TRANSPARENT BASE		*	
SCULPTURE MATERIALS				
Activa Products	ART PLASTER		*	
Activa Products	INSTAMOLD		*	
Activa Products	PERMASTONE		*	
Active Products	RIGID WRAP		*	
American Art Clay	AMACO FLEXWAX 120		*	
American Art Clay	AMACO CARVING WAX		*	
Hunt Manufacturing	BIENFANG PLASTER OF PARISCRAFT II		*	
JCS Incorporated	MAK 'A MOLD MOLDING COMPOUND		*	
JCS Incorporated	MASTERPIECE CASTING COMPOUND		*	
JCS Incorporated	MASTERPIECE QUICK SET CASTING COMPOUND		*	
Polyform Products Co.	SCULPEY DILUENT		*	
Rose Art Industries	GARGOYLES ACTIVITY CASE LIQUID STONE		*	
Skullduggery, Inc.	PERFECTCAST		*	
SOLVENTS				
Martin/F. Weber Co.	TURPENOID NATURAL		*	
Winsor & Newton	ARTISTS' ACRYLIC VARNISH REMOVER			*

Some products in this line do not bear
the CP, AP or Health Label (Non-Toxic) Seal.

-25-

TABLE 2   (continued)

**PRODUCTS AUTHORIZED TO BEAR THE
HL/CR HEALTH LABEL (CAUTIONS REQUIRED) SEAL OF
THE CERTIFIED PRODUCTS AND CERTIFIED LABELING BUREAU OF
THE ART & CREATIVE MATERIALS INSTITUTE, INC. © 1997
100 Boylston Street, Suite 1050, Boston, MA 02116 617/426-6400**

SPECIFIC LABELING FOR TOXIC
INGREDIENT(S) AS REQUIRED
BY THE TOXICOLOGIST.

APRIL 1997

Products bearing the Health Label (Cautions Required) Seal (HL/CR) of The Art & Creative Materials Institute, Inc. (ACMI) are certified in a program of toxicological evaluation by a medical expert to be properly labeled. This program is reviewed by ACMI's Toxicological Advisory Board. These products are certified by ACMI to be labeled in accordance with the chronic hazard labeling standard, ASTM D-4236, and Federal law, P.L. 100-695. Products bearing the Health Label (Cautions Required) Seal bear appropriate ingredient and cautionary labeling and safe use instructions. Non-Toxic products with the Health Label (Non-Toxic) Seal bear the wording Non-Toxic or No Health Labeling Required and are located at the front of this list with the other non-toxic (CP and AP) products. Be sure to purchase products that bear the ACMI Seals!

PRODUCTS AND MANUFACTURERS	BRAND NAMES

ADHESIVES

Glues

American Art Clay	FRIENDLY PLASTICS GOOP
Cascade Sales & Mfg.	CASCADE GLITTER GLUE (AEROSOL)
Cascade Sales & Mfg.	CASCADE SUPER U-200
Cascade Sales & Mfg.	CASCADE U-2 SPRAY
Delta Tech. Coatings	CERAM DECOR STENCIL ADHESIVE SPRAY
Delta Tech. Coatings	DELTA'S STENCIL MAGIC ADHESIVE SPRAY
Elmer's Products/Borden	ELMER'S CARPENTER'S EXTERIOR WOOD FILLER
Elmer's Products/Borden	ELMER'S CLEAR HOUSEHOLD CEMENT
Elmer's Products/Borden	ELMER'S CRAFT BOND METAL & PLASTIC CEMENT
Elmer's Products/Borden	ELMER'S CRAFT BOND NO WRINKLE RUBBER CEMENT
Elmer's Products/Borden	ELMER'S EPOXY CEMENT (TUBE & SYRINGE)
Elmer's Products/Borden	ELMER'S EPOXY RIBBON
Elmer's Products/Borden	ELMER'S FILL 'N FINISH FOR DARK WOOD
Elmer's Products/Borden	ELMER'S FILL 'N FINISH FOR LIGHT WOOD
Elmer's Products/Borden	ELMER'S FLAMMABLE CONTACT CEMENT
Elmer's Products/Borden	ELMER'S HEAVY GRIP CEMENT
Elmer's Products/Borden	ELMER'S METAL MENDER CEMENT
Elmer's Products/Borden	ELMER'S MODEL & HOBBY CEMENT
Elmer's Products/Borden	ELMER'S NO WRINKLE RUBBER CEMENT
Elmer's Products/Borden	ELMER'S PROBOND POLYURETHANE GLUE
Elmer's Products/Borden	ELMBER'S PROFESSIONAL CONTACT CEMENT
Elmer's Products/Borden	ELMER'S RUBBER CEMENT
Elmer's Products/Borden	ELMER'S STIX-ALL
Elmer's Products/Borden	ELMER'S SUPER-FAST EPOXY CEMENT (TUBE & SYRINGE)
Elmer's Products/Borden	ELMER'S SUPER GLUE
Elmer's Products/Borden	KRAZY GLUE ALL PURPOSE
Elmer's Products/Borden	KRAZY GLUE FINE DETAIL FORMULA WITH EXTENDER TIPS
Elmer's Products/Borden	KRAZY GLUE LEATHER FORMULA
Elmer's Products/Borden	KRAZY GLUE NO RUN GEL
Elmer's Products/Borden	KRAZY GLUE PLUS AUTO/MARINE FORMULA WITH SURFACE PREP
Elmer's Products/Borden	KRAZY GLUE PLUS GENERAL REPAIR FORMULA WITH SURFACE PREP
Elmer's Products/Borden	KRAZY GLUE PLUS PORCELAIN/CERAMIC FORMULA
Elmer's Products/Borden	KRAZY GLUE PUSH-N-PULL PEN
Elmer's Products/Borden	KRAZY GLUE SKIN GUARD FORMULA
Elmer's Products/Borden	KRAZY GLUE SKIN GUARD GEL
Elmer's Products/Borden	KRAZY GLUE SKIN GUARD PUSH-N-PULL PEN
Elmer's Products/Borden	KRAZY GLUE WOOD FORMULA
Elmer's Products/Borden	KRAZY GLUE WORKSHOP
Elmer's Products/Borden	WONDERBOND PLUS SUPER GLUE
Fiebing Company	FIEBING'S TANNERS BOND ADHESIVE
Sanford Corporation	GRIPPIT
Sanford Corporation	RUBBER CEMENT
Union Rubber, Inc.	BEST-TEST OFFICE RUBBER CEMENT
Union Rubber, Inc.	BEST-TEST ONE COAT CEMENT
Union Rubber, Inc.	BEST-TEST PAPER CEMENT
Union Rubber, Inc.	BEST-TEST RUBBER CEMENT

Polymer

Elmer's Products/Borden	ELMER'S CRAFT BOND MULTI-PURPOSE SPRAY
Elmer's Products/Borden	ELMER'S SPRAY ADHESIVE
M. Grumbacher, Inc.	ACCENT SPRAY ADHESIVE
Humbrol Limited	CLEARFIX

AIRBRUSH COLORS, MEDIUMS & ACCESSORIES

Badger Air-Brush Co.	PROPEL
Winsor & Newton	AIRBRUSH CLEANER
Winsor & Newton	DESIGNERS BRILLIANT WATERCOLOURS ##

BLOCK PRINTING INKS & MEDIUMS

Oil Base

Daler-Rowney	ROWNEY BLOCK PRINTING OIL COLOUR MEDIUM
Graphic Chemical & Ink	GRAPHIC ROSE MADDER

BRUSH CARE PRODUCTS

Fiesta Colors	OIL BRUSH CLEANER
M. Grumbacher, Inc.	ACCENT BRUSH CLEANER #659
M. Grumbacher, Inc.	BRUSH & HAND CLEANER
Holbein Works Ltd.	BRUSH CLEANER S
Loew-Cornell	BETTER WAY BRUSH CLEANING FLUID & ODORLESS THINNER
Loew-Cornell	ODORLESS BRUSH CLEANER & THINNER
Martin/F. Weber Co.	WEBER SILICONE BRUSH CLEANER
Plaid Enterprises	BRUSH PLUS
Plaid Enterprises	STENCIL DECOR BRUSH CLEANER

CERAMICS, SPECIALTY PRODUCTS

American Art Clay	AMACO EXTERIOR BRUSH 'N LEAF
American Art Clay	AMACO INTERIOR BRUSH 'N LEAF
American Art Clay	AMACO ENAMELING OIL
American Art Clay	AMACO KILN CEMENT
American Art Clay	AMACO KILN SEAL
American Art Clay	AMACO PLASTER SEPARATOR
American Art Clay	AMACO RUB 'N BUFF
American Art Clay	AMACO SP-OVERDRIFT
American Art Clay	AMACO SP-400 WHITE PEBBLE
American Art Clay	AMACO STAIN 'N BUFF
Caldex Enterprises	#803 OLD WORLD ART SATIN SEALER
Caldex Enterprises	#804 OLD WORLD ART ANTIQUING GLAZE
Ceramichrome, Inc.	FLINT
Ceramichrome, Inc.	GLOSS BRUSH-ON SEALER
Ceramichrome, Inc.	KILN WASH
Ceramichrome, Inc.	MENDSWARE
Ceramichrome, Inc.	SODIUM SILICATE
Ceramichrome, Inc.	STAIN MEDIA
Ceramichrome, Inc.	TRANZMASK
Ceramichrome, Inc.	TWINKLE DUST
Ceramichrome, Inc.	WHITE GLOSS BROCADE
Fiesta Colors	CRYSTAL SAND
Gare, Inc.	5100 ADORN
Gare, Inc.	BLEND-A-GLAZE
Gare, Inc.	5001 SEAL
Gare, Inc.	THICK-N-ETCH
Gare, Inc.	THICKEN-IT
Minn/Midwest Clay	EGYPTIAN PASTE (POWDER)

CLAYS

Modeling (Self-Hardening)

American Art Clay	AMACO BEESWAX

Powdered Sculpting & Modeling Mediums

American Art Clay	AMACO CREA-STONE
American Art Clay	AMACO MIX-A-MOLD

Some of the products in this line bear the
CP, AP or Health Label (Non-Toxic) Seal.

TABLE 2   (continued)

PRODUCTS AND MANUFACTURERS	BRAND NAMES

CLAYS (continued)

Ceramic

American Art Clay	AMACO COARSE GROG
American Art Clay	AMACO EGYPTIAN PASTE #70
American Art Clay	AMACO MEDIUM GROG
American Art Clay	AMACO STONEWARE WITH GROG #48 (DRY)
American Art Clay	AMACO WHITE ART #25 (DRY)
A.R.T. Studio Clay	CINNAMONSTONE II (DRY)
A.R.T. Studio Clay	ORANGESTONE #519
Ex-Cel, Inc.	EXCEL TERRA COTTA (DRY)
Minn/Midwest Clay	COLORED PORCELAIN ##
Minn/Midwest Clay	S SERIES COLORED ##
Minn/Midwest Clay	M SERIES COLORED ##
Minn/Midwest Clay	NO. 3 WHITE STONEWARE ##

Ceramic Casting Slip

American Art Clay	AMACO 67S
American Art Clay	AMACO DS 46 (POWDER)
American Art Clay	AMACO DS-225 (DRY)
American Art Clay	AMACO PORCELAIN #1
A.R.T. Studio Clay	LOW FIRE RED #512
A.R.T. Studio Clay	ORANGESTONE #519
Minn/Midwest Clay	MC #3 (POWDER)
Minn/Midwest Clay	MC #5 (POWDER)
Minn/Midwest Clay	MC LIGHTONE (POWDER)

CRAFT MATERIALS, MISCELLANEOUS

American Art Clay	COTTON PRESS MOLD RELEASE
Arts Encaustic Internat'l	ENCAUSTIC WAXES

DETERGENT CLEANERS

Dixon Ticonderoga	WHITE SYSTEM LIQUID WHITE BOARD CLEANER
General Pencil Co.	KISS OFF STAIN REMOVER
Kuretake Co., Ltd.	ZIG SPRAY CLEANER
Puresol, Inc.	AQUASOL
Quartet Manufacturing	QUARTET MARKER BOARD CLEANER

DRAWING & WRITING INSTRUMENTS & ACCESSORIES

Professional Drawing Pencils

NES Arnold Inc.	SCOLA VELVAWAX ##

DRAWING & LETTERING INKS & MEDIUMS

Non-Waterproof

Holbein Works Ltd.	SUMI
Kuretake Co., Ltd.	KURETAKE SHUEKI
Royal Talens	ECOLINE ##
Yasutomo & Co.	SUMI STICK

Technical

Pelikan USA	PELIKAN DRAWING INK A ##
Pelikan USA	PELIKAN DRAWING INK FT
Salis International	DR. PH. MARTIN'S PEN-WHITE

Waterproof

Daler-Rowney	F. W. ARTISTS ##
Daler-Rowney	LUMA BLEED PROOF WHITE
Empire Berol USA	ELEMENTS CORRECTION PEN
Empire Berol USA	PEDIGREE LIQUID TYPE FIX
Holbein Works Ltd.	HOLBEIN ##
Kuretake Co., Ltd.	KURETAKE NOUBOKU SHOGEI
S. K. Merchandising Corp.	POTPOURRI CORRECTION FLUID
S. K. Merchandising Corp.	POTPOURRI CORRECTION PEN
Winsor & Newton	ARTISTS' DRAWING ##
Yasutomo & Co.	COLORED SUMI INKS
Yasutomo & Co.	SUMI INK KF

ETCHING INKS & MEDIUMS

Inks

Daniel Smith, Inc.	DANIEL SMITH ETCHING INKS ##

Mediums

B & B Etching Products	DIP N' ETCH
B & B Etching Products	ETCHING CREME
B & B Etching Products	GOLD-OFF
Graphic Chemical & Ink	GRAPHIC STOP OUT VARNISH
Graphic Chemical & Ink	GRAPHIC UNIVERSAL ETCH HARD

PRODUCTS AND MANUFACTURERS	BRAND NAMES

ETCHING INKS & MEDIUMS (continued)

Mediums (continued)

Graphic Chemical & Ink	GRAPHIC UNIVERSAL ETCH SOFT
Daniel Smith, Inc.	DANIEL SMITH ANTI-SKIN SPRAY (PUMP)
Daniel Smith, Inc.	DANIEL SMITH ASPHALTUM POWDERED
Daniel Smith, Inc.	DANIEL SMITH FLASH OIL 470
Daniel Smith, Inc.	DANIEL SMITH LIQUID ASPHALTUM
Daniel Smith, Inc.	DANIEL SMITH MIRACLE GEL REDUCER
Daniel Smith, Inc.	DANIEL SMITH PROCESS ETCHING INKS ##
Daniel Smith, Inc.	DANIEL SMITH WHITING

FIXATIVES

Cascade Sales & Mfg.	CASCADE FABRIC STIFFENER
Cascade Sales & Mfg.	CASCADE FLOWER CLEANER
Cascade Sales & Mfg.	FABRIC STIFFENER
Chartpak	CHARTPAK NO ODOR WORKABLE SPRAY
Daler-Rowney	ROWNEY
Daler-Rowney	ROWNEY LOW ODOUR PERFIX (AEROSOL)
Delta Tech. Coatings	STA SET & SPRITZER BY DELTA
Martin/F. Weber Co.	BLUE LABEL REWORKABLE (LIQUID & AEROSOL)
Pebeo of America	MATT PHOTO SPRAY
Pebeo of America	PASTEL FIXATIVE
Pebeo of America	PASTEL FIXATIVE SPRAY
Pebeo of America	SOLVENT GOUACHE VARNISH SPRAY
Plaid Enterprises	FLAT MATTE FIX-IT (AEROSOL)
Plaid Enterprises	MATTE FIX-IT (AEROSOL)
Royal Talens	TALENS CONCENTRATED (AEROSOL)
Royal Talens	TALENS FOR CHARCOAL
Royal Talens	TALENS FOR PASTELS
Salis International	DR. PH. MARTIN'S SPECTRA-TEX
Sennelier Beaux Arts	DELACROIX FIXATIVE (LIQUID & AEROSOL)
Sennelier Beaux Arts	LATOUR FIXATIVE (LIQUID & AEROSOL)
Sennelier Beaux Arts	OIL PASTEL FIXATIVE (LIQUID & AEROSOL)

GESSOS & PAINTING GROUNDS

Golden Artist Colors	GAC ABSORBENT GROUND
Maimeri USA	MAIMERI BLACK GESSO
Maimeri USA	MAIMERI GESSO
Daniel Smith, Inc.	DANIEL SMITH WORLD'S BEST GESSO

GLAZES (CERAMIC)

Glazes

American Art Clay	AMACO ALLIGATOR ##
American Art Clay	AMACO CRYSTALTEX ##
American Art Clay	AMACO DECO
American Art Clay	AMACO ENGOBES ##
American Art Clay	AMACO F SERIES ##
American Art Clay	AMACO LOW FIRE CRACKLE ##
American Art Clay	AMACO LUSTRE & METALLIC
American Art Clay	AMACO MAJOLICA GLOSS ##
American Art Clay	AMACO MATT (LM SERIES) ##
American Art Clay	AMACO OPALESCENT ##
American Art Clay	AMACO SAHARA HIGH FIRE DRY (HF SERIES) ##
American Art Clay	AMACO SAHARA HIGH FIRE LIQ. (HF SERIES) ##
A.R.T. Studio Clay	FIREWARE - FW 2000 SERIES ##
A.R.T. Studio Clay	GLAZEWORKS LEADFREE LOW-FIRE GLOSS - FW 2000 SERIES ##
A.R.T. Studio Clay	GLAZEWORKS LEADFREE MAJOLICA - MK2900 SERIES ##
A.R.T. Studio Clay	NERO (CONE 5) ##
A.R.T. Studio Clay	NERO (CONE 6) ##
Borden, Inc.	FAUX FINISHES
Ceramichrome, Inc.	ART ##
Ceramichrome, Inc.	CRYSTAL
Ceramichrome, Inc.	DECO-PAQUE
Ceramichrome, Inc.	GLOSS ##
Ceramichrome, Inc.	KRACKLE
Ceramichrome, Inc.	MATT
Ceramichrome, Inc.	OK DINNERWARE GLOSS
Ceramichrome, Inc.	PORCELAIN CLEAR
Ceramichrome, Inc.	SPECIALTY ##
Ceramichrome, Inc.	SPECKLED ##
Ceramichrome, Inc.	TESSERAE
Gare, Inc.	GARE CRYSTAL GLAZES
Gare, Inc.	GARE GLOSS ##
Gare, Inc.	GARE OPAQUE GLOSS

Some of the products in this line bear the CP, AP or Health Label (Non-Toxic) Seal.

-2-

TABLE 2   (continued)

PRODUCTS AND MANUFACTURERS	BRAND NAMES
GLAZES (CERAMIC) (continued)	
Glazes (continued)	
Gare, Inc.	METALLIC
Gare, Inc.	POLISHED STONE ##
Gare, Inc.	STARLIGHT COLORS ##
Mid-South Ceramic Sply.	OPULENCE C/6 (POWDER)
Minn/Midwest Clay	HIGH RANGE STONEWARE MATT/HHM SERIES
Minn/Midwest Clay	HIGH RANGE STONEWARE OPAQUE GLOSS/HHG SERIES
Minn/Midwest Clay	MED-RANGE STONEWARE MATT/ HM SERIES (LIQUID) ##
Minn/Midwest Clay	LOW FIRE MATT ##
Minn/Midwest Clay	MATT EARTHENWARE/M SERIES (LIQUID) ##
Minn/Midwest Clay	MATT EARTHENWARE/M SERIES (POWDER)
Minn/Midwest Clay	MEDIUM RANGE STONEWARE EARTHSTONE/HE SERIES (LIQUID)
Minn/Midwest Clay	MEDIUM RANGE STONEWARE EARTHSTONE/HE SERIES (POWDER)
Minn/Midwest Clay	MEDIUM RANGE STONEWARE MATT/HM SERIES (POWDER)
Minn/Midwest Clay	MED-RANGE STONEWARE TRANSPARENT/ HT SERIES (POWDER)
Minn/Midwest Clay	OPAQUE GLOSS EARTHENWARE/ G SERIES (LIQUID) ##
Minn/Midwest Clay	OPAQUE GLOSS EARTHENWARE/ G SERIES (POWDER)
Minn/Midwest Clay	OPAQUE GLOSS MID-RANGE STONEWARE/ HG SERIES (LIQUID) ##
Minn/Midwest Clay	OPAQUE GLOSS MID-RANGE STONEWARE/ HG SERIES (POWDER) ##
Minn/Midwest Clay	SLIP GLAZE ##
Minn/Midwest Clay	TRANSPARENT EARTHENWARE/ T SERIES (LIQUID) ##
Minn/Midwest Clay	TRANSPARENT EARTHENWARE/ T SERIES (POWDER)
Seattle Pottery	DARK BLUE-SP 9
Seattle Pottery	DEEP BLUE-SP 24
Seattle Pottery	GREEN MOTTLED-SP 4
Seattle Pottery	LIGHT BLUE MOTTLED-SP 5
Seattle Pottery	NICKEL BROWN-SP 26
Seattle Pottery	TURQUOISE GREEN-SP 18
Sherry's Western	WESTERN CLEAR #1000
Sherry's Western	WESTERN COLORED TRANSPARENT GLOSS
Sherry's Western	WESTERN 900 SERIES
Spectrum Glazes	GLOSS
Spectrum Glazes	GREEN LINE ##
Spectrum Glazes	HIGH FIRE 1100 SERIES (LIQUID) ##
Spectrum Glazes	HIGH FIRE 1200 SERIES (LIQUID) ##
Spectrum Glazes	SATIN ##
Spectrum Glazes	TEXTURE ##
Underglazes	
American Art Clay	AMACO DECORATING CRAYONS ##
American Art Clay	AMACO LIQUID UNDERGLAZES ##
American Art Clay	AMACO SEMI-MOIST DECORATING COLORS ##
American Art Clay	AMACO SUN STROKES
American Art Clay	AMACO VELVET-1-STROKE ##
American Art Clay	AMACO VELVETS ##
Ceramichrome, Inc.	BEAUTY-FLO OPAQUE ##
Ceramichrome, Inc.	BRITE-STROKES
Ceramichrome, Inc.	SPECIALIZED
Ceramichrome, Inc.	STONEWARE-LIKE
Gare, Inc.	GARE ##
Gare, Inc.	GARE ONE-STROKES ##
Minn/Midwest Clay	MINNESOTA ##
Minn/Midwest Clay	MINNESOTA/MIDWEST ##
Minn/Midwest Clay	POTTER'S PEN REFILLS ##
Overglazes	
American Art Clay	AMACO GLASS & METAL ENAMEL DECORATING COLORS
American Art Clay	AMACO OPALESCENT VERSA COLORS
American Art Clay	AMACO SEMI-MOIST DECORATING COLORS
American Art Clay	AMACO VERSA COLOR
American Art Clay	AMACO WATER BASED VERSA COLORS ##
GLITTER	
Cascade Sales & Mfg.	GLITTERAMA SPRAY

PRODUCTS AND MANUFACTURERS	BRAND NAMES
GRAPHIC MASKING LIQUIDS	
Creative Art Products	SHIVA LIQUID MASQUE CLEANER
Fluorographic Services	COL-TEC MASKING INK
Fluorographic Services	FLUORO MASKING INK
LITHO INKS & MEDIUMS	
Daniel Smith, Inc.	DANIEL SMITH FRENCH CHALK
Daniel Smith, Inc.	DANIEL SMITH PUMICE POWDER
Stones Crayons	STONES LIQUID TUSCHE
Stones Crayons	STONES PASTE TUSCHE
MARKERS	
Audio Visual	
Chartpak	AVP AUDIO VISUAL ##
Graphic Art	
Chartpak	OPAQUING PEN
Fluorographic Services	COL-TEC REMOVER, BRUSH TIP
Kuretake Co., Ltd.	ZIG KURECOLOR REFILL INK
Metallic	
Yasutomo & Co.	Y&C METALLIC MARKER (GOLD - BROAD NIB ONLY)
Permanent	
Pentel of America	PENTEL 100W-S WHITE MARKER
Staedtler, Inc.	LUMOCOLOR CORRECTION 319
Staedtler, Inc.	LUMOCOLOR PERMANENT 313, 314, 317, 318
Writing	
Kuretake Co., Ltd.	ZIG WHITE PEN
Yasutomo & Co.	NIJI STYLIST
MEDIUMS & VARNISHES, ACRYLIC/POLYMER	
Mediums	
Binney & Smith	LIQUITEX MARBLING
Colart/International	POLYFLASHE TRANSPARENT
Daler-Rowney	ROWNEY CRYLA TENSION BREAKER
Fiesta Colors	CRACKLE
Fiesta Colors	KLEER HY-GLOSS
Fiesta Colors	KLEER MATTE
Golden Artist Colors	ACRYLIC FLOW RELEASE
Golden Artist Colors	GLAZING
Golden Artist Colors	MSA GEL
Golden Artist Colors	POLYMER 400, 900
Pebeo of America	ACRYLIC DIFFUSER
Pebeo of America	ACRYLIC RETARDER
Maimeri USA	MAIMERI ACRYLIC MODELING PASTE
Maimeri USA	MAIMERI COARSE ACRYLIC PUMICE
Maimeri USA	MAIMERI FINE ACRYLIC PUMICE
Maimeri USA	MAIMERI GEL MEDIUM
Maimeri USA	MAIMERI GLOSS MEDIUM
Maimeri USA	MAIMERI HEAVY GEL GLOSS
Maimeri USA	MAIMERI HEAVY GEL MATTE
Maimeri USA	MAIMERI MATTE GEL
Maimeri USA	MAIMERI MATTE MEDIUM
Maimeri USA	MAIMERI RETARDER MEDIUM
Maimeri USA	MAIMERI VOLUME
Turner Colour Works	NEO COLOUR OVERLAY
Varnishes	
Daler-Rowney	ROWNEY CRYLA SOLUBLE GLOSS
Daler-Rowney	ROWNEY CRYLA SOLUBLE MATTE
Golden Artist Colors	POLYMER (GLOSS, MATTE & SATIN)
Golden Artist Colors	HARD MSA (GLOSS, MATTE & SATIN)
Golden Artist Colors	MSA (GLOSS, MATTE & SATIN)
M. Grumbacher, Inc.	ACCENT POLY VARNISH - GLOSS & SATIN
J. W. Etc.	EXTERIOR VARNISH GLOSS
J. W. Etc.	EXTERIOR VARNISH SATIN
Martin/F. Weber Co.	JENKINS STA-BRITE (AEROSOL)
Martin/F. Weber Co.	BOB ROSS FINISHING SPRAY VARNISH
Martin/F. Weber Co.	WEBER SYNVAR (LIQUID & AEROSOL)
Pebeo of America	SOLVENT BASED UV-ABSORBER
Plaid Enterprises	SUPERSHINE (AEROSOL)
Plaid Enterprises	TREASURE CRYSTAL COAT
Royal Talens	TALENS PROTECTING SPRAY

Some of the products in this line bear the
CP, AP or Health Label (Non-Toxic) Seal.

-3-

TABLE 2   (continued)

PRODUCTS AND MANUFACTURERS	BRAND NAMES

MEDIUMS & VARNISHES, ACRYLIC/POLYMER (continued)

Varnishes (continued

Royal Talens	TALENS REMBRANDT ACRYLIC GLOSSY (LIQUID & AEROSOL)
Royal Talens	TALENS REMBRANDT ACRYLIC MAT (LIQUID & AEROSOL)

MEDIUMS & VARNISHES, ALKYD & OIL

Driers

Binney & Smith	LIQUITEX COBALT SICCATIVE
M. Grumbacher, Inc.	COBALT
M. Grumbacher, Inc.	JAPAN
Holbein Works Ltd.	JAPAN GOLD SIZE
Lefranc & Bourgeois	COURTRAI DRIER, BROWN
Lefranc & Bourgeois	COURTRAI DRIER, WHITE
Martin/F. Weber Co.	WEBER JAPAN
Pebeo of America	COBALT SICCATIVE
Pebeo of America	COURTRAI SICCATIVE
Pebeo of America	SICCATIVE MEDIUM
Daniel Smith, Inc.	DANIEL SMITH COBALT DRIER
Winsor & Newton	JAPAN GOLD SIZE

Oils

Fiesta Colors	#8 NATURAL
Holbein Works Ltd.	PAINTING
Holbein Works Ltd.	SPIKE LAVENDER OIL
Martin/F. Weber Co.	BOB ROSS OIL PAINTING
Martin/F. Weber Co.	WEBER LIGHT DRYING
Martin/F. Weber Co.	WEBER OIL PAINTING
Sennelier Beaux Arts	COOKED LINSEED OIL

Painting Mediums - Gels

Binney & Smith	LIQUITEX PERMAGEL
Chroma Acrylics	ARCHIVAL SMOOTH
Daler-Rowney	ROWNEY GEL MEDIUM
Daler-Rowney	ROWNEY ALKYD WHITE
M. Grumbacher, Inc.	ZEC
Holbein Works Ltd.	PAINTING MEDIUM JELLY
Martin/F. Weber Co.	WEBER RES-N-GEL
Pebeo of America	COATING MEDIUM
Pebeo of America	FLORENTINE MEDIUM
Pebeo of America	FRAGONARD GEL MEDIUM
Royal Talens	REMBRANDT PAINTING PASTE

Painting Mediums - Liquids

Binney & Smith	LIQUITEX ALL-PURPOSE
Binney & Smith	LIQUITEX DAMAR SOLUTION HEAVY
Binney & Smith	LIQUITEX KOPAL
Binney & Smith	LIQUITEX RAPID SET OIL
Chroma Acrylics	ARCHIVAL CLASSIC
Chroma Acrylics	ARCHIVAL FAT
Creative Art Products	SHIVA COPAL
Creative Art Products	SHIVA PAINTING, LIGHT
Daler-Rowney	ROWNEY #700
Daler-Rowney	ROWNEY ALKYD
Daler-Rowney	ROWNEY LIGHT DRYING OIL
M. Grumbacher, Inc.	ALKYD
M. Grumbacher, Inc.	COPAL
M. Grumbacher, Inc.	OIL I
M. Grumbacher, Inc.	OIL II
M. Grumbacher, Inc.	OIL III
Holbein Works Ltd.	COPAL OIL
Holbein Works Ltd.	QUICK DRYING
Lefranc & Bourgeois	COLOURLESS PAINTING
Lefranc & Bourgeois	FLEMISH
Lefranc & Bourgeois	VENETIAN
Martin/F. Weber Co.	DOROTHY DENT
Martin/F. Weber Co.	JENKINS HAPPY
Martin/F. Weber Co.	WEBER COPAL
Martin/F. Weber Co.	WEBER RESIN OIL
Pebeo of America	ODORLESS MINERAL SPIRIT
Pebeo of America	PAINTING MEDIUM
Royal Talens	TALENS REMBRANDT
Royal Talens	TALENS REMBRANDT QUICK DRYING
Royal Talens	TALENS SICCATIVE DARK (DE HARLEM)
Royal Talens	TALENS SICCATIVE DE COURTRAI
Royal Talens	VAN EYCK
Sennelier Beaux Arts	OIL PAINT BINDING MEDIUM
Daniel Smith, Inc.	DANIEL SMITH PAINTING MEDIUM
Winsor & Newton	BLENDING & GLAZING
Winsor & Newton	LIQUIN

PRODUCTS AND MANUFACTURERS	BRAND NAMES

MEDIUMS & VARNISHES, ALKYD & OIL (continued)

Painting Mediums - Liquids (continued)

Winsor & Newton	OIL PRIMER
Winsor & Newton	OIL VEHICLE #1
Winsor & Newton	OIL VEHICLE #2
Winsor & Newton	OPAL
Winsor & Newton	ARTISTS

Varnishes

Binney & Smith	LIQUITEX DAMAR PICTURE (LIQUID)
Binney & Smith	LIQUITEX MATTE PICTURE
Binney & Smith	LIQUITEX RETOUCHING (LIQUID)
Binney & Smith	LIQUITEX SOLUVAR GLOSS PICTURE (LIQUID)
Binney & Smith	LIQUITEX SOLUVAR MATTE PICTURE (LIQUID)
Cascade Sales & Mfg.	CLEAR GLAZE (AEROSOL)
Chroma Acrylics	ATELIER SATIN FINISHING
Creative Art Products	SHIVA CASEIN
Creative Art Products	SHIVA DAMAR
Daler-Rowney	ROWNEY DAMAR
Daler-Rowney	ROWNEY #800
Daler-Rowney	ROWNEY GOLDFINGER
Daler-Rowney	ROWNEY MATT
Daler-Rowney	ROWNEY MATWAX PICTURE
Daler-Rowney	ROWNEY RETOUCHING
Duro Art Industries	DURO DAMAR
M. Grumbacher, Inc.	ACRYLIC PAINTING (AEROSOL)
M. Grumbacher, Inc.	DAMAR GLOSS (AEROSOL)
M. Grumbacher, Inc.	DAMAR MATTE (AEROSOL)
M. Grumbacher, Inc.	DAMAR RETOUCH (AEROLSOL)
M. Grumbacher, Inc.	PICTURE & OIL PAINTING - GLOSS (AEROSOL)
M. Grumbacher, Inc.	PICTURE & OIL PAINTING - MATTE (AEROSOL)
Holbein Works Ltd.	DAMMAR PAINTING
Holbein Works Ltd.	DAMMAR RETOUCHING
Holbein Works Ltd.	GLAZING
Holbein Works Ltd.	MASTIC
Holbein Works Ltd.	PICTURE COPAL
Holbein Works Ltd.	TABLEAU PICTURE
Holbein Works Ltd.	WHITE MAT
Humbrol Limited	HUMBROL SUPER ENAMEL VARNISH
Lefranc & Bourgeois	BLACK SATIN FOR ETCHING
Lefranc & Bourgeois	BLACK STOPPING OUT
Lefranc & Bourgeois	DUROZIEZ HARLEM DRYING
Lefranc & Bourgeois	DUROZIEZ RETOUCHING, BLACK FLUID
Lefranc & Bourgeois	FINEST DAMAR
Lefranc & Bourgeois	J. G. VIBERT PAINTING
Lefranc & Bourgeois	J. G. VIBERT PICTURE
Lefranc & Bourgeois	J. G. VIBERT RETOUCHING
Martin/F. Weber Co.	WEBER DAMAR
Martin/F. Weber Co.	WEBER MATVAR
Martin/F. Weber Co.	WEBER SPHINX RETOUCH
Martin/F. Weber Co.	WEBER SYNVAR (LIQUID)
Pebeo of America	CRYSTAL
Pebeo of America	DAMAR PICTURE
Pebeo of America	MATTE PICTURE (LIQUID & AEROSOL)
Pebeo of America	PAINTING
Pebeo of America	PICTURE
Pebeo of America	RETOUCHING
Pebeo of America	SATIN FINISH PICTURE
Pebeo of America	SUPERFINE PICTURE (LIQUID & AEROSOL)
Pebeo of America	SUPERFINE RETOUCHING (AEROSOL)
Royal Talens	TALENS DAMMAR PICTURE GLOSSY
Royal Talens	TALENS DAMMAR PICTURE MAT
Royal Talens	TALENS REMBRANDT PICTURE GLOSSY (LIQUID & AEROSOL)
Royal Talens	TALENS REMBRANDT PICTURE MAT (LIQUID & AEROSOL)
Royal Talens	TALENS REMBRANDT RETOUCHING (LIQUID & AEROSOL)
Sennelier Beaux Arts	33% DAMAR
Sennelier Beaux Arts	ALCOHOL-BASED RETOUCHING
Sennelier Beaux Arts	BRONZING
Sennelier Beaux Arts	ETCHING
Sennelier Beaux Arts	EXTRA-FINE PAINTING
Sennelier Beaux Arts	FINAL MATT
Sennelier Beaux Arts	FINE PAINTING
Sennelier Beaux Arts	GLOSSY ACRYLIC
Sennelier Beaux Arts	GOUACHE
Sennelier Beaux Arts	ISOLAN
Sennelier Beaux Arts	PURE MASTIC

Some of the products in this line bear the CP, AP or Health Label (Non-Toxic) Seal.

-4-

TABLE 2   (continued)

PRODUCTS AND MANUFACTURERS	BRAND NAMES	PRODUCTS AND MANUFACTURERS	BRAND NAMES

MEDIUMS & VARNISHES, ALKYD & OIL (continued)

Varnishes (continued)

Sennelier Beaux Arts	SATIN ACRYLIC
Sennelier Beaux Arts	TURNER PAINTING
Sennelier Beaux Arts	TURNER RETOUCHING
Sennelier Beaux Arts	WATERCOLOR
Daniel Smith, Inc.	DAMAR
Daniel Smith, Inc.	DANIEL SMITH PICTURE VARNISH GLOSS
Daniel Smith, Inc.	DANIEL SMITH PICTURE VARNISH MATTE
Winsor & Newton	DAMAR
Winsor & Newton	DAMAR RETOUCHING
Winsor & Newton	EXTERIOR
Winsor & Newton	GRIFFIN PICTURE
Winsor & Newton	WAX
Winsor & Newton	ARTISTS GLOSS
Winsor & Newton	ARTISTS MATT
Winsor & Newton	ARTISTS RETOUCHING

MEDIUMS & VARNISHES, MULTI-PURPOSE

Eberhard Faber	FIMO GLOSS VARNISH
Eberhard Faber	FIMO MATT VARNISH
M. Grumbacher, Inc.	DAMAR VARNISH
M. Grumbacher, Inc.	MATTE VARNISH
M. Grumbacher, Inc.	PICTURE VARNISH
M. Grumbacher, Inc.	RETOUCH VARNISH
Maimeri USA	MAIMERI MATTE WATER BASED PICTURE VARNISH
Maimeri USA	MAIMERI WATER BASED PICTURE VARNISH
Pebeo of America	BLACK GUTTA
Pebeo of America	COLORLESS SOLVENT BASED GUTTA
Pebeo of America	DILUENT PEBEO SILK
Pebeo of America	GOLDEN GUTTA
Pebeo of America	PATINA VARNISH
Pebeo of America	SILVER GUTTA
Pebeo of America	STAIN GLASS VARNISH
Pelikan USA	PELIKAN GRAPHIC WHITE
Sennelier Beaux Arts	DIFFUSING AGENT
Sennelier Beaux Arts	PRESERVATIVE AGENT
Daniel Smith, Inc.	DANIEL SMITH ALUMINUM SULFATE (ALUM)

MEDIUMS & VARNISHES, WATER COLOR

Daler-Rowney	ROWNEY ART MASKING FLUID
Daler-Rowney	ROWNEY POSTER & WATER COLOR VARNISH
Pebeo of America	SOLVENT GOUACHE VARNISH
Pebeo of America	WATER COLOR WHITE VARNISH
Royal Talens	TALENS VARNISH FOR DESIGNER COLORS GLOSSY
Royal Talens	TALENS VARNISH FOR DESIGNER COLORS
Royal Talens	TALENS VARNISH FOR WATERCOLORS MAT
Sennelier Beaux Arts	GOUACHE BINDING MEDIUM
Sennelier Beaux Arts	LIQUID GUM ARABIC
Sennelier Beaux Arts	OX GALL
Daniel Smith, Inc.	DANIEL SMITH POWDERED GUM ARABIC
Winsor & Newton	GUM ARABIC SOLUTION
Winsor & Newton	LIQUID OX GALL

PAINTS

Acrylic, Artists

Binney & Smith	LIQUITEX CONCENTRATED ARTIST COLORS ##
Binney & Smith	LIQUITEX TUBE COLORS ##
Caldex Enterprises	BON ARTISTE ##
Ceramichrome, Inc.	DECOART WOOD-TIQUES
Chroma Acrylics	ATELIER ##
Daler-Rowney	ROWNEY CRYLA ARTISTS ##
Daler-Rowney	ROWNEY CRYLA FLOW ##
Golden Artist Colors	FLUID ##
Golden Artist Colors	GOLDEN ##
M. Grumbacher, Inc.	ARTISTS' ACRYLIC JAR COLORS ##
M. Grumbacher, Inc.	GRUMBACHER ##
M. Grumbacher, Inc.	FINEST ACRYLIC COLORS ##
Holbein Works Ltd.	HOLBEIN ACRYLA ##
Humbrol Limited	HUMBROL METAL COTE
Maimeri USA	MAIMERI AQUA SERIES #10
Maimeri USA	MAIMERI BRERA ##
Maimeri USA	MAIMERI POLYCOLOR SERIES #12
Pebeo of America	EXTRA FINE ACRYLIC ##
ShinHan Art Materials	SHINHAN ACRYLIC COLOR ##
Turner Colour Works	ACRYL COLOR ##
Turner Colour Works	ACRYL GOUACHE ##
Winsor & Newton	ARTISTS COLOURS ##

PAINTS (continued)

Alkyds

Winsor & Newton	GRIFFIN ##

Caseins

Pelikan USA	PELIKAN PLAKA FLUORESCENT ##
Pelikan USA	PELIKAN PLAKA STANDARD SHADES

Ceramic Stains, Solvent Base

Caldex Enterprises	BON ARTISTE ANTIQUING
Ceramichrome, Inc.	MINERAL SPIRIT
Ceramichrome, Inc.	SOFTEE MINERAL SPIRIT
Ceramichrome, Inc.	TOUCH 'N GLO WAX
Pebeo of America	CERAMIC COLOR
Pebeo of America	DILUENT CERAMIC
Pebeo of America	SOLVENT BASED STAIN GLASS
Pebeo of America	VITRAIL SOLVENT

Ceramic Stains, Water Base

Gare, Inc.	COLOR WASH SPARKLE

Designer Colors (Gouache)

Daler-Rowney	ROWNEY DESIGNERS ##
Daler-Rowney	ROWNEY POSTER COLOURS ##
Holbein Works Ltd.	DESIGNERS' COLORS ##
Holbein Works Ltd.	HOLBEIN ACRYLA ##
Lefranc & Bourgeois	LINEL 35GT ##
Lefranc & Bourgeois	LINEL 650 ##
Maimeri USA	MAIMERI DESIGNER'S GOUACHE EXTRAFINE
Maimeri USA	MAIMERI STUDIO GOUACHE
Nicker Colour Co., Ltd.	NICKER ##
Nicker Colour Co., Ltd.	NICKER ACRYLIC GOUACHE ##
Pebeo of America	DESIGNERS' GOUACHE T7 ##
Pelikan USA	PELIKAN DESIGNERS' COLORS
Pelikan USA	PELIKAN GRAPHIC WHITE
Royal Talens	EXTRA FINE ##
Turner Colour Works	DESIGN COLOUR ##
Turner Colour Works	POSTER COLOUR ##
Turner Colour Works	TURNER DESIGN ##
Winsor & Newton	DESIGNERS ##
Winsor & Newton	PROCESS

Dyes

American Art Clay	BATIKIT COLDWATER FABRIC
Pebeo of America	PEBEO SILK

Enamels

Humbrol Limited	HUMBROL GLOSS SUPER ENAMEL
Humbrol Limited	HUMBROL MATT SUPER ENAMEL
Humbrol Limited	HUMBROL SATIN SUPER ENAMEL
Humbrol Limited	HUMBROL SUPER ENAMEL FLUORESCENT
Humbrol Limited	HUMBROL SUPER ENAMEL METALLIC
Pelikan USA	PELIKAN PLAKA LACK (NON-METALLIC)
Plaid Enterprises	GREAT GLASS FLOW ON GLASS STAIN
Thompson Enamel	T3 ENAMELS FOR ALUMINUM
Thompson Enamel	T4 VITREARC ENAMELS FOR GLASS ##
Thompson Enamel	T13 ENAMELS FOR STAINED GLASS ##

Fabric

Delta Technical Coatings	DELTA STARLITE ##
NASCO International	FABRI-PAINT ##
Pebeo of America	FLUO SETACOLOR
Pebeo of America	SETACOLOR OPAQUE
Pebeo of America	SETACOLOR TRANSPARENT
Rock Paint Distrib'g	HANDY ART ##
Sennelier Beaux Arts	GUTTA SERTI
Triarco Arts & Crafts	TRI-FAB ##

Metallic

Daler-Rowney	ROWNEY GOLDFINGER
M. Grumbacher, Inc.	ACCENT LEAFING PAINT

Oils

Binney & Smith	LIQUITEX ARTIST ##
Binney & Smith	LIQUITEX TEXTURE WHITE UNDERPAINT
Camlin Limited	CAMEL ARTISTS' OIL COLOURS ##
Daler-Rowney	GEORGIAN ##
Da Vinci Paint Co.	DA VINCI FIRST QUALITY ARTISTS' ##
Daler-Rowney	ROWNEY ARTISTS ##

Some of the products in this line bear the CP, AP or Health Label (Non-Toxic) Seal.

TABLE 2   (continued)

PRODUCTS AND MANUFACTURERS	BRAND NAMES	PRODUCTS AND MANUFACTURERS	BRAND NAMES

PAINTS (continued)

PAINTS (continued)

Oils (continued)

Fostport, Inc.	YARKA FINE ##
M. Grumbacher, Inc.	GAINSBOROUGH ##
M. Grumbacher, Inc.	M.G. UNDERPAINTING WHITE
M. Grumbacher, Inc.	PRE-TESTED ARTISTS' ##
Holbein Works Ltd.	HOC ##
Lefranc & Bourgeois	401 EXTRA-FINE ARTIST'S ##
Lefranc & Bourgeois	104 FINE ##
Maimeri USA	MAIMERI ARTISTI EXTRAFINE OIL COLOURS ##
Maimeri USA	MAIMERI CLASSICO FINE OIL COLOURS ##
Maimeri USA	MAIMERI PURO SUPERIOR OIL COLOURS ##
Martin/F. Weber Co.	PERMALBA ##
Pebeo of America	FRAGONARD OIL COLORS ##
Pebeo of America	STUDIO OIL COLOURS ##
Royal Talens	REMBRANDT ##
Royal Talens	VAN GOGH ##
H. Schmincke & Co.	BRONZES
H. Schmincke & Co.	MUSSINI RESIN-IN-OIL COLOURS, SERIES 10 ##
Schoenfeld & Co.	LUKAS SORTE 1 ##
Sennelier Beaux Arts	SENNELIER EXTRA FINE OIL COLORS ##
Daniel Smith, Inc.	DANIEL SMITH AUTOGRAPH SERIES OIL COLORS ##
Daniel Smith, Inc.	DANIEL SMITH LUMINESCENT OIL COLORS ##
Daniel Smith, Inc.	DANIEL SMITH ORIGINAL OIL COLORS ##
Winsor & Newton	ARTISTS FOUNDATION WHITE
Winsor & Newton	ARTISTS ##
Winsor & Newton	WINTON ##

Pigments, Dry Ground

Golden Artist Colors	GOLDEN
M. Grumbacher, Inc.	GRUMBACHER ARTISTS' ##
Holbein Works Ltd.	HOLBEIN ARTISTS' ##
Kremer Pigments	KREMER GREEN PIGMENTS ##
Kremer Pigments	KREMER YELLOW/ORANGE PIGMENTS ##
Sennelier Beaux Arts	SENNELIER DRY PIGMENTS ##
Daniel Smith, Inc.	DANIEL SMITH DRY PIGMENTS ##
Daniel Smith, Inc.	DANIEL SMITH EXTENDERS & MISC. PIGMENTS ##
Winsor & Newton	ARTISTS ##

Spray

Back Street, Inc.	ANITA'S PEARL SPRAY
Back Street, Inc.	ANITA'S POTTERY COAT
Cascade Sales & Mfg.	LUSTER PEARLS
M. Grumbacher, Inc.	ACCENT COUNTRY COLORS
M. Grumbacher, Inc.	ACCENT COUNTRY MANOR
M. Grumbacher, Inc.	IMPERIAL ANTIQUE GOLD
Plaid Enterprises	FOLK ART CLEAR COAT GLAZE
Plaid Enterprises	FOLK ART PEARL GLAZE
Plaid Enterprises	PORCELAIN BISQUE-IT

Tempera, Egg

Daler-Rowney	ROWNEY ##

Tempera, Liquid

ShinHan Art Materials	SHINHAN POSTER PAINT ##

Textile

Pebeo of America	CLEAR COUPURE SETACOLOR
Pebeo of America	THICKENER SETACOLOR

Vinyls

Lefranc & Bourgeois	FLASHE
Turner Colour Works	NEO COLOUR ##

Water Colors, Dry Pan

Yasutomo & Co.	SUMI ##

Water Colors, Powder

H. Schmincke & Co.	TRO-COL BRONZES
Daniel Smith, Inc.	DANIEL SMITH METALLIC WATERCOLORS

Water Colors, Semi-Moist

Daler-Rowney	ROWNEY ARTISTS ##
Fostport, Inc.	YARKA PROFESSIONAL ##
LYRA-Bleistift-Fabrik	LYRA AQUA COLOR (STICK)
Royal Talens	REMBRANDT ##
Schoenfeld & Co.	LUKAS ##
Winsor & Newton	ARTISTS ##

Water Colors, Tube

Creative Art Products	SHIVA ARTISTS' ##
Da Vinci Paint Co.	DA VINCI ARTISTS' ##
Daler-Rowney	ROWNEY ARTISTS ##
M. Grumbacher, Inc.	FINEST ##
Holbein Works Ltd.	HOLBEIN ##
Lefranc & Bourgeois	AQUARELLE 600 ##
Maimeri USA	MAIMERI ARTISTI EXTRAFINE
Maimeri USA	MAIMERI STUDIO FINE
Pelikan USA	PELIKAN CHINESE WHITE
Royal Talens	REMBRANDT ##
Schoenfeld & Co.	LUKAS MOIST ARTISTS' ##
Sennelier Beaux Arts	SENNELIER EXTRA FINE WATERCOLORS ##
ShinHan Art Materials	SHINHAN WATER PAINT ##
Daniel Smith, Inc.	DANIEL SMITH EXTRA FINE ##
Winsor & Newton	ARTISTS ##
Winsor & Newton	COTMAN ##

PHOTO EMULSIONS

Fluorographic Services	GUIDE-LINE DISCHARGE SPRAY

RESTORATION/CONSERVATION PRODUCTS

M. Grumbacher, Inc.	OIL PAINTING RESTORER
Martin/F. Weber Co.	WEBER CLEANING SOLUTION
Martin/F. Weber Co.	WEBER SALAMANDER RESTORATIVE
Royal Talens	TALENS ANTIQUE COLOUR
Royal Talens	TALENS ANTIQUE PASTE
Sennelier Beaux Arts	COLOPHONY
Sennelier Beaux Arts	GUM ARABIC

SCREEN PRINTING INKS & MEDIUMS

Accessories

Creative Art Products	DICK BLICK DIAZO SENSITIZER
Hunt Manufacturing	SPEEDBALL PHOTO EMULSION REMOVER
Hunt Manufacturing	SPEEDBALL SENSITIZER

SOLVENTS

Binney & Smith	LIQUITEX ARTIST RECTIFIED TURPENTINE
Binney & Smith	LIQUITEX PERMTINE
Elmer's Products/Borden	KRAZY GLUE REMOVER
Caldex Enterprises	BON ARTISTE ANTIQUING THINNER
Ceramichrome, Inc.	DECOART AMERICANA ANTIQUING SOLVENT & CLEANER
Ceramichrome, Inc.	GALAXY GLAZE SEALER
Ceramichrome, Inc.	THINNER & CLEANER
Creative Art Products	DICK BLICK ACRYLIC REMOVER
Creative Art Products	SHIVA RECTIFIED TURPENTINE
Creative Art Products	SHIVA SIGNA-TURP ODORLESS THINNER
Creative Art Products	SHIVA VENICE TURPENTINE
Creative Art Products	SPEEDY SQUEEGEE FILM & FILTER
Creative Art Products	SPEEDY SQUEEGEE SCREEN WASH
Daler-Rowney	ROWNEY OIL PAINTING THINNERS - LOW ODOUR
Daler-Rowney	ROWNEY TURPENTINE
Dhanes Company	DHANES TURPENTINE
Duro Art Industries	DUROTINE ODORLESS TURPENTINE SUBSTITUTE
Graphic Chemical & Ink	GRAPHIC DENATURED ALCOHOL
Graphic Chemical & Ink	GRAPHIC MINERAL SPIRITS
Graphic Chemical & Ink	GRAPHIC NAPHTHA
Graphic Chemical & Ink	GRAPHIC STOP OUT VARNISH REMOVER
Graphic Chemical & Ink	GRAPHIC TYPE & BLOCK WASH
M. Grumbacher, Inc.	GRUMTINE
M. Grumbacher, Inc.	PRETESTED ODORLESS THINNER
M. Grumbacher, Inc.	TURPENTINE
Holbein Works Ltd.	HOLTINE-SPIRIT OF PETROLEUM
Holbein Works Ltd.	LESOLVENT DE'COLORE
Holbein Works Ltd.	SPIRIT OF TURPENTINE
Holbein Works Ltd.	VENETIAN TURPENTINE
Martin/F. Weber Co.	BOB ROSS ODORLESS THINNER
Martin/F. Weber Co.	WEBER PURE GUM SPIRITS OF TURPENTINE
Martin/F. Weber Co.	WEBER TURPENOID

Some of the products in this line bear the
CP, AP or Health Label (Non-Toxic) Seal.

-6-

TABLE 2   (continued)

PRODUCTS AND MANUFACTURERS	BRAND NAMES
SOLVENTS (continued)	
Pebeo of America	PETROLEUM SPIRIT
Pebeo of America	SOLVENT FOR GUTTA
Pebeo of America	TURPENTINE
Plaid Enterprises	TREASURE CRYSTAL COAT THINNER
Royal Talens	TALENS CLEANER
Royal Talens	TALENS TURPENTINE RECTIFIED
Royal Talens	TALENS VENETIAN TURPENTINE
Royal Talens	TALENS WHITE SPIRIT
Sanford Corp.	THINNER FOR RUBBER CEMENT & GRIPPIT
Daniel Smith, Inc.	DANIEL SMITH CITRUS PAINT THINNER
Daniel Smith, Inc.	DANIEL SMITH DANCOLITE
Daniel Smith, Inc.	DANIEL SMITH LITHOTINE
Daniel Smith, Inc.	DANIEL SMITH ODORLESS MINERAL SPIRITS
Daniel Smith, Inc.	DANIEL SMITH 100% PURE GUM TURPENTINE
Daniel Smith, Inc.	DANIEL SMITH ROLLER & PLATE WASH
Union Rubber, Inc.	BEST KLEAN
Union Rubber, Inc.	BEST TEST SAFE KLEAN
Union Rubber, Inc.	BESTINE SOLVENT & THINNER
Winsor & Newton	OIL OF SPIKE LAVENDER
Winsor & Newton	PAINT THINNER (LOW ODOR)
Winsor & Newton	TURPENTINE
SPRAY SEALERS	
Caldex Enterprises	BON ARTISTE CLEAR ACRYLIC
Caldex Enterprises	BON ARTISTE MARVEL GLAZE
Caldex Enterprises	BON ARTISTE MATTE CLEAR FIXATIVE
Ceramichrome, Inc.	DECOART AMERICANA GLOSS
Ceramichrome, Inc.	DECOART AMERICANA MATT
Ceramichrome, Inc.	PORCELAIN-LIKE
Ceramichrome, Inc.	TRUE GLOSS
Ceramichrome, Inc.	TRUE MATT
Chartpak	CHARTPAK CLEAR GLOSS
Creative Art Products	DICK BLICK GLOSS ACRYLIC
Creative Art Products	DICK BLICK MATTE
Creative Art Products	SHIVA REPOSITIONABLE ADHESIVE (AEROSOL)
Delta Tech. Coatings	DELTA CLEAR ACRYLIC GLOSS FINISH
Delta Tech. Coatings	DELTA CLEAR ACRYLIC SATIN FINISH
Delta Tech. Coatings	DELTA STENCIL MAGIC TOP COAT
Duro Art Industries	DURO WORKABLE MATTE FIXATIVE
Gare, Inc.	GAREOSOL CERAMIC NON-FIRED SPRAY FINISHES
M. Grumbacher, Inc.	MYSTON WORKABLE FIXATIVE
M. Grumbacher, Inc.	TUFFILM FINAL FIXATIVE - GLOSS
M. Grumbacher, Inc.	TUFFILM FINAL FIXATIVE - MATTE
Plaid Enterprises	FOIL SEALER
Plaid Enterprises	FOLK ART ACRYLIC SEALER
Plaid Enterprises	FOLK ART CLEARCOTE HI-SHINE
Plaid Enterprises	HIGH GLOSS FIX-IT

Some of the products in this line bear the
CP, AP or Health Label (Non-Toxic) Seal.

-7-

TABLE 2   (continued)

REFERENCES

Alexander, J. "We Need Arts in Our Schools' Lives, says NEA Chief." *San Jose Mercury News.* June 11, 1995.

Alkema, C. J. *Alkema's Scrap Magic.* New York: Sterling Publishing, 1976.

———. *Art for the Exceptional.* Boulder, CO: Pruett Publishing, 1971.

———. *The Complete Crayon Book.* New York: Sterling Publishing, 1974.

Anderson, R., Manoogian, S. T., and Reznick, J. S. "The Undermining and Enhancing of Intrinsic Motivation in Preschool Children." *Journal of Personality and Social Psychology* 34 (1976): 915–922.

Arnheim, R. "Child Art and Visual Thinking." In *Child Art: The Beginnings of Self-Affirmation,* edited by H. P. Lewis. Berkeley, CA: Diablo Press, 1973.

Bland, J. C. *Art of the Young Child.* New York: Museum of Modern Art, 1968.

Bos, B. *Don't Move the Muffin Tins: A Hands-off Guide to Art for the Young Child.* Roseville, CA: Turn the Page Press, 1978.

Bredekamp, S., ed. *Developmentally Appropriate Practice in Early Childhood Programs Serving Children from Birth through Age Eight.* Washington, D.C.: National Association for the Education of Young Children, 1987.

Bredekamp, S. "Reflections on Reggio Emilia." *Young Children* 49 (1993): 13–17.

Brittain, W. L. *Creativity, Art, and the Young Child.* New York: Macmillan, 1979.

———. "Some Exploratory Studies of the Art of Preschool Children." *Studies in Art Education* 10 (1969): 14–24.

Brookes, M. *Drawing With Children.* Los Angeles: J. P. Tarcher, 1986.

Buton, L., and Kuroda, K. *Artsplay.* Reading, MA: Addison-Wesley, 1981.

Chapman, L. H. *Approaches to Art in Education.* New York: Harcourt Brace Jovanovich, 1978.

Chenfeld, M. B. *Creative Activities for Young Children.* New York: Harcourt Brace Jovanovich, 1983.

Chernoff, G. T. *Clay-Dough Play-Dough.* New York: Scholastic Book Services, 1974.

Cherry, C. *Creative Art for the Developing Child.* 2d ed. Belmont, CA: Fearon, 1990.

Clemens, S. G. "Art in the Classroom: Making Every Day Special." *Young Children* 46 (1991): 4–11.

Cole, E., and Schaefer, C. "Can Young Children Be Art Critics?" *Young Children* 45 (1990): 33–38

Cook, R. E., and Armbruster, V. B. *Adapting Early Childhood Curriculum.* St. Louis: Mosby, 1983.

Debelak, M., Herr, J., and Jacobson, M. *Creating Innovative Classroom Materials for Teaching Young Children.* New York: Harcourt Brace Jovanovich, 1981.

DeBono, E. *Lateral Thinking: A Textbook of Creativity.* London: Ward Lock Educational, 1970.

Dennis, W. *Group Values through Children's Drawings.* New York: John Wiley and Sons, 1966.

Derman-Sparks, L. "Anti-Bias Curriculum Challenges Diversity." *School Safety* 3 (Winter 1989): 10–13.

Derman-Sparks, L., and ABC Task Force. *Anti-Bias Curriculum: Tools for Empowering Young Children.* Washington, D.C.: NAEYC, 1989.

Derman-Sparks, L., Gutierrez, M., and Phillips, C. B. *Teaching Young Children to Resist Bias: What Parents Can Do.* Washington, D.C.: National Association for the Education of Young Children, n.d.

Dewey, J. *Art As Experience.* New York: Capricorn Books, 1958.

DiLeo, J. H. *Children's Drawings As Diagnostic Aids.* New York: Brunner/Mazel, 1973.

———. *Young Children and Their Drawings.* New York: Brunner/Mazel, 1970.

Dimondstein, G. *Exploring the Arts of Children.* New York: Macmillan, 1974.

Dyson, A. H. "Appreciate the Drawing and Dictating of Young Children." *Young Children* 43 (1988): 25–32.

———. "The Emergence of Visible Language: Interrelationships between Drawing and Early Writing." *Visible Language* 6 (1982): 360–381.

———. *Multiple Worlds of Child Writers: Friends Learning to Write.* New York: Teachers College Press, 1989.

———. "Puzzles, Paints, and Pencils: Writing Emerges." *Educational Horizons* 64 (1985): 13–16.

———. "Symbol Makers, Symbol Weavers: How Children Link Play, Pictures, and Print." *Young Children* 45 (1990): 50–57.

———. "Transitions and Tensions: Interrelationships between the Drawing, Talking, and Dictating of Young Children." *Research in the Teaching of English* 20 (1986): 379–409.

Eberle, R. F. *Scamper: Games for Imagination Development.* Buffalo, NY: D.O.K. Publishers, 1971.

Edwards, B. *Drawing on the Right Side of the Brain.* Los Angeles: J. P. Tarcher, 1979.

Edwards, C., Gandini, L. and Forman, G. (Eds.). *The Hundred Languages of Children: The Reggio Emilia Approach to Early Childhood Education.* Norwood, NJ: Ablex, 1993.

Edwards, L. C., and Nabors, M. L. "The Creative Arts Process: What It Is and What It Is Not." *Young Children* (1993): 77–81.

Eisner, E. W. *Cognition and Curriculum—A Basis for Deciding What to Teach.* New York: Longman, 1982.

———. "What We Know about Children's Art—And What We Need to Know." In *The Arts, Human Development, and Education,* edited by E. W. Eisner, pp. 5–18. Berkeley, CA: McCutchan, 1976.

Emberley, E. E. *Ed Emberley's Drawing Book: Make a World.* Little, 1991.

———. *Drawing Book of Animals.* Little, 1973.

———. *Ed Emberley's Big Green Drawing Book.* Little, 1979.

———. *Ed Emberley's Big Orange Drawing Book.* Little, 1980.

———. *Ed Emberley's Big Purple Drawing Book.* Little, 1981.

———. *Ed Emberley's Christmas Drawing Book.* Little, 1989.

———. *Ed Emberley's Drawing Book: Make a World.* Little, 1972.

———. *Ed Emberley's Drawing Book of Faces.* Little, 1975.

———. *Ed Emberley's Great Thumbprint Drawing Book.* Little, 1977.

———. *Ed Emberley's Picture Pie: A Book of Circle Art.* Little, 1984.

———. *EE Second Drawing Box.* Little, 1990.

Erikson, E. H. *Childhood and Society.* New York: Norton, 1963.

Feeney, S., and Moravcik, E. "A Thing of Beauty: Aesthetic Development in Young Children." *Young Children* 42 (1987): 7–15.

Fiarotta, P., and Fiarotta, N. *Sticks and Stones and Ice Cream Cones.* New York: Workman Publishing Company, 1974.

Fisher, E. F. *Aesthetic Awareness and the Child.* Itasca, IL: F. E. Peacock, 1978.

Fowler, V. *Paperworks.* Englewood Cliffs, NJ: Prentice-Hall, 1982.

Frank, M. *I Can Make a Rainbow.* Nashville, TN: Incentive Publications, 1976.

Furrer, P. J. *Art Therapy Activities and Lesson Plans for Individuals and Groups.* Springfield, IL: Charles C. Thomas, 1982.

Galin, D. "Educating Both Halves of the Brain." *Childhood Education* 53 (1976): 17–20.

Gandini, L. Fundamentals of the Reggio Emilia Approach To Early Childhood Education. *Young Children* 49 (1993): 4–8.

Gardner, H. *Artful Scribbles: The Significance of Children's Drawings.* New York: Basic Books, 1980.

———. *The Arts and Human Development.* New York: Wiley, 1973.

———. "Children's Sensitivity to Painting Styles." *Child Development* 41 (1970): 813–821.

———. *Multiple Intelligences: The Theory in Practice.* New York: Basic Books, 1993.

Garvey, C. *Play.* Enlarged edition. Cambridge, MA: Harvard University Press, 1990.

Genishi, C. "Art, Portfolios, and Assessment." *Scholastic Early Childhood Today* (October 1993): 67.

Getty Center for Education in the Arts. *Beyond Creating: The Place for Art in America's Schools.* A report by the Getty Center for Education in the Arts. Santa Monica, CA, April, 1985.

———. *Education in Art: Future Building.* Proceedings of a National Invitational Conference. Los Angeles, CA, 1989.

Getzels, J., and Jackson, P. *Creativity and Intelligence.* New York: John Wiley and Sons, 1962.

Golomb, C. *Young Children's Sculpture and Drawing—A Study in Representative Development.* Cambridge, MA: Harvard University Press, 1974.

Goodenough F. L. *Measurement of Intelligence by Drawings.* New York: Arno Press, 1975.

Goodnow, J. *Children Drawing.* Cambridge, MA: Harvard University Press, 1977.

Guilford, J. P. *Way Beyond the IQ.* Buffalo, NY: The Creative Education Foundation, 1977.

Hardiman, G. W., and Zernich, T. *Art Activities for Children.* Englewood Cliffs, NJ: Prentice Hall, 1981.

Harris, D. B. *Children's Drawings As Measures of Intellectual Maturity.* New York: Harcourt, Brace and World, 1963.

Hartley, R. E., Frank, L. K., and Goldenson, R. M. *Understanding Children's Play.* New York: Columbia University Press, 1952.

Haskell, L. L. *Art in the Early Childhood Years.* Columbus, OH: Charles E. Merrill, 1979.

Herberholz, B., and Hanson, L. *Early Childhood Art.* 4th ed. Dubuque, IA: Wm. C. Brown, 1990.

Hohmann, M., and Weikart, D. P. *Educating Young Children.* Ypsilanti, MI: High/Scope Press, 1995.

Hoover, F. L. *Art Activities for the Very Young.* Worcester, MA: Davis Publishing, 1961.

Indenbaum, V., and Shapiro, M. *The Everything Book for Teachers of Young Children.* Livonia, MI: Partner Press, 1983.

Jalongo, M. R. "The Child's Right to the Expressive Arts: Nurturing the Imagination As Well As the Intellect." *Childhood Education* 66 (1990): 195–201.

Jameson, K. *Art and the Young Child.* New York: Viking Press, 1970.

Janson, H. W., and Janson, D. J. *Janson's Story of Painting.* New York: Harrison House/Harry N. Abrams, 1984.

Johnson, M. *Teach Your Child to Draw.* Los Angeles: Lowell House, 1990.

Jones, S. *Learning for Little Kids.* Boston, MA: Houghton Mifflin, 1979.

Kaagan, S. S. *Aesthetic Persuasion: Pressing the Cause of Arts Education in American Schools.* A Monograph for The Getty Center for Education in the Arts. Santa Monica, CA, 1990.

Kamii, C., and DeVries, R. *Physical Knowledge in Preschool Education: Implications of Piaget's Theory.* Englewood Cliffs, NJ: Prentice-Hall, 1978.

Karnes, M. "Art for Children with Special Needs." *Scholastic Early Childhood Today* (1993): 63.

Katz, L. "Impressions of Reggio Emilia Preschools." *Young Children* 45 (1990): 11–14.

———. "What Should Young Children Be Learning?" *ERIC Digest* (1987). Urbana, IL: ERIC Clearinghouse on Elementary and Early Childhood Education.

Kellogg, R. *Analyzing Children's Art.* Palo Alto, CA: Mayfield Publishing, 1969.

———. *Children's Drawings/Children's Minds.* New York: Avon Books, 1979.

———. "Stages of Development in Preschool Art." In *Child Art: The Beginnings of Self-Affirmation,* edited by H. P. Lewis. Berkeley, CA: Diablo Press, 1973.

Kellogg, R., and O'Dell, S. *The Psychology of Children's Art.* San Diego: CRM-Random House, 1967.

Kohl, M. A. *Scribble Cookies and Other Independent Creative Art Experiences for Children.* Bellingham, WA: Bright Ring Publishing, 1985.

Kramer, E. *Art As Therapy with Children.* New York: Schocken Books, 1974.

Kristeller, J. "Creating Curriculum As a Workshop." *Scholastic Early Childhood Today* (November/December 1994): 58–60.

Langer, S. K. *Philosophy in a New Key.* Cambridge, MA: Harvard University Press, 1957.

Lansing, K. M. *Art, Artists, and Art Education.* New York: McGraw-Hill, 1969.

Lasky, L., and Mukerji, R. *Art: Basic for Young Children.* Washington, D.C.: National Association for the Education of Young Children, 1980.

Lepper, M. R., and Greene, D. "Turning Play into Work: Effects of Adult Surveillance and Extrinsic Rewards on Children's Intrinsic Motivation." *Journal of Personality and Social Psychology* 31 (1975): 479–486.

Lessen-Firestone, J. "The Trials of Testing." *Scholastic Early Childhood Today* (March 1995): 23.

Lewis, H. P., ed. *Child Art—The Beginnings of Self-Affirmation.* Berkeley, CA: Diablo Press, 1973.

Linder, T. W. *Early Childhood Special Education.* Baltimore, MD: Paul H. Brooks, 1983.

Linderman, E. W., and Heberholz, D. S. *Developing Artistic and Perceptual Awareness.* Dubuque, IA: Wm. C. Brown, 1974.

Linderman, E. W., and Linderman, M. *Arts and Crafts for the Classroom.* New York: Macmillan, 1984.

Lowenfeld, V. "On the Importance of Early Art Expression." In *Viktor Lowenfeld Speaks on Art and Creativity,* edited by W. L. Brittain, pp. 20–27. Washington, D.C.: National Art Education Association, 1968.

Lowenfeld, V., and Brittain, W. L. *Creative and Mental Growth.* New York: Macmillan, 1987.

MacKinnon, D. W. "The Nature and Nurture of Creative Talent." *American Psychologist* 17 (1962): 484–495.

Malaguzzi, L. Translated by L. Gandini. "For an Education Based on Relationships." *Young Children* 49 (1993): 9–12.

Martin, S. *Observation and Portfolio Assessment in Early Childhood.* Don Mills, Ontario: Addison-Wesley, 1994.

Marzolla, J. *Supertot—Creative Learning Activities for Children from One to Three and Sympathetic Advice for Their Parents.* New York: Harper & Row, 1977.

Mattil, E. L., and Marzan, B. *Meaning in Children's Art.* Englewood Cliffs, NJ: Prentice-Hall, 1981.

McFee, J. K. *Preparation for Art.* Belmont, CA: Wadsworth, 1970.

McNeill, E., Allen, J., and Schmidt, V. *Cultural Awareness for Young Children.* Reading, MA: Addison-Wesley, 1991.

Moll, P. B. *Children and Scissors—A Developmental Approach.* Tampa, FL: Hampton Mae Institute, 1985.

Montessori, M. *The Absorbent Mind.* New York: Holt, Rinehart and Winston, 1967.

Moyer, J. "Whose Creation Is It, Anyway?" *Childhood Education* 66 (1990): 130–131.

National Association for the Education of Young Children (NAEYC). "Guidelines for Appropriate Curriculum Content and Assessment in Programs Serving Children Ages 3 Through 8." *Young Children* 46 (1991): 21–38.

Naumberg, M. *An Introduction to Art Therapy.* New York: Teachers College Press, 1973.

Neugebauer, B., ed. *Alike and Different—Exploring Our Humanity with Young Children.* Redmond, WA: Exchange Press, 1987.

New, R. "Cultural Variations on Developmentally Appropriate Practice: Challenges to Theory and Practice." In *The Hundred Languages of Children: The Reggio Emilia Approach to Early Childhood Education,* edited by C. Edwards, L. Gandini and G. Forman, pp. 215–232. Norwood, NJ: Ablex, 1993.

———. Excellent Early Education: A City in Italy Has It. *Young Children* 45 (1990): 4–10.

Newman, E. "Yani: The Brush of Innocence." *Bay Area Parent* (April, 1990): 24–26.

Parnes, S. J. *Creative Behavior Guidebook.* New York: Charles Scribner's Sons, 1967.

Piaget, J. "Art Education and Child Psychology." In *Education and Art,* edited by E. Ziegfeld. Switzerland: UNESCO, 1953.

———. *Mental Imagery in the Child.* New York: Basic Books, 1971.

———. *Play, Dreams, and Imitation in Childhood.* New York: W. W. Norton, 1962.

Piaget, J., and Inhelder, B. *The Child's Conception of Space.* London: Routledge and Kegan Paul, 1956.

———. *The Psychology of the Child.* Translated by H. Weaver. New York: Basic Books,

Pica, R. *Experiences in Movement with Music, Activities, and Theory.* Albany, NY: Delmar, 1995.

Pile, N. F. *Art Experiences for Young Children.* New York: Macmillan, 1973.

Rubin, J. A. *Child Art Therapy.* New York: Van Nostrand Reinhold, 1978.

Russell, I., and Waugaman, B. "A Study of the Effect of Workbook Copy Experiences on the Creative Concepts of Children." Cited in V. Lowenfeld and W. L. Brittain, *Creative and Mental Growth.* Research Bulletin, Eastern Arts Association, 3, (1).

Safford, P. L. *Integrated Teaching in Early Childhood: Starting in the Mainstream.* West Plains, NY: Longman, 1989.

Saracho, O. N., and Spodek, B., eds. *Understanding the Multicultural Experience in Early Childhood Education.* Washington, D.C.: National Association for the Education of Young Children, 1983.

Schirrmacher, R. "Child Art." In *Toward a Theory of Psychological Development,* edited by S. Modgil and C. Modgil, pp. 733–762. Windsor, England: National Foundation for Educational Research, 1980.

———. "Talking with Young Children about Their Art." *Young Children* 41 (1986): 3–7.

Scott, L. B., May, M. E., and Shaw, M. S. *Puppets for All Grades.* New York: The Instructor Publications, 1972.

Shallcross, D. J. *Teaching Creative Behavior.* Englewood Cliffs, NJ: Prentice-Hall, 1981.

Silberstein-Storfer, M., and Jones, M. *Doing Art Together.* New York: Simon and Schuster, 1982.

Smith, N. R. *Experience and Art. Teaching Children to Paint.* New York: Teachers College Press, 1983.

———. "The Visual Arts in Early Childhood Education: Development and the Creation of Meaning." In *Handbook of Research in Early Childhood Education,* edited by B. Spodek, pp. 295–317. New York: The Free Press, 1982.

Spodek, B., Saracho, O. N., and Lee, R. C. *Mainstreaming Young Children.* Belmont, CA: Wadsworth, 1984.

Striker, S. *Please Touch—How to Stimulate Your Child's Creative Development.* New York: Simon and Schuster, 1986.

Szekely, G. "An Introduction to Art: Children's Books." *Childhood Education* 66 (1990): 132–138.

Taunton, M. "Reflective Dialogue in the Art Classroom: Focusing on the Art Process." *Art Education* 37 (1984): 15–16.

Taunton, M., and Colbert, C. "Artistic and Aesthetic Development: Considerations for Early Childhood Educators." *Childhood Education* 61 (1984): 55–63.

Topal, C. W. *Children, Clay and Sculpture.* Worcester, MA: Davis Publications, 1983.

Torrance, E. P. *Creativity.* Washington, D.C.: National Education Association, 1963.

———. *Guiding Creative Talent.* Englewood Cliffs, NJ: Prentice-Hall, 1962.

———. *Minnesota Tests of Creative Thinking.* Minneapolis, MN: University of Minnesota Bureau of Educational Research, 1963.

———. *Rewarding Creative Behavior: Experiments in Classroom Creativity.* Englewood Cliffs, NJ: Prentice-Hall, 1965.

———. *The Search for Satori and Creativity.* Buffalo, NY: The Creative Education Foundation, 1979.

———. *Torrance Tests of Creative Thinking: Technical-Norms Manual.* Lexington, MA: Personnel Press, 1966.

Torrance, E. P., and Myers, R. E. *Creative Learning and Teaching.* New York: Harper and Row, 1970.

Uhlin, D. *Art for Exceptional Children.* Dubuque, IA: Wm. C. Brown, 1979.

Wachowiak, F. *Emphasis Art.* New York: Harper and Row, 1985.

Wallach, M. A., and Kogan, N. *Modes of Thinking in Young Children.* New York: Holt, Rinehart and Winston, 1965.

Wankelmen, W. F., Wigg, P. R., and Wigg, M. K. *A Handbook of Arts and Crafts.* Dubuque, IA: Wm. C. Brown, 1974.

Weikart, D. L., Rogers, C., Adcock, C., and McClelland, D. *The Cognitively Oriented Curriculum: A Framework for Preschool Teachers.* Washington, D.C.: National Association for the Education of Young Children, 1971.

Wolf, A. D. "Art Postcards—Another Aspect of Your Aesthetics Program?" *Young Children* 45 (1990): 39–43.

———. *Child-Size Masterpieces.* Altoona, PA: Parent-Child Press, 1986.

———. "Hands On Art." *Montessori Today* (May/June, 1988).

———. *Mommy, It's a Renoir!* Altoona, PA: Parent-Child Press, 1984.

Wolf, J. "Singing With Children Is a Cinch!" *Young Children* 49 (1994): 20–25.

clay, 266–69
color blocks, edible, 156
finger paint, 142–43
gingerbread children, 208
glue, 87
orange drink, 156
paint, 136
papier-mâché, 290
paste, 86–87
plaster, 291
play dough, 266–69
popsicles, 205
potpourri, 201
sidewalk chalk, 202
snow sherbert, 205
soap bubbles, iridescent, 193
Recording, 348
  observing and, 351–55
Record player art, 65
Recycled junk print, 166–67
Redefinition, 9
Reggio Emilia, 185–86
Resist art, 208–10
Reznick, J. S., 235
Roll a can painting, 146
Roll a line design, 144
Roller printing, 165
Rub-a-dub-rub activity, 65
Run, mark, run activity, 63
Russell, I., 237

Safety shapes activity, 158–59
Safford, P. L., 96
Salad spinner art, 170
Salt
  paint, 136
  sculpture, 289
Sampling
  event, 354
  time, 353–54
Sand
  pendulum, 90
  play, 44–46
Sandpaper
  art, 63
  designs, 333
  feel, 198
  shapes, 158
Scene in a box activitiy, 288–89
Scent bottles, 200–201
Schaefer, C., 221
School, 11, 12
Science, art activities and, 277–80

Scissoring, 74–77
Scissors, 75–76, 84–86, 88. *See also* cutters
Scraped print, 169–70
Scribbling, 58, 61
Sculpture, 285, 287, 288, 289, 291
Secret message activity, 210
Self-direction, 9
Self-feeling, 9
Sendak, Maurice (Bernard), 184
Senses, 192, 194
Sensory experiences, 192–210, 213–14
  auditory, 196–98
  baric, 206
  chromatic, 202–4
  at a glance, 194
  gustatory, 201–2
  olfactory, 200–201
  sterognostic, 205–6
  table for, 200
  tactile, 198–200
  thermic, 204–5
  visual, 193–94
Sensory literacy, 187
Sensory motor stage, 80
Seriation art, 277
Seuss, Dr., 184
Sewing
  accessories, 337
  activities, 333–34
  simple, 333–34
Sex roles, 11, 12
Shade, 155
Shake a painting, 145
Shape(s), 157–60
  activities, 158–60
  characteristics of, 158
  movement, 207–8
  spatter paint, 159
  stamps, 159
Shoe polish resist, 209–10
Sidewalk chalk, 62
Signs, 159
Silly putty, 268
Singing, 53–54
Sketching, 61–62
Slobodkina, Esphyr, 157, 184
Small, David, 51
Smith, N. R., 327
Smocks, 304–5
Snacks, 201–2
Snowflakes (paper), 240–41
Snow sherbert, 205
Soap

bubbles, iridescent, 193
crayons, 60
paint, 136
painting, 144
and sawdust clay, 267
sculpture, 288
suds sculpture, 288
Social development, 77
Social studies, art activities and, 282–84
Society, 11,12
Society for the Prevention of Blindness, 88–89
Sociodramatic play, 43,44
Soda and cornstarch clay, 267
Sound(s)
  around us, 197
  containers, 197–98
  detectives, 197
Space, 161–62
  activity, 162
  artist's use of, 162
  types of, 162
Special-needs children
  art activity suggestions for, 95–96
  rights of, 95
Sponge
  painting, 161
  printing, 165
Spool sculpture, 287
Spray bottle
  resist, 210
  watercoloring, 188
Sprinkle a picture activity, 88
Squeeze and dribble painting, 144
Squeeze and sprinkle painting, 154
Squeeze a sculpture activity, 291
Squeeze, mash and taste activity, 208
Stabiles, 322–23
Staplers, 88
Starch and yarn art, 90–91
Stars (paper), 240–41
Steig, Willilam, 51
Stencil, 162, 170
Sterognostic sense, 205–6
Stick art, 154
Straw painting, 144
Streamers, 285
String
  collage, 223
  design, 276
  painting, 144
  printing, 167
Stringing art, 89
Structure of the intellect, 22